THE VINDOLANDA WRITING-TABLETS

(TABULAE VINDOLANDENSES II)

THE VINDOLANDA WRITING-TABLETS

(TABULAE VINDOLANDENSES II)

by

ALAN K.BOWMAN AND J.DAVID THOMAS

with contributions by

J.N.ADAMS

Published for the Trustees of the British Museum

by

BRITISH MUSEUM PRESS

Published by British Museum Press
a division of
British Museum Publications Ltd.
46 Bloomsbury Street, London WC1B 3QQ

British Library Cataloguing in Publication Data
A catalogue record for this book is
available from the British Library

IBSN 0-7141-2300 5
Jacket design by Andrew Shoolbred

Printed and bound in Great Britain by
Henry Ltd., Dorchester, Dorset

CONTENTS

PREFACE

This volume contains editions of all the wooden leaf writing-tablets with ink texts discovered at Vindolanda in the excavations of 1985-9, together with re-editions of almost all the leaf tablets excavated in the 1970s and published by the present authors in 1983 (Bowman and Thomas (1983)). When the material from the 1980s began to come to light, we announced our intention to publish a complete corpus of all the Latin texts from Vindolanda (Bowman and Thomas (1986)), but that has proved impossible for two reasons. The first is that excavation was resumed in 1991, after an interval of two years, and a small number of leaf tablets and a larger number of stilus tablets have been found in the seasons of 1991, 1992 and 1993. We have been unable to include any of these in the present volume. The second reason is that it is evident that the now considerable number of stilus tablets requires prolonged study and any attempt to include them in the present volume would have delayed its appearance for a number of years. A significant number of the stilus tablets - perhaps as many as 30 out of a total of well over 100 - contain substantial amounts of writing, although some may be palimpsests. In virtually all cases the incised texts are difficult to see and it is clear that it is essential to find some means of improving their visibility and legibility. Photographic techniques (see *VRR* II, 107-8) have not so far made significant improvements. Nor have we been able to achieve any appreciable progress using computer-based methods of image-enhancement. The latter would seem to offer the best hope of advance, but the adaptation of existing techniques to these tablets is time-consuming and expensive. The notes which we have included in this volume on the readings of texts on stilus tablets relate only to addresses which are relatively clearly visible and legible. Some of the stilus tablets contain notations written in ink on the edge of the tablet but these need further study and we have not attempted to include them in this volume.

The task of editing the ink texts has been laborious and time-consuming and we are acutely conscious that these editions are still far from perfect. The fact that we think that it has been possible to improve the readings and interpretations of the tablets published in 1983 has made us aware that there must be further room for improvement in many of the texts in the present volume and that improvement is made possible by the accretion of new material from related contexts and from other sites. It would hardly have been possible to read these texts at all without the excellent infra-red photographs taken by Alison Rutherford, formerly of the School of Medicine, University of Newcastle upon Tyne. We are also very grateful to Dave Webb, of the British Museum's Photographic Service, for the plates which are reproduced in this volume. We have worked almost entirely from the photographs and it should be emphasised that, in contrast to papyri, the presence of marks which may be either dirt or ink is a constant source of difficulty. In some cases, but not all, recourse to the original tablet has enabled us to decide whether a mark is or is not ink. We hope, at least, that we have clearly indicated our doubts about readings and interpretations and that other scholars will be able to make further improvements in the course of time. The original tablets and the infra-red photographs remain available for study in the British Museum.

The sheer quantity of material should be stressed. We here present full editions of 194 texts from the 1980s. The contribution which this represents to the corpus of Latin documents and letters from the first three centuries of our era may be gauged from the fact that Cugusi's *Corpus epistularum latinarum* (*CEL*) contains about 170 letters (excluding those from Vindolanda published in *Tab.Vindol.*I and our subsequent articles) which may be assigned to the period before AD 300, but many of these preserve no more than an address; we are here adding another 144, not to mention our 156 new *descripta*, many of which are as substantial as some of the letters in *CEL*.

Although photographs of the ink tablets were made available to us from 1986 onwards, the bulk of the work involved in preparing this volume was accomplished between 1989 and 1993. We have incurred a large number of debts to individuals and to institutions which it is a pleasure to acknowledge. We are grateful to the Vindolanda Trust and more particularly to its Director, Robin Birley, for the opportunity to work on this fascinating and important material and for his constant encouragement and help. The British Museum has now acquired the tablets and Drs. Ian Longworth and Tim Potter, of the Department of Prehistoric and Romano-British Antiquities, have been unfailing in their support, encouragement and practical assistance, as have other members of their staff. We are also grateful to the staff of British Museum Publications Ltd., particularly Celia Clear, for their encouragement and help; and to Harold Frayman for his willingness to respond to our need for technical help in word-processing.

Our academic debts are numerous. It is a pleasure to acknowledge the substantial contribution made by Professor J.N.Adams, of the University of Manchester. This is not limited to those many points on which we have quoted his comments verbatim; we have benefited from his advice on a wide variety of linguistic matters. In November, 1986 and March, 1989 we held seminars in Oxford, at which several of these texts were discussed. We are most grateful for the advice and comments of the participants: J.N.Adams, A.R.Birley, E.Birley, R.E.Birley, S.S.Frere, M.W.C.Hassall, J.C.Mann, F.Millar, P.J.Parsons, T.W.Potter, N.B.Rankov, J.R.Rea, M.M.Roxan, the late Sir Ronald Syme, R.S.O.Tomlin, J.J.Wilkes. The financial support of the Trustees of the Haverfield Bequest and the Craven Fund, University of Oxford, enabled us to hold these seminars and was much appreciated. We have had valuable help from Anthony Birley, Mark Hassall, Barri Jones and Margaret Roxan over a long period of time. Roger Tomlin and John Rea have read and commented on substantial portions of the text. John-Peter Wild, Carol van Driel-Murray, Chris Howgego, Helen Whitehouse and Roger Ling have responded generously to our enquiries on various points. We have both given lectures and seminars on the tablets at a variety of universities and academic conferences. Members of our audiences have frequently made useful comments and suggestions which have found their way into our commentaries. We hope that they will accept a general acknowledgement and understand that it has not been possible to mention them all individually.

We are most grateful to Mr. H.A.Orr-Ewing for his generous assistance in meeting some of the costs incurred in the preparation of this volume. Christ Church, Oxford and the University of Durham have afforded us financial and material support over many years and the former enabled Dr. Bowman to make use of the services of a Research Assistant, Dr. N.P.Milner, during a period of heavy administrative burdens; the bibliographical work accomplished by Dr. Milner was extremely meticulous and helpful. Dr. Bowman is also grateful to the Master and Fellows of Trinity College, Cambridge for the invitation to deliver the Lees Knowles Lectures in Military History in autumn, 1988; and to the British Academy which awarded him the Marc Fitch Research Readership in 1991-3, without which the completion of this volume would certainly have taken longer.

As a suitable form of abbreviation for reference to the texts in this volume we suggest: *Tab. Vindol.*II.

Christ Church, Oxford (A.K.B.) September, 1993
University of Durham (J.D.T.)

LIST OF ILLUSTRATIONS

TEXT FIGURE

Fig. 1 Table of letter-forms: page 53

PLATES

LIST OF ABBREVIATIONS

Standard abbreviations for periodicals which are used in this book may be found in *L'année philologique*. Abbreviations for editions of papyri are listed in E.G.Turner, *Greek papyri, an introduction* (2nd ed., Oxford, 1979) and J.F.Oates, R.S.Bagnall, W.H.Willis, K.A.Worp, *Checklist of editions of Greek papyri and ostraca* (4th ed., Atlanta, 1992).

AJ	F.F.Abbott, A.C.Johnson, *Municipal administration in the Roman empire*. Princeton, 1926
ANRW	H.Temporini, W.Haase (ed.), *Aufstieg und Niedergang der römischen Welt*. Berlin, 1972-
AS	A.Holder, *Altceltischer Sprachschatz*. Leipzig, 1896-1913
BL	F.Preisigke *et al.*, *Berichtigungsliste der griechischen Papyrusurkunden aus Ägypten*. Berlin/Leipzig and Leiden, 1913-
CEL	P.Cugusi, *Corpus epistularum latinarum papyris, tabulis, ostracis seruatarum*. Florence, 1992
CGL	G.Goetz, *Corpus glossariorum latinorum*. Amsterdam, 1965
ChLA	A.Bruckner, R.Marichal, *Chartae latinae antiquiores*. Olten/Lausanne, 1954-
CLA	E.A.Lowe, *Codices latini antiquiores*. Oxford, 1934-66
CPE	H.-G.Pflaum, *Les carrières procuratoriennes équestres sous le haut-empire romain*. Paris, 1960/1 (Suppl. 1982)
CPL	R.Cavenaile, *Corpus papyrorum latinarum*. Wiesbaden, 1958
Doc.Masada	H.M.Cotton, J.Geiger, *Masada II, The Yigael Yadin excavations 1963-1965, Final reports, The Latin and Greek documents*. Jerusalem, 1989
Ed.Diocl.	S.Lauffer, *Diokletians Preisedikt*. Berlin, 1971
*EJ*²	V.Ehrenberg, A.H.M.Jones, *Documents illustrating the reigns of Augustus and Tiberius*. 2nd ed., Oxford, 1976
LAN	H.Reichert, *Lexicon der altgermanischen Namen*. Vienna, 1987-90
LC	I.Kajanto, *The Latin cognomina*. Helsinki, 1965
LE	W.Schulze, *Zur Geschichte lateinischer Eigennamen*. Berlin, 1904
LS	C.T.Lewis, C.Short, *A Latin dictionary*. Oxford, 1879
LSJ	H.G.Liddell, R.Scott, H.S.Jones, *Greek-English lexicon*. 9th ed., Oxford, 1940
LVL	O.Gradenwitz, *Laterculi uocum latinarum*. Leipzig, 1904

NPEL	A.Mócsy, *Nomenclator prouinciarum Europae latinarum et Galliae Cisalpinae*. Dissertationes Pannonicae III.1. Budapest, 1983
O.Bu Njem	R.Marichal, *Les ostraca de Bu Njem. Libya Antiqua*, Suppl.9. Tripoli, 1992
O.Claud.	J.Bingen *et al.*, *Mons Claudianus, ostraca graeca et latina*, I. IFAO, Documents de fouilles 29. Cairo, 1992
O.Flor.	R.S.Bagnall, *The Florida ostraca: documents from the Roman army in Upper Egypt*, Greek, Roman and Byzantine Monographs 7. Durham, N.C., 1976
OLD	P.Glare (ed.), *Oxford Latin Dictionary*. Oxford, 1968-82
O.Wâdi Fawâkhir	O.Guéraud, "Ostraca grecs et latins de l'Wâdi Fawâkhir", *Bulletin de l'Institut Français d'Archéologie Orientale* 49 (1942), 141-96
P.Diog.	P.Schubert, *Les archives de Marcus Aurelius Diogenes et textes apparentés*. Bonn, 1990
P.Dura	C.B.Welles, R.O.Fink, J.F.Gilliam, *The excavations at Dura-Europus, Final Report V, Part I: the parchments and papyri*. New Haven, 1959
PLP	R.Seider, *Paläographie der lateinischen Papyri*. Stuttgart, 1972-81
PME	H.Devijver, *Prosopographia militiarum equestrium quae fuerunt ab Augusto ad Gallienum*. Leuven, 1976-87
PNRB	A.L.F.Rivet, C.Smith, *The place-names of Roman Britain*. London, 1979
P.Qasr Ibrîm	M.E.Weinstein, E.G.Turner, "Greek and Latin papyri from Qasr Ibrîm", *JEA* 62 (1976), 115-30
RE	A.F.Pauly, G.Wissowa, *Real-Encyclopädie der klassischen Altertumswissenschaft*. Stuttgart, 1894-
RIB I-II	R.G.Collingwood, R.P.Wright, *The Roman inscriptions of Britain*. Oxford, 1965-
RMD I	M.M.Roxan, *Roman military diplomas 1954-77*. University of London, Institute of Archaeology, Occasional Publication no.2, 1978
RMD II	M.M.Roxan, *Roman military diplomas 1977-84*. University of London, Institute of Archaeology, Occasional Publication no.9, 1985
RMLW	R.E.Latham, *Revised medieval Latin word-list from British and Irish sources*. Oxford, 1965
RMR	R.O.Fink, *Roman military records on papyrus*. Cleveland, 1971
RNGCL	H.Solin, O.Salomies, *Repertorium nominum gentilium et cognominum latinorum*. Hildesheim, 1988
Tab.Sulis	R.S.O.Tomlin, "The curse tablets", in B.Cunliffe (ed.), *The temple of Sulis Minerva at Bath, Volume 2. The finds from the sacred spring*. Oxford University Committee for Archaeology, Monograph 16, 1988, 4-277

*Tab. Vindol.*I	A.K.Bowman, J.D.Thomas, *Vindolanda: the Latin writing-tablets*, Britannia Monograph 4. London, 1983
TLL	*Thesaurus linguae latinae*. Leipzig, 1900-
VRR I	*Vindolanda Research Reports, New Series*, Vol.I, *The early wooden forts. Introduction and analysis of the structures*. Hexham, 1994
VRR II	*Vindolanda Research Reports, New Series*, Vol.II, *Reports on the auxiliaries, the writing tablets, inscriptions, brands and graffiti*. By E.Birley, R.E.Birley, A.R.Birley. Hexham, 1993
VRR III	*Vindolanda Research Reports, New Series*, Vol.III, *Preliminary Reports on the leather, textiles, environmental evidence and dendrochronology*. Hexham, 1993

PART I INTRODUCTION

I. THE ARCHAEOLOGICAL CONTEXT

It is necessary to begin by considering the context in which these writing-tablets were found. The archaeology at Vindolanda has its own story to tell and it can be reviewed only very briefly here. R.E.Birley's analysis shows that in the early forts at Vindolanda which have given us the writing-tablets five periods of occupation can be identified; the dates assigned to these periods are subject to the *caveat* which must always be applied to such indications. The earliest fort begins *c.* AD 85 and terminates *c.* AD 92 (Period 1); the fort is then enlarged and Periods 2 and 3 run down to *c.* AD 102/3 (Period 2 *c.* AD 92-97, Period 3 *c.* AD 97-102/3); after a short hiatus, Period 4 perhaps begins in AD 104 and takes us to about AD 120; the occupation of Period 5 lies between the years *c.* AD 120 and 130.[1]

The excavations of 1985-9 have examined the southern part of the central range on and adjacent to the *via principalis* of the enlarged fort.[2] The most important structures of Periods 2 and 3 are the timber buildings which fronted the street on the east side. These buildings certainly formed part of the *praetorium*, the residence of the commanding officers of units stationed at Vindolanda during Periods 2 and 3, the latter phase a rebuilding of a substantially higher quality than the former. The main living quarters of the officers and their families probably lay beneath the later stone fort and are now inaccessible. The rooms at the southern end of the west side, which have been excavated, seem to include a large yard, a kitchen and storeroom, and may have been devoted to the domestic services and organisation of the household. During Period 4 the area of the earlier *praetorium* seems to have been occupied by a barrack-block, the southern end of which was sealed off from the rest, perhaps to form the living-quarters of the centurions or *optiones*. The function of the building of Period 5 is more problematic. It seems likely to have been a workshop (*fabrica*), but it is perhaps worth bearing in mind that at Valkenburg the functions of barrack accommodation and workshop facility seem to have been combined in part of one building or complex.[3]

---

[1] See *VRR* I. The period shortly after AD 90, from which the earliest of the writing-tablets appear to derive, may be crucial in the establishment of the pre-Hadrianic, Stanegate frontier. G.D.B.Jones (1990) argues that the enlargement of the fort at Vindolanda probably fits into a pattern which is repeated elsewhere at important sites in the frontier region and it suggests that this phase of construction was the central feature of a new direction in Roman policy. This will have been initiated shortly after the decision was taken, late in the 80s, to abandon the greater part of the territory in Scotland which Agricola's last campaigns covered.

[2] See *VRR* II, 10-15 and Figs. 1-5. It should be noted that we have used Roman numerals to designate the rooms since we believe that this is how they are marked on the archaeological site plans (see *VRR* I). As a consequence, in order to avoid confusion, we use arabic numerals to refer to the periods of occupation. At the time of going to press, the site plans were not available for reproduction in the present volume.

[3] See Glasbergen and Groenman-van Waateringe (1974), 11, 25.

The writing-tablets were deposited in layers of bracken and straw flooring in successive occupation levels in the buildings and on the street outside. These deposits, some of which show signs of incineration, look like the result of dumping of rubbish and contain a wide variety of other organic remains and artefacts. The location of the early finds suggested that the presence of organic remains, in particular human urine and excreta, might have been significant in creating chemical conditions crucial for the preservation of the wooden tablets.[4] As the excavations progressed, however, tablets were found in areas where these conditions did not obtain and it now seems likely that the damp, anaerobic environment is sufficient to account for the preservation, as it seems to be elsewhere, notably at Carlisle.[5]

Writing-tablets have been found in all the phases of occupation identified in the pre-Hadrianic area. A small number of tablets were found in the ditch on the west side of the Period 1 fort, lying under the west front of the Period 2 building. Although it is not impossible to envisage documents being deposited outside the fortification, it now seems more open to doubt that this material was the product of the earliest fort and it is more likely that it was part of the debris from Period 2.[6] Most of the writing-tablets have been found in contexts which unambiguously associate them with Periods 2, 3, 4 and 5, from *c.* AD 92 onwards. The great majority of the tablets cluster in Periods 2 and 3, both on the street (WVIA) and in the adjacent *praetorium* structures to the east. The tablets are scattered in these rooms and on the street. Signs of burning on some of the tablets might suggest that they were carried out as rubbish from the inner rooms and taken to bonfires on the street when these buildings were abandoned or rebuilt; R.E.Birley has kindly informed us that the site of the bonfire in which the tablets were burned was discovered near the south gate in the excavation of 1993.[7]

The deposit at Vindolanda contains a mixture of letters and documents, personal and administrative, which were deposited as the area in the central southern sector of the enlarged fort was rebuilt or re-occupied in successive phases. The dating of these levels and the assignation of particular tablets or groups of tablets and other artefacts to specific levels and locations is a complex matter which is discussed in the archaeological reports and need not be repeated in detail here.[8] It may be useful, however, to emphasise some points which are particularly relevant to the tablets. We have only two pieces of evidence in the texts themselves which help us to date the tablets. **225** (Period 3) refers to the governor (Neratius) Marcellus who is known to have been in office in AD 103 and thus only suggests an approximate date. This text has an additional importance, however, since the handwriting

---

[4] See *Tab.Vindol.*I, pp.22-4.

[5] See now *VRR* III, 116. There is no indication of such conditions at Carlisle, the only other place where significant quantities of leaf-tablets written in ink have been found, see Caruana (1992), 68-70, Tomlin (1992).

[6] Note that some tablets were found at Carlisle in a silted hollow in cobbles overlying a ditch, Tomlin (1992), 147, note 32. In Bowman and Thomas (1991) we accepted the attribution of **154** to Period 1 and discussed the possible connection between the earliest fort and the First Cohort of Tungrians. These remarks should now be discounted.

[7] Cf. *VRR* II, 10-11.

[8] See especially *VRR* I. Our concordance (below, pp.367-77) gives the essential information for each of the published texts. For a complete list of tablets see *VRR* II, 109-22.

associates it quite clearly with the correspondence of Flavius Cerialis. The internal textual evidence thus reinforces the archaeological, and we can locate Cerialis and his correspondence firmly in Period 3, the end of which, according to the dendrochronological evidence, was in or not long after AD 103.[9] Much of this correspondence was found in Room IV, the yard fronting the street (Room VIA) and the street itself (WVIA). The second piece of evidence is more precise. **186**, assigned to Period 4 (Room IV), is dated by the consuls of AD 111, but the textual evidence of this document does not provide any links or associations with any other texts.

Our approach to the chronology of the tablets as a whole is somewhat different from that adopted by A.R.Birley in his survey.[10] Since there are, quite understandably, a significant number of tablets in which the content does not fit the archaeological context to which they are assigned, and it is a well-known fact of archaeological life that objects are not infrequently found in strata where they do not belong, we have preferred not to group the tablets by period. We have taken the evidence of period and location as general indicators and not as proof of association with a particular person or group of texts or as a basis for reading or interpreting a text in a particular way. Thus, it is quite likely that a large number of the tablets assigned to Period 3 belong to the papers of Flavius Cerialis and we think it consistent with the available evidence to refer some of the details in the accounts to the domestic administration of his household; for example, the inventory of kitchen equipment (**194**) was found in a room which has been identified as a kitchen (Room VIII). The content of the group of tablets discovered in Room XIV of the Period 4 building (**180-2**, **343**, **344**) is consistent with the view that they come from residential quarters of centurions or *optiones*, but we would not wish to argue that any text found in that location *must* be identified with or refer to the activities of such officers. Conversely, we have avoided taking the position that because a particular tablet is attributed to Period 4, for instance, it cannot belong with the correspondence of Flavius Cerialis.[11]

Apart from the phenomena noted above, we cannot specify, beyond the broad chronological limits, for how long and with what system the texts were stored, and the patterns of deposit when they were discarded. The archaeology at Vindolanda serves us much better than in many places (Masada, for example, where we simply do not know how, why or by whom the material was collected[12]), but we remain very mindful of the principle most elegantly expressed by Bingen in discussing the excavation of ostraca at Mons Claudianus:

> "Sur le plan historique, un ostracon de l'an 14 de Trajan fixe à un moment précis l'existence d'un acte humain générateur de relations humaines à un endroit que nous pouvons fixer avec plus ou moins de précision. Sur le plan

---

[9] *VRR* III, 120-4.

[10] *VRR* II, 18-72.

[11] Cf. above, note 6. R.E.Birley has informed us that the excavations of 1992 have yielded a number of fragmentary and decomposed ink tablets from a Period 6 context (*c.* AD 180), including one with an address to Flavius Cerialis. For an equally telling example from a different area and period see Franklin (1985), 6, note 17.

[12] *Doc.Masada*, pp. 18-20.

de la fouille, l'endroit de la découverte est bien connue, mais c'est le moment où le document a rejoint ce point précis qui est incertain."[13]

It is worth noting, however, that the lateral range of the deposit presents less of a problem. If the tablets were collected and transported within this small area, it need not worry us unduly if fragments of what appears to be the same document or letter were found several metres apart.

It is important to emphasise that the area in which the tablets were found cannot have been the location of the official record-office of the fort, which will have been situated within the headquarters building (*principia*) in the central sector of the site. Sometimes, no doubt, the contents of the *tabularium* (record-office) will have been dumped or destroyed, sometimes moved when the unit which generated them was transferred. There is clearly a deposit of records from the *tabularium* at Bu Njem and we must owe the preservation of papyri from the archives of the Twentieth Cohort of Palmyrene Archers, stationed at Dura-Europos on the Euphrates in the mid-third century AD, to the fact that the fort was captured by the Persians in the 250s.[14]

At Vindolanda we have a sample of the written material which ended up in the commanding officers' residence or was generated there, or in the later barrack-block and workshop - in many ways a much more varied and potentially interesting mixture than that at Bu Njem. Some, at least, of the tablets found in the *praetorium* may bear some relationship (we cannot tell precisely what) to records in the *tabularium*.[15] Although there are some suggestive groupings of tablets, we cannot now discern whether any precise filing-system lay behind the keeping of letters and documents in these buildings. Some of the stilus tablets have notations on the edge which we would expect to identify the nature of their contents and it may be that these will offer some helpful indications.[16] For the present, we are not able to make a clear distinction in the pattern of preservation between letters and documents.[17] The range of subject-matter and content is truly astonishing, especially in the context of the frontier area of a province which had no long history of urban or literate culture. As at Vindolanda, the indications are clear that this phenomenon is also found in the early phases of the Roman presence at Carlisle.[18]

There is little to add on the subject of the technical matters discussed with reference to the tablets found in the 1970s. The patterns of legibility in the ink tablets do not vary significantly from our earlier description and we remain virtually completely dependent on

---

[13] *O.Claud.*, pp.20-1.

[14] *O.Bu Njem*, pp.5-10, *P.Dura*, pp.3-4.

[15] We note that at Bu Njem 4 official reports which originated in the *principia* were found in the *praetorium*, *O.Bu Njem*, p.5.

[16] Cf. Tomlin (1992), 148, note 34.

[17] Caruana (1992), 68-70 notes that at Carlisle legal documents were found inside the fort whereas the majority of texts found outside it were letters.

[18] Caruana (1992), 68-70, Tomlin (1992). It may be noted that despite the large quantities of leather found at Vindolanda (*VRR* III, 1-75) there is no report of an example of a pouch for writing-tablets, for which see Baatz (1983). For possible references to writing-tablets in the texts see **217**.ii.1, **283**.6.

very fine infra-red photographs.[19] As ever, the problem with these is to distinguish those marks which are ink from those which are not, a difficulty to which we often refer in the notes to our readings. There are several cases in which we feel that technical improvements might offer better legibility, but the likely expense and length of time involved in the necessary experimentation is great. Computer-based techniques of image enhancement would seem, in particular, to offer a way forward. We were fortunate to be able to call upon some expertise in this area but were only able to experiment with the photographs. It is fair to say that it proved possible to obtain a better image of text which we had already been able to see and read but we did not succeed in producing an image which enabled us to see or to read text when we had previously been unable to do so.[20] It may well be that producing digitised images directly from the original tablets would give better results, but at present this involves too many practical problems. This is likely to be the most promising way forward with the stilus tablets.[21]

[19] For conservation and photography see *VRR* II, 15-6, 103-6.

[20] We are grateful to Dr.W.J.Fitzgerald, Mr. A.C.Kokaram and Mr.J.A.Stark of the Department of Engineering, University of Cambridge, for their efforts in this area.

[21] On the photography of the stilus tablets see *VRR* II, 107-8.

II. THE ROMAN ARMY

The tablets offer some evidence for military units and their personnel at Vindolanda and elsewhere but it is especially important to re-emphasise that, with one exception, the individual texts themselves are not susceptible to precise dating and caution is therefore needed when discussing the chronology.[1]

Military units

In interpreting the evidence of the tablets from the 1970s, we suggested that in the mid-90s Vindolanda was occupied by the quingenary Eighth Cohort of Batavians and that it was succeeded towards the end of the period *c.* AD 95-105 by the First Cohort of Tungrians, which may have remained in occupation for some years thereafter.[2] This interpretation can now be revised and amplified, beginning with the removal from the record of the Eighth Cohort of Batavians, since the evidence which has accumulated subsequently makes it clear that the numeral should have been read as *viiii* rather than *viii*.[3]

The evidence of the tablets now indicates the certain or possible presence of three cohorts, or parts thereof, at Vindolanda, the First Cohort of Tungrians, the Third Cohort of Batavians and the Ninth Cohort of Batavians. The strength report of the First Cohort of Tungrians (**154**) shows that the unit was based at Vindolanda and the archaeological context of this tablet and of the correspondence of its prefect, Iulius Verecundus, indicates that it was there in the earlier part of the pre-Hadrianic period. The attribution of the strength report to Period 1 now seems less likely than was once thought and we prefer to regard this particular piece of evidence as attributable to Period 2 and hence to the last decade of the first century AD. If this is correct, the Tungrian cohort will have garrisoned Vindolanda after the enlargement of the fort.[4] The strength report shows that its nominal strength was 752, including 6 centurions, but of these only 296 were present at Vindolanda when the report was compiled. The absentees included a contribution of 46 *singulares legati*. It is probable that

---

[1] See above, pp.18-9.

[2] *Tab. Vindol.*I, p.48.

[3] On the Ninth Cohort of Batavians see further, below. Our caution in Bowman and Thomas (1987), 134 (cf. A.R.Birley (1990a), 19) has not been justified by subsequent evidence. It should be noted that the citation there of a *cohors vii* (in **137** = Inv.no.85.199.a) is unfortunately a misprint for *viii*. We had envisaged the possible presence of an Eighth Cohort, as well as the Ninth, but there is no evidence for this; but since there clearly was a series of Batavian cohorts it is not impossible that an Eighth Cohort of Batavians existed at this time.

[4] To a maximum size of 7 acres or 2.7 ha., see *VRR* II, 3. On this unit see also Smeesters (1977), *VRR* II, 5-7.

the unit was in the process of being enlarged from quingenary to milliary (it is attested as such in the diploma of 103[5]), but there can be no doubt that the enlarged fort will have contained other units or part of units as well; the evidence for the splitting of units and the combination of parts of different types of unit which is accumulating makes it clear that the notion that a fort was garrisoned by one particular unit is far from realistic.[6] It is likely that the Tungrian cohort was at Vindolanda also in the period after AD 100. A diploma found at Vindolanda and dating to AD 146, which belongs to a member of the unit who will have been recruited *c*. AD 122, shows that it is likely to have been at Vindolanda around this time.[7] It is certainly mentioned in a letter attributed to Period 4 which implies that it was at Vindolanda (**295**). The argument that it left Vindolanda and returned after a period of absence is hypothetical and cannot be supported by the one-fort-one-unit pattern. Part of it, at least, may have been there (perhaps coming and going) throughout much of the period *c*. AD 90-120. Some of the names which occur in texts attributed to the later part of the period would suit a Tungrian unit.[8]

There is evidence in the tablets for two cohorts of Batavians, the Ninth and the Third, which may well have been two of the units which fought with Agricola at Mons Graupius.[9] The Ninth Cohort is attested on several occasions, mainly on tablets which are attributed to Period 3, or which may safely be assigned to the later 90s or early 100s, and there can be no doubt that it formed the main part or a major part of the garrison at Vindolanda at this time.[10] There are far more attestations for this unit than for any other in the tablets. In discussing the earlier evidence for the unit (then identified as the Eighth Cohort), we suggested that it might have been a quingenary *cohors equitata*, basing this mainly on the number of 343 men attested as working in the *fabricae* (**155**) and on the repeated mention of barley in an account (**190**). This no longer seems such an attractive hypothesis, and in view of the fact that there is no other direct evidence for the strength or nature of the unit in this period we think the matter is best left open.[11] It is unclear when the unit left

---

[5] *CIL* 16.48 = *RIB* II 2401.1.

[6] See Maxfield (1986), 59, Frere and Wilkes (1989), 120-1, Jones (1990), cf. Hassall (1983). *VRR* II, 6-7 suggests that the members of the First Cohort of Tungrians who were at Coria were new recruits undergoing intensive training.

[7] *RMD* II 97 = *RIB* II 2401.9. For evidence of its presence at Carrawburgh and Castelcary see *Tab.Vindol.*I 30.i.4 note.

[8] There is a possible reference to a Tungrian unit in **315**, perhaps *cohors i* or *cohors ii*, but it seems unlikely that the unit there mentioned was stationed at Vindolanda. *VRR* II, 23 quotes *]cho Tung* in the address on a stilus tablet (Inv.no.87.787) but the reading is far from secure.

[9] Tacitus, *Agr*. 36. See *VRR* II, 7-9, Strobel (1987). Holder (1980), 110-1 appears to envisage two separate series of Batavian units, the first consisting of nine milliary units and the second of nine other (presumably quingenary) cohorts.

[10] E.g. **127**, **135**, **137**, **271**, **281**, **282**, **284**. See also the inscriptions *CIXB* on the leather offcuts, *VRR* II, 92, nos.1-2.

[11] The argument, reviewed and accepted in *VRR* II, 7, that the Batavian cohorts had been raised to milliary strength by the closing years of Domitian's reign seems to us very hypothetical. *RMD* I 46 shows that it was milliary by AD 153.

Vindolanda; tile stamps which name the unit have been found at Buridava in Moesia Inferior and these have been dated to the period between the first and second Dacian Wars (*c.* AD 102/6).[12]

There are two texts which refer to the Third Cohort of Batavians - one addressed to someone connected with the unit and the other probably referring to the fact that Cerialis, prefect of the Ninth Cohort, had received letters from a centurion of the Third. This suggests the presence of part or all of the unit, or individuals belonging to it, at Vindolanda at some point in the late 90s - early 100s, but this does not constitute strong evidence that the unit was actually based at Vindolanda.[13] A diploma shows the Third Cohort of Batavians at milliary strength in Raetia in AD 107.[14]

An account which is attributed to Period 4 (**181**) mentions a debt owed by *equites Vardulli* and this suggests the presence of a detachment of the Spanish *cohors I Fida Vardullorum equitata ciuium Romanorum*, attested in Britain in AD 98 and known to be milliary in AD 122.[15] Another account of the same period records a dispensation of wheat to *militibus legionaribus* [sic] (**180**.22-3); whether they were at Vindolanda or simply in the surrounding region, in which the supplier of wheat was operating, remains uncertain, but their presence in a period of important activity in the frontier region is hardly surprising.

Finally, it should be stated that we would not wish to claim evidence in the tablets for an *ala Vocontiorum*. The reference on which this claim is based (**316**) seems to us most likely to be an instance of the personal name Vocontius.[16] It should be noted, however, that two letters addressed to a decurion named Lucius (**299-300**) and one military document mentioning a *turma* (**159**) offer firm evidence for the presence of cavalry at Vindolanda.

Units stationed elsewhere than Vindolanda, apart from the *singulares legati* and other detachments from the First Cohort of Tungrians (see **154**), are represented only in a letter from a legionary *aquilifer*, almost certainly of *legio II Augusta*, to someone at Vindolanda (**214**, cf. **281**.back 4 note). It must be emphasised, however, that despite the lack of named units there is a great deal of evidence for communication and contact between Vindolanda and units and personnel at other important military stations, such as Carlisle, Catterick, Ribchester, Corbridge and Binchester (see below, p.35).

Personnel

The list of persons attested, which is appended at the end of this chapter, summarises the evidence for people at Vindolanda (A) and elsewhere (B).

---

[12] See Strobel (1987).

[13] **311** back, **263**. In view of the pattern of deposit of letters received by people elsewhere (see below, pp.43-5), and the fragmentation and movement of units attested by **154**, the Third Cohort might not have been stationed there at all. The recipient of **311** might have spent only a short time at Vindolanda, cf. **311**.back 1 note.

[14] *CIL* 16.55.

[15] *CIL* 16.43, 69, cf. *VRR* II, 5.

[16] Cf. *VRR* II, 4. It should be noted that even if it could be understood as referring to the *ala*, or members of it, it does not however imply a presence at Vindolanda.

At Vindolanda

The column designated (A) includes people who appear in accounts and documents which we assume were generated at Vindolanda, and addressees of letters which are not either drafts written at Vindolanda or letters apparently received elsewhere by people who may have been at Vindolanda at the time when they disposed of them (see below, pp.43-5). It should be noted (1) that we have not attempted to arrange the material chronologically and (2) that we have only included as military personnel (no.9) those for whose status there is explicit or substantial implicit evidence.[17] Many cases remain doubtful and, in view of the evidence for movement of personnel and fragmentation of units, we are reluctant to conclude that a soldier attested, for example, in a text attributed to Period 2 must belong to the First Cohort of Tungrians because that unit is known to have been at Vindolanda in that period. There are certainly a large number of people in the "unknown" category who will in fact have been officers or soldiers.

The prefects of auxiliary units may not have been at Vindolanda for more than a few years. We may begin by observing that only two named individuals are clearly attested as *praefecti* of specific units: Iulius Verecundus, prefect of the First Cohort of Tungrians, and Flavius Cerialis, prefect of the Ninth Cohort of Batavians. It is probable that the first unit was at Vindolanda during the earlier part of the 90s and the second during the later years of that decade and for a short time after AD 100 (see above, pp.22-4). Iulius Verecundus' names alone are far too common to tell us anything about him or his origin. The statement of Tacitus that Batavian units in the Roman army were commanded by their own *nobiles* fits very well the evidence for Flavius Cerialis' command of the Ninth Cohort. His *gentilicium* shows enfranchisement in the Flavian period and the *cognomen* Cerialis clearly suggests a connection with Petillius Cerialis, the general who suppressed the Batavian revolt of AD 69-70. It is possible that Cerialis' father was rewarded with citizenship for loyalty to Rome in this revolt, but also possible that it was Cerialis himself who was thus rewarded at a young age and commanded the Batavian unit at Vindolanda in his 40s.[18] It may be that the Tungrian units, which unusually for milliary cohorts were commanded by prefects rather than tribunes until the third century, shared this tradition of local commanders, but there is no direct evidence.[19] Finally, it is unclear whether we should expect such local *nobiles* to have been assimilated into the pattern of relatively short tenure of posts in the equestrian *militiae* or to have held their commands for longer periods of time.[20]

Of the other prefects whom we can identify with some degree of confidence only one can probably be connected with a specific unit: Priscinus may have commanded the First Cohort of Tungrians, perhaps after rather than before AD 100 since the letters addressed to him are archaeologically attributed to Period 4. Hostilius Flavianus is perhaps the recipient of an application for leave like those directed to Flavius Cerialis, but perhaps slightly earlier.

---

[17] For a survey of the personnel period by period see *VRR* II, 18-72, but there are some differences in the readings of personal names (see below, pp.363-5). By "substantial implicit evidence" we mean, for example, applications for leave (**166-77**), which could only have been submitted by soldiers.

[18] Tacitus, *Hist.* 4.12, cf. A.R. Birley (1991), 97, *VRR* II, 7-9. That the practice of appointing local élites continued is not necessarily incompatible with the notion of "detribalisation" after the Batavian revolt, for which see Brandt and Slofstra (1983), Roymans (1990), 268-70.

[19] Strobel (1987), 289-90 , *VRR* II, 8.

[20] E.Birley (1988), 147-64.

On the face of it, this might suggest that he was Cerialis' predecessor as prefect of the Ninth Cohort of Batavians, but there are obviously other possible explanations and it is perhaps unwise to insist on the presence of only one unit commander at a time.[21] Flavius Genialis was probably also a *praefectus* and the balance of the evidence points to his presence at Vindolanda in Period 2; he too might have been a predecessor of Cerialis, or prefect of another unit.[22] Vettius Severus, the recipient of a letter attributed to Period 2 (**305**), might also be a prefect but the reading of the title is very uncertain. For Veranius we have only the bare title of *praef(ectus) coh(ortis)*, in a text attributed to Period 3 (**319**). There are others whose Roman *gentilicia* might suggest equestrian officer status, but in no case is there any positive evidence: for example, Licinius Asper (**224**), M.Cocceius Velox (**352**), ..scinius Ni...(?) (**325**).

There are several other named individuals who can be shown or presumed to have been officers at Vindolanda. The evidence for a *beneficiarius*, surely *praefecti* rather than *consularis*, is a very welcome addition to the meagre epigraphic record for Britain.[23] The individual centurions, the *optiones* and the decurion require no particular comment, but it should perhaps be borne in mind that the units to which they belonged may have been at Vindolanda for a number of years or on more than one occasion and we have therefore not attempted to list them by the periods to which the relevant texts are attributed. Once again, the list of persons of unknown status will certainly contain some centurions and "senior non-commissioned officers". The group of texts attributed to the building of Period 4 may concern some centurions and/or *optiones* and one account certainly includes the names Firmus and Spectatus as people who were in a position to give instructions about dispensing supplies of wheat (**180**.5, 23). One individual who is very likely to have been of similar status is Cassius Saecularis, addressed in warm and intimate terms by a legionary *aquilifer*, and concerned with supplies of timber and food (**213-5**).

The names and positions of some other functionaries are of some interest. The *medicus* (a medical orderly or a doctor) and *ueterinarius* are well-attested as members of the army's medical service (**156, 181**).[24] A *uexillarius* is mentioned in a context which suggests that he might have been a member of the group of cavalry from the *cohors I Fida Vardullorum* (**181**, see above).[25] The *cornicen* (**182**.i.1) is also to be expected in the

---

[21] The application to Flavianus: **172**. Hostilius Flavianus is a correspondent of Flavius Cerialis in **261** and, as such, is very likely to be somewhere other than Vindolanda.

[22] Genialis is suggested as a possible predecessor for Cerialis, *VRR* II, 9, 30. For Cassius Saecularis see below. Of the other people identified or suggested as prefects in *VRR* II, 41, 45-6, Flavius Similis (**235**, **254**, **286**) was certainly elsewhere; Pacatus (Inv.no.88.923, stilus tablet) does not seem to have a title surviving or at any rate legible; Vindex (**260**) is entirely speculative; Paternus is probably a "ghost-name" (**283** may be addressed to Cerialis and *Tab.Vindol.*I 61 = **531** is completely uncertain); [Perp]etuus relies on traces in **177** which are far too exiguous to suggest a restoration with any confidence; Vocusius Africanus (**315**) was probably not at Vindolanda (see below) - this name cannot be read in **300** and the reading in Inv.no.87.725 (stilus tablet) is very uncertain.

[23] Schallmayer *et al.* (1990), 1-22; for role and activities see Rankov (1986).

[24] Davies (1989), 209-36, Dixon and Southern (1992), 223-9, *VRR* II, 34, but note that the same *medicus* is probably not attested in **207**.11 (see note).

[25] Cf. *Tab.Vindol.*I 65.2 = **535**. For auxiliary *uexillarii*, Breeze (1974), 282-6.

auxiliary context.[26] Less easy to explain are the unnamed *curatores* who appear in routine reports (**127-8**), a term which in infantry units seems normally to indicate a special responsibility rather than a regular career post; they were perhaps therefore in charge of small groups of soldiers performing particular tasks.[27] The *scutarii* are likely to have been involved in the manufacture or repair of weapons and might well be classed as *immunes* (**160**.A.4, **184**.ii.21).[28] It is more difficult to know what to make of a *balniator*, a *ceruesarius* and a *uector* (**181**.8, **182**.ii.14, **183**). The first is presumably a bath-attendant; the term does not appear to occur in the military context and elsewhere frequently refers to slaves.[29] The second is a brewer (and retailer?) of beer, and the role of the transporter is obvious. What is not so obvious is whether they were actually military personnel or civilians. We envisage some civilian presence in the region of Vindolanda at this time (see below) and it is perhaps relevant to note the possible evidence in the tablets for a *ueteranus* (**187**.i.11), perhaps given added weight by the fragmentary military diploma found at Vindolanda.[30]

About the lower ranks little can be said. It should be noted that we include in our lists as *milites* or *equites* only those specifically attested as such or occurring in texts, such as requests for leave, which guarantees that they were military personnel. It should be emphasised that our approach differs from that of A.R.Birley[31] in two important respects: (1) since we are convinced of a significant civilian presence, we do not assume that people are necessarily "members of the garrison" unless there is some direct or substantial indirect evidence; (2) we do not divide the material according to period of attribution and we suggest that it is likely that soldiers serving for up to 25 years in units which may have been at Vindolanda more than once or for a considerable number of years might turn up in texts from different periods. There are sure to be a large number of soldiers in the list of those of unknown status and there is a significant degree of doubt over whether some of the individuals attested were at Vindolanda or elsewhere - to put it bluntly, the context is frequently ambiguous.

Elsewhere

The column designated (B) includes people who can be shown or assumed to be somewhere other than Vindolanda. Only one provincial governor is named, (L. Neratius) Marcellus (**225**.14-5), but there are other references to an unnamed *consularis* (**248**.ii.9-10, **295**.i.5), one to the *legatus*, which must also refer to the governor, the *legatus Augusti pro praetore* (**154**.5), and a petition or appeal to a person of whom the term *maiestas* is used; this is very likely to be intended for the governor (**344**). Other officers of high rank may include Ferox who may have been a *legatus legionis* (**154**.6), and the Crispinus addressed

---

[26] See Speidel (1984), 40-2.

[27] See *O.Flor.*, p.24.

[28] See Bishop (1985), 11.

[29] See *TLL* II 1703-4. For duties connected with military baths see e.g. *RMR* 9, 52.b.8, *O.Bu Njem*, Index 5, s.v. *balneum*. For baths at Vindolanda see **155**.3 and **322**.2 note.

[30] For civilians see our remarks in the introduction to **180**, Casey (1982), Jones (1984), and cf. Peacock (1992), 17. Diploma: *RMD* II 97 = *RIB* II 2401.9.

[31] *VRR* II, 18-72.

respectfully by Flavius Cerialis may well be an officer of senatorial status, perhaps a tribune (**225**.1). Finally, there is the important evidence for the presence of a *centurio regionarius* at Luguvalium in this period (**250**.i.8-9).

There are several people who can certainly be identified as equestrian officers, but evidence for units and stations is practically non-existent. Oppius Niger is probably in command of a unit at Bremetennacum (**295**) and Vocusius Africanus may be in command of either the First or Second Cohort of Tungrians (**315**). Aelius Brocchus and Caecilius September, both correspondents of Flavius Cerialis, and the latter probably also of Priscinus, are known from inscriptional evidence; September (**252-3**, **234**, **298**) was in Syria at an earlier date, Brocchus (**233**, **243-8**, **234**) in Pannonia later. Hostilius Flavianus may be attested at Vindolanda and in a posting elsewhere (**172**, **261**), and we note the difficult evidence for Flavius Genialis, who might well have been an equestrian prefect, perhaps also occurring at Vindolanda and elsewhere (**217-24**, **256**). Others may be identified as likely *praefecti* by the use of the terms *collega* and *frater* in correspondence with a known *praefectus* (**259**, **260**, **345**), or by association with an equestrian officer in the address of a letter (**248**).[32] Amongst those of unknown status, there are undoubtedly some equestrian commanders, perhaps most readily to be sought amongst those with the common *gentilicia*, Iulius, Claudius, Flavius;[33] but the strong possibility of having (e.g.) legionary officers and centurions holding these *gentilicia* means that individual cases cannot be pressed or used as a basis for further hypotheses.

The known centurions and decurions are again a small group. It is noteworthy that Clodius Super, one of Cerialis' correspondents who is probably a centurion, addresses the prefect in familiar tones and we think that this can be explained by the supposition that he was of similar social status, i.e. a centurion *ex equite Romano* and probably a legionary centurion (**255**). We suspect that among those at places other than Vindolanda whose position is unknown, there may be many centurions and decurions, since letters coming to Vindolanda might be expected to emanate from people with some administrative military responsibility; but the general nature of activities of presumed officers such as Curtius Super and Severinus (**213**, **215**.ii.3) can, once again, be regarded only as a basis for hypothesis.

Of the other military personnel, the most interesting are Vittius Adiutor, the legionary *aquilifer* very probably of the *legio II Augusta* based at Caerleon (**214**), and Veldedeius, the *equisio consularis*, who may have had some position of responsibility for animals attached to the governor's retinue (**310**). Given the movement of groups and individuals attested in the tablets, it is possible that Adiutor was not at Caerleon when he wrote to Saecularis.[34] As for Veldedeius, the letter addressed to him (**310**) seems to have been sent to London, but there is no reason to doubt that he may at some time have been at Vindolanda, where the letter was deposited. Virilis the *ueterinarius* mentioned in the letter was presumably also in

---

[32] Valerius Niger rather than Oppius Niger may be the co-author of **248** (see introduction and cf. **465**).

[33] *VRR* II, 9 notes that in general one does not not expect to find Flavii holding equestrian commands before the reign of Trajan.

[34] We prefer to read the *gentilicium* as Vittius, not Vettius as suggested by A.R.Birley (1990b), see **214**, introduction.

or near London.[35] The *duplicarius* named Cessaucius Nigrinus (?) received a letter at a place which was probably very close to Vindolanda and may have been based there and out-stationed (**312**).[36]

Soldiers and Civilians

When we come to consider the people attested in the tablets who did not hold military posts, the clearest evidence relates to members of officers' families and slaves.[37] The presence of officers' wives is most clearly illustrated by the correspondence of Sulpicia Lepidina, wife of Flavius Cerialis, who receives letters from at least two different women, one certainly and the other perhaps the wife of an officer (**291-4**). There is at least one other letter between female correspondents, as well as one addressed to Flavius Cerialis by a woman (**324**, **257**). Requests by authors of letters that recipients should pass on greetings to people with female names further emphasise the presence of women in the military ambit, some of them surely below the equestrian officer level and thus not permitted to contract legal marriages (**310**, **353**, cf. **346**); one such may be concealed in a reference to a *contubernalis* (**181**.14). The presence of officers' wives in the *praetorium*, surprising though it may at first have seemed, must now be accepted as common, if not routine. The only unambiguous evidence for children in the tablets relates to the equestrian officer class (**291**).[38] The status of women connected with men of other ranks is less clear cut, but the evidence of the tablets themselves does not necessarily presuppose their presence within the fort, as opposed to an adjacent settlement.

The presence of slaves is also clearly attested.[39] Candidus the slave of Genialis is the recipient of a letter from a slave named Severus, and Rhenus the slave of Similis sends a letter to Primigenius who was no doubt also a slave (**301**, **347**). Genialis is an equestrian officer and Similis is likely also to be one. Primigenius might be a slave of Flavius Cerialis and we may also have letters addressed to a slave of the prefect Iulius Verecundus and to another slave of Genialis named Albiso (**302**, **303**). The evidence of nomenclature is not an infallible guide to status but some examples in letters (e.g. **311**) are suggestive and the name Privatus in one of the accounts is very likely to belong to a slave involved in domestic duties in the *praetorium* (**190**). It is possible that a separate bathing establishment was maintained for slaves in the fort (**322**). Although it is known that soldiers below the equestrian officer level kept slaves, the only probable evidence for this in the tablets concerns a centurion who will have been somewhere other than Vindolanda (**255**).

The case for the presence of freeborn civilians at or near Vindolanda is more difficult to evaluate. The role of independent civilian traders and contractors in the ambit of the army

---

[35] We cannot accept the suggestions about the relationships between the people and their units made at *VRR* II, 36-7 since these are based on the supposition that the letter was written at London and sent to Vindolanda (see below, pp.43-5).

[36] We do not agree with the reading of the *cognomen* as *Morin[o*, suggested by A.R.Birley (1991), 92, cf. *VRR* II, 37.

[37] For archaeological evidence for the presence of women see *VRR* III, 44-6.

[38] For some comparable evidence for women see Allason-Jones (1989), ch.4. We do not believe that the term *pueri* which is used in **255**.i.7 and **260**.7 refers to children (see notes *ad locc.*).

[39] On this topic see Speidel (1989).

has long been recognised and although it is unsafe to rely on analogy with other, more developed areas, it is not difficult to imagine their presence, perhaps in small numbers, in the northern frontier zone even at this early date.[40] It is, however, very difficult to demonstrate beyond doubt the civilian status of particular individuals and unsafe to infer it from their function or activity; we have already raised the question with reference to a *balniator*, a *ceruesarius* and a *uector*, who could perhaps be either military or civilian, and the same may be true of people performing agricultural tasks (**180**).[41] We had earlier suggested that Metto and Aduectus, the sender and the recipient of wagon parts (**309**), and Octavius and Candidus, the dealers in cereals and leather (**343**), might be civilian traders or contractors, but the case is not compelling.[42]

In our view, the most persuasive evidence for civilian presence lies in **180** and **344**, two texts written on one tablet or set of tablets. The anonymous writer of the account is clearly also the person who wrote the letter or draft petition; there is no doubt about the identity of the hands. The author of the petition describes himself as an innocent man from overseas (*hominem trasmarinum et innocentem*) and the whole tone of the appeal suggests a civilian suffering maltreatment at the hands of the military. Unless the writer was drafting this on behalf of someone else, it follows that the compiler of the wheat account, who was presumably a dealer and tradesman, is likely to have been the maltreated civilian.[43] If this is so, it might lend weight to the hypothesis that other persons appearing in the group of tablets which includes this and the letter of Octavius (**343**) are also civilians, but it is impossible to decide how far such hypotheses can be pressed. We can only conclude that the case for the presence of some civilians is, in principle, quite strong.

Origins

Some attention has already been devoted to the question of the ethnic identity and origins of the people who appear in the writing-tablets.[44] In general it is to be emphasised that the firm evidence for the presence of Batavian and Tungrian units at Vindolanda means that we should expect to find a preponderance of personnel, including officers (see above, p.25), from the area of Gallia Belgica and Germany in which these units were originally recruited.[45] Beyond that, we assume that origins are likely to lie in the western empire, perhaps with some representation for Italy (obviously so in the case of the high-ranking officials such as the governor and the legionary legates), but the nomenclature of individuals

---

[40] Middleton (1979), Casey (1982), Breeze (1984).

[41] Cf. Tomlin (1992), 150, note 50 on the term *sesplasiarius*.

[42] If so, we are left with the need to explain the presence of such documents inside the fort; perhaps compare Caruana (1992).

[43] *VRR* II, 59 seems to suggest that the complainant is regarded as a soldier.

[44] A.R.Birley (1990a), (1991), *VRR* II, 18-72.

[45] We have therefore relied very heavily on the evidence assembled in *NPEL* in our attempts to read, interpret and explain the personal names in the tablets. Also useful for this region are *LAN* and Weisgerber (1968) and (1969).

is often too commonplace to allow us to be specific, and only in one case, that of Sabinus from Trier (**182**.i.4), do we have clear evidence of a place of origin.[46]

The evidence for the Roman *gentilicia* may be appreciated from a survey of the List of Persons. The frequency with which Flavius and Claudius occur requires no explanation other than the obvious, and these names often indicate citizens of provincial origin. Iulius tends to be held by legionaries rather than auxiliaries in Britain,[47] but Iulius Verecundus is a prefect of an auxiliary cohort (**154**, **210-2**). Sulpicia (**291**) and Cocceius (**352**) probably indicate citizenship acquired by the individual or an ancestor in the reigns of Galba and Nerva, but our one example of Aelius (**233**, **243-8**) is certainly pre-Hadrianic. Others such as Vettius, Cassius, Caecilius, Hostilius in themselves indicate very little. We are reluctant to suggest unattested *gentilicia* unless the reading is certain, but there is one clear case in Cessaucius (**312**) and another, Celonius (**345**), may connect with an inscription from Rovenich. There are some uncommon names and formations which are known elsewhere.[48]

The *cognomina* are in general more informative and, apart from the very common examples which we here omit,[49] may be considered by type and by the region from which they derive. Celtic and Germanic names and formations are, as we would expect, common. We make no pretence to expertise in the matter of classification or in the very difficult philological and linguistic problems which these names raise, and in view of the generally poor attestation of such names it is not surprising that many examples cannot be precisely paralleled.[50] We hope, at least, to have presented the evidence with sufficient clarity for the experts in these fields to analyse it.

As fairly typical examples of names of "Celtic" type which are otherwise attested or reasonably closely paralleled we can cite Andecarus and Sautenus (**182** back i.5, cf. **188**.7), Atto (**308**, **345**), Albiso (**303**), Brigio (-nus) (**188**, **250**), Saco (**309**), Veldeius or Veldedeius and Velbuteius (**310**), Sattua (**346**), Metto (**309**) and Gavo (**192**, **207**). We note that, as with many other names, the common *cognomina* Buccus (**176**) and Exomnius (**182**.ii.13) are variously regarded by the modern authorities as Celtic or Germanic.[51]

The names which seem most obviously Germanic are Chrauttius and Thuttena (**310**), both unattested. No doubt there are others which could be Germanic in origin, e.g. the unattested Gannallius (**169**) and very rare Uxperus (**182**.ii.24). Insofar as we have been able to parallel the names (other than those which are universal) or some of the linguistic elements in them, however, we find them turning up in Gallia Belgica, the remainder of Gaul, the Danube lands and Spain, sometimes in more than one of these areas. There is no reason why Vindolanda should not have seen the presence of people from all these places at some point,

---

[46] For the alleged "Morinian" of **312** see above, note 36. The name Rhenus (a slave, **347**) is too vague to be very helpful.

[47] Tomlin (1992), 151.

[48] E.g. Vocusius (**316**), Frontinius (**343**.iv.38-9), see A.R.Birley (1991), 91.

[49] Some statistics may be found in the lists in *VRR* II, 18-72.

[50] The classification of such names presents serious difficulty and the standard works are frequently unsure whether they are Celtic or Germanic. We rely largely on *AS* (which is now very old), *LAN*, Evans (1967), Weisgerber (1968) and (1969). See also Tomlin's remarks in *Tab.Sulis*, passim.

[51] *AS*, *LAN*. On Buccus see however André (1991), 37.

given the presence of units from Gallia Belgica and Spain, but it is often impossible to be sure in individual cases. Thus, but not exhaustively: for Spain, possibly Valatta (**257**), Andle... (**188**), either or both of the names beginning with Tag- (**181**.14, **184**.i.3). The Danube lands: Ucen(i)us, Butimas, Gambax (**184**), Ircucisso (**182**.i.5), Huep- (Vep-?, **184**.ii.27). One point which is to be emphasised is that we have no direct evidence in the tablets for individual native Britons, although some (either military recruits or traders) could in principle be concealed behind Celtic or Germanic names of this type which we would not expect to be able to distinguish from continental examples.[52]

Finally, there is a certain amount of evidence for Greek names: Elpis (**346**), Gleuco (**343**.iv.44), Paris, Corinthus (**311**), Hermes (**487**), Trophimus (**341**). This is not so surprising as it might at first appear, for Greek names are quite well attested in Gallia Belgica and are even to be found among the German soldiers of the imperial bodyguard.[53] Some of the Greek names in the Vindolanda tablets might suggest a servile context but in no case is this clearly demonstrable and it is certainly not a necessary conclusion.

Activities

Our survey of the military activities recorded in the tablets deals with four main topics: general organisational role and the administration of units and personnel; the administration, use and manufacture of goods and supplies; communications; judiciary and policing role.

For the general organisational role of the army in the frontier region, two brief items of evidence need to be noted. First, the reference to the organisation of a census (**304**), which should certainly be regarded as an activity which often involved military personnel in newly acquired territory. Second, the presence of a *centurio regionarius* at Luguvalium (**250**) who must certainly have been a key figure in the organisation of this sector of the frontier and may, indeed, himself have been involved in the census-taking operation.

There is a good deal of evidence for the administration of units and personnel but, perhaps not surprisingly given the nature and location of the deposit, virtually none for pay-records or rosters of individuals and their duties, so well represented in the papyri from Egypt and Dura-Europos. The complete strength report of the First Cohort of Tungrians (**154**) is uniquely important and indicates a degree of fragmentation of units which is surely a very important characteristic of the frontier zone at this period. Other reports indicate the dispositions of particular groups performing specific functions (**155-7**, see further below) and may be compared with the "rapports journaliers" found at Bu Njem.[54] A list of individuals (**161**) is fragmentary and uninformative. We may note the request that some individuals whose names are lost should be removed from a list (**345**), and it is worth emphasising the inclusion in the strength report (**154**) of categories of men unfit for service. Medical facilities were available at Vindolanda which had its own hospital, and there is also a reference to a *ueterinarius* (**155**, **181**).

---

[52] For a general reference to Britons see **164** and cf. **344**, introduction. We see no reason to regard Lucco (**180**.27, 30) as a British recruit (*VRR* II, 64).

[53] Hermes, for example, is attested 8 times in Gallia Belgica according to *NPEL*. For the imperial bodyguard see e.g. Alkimachus, Phoebus, Pothus, in Bellen (1981).

[54] *O.Bu Njem* 1-62.

A striking novelty is the large number of reports with the *renuntium* heading, clearly made at regular intervals, perhaps daily; these were submitted by *optiones* and seem to be straightforward checks on personnel and equipment (**127-53**). One unfortunately incomplete letter appears to refer to the occurrence of a *numeratio* at Vindolanda, but it is unclear whether this is a "pay-parade" or a muster of a more general kind (**242**). Some new light is cast on Vegetius' statement about the care with which leave was granted and recorded by a group of applications for leave submitted by individuals to the prefect of the unit (**166-77**). There may be two references to deserters, both in lacunose contexts (**226**, **320**), and another perhaps to a malcontent who was at large in the region and posing a threat to someone's peace of mind (**256**).

Three letters in particular illustrate the way in which individual careers might be affected or influenced by contacts: two letters which shed some light on the connections of Flavius Cerialis, prefect of the Ninth Cohort of Batavians, with the provincial governor and perhaps with another superior officer (**248**, **225**), and one recognisable example of *litterae commendaticiae*, for someone probably called Brigionus, a romanised Celtic name, who might be of humble station (**250**). This is the closest we come to having direct evidence for recruitment of local Britons into units originally raised elsewhere. A note which describes the fighting characteristics of the Britons (**164**) might possibly be relevant if it was compiled by or for someone who was interested in recruitment (units of Britons were certainly being raised at this time).[55]

The administration of goods and supplies is more abundantly attested than any other aspect of military activity, thanks to the large number of accounts, and here we can only indicate some of the more interesting items of evidence, excluding those which we consider more relevant to the domestic administration of the *praetorium* (see below, p.119). It is in general compatible with the picture of the Roman army "managing the supply of its own specialised requirements, an intermediate stage between importing its own supplies into newly occupied territory and the full economic integration of the frontier region".[56]

There is a good deal of evidence for procurement and dispensation of food supplies, a central feature of the papyrological documentation from Egypt.[57] Wheat is distributed to individuals and groups who might have been scattered about in the vicinity of the fort in a variety of positions and tasks (**180**). Trade on a fairly large scale in the cereal known as *braces* is attested and it is more than likely that such activities involved military officers, civilian traders and local Britons at different stages (**343**, **348**). There are also signs of the provision of beer probably brewed locally (**182**, **186**, **190**), for which the *braces* may well have been the basis, and of meat products (**182**, **191**). There can be no doubt that such staples were supplied by a combination of purchase and direct production under military supervision (**180**, **183**) and the record of revenues of the fort (**178**) is interesting. By-products such as tallow (*sebum*, **184**) could also be produced locally. More exotic items, such as pepper (**184**), indicate the vital role of imports, presumably available for purchase as additional luxury items.

---

[55] See **164**, introduction. We do not regard the writer of **344** as a locally recruited Briton, but as a civilian.

[56] Ferris and Jones (1991), 103.

[57] *RMR* 74-81, *O.Claud.*, *passim* and cf. *O.Bu Njem*. For a survey of the subject for northern England see most recently Higham (1991) and cf. Dickson (1989).

Clothing supplies are also documented, for which it is less likely that Vindolanda will have been a primary producer, although it probably possessed the facilities for refurbishment and repair. The despatch and receipt of tunics and other kinds of cloaks and garments is well-attested (**207**, **255**), and there are signs of the provision and repair of footwear in the form of the boot called *coturnus* (**184**), the purchase of 100 nails for boots *clauos caligares* (**186**), and perhaps in the activities of *sutores* in the workshops (**155**). It is possible that some tanning was done at Vindolanda but in any case the clear evidence for contact between Vindolanda and Catterick in the context of the supply of hides is very significant and underlines the role of the latter as a major manufacturing base for leather (**343**).[58]

Concern with military equipment of various kinds and with the raw materials from which they could be made is attested. Two accounts refer to the purchase of iron, although the use to which it was put is not clear (**182**, **183**). Large quantities of sinew (*neruum*, **343**) might be intended for the manufacture of catapults or *ballistae*, and it is possible that the use of the term *membra* (**198**) has something to do with such machinery. The manufacture or repair of tents might also be attested (**155**.10), to which the provision of goat-skins might be relevant (**309**), although a variety of uses could be envisaged. Metal-working facilities must have been available and the repair (and possibly manufacture) of weaponry could have taken place at Vindolanda, although it is unclear on what scale (**160**, **184**.ii.21). Finally, we should note the evidence for the despatch to Vindolanda of large quantities of vehicle components - axles, spokes, seats etc. - which were evidently made elsewhere (**309**).

It hardly needs emphasising that building was an important element in the activities of the army at all times and might be expected to bulk large in the period of consolidation in the frontier region. Groups of soldiers and building specialists are attested at Vindolanda constructing a bath-house, a hospital (*ualetudinarium*) and a guest-house or residence (*hospitium*), and there may be a reference to the construction of a bridge elsewhere (**155**, **156**, **258**). Raw materials needed to be collected or processed: lead, rubble, clay for wattle fences, lime to be burned (**155**, **156**), and attention is paid to the purchase and storage of supplies of timber (**181**, **215**). Three texts are concerned with matters relevant to the transport of stone, requiring the organisation of animals and wagons, perhaps on a large scale (**314-6**).

As a whole, the evidence from Vindolanda reinforces and illustrates in detail the summary picture of military requirements in the frontier zone, recently catalogued as: land for military installations and surveillance posts, *territoria* providing agricultural and pasture land, as well as timber and fuel, stone quarries and mines for metal-ores.[59]

The evidence for concern with transportation underlines another very important aspect of the military presence: the way in which the army affected the distances over which economic activities and transactions took place. Our most explicit evidence concerns the contact between Vindolanda and Catterick (**343**, cf. **185**), but references to London, which must have been the port of entry for the luxury goods found at Vindolanda, and to Gaul are equally suggestive (**154**, **310**, **255**). The presence of the letters themselves and the range of places mentioned is our best evidence for the high degree to which military posts on the northern frontier were integrated into the communication network, with important consequences for our view of the military and economic organisation of the region.

---

[58] *VRR* III, 1-75, Burnham and Wacher (1990), 111-7.

[59] Higham (1991), 95-6.

The list of identifiable place-names includes many of the major sites in the northern military command and gives us a good guide to the range of contact: Luguvalium (**211**, **250**), Coria (**154**, **175**), Coria Textoverdorum (?) (**312**), Bremetennacum (**295**), Eburacum (Inv.no. 575, stilus), Isurium, Vinovia, Cataractonium (**185**, **343**), Londinium (**154**, **310**), perhaps Lindum (**295**). Economic contact is explicit in the case of Cataractonium but it is surely an implicit and ubiquitous general feature of the communication network which is, perhaps incidentally, well illustrated by a record of expenses on a journey between Vindolanda and Catterick (**185**) and by the despatch of clothing, money or a gift of oysters (**346**, **312**, **299**). There are, unfortunately, also several place-names which we cannot identify, including *Ulucium* (**174**), *Cordonoui* (or *-uae* or *-uia*?) (**299**), and *Briga* (**190**, **292**). The evidence for the movement of small groups of soldiers and the carrying of letters (**252**, **263**, **300**, **295**) is sufficient testimony to the use of the military roads and the postal service. This makes explicit what is implicit in the character of the collection as a whole - the accumulation at Vindolanda (which was surely not unique, as the discoveries at Carlisle now demonstrate[60]) of a large quantity of correspondence coming from a variety of places; no source outside Britain can be identified but there is incidental evidence for contact with Gaul and with Rome (**255**, **283**).[61]

Finally, there is a small but important quantity of evidence for broader aspects of the administration of justice. The possible evidence for concern with deserters has already been noted. More formal action is attested in **344** which shows a victim of brutal treatment, perhaps at the hands of a centurion, complaining, surely to the provincial governor, after having failed to make contact with the prefect of the unit, his *beneficiarius* and perhaps the other centurions.[62] Flavius Cerialis may have received a number of petitions, brought to him by a man named Cluvius Faber (**281**). Another fragmentary text appears to concern the theft of a *balteus* and may have been dealt with internally at Vindolanda (**322**). We can hardly expect to find evidence for the formal aspects of a judiciary system as it existed in the towns of the more romanised provinces, but the provincial governor will obviously have exercised the full necessary range of judiciary powers. A very interesting but fragmentary draft of a text which uses the word *cognitionem* may be relevant here (**317**) but no further detail can be extracted.

LIST OF PERSONS

The following list includes all people attested in the tablets, military and non-military (but not all attestations of each individual, for which Index II should be consulted). It should be noted that in many cases included in the unknown category (No.10) there is uncertainty about status; many were certainly military, some may have been slaves. Likewise, the placing of individuals at Vindolanda or elsewhere is by no means always certain and often represents only a best guess. Further discussion of such details may be found in the commentaries on the texts, *ad locc.*

---

[60] Tomlin (1992).

[61] Cf. **154**.12 note.

[62] For the role of the *beneficiarius* see Rankov (1986).

A. Vindolanda	B. Elsewhere
1. Consularis	
None	Marcellus **225**
2. Legatus legionis	
None	Ferox **154**
3. Centurio regionarius	
None	Equester, Annius **250**
4. Praefecti	
Cerialis, Flavius **225-90**	Africanus, Vocusius **315**
Flavianus **172**	Brocchus, Aelius **233**, **243-8**, **291-2**
Genialis, Flavius **217-24**, **301**	Flavianus, Hostilius **261**
Priscinus **173**, **295-8**	Genialis, Flavius **256**
Veranius **319**	Iustinus **260**
Verecundus, Iulius **154**, **210-2**, **313**	Iustus, Celonius **345**
	Niger, Oppius **249**, **295**
	Niger, Valerius ? **248**, **465**
	Pastor **259**
	Rufinus ? **177**
	September, Caecilius **234**, **252-3**, **298**
5. Beneficiarius	
Lu... **180**	None
6. Centurions	
Crescens **128**, **148**	Fortunatus **351**
Cuselus ? **172**	Imber, Furius ? **258**
Equester **263**	Super, Clodius **255**
Exomnius **182**	Vocontius **316**
Felicio **138**, **166**, **168**, **182**, **193**	
Frum... **160**	
Tullio **184**	
T]utor ? **183**	
Ucen(i)us **184**	
Vern... **171**	
Voturius ? **180**	

7. Optiones

Arquittius **128**
Candidus **146**, **148**
Iustinus **129**
Verecundus **127**
Marcus ? **207**

8. Decurions

Lucius **299-300**
Atto **345**
Masculus ? **505**
Verus, Claudius **284**
Vitalis **263**

9. Other military personnel

Agi... **184**
Agilis **329**
Alio, *ueterinarius* **181**
Ammius **184**
Arcanus, *miles* **162**, **333** ?
Atrectus, *ceruesarius* **182**
Aventinus **172**
Buccus **176**
Butimas **184**
C]aledus **184**
Crispus **295**
Expeditus ? **171**
Frontinus, *eques* **300**
Furio Stiponis ? **184**
Gambax Tapponis **184**
Gannallius **169**
Huep... **184**
Ingenuus, *ueteranus* **187**
Luca (?), *uector* **183**
Lucius, *scutarius* **184**
Marcus, *medicus* **156**
Messicus **175**
Messor **184**
Rufinus **160**
Tagamatis, *uexillarius* **181**
Tagarminis **184**
Tullio Carpentari **184**
U]xperus **184**
Vitalis, *balniator* 181
...danus **166**
Adiutor, Vittius, *aquilifer* **214**
Faber, Cluvius **281**
Lib(e)rinus ? **319**
Nigrinus ?, Cessaucius, *duplicarius* **312**
Quotus ? **310**
Veldedeius, *equisio consularis* **310**
Virilis, *ueterinarius* **310**

10. Unknown

Acranius **181**
Adiutor ? **199**
Advectus **309**
Albinus **161**
Andecarus **182**
Andle... **188**
Aquilio ? **451**
Ascanius **183**
Atto **308**
Audax **186**
Brigio **188**
Caecus ? **506**
Candidus **343, 180, 181, 183**
Cogitatus **311**
Corinthus **311**
Crescens **180**
Diligens **311**
Expeditus **161**
Fadus **321**
Feni... **206**
Festus **161**
Fin..., Cessius ? **494**
Firmus **343, 180**
Fruendus ? **187**
Fuscus **161, 206** ?
Gracilis **186**
Huete... **187**
Ianuarius ? **343**
Ingenuus **181**
Ircucisso **182**
Iustus, Macrius ? **180**
Lucco **180**
Macrinus **180**
Mansue... **188**
Masuetus **187**
Ni...., ...scinius ? **325**
Paris **311**
Primus **181**
Primus Luci **180**
Rhenus ? **346**
Sabinus **182**
Saecularis, Cassius **213-6**
Sanctus **182**
Sautenus **182**
Saute... **188**
Amabilis **180**
Asper, Licinius **224**
Ato ? **320**
Atto ? **308**
Brigionus **250**
Candidus **312**
Chrauttius **310**
Conianus, Flavius **296**
Crispinus **225**
Crispinus, Grattius **225**
Dio **405**
Fatalis **343, 349**
Firminus **297**
Fontanus **325**
Frontius **343**
Gavo **192, 207, 218**
Genitor **256**
Gentilis ? **217**
Gleuco **343**
Gramaseus ? **451**
Hermes **487**
Iulius, Frontinius **343**
Karus, Claudius **250-1**
Marinus **343**
Metto **309**
Natalis **312**
Octavius **343**
Paratus ? **301**
Paternus **218**
Placidus **262**
Popa, Claudius **350**
Priscus **420**
Proculus, Flavius **219, 444** ?
Publicus ? **320**
Rubr... ? **320**
Saco **309**
Severinus **215**
Severus **349**
Similis, Flavius **235, 254, 347**
Singularis ? **275**
Sollemnis **311**
Super ? **334**
Super, Curtius **213**
Tranquillus **196**
Trophimus **341**

Sene... **188**
Settius **161**
Severus, Vettius **305**
Similis **186**
Spectatus **180**, **343**
Tertius **343**
Tetricus **181**, **346**
Valentinus ? **187**
Varia... **182**
Vattus **182**
Velox, M.Cocceius **352**
Verecundinus ? **161**
Victor, Felicius **180**
Victor **182**
Viddi... ? **187**
Vindex **260**
Tullio **312**
Valentinus **255**
Velbuteius **310**
Viriocius ? **312**
]ustus **490**

11. Women

Crispa Polionis **187**
Elpis ? **346**
Lepidina, Sulpicia **291-4**
Pacata **353**
Marcia **464**
Pacta ? **320**
Paterna ? **294**
Sattua **346**
Severa, Claudia **244**, **291-3**
Thuttena **310**
Valatta **257**
...inna (?) **324**

12. Slaves

Albiso **303**
Allatus ? **190**
Candidus **301**
Primigenius **347**
Privatus **190**
Privatus **303**
Rhenus **347**
Severus **301**

III. THE FORMAT OF THE TABLETS

In describing the discovery and excavation at Vindolanda of wooden leaf tablets with ink writing in the 1970s we suggested that such finds might be more frequent in the future.[1] It is Vindolanda itself which has fulfilled this prediction most spectacularly, as the contents of the present volume show, but tablets of this type from the Flavian period have been discovered at two other important military sites in Britain - Caerleon and Carlisle.[2]

The very large number of wooden leaf tablets found in the excavations of the 1980s and their continued preponderance compared to the number of stilus tablets confirms the view that their use must have been very widespread and that this medium was the counterpart of papyrus at least in the north-western provinces of the empire.[3] The practice of scoring and folding the leaves and the frequent presence of notches and tie-holes, which writers often avoid, shows that the tablets were manufactured in this way before the texts were written. It is interesting to note that there are two tablets with writing by the same hand which have distinctive semi-circular notches in the left margin; if these belong to the same letter it must have been written on more than one leaf, but it is perhaps more likely that they are from two different letters written on leaves from the same batch (**214**, **216**).[4] Discussion of the new evidence concerning the format of the leaf tablets can be divided as before, treating the letters and the documents and accounts separately.[5]

Letters

From the point of view of format the letters perhaps offer the more interesting evidence. In the layout which occurs most commonly the leaf is used with the broad dimension running horizontally and the writing along the grain. The broadest examples we have found are of the order of 250mm.[6] The text is normally written in two columns, the

---

[1] *Tab.Vindol.*I, p.24; cf. *VRR* II, 10.

[2] Caerleon: Tomlin (1986). Carlisle: Tomlin (1992), 146, note 30, 150-3. For leaf tablets from Lechlade see *Tab.Vindol.*I, p.35.

[3] Cf. Locher and Rottländer (1985). Much of the material in this section is also discussed by Bowman (1994b).

[4] There are similar notches in Inv.no.87.809 (no legible writing).

[5] See *Tab.Vindol.*I, pp.37-44. It should be noted that we are now cautious about the application of the term "official" to the documents, see p.73, below.

[6] We have no example of a letter written across the grain; we think that **495** is more likely to be a document than a letter (cf. *VRR* II, 28). For some scale drawings indicating the dimensions see *VRR* II, 14.

first on the left-hand side of the leaf, the second on the right, the first often having longer lines than the second and extending beyond the centre of the leaf. The leaf is scored vertically down the centre and folded, forming a diptych. This is what we previously described as the "letter format" and it bears emphasising that it is used in a great number of letters which evidently came from a variety of different places.[7] The address is normally written on the back of the right-hand half of the diptych (see below). The two-column format has parallels in Greek letters, but it is extremely rare; indeed, it is very uncommon to find a Greek letter on papyrus written in more than one column. In papyrus letters, too, it is conventional to write the address on the back but normally along the fibres at a right-angle to the writing on the front. The two-column format may well be commoner in Latin papyrus letters but so few examples survive (and those biassed towards the military context) that it is impossible to be sure.[8]

This arrangement is, however, not universal and the variations are interesting. A letter with the opening on a right-hand portion may be either very short or may be continued on another leaf (**243**). A letter may be written on two or three leaves, folded together; the first part of a letter from Claudia Severa is written in one column across the whole diptych, the remainder in two columns on two further leaves and the closing greeting is actually on the back of the middle leaf (**292**). A letter with a closure on what appears to be a left-hand half may have been written on more than one diptych (**247**). Octavius writes to Candidus on two leaves, two columns on each leaf, but the sequence runs from right to left and the easiest explanation of this is that Octavius was a left-hander (**343**); placing the first column on the right would enable him to see what he had written as he moved on to the second column at the left. Some writers conclude their text by writing at a right-angle down the left-hand margin, usually between the columns (**302**, **311**), but in one case in the margin beside the first column (**316**); others continue on the back of the leaf (**305**, **307**, **340**).

As to other features of the layout and appearance of the text, the heading is usually written on the first two lines of the left-hand column with *salutem* or *suo salutem* on line 2 and justified at the right.[9] There are, again, a few interesting exceptions. On one occasion the whole address is written in the first line (**212**); on another *salutem* seems to be more or less in the centre of line 2 (**275**); a third appears to have *suo* justified at the left and *salutem* justified at the right (**250**). Two examples have more effusive openings occupying (probably) five and three lines respectively (**214**, **310**).[10] The first line of the message proper is more

---

[7] This use of the whole leaf for letters appears to be so nearly universal that we feel justified in assuming it in the case of an individual example even when we have only one half, or part of one half of the leaf. Thus, in the introductions to the letters, a fragment is often described as belonging to the left-hand or the right-hand half of a diptych. Where the content gives no clue, the position of notches and/or tie-holes may make it clear which half of the diptych we have.

[8] Columns, *P.Oxy*. XVIII 2192, *P.Wisc*. II 84 (3 columns of which the first is almost wholly lost). Latin letters, *ChLA* V 300, X 452, 457, XI 487; but X 452 is written in three columns and the same could be true of all the others.

[9] For a comparable example on papyrus see *P.Oxy*.I 32 = *ChLA* IV 267.

[10] **214** is incomplete. Note that in **310** *-mam salutem* in line 3 is right justified as it also is in **311**.i.2.

often than not indented, with an enlarged initial letter,[11] and the subsequent lines are often further indented. Occasionally the first line of the second column begins further to the left than the subsequent lines (e.g. **215**).

Some of the letters found at Vindolanda did not come from other places. The correspondence of Flavius Cerialis includes examples written by him which we have described as drafts or file copies (**225-41**). Our conception of a draft is based on **225**, in which the name of the sender, certainly Flavius Cerialis, is omitted from the heading. Both sides of the leaf are used and there are several erasures; we think that this hand, which occurs in 8 texts (**225-32**), is that of Cerialis himself; it is just conceivable that **226** contained drafts of at least two separate letters. There is another draft with erasures which we are unable to assign to any group of letters (**317**) and another which was found in the Period 4 barracks (**344**). The latter is a draft of a petition or letter and is written on three sections of a leaf or leaves which have an account on the other side (**180**); since its beginning is missing, it must have commenced on another leaf. Our notion of a "file copy" is best exemplified by **234** which has a clear instance of the correction of a dictation error (see note to ii.2). This is a letter from Flavius Cerialis with the opening address in its full form but lacking a closure and an address on the back. Another example has a brief account written across the grain from top to bottom on the right-hand portion; this is likely to be an earlier text which was re-used for the letter (**233**). We regard the lack of an address on the back or outside of the leaf as an essential feature of both drafts and file copies and for this reason we prefer to regard one example of a letter from Cerialis which includes this element (as well as a closure) as a letter which was sent to someone elsewhere and brought back to Vindolanda by the addressee (**242**). As the dictation error in **234** suggests, the distinction between "drafts" and "file copies" is not completely clear-cut and involves an element of arbitrary judgement on our part. Furthermore, one could easily envisage a "draft" being used as a file copy after the final version had been despatched.

One of the most important features of the evidence in the letters concerns the form and content of the addresses written on the back of the leaves. As has been stated, letters were nearly always written in two columns and addresses were written on the back of the right-hand side of the leaf which normally contained the second column. We have noticed only one exception to this: **319** appears to have the address on the back of the left-hand side of the letter, though as only a fragment remains, there may be some special explanation for this.[12] In **221** the address on the back is upside down in relation to the writing on the inner faces. **343** is also anomalous: it has on the back of one of its two leaves the word *Vindol* (on which see below), but there is no sign of the name of the addressee on the remainder of the leaf.

---

[11] See Parkes (1992), 10, who discusses this feature, for which he uses the term *littera notabilior*, in inscriptions and literary papyri.

[12] In many instances we have insufficient evidence to know whether it is the left-hand or right-hand side of a tablet which is preserved. In all cases we have assumed that if there is an address on the back it is the right-hand side of the letter on the front which survives, cf. note 7, above.

As a minimum an address consisted of the name of the addressee in the dative.[13] Usually the name consists of both a *gentilicium* and a *cognomen*. The addition of a *praenomen* is most unusual and occurs only in **352**. It is almost as rare to find the *gentilicium* omitted. Except in the case of slaves or probable slaves, this omission is only found in **299**, **310** and (probably) **250**. As a further aid to identification a title or other description was often added; thus in the case of Cerialis it is usual to find him described as *praef(ecto)* or *praef(ecto) coh(ortis)*. Much more rarely is the name of the unit given as well (**242**, **248**?, **263**, **271**, **281**, **284**, **311**). Verecundus is described as *praef(ecto) coh(ortis)* in **210** and **211**. Other ranks or positions are mentioned in **299**, **310** and **312**. Cerialis' wife is addressed by her full name in **291** and **292**, with the name of her husband added. Similarly slaves are addressed by their own name plus the name of their owner (e.g. **301**). The name of the addressee is usually, but by no means always, written in elongated letters, to which we have given the name "address script" (see below, p.52). This script is not used for any further description of the addressee nor is it used for either of the other two parts of the address, which we are about to discuss.

The first of these is the name of the sender. This is found in nearly half of the tablets and may of course have occurred much more frequently and simply not have survived. It is written below the address proper, usually in the bottom left-hand part of this half of the tablet. It is frequently written diagonally upwards, starting in the corner. It begins with the preposition *a/ab* followed, usually, by the sender's *gentilicium* and *cognomen*.[14] The *gentilicium* can be omitted: for examples other than those involving slaves see **260**, **263**, **310**, **312**; Severa also omits her *gentilicium*, see **291-3**. To the name a title may be added (**215**, **255**, **258**, **263**, **284**) or the word *collega* (**210**, **260**, **341**, **345**);[15] *fratre* is found only in **310**. Slaves give their owner's name plus *seruo* (**301**, **347**). In **292** Severa may add her husband's name, and other tablets probably record the unit in which the sender was serving (**281**, **299**, **319**).

Very occasionally there is one further element in addresses, the occurrence of a place-name. This happens only four or five times in the tablets published in this volume: **310** has *Londini*; **312**, *Coris* with some further description (see note *ad loc.*); **338** and **343**, *Vindol* (i.e. an abbreviated form); **271** may also have a place-name on the back. This has given rise to some controversy, since we should naturally expect an address to state the place to which a letter is being sent, but the case in which the place-names occur is locative.[16]

Before attempting to resolve this problem we must look at the other evidence from Vindolanda. One other wooden leaf-tablet (Inv.no.1022) has on the back *Vindolande* (= the

---

[13] For a general discussion of the formulae of addresses used in Latin letters see Cugusi (1983), 64-7. For illustrations of comparable examples on papyrus see *P.Dura*, Plate XXXIII.1-6, *P.Oxy*.I 32 = *ChLA* IV 267, a Latin letter to a tribune from a *beneficiarius*. On the texts from Vindolanda cf. also R.E.Birley (1990), 10-11.

[14] Only a handful of the addresses in *CEL* give the name of the sender, though there is at least one example from each of the three major areas, Vindonissa, Egypt (note particularly *CEL* 169 = *P.Oxy*.I 32 = *ChLA* IV 267) and Dura; see further Cugusi (1983), 66-7 and his comments on *CEL* 16 verso.

[15] *collega* is also used in *CEL* 177 = *P.Hib.* II 276, from Egypt.

[16] This is unequivocal in the case of *Londini* (**310**), which was the first text with a place-name to be published (Bowman, Thomas and Adams, 1990); in fact, as we shall see, all examples are to be understood as locatives.

locative form *Vindolandae*),[17] and addresses are legible on at least five of the stilus tablets: Inv.no.689, which also reads *Vindolande*; Inv.no.722, *Coris*; Inv.no.851, *Vinouis*; Inv.no.836, *Cataractonio* and Inv.no.575, *Eburaci*.[18] In every case the place-name comes first, at the head of the address, before the name of the recipient; in two cases (**343** and Inv.no.1022) it is written diagonally across the top left-hand corner. Further examples from other sources are to be found in *CEL*. We are quite certain that in every case the place-name is locative.[19]

This evidence would seem to compound the problem. It obviously makes sense for letters found at Vindolanda to have the name Vindolanda as part of their address (as happens in four of the ten examples cited); but it is not obvious why the case should be locative rather than accusative. If the places are to be explained as those from which the letters were being sent, we can understand why letters found at Vindolanda bear the place-names *Londini*, *Eburaci*, etc.; but, apart from the objection that an address should state where a letter is going to rather than the place from which it has come, such an explanation will not do for the four letters with Vindolanda on the back. One then has to fall back on the implausible notion that such letters were drafts or copies which were never sent.[20]

The solution to our problem, we believe, is supplied by evidence from outside Vindolanda. Firstly, in a number of tablets from Vindonissa the address begins with the word *dabis*;[21] this is true also of a stilus tablet from Carlisle and may occur in one of the stilus tablets from Vindolanda.[22] This suggests the possibility that such a word is to be understood with all addresses, which therefore mean something like "Deliver to NN".[23] It then becomes easy to understand that, where a place-name was added, the sense would be "Deliver to NN at [place]", thus accounting for the locative. Against this it may be argued that the word order is wrong - that the place-name ought in that case to follow the name of the recipient. Here we may call upon the evidence of another Carlisle stilus tablet addressed to a certain Tertius, where, *after* the name of the recipient, we read *Lugualio* [sic].[24] If that does not seem conclusive, we believe the evidence of yet another Carlisle stilus tablet puts the matter

---

17 *VRR* II, 61 and Plate XV.

18 For the last two see fig.6 in *VRR* II, 26. On the readings see Appendix, pp.364-5.

19 Notwithstanding Cugusi's contrary view (e.g. in his notes on *CEL* 14.1 and 87 verso).

20 *VRR* II, 61.

21 The Vindonissa tablets are now most conveniently accessible as *CEL* 16-71. On tablets where the address begins *dabis* (often *dabes* at Vindonissa), see *CEL* II, p.41. We do not think it likely that **445** has an address in this form.

22 *Britannia* 19 (1988) 498 no.33 and fig.8 = *RIB* II 2443.3. *Tab.Vindol.*I 107.

23 Future for imperative. Note that the imperative *da* is used in one tablet from Vindonissa (*CEL* 38); *CEL* 142.68 (= *P.Mich.*VIII 468) is alleged to read *tr]ạḍ[e*, and *CEL* 243 (= P.Oxy.XVIII 2193), from a later period, reads *redde*.

24 *Britannia* 19 (1988), 496 no.32 and fig.7 = *RIB* II 2443.4; the drawing suggests the possibility that the preceding word may be abbreviated (*bra..car*) and that we actually have *Luguualio*. We wonder whether the first word in *Britannia* 19 (1988), 498 no.34 = *RIB* II 2443.6, transcribed by Tomlin as *ḳimio*, is also a place-name. For the position of the place-name after the name of the recipient cf. also **311**.back 1 note.

beyond all reasonable doubt. The address on this tablet reads (before the name of the addressee) *Trimontio ạut Luguạ[l]io* [sic].[25] This is a conclusive piece of evidence since it clearly cannot refer to the place of writing and *must* refer to the places *to* one of which the letter was to be delivered (i.e. the sender was uncertain whether the addressee was at Trimontium or Luguvalium). Theoretically one could argue that the function of these place-names was not always the same, sometimes indicating the place where the letter came from and on other occasions the place to which it was being sent;[26] this in our opinion is a counsel of despair.[27] We must surely try and find a solution which accommodates all examples of the occurrence of these place-names and such a solution we believe we have now given. It may be added that this solution is also consonant with the evidence of the addresses in Greek letters on papyrus. There are several examples which contain instructions for delivery, with and without the imperative ἀπόδος; in several of these the personal name (dative) is preceded by εἰς plus place-name (accusative).[28]

This leaves only the oddity that six of the ten examples of letters found at Vindolanda quoted above record a place other than Vindolanda, and the need to explain why letters written for delivery at York, London, etc. should have ended up at Vindolanda. The explanation must simply be that they were received by their addressees at York, London or wherever and that subsequently the recipients came to Vindolanda bringing their correspondence with them. In view of the fragmentation of units and the movement of personnel attested in the Vindolanda tablets and elsewhere this is not difficult to believe.

It is important to emphasise the value and importance of the evidence for the physical characteristics and appearance of the Latin letter. The papyri from the Roman east supply little such evidence and the literary letters of Cicero, Pliny and Fronto give us none. Although there is a good deal of ancient evidence for the principles and practice of epistolography,[29] there is no ancient text which describes the characteristics of the layout of a letter. An important development may have been initiated by Julius Caesar who sent letters to the senate *quas primum uidetur ad paginas et formam memorialis libelli conuertisse, cum antea consules et duces non nisi transuersa charta scriptas mitterent* ("which he seems to have been the first to change to the form of a paginated notebook whereas previously consuls and generals had only sent despatches written with the roll rotated through 90 degrees").[30] The relationship between these features of layout in our Vindolanda letters and the layout of a "literary" letter is of major interest but must be left open. What is important,

---

[25] *Britannia* 19 (1988), 496 no.31 and fig.6 = *RIB* II 2443.10. This is Tomlin's reading; here *Lugu[u]/ạlio* is perhaps possible.

[26] Cf. R.E.Birley (1990), 10-11 and *VRR* II, 19-20.

[27] Nevertheless, this seems to be the view taken by Cugusi; see his comments referred to in note 19 above, and his note to *CEL* 37 (cf. also his note to *CEL* 87). This text reads *dabis Vịndoinsa[* where, despite Cugusi, we must surely adopt Marichal's reading *Vindoinsa[e]*, i.e. the letter was to be delivered *at* Vindonissa (a meaning which Cugusi also accepts). Cf. *CEL* 35, which reads *dabis Atico Luciano qui est in Girece Vindoinsa.*

[28] E.g. *BGU* IV 1079 (= *SP* I 107), *SP* I 111, *BGU* II 423 (= *SP* I 112); it is perhaps particularly relevant that the last item is a letter from a sailor in the fleet at Misenum.

[29] See Cugusi (1983), 43-145.

[30] Suetonius, *Iul.* 56.6, cf. Turner (1978), 32.

as with documents, is the relative uniformity of convention; correspondents knew what to expect to see and this is a vital part of the development of a "grammar of legibility".[31]

Documents and accounts

Since we now have a greater range of types of document it is perhaps not surprising that we also have a much larger number of ways in which the leaves were used. The folded diptych, which is so common in the letter format, is employed. In the most notable example (**154**) it is used *transversa charta* but it should be noted that this diptych is very much larger than any other example. Another example, also a large tablet (**161**), exhibits the familiar notches and tie-holes. **164**, which may be a memorandum of a military nature, is also written across the grain and it is to be noted that the text is in narrative form unlike other texts written across the grain. Reports detailing the activities of groups of soldiers are written along the grain possibly only on half-leaves (**155-7**) and this is also consistently the format of the reports with the *renuntium*-heading (**127-53**) as well as the applications for leave (**166-77**).

The accounts which were found in the 1970s led us to expect that texts of this form were likely to be written in narrow columns *transversa charta* and there are indeed several more examples (e.g. **181**, **185**, **194**, **196**). Although there is no clear example of another concertina-form notebook like **190**,[32] **180** may be a triptych which has been folded concertina fashion; this contains an account written *transversa charta* on one side and a letter or petition written along the grain on the backs of two of the three sections. There are several examples of short accounts written along the grain, perhaps on half-leaves (e.g. **178**, **193**). More interesting are two unusual examples written along the grain, one with an account in two columns like a letter (**182**), the other in three columns of which the middle one straddles the central fold (**184**); on both these accounts the text appears to continue on the back of the leaf. It is clear that there was no standard format to which the writers of these reports and accounts (which we assume were all produced at Vindolanda) were confined, but there is what might be described as a broad commonality of convention in the use of the wooden leaves.

Stilus tablets

Although we are here excluding the Vindolanda stilus tablets (of which there are over 100 from the 1980s) from detailed consideration, it is appropriate to mention a recent survey containing material which has appeared since 1983 and to list a few recent items of particular interest.[33]

---

[31] The phrase is taken from Parkes (1991), 2. The question of layout is considered by Bischoff (1990), 27-30 but only with reference to books. The very small amount of literary evidence is cited by Cugusi (1983), 30. Since there is virtually no literary evidence for the appearance of letters, examples written on tablets and papyri are of the utmost importance. On the whole topic see further Bowman (1994b).

[32] On this see Tjäder (1986), 301.

[33] Vindolanda, *VRR* II, 12-5. *Tab.Vindol.*I, pp.34-5. British examples collected in *RIB* II 2443. Survey: Marichal in Lalou (ed. 1992), discussing the format of multi-leaved sets of tablets; cf. also Pintaudi and Sijpesteijn (1989), Caruana (1992). Stilus tablets from Carlisle: *Britannia* 22 (1991), 299-300, nos.24-5, cf. *Britannia* 23 (1992), 323; Tomlin (1992), 146-50; Caruana (1992), 68-70. Egypt: a stilus tablet with an ink text, Devijver, Harrauer and Worp (1984/5). Vindonissa: M.A.Speidel (1987), (1991), (1992), and cf. Tomlin (1992), 148 note 33, no.2.

IV. PALAEOGRAPHY

In *Tab. Vindol.*I we devoted a chapter of the introduction (pp. 51-71) to a detailed discussion of various aspects of the palaeography of the tablets there published. Our main purpose was to indicate all features of palaeographical interest (especially in the letter-forms). In addition we attempted to relate the new information which the tablets provided to the known palaeographical background, in particular to the vexed question of the development of Old Roman Cursive (ORC) into New Roman Cursive (NRC).[1] We do not propose to consider this problem further here, other than to refer to Tjäder (1979). In this important article Tjäder suggests that Roman script had developed by at any rate the first century AD two different variants, an official script (the one used in military documents) and a private script. He believes that the official script did not lead to any further developments, and that it is to the private script that we must look for those features which were to be significant for the change to NRC in the third century. He further suggests that alongside these two scripts there also existed a "popular" script, written by semi-literates, which influenced the private script and so contributed to the development of NRC.[2]

Since *Tab. Vindol.*I was published a new handbook of Latin palaeography has appeared with a brief discussion of Latin handwriting in the classical period.[3] There have been sporadic publications of individual Latin papyri and ostraca from Egypt written in ORC,[4] as well as an edition of fragments of papyri and ostraca in Latin recovered at Masada, which are close in date to our tablets.[5]

Special mention should be made of two publications of extensive collections of

---

[1] Various labels have been used for the script we call ORC: Capital Cursive, Ancient Roman Cursive, etc. Mallon (1952) preferred the expression "l'écriture commune classique"; Cencetti (1950) and Tjäder (1979) similarly prefer to speak of "scrittura usuale". Since many examples of ORC (in our tablets and elsewhere) show few cursive features, there is a certain logic in this. However, we have decided to retain the terminology we used previously. In any case there is no doubt as to the *type* of script to which all these studies refer.

[2] In part this hypothesis was already put forward by Cencetti (1950); Tjäder develops it further, especially by introducing the concept of a "popular" script, an idea he derives from studies by Petrucci (cf. *Tab. Vindol.*I, pp.58-9). He repeats his views in a more summary fashion in Tjäder (1986), his important review of *Tab. Vindol.*I. Here he argues that the most important letters are *a*, *b*, *d*, *n*, *p*, *q* and *u*, "of which *a*, *b*, *n* and to some extent *p* are particularly crucial" (p.299). The letters he considers important should be compared with those analysed in Casamassima and Starez (1977). For a description of their views see *Tab. Vindol.*I, p.57, and Tjäder (1977), 139-41.

[3] Bischoff (1986), 76-89 = Bischoff (1990), 54-63.

[4] E.g. a few ostraca in Latin are to be found in *O. Claud.*

[5] *Doc. Masada* 721-38, 750-71. On the palaeography see Thomas, ibid. 27-31.

material written, mostly or entirely, in ORC and which are not from places in the eastern half of the Empire: the ostraca from Bu Njem and the curse tablets from Bath. In both cases the editors have accompanied their editions with very detailed discussions of the palaeography, especially the letter-forms.[6] Unfortunately neither of these collections offers close parallels for the Vindolanda material. It is obvious that the writers of the curse tablets (which in any case are somewhat later in date than our tablets) will have used a different technique for inscribing lead from that used for writing on wood (even though they demonstrably were attempting to use the same basic letter-forms). Writers in ink on ostraca will no doubt have used much the same technique as the writers of our tablets, but the Bu Njem collection dates from the middle of the third century, by which time ORC was noticeably different from its various forms around AD 100. Also worth mentioning is the edition of painted inscriptions found in SE Spain, since these inscriptions are mostly in ORC and here also the editors give a thorough discussion of the palaeography of their material.[7] Again, however, the technique used must have differed somewhat from that used for writing with a pen on wood.[8]

Capital script

The best example of this in the tablets is the line of Virgil (**118**; Plate I). The letter-forms resemble those in the script usually known as Capitalis Rustica.[9] This is especially true of *A*, with the elaborate thick stroke at the foot of the left-hand diagonal. Note also the forms of *R*, *V* and *D*. *P* is not in the usual capital form, though such a form, which is much closer to that of ORC and lacks the bow, is sometimes found in capital scripts of this period. For the very remarkable form of *E* see the introduction to this tablet.

Capital letter-forms are to be seen in the few letters preserved in **119**, in **121** (here mixed with cursive forms), in **162** and **163**, certainly military documents of some kind, in the consular date of **186** and, much the most surprisingly, in the lines in the margin of **206**. This text appears to be a normal account and yet has these two lines in capital script added. It was of course common for military documents to be written in a mixture of capital and cursive scripts (a recently published example is *Doc.Masada* 722), the capital script being used for the most part in headings. We need not therefore be surprised that capital script is used for the date in **186**. But these instances are in no way a reasonable parallel for **206**.

The above documents are all more or less bilinear and, apart from **118**, the individual letter forms need little comment. Note the long tail to *Q* in **119**, the rather crude forms in **186** (where *R* is close to the cursive form), the tiny *O* in **163**, and the use of serifs here and in **162**; this last document shows forms approaching those of Capitalis Rustica. The form of *S* in **206** is remarkable: it is little more than a straight diagonal stroke.

---

[6] Ostraca from Bu Njem: *O.Bu Njem*, pp.16-45; Bath curse tablets: *Tab.Sulis*, pp.84-94.

[7] See Stylow and Mayer Olivé (1987).

[8] There is some similarity with painted inscriptions from Pompeii; cf. also those painted on wine jars found at Masada, *Doc.Masada*, pp.133-77.

[9] For the normal letter forms see Bischoff (1986), fig.1 on p.79 = Bischoff (1990), 56, where there is a brief discussion of the script (for which Bischoff prefers the term Capitalis).

Cursive script

We have not attempted to classify the various types of ORC which appear in the tablets in the way that others have done.[10] We would, however, emphasise the great variety of scripts occurring. The military documents are on the whole written in rather similar versions of ORC, competent hands of what may be called a normal type. This is only what we should expect. But even here there are surprises, notably the remarkably elegant **152**.[11] The letters, again as would be expected, show a much greater variety of scripts. Some are remarkably elegant, whereas others are much cruder (contrast, for example, the elegance of **291** with the clumsiness of **310**). One notable feature is the way some scripts give an impression of bilinearity (e.g. **302**), whereas many others, though using what are essentially the same letter-forms, have exaggerated ascenders and descenders (e.g. **233**, **248**, **265**). Most are written in an upright fashion, but others slope to the right (e.g. **213** and **215**). Some writers seem to eschew ligatures altogether; most use ligature very occasionally, but in a few texts it is common (e.g. **213**, **225**, **313**, **343**). Often the scripts which are palaeographically the most interesting, since the most idiosyncratic, are those in which the sender of a letter has appended the final greeting in his or her own hand; or those which are mere drafts of which a professional scribe would no doubt later have produced a fair version.

The palaeographical information provided by the new tablets has not caused us to modify our view that the evidence from Vindolanda strongly suggests that Latin writing throughout the empire in about AD 100 was all much the same; indeed the new information merely serves to strengthen our previous impression.

In our earlier publication we examined in detail the handwriting found in those tablets written in ORC (the vast majority), considering in particular all the various letter-forms and the use of ligatures. We have not felt it necessary to repeat here all that was said before. The comments which follow are to be understood as complementary to those made in *Tab. Vindol.*I, superseding them and adding to them where the new material gives significant new information or causes us to modify our earlier views.

The letter-forms[12]

a The vast majority of occurrences are in the form shown in col.1; the left-hand diagonal is not infrequently extended well below the line and may end in a curve. The form illustrated in col.2 occurs in several tablets, usually together with that in col.1 (e.g. **181**, **218**, **224**, **252**, **344**, **345**), and may reasonably be considered a survival of an older form. The extra stroke may be just a curve on the end of the right-hand diagonal (e.g. **321**; see also address script, below) or may be quite long (e.g. **324** and especially **186**); in one or two instances, notably **169**, **312**.back, **325**, **330**, cf. **139**, **181**.7 and **258**, it is written across the angles between the diagonals, so that the letter superficially resembles a capital. We have found no

---

[10] Notably Marichal; in *ChLA* VI-IX where he re-edits all the papyri from Dura, he classifies the scripts used in them into four broad categories (see IX, pp.15-8). See also his classification of the scripts in the Bu Njem ostraca, *loc.cit.* in note 6. On Tjäder's classification of ORC scripts into "private" and "official" see his article cited above.

[11] We already drew attention to the script of this tablet in *Tab. Vindol.*I, p.53 (cf. Tjäder (1986), 298, who describes it as "clearly a book hand"). It is astonishing that it should now turn out to be no more than a routine military report.

[12] References in what follows are to fig.1 on p.53. In addition, for the letter-forms used in ORC and NRC, see Bischoff (1986), 88, fig.5 = Bischoff (1990), 64; cf. *Tab. Vindol.*I, p.54, fig.10.

further instances of the very interesting form of the letter found in **341** (see fig.11.3 in *Tab. Vindol.*I, p.58) and already commented on in *Tab. Vindol.*I, pp.61-2, nor even of the form found in **225**.22, *amicis*, which is on the way towards this 'uncial' type of *a*.[13] For ligature with *l* and *u* see below.

b All examples in our tablets are of the standard ORC type. There is a squat variety and one with a very tall ascender, but none shows the loop or bow at the right of the hasta as was to become the norm in NRC. The loop may in fact be written under the hasta (e.g. **158** and **310**) so as to give an impression of an NRC *b* but the letter is still formed in the normal ORC manner.[14]

c The form which resembles a modern c is shown in col.1 and the more usual form, in two strokes, in col.2. In this form the top stroke may be extended considerably.

d Of the two forms that in col.1 may reasonably be considered the older, since that in col.2 is very like the one which was to be used in NRC. Both occur regularly throughout the tablets with perhaps a tendency for the form in col.1 to predominate in the documents and that in col.2 to be more common in the letters. It is noteworthy that a few tablets show the same writer using both forms, e.g. **255** and **294**; also **218**, where the letter is always made in a single movement (as is sometimes the case elsewhere for *d* in the form shown in col.1). The form in col.2 naturally easily ligatures to the right.

e The form in col.1, normally made in three strokes but occasionally in four (e.g. **152**), is obviously very close to the capital; the top stroke is often extended. The form in col.2, in two strokes, is much the most common. Only rarely, if at all, do we find the very cursive single-stroke version shown in col.3 in the body of a letter (possibilities are **266**.1, **323**.1 and **328**.1). However, it is not at all uncommon in closing greetings, see **247**, **285**, **295**, **301**, **310**; note also the draft letters **225**, **227** and **317**, and the names of the senders on the backs of **263** and **298**. In *Tab. Vindol.*I we referred to a form in two halves (p.63), which we considered distinctive for the development of this letter into its NRC version. We are no longer confident that this form of *e* occurs in any of our tablets.[15]

f There is a very remarkable form in **180** and **344** (the work of the same writer) in which the top stroke is entirely missing. A similar form seems to occur in **186**.19 and 22.

g The same writer uses a rather odd form of *g* in two curves, rather like some forms of *s* (**180** and **181**). The tail of the letter can differ in different scripts; it is often somewhat prolonged, e.g. **178** and **343**, cf. **307**.a.2.

h The form shown in col.1, which is obviously close to the capital form, occurs several

[13] This type of *a* is found at Bu Njem, *O Bu Njem*, p.22.

[14] Note also **348**, where the loop appears to come at the *right* of the hasta (though again the basic form of the letter is not altered). On the occurrence of *b* in the NRC form as early as the first century AD see Petrucci, cited in *Tab. Vindol.*I, p.51, note 3.

[15] See further the introduction to **263** and ii.1 note.

times (e.g. in **143**, **260**.back, **299**, cf. **218**), but less frequently than that shown in col.2. This latter form often has the horizontal stroke extended, sometimes but not always in order to facilitate ligature. This second stroke may be ligatured to the first stroke, in which case it starts at the foot of the upright (e.g. **168**, **196**.15, **236**, **245**.back, **347**.a.1).

i The short form (col.1) frequently has a noticeable serif at top right, so that the letter can readily be confused with *p* or even *t*. The long form is commonest at word ends (often here in the ligature *bi*) and at the beginning of words, but is by no means confined to these usages. The form of the letter bears no apparent relationship to the length of the vowel.

l Both the forms illustrated occur frequently (the former usually with serifs) and some writers use either form indifferently (e.g. **297** and **316**). The form in col.2 can be quite tall and can also descend well below the line, often in a diagonal direction.[16] *l* is frequently found in ligature with a following *a*, in which case it is often written above the level of the other letters (see **192**.4, **299**.i.1, **315**.2, etc).

m The basic form, as illustrated in col.1, can in fact be made in two, three or four strokes, of which the last is sometimes horizontal. The form in col.2 is perhaps made rather differently and this may be significant for the later development of the NRC form. It is rare in the tablets and usually confined to ligatures in closing greetings (see **247**, **248**, **258**, **288**).

n The forms illustrated in col.1 and col.2 occur with equal frequency throughout and very often in the same tablet (e.g. **164** and **292**). In both varieties the stroke joining the two uprights may project a long way to the left. The form in col.3, which is probably made differently from that in col.2, is rare and, like the form of *m* in col.2, is usually found only in closing greetings; see **247**, **248**, **258**, **288**.[17]

o Nearly always made in two halves, as illustrated. The second stroke can curve the "wrong" way, when the letter can resemble *c*, see, e.g., **233**, **310**.i.11, **312**; it can also resemble one form of *d*, cf. especially **302**.3. In this version it often ligatures with a following letter, especially with *r*.

p The form in col.2 is only found rarely, notably in **151**, **324**, **258** (second hand) and **262** (where the normal form also occurs).[18] A form which approaches this is to be seen in **186**.9 and in the name of the sender in **341**.

q The form in col.1 is no doubt the older form, but it is our impression that it occurs in our tablets more or less as frequently as the form in col.2, though there is probably a tendency

---

[16] Our remark in *Tab.Vindol.*I, p.64 that there was no good example of this feature, no longer holds true; see, e.g., **261** and **265**.

[17] This form may well be significant for the development of the letter into its NRC form as Tjäder (1979), 53-6 and (1986), 299 argues (in the former article, but not the latter, he couples it with the form of *m* illustrated in col.2). He regards it as the private form, which is supported by its occurrence in closing greetings in our tablets.

[18] Tjäder (1979), 51-2 and (1986), 299 regards this as an example of the "popular" form; it is noteworthy therefore that in our tablets it is found in one of the military documents (**151**).

for the documents to use the form in col.1 and for the letters to use that in col.2.[19] It may be significant that (unlike *d*) we can quote no clear instance of the same writer using both forms, though this may occur in **255** (contrast ii.11 with *q* elsewhere) and **300**.i.4 and ii.8.

r There is no apparent basic difference in any of the occurrences of this letter in our tablets, although the top stroke in one or two writers is so curved as to illustrate clearly the derivation of the cursive from from the capital (see **138**, **186**, **204**.b.1, **215**.5, **324**). The descender can be prolonged to a considerable extent and usually curves at the foot.

s Again there is, we think, only one basic form in our tablets, though this can be made in one or, much more often, in two strokes; the single stroke version can be almost a straight diagonal line (cf. the remarks above on the capital script in **206**). On the *us* ligature see below.

t Note the ligature with following *i* in **180**.5 and 11, where an extra link stroke is used.

u The forms illustrated in col.1, col.2 and col.3 are all common and sometimes occur alongside one another in the same tablet (e.g. **184**, **213**, **310**, **316**). The form in col.3 is no doubt basically the same as that in col.2, but that in col.1 may be different.[20] The form in col.3 is occasionally flattened out into an almost straight line when used in ligatures (*ua*, *um*, *ur*), e.g. **245**, **255**.4, **294**.3, **315**. In ligatures with following letters, especially *a* and *s*, *u* can lose its right-hand half, e.g. *oua* **193**.5, *tuam* **274**, several occurrences in *uale* written by a second hand, and once with *ualere* used in the body of a letter, **311**.i.3; for *us* cf. **248**.3 and **291**.9, and for *ur* **291**.7.[21]

Address script

It was usual, though not universal, to write the name of the addressee on the back of a letter in very tall, elongated, spindly writing; see the examples illustrated in Plates XV, XX and XXV. This type of script is paralleled in letters from Egypt and from Dura-Europos.[22]

This is not a capital script.[23] Of the letters which differ most in capital and cursive scripts, *b* and *q* do not occur in our addresses, but *r* is common and is clearly in the cursive form, as is *d*. The same is true, though less noticeably, of the other letters. It is, however, interesting that the writing gives the impression of being similar in most (though not all) of

---

[19] To some extent therefore the tablets may support Tjäder (1986), 300, where he suggests that the form in col.1 is the official form and that in col.2 the private form ["As a counterpart to *d* the *g* will be of interest" is a misprint for "As a counterpart to *d* the *q* will be of interest"].

[20] Tjäder (1986), 299 regards the form in col.1 as the private form. Again there is probably a tendency for writers of the documents to prefer the form in col.3 and for the form in col.1 to be commoner in the letters. However, a more striking tendency, we think, is for the more elegant writers to avoid the form in col.1.

[21] In *Tab. Vindol.*I, p.67 we commented that the ligature *us* was likely to have been derived from the way these letters are often written as a conjoint letter in inscriptions. Tjäder (1986), 300 rightly points out that it is at least as likely that the influence was the other way.

[22] See the papyri cited on p.42, note 13.

[23] Cf. *ChLA* IX, p.16.

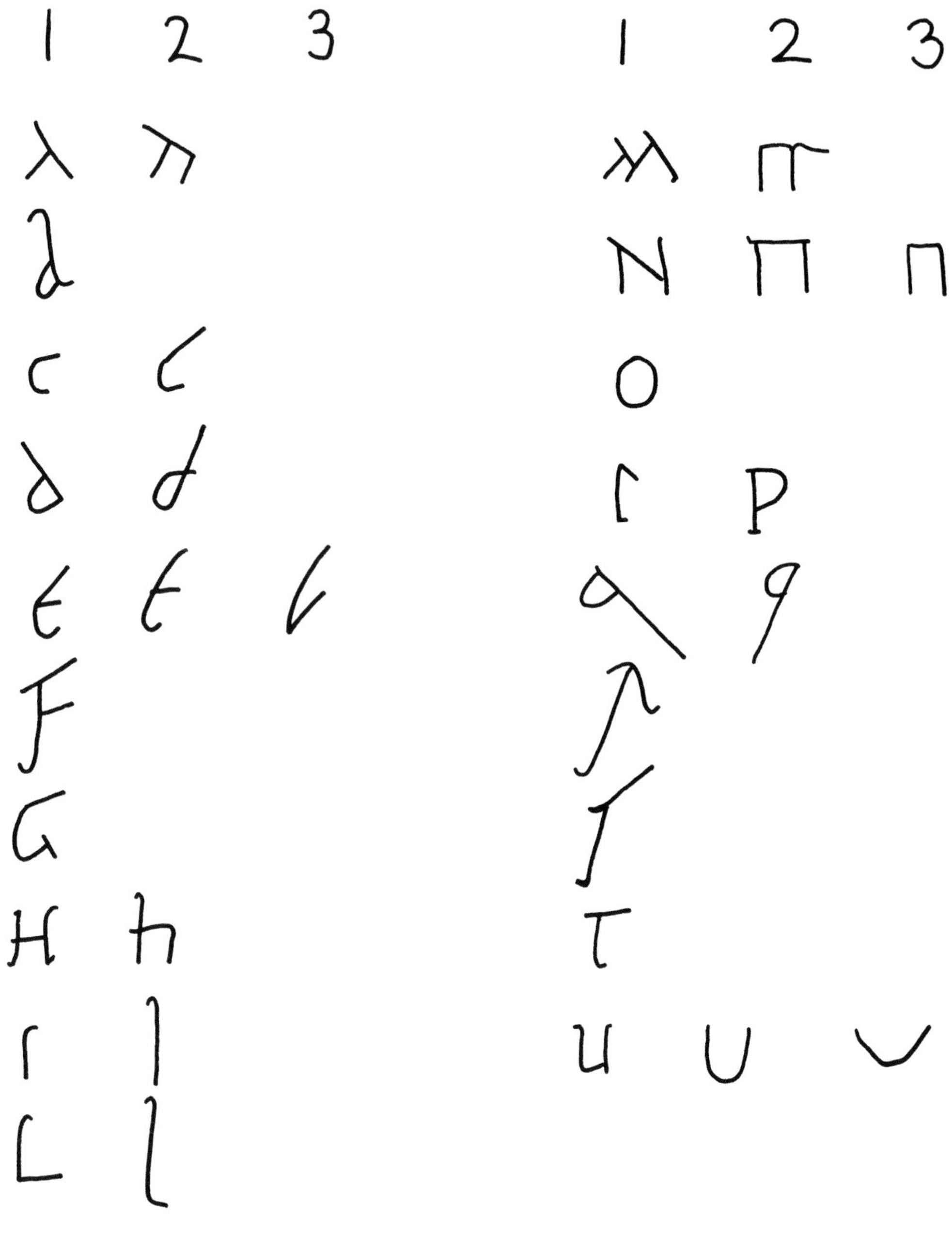

Fig.1 TABLE OF LETTER-FORMS

the examples preserved (e.g. in the hooks at the top of both strokes of *u* and at the top and bottom of *i*), even when the script used on the other sides is dissimilar. Attention may be drawn to *a* which often has a curve at the foot of the right-hand stroke (cf. the form illustrated in col.2 of fig.1).

Abbreviations and symbols[24]

On the whole abbreviation is not frequent in the tablets. When it does occur it is often not marked at all (a practice which is well attested from Latin papyri); thus virtually all occurrences of *coh* and *praef* have no mark to indicate the abbreviation, and there is hardly ever an indication of abbreviation in dates. When it *is* marked this is nearly always done either by a medial point following (i.e. a dot identical to that used for interpunct) or by a superscript bar, e.g. over *n* for *noster* or *numerus*. Special mention may be made of the abbreviation of the *gentilicium* Claudia written as *Cl* followed by a medial point (**291**),[25] the possible abbreviation *p(er)* in **118**, and the probable abbreviation of *qui* in the official reports (**127-53**), which is unmarked except in **139** and possibly **145**. These instances are all referred to further in the notes to the individual texts. Note also the abbreviation of *Bat(auorum)* on the back of **284** (cf. **242**), marked by raising the *t*. *s* = *semis* is, strictly speaking, an abbreviation, but is discussed below, with symbols.

Symbols for only two monetary denominations appear in the tablets, the *denarius* and the *as*. The *denarius*-symbol is in the standard form which is virtually universal, a large X with a horizontal bar through the centre; there are, however, several texts in which the horizontal stroke does not transect the X but appears as a tick at the centre left.[26] The *as*-symbol is a longish vertical which slants to the right and has a short, more or less horizontal tick placed centrally at the left.[27] This probably occurs five times in **186**. In **301**.i.4 we have a similar symbol but with a top-stroke which makes it look more like *s* with a tick at the left; the context strongly suggests, however, that it must be the *as*-symbol.

As for the fractions of the *denarius*, the large *s* = *s(emis)* appears frequently; it may also be used of the *as* (see below) and can be used of the *modius* too (e.g. **190**). There is one symbol which we have not been able to parallel and which occurs fairly frequently in a position which makes it certain that it must be a fraction of the *denarius*, presumably a quarter in view of the fact that the largest number of *asses* appearing in such contexts is three (**185** passim, **187**.i.10, **193**.5, **202**.a.2, **206**.3); this looks like a shallow reversed *c* or a longish *i* curling to the left with a short superscript bar. It is perhaps not so very surprising that this has not hitherto occurred in Latin cursive since almost all the texts in which such symbols occur are in papyri from Egypt which employ an idiosyncratic method of calculating in *denarii* and obols.[28] In **184**.i.15 we might have a different *quadrans* symbol, which looks

---

[24] For a full list of abbreviations see Index V.

[25] Contrast the ostraca from Bu Njem, where it is normal to abbreviate the more common *gentilicia* (*O.Bu Njem*, p.39).

[26] Consistently in **182** and **493**, also in **179** and **343**.ii.22. Manzella (1987), 157, note 394 quotes examples of the symbol without the bar.

[27] Something close to this is recognised by Cagnat (1914), 34, cf. also Castrén and Lilius (1970), 157-9, 164, 168, 174. A cursive *a* is used as an abbreviation in *P.Oxy*.IV 737 and elsewhere.

[28] E.g. *RMR* 68-73.

like a *c* with an extended top-stroke.[29] The symbol in **193**.4 following the reversed *c* with bar which we think represents a quarter-*denarius*, looks like a long *i*; the context is abraded and difficult and we do not know what it represents - perhaps a quarter-*as*.

Accounts which reckon in *denarii* and *asses* use the *denarius* symbol and denote the number of *asses* with short, horizontal ticks to a maximum of three. This is best illustrated in **182**. We assume that allowance must be made for the style of individual hands and think that it is legitimate to see the short horizontal with two curly ticks below it in **184**.ii.20 as a variation of the symbol for 3 *asses*. There are also several instances in which one tick, which can point up or down or curl, follows *s* = *s(emis)* (e.g. **179**, **184**.i.17), sometimes virtually joined; we interpret this as half a *denarius* and one *as* rather than an idiosyncratic form of *s*.[30] **186** is the only account which reckons in *asses* alone and it seems to represent the numerals 1 and 2 by ticks and those over 3 by digits.

We may also have symbols for fractions of the *as* but these naturally do not conform to the fractional weights which are normally identified.[31] These symbols can be seen most clearly in **182**. In line i.2, after the horizontal tick denoting one *as*, we might have a small *s* followed by a sickle- or 7-shaped sign; these are perhaps most naturally to be identified as a half and a quarter of an *as* respectively; the small *s* and the sickle-shaped sign might also occur in i.9 and the latter in line 5 on the back.

As for the measures, the only symbol which needs to be noted here is the large *s* = *sextarius*, which is very common. There is a notable variant in **193**.3 and 4 where it has a horizontal stroke through the vertical; this is attested in inscriptions,[32] but a particular reason for its appearance here may be that the writer wanted to differentiate it from *s* = *s(emis)* which follows it in both cases.

Finally, we should note the centurial symbol which is used for *centurio* and *centuria*, as elsewhere. Allowing for individual variations, this is recognisable in its common form which can look like a sickle or a figure 7 or a reversed *C*.[33] We have noted two interesting variants: in **138**.2 it is written like a figure 7 with a dot in the angle formed by the strokes;[34] in **182**.ii.13 it is more like a reversed *C* with a long tail and it has a horizontal tick in the middle at the left.

Numerals

Numerals are often marked out by the addition of a superscript bar, sometimes with

---

[29] Cf. *ChLA* V 304.a.28. See also *RMR* 73.i.17 (= *ChLA* III 208), with Fink's note *ad loc.*, Marichal (1988), 47.

[30] Cf. *CIL* III^2, p.953 no.XV, pag. posterior, line 25.

[31] Cagnat (1914), 33, Manzella (1987), 158 and fig. 202, Marichal (1988), 47. Cagnat lists the notations for the fractions of the *as*. We note the remark of Fink, *RMR* 556: "it is obvious that, aside from standard abbreviations ..., most of the following [*sc.* abbreviations and conventional symbols] were devised by the clerk on the spur of the moment to suit his own convenience"; this is perhaps an overstatement of the degree of anarchy but there seems to us to be some truth in it.

[32] See Gordon (1958-65) IV, p.61.

[33] See Manzella (1987), 151 and figs.181-3.

[34] Gordon (1958-65) IV, p.61 cites a sickle-shaped symbol, open-facing to the right with a dot underneath it.

hooks at left and right, so that the mark is saucer-shaped. It is interesting that in almost every case the number of the cohort is marked in this fashion (**143** is an exception), whereas other numbers, especially dates, are never marked in this way. In **263**.ii.5 and **295**.i.4 the number of the cohort is marked both by a superscript bar and the addition of dots before and after the figure. Marking out numbers in this way is a regular feature of Latin script, the intention being no doubt to alert the reader to the fact that *i*, *l*, *x* etc. are not to be treated as letters but as figures.

In the numbers *iii* and *iiii* the figures usually have marked serifs and join together, a common feature of numbers in Latin papyri. Noteworthy is the writing of *iiii* and *iii* in the dates in **178**, **200** and **291**.i.3, where the first figure is much taller than those following.[35]

Subtractives are used only very occasionally, e.g. **182**.i.4, **185**.28. The appearance of different conventions in one and the same text (**154**.5, *xlvi*; **154**.16, *xxxxv*) is noteworthy but by no means unparalleled (see note to lines 5-6).[36] There is no occurrence of *iv* in the tablets, *iiii* is always used. Similarly it was usual to write *viiii*, though *ix* is found in **180**.21. The number of the Batavian cohort is always given in the form *viiii*.[37]

Punctuation and lectional signs

It is well known that the Romans punctuated their writing under the early Empire by the use of a medial point between words (interpunct); it is also well known that they came to abandon this practice.[38] In inscriptions it is still found in use, though rarely, into the third century, but in Latin papyri it ceased to be used early in the second century.[39] In first-century papyri, both literary and documentary, it is often found, sometimes used regularly but more often only used here and there.

With respect to the Vindolanda tablets it must be stressed that a great many apparent dots occur on the photographs many of which are certainly not ink. In other cases we cannot be sure which are and which are not ink (and recourse to the originals does not always help). In consequence we are often unsure whether or not an apparent dot after a word is to be treated as interpunct or not. That said, the impression we gain from our tablets is that they fit very well into the known picture. Only a minority of writers use interpunct, and there may well be none at all in the military documents;[40] possible exceptions are **135**.1 (but this may have a different purpose, see p.57) and **160**.[41] It is rare to find interpunct used consistently;

---

[35] A similar practice was followed in writing numerals at Bu Njem, see *O.Bu Njem*, pp.38-9.

[36] See Marichal (1988), 41-6.

[37] Contrast *VRR* II, 92, nos.1-2.

[38] On punctuation in the classical period see esp. Müller (1964); cf. Wingo (1972) and Habinek (1985), 42-88. For a recent brief discussion see Parkes (1992), 9-19, esp. 10.

[39] Marichal, *ChLA* XI 493, introduction, quotes *ChLA* V 278 = *P.Mich*.VII 433 of AD 110 as the latest dated example. Cugusi, *CEL* I, p.7, quotes *CEL* 152 (= *ChLA* IX 397) of AD 140 for the use of interpunct, but we do not think it occurs in this text.

[40] Seider (1983), 139 states that interpunct never occurs in military papyri.

[41] For this purpose we do not regard requests for leave as military documents nor, necessarily, any of the accounts; interpunct is found in some texts in both these categories.

more commonly it occurs only here and there within a text. This confirms the received opinion that interpunct was on the way to dying out altogether by *c*. AD 100.[42] Interpunct occurs in the following texts:[43] **120**, **164**, **175**, **196**, **208**, **211**, **216**, **238**, **242**, **266**, **297**, **311**, **315**, **323**, **326**, **330**, **339**, **345** and **351**. Of these, however, only **164**, **175**, **196**, **238**, **266**, **297**, **323**, **330** and **345** use interpunct frequently. In addition there are some ten or eleven texts in which interpuncts may or may not occur.

The other way to indicate word division is by leaving spaces between words. This is not a normal feature of Latin papyri and it is perhaps surprising that it does occur here and there in the tablets. Good examples are **152**, **225**, **311**, **314**, **322** and **335**. In medieval manuscripts, after word division became the norm, it was usual to leave no space between a monosyllable and the word following. This practice does not seem to be observed in our tablets, not even when the monosyllable is a preposition.

A further feature which needs mentioning is the occurrence of a diagonal mark, exactly like an apex mark (see the following section), after *salutem*. If this occurred only once we should simply dismiss it as having no significance. But the fact that it probably occurs no less than four times must give us pause: see **234**, **243**, **248** and (the clearest example) **265**. In the position where it occurs it cannot be intended as an apex over a vowel and should perhaps be understood as marking the end of a section of a letter (in fact the opening section).[44] In this connection we should also draw attention to the medial point after the date in **135**.1; this seems unlikely to be interpunct (it is not normal at line ends and is not used elsewhere in the text) and may be intended to mark off the date from the text following. There may well be a similar indication of the end of a section of a text in **146**.1, see the note *ad loc*.[45]

A lectional sign which occurs fairly frequently in the tablets is the apex mark, made as a more or less oblique stroke. It must be stressed, however, that some, perhaps many, uses of apices may not show up on our photographs - this is especially true of addresses on the backs of letters - and in other places we cannot be sure whether a mark is or is not an apex.[46] With that proviso, the list of certain and possible examples is as follows:

Apices over long vowels
194 *laterarió*
194 *compendiárium*
196 *á Tranquillo*
196 *á*
196 *Brocchó*

---

[42] The best survey of the evidence is by Parsons in Anderson, Parsons and Nisbet (1979), 131, note 43.

[43] We exclude the use of medial point to indicate abbreviation or a figure.

[44] The use of oblique marks and other marks to indicate sense breaks, i.e "true" punctuation (as distinct from word interpunct), in papyri and inscriptions from the period of the early empire is discussed by Müller (1964), 46-50 and Habinek (1985), 68-81. The most interesting papyrus is P.Iand. V 90 = *PLP* II.i 1 (Cicero, 1st cent. BC/AD), on which see also Parkes (1992), 12 (these marks are sometimes called *virgulae*); see also the works cited in note 38, above. There is an apparent example in *ChLA* X 442.9.

[45] For the apparent mark at the end of line i.3 in **291** see note 48, below.

[46] Cf. p.56 above, on punctuation.

212 *Verecundó*
212 *suó*
215 *aequó* ?
215 *Cassió*
221 *Fláuio*
234 *Octóbres*
239 *Fláuius*
239 *suó*
242 *numerátioni*
243 *suó*
243 *fráter*
245 *-ró*
248 *óptamus*
248 *tú*
255 *Flauió*
261 *suó*
263 *tuó*
265 *fráter*
265 *sácrifició* (the *o* is long but the *a* short)
265 *uoluerás*
291 *rogó* [47]
291 *interuentú*
291 *salutá*
291 *Seuerá* ?
292 *Brocchó*
292 *uná*
292 *quaé* ?
301 *-ó* ?
304 *censús* ?
305 *Vettió*
305 *Seueró*
307 *exoró*
310 *suó*
311 *cupió*
311 *putó*
311 *scribó*
311 *rogó*
311 *nómina*
319 *Veranió*
319 *suó*
324 *-inná*
330 *uiaticó* ?
330 *meó*
371 *amá* ? (the final *a* could be short)

---

[47] We have reckoned all cases of final *o* in the first person singular verb as long but it should be noted that this vowel was sometimes shortened in Latin of the imperial period, see Leumann (1977), 110, 514.

402 *P]ris[c]ó* ?
456 *]..nátore[*
464 *Marciá* (the final *a* could be short)
479 *]ná*
479 *á*
479 *lạṇ.ḅá*
479 *]ó*
479 *]ló*
479 *]nestú* ?
499 *-á*
499 *-ó*
513 *-ó*

Apices over short vowels
175 *rógo*
175 *Córis* ?
197 *-neariá*
198 *]..brá*
198 *membrá*
207 *sagá*
265 *Kálendarum*
265 *sácrifició* (the *a* is short)
291 *Seuerá*
291 *faciás*
291 *facturá* [48]
292 *necessariá*
292 *acturá* ?
391 *ád* ?

It is worth noting that there is no instance of the use of an apex in a military document.[49]

The use of apices in Latin inscriptions and papyri has been the subject of two recent articles by Kramer and Flobert.[50] Kramer discusses the shape the apex mark takes (in papyri it is always straight and looks much like an acute accent), the period of time over which apices are attested (from the 1st century BC to the 2nd century AD in inscriptions, but as late as the third century in papyri), and the reasons for their use: he seems to believe that the use

[48] This text also has an oblique stroke after *diem* in i.3, like an apex or the mark found after *salutem* in some texts (see above, p.57). Here it cannot be an apex or serve as punctuation. In some texts a final *m* has its last stroke raised so as to be horizontal or even to slope upwards, but this is hardly a convincing explanation in the present instance and we should perhaps just suppose that we have an accidental stroke without significance.

[49] Cf. p.56, above, on the use of interpunct (and for the definition of "military document" for this purpose).

[50] Kramer (1991), Flobert (1990); see also Marichal *ChLA* XI 493, introduction (p.37). For inscriptions see also A.E.Gordon and J.S.Gordon (1957), 148-9. In addition to papyri and inscriptions apices can occur on ostraca; see e.g. *O.Claud.* 2 and 135.

of apices depended more or less on the whim of the individual writer (his word is "fakultativ").[51]

Kramer, however, does not go into details, in contrast to Flobert, who gives a statistical analysis of a selection of inscriptions, indicating the nature of the syllable on which the apex is placed (open/closed, stressed/unstressed) and its position in the word (initial/medial/final).[52]

Of the 75 examples of apices in the Vindolanda texts 61 are on vowels in final syllables or on monosyllables, about 80%. Flobert too, in the material he examined, noted a significant proportion of examples on final vowels (up to 49%), but not such a striking proportion as in the Vindolanda material.[53] Of the 14 falsely placed apices (i.e. those on short vowels), 9 are on vowels in final syllables, about 65%, a somewhat smaller proportion than in the case of the correctly placed apices. The figures suggest almost a mechanical habit of placing apices (if they were used at all) on final vowels, regardless of whether those vowels were long or short. But apices are not placed willy-nilly on final vowels. It is striking that certain words or word-forms repeatedly have an apex on their final vowel, a fact which further demonstrates the importance of conventions of writing which one can no longer understand: *suó* 6 times (cf. *tuó* once, *meó* once), first-person singular present verb-forms (*rogó*, *exoró*, *cupió*, *putó*, *scribó*, *rogó*), dative and ablative forms of second-declension nouns (*Brocchó*, *Verecundó*, *Cassió*, *Flauió*, *Vettió*, *Seueró*, *uiaticó* (?)). A high proportion of apices on short vowels are on a final *a* (8 out of 14). 32 of the 61 correctly placed apices are over final *o*, and another 12 are over final *a*. *a* and *o* have a similar capacity, it seems, to attract an apex, particularly if they are in final position. It is not simply the length of the vowel which is influential. The letter (regardless of the length of the phoneme which it represents) and its position in the word have to be taken into account.

As for apices which are not on final vowels, we find that in most cases the apex is on the vowel which bears the stress accent. Long vowels: *compendiárium*, *Fláuio*, *Octóbres*, *Fláuius*, *numerátioni*, *fráter* (twice), *nómina*; 7 examples, i.e. all but one of the apices on long vowels which are not on final syllables. Short vowels: *rógo*, *Córis* (?). Flobert too has noted a marked tendency for the apex to be used on stressed vowels. There is evidence that short vowels under the accent tended to be lengthened,[54] and that tendency may help to explain a form such as *rógo*. Does *sácrifició* offer evidence that there was a secondary stress on the *a*?

It is also worth noting that it is particularly common to find final *o* marked with an apex when it is being used in the address in the prescript of a letter or in an address on the back of a letter. This is only what we would expect. The use of an apex in this position continues in papyrus letters into the third century, well after the use of the apex elsewhere

---

[51] One problem is that Quintilian's "rule" (1.7.2) that apices should only be used to avoid confusion, seems never to have been observed in practice: see Kramer (pp.142-3), "Wenn Apices verwendet werden, dann sind einige Langvokale mit ihnen versehen, die meisten aber nicht, ohne dass es einen erkennbaren sprachlichen Grund für die Verteilung gäbe" (142-3).

[52] We are most grateful to Professor Adams for the detailed observations which follow.

[53] Flobert (1990), 103, 104, 105.

[54] See Consentius, *GL* V, p.392, line 3.

had been abandoned.[55] As has been indicated, Flobert's analysis naturally takes account of the use of apices over short vowels in inscriptions.[56] We know of no such analysis for Latin papyri,[57] but have noted two probable examples of its occurrence, both in letters: *P.Köln* III 160.7[58] and *P.Qasr Ibrîm* 30.[59] This is clearly a subject which will repay further study and one for which the evidence of the tablets will be of great value.[60]

[55] See Kramer (1991), 142, and Marichal, *loc.cit.* in note 50. Kramer describes this use as having a "Reliktcharakter" comparable to the survival of iota adscript in addresses of Greek papyrus letters long after the use of iota adscript elsewhere had ceased.

[56] Flobert (1990), esp. pp.106-7. See also J.S.Gordon and A.E.Gordon (1957), 148-9, mentioning "eight to twelve examples" occurring in Gordon (1958-65).

[57] Kramer (1991) does not mention this phenomenon.

[58] *epistolám*; see the editor's note for an explanation of why this is unlikely to be the ablative *epistola m[ea.*

[59] The edition prints *VARÍUS*, on which the editors offer no comment. The accompanying plate (Plate XVIII) shows only *]´IUS* which might easily represent *Várius*; but even so the apex mark, if that is what it is, would be over a short vowel.

[60] Cf. the comments by Petersmann (1992), 287, on the *ed.pr.* of **291**, that the use there of apices over short vowels suggests "dass allgemein das Gefühl für Quantitäten bereits im Schwinden begriffen war".

PART II THE TEXTS

CONVENTIONS

It should be noted that the line numeration is continuous in texts which are complete; in incomplete texts each column and any text on the back of the tablets is numbered separately. Unless otherwise noted the text is written along the grain of the wood; the symbol "↓" indicates that the grain of the wood runs vertically, i.e. that the text is written across the grain. In addition, the following conventions are employed in the presentation of the texts:

i, ii: designate separate columns of text following the original layout.
. . . : indicates that the text is broken or incomplete at the top or bottom.
m^1, m^2: distinguish different hands in the text.
[ ]: indicates a lacuna in the text.
[*c.4*]: estimate of the number of letters missing in a lacuna.
uacat: a space left by the scribe on the tablet.
⟦abc⟧: letters crossed out or erased by the scribe.
⌜abc⌝: letters or words added by the scribe above the line.
<abc>: letters erroneously omitted by the scribe.
{abc}: superfluous letters written by the scribe.
ạḅc̣: doubtful or partially preserved letters.
... : represents traces of letters visible on the tablet which have been left unread.
praef(ecto), *(centurio)*: expansion or resolution of an abbreviation or symbol.

LITERARY AND SUB-LITERARY TEXTS
(Nos. 118-121)

Of the four texts which follow only the first (**118**) is unquestionably literary. However, we consider that the possibility that the other three are of a literary character is sufficiently strong to justify their inclusion in this section. All four tablets are assigned to the *praetorium* of Period 3. The appearance of Latin literature in a Roman military context and especially the equestrian officer milieu is not surprising (cf. *Doc.Masada* 721, Anderson, Parsons and Nisbet (1979), *O.Claud.* 190), and the occurrence of a line of the *Aeneid* would not be unexpected.

118

Inv.no.85.137. 100 x 15 mm. Plate I. Bowman and Thomas (1987), no.1, Plate XV. R.E. Birley (1990), 31 and fig.25. *VRR* II, Plate V.

The tablet survives in two joining fragments; it is incomplete at the top and the bottom, but appears to be complete at both sides. On one side is a draft of a letter (**331**) and on the other a line of Virgil. We have assumed that the letter was never sent and, once discarded, was used for writing the line of Virgil. Hence we have designated the letter the front, and the Virgil the back; but it is not impossible that the sides were used in the reverse order. Another example of a letter on the other side of a literary text is to be found in a Hamburg papyrus which, since it is a Latin papyrus from Egypt, is no doubt also from a military milieu. On one side, probably the recto, is a piece of mime written in capitals (*P.Hamb.*II 167 = *PLP* II.1 6); on the other is the beginning of a letter of recommendation (*ChLA* XI 493). However, the writer has apparently attempted to begin the letter more than once and writes for the most part in an elegant cursive; therefore we agree with Marichal that this is not a real letter but a writing exercise.

. . . .

INTEREA PAVIDAM VOLIṬANS P̣ỊNNA
ṬA . ṾBEM *m*² seg̣ . *uacat*

. . . .

It is quite certain that the first hand was attempting to write the verse *Aeneid* 9.473: *interea pauidam uolitans pinnata per urbem*. It is well known that Virgil was extensively used for elementary instruction and it may well be that the present tablet was likewise used in instruction, perhaps in the family of the commanding officer. While it is not possible to establish that this tablet belongs to the papers of Flavius Cerialis, it was certainly found in the same context and there is good evidence for the presence of children in the *praetorium* at Vindolanda (see *VRR* III, 45). It may have been written out simply as a writing exercise, even though such exercises normally contain more letters of the Latin alphabet than are to be found in the present line of Virgil. It is difficult in fact to see what other purpose it can have served - the line itself does not seem capable of conveying any coherent message and is not even a complete sentence.

Among other examples of lines of Virgil found in documents from a military context we have noted the following. (1) *P.Tebt.* II 686 = *ChLA* V 304 = *PLP* II.1 11: the first two lines of *Georgic* 4 written six times on a discarded account; assigned to the second century. (2) *Doc.Masada* 721: *Aeneid* 4.9 with a portion of an unidentified hexameter on the other side; of necessity not later than AD 75. (3) *O.Claud.* 190: *Aeneid* 1.1-3; early second century. The first of these texts is clearly a writing exercise and the second may be. Further examples of Virgil used for this purpose in the early Roman period are: (4) *P.Hawara* 24 = *PLP* II.1 7: on one side *Aeneid* 2.601 and on the other part of *Aeneid* 4.174, both copied several times (on this text see also our comments on **120**); it is usually assigned to the later first century AD. (5) *P.Oxy*.L 3554 = Cockle (1979): *Aeneid* 11.371-2 copied out several times on the back of a Greek document; this is also assigned to the later first century. We should also compare *PSI* XIII 1307 (= *ChLA XXV* 786 verso), a first-century writing exercise, on the back of a military document, with the two words *AENEAS DARDANIAE*, words which are undoubtedly Virgilian even though they do not form part of any known line of Virgil; and *RIB* I 1954, an altar with the inscription *AVREA PER CAẸḶỤM VOLITAT VICTORIA PENNIS*; again, this is not a known piece of Virgil, but it is reminiscent of *Aeneid* 4.700 (as the editors point out), as well as bearing some similarity to our Vindolanda text. In addition it is worth comparing several inscriptions painted in red on a cave-wall in south-east Spain, datable to the imperial period (1st-3rd centuries AD), see González Blanco (1987). Several of these are in verse and are clearly Virgilian, even though they do not exactly reproduce known lines of Virgil; see especially Panel III which the editors describe (p.223) as an "adaptación de la *Eneida* de Virgilio" (lines 1.139, 166-7, 310-11, 3.229-30).

It is of considerable interest to find evidence for such knowledge of Virgil in northern Britain at this date. We know that Virgil's work was widely known during the first century from various pieces of evidence; e.g., in addition to the above, the fragment of the *Eclogues* from Egypt, P.Narm.inv.66.362 (Gallazzi (1982), not a writing exercise); and the numerous Virgilian graffiti from Pompeii (Della Corte (1940) lists over fifty examples). The standard work on the diffusion of Virgil in the Roman world is Hoogma (1959). For a more recent study see Horsfall (1981), esp. 48-51; in view of the evidence of the present text it is noteworthy that Horsfall should stress the rarity of quotations from the later books of the *Aeneid*. See also the discussion by the editors of *Doc.Masada* 721.

The text is equally interesting from a palaeographical point of view. The first line is written in a bilinear capital script. The letters *I*, *N*, *R*, *A*, *V*, *D*, *M*, *O* and *L* are in the so-called *Capitalis Rustica*, with much use of serifs and a noticeable attempt to differentiate thick and thin strokes. *T* is also capital in form though less carefully made, and the last six letters of the line are all somewhat less elegantly written. *S* of *VOLITANS* is particularly crude and is closer to the form sometimes found in Old Roman Cursive than to the capital form; it may be followed by interpunct, but this is uncertain and does not occur elsewhere in this tablet. *P*, however, is not in the normal capital form since it lacks the loop at the top;

this form is normal in ORC, but it is sometimes found in more literary scripts, e.g. the famous Gallus papyrus (Anderson, Parsons and Nisbet (1979)). The most remarkable letter is *E*: it occurs twice in this line and at least once in the second line and always in a form which resembles \\. It is often written thus in stilus tablets and in graffiti (for a Pompeian example see the alphabet shown in Plate V, no.2, in Mallon, Marichal and Perrat (1939)). We know of no example of this form of *E* in Latin written on papyrus or parchment or in any other of the leaf tablets from Vindolanda. Apparently, however, it does occur in an ostracon from Mons Claudianus written in ink (unpublished; we are grateful for this information to Hélène Cuvigny). It is also found in the painted inscriptions from Spain mentioned above, see, e.g. II/5 (p.204), along with the normal capital *E*.

The writing in line 1 continues up to the edge of the tablet, but since this edge corresponds to the left-hand edge of the front, and since there there is a blank space before the first word, we may be confident that nothing has been lost after *PINNA*. It is likely therefore that the writer continued the word on the next line and there is indeed no difficulty in reading the first two letters in this line *TA*, written in the same capital form as in the first line. Thereafter serious difficulties begin. What we require to follow is *per urbem* and *BEM* has certainly been written; *E* is in exactly the same form as in line 1, but *M* is much more cursively written, and *B* is not in the capital form but in the usual cursive form of ORC; it noticeably does not conform to the bilinearity of the other letters. What is between *TA* and *BEM* is a problem, since only two letters can have been written, not the five we require. The letter before *BEM* is most like *V*, though it is made differently from the way this letter is written in line 1 and is much more like a modern U (for a capital script with *V* made in two different forms cf. *O.Claud.* 190, Plate XXXIII, *VIRUMQVE*; cf. also the Gallus papyrus, Anderson, Parsons and Nisbet, (1979)). We could therefore read *VBEM* and suppose that the writer had blundered by omitting *R*; such blunders are naturally very common in writing exercises and most of the texts cited above contain similar errors. Before this, after *TA*, what is written most resembles *B*, for which no explanation occurs to us. Tentatively we suggest that it is to be read *P* (made as in line 1) with a diagonal stroke above it placed there to indicate the abbreviation *p(er)*. This would at any rate enable us to complete the line of the *Aeneid*, but we cannot quote a parallel for such an abbreviation of *per*. The only alternative we have thought of is to read this line *TAP̣ẸBEM*, taking *PEBEM* as a blunder for *PE<R VR>BEM*; but this leaves the mark over the supposed *P* unexplained and the letter following appears to have a connecting stroke joining the two verticals. It is of course possible that the line of Virgil was left uncompleted. (On the palaeography of this text see also above, p.48).

After this we have three or four letters written by a different pen and in a very different, much more cursive, hand. The first two letters are certainly *se*. This is therefore not an attempt to start the next line of *Aeneid* 9. The next letter is either *g* or *c*, and there seem to be traces of at least one more letter. In *VRR* II, 38 it is suggested that we should read this *segn(iter)* or the like and interpret it as the teacher's comment on a pupil's exercise ("slack"). *seg* is the most obvious reading but we think *sec* also possible, perhaps followed by *u*; *secuntur* (= *sequuntur*) might make sense in the context, but there is no clear trace of any writing after *sec̣ụ*.

119

Inv.no.85.183.a. 62 x 73 mm. Plate II.

Two joining fragments with writing on both sides. The side which is likely to have been the front is probably complete at the foot but is less likely to have been complete at the top; it is complete at the right but not the left. Most of this side is taken up with four lines of shorthand, for which see **122**. At the foot, and almost certainly upside down in relation to the shorthand, is part of one line:

QVIN[

On the back, in the same hand, we read:

QVỊN *traces?* [
QVINTIA [

The rest of the tablet is not blank but the ink which survives does not look like writing and is perhaps best described as pen trials; there are some such ink marks after *QVINTIA* in line 2, but they do not resemble letters. We are confident that this is to be classed as a writing exercise, both because of the repetition and because it has been written on a tablet which was previously used for another purpose and was no doubt then discarded. It was a commonplace to use lines from literature for such purposes, which is one reason for thinking that this text may be literary. The other reason is the hand in which it is written: it is a capital script, not unlike the script of **118** and possibly the work of the same writer. *I*, *N*, *T* and *A* are very similar, but *V* is made in a more rounded form, and the writing in general is not as elegant as **118**. *Q* breaks the bilinearity with a long diagonal descender, especially noticeable in line 1 on the back.

Quintia must be a name; we have considered the possibility that it is the start of the longer name Quintianus, but the ink marks after *QVINTIA* in line 2 on the back do not support this. We therefore suggest the possibility that we have an attempt to write the first line of Catullus 86, which begins: *Quintia formosa est multis*. It is worth noting that Catullus is an author not represented in the literary papyri (see Pack (1965)).

120

Inv.no.86.409. 66 x 24 mm. Plate I.

A fragment of a leaf containing part of two lines. It is complete at the right and, probably, at the foot. The back is blank.

The reason for suggesting that this text may be literary is entirely palaeographical. The hand in which it is written is remarkable for being much more elegant than is normal in the tablets. It reminds one forcibly of *P.Hawara* 24 = *PLP* II.1 7, which has on one side a line of Virgil used as a writing exercise; see Turner (1957), Dow (1968), Seider (1976), esp. 133-6 and 165-72. All agree in assigning the papyrus to the later first century AD, thus making it more or less contemporary with our Vindolanda text. As in our text, the letters in *P.Hawara* are a mixture of capitals and cursives. All the letters are similar or very similar to those in the Vindolanda text; note especially the very tall ascender to *b* (made in the cursive form), *u* with the left stroke a diagonal and the right almost vertical, and *r* in the cursive form but with a very short descender. Other literary texts from the late first century BC and the first century AD, whether writing exercises or not, which may be compared are: the Gallus papyrus (Anderson, Parsons and Nisbet (1979)), *P.Iand.* V 90 = *PLP* II.1 1, *Doc.Masada* 721 and *P.Oxy.*L 3554 (= Cockle (1979)). We therefore think there is some reason to class the present text as literary, but we have not succeeded in identifying it with any known piece of Latin literature. There is no reason to think it was a writing exercise and it is certainly possible that it is just a fragment of an ordinary private letter, over the writing of which the writer took more than usual care.

. . . . .

]ạlḷ.ṇ.[.].[
]ibi · soluerẹṇt

1. The first surviving letter could equally well be *r*, but if *ll* follows we must read *a*; in either case it is made in a cursive not a capital form, with a very long descender (*r* in line 2 has only a short descender; *P.Hawara* has *r* made with a long descender on the verso). *l* appears certain for the next letter and very probable for the letter thereafter; on both occasions it is made in the capital form, as it is in line 2. The next letter is very unclear; it looks most like *o* but, if so, it is much smaller than *o* in the next line. After *n*, which is reasonably secure, we have the foot of an upright, most probably *i* or *t*. After a gap a long diagonal survives, but the ink is preserved in such a way that it is impossible to be certain whether this diagonal belongs to this line or the line below. If it belongs to line 1 it must be the tail of *q* or, less probably, *g*; for *q* with such a tail cf. *P.Iand.*V 90 and *Doc.Masada* 721; *g* is written with a long tail in *P.Hawara*. Two or three letters may have been lost after this.

2. Between the lines is an almost horizontal line of ink, cutting through the top of *b*. This can hardly be anything other than the tail of *q* from the lost part at the left of line 1. *b* is made in the normal cursive form, with a very tall ascender. There is clear interpunct after *ibi*. *s* following is not in the normal capital form, since it lacks the stroke at the foot which would usually complete the letter; however, it is closer to this form than to the ordinary cursive form. *o* is large and *u* is made in a *v*-form, much like the form found in **118**. *e* is narrow and in a capital form; it is made in much this form in all the texts referred to above. If the diagonal referred to in the note to line 1 belongs to this line, it can only have been a long leading-in stroke to the oblique of *n*; this exaggerated leading-in stroke is occasionally found, e.g. in *P.Iand.*V 90 and, less noticeably, in *P.Hawara*.

121

Inv.no.85.119.a. 65 x 40 mm. Plate I. *VRR* II, Plate V.

A small fragment, complete at left and foot. It contains the bottom and left part of a drawing (unless this is mere idle doodling). Another drawing in the tablets is to be found in Inv.no.87.616 = *VRR* II, Plate XVIII. That tablet contains no writing, whereas the present tablet preserves a number of letters. It appears to begin with three upright strokes (rather like the numeral *iii*); we then have some letters of which the first two are certainly *be*, and it is likely that *ll* follows, perhaps in turn followed by *i*. After this there seem to be three more uprights before the letter *r*, probably followed by *e*. There is then a small space before some more marks which do not look like letters; at this point the tablet breaks off. As can be seen from the plate, all the uprights have long arching strokes projecting up from their tops and crossing one another (an attempt to draw a tent?). Below this, considerably inset from the left margin, we have two or three large letters of which the first is *c* or *g*. In line 1 *b* is written in the cursive form, whereas *e* and *r* are in the normal capital form. In *VRR* II, 38 it is suggested that we should read *belli por* in the first line and *cla* in the second; and it is further suggested that this may be "another Virgilian effort, recalling *Aeneid* 1.294, *claudentur Belli portae*. The drawing could be a doodle intended to represent the Gates of War". It is difficult, however, to reconcile the traces after *belli* with the reading suggested; it seems more likely that the first three strokes, which are connected to the drawing, are not letters, and the reading thereafter is almost certainly *re*. If we are to pursue this idea further (and, as is pointed out in *VRR*, the tablet was found in close proximity to **118**), perhaps a more likely Virgilian quotation is *Aeneid* 12.567, *causam belli regna ipsa Latini*. The first line might read *belli re* and the first letter in the second line could well be *g*. It is perhaps just possible that what is written thereafter is a botched attempt to write *na*, after which the writer abandoned his efforts.

SHORTHAND TEXTS
(Nos. 122-126)

The five texts described below clearly belong together and seem to be written in a combination of letters and symbols. Rather than regarding them as normal script written extremely cursively, we feel confident that they are in fact examples of Latin written in shorthand.

The evidence for the knowledge of shorthand in the late Republic and early Empire is surveyed in detail by Boge (1973), 47-68. Boge accepts the traditional theory that shorthand was a discovery of Cicero's freedman Tiro. Others have been less inclined to accept this at its face value (e.g. Coles (1966)). In the most recent study of the subject, Teitler (1985), 28-9 and 172-3, s.v. TIRO, leaves the question open. What is important is that there is general agreement that shorthand was known and used in the Roman world by at least the middle of the first century AD (the evidence of Seneca, *Apoc.* 9.2, would appear to be decisive). Since our tablets have been found in a military context it is relevant to note that Vegetius 2.19, in discussing *litterati milites*, remarks that in some cases when recruiting troops, in addition to examining their physical condition, *notarum peritia, calculandi computandique usus eligitur* (although Teitler (1985), 210-11 thinks that *notae* might simply mean the "letters of the alphabet"). Further evidence for the use of shorthand in military circles is provided by *Digest* 29.1.40 (Paulus). In general on the *litterati milites* see Teitler (1985), 44-9, who regards the presence of shorthand writers in the army as certain by the third century.

The history of shorthand in the classical and early medieval periods is summarised in Bischoff (1986), 110-2 and (1990), 80-2 (where the numbering of the footnotes is incorrect). He gives a good bibliography in (1986), 316-317 (see also (1990), 244). Add now P.F.Ganz (ed. 1990), a collection of articles of which the most relevant for our purposes is that by D.Ganz, pp. 35-51.

So-called Tironian notes are preserved in a number of Latin manuscripts of the Carolingian period, see Schmitz (1893). A recent collection of the various signs is to be found in Costamagna, Baroni and Zagni (1983). In what is still the most thorough treatment of the subject, Mentz (1944), three different systems are analysed: System A = the so-called Tironian notes. These are to be seen in use in Merovingian and Carolingian charters from the seventh century onwards and in manuscripts of the ninth and tenth centuries. System B and System C are only attested in papyri from Ravenna, the earliest evidence being from the sixth century; they both use a syllabic system, different from the system employed for true Tironian notes. On them see Tjäder (1954-82), I 128-9, and II 260 (note 29 to P.30, 91). Earlier than the above is the use of shorthand symbols at the head of an inscription which records a *constitutio* of AD 362 (*CIL* 3.459). Cf. also P.Reinach inv.2140 = *CLA* V 699, assigned to the fourth or fifth century.

The relationship between these systems and the shorthand in use during the early Empire is unknown. See Ganz's remark, (1990), 37, that "Traditionally this vocabulary [i.e. the system of shorthand used in the classical period and in late antiquity] has been identified with the commentaries which are preserved in the *Commentarii Notarum Tironian[ar]um*... However, our earliest evidence for the use of shorthand in official documents reveals that the elaborate shorthand system taught by the *Commentarii* was not used by the urban bureaucracy of Ravenna". Whether the tachygraphic writing on our tablets represents Tironian notes as known from the Carolingian period (Mentz's System A), or whether, as we think less likely, it represents either of those known from Ravenna, or whether it represents something different from any of the known systems, we do not feel competent to judge. It would, we feel, be hazardous in the extreme to attempt any transcription of these tablets. Even if they are essentially the same as the attested Tironian notes, we can hardly suppose that the signs would have been made in the same way 500 or more years earlier and on a different medium. Hitherto the idea that the Romans were acquainted with shorthand in the classical period has been no more than a conclusion drawn from the literary evidence and from the existence of inscriptions referring to *notarii* and the like. The importance of the tablets from Vindolanda is that they provide documentary confirmation that shorthand was used in military circles on the frontier of the Roman world by about AD 100.

As we have not offered any transcription, we include plates of the better preserved examples. We should warn the reader that in some cases the "writing" is so enigmatic that we cannot be sure that the plates present the tablet the right way up. For other possible examples see **376** and **401**.

122. Inv.no.85.183.a. 90 x 36 mm. Plate II. R.E.Birley (1990), fig.28. Two joining fragments, on one of which is **119**. Complete at the right. Substantial remains of four lines.

123. Inv.no.86.371. 90 x 114 mm. Plate III. Two joining fragments, probably complete at left and right. Side A preserves remains of two lines; Side B preserves one line only. Both are written along the grain. We are less certain than in the case of the other tablets in this section that **123** is in shorthand, especially Side B.

124. Inv.no.86.474. 60 x 14 mm. On Side A, written along the grain, remains of two lines; on Side B, written across the grain, traces of at least three lines.

125. Inv.no.87.515. 47 x 85 mm. A substantial fragment mostly blank, but with remains of two lines written across the grain on each side.

126. Inv.no.87.684. 28 x 75 mm. Plate III. On Side A (illustrated in the Plate) the beginnings of seven lines written across the grain. On Side B somewhat abraded remains of seven lines across the grain.

MILITARY DOCUMENTS
(Nos. 127-177)

The texts grouped under this rubric are, apart from the reports with the *renuntium*-heading and the requests for leave (see below), a miscellaneous collection. Some of these documents may have belonged to, or been preserved with, groups of letters associated with individuals; there is an obvious possible connection, for instance, between **154** and the correspondence of Verecundus (**210-12**); the *renuntium* texts, almost all of which are attributed to the Period 3 *praetorium*, might belong with the papers of Flavius Cerialis, as do several of the requests for leave (**166-77**). It is important to emphasise, however, that we cannot identify these documents as belonging to the official archives of the unit or units stationed at Vindolanda. In this respect there is a clear contrast with the papyri from Dura-Europos and the ostraca from Bu Njem, all or some of which quite clearly do belong to official archives. It is, of course, possible that some of the Vindolanda tablets may be copies of archive documents and it should be borne in mind that two of the official reports originating in the *tabularium* at Bu Njem were actually found in the *praetorium* (see *O.Bu Njem*, pp.5-10).

(a) Military reports with *renuntium*-heading

Five fragmentary texts in this category were edited and discussed by Bowman and Thomas (1987), no.2.A-E (and cf. Bowman and Thomas (1991), 65). They are clearly formulaic reports and we have been able to identify a total of 27 texts which are certainly or probably of this type (for other possible examples see **165**, **393**, **410**, **453**, **458**, **511**, **545**). Of the 23 tablets which were found in the excavations of the 1980s, 21 are attributed to Period 3 and the *praetorium*. **136** is attributed to Period 2 (Room C) and **128** is attributed to Period 4 (Room III); in view of the location of the others, however, the inevitable margin of error in attribution, and the tendency of objects to move between strata (see above, p.19), no conclusion can be drawn with confidence about the aberrant examples. 12 of the 21 tablets from Period 3 were found on the *via principalis* adjacent to the courtyard designated as Room VIA (**129, 132**, **133**, **134**, **135**, **137**, **138**, **140**, **141**, **142**, **145**, **146**); 7 in the courtyard (**130**, **131**, **139**, **147**, **148**, **149**, **150**); and 2 by the South Gate (**143**, **144**). These groupings are suggestive of the process of dumping or disposal of out-of-date material; compare the 9 *commeatus* applications from the 1980s attributed to Period 3, of which 7 were found on the *via principalis*. If the reports of this type are confined to Period 3, the group might be connected with Flavius Cerialis and belong to his files, but this we cannot demonstrate.

It is noteworthy that all the texts are written along the grain of the wood, as are several other brief military reports (**155-7**). In only one case (**145**) does it seem that the text was written on a diptych and in that instance not in columns, but across the fold (cf. **292**).

There are notches and tie-holes in **137**. Some of the texts were certainly not justified at the right. As for the hands, it is striking and important that no two are certainly or even very probably by the same hand; the only possibilities for identity seem to be **136** with **138** and **150** with **153** but neither connection is at all certain. In this respect the contrast with the "rapports journaliers" from Bu Njem and several of the groups of ostraca from Mons Claudianus is striking (*O.Bu Njem*, pp.41-5, *O.Claud.* 48-82). Since the closing formula is always, as far as we can tell, written by the same hand as the remainder of the text, we are probably justified in concluding that most or some of these reports were written by the *optiones* who submitted them (cf. Bowman (1991) and (1994b)), although in three cases they appear to have been delivered by someone else (**127**, **128**, **129**); we note that two reports by an *optio* named Candidus (**146**, **148**) are written in different hands, but the name is a very common one indeed. Like the applications for *commeatus* (**166-77**), these are not *pro forma* chits, but the comparative uniformity of the laconic formulae and the regular use of the idiosyncratic *q(ui) uidebunt* (see below) suggests that the writers are following an exemplar.

Although we have by no means solved all the problems of reading and interpretation, the formulaic elements in the texts can now be more securely identified and understood. We first offer some comments on the formulae and the variations, before considering the general characteristics and significance of the reports.

Date. The reports are dated by month and day and there is no reason to doubt that all reports began thus (although **130** is an oddity). The date is preserved at least partially in 13 texts and there are month-names in **127** (probably June), **130** (January/?February), **132** (June), **133** (December/February), **135** (probably March), **136** (April), **143** (December), **151** (July). It is striking that there is no example in the months August-November but this may well be pure chance.

renuntium. This is once written as *renutium* (**136**). It occurs immediately after the date in 9 examples (**127**, **131**, **133**, **135**, **136**, **140**, **143**, **147**, **149**; **130** again appears to be an oddity) and there is no problem in supplying or restoring this pattern in all the others. The lexica cite two examples of *renuntius* meaning "reporter" (Plautus, *Trin.* 254, *C.Th.* 3.7.1). It might be explained grammatically as a noun meaning "report" in the accusative case as the subject of an implied verb (cf. p.120 below). The construction with the name of the unit following in the genitive is paralleled in *RMR* 64.1, *Pridianum coh(ortis) I Aug(ustae) pr(aetoriae) Lus(itanorum) eq(uitatae)*.

coh(ortis) viiii Batauorum. This is found in 14 texts but only 3 examples are complete (**134**, **135**, **143**, cf. **127**, **137**). *coh(ortis)* is abbreviated in all cases except one (**127**). The numeral is wholly or partly lost in 7 cases (**130**, **132**, **133**, **139**, **140**, **144**, **149**) and *Batauorum* is wholly lost in 3 (**132**, **144**, **149**). We have now abandoned our earlier belief that there might also be evidence for an Eighth Cohort (Bowman and Thomas (1987), 133, cf. above, pp.22-4) and in no case do we now doubt that the Ninth is the unit concerned (in **128** and **136**, the only examples not attributed to Period 3, the name of the unit is lost).

omnes. We originally suggested that the next word might be *immunes*, those exempt from regular duties, but we no longer believe this to be the case. With some hesitation and a great deal of caution we suggest that what we have is *omnes*, which makes good sense. We cannot be sure that we have the same word in all examples and in no case can *omnes* be read with absolute certainty. For the individual readings see the notes *ad locc.* in **127**, **130**, **135**, **137**, **142**, **149**, **150**.

ad locum/loca. The singular is found in 4 texts (**130** twice, **139**, **140**, **151**) and the plural in 7 (**127**, **134**, **135**, **141**, **142**, **145**, **149**), but there is no obvious difference in meaning. The word should presumably be taken to mean military stations or posts (see Breeze and Dobson (1987), 140-1) rather than local tribal meeting-places (see S.S.Frere, *Britannia* 11 (1980), 422-3 against *PNRB* 212). We note that *OLD*, s.v. *ad*, 18b translates the phrase *ad locum* "at duty stations", citing Livy, 27.27.2, *ut ad locum miles esset paratus*. It is also used as a synonym of *castellum* (cf. **178**.1) and of a *castrum* [sic], see *TLL* VII.2 1582.25.

q(ui) uidebunt. This is very problematical. What is written is *quidebunt*; it occurs in full in 6 texts (**130**, **134**, **135**, **139**, **145**, **150**) and is probable elsewhere. The reading is inescapable but difficult to explain. We have considered understanding it as one word, *quidebunt* (cf. Bowman and Thomas (1987), 134-5), but we can see no way of explaining this linguistically. Since confusion between 3rd person plurals of 2nd and 3rd conjugation verbs does occur in vulgar Latin (e.g. *ualunt* for *ualent*, see *CEL* 142.40 note, and Adams (1977), 51) we could understand it as *debent* (see *VRR* II, 33) although we have not found the form attested for this verb; but it is still difficult to construe it and to see what it would mean. In Bowman and Thomas (1987), 134-5 we noted that there might be an abbreviation mark after *q* in one example (**139**.2). We now think that this should be taken seriously as an abbreviation for *q(ui)*. That the abbreviation is not elsewhere marked is not a serious difficulty given the erratic use of such marks in the Vindolanda texts; it is possible that it is also marked in **145**. This will then be followed by the future verb *uidebunt* in the sense of "see to" (see *OLD*, s.v. 19).

et impedimenta (sometimes *inpedimenta*). This is found certainly or very probably in 14 examples (**127**, **130**, **134**, **135**, **137**, **139**, **142**, **145**, **146**, **149**, **150**, **151**, **152**, **153**) and is no doubt universal. It has various meanings in a military context but it is perhaps most likely to refer to baggage, kit or equipment (see *TLL* VII.1 530, cf. Caesar, *BG* 6.35.1). *impedimenta* is followed by a *uacat* in **134**, **139**, **145** and **146**. More problematic are **127**, **130**, **135**, **138** and **150** (see the notes *ad locc.*). The reading of **127**.4 is difficult (see note *ad loc.*) but this is the only instance in which the traces are substantial enough to allow us to hazard an interpretation; if we have an abbreviation *pr*, we can only suggest that it might represent *pr(aesentia)* ("they will see to the baggage which is present").

renuntiauit. This is found in **139**, **146**, **148**, **152** and presumably in **137** and **138**. In **127**, **128** and **153** we have *renuntiauerunt*. No doubt the verb was universal. In most cases it begins a new line, sometime after a *uacat* of one line; this is not the case in **138** and may not be true of **130** and **135**. The verb is followed by a name in **146** and **152** and by a name + *optio* + (century of) [name] in **137**, **138** and **148**. There is no reason to doubt that every report had a comparable statement. There are important variations in **127** and **128**, where (a) the *optiones* are not named but the subjects of the verb are not only *optiones*, but *optiones et curatores* and (b) there is an additional statement in the form of the verb *detulit* followed by a name, which must refer to the person who physically delivered the report to its destination; this also appears in **129** and we note that the word is used for submission of a *pridianum* in *ChLA* XI 501. Given the fragmentary state of many of the texts it is obviously possible that these elements will have appeared in more than three examples. It seems probable that we have two alternative forms of closure: either *renuntiauit* + name of *optio* + century of [name], or *renuntiauerunt optiones* (*et curatores*, no doubt) without names, followed by the *detulit* formula.

A reconstruction and translation of the full form of this type of report, as we understand it, would run as follows: *iii Idus Martias. renuntium coh(ortis) viiii Batauorum. omnes ad loca (-um) q(ui) uidebunt et impedimenta [?praesentia] renuntiauit Candidus optio (centuriae) Felicionis*, **or** *renuntiauerunt optiones et curatores. detulit Iustinus optio (centuriae) Crescentis*; "13 March. Report of the 9th Cohort of Batavians. All who ought to be at their posts are there, and they will see to the baggage, which is present (?). Candidus, *optio* of the century of Felicio, submitted the report [**or** The *optiones* and *curatores* submitted the report. Iustinus *optio* of the century of Crescens delivered it]." As this volume was about to go to press R.E.Birley kindly informed us that he has excavated another, complete example of this type of report in a Period 3 context (Inv.no.1418). The reading of the text confirms our reconstruction and is as follows: *xvii K Maias / renuntium / coh vịịịi Batauo/rum omnes ad lọc̣a qui/debunt et inpedimenta / renuntiarunt optiones / et curatores / detulit Arcụittius optio / (centuriae) Cresc̣ẹntis*; cf. in particular **127-8**.

As for the general significance of these texts, we can only suggest that they are routine regular reports made by the *optiones* who were required to inspect and verify that all personnel and equipment was "present and correct". These may have applied to the fort at Vindolanda itself, or perhaps to small groups, either outposted to nearby fortlets possibly under the command of *optiones* (see **154**.16 note), or engaged in special tasks under the supervision of *curatores*, or both. There is no evidence elsewhere for reports in this form but the danger of arguing from silence to the conclusion that this procedure was peculiar to the Ninth Cohort of Batavians is obvious. There may be some support for the widespread existence of such reporting procedures in the evidence of Polybius for the organisation of the army of the Republic (6.34.7-36.9): the guards on night-duty receive written *tesserae* before going to their posts and the men chosen by the *optiones* to inspect the guards get written orders from the tribune, visit the posts collecting the *tesserae* from the guards and deliver them to the tribune at daybreak.

We note Fink's remark (*RMR*, p.181) on *pridiana*, that they are "the one sort of military record known to have a specific technical meaning". It would appear that the *renuntius* (?) is a second example.

(b) Miscellaneous documents

There are seven texts which may be described as military reports of one sort or another. Of these, the most extensive and most important is **154**, the strength report of the First Cohort of Tungrians. Although the nature of this document is clear enough, we do not find it easy to offer for this or for the other reports a precise classification of the sort suggested by Fink, *RMR*, pp.179-82, cf. Bowman and Thomas (1991), 62-6. There are four texts which may be daily reports (**155-8**) recording the activities of groups of personnel on a particular day; the term βιβλίον ἐφήμερον (Appian, *BC* 5.46) might be appropriate to these and they do bear some resemblance to the "rapports journaliers" from Bu Njem (*O.Bu Njem* 1-62). It is noteworthy that, unlike **154**, they are written along the grain of the wood and parallel to the long edge of the leaf, perhaps on a half-diptych. Another fragmentary report appears to concern a *turma* (**159**). It should be noted that we have no records of the movements of small groups and individuals like the "comptes-rendus" from Bu Njem (*O.Bu Njem* 67-73, cf. Tomlin (1986)). Of the remainder, **163**, in a capital hand, may be the heading of a list and **162** could be something similar. **164**, describing the fighting characteristics of the native Britons, may be a memorandum sent to a unit commander. **161** might be a straightforward list of names of military personnel.

For other texts which are possibly military documents see **365**, **367** and **491**.

(c) Applications for leave

This group of 12 texts (**166-77**) contains applications for leave (*commeatus*). The small amount of evidence for leave in the Roman army has been discussed by Bagnall (*O.Flor.*, pp.19-20), Speidel (1985) and Davies (1989), 67. It is evident that this was a regular provision, although given sparingly and only for good reasons according to Vegetius 2.19: *quando quis commeatum acceperit uel quot dierum, adnotatur in breuibus. tunc enim difficile commeatus dabatur, nisi causis iustissimis adprobatis* (cf. Suetonius, *Galb.* 6, *pari seueritate interdixit commeatus peti*). The documentary evidence from Egypt includes reasons for a grant of leave, indicating the purpose for which it was requested (*P.Wisc.*II 70, *ChLA* XI 467), a pass showing the length of time for which it was granted (*O.Flor.* 1), and an indication that a soldier serving in Bostra expected to be able to get leave for long enough to visit his family in Egypt (*P.Mich.*VIII 466) and an instance of an application for leave being refused (Karlsson and Maehler (1977), no.1.16-7). For additional references see: Vegetius 3.4, *Digest* 49.16.12.1, 14, *RMR* 9.2m, n, 24b, 34-7, 47.ii.18-9, 53b.6-7, *P.Oxy.*XIV 1666, *SB* VI 9272 = *JJP* 9-10 (1955- 6), 162 no.2, *ChLA* XI 467, 500, *O.Claud.* 137.

The applications from Vindolanda add a new category of evidence. Although most of the texts are mere fragments, we have no reason to doubt that, apart from **175** in which the order of words is quite different, all the texts follow the same formula: *rogo domine* (name) *dignum me habeas cui des commeatum*; the only variations are the omission of the name of the recipient in **176** and the addition of *te* after *rogo* in **173**. The name following *domine* is preserved in 8 texts; 6 of them have *Cerialis* (**166-71**), the others appear to have *Flauiane* (**172**) and *Priscine* (**173**). The use of *dare* with *commeatus* in this sense is several times attested, e.g. Festus, *Verb.* 277.27 (= p.345.3 Lindsay), *commeatus dari dicitur, id est tempus, quo ire et redire qui possit*, Livy, 21.21.6, *si quis uestrum suos inuisere uolt, commeatum do* (said by Hannibal). For *rogo domine dignum me habeas* we should compare the text published by Speidel and Seider (1988) (= *CEL* 149), *rogo domine [dig]num me iudices ut pr[obe]s militem in cohorte u[t po]ssim* etc. Before *rogo domine* etc. 6 texts (**166**, **168**, **169**, **171**, **172**, **176**) have the name of the applicant with his unit subdivision, without the name of the addressee or *salutem*. Of the other texts **170** is almost certainly blank before *rogo*, and the same may be true of **167** and **173**. However, it is clear that the hand responsible for writing the name of the applicant is always the same as that which wrote the body of the request; therefore these requests did not simply exist as *pro forma* chits on which a blank was left for the name of the applicant to be inserted (as is the case in *O.Flor.* 1, and compare *O.Claud.* 48-82). It is also noteworthy that, although for the most part only small fragments are preserved, the hand is very probably different in every one of the examples (only **169** and **174** are at all similar). After the formula quoted above, in **174** and **175** the place at which the leave is to be taken is added and the same is likely to be the case in **176** (cf. **171**); the other texts all break off before this point but it is probable that this information was included in all applications. After this, it is possible that the purpose for which the leave was requested might be stated (see **176** and cf. *P.Wisc.*II 70, *ChLA* XI 467, but contrast **174** and **175**). If we are correct in believing that **177** is another such application it might add a request for the commanding officer at the place which the applicant was to visit to be informed. The applications do not mention the length of time involved, which suggests that this would be fixed by the authorities on the basis of the place and reasons specified; note the phrase *finitum commeatum* in *ChLA* XI 500, which must mean "limited furlough", see Speidel (1985), 283. There is no clear case of an application being written on a double leaf, like a letter; **174** has a notch in the left edge, as may **170** and **172**. Since these applications were not as personal as letters it may have been the custom to write them on open half-leaves. **175** has something on the back indicating the name of the applicant.

Most of the applications are attributed to Period 3, and six of these mention the name of Cerialis as the recipient. Of these, three (**168**, **169**, **170**) were found in the *via principalis*, adjacent to the courtyard designated as Room VIA, and it may well therefore be the case that three other examples from the same location, in which the name of the recipient is not preserved (**174**, **175**, **176**), were also directed to him; **177** was also found in the same area. The other two tablets from Period 3 come from Room IV (**166**) and the courtyard, Room VIA (**167**). **172** is attributed to Period 2 and directed to Flavianus (perhaps Hostilius Flavianus, known as a correspondent of Cerialis from **261**); **173** is probably directed to Priscinus who was at some time probably prefect of the First Cohort of Tungrians. It therefore seems likely that Flavianus was also a prefect and that such applications were, at Vindolanda at least, normally addressed to the unit commander.

127

*Tab. Vindol.*I 12. Plate IV.

This leaf, which appears to be intact at the top, bottom and right, contains a version of the report which is paralleled only in **128** and probably **129** (but see above, p.76). The text is very abraded throughout.

] ̣ Iu ̣[ ]
[renunti]ụṃ cḥọṛtis viiii
[Batauor]ụṃ ọṃṇes ad loca
[q(ui) uideb]ụṇṭ et inpedimenta ̣ṛ
] *uacat*
[*uacat?* renu]ṇṭịạuẹrunt optiones
[et] cuṛạṭọṛẹṣ *uacat*
[detul]ịṭ Verecundus opṭịọ
[*c.5*] ̣ ̣ ̣ ̣ ̣ ̣

1. The first trace after the break looks like the top of *s*. Therefore perhaps *Idu]ṣ*, which is normally not abbreviated in these reports (**135**.1, **136**.1), or *Nona]ṣ*. The last trace is compatible with *n*, suggesting *Iuṇ[ias*; the tablet is intact after this but no trace of ink survives. If our reconstruction is correct, the remainder of this line will have been left blank (cf. **135**).

2. The traces at the beginning of the preserved part of the line are very faint indeed and the reading can only be said to represent what we assume to have been there.

cḥọṛtis viiii: an apparent vertical after *c* is probably dirt rather than ink. For *chortis* cf. **396**. The numeral has a superscript bar.

3. *ọṃṇes*: the last two letters are certain and *ṃṇ* is possible, but the preceding traces are wholly unclear. The remainder of the line after *loca* was left blank.

4. *inpedimenta*: for the use of *in-* for *im-* cf. **134**, **145**, **146**, **152**. The apparent traces

following this are problematical. The word is followed by a *uacat* in **134**, **139**, **145** and **146** (in the last case there may well be a punctuation mark at this point). In **130** and **135** the slight traces could be part of *renuntiauit* (see the notes *ad locc.*). This leaves **138**, where what is written before *renuntiauit* is not the end of *impedimenta*, and **150**.3 where there *might* be traces of a letter before the break. In the present instance there appear to be traces of three letters running up to the edge of the leaf, but the first might be a crack in the surface of the wood. Of the two remaining traces the second is *a* or *r*, the first could be *t*, *c* or *p*. The best solution we can suggest is that we have *pr* as an abbreviation of *pr(aesentia)*. For the use of *praesum* of inanimate objects see *P.Mich.*VIII 471.17-18 (= *CEL* 146), *quo tempus autem ueni omnia praefuerunt et lana et (linum?)*.

6-7. The words on line 6 are not quite properly aligned but this may be due to differential shrinkage of the fragments. Line 7 appears to be slightly inset, as perhaps is line 9 in comparison to line 8. For *curatores* see **128**.2 note.

9. There are traces of about 6 letters which presumably belong to the name of the century. They are compatible with the reading *Cres]c̣ẹṇṭịṣ* (see **128**.5 and cf. **148**.2 note) but cannot be said to compel it. There would be room for the centurial sign (but hardly the full word) in the lost portion. Since **127** and **128** appear to have the same formula at the end, it is possible that *(centuriae) Cres]c̣ẹṇṭịṣ* should be restored here.

128

Inv.no.85.242.a. 75 x 36 mm.

A fragment of a leaf which is complete at the right-hand edge and perhaps at the foot. It contains a report made by an *optio* named Arquittius in a form which is paralleled in **127** (see also above, p.76).

. . . .
ṛenụnṭịạ[ue]ṛ[unt optio-
nes et curatores
detulit Arquittius optiọ
(centuriae) Crescentis

2. *curatores*: the term occurs as a rank or regular position in units with cavalry, see Breeze (1974), 282-3, *RMR* 47.i.7, *CEL* 82 (= *ChLA* X 431). Elsewhere, it probably denotes a specific function or task rather than a regular rank (Gilliam (1986), 109-13, *O.Flor.*, p.24) and this may well be the case here. If we had the local equivalent of *curatores praesidii* (see *O.Flor.*, *loc. cit.*), they might be in charge of small detachments outposted to local fortlets (cf. **154**.16 note and introduction).

3. *Arquittius*: for this name as a *gentilicium* see *LE* 126, 403; it does not seem to occur as a *cognomen*.

4. For a century of Crescens see **148**.2 and note. The name is very common.

129

Inv.no.85.224. 102 x 42 mm.

A fragment containing the end of a report, probably in the same form as **127** and **128** (see also above, p.76).

. . . .
[de]tuliṭ Iụṣtiṇụṣ optio
(c̣ẹṇṭụṛịạẹ) *traces*

130

Inv.no.85.053.a. 66 x 33 mm. Plate VII.

Three joining fragments which belong to a single leaf. It is certain that the left-hand edge of the leaf is preserved and virtually certain that the top is also. It is probable that not more than about three letters are missing at the right in lines 3 and 5. At the foot we have lost the name(s) of the reporting officer(s). There are possible traces of writing on the back of the leaf.

The nature of the text is not in doubt but it poses problems to which we cannot offer any satisfactory solution, whether we suppose we have the conflation of two reports, a single text with some correction or addition by a second hand, or a palimpsest. We are confident that what survives is written in at least two hands, one hand responsible for lines 3, 5 and 6, and a different hand for line 4. So little remains of lines 1 and 2 that we are not sure whether they are written in the hand responsible for lines 3, 5 and 6, or the one responsible for line 4, or indeed whether both are in the same hand. However, the form of *e* in line 2 is strikingly different from the form in lines 5 and 6.

Two possible solutions occur to us. (a) Lines 1-2 contain a double date, the first the date of submission followed by *renuntium*, then perhaps by a preposition and a second date to which the report relates; after this the pattern would be regular except that a second hand has inserted line 4. The problem with this is that the inserted line does not correct what had already been written, since there is no sign of deletion, and does not appear to add anything new, but merely to repeat what is already stated in line 5 (but cf. the note to line 4). (b) If we ignore lines 2 and 4 we have a normal report in lines 1, 3, 5 and 6. We should then have to suppose that we have a poorly erased text in lines 2 and 4 (in which case a *first* hand wrote these two lines before a *second* hand wrote lines 1, 3, 5 and 6). We then need to explain the traces at the left in line 2 as not belonging to this line but to the feet of letters from the date in line 1 (e.g. the first two traces might be the foot of *p̣ṛ(idie)*); line 2 would then be aligned with line 4 (where no traces are visible at the left) and the figure in the date would be either *[x]v* or *[xi]v*. Here the problem is that, if the normal pattern was followed, we then have to suppose that line 2 contained, after the date, *renuntium coh viiii batauorum omnes*. This would not only make this line more than twice the width of lines 1, 3 and 5, but it would also make it much broader than any other tablet in this group. On balance we are inclined to favour the second solution, but certainty is obviously impossible.

[*c.4* Fe]ḅ[r]uariaṣ ṛ[enuntium
m^2? *traces* [*c.4*]v K(alendas) Februạạṛ[ias
m^1 coḥ(ortis) [viiii] Ḅatauorum ọm[nes
m^2? [*c.8*] ad locum q̣.....bụṇ[
m^1 ad loc̣uṃ q̣(ui) uiḍebunt eṭ [im-
pedimenta .[
. . . .

1-2. Our restoration is reasonably secure if the high trace at the broken edge is ink (it is likely to be *ḅ* and thus excludes *Ian]uariaṣ*). If we have a late or retrospective report beginning with the date of submission in line 1 and the date to which the report relates in line 2, we might have *ṛ[enun-* at the end of line 1 and *tium*, perhaps followed by *ad* at the beginning of line 2. For an alternative explanation of the traces at the start of this line see the introduction.

3. *ọm[nes*: although the first letter is not clear, we are reasonably confident that we can read *ọ* (rather than *i*, i.e. *ịm[munes*); see the introduction to this section.

4. After *locum* we expect *quidebunt* but only *q* and *b* are certain. The traces after *q* are so faint that they present no serious obstacle to the reading *ui*, and those after *b* can be said to be compatible with *un[t*; however, the traces between *q̣ụị* and *bụṇ[t* seem to require three if not four letters and are very hard to reconcile with *de*. If we are to look for a future indicative *ạbụṇ[t* is not easy but slightly less of a problem than *ẹbụṇ[t*.

6. There is a broken letter, which could be *r*, at the end of the line. This points to *ṛ[enuntiauit* (*-uerunt*), with the name(s) of the *optio(nes)* on a following line. Elsewhere, however, except for **138** (and possibly **135**), *renuntiauit/-uerunt* begins a new line, often with a *uacat* after *impedimenta*. Other possibilities are *n* or *p*, the latter suggesting that we may have the same word here as in **127**.4 (where see note).

131

Inv.no.85.101.a. 38 x 20 mm.

It is worth noting that the writing does not follow the grain and slopes downwards. Unusually, the second line begins further to the left than the first.

pr(idie) Noṇ[as
renunt[ium
. . . .

132

Inv.no.85.105. 31 x 14 mm.

x K(alendas) Iulias [

coh(ortis) vii[
traces
. . . .

2. The beginning of a superscript bar over the numeral is visible.

3. The traces cannot be read as *omnes*. Perhaps *a]ḍ ḷọc̣ụṃ*, although this would necessitate *omnes* in line 2 and would make it rather long.

133

Inv.no.85.123. 37 x 25 mm.

]ụarịas reṇ[untium
B]atauoruṃ [
traces
. . . . . .

3. Traces of the tops of a few letters are visible but they are too slight to enable us to offer a reading.

134

Inv.no.85.135. 110 x 22 mm.

There is no trace of a line lost at the top but the normal pattern would require one, which will have contained the date.

. . . .
renuntiuṃ c̣ọh(ortis) viiii Ḅaṭaụọ-
rụṃ ọṃṇẹṣ ạḍ ḷọc̣ạ q(ui) ụịḍe-
bunt et inpedimenta *uacat*
. . . .

1. There is probably a superscript bar over the numeral.

2. This line is very badly abraded and can only be read by analogy with the known pattern. Nothing except the first and last letters of the line is at all certain.

135

Inv.no.85.168. 70 x 20 mm. Plate VI. Bowman and Thomas (1987), no.2A. R.E.Birley (1990), Fig.20. *VRR* II, Plate VI.

The hand in which this report is written is of good quality. The top and right-hand margin are preserved intact and the largest of three detached scraps supplies part of lines 3-4. The second and third scraps contain part of the date in line 1. It is noteworthy that the date stands alone in line 1, with a medial point and a *uacat* following. The other side of the leaf contains four lines of a text written in a tiny script, the nature of which we have not been able to elucidate (**394**).

[*c.3*] Idus Ma[ ]ạs ·
[renunti]ụm coh(ortis) viiii Batauorum
ọmṇẹ[s ad] ḷoc̣a q(ui) uidebunt et impe-
ḍimeṇ[ta *c.7*]ạ[
. . . .

1. *Id]ụs*, *ed. pr.* One of the small fragments can now be seen to supply the beginning of *Idus*, with *us* and the beginning of the month-name on another. The position of these scraps, which can have had no more than four letters before what survives, was probably far enough to the left to make *Ma[rti]ạs* the more probable reading.

3. *ịṃṃ*, *ed. pr.* The word *omnes* is what we now expect at the beginning of the line and it is not difficult to read the first three letters; the trace before the break is compatible with *ẹ*. The loss implied by the previous line would just about accommodate the three more letters needed before *ḷoc̣a*. In the latter, *c* is curiously written almost exactly like *p* in *impe-* at the end of the line.

4. The trace at the right-hand end of the line which is signalled in the *ed. pr.* may not be ink. There is, however, a trace in the middle of the line which is probably the top of *a*. This would permit the restoration *renunti]ạ[u-*. Another possibility is that we have the same addition as in **127**.4 (cf. **130**.6); *[praesenti]ạ* is perhaps not too long for the available space.

136

Inv.no.85.176. 115 x 20 mm. Bowman and Thomas (1987), no.2B.

In this fragment the *e* in *renutium* is of some palaeographical interest, having an emphatic oblique ascender, as also in *Apriles*, though not so marked; in the latter we have an unexpectedly tall *p*, a phenomenon which is usually confined to initial letters.

vi Idus Apṛiles renutium
].[
. . . .

1. *renutium*: see the comment by Adams in Bowman and Thomas (1987), 133.

137

Inv.no.85.199.a. 57 x 80 mm.

This leaf is complete at the top and the left-hand side and probably also at the foot. The left-hand margin has the remains of two v-shaped notches and two tie-holes. On the photograph of this text it is particularly difficult to be sure which marks are ink and which are to be ignored.

pṛ(idie) Ịḍụṣ [
c̣ọh(ortis) viiiị Bạ[tauorum
ọṃṇẹṣ ạ[d
et impẹ[dimenta
renunṭ[iauit
ọptio (c̣ẹṇṭụṛịạẹ) . . [

1. The second letter seems to have a long descender which would only allow the reading *pṛ*.

2. There is the usual saucer-shaped mark over the numeral. The numeral could be read as *viii* (see our comment on this text in Bowman and Thomas (1987), 134 where, unfortunately, *vii* is a misprint for *viii*), but the evidence for the Ninth Cohort and the lack of evidence for an Eighth makes us prefer the more difficult reading.

3. *ọṃṇẹṣ*: *es* is a good reading and *n* before it suits the traces, but the reading of the first two letters is far from secure.

6. After the centurial sign, which is very abraded, we may have *Kạ.[* (but not *Kaṛ[i*), or *Ḷ..[*.

138

Inv.no.85.206. 69 x 25 mm.

This fragment exhibits some deviation from the normal formula.

. . . .
]. . . renunṭịạ[uit
]. optio (centuriae) Felicionis

1. It is not clear what preceded the verb. It is certainly not the end of *impedimenta* since the last letter cannot be *a*. It might be *c*, although we would expect to see the top of it if it were, but neither *ḥọc̣* nor *h]ạẹc̣* is persuasive. It looks more like *i* which suggests a genitive (cf. **127**.4 note).

2. The tiny scrap with traces of two letters followed by *op̣* appears to belong to this line. It is noteworthy that the centurial sign is written with a dot in the angle of the strokes, so placed that it cannot be intended as an interpunct after *op̣tio*. We have not found this anywhere else in the tablets. For the century of Felicio see **166**.1 note.

139

Inv.no.85.260. 76 x 37 mm. Plate IV. Bowman and Thomas (1987), no.2C.

This fragmentary report is written in a good, regular hand. The serifs on *i* and the form of *a* in *impe]ḍimenta* are noteworthy; in the latter *ḍi* may be a ligature.

. . . .
B]ạṭạuorum
ad] locum q(ui) ụidebunt
[et impe]ḍimenta *uacat*
uacat
[renu]ṇṭiauiṭ [
. . . .

2. There is an apex-like mark over *q* which we take to indicate the abbreviation of *qui* (see above, p.75). This is the only clear example of a marked abbreviation of this word (cf. **145**).

4. There is a mark at the left-hand edge which, if it is ink, may be an ascender from a line below.

140

Inv.no.85.276. 30 x 38 mm.

]. . reṇụṇ-
[tium coh(ortis) vi]iii Bata-
[uorum omn]ẹs ad locuṃ
[q(ui) uidebun]ṭ et [
. . . .

1. The traces at the left must be the end of the date. If we have *]ụṣ*, it can only have been *Aprilib]us*; but *]ṛịṣ* is also a possible reading.

2. The numeral has a superscript bar.

141

Inv.no.85.282.a. 50 x 14 mm. Bowman and Thomas (1987), no.2D.

It is noteworthy that the writing slopes upwards in relation to the grain of the wood (cf. **131**). The very small *o* in *ḷọca* and the serifs on *i* are of palaeographical interest.

. . . .
[r]enuntiuṃ c̣[oh(ortis)
[om]ṇes ad ḷọca q(ui) uịde[bunt
. . . .

142

Inv.no.85.309.b. 67 x 30 mm.

. . . .
traces
ọṃṇẹṣ ạ[d loc]ạ q(ui) ụ[idebunt
et impedim[enta
. . . .

2. The reading is very uncertain but the traces are compatible with the normal pattern.

143

Inv.no.85.328. 97 x 21 mm. Bowman and Thomas (1987), no.2E and Plate XVB.

viiii K(alendas) Ianuarias renun-
ṭịụm coh(ortis) viiii Baṭạuorum
. . . .

2. This line must begin with a tall *t* of which the cross-bar has been lost.

144

Inv.no.85.334. 43 x 10 mm.

A fragment in which the numeral should presumably be restored as *viiii* and which may possibly belong to one of the other reports (but it might be from a document of a different type). It has a capital form of *h* and a superscript bar over the numeral.

. . . . . .
coh(ortis) viii[
. . . . . .

145

Inv.no.86.341. 81 x 14 mm.

. . . .

traces?
ạḍ ḷọca q(ui) uidebunt et inpẹ-
ḍịṃenta *uacat*

. . . .

2. There might possibly be an abbreviation mark after *q*, cf. **139**.
3. There is a dark oblique stroke after *-dimenta* which is unlikely to be ink.

146

Inv.no.86.343. 76 x 28 mm.

This fragment is complete at the left- and right-hand margins. The back contains remains of three lines, much abraded and perhaps erased, written across the grain.

. . . .

et inpedịmenta *uacat*
uacat
[renun]ṭịauit Candidus

. . . .

1. The marked serif on *i* and the form of *n* following are interesting. There are two marks at the end of the line, one horizontal and one oblique like an apex. It is not clear whether either or both of these are ink and, if so, deliberate marks of punctuation (see above, p.57 and cf. **248**.i.2 note).

2. For the name Candidus in these reports see **148**.1. The name is very common (cf. **181**.2) and it is possible that these are two different men. Unfortunately the name of the century to which the Candidus of **146** belongs is not preserved.

147

Inv.no.86.360. 75 x 20 mm. Plate III.

This report is written in a very large and elegant script.

].[....]ṣ [r]ẹṇuntium

. . . .

1. We would expect to see something of the *e* if the month-name ended *-es*. *Idu]ṣ* (or *Nona]ṣ*) *[Maia]ṣ* would fit the traces and the spacing.

148

Inv.no.86.426. 78 x 33 mm.

One of two reports, in different hands, submitted by an *optio* named Candidus (see **146**). Given the commonness of the name it is not safe to assume identity since the name of the century to which the Candidus of **146** belonged is lost.

. . . .
uacat
ṛenuntiauit Candidus optio
[ce]ṇṭụṛịạẹ Crescẹṇṭịṣ
uacat

1. *ṛenuntiauit* has a very tall *e*, and the initial *o* of *optio* is also large.
2. *ce]ṇṭụṛịạẹ*: the traces at the beginning of the line are difficult but compatible with the reading. There is no other certain example in which the word is written out in full (but see **316**.6 note and **242**.i.3 note).

149

Inv.no.86.428. 61 x 23 mm.

This fragment is complete at the left margin and there survives a trace of a descender from the first line which must have contained only the date.

].[
renuntium coh(ortis) v[
. . .ẹṣ ad loca q(ui) uiḍẹ[bunt et impe-
ḍ[imenta
. . . .

2. *coh*: *c* has an abnormally long top-stroke which covers the two letters following, cf. perhaps **168**.4.
3. The traces surviving at the beginning of this line are very abraded. Probably we simply have *ọṃṇẹṣ*, slightly inset; there seems to be insufficient room for *rum omnes*.

150

Inv.no.86.479. 54 x 17 mm.

This fragment is probably intact at the left-hand margin. The text must have been written in short lines and the hand is a crude one; the feet of *t* and *p* are noteworthy.

. . . .
ọmṇẹṣ aḍ ḷ[
q(ui) uidebun[t et im-
pedimenta ̣[
]̣ ̣[
. . . .

1. There is rather more space than we would expect between *m* and *ṇ* in *ọmṇẹṣ*, but despite the loss of the tops of all the letters we are reasonably confident of the reading.

3. It is not certain whether there is the trace of a letter at the right before the tablet breaks off (cf. **127**.4 and note). Normally *renuntiauit* would begin a new line.

4. The traces are too uncertain to offer a reading.

151

*Tab. Vindol.*I 2, Plate I, 5.

With the evidence of the tablets found in the 1980s, there is no difficulty in recognising the category to which this text belongs and the unit involved as the Ninth Cohort of Batavians, despite the fact that a break in the leaf makes the reading of the numeral by no means straightforward (see line 2 note). The script has a number of serifs - *l* is a particularly emphatic example.

pr(idie) Nonas Ịuliạ[s
vịiii Baṭ[auorum
ad locuṃ [
ẹṭ imped[imenta
. . . .

1. This line must have contained *renuntium* and, unusually, *coh(ortis).*

2. The numeral has a superscript bar. A close examination of the original supports the reading *viiii* (against our remark in Bowman and Thomas (1987), 134, cf. A.R.Birley (1990a), 19).

152

*Tab.Vindol.*I 47, Plate X, 3. *CEL* 114.

This fragment of text can now be recognised, perhaps surprisingly in view of the elegance of the hand (see Thomas (1976), 41), as a report of this type.

. . . .
bunt et inpẹ[dimenta
ṛẹ[n]ụṇtiauit ạ .[
. . . .

1. *inpọ[*, *ed. pr.* The last letter is a mere trace at the broken edge. There is no doubt about the *n*, however, and this form is paralleled in **127**.4, **145**.2-3, **146**.1.

2. *ạ .*: presumably the beginning of the name of the *optio*. The first letter might alternatively be *d*. *C]ạṇ[didus* (cf. **148**) does not seem possible.

153

*Tab.Vindol.*I 66. *CEL* 132.

. . . .
traces
]nt et impediṃ[
] ṛẹnuntiauerṛ[unt
. . . .

2. *]nt*: there are no visible traces preceding but *uidebu/nt* is an impossible word division and we must assume that at least *bu* has disappeared. This implies between lines 2 and 3 a division *impediṃ[en-/ta*. Note that **127** has something between *impedimenta* and *renuntiauerunt* (see line 4 note).

154

Inv.no.88.841. 86 x 394 mm. Plate V. Bowman and Thomas (1991), 62-73 and Plate VIII. *VRR* II, Plate II.

A diptych on which the text is written across the grain of the wood; R.E.Birley informs us that this leaf is cut from oak. Only two lines of text run over on to the second half of the diptych, the great majority of which is apparently blank. There is one physical characteristic of the text which deserves special emphasis - the sheer size of the diptych; with the single exception of **161** which was found in close proximity, it is very large by comparison with all the other leaf tablets, which are no more than half its size. Given that almost half of the piece is blank, however, it cannot be envisaged that it was cut especially for this text, so we must conclude that it is merely accidental that almost no other leaves of this dimension have survived. The text is complete, although badly abraded in the middle section. The back of the tablet is blank.

The hand is a typical example of Old Roman Cursive of this period. It is competent without showing any pretensions to elegance. There is some use of ligature but this is found only rarely. We have noticed nothing unusual in any of the letter forms. It is possible that the same hand may be responsible for **161**.

The text is a strength report of the First Cohort of Tungrians. There are three main elements. The heading contains the date, name of the unit, name of the commanding officer and the total strength of the unit. Then follows a list of those absent on detached duties, a total of the absentees and a total of the remaining *praesentes*. Then we are given the number of the *praesentes* who are unfit for active service, broken down into categories. This section concludes with the total of *ualentes*, obtained by subtracting the number of the unfit from the number of *praesentes*. In the *ed. pr.* we discussed the location of the tablet in the Period 1 Ditch and noted that the name of the prefect of the unit, Iulius Verecundus, suggested a connection with other documents in which this officer is named (see **210-12**). It now appears much more likely that the material in this ditch was produced by the occupants of Period 2 (see *VRR* II, 23), which would place the presence of Iulius Verecundus and the First Cohort of Tungrians at Vindolanda in the years *c.* AD 92-7.

Apart from being the only document of its kind from Britain, this text provides us with our only known example of a strength report of an auxiliary *cohors milliaria peditata*. For a full discussion of the classification of military reports see the introduction to the *ed. pr.* (to the references in (4), pp.64-5, should be added *ChLA* XI 497, a fragment of a roll of a *cohors equitata*, with summary of strength at the bottom). It is evident that **154** cannot be straightforwardly classified as a *pridianum*: the date is inappropriate and it does not list accessions, losses and absentees in the appropriate form. Nor does it appear to be a daily report, although it does list those who are unfit for service and might, in the abraded section in the middle, specify what some of the detachments were doing. The documents which it most resembles fall into the "monthly summary" category of *RMR* (see Bowman and Thomas (1991), 64) but there is no doubt that the Vindolanda report does not fall on the first of a month. It is perhaps best to regard it as an example of an interim strength report from which a *pridianum* could eventually be compiled. We might go further and suggest that the "monthly summary" and the *pridianum* should perhaps be regarded as complementary types of document within the same category. It is also worth bearing in mind that the archaeological context of the Vindolanda tablet gives us no reason to suppose that this document went into the official archives of the unit - it is perhaps more likely to have been an interim report compiled for the commanding officer. There is some support for this in the text itself. In several places the numbers are rather crushed in, as if that part of the information was added after the outline of the report had been drafted and we are inclined to think that the left-hand side of lines 5-15 was written first, before the numbers were added at the right.

It should be noted that the readings of all the numerals are not absolutely certain (see notes to lines 3, 7, 17, 19, 26) but the orders of magnitude are certainly correct and the margin of error applies only to digits below 10. With this proviso, the dispositions may be tabulated as follows:

Line 3	Total	752	inc. 6 centurions

Absentees:

Line 5	Singulares	46	
Line 7	Coria	337	inc. 2 centurions (?)
Line 9	Londinium	1	centurion (?)
Line 10	...	6	inc. 1 centurion
Line 12	...	9	inc. 1 centurion
Line 14	...	11	
Line 15	...	1	
Line 16	...	45	
Line 17	Total	456	inc. 5 centurions

Present:

Line 19	296		inc. 1 centurion
Of whom there are:			
Line 25	Unfit	31	
Line 26	Healthy	265	inc. 1 centurion

The first point which calls for comment is the overall strength of the unit and the number of centurions. The First Cohort of Tungrians was a peditate milliary unit which, according to orthodox dogma based on the statement of Hyginus 28, should have had 10 centuries. Although there is no positive proof of the notion that the centuries will have been 80 strong (see Frere and Wilkes (1989), 118), the figure of 752 is tolerably close to a notional strength of 800. There can be, however, no possible doubt that the Tungrian cohort had only 6 centurions. There is good evidence for the existence of only 6 centuries in *equitate* milliary cohorts (such as the Twentieth Cohort of Palmyrenes) and it has been supposed that they might consist of 6 centuries of 140/150 each plus 5 *turmae*; scholars differ in their views of how such an arrangement might have evolved (see Hassall (1983), 99-100). There is nothing in our Vindolanda text to indicate the size of the centuries. Six centuries in a notional strength of 800 would give us an approximately 130-strong century, but the dispositions of the unit listed in our text do not support such a figure. It may simply be that during a period of transition when the size of the unit fluctuated somewhat (being brought up to milliary size in the 80s and then reduced to quingenary between 103 and 122) it proved impractical to maintain a strictly "correct" number of constituent centuries (cf. *VRR* II, 6-7). If we have read the figures correctly, it is striking that only 3 of the 6 centurions are in charge of major sections of the unit, one at Vindolanda and 2 (?) at Corbridge (see below, line 15 note); of the remaining 3, one is at London on his own and the other 2 are in charge of 6 and 9 men respectively. Again, this may reflect the tendency to make *ad hoc* arrangements in frontier regions during periods of flux. Even so, given the small amount of documentary evidence for the actual size and organisation of auxiliary units, it is striking that almost all of it diverges in some degree from what orthodoxy regards as the norm.

The details of the disposition of the unit are also remarkable. The 46 *singulares legati* will have been the contribution of *pedites* made by the Tungrian unit to the governor's guard (see line 5 note). Then there are 337, by far the largest single group, stationed "*coris*". There is every likelihood this is Corbridge and this is the strongest single piece of evidence relevant to the debate about its Latin name - it was probably simply *Coria* (see line 7 note). It is remarkable that this large section of the unit, which outnumbers that left behind at Vindolanda, is probably under the command of just two centurions, possibly only one. Following this we apparently have a single centurion in London, presumably on some special mission or message (for another connection between Vindolanda and London see **310**). The postings or activities of the following four groups are unfortunately impossible to elucidate; only the last is sizeable, consisting of 45 men (with no centurion). We have considered the possibility that these were *thetati* (the deceased), but this is the wrong position in the text for such an entry (at *RMR* 63.ii.11 they are included among losses, not absentees, and at *P.Brooklyn* 24.ii.5, Thomas and Davies (1977), they are the last entry before *summa qui decesserunt*). The number might be suitable as a detachment for garrisoning one of the Stanegate fortlets, but then it would be odd to find it lacking a centurion in command. Finally, it is worth noting that of the almost 300 who remained at Vindolanda, with one centurion, more than 10% were unfit for service; this text is unique in dividing them into categories, *aegri*, *uolnerati* and *lippientes*.

The most striking feature is the division of the unit into two major sections of which the larger was away from base at Corbridge. This strength report attests a degree of fragmentation which is by no means unique; accumulating evidence suggests, indeed, that it might well have been relatively normal, at least on the British frontier at this period. Corbridge may be a case in point (see line 7 note). This text supports evidence which has accumulated in the last two or three decades strongly militating against any notion that units would remain in relatively permanent garrisons constructed for them according to a model which can be reconstructed on the basis of the composition of particular types of units (see Maxfield (1986), 59).

↓ xv K(alendas) Ịuṇias n(umerus) p(urus) [co]ḥ(ortis) ị Tụngrọ-
ṛụṃ cui prae<e>st Iulius Vere-
c̣ụndus praef(ectus) dc̣c̣lịị in is (centuriones) vi
ẹx ẹis absentes
singulares leg(ati) xlvi
officio F̣ẹrocis
Coris c̣c̣cxxxvịị
ịn is (centuriones) ịị
Londinio (centurio) [i]
uaṣ..aḍ[*c.4*]...apaḍụṇ...
in is (centurio) i
]ạc̣.........ạllia viiii
in is (centurio) i
...c...ịpẹndiaṭuṃ xi
ịṇ.ạ ị
xxxxv
ṣụṃma absentes ccccḷvị
in is (centuriones) v
reliqui praesenṭes cclxxx̣x̣ṿị
in is (centurio) i
ẹx eis
aegri xv
uolnerati vi
ḷịppientes [x]

summa eoṛ[um]		x̣xxi
reliqui ualent[es		cc]lx̣ṿ
	in [is (centurio) i]	

"18 May, net number of the First Cohort of Tungrians, of which the commander is Iulius Verecundus the prefect, 752, including centurions 6

of whom there are absent:	
guards of the governor	46
at the office of Ferox	
at Coria	337
	including centurions 2 (?)
at London	centurion 1 (?)
...	6
	including centurion 1
...	9
	including centurion 1
...	11
at (?) ...	1 (?)
	45
total absentees	456
	including centurions 5
remainder, present	296
	including centurion 1
from these:	
sick	15
wounded	6
suffering from inflammation of the eyes	10
total of these	31
remainder, fit for active service	265
	including centurion 1."

1-3. None of the elements in the heading is unexpected but as a whole it is not precisely comparable to the headings of other military documents, of which comparatively few survive intact. That of *RMR* 64, the *pridianum*, has much more detail including the consular date and the station. The morning report from Dura (*RMR* 47) has a more detailed breakdown of the cohort, followed by the password. Reports of other types have less detail. *RMR* 62 ("monthly summary") has simply the date followed by the number of *equites*; in the daily reports from Bu Njem (*O.Bu Njem* 1-62) the date is followed by a bare number; **155** has a date followed by *fạbṛịcis h(omines) cccxxxxiii*; **156**.1 has no total after the date heading.

xv K(alendas) Ịuṇịas: the date suggests no obvious connection with *pridiana*. It must reflect the state of the unit at the period of maximum military activity (early summer). Gilliam's view ((1986), 263-72) that strength reports were made at intervals (probably monthly) throughout the year and then summarised at the end of the year seems to us persuasive. But our Vindolanda strength report would then have to be seen as an internal, interim report from which the monthly *pridianum* was compiled. It is difficult to find any evidence for regularity in dates. *RMR* 66 b.ii.9 ("unclassified") records the strength of the Twentieth Cohort of Palmyrene Archers at *xv Kal(endas) Octobr(es)*, followed by a string of dates against which is entered *n(umerus) p(urus) mansit*. In the so-called Moesian *pridianum* Fink originally read *xv K(alendas) Octobres* (*RMR* 63.i.23 note) but Marichal (*ChLA* III 219) prefers *xvi* (see his note *ad loc.*); the facsimile seems to support this reading which Fink has accepted in *RMR*.

1. There are difficulties in reading what follows the date. *n* with a superscript bar is clear. The next letter looks like *o*, but *p* (or *c*) is also possible and parallels (e.g. *RMR* 47.i.1, ii.1, 50.i.5, *ChLA* X 454, XI 479) make it virtually certain that we must here have the expression *numerus purus*; it is not clear whether the superscript bar extends beyond the *n* but *n p* is the usual abbreviation for this expression and it is certain that *purus* cannot have been written in full in our text (*O.Bu Njem* 57.1 may have *n(umerus) pur(us)* but the reading is doubtful). The next clear letter is a *t*; before this we might have another *t*, but it can just be read as *i* with a superscript bar (i.e. the number one), and before this we might read part of *h* in the capital form. What we expect here is the name of the unit and the only possibility we can envisage is *coh(ortis) i Tungrorum*, which fits the other evidence for the identity of units in this area at this period. After *t* it is very difficult to read *u*; then *n* is clear; the next letter looks most like a square *o* but may be read as *g* if we assume that the tail is no longer visible; then *r* is clear; of the rest of *tungrorum* all that can be said is that the reading would at least suit the meagre remaining traces. All in all, the reading is palaeographically fragile, but the historical evidence makes it overwhelmingly probable that it is correct. For recent evidence for the unit's presence in Britain see *Britannia* 18 (1987), 369, no.10, an undated inscription from Housesteads reading *coh(ors) I Tu(ngrorum)*; *Britannia* 19 (1988), 502, no.70 (a spear-head from Vindolanda, after AD 120, with a punched inscription reading *tung*).

2. *prae<e>st*: this haplography is also found in *ChLA* XI 501.5.

2-3. *Iulius Verec̣ụndus*: for other texts concerning this prefect see **210-12.**

3. *praef*: unusually for a milliary cohort, the First Tungrian was regularly commanded by a prefect rather than a tribune, see Smeesters (1977), *VRR* II, 8.

dc̣c̣lịị: the first two digits are relatively clear. Thereafter the readings are more conjectural. Palaeographically, we cannot exclude *dc̣c̣c̣ḷ*, but since the number in line 17 is clearly 450+ and that in line 17 250+, a number in the 700s is required. It would be possible to read *dcclx̣ị* but the reading we have adopted fits more easily with the other numbers.

in is: *is* could be explained as a contracted form of *iis* (cf. *coris* < *coriis* (line 7 note)). In lines 4 and 21, however, the writer uses the form *eis* with *ex*. Would he have written one form of the ablative plural of *is* with *in*, but another with *ex*? Contrast *ChLA* X 454 which has *in eis* in line 12 and *ex eis* in line 40. It is obviously possible that *is* represents *his*, with loss of *h* (for *in his* see, e.g., *O.Bu Njem* 5.3, 13.2). But since one cannot be certain that the writer would not have alternated between *in i(i)s* and *ex eis*, the form he intended in *is* should be left open. *i(i)s* and *(h)is* are later hopelessly confused in manuscripts (see *TLL* VI.3 2692.25) and the ambiguity of this form illustrates the reason.

(centuriones) vi: there is no doubt about the reading and the number is guaranteed by the individual dispositions and the total given below. This is a major surprise. For the difficulties involved in assessing unit strength and organisation see the introduction. If this strength report is to be dated in the early 90s it may attest the Tungrian unit at a time when its enlargement and reorganisation were still uncompleted (cf. *VRR* II, 6-7).

5-6. *leg*: this is not an easy reading - the last letter looks more like *s* than *g*, but the sense renders *leg(ati)* inescapable. We are in some doubt as to how we should interpret these lines. It is worth comparing *RMR* 63.ii.25, *singulares fabi iusti legat in is carus dec e[*, Fabius Iustus being the governor of the province; that is followed (line 26) by *officii latiniani proc aug* and on that basis we might expect that our *officio Ferocis* refers to a detachment serving with the procurator. However, we do not think there are any traces of ink visible at the end of line 6 and it is very unlikely that ink would not show up at this point where the tablet is less abraded than on the left. We are therefore inclined to suggest that we should take the two lines as a single entry, see further below.

On the *singulares* in general see Speidel (1978), and on the British *singulares*, Appendix I, 126-9, Davies (1976), Hassall (1973), 231-7, *Britannia* 19 (1988), 496. The provincial governor's corps of *singulares* consisted of 500 *pedites* and 500 *equites*. The contribution of the First Cohort of Tungrians to this corps was 46 *pedites*. It is generally agreed that the *singulares* of the governor of Britain were based in London at the Cripplegate fort (Hassall (1973)). They might be employed on special duties (see Speidel (1978), 44).

xlvi: the numeral is here written *xlvi* whereas in line 16 a number in the forties is written in the more usual form *xxxxv*. The reading seems secure, however, and the use of both conventions in the same document can be paralleled in *RMR* 68.ii.19, 31, 69.18, 25a.

officio Ferocis: the location of this group of *singulares* depends on the interpretation of this phrase. If Ferox is some official other than the governor to whom the *singulares* were detached we would expect him to be high-ranking. One possibility is that he was a legionary legate, to whom some of the governor's *singulares* were attached (*leg(ati)* without further qualification must surely refer to the provincial governor). It is a difficulty, but perhaps not a decisive one, that an inscription of the reign of Trajan proves that a *legatus legionis* could have his own *singulares* (*AE* 1969/70, 583.6-7 = Speidel (1970), cf. *id.* (1978), 78-9). Ferox is not a common cognomen. The two consuls of this period who bear it are Cn. Pompeius Ferox Licinianus (suff. 98) about whom nothing else is known and Iulius Ferox (suff. ?99, *PIR*^{2} I 306), who had held a provincial governorship at some time before the date of Pliny, *Ep.* 10.87 (i.e before *c.* AD 110), in which post he is said to have recognised the merits of Nymphidius Sabinus. The chronology of his career suggests the possibility that he might have held a legionary legateship *c.* AD 90 and the most likely unit would surely be *legio IX Hispana*, based at York. The archaeological context of the tablet seems to rule out the possibility that the reference is to Iulius Ferox as provincial governor, a post which he could, in theory, have held *c.* AD 105, where there is ample room in the *fasti* between Neratius Marcellus and Metilius Bradua (see A.R.Birley (1981), 87-94). If lines 25 and 26 of *RMR* 63.ii are also a single entry the troops at the *officium* of the procurator Latinianus will also be *singulares* and the parallel will be all the more striking.

officium: compare *P.Brooklyn* 24.iii.10 (Thomas and Davies (1977)), *officio epistrategi theb..os*.

7. *coris*: this can hardly be anywhere other than Corbridge and it provides the clearest piece of evidence relevant to the long-standing doubt about the Latin name of the site. The natural assumption must be that it was *Coria* and that *Coris* is a locative form, = *coriis*. The contraction of *-ii-* is standard by this time in all but the most formal writing. For Vindolanda see **343**.i.9, *Tab.Vindol.*I, p.73 and cf. Adams (1990a), 235. We may have the uncontracted form in **412** and the contracted form again in **175**.3. In **312**.back 1 we may have *coris* followed by an ethnic or tribal name, referring to a different place (see note *ad loc.*). The root *corio-* is Celtic, *AS* I 1126, cf. *PNRB* 317-9. In the case of some place-names there may

have been interference from the Latin *curia*, as *PNRB* suggests, but obviously not in this name. The form of the locative shows that Latin speakers interpreted *Coria* as a neuter plural. Hind (1980) argues for Corioritum as a Roman adoption for the successive bases and forts at Corbridge.

cccxxxvii: only the reading of the last two digits of the numeral is open to any serious doubt, so the figure must be well in excess of 300 and it is very surprising to find almost half of the strength of the Tungrian cohort at Corbridge in the charge of only two centurions (see note to line 15). There are no solid clues as to the nature of the garrison of the early forts at Corbridge (Phases 1a and 1b), see Bishop and Dore (1988), 129. Fort 1a may be about 13 acres in area, larger than the standard auxiliary cohort-sized fort, but smaller than a legionary fortress, and it seems to fit into the pattern of the so-called "vexillation fortress", see Frere and St. Joseph (1974), 6-7. There is no doubt, therefore, that the section of the Tungrian cohort will have been only one element in the garrison of Corbridge at this time.

8. *(centuriones) ii*: for the reading of the numeral see note to line 15.

9. The entry seems to suggest one single centurion at London, see note to line 15, but no trace of a numeral survives after the centurial sign. For contacts between Vindolanda and London, see **310**.back 1 and introduction, and cf. our note to lines 5-6, above.

10-16. These lines present major problems of reading and interpretation, mainly because of severe abrasion of the writing at the left-hand side. It is clear from the figures at the right that the entries concern small detachments of troops. We might expect simply to have place-names at the left, as we have in lines 7 and 9, but the amount of writing in lines 10, 12 and 14 seems too great for this, unless all the names were composite ones such as *Isurium Brigantum*. Any attempt to elucidate these lines on this assumption is further hampered by the high degree of probability that the place-names, if that is what we have, are unknown.

A second possibility is that the entries describe the activities of different groups, such as we find, for example, in *RMR* 63.ii.27-37, sometimes with places specified. Lines 10 and 14 seem more likely to be of this type than the other entries.

10. The first three letters seem relatively clear and suggest the beginning of a place-name, though there is no known name in the region which begins like this. A short place-name followed by *ad* plus gerund(ive)?

12. In the *ed.pr.* we rejected the reading *Gallia* but we now think that it is at least a possibility, cf. **255**.i.3-4.

14. The traces invite the reading *stipendiatum* or something like it and one could adduce *stipendiari* in Pliny, *NH* 6.68 ("to serve for pay under"), cf. *ad opinionem stip* and *ad opinionem peten* (*RMR* 66 b.i.29-30, ii.1) and *[ad opin]ionem peten(dam)* in the Caerleon tablet, Tomlin (1986); see Davies (1967). Then we would have a reference to a group which had gone off to collect pay; Tomlin suggests (*op.cit.*, note to line 1) that the size of such a party for a *cohors milliaria* would be about 30 men, but this is not decisive against such an interpretation of the entry in the Vindolanda text. The much greater problem is that *stipendiatum* is hard to explain grammatically.

15. The length of line makes it look as if we simply have a place-name and *]in.a*, possibly *]inna*, would be suitable, though it does not look like a locative; but other readings are possible. What we have read as the digit *i* might, alternatively, be read as a centurial sign. The same possibility exists in line 9 (see note) and both entries need to be considered against the reading of the number of centurions in line 8 and the fact that we must arrive at the total number of five absent centurions (line 18). It is conceivable that we have only one

centurion at Coria (line 8), one in London and one in line 15. The traces in line 8 favour *ịị*, however, and the character in line 15 looks very much like the numeral at the end of line 13; whereas that in line 9 is much more sharply angled.

16. Given the lack of any trace at all at the left of line 16, it is difficult to know what to make of the entry as a whole. Perhaps the entry at the left was very short and has left no trace. We have considered and rejected the possibility that this refers to *thetati* (deceased). Forty-five soldiers would perhaps be an appropriate force for the garrison of a small outpost. It is worth noting that the writer has left a noticeably larger than usual space after line 16, where the detailed account of the *absentes* ends.

17. The reading of the first five digits of the numeral is beyond any reasonable doubt. *ṿ* is probable after this but nothing thereafter can be read securely. The number of *absentes* must be between 450 and 459. For *summa absentes* cf. *RMR* 50.1.6, 12, 63.ii.23, 38.

19. The reading of the first five digits of the number is secure, so we must have at least 270 *praesentes*. The small figures depend on calculation.

22-5. Daily reports from Bu Njem (*O.Bu Njem* 1-62) include entries for *aegri* and name the individuals. See also *RMR* 63.ii.44 and *ChLA* X 443.ii.3. What is remarkable in our Vindolanda text is that the unfit are broken down into categories and comprise, in all, over 10% of the *praesentes*. See the note by Jackson (1990a), 13 and note also *Doc.Masada* 723.

24. *ḷịp̣p̣ientes*: palaeographically, the reading of the first four letters is unclear but the traces are compatible with the reading suggested. The term refers to chronic general inflammation of the eyes. See Kind, *RE* XIII (1927), 723-6, Jackson (1988), 82-5, Boon (1983), Jackson (1990a), (1990b), and cf. *RIB* II 2446, A.R.Birley (1992).

26. We can find no parallel in strength reports for the recording of the *ualentes*, but the reading is not in doubt. The numeral cannot be read in full, however, and the restoration is based entirely on arithmetical calculation.

27. We can see no clear sign of writing below this, and we might well expect the document to end at this point. The lower half of the second section of the leaf, on which lines 26-7 are written, is clearly blank, but there are possible traces of two or three lines below line 27.

155

*Tab.Vindol.*I 1, Plate I, 1.

Military reports of this general type also occur in **156** and probably **157**. Both these texts are written along the grain of the wood, as is **155**. If the archaeological attribution to the earlier part of the 90s is correct (see the introduction to the *ed. pr.*), the number of men reported in the *fabricae* (343) should perhaps be compared to the total of 265 men of the First Cohort of Tungrians who were at Vindolanda and fit for service (**154**). This would suggest the presence of part of at least one other unit at Vindolanda in this period. This text may be compared with the daily reports in *O.Bu Njem* 1-62 and with *ChLA* X, 409, details of duties in a legionary *fabrica* of the second/third century AD. See also the discussion in Bishop (1985).

vii K(alendas) Maiạs fạbṛịcis h(omines) cccxxxxiii
ex eịṣ suṭores *uacat* xii
ṣ[tr]ụctọṛẹṣ ad balṇeum xviii
[a]d plumbụm *uacat* [
[a]ḍ .ạṛ.[
[..]..a[ ] ụaletudinar[
ad furnaceṣ [
ad lutum [
tectores [
...apil.[
ạḍ cae[
[.]..b[
ad p.[
cum[
. . . .

"25 April, in the workshops, 343 men.
of these: shoemakers, 12
builders to the bath-house, 18
for lead ...
for ... wagons (?) ...
... hospital ...
to the kilns ...
for clay ...
plasterers ...
for ... tents (?) ...
for rubble ...
..."

1. In the *ed. pr.* we were unable to cite a certain parallel for *h* = *h(omines)*; it can now be seen that it also occurs in **157**.2, 3. Note, however, *ChLA* V 305 = *P.Teb.*II 433, where *hom(ines)* occurs three times in an account. Despite the fact that the word *homo* is attested with the meaning "workman" and "soldier" (*TLL* VI.3 2889.14, 43), Marichal doubts whether this account is a military or administrative document and suggests that it might be a writing exercise. The evidence of the Vindolanda texts should be sufficient to allay such doubts.

3. *ṣ[tr]ụctọṛẹṣ*: cf. **156**.3 which is sufficient to resolve any doubt about the reading here. See Marichal's note in *O.Bu Njem*, p.81, where he suggests that the word does not indicate a specialist craftsman.

5. *a]ḍ p̣ịc̣ạrị[am* was suggested in the *ed. pr.* We now think that *a]d ḳaṛ.[* is possible and perhaps better. This would presumably be most likely to be a reference to wagons (cf. **343**.ii.17-8, **316**.2).

6. Perhaps a reference to the building of a hospital, cf. **156**.2-3 (where *hospitium* = "residence"). The presence of such a facility at Vindolanda is clearly implied by **154**.21-5.

7. In the *ed. pr.* we suggested that these might be kilns for firing clay. See now also **156**.4, *a]ḍ lapidem flạṃṃạndum*.

8. *lutum*: cf. **156**.5.

10. We now feel less dubious about reading *ạḍ* at the start where the surface is very abraded (cf. our note in the *ed. pr.*), and it would match the entries in lines 4, 5, 8 and 11. If that is possible we might have *p̣apilị[ones* ("tents", see *LS*, s.v.II) to follow; for possible evidence of the repair of tents at Vindolanda see *VRR* II, 93-4.

11. *cae[mentum* seems likely in the context. Loose rubble is perhaps indicated, cf. Pliny, *Ep.* 10.39.4, *quia sint caemento medii farti nec testaceo opere praecincti.*

156

Inv.no.85.248. 96 x 30 mm.

Ten joining fragments of a leaf which contain the beginning of a report of the same general type as **155** and **157**. It is dated 7 March and reports the activities of three groups of men, one building a *hospitium*, a second working at lime-kilns and a third to get clay for making wattle fences for the *castra*. This may all relate to routine construction work.

Nonis Martiị[s] *uacat*
missi ad hospitị[u]ṃ c̣ụṃ Mạrco medico
faciendum ṣtructores ṇ(umero) xxx
[a]ḍ lapidem flạṃṃạndum ṇ(umero) xviiiị
[a]ḍ lutum uiṃ[ini]ḅus castroruṃ facien-
[dum] *traces*
. . . .

"7 March
sent with Marcus, the medical orderly, to build
the residence, builders, number 30
to burn stone, number 19 (?)
to produce clay for the wattle fences of the
camp ..."

1. After the date heading, **155**.1 records a total number of men in the *fabricae* but there is no corresponding entry here.

2. *hospitị[u]ṃ*: in a military context the word normally means the residence of a particular officer or a soldier's billet in a civilian house (see *P.Dura* 107.i.22 and note, Adams (1992b), 5). The building at Vindolanda is surely in the fort but it is not specified as being assigned to an individual; perhaps it is simply a residence used as a guest-house (see *TLL* VI.3 3037). Despite the reference to the *medicus* (see below), this surely can have nothing to do with a hospital (for the *ualetudinarium* at Vindolanda see **155**.6).

c̣ụṃ Mạrco medico: there is no serious doubt about the reading of the name and title. What precedes it is very dark on the photograph; we might expect *cum* (cf. *ChLA* XI 454.32-4, **155**.14), for which there may be room if we suppose that the pieces did not fit flush at this point, thus allowing for the loss of *u* and most of *m* at the end of the preceding word. For *medici* in the army see Davies (1989), 213-4 and cf. *CEL* 57 (Vindonissa), *CEL* 14

(Valkenburg). Marcus can quite well be used as a *cognomen*, *P.Brooklyn* 24.ii.13 and note (Thomas and Davies (1977)); cf. **184**.ii.21, **207**.11.

3. *ṣtructores*: cf. **155**.3 and note. What is before the numeral is obscured by dirt and the corresponding point in line 4 is badly abraded. We may have nothing at all (as in **155**) but if the mark in line 3 is ink it looks more like *n(umero)* than *h(omines)*, which we might expect in view of in **155**.1 and **157**.

4. There is some abrasion in this line but we are confident of the reading. After *lapidem*, which is certain, *fl* is clear, then *ạṃ* are bare traces, but the remainder of the word looks very good and makes excellent sense. This group is likely to be dealing with lime (cf. **314**.2 and note the entry *ad furnaceṣ* in **155**.7). For quarrying in this region see **314** introduction, Jones and Mattingly (1990), 217 and map 6.37. For a brief description of the chemistry of the process, Rosenfeld (1965), 192.

5-6. *lutum*: see **155**.8. For *faciendum* cf. Cato, *Agr*. 14.3, *terram unde lutum fiat*. For clay deposits in the area see *VRR* I.

uiṃ[ini]ḅus: *ui* and *ḅus* are certain, despite the loss of the bottom of *b*, and the restoration fits the space and makes excellent sense; cf. Tacitus, *Ann*. 12.16, *moenis non saxo sed cratibus et uimentis aduersum inrumpentis inualida*. It seems likely, though it is impossible to be sure, that *castroruṃ* refers to Vindolanda itself, rather than some neighbouring fortlet.

157

Inv.no.86.364. 59 x 13 mm.

Evidently a report of the same general type as **155** and **156**.

. . . .

traces

].ẹum faciendum ḥ(omines) xxxxvi

].ẹc̣ṭẹṣạ.... h(omines) xviii

. . . .

2. At the beginning neither *bal]ṇẹum* nor *plu]ṭẹum* (cf. **309**.i.11) is attractive. For *h(omines)* see **155**.1 and note. It is noteworthy that this is not aligned with the corresponding entry in line 3.

3. There is some dirt adhering to the surface which obscures the writing. Perhaps .*ẹc̣ṭẹṣ ạḍ*....

158

Inv.no.85.190. 35 x 14 mm.

A fragment of the top left-hand corner of a leaf containing the beginning of what was probably a report similar to **155** and **156**.

pr(idie) K(alendas) Octobres [
ad ..[
. . . .

2. After *ad*, *ṭ.[* is a feasible reading.

159

Inv.no.85.048.a. 30 x 53 mm.

A fragment of the top left-hand corner of a leaf, complete only at the top and left. The space between the top edge and the first line of writing suggests that we might have the beginning of the document. The text is difficult to classify, not least because so little of it survives. It might be part of an account but it does not look like the other accounts which seem to relate to military units and it has no date. It is noteworthy that lines 4 and 6 are indented by a considerable amount. The fact that it refers to a *turma* indicates the presence of cavalry at Vindolanda.

↓ turm.[
hordiaṛ[
.x̣.ḷ.ạṣ[
ẹxe.[
penes tuṛ[
xx[
..[
. . . .

1. *turm.[*: there is a tiny trace at the broken edge of the leaf which is compatible with *a*. Presumably a reference to a *turma* and, if a heading, perhaps followed by a name, cf. **184**.i.1. There is a reference to a *conturmalem* in **329**.

2. *hordiaṛ[*: the letter at the break can comfortably be read as *r* but not as *t*; *hordiaṭ[or(es)* (cf. *RMR* 47.ii.5) is therefore excluded and the most likely restoration is *hordiaṛ[ia* or a cognate. This term occurs in *Doc.Masada* 722.6 and 13 where it means "barley-money" deducted from the *stipendium* of cavalrymen (see note *ad loc.*).

3. Perhaps a number (*ix* or *lx*?) at the beginning, but *x* does not compare well with the example in line 4 where it is certain.

4. *ẹxe.[*: the trace at the edge is compatible with *m* but certainly cannot be *r*. *exemplum* does not seem to offer much hope and the only other entry in the index of *RMR* is *exeṃ* (54.d.2, where Fink suggests that it might be part of the verb *eximo*); we might have *exeṃ[pti* here, cf. *OLD*, s.v.5b. Alternatively, we might have two words.

5. *penes* normally governs a personal noun, but *OLD*, s.v.1 has examples of its use with non-personal nouns, and in any case a *turma* is a collection of people. Therefore perhaps *penes tuṛ[mam* plus name?

6. *xx* is presumably a number but there is no indication whether it refers to men, money or commodities.

7. The reading may again be *xx* but this line is not indented (see introduction); perhaps compare line 3.

160

*Tab. Vindol.*I 3, Plate I, 6 and 7.

A leaf with writing on both sides, perhaps a document recording the activities of workmen. The order of the text is uncertain and our designation of the sides as A and B is therefore arbitrary. The text appears to record names in the nominative, followed by a trade and the century to which they belong, then adding the work on which they are engaged. This has been discussed by Bishop (1985) in connection with the manufacture of weapons and military equipment; note the archaeological evidence for the manufacture or repair of metal objects at Vindolanda (see *VRR* I). There is occasional use of interpunct.

A.

. . . .
↓ *traces?*
⟦] ẹm[⟧
⟦].riu..[⟧
⟦]utariuṣ [⟧
]arium · [
]us adiuụ[
⟦]arium [⟧
]s fabeṛ · (centuriae) ụ[
].um glaḍị.[
]uṣạs (centur-) fru[
⟦].tralem [⟧
⟦].s faber [⟧
⟦]rruṃ[⟧
m[2]]ṭ qṣ ẹ.[
. . . .

B.

. . . .
m[1] ⟦].eṇị ạ[⟧
⟦]ịụṣ · (centur-) .[⟧
⟦].ụṣ ṃạ.ṛị.[⟧
⟦].uus faber [⟧
]..am..[
]s · Rufiṇi [
].ạ.ẹạṇ.[
traces
].. faber [
⟦]atorium [⟧

ↄ]. frumeṇ[
]ạ. . am[
] (centur-) frum[
]m [
trace
. . . .

A.4. Cf. **184**.ii.21, *Luc̣ius scutarius* and *CEL* 26 (Vindonissa).

6. There are many possibilities, including *adiuụ[andum* and *ad iuụ[encos*, cf. **180**.33.

8. In the *ed. pr.* these words were transcribed as belonging to two separate lines. It now seems to us that the join between the two pieces of the leaf is close enough to take them as one line; the *r* is rather odd, but not impossible. For the century compare **184**.i.1. On *faber* see *O.Bu Njem*, pp.80-1.

9. Since *glaḍị.* cannot be preceded by a name, we prefer to envisage a reference to swords rather than some case of *gladiarius*; since *]ḍum* cannot be read, we do not have *ad* plus gerund(ive).

10. *]uṣạs*: perhaps the end of a name; *NPEL* lists Attusas, Beusas, Nausas.

fru[: see also B.11, 13. Perhaps "N of the century of Fru..."; for a name beginning with these letters (but probably not Frumentius, which occurs in *RIB* I 2109) see **187**.i.3.

11. Perhaps *de]x̣ṭralem*, an axe or hatchet, but the only example we can find (Isidorus 19.19.11) is late. Adams points out that *dextralis* goes into some Romance languages, including Spanish (Meyer-Lübke (1911), 2620) and that Isidorus would therefore have got it from contemporary usage rather than earlier Latin.

13. Possibly a reference to a *carrus*, cf. **343**.ii.17-8.

14. As a possible parallel we note that *ChLA* XI 497 has 5 lines added at the foot in a second hand, the last of which is read *ṣ(unt) q(uo)q(ue b(ene)f(iciarii) ii*. The first trace in this line might be *s* but *t* is preferable; thereafter we cannot read *qq* but we now prefer *qṣ* to *qp̣* of the *ed. pr.*

B.1 The first trace does not permit *(centuria) u]c̣eṇị*, cf. **184**.i.1.

2. After the centurial sign we cannot read *f* or *u*.

3. We might have the name Macrinus here.

4. *].ḷius*, *ed. pr.* We might have e.g. *Inge]ṇuus* (cf. **187**.i.11) or another name with this ending.

6. We cannot read a centurial sign before *Rufiṇi*.

161

Inv.no.88.837. 175 x 61 mm.

The left-hand portion of a very large diptych (compare **154**) with two notches and two tie-holes in the left-hand edge. At the left there are remains of perhaps 12 lines written along the grain. The text may be a simple list of names, cf. **365**, **367**, **491**, *P.Quseir al-Quadim* 18 (Bagnall (1986)); the surface is abraded at the right and if there was any writing in this area, which one might expect if it were an account, it has completely disappeared. The hand looks similar to that of **154**; since the two tablets were found in close proximity it is possible that this is a list of soldiers of the *cohors i Tungrorum*. Of the names we have deciphered, almost all of which are common, only Expeditus, Fuscus and Verecund..... might occur elsewhere, the first in a request for leave attributed to a different period (**171**.a.1 and note), the second in an account (**206**.back 5) and the third in **457**.

. . . .
traces of 2 lines
Fuscus
Sẹttius
Ẹxpediṭuṣ
Albinus
Verecund. . . . .
. .le.
Feṣṭus
traces of ?3 lines
. . . .

1. It is possible that this line commences slightly further to the left than the subsequent lines and that it begins with a centurial sign (cf. **184**.i.1).

4. The name looks most like *Sẹttius* but the cross-bar of *e* may be illusory; the alternative is *Sịttius*. Both names are listed as *gentilicia* in *RNGCL*.

5. *Ẹxpediṭuṣ*: the first letter is obscured by dirt but the reading is inescapable.

7. *Verecund*. . . . .: although the end of the name is abraded there is no doubt that there is more than *Verecundụṣ*; *optio* (cf. **127**.7) is not possible. *NPEL* lists Verecundinus as a *cognomen* (3 instances) and Verecundinius as a *gentilicium* (5 instances in Gallia Belgica); it is likely that we have one of these but the traces are so abraded that it is impossible to be sure which is a more plausible reading.

8. This is difficult because of the grain of the wood; it seems to end in *-les*, although *C̣eleṛ* (so *VRR* II, 25) should perhaps not be ruled out.

162

Inv.no.85.244. 33 x 86 mm. Plate in Lalou (ed. 1992), 208.

A fragment of a leaf containing two words written in a good capital hand. It is possible that it is some sort of "tag", merely recording the name of a soldier. Alternatively it might refer to an intelligence agent or *explorator* of some sort (see note to line 2).

↓ MILES
ARCANỤ[
uacat

2. Presumably *Arcanụ[s* is to be restored, to agree with *miles*. Arcanus is registered as a *cognomen* in *RNGCL*; it probably occurs as such in **333** and it may well be a name here; on the other hand, if that were the case, we might expect the words in the reverse order. The

only use we have found of the word *arcanus* in a military context is in Ammianus 28.3.8, where he describes military spies or secret agents: *inter haec tam praecipua, arcanos* [the ms. reading is *areanos*] *genus hominum a ueteribus institutum ... a stationibus suis remouit ... id enim illis erat officium, ut ultro citroque, per longa spatia discurrentes, uicinarum gentium strepitus nostris ducibus intimarent* (cf. Mann (1974), 40, note 50). Activities of this sort are certainly attested earlier (see *P.Mich.*VIII 469.24 note (= *CEL* 144), *ChLA* I 7 = *RMR* 9.15.e, Rankov (1987), 246 and cf. **164**, introduction) and it is noteworthy that Ammianus describes the *arcani* as a longstanding institution. If this were the meaning of the word in the Vindolanda text it would not make its purpose any clearer; could it be an "identity card" carried by someone moving around the countryside in "plain clothes" (*pagano cultu*, cf. *RMR* 9.15.e) to be produced if he were challenged by other Roman military personnel?

163

*Tab.Vindol.*I 11, Plate III, 4

This text is written across the grain and is perhaps the heading of a list of *optiones*. For the capital script cf. **162**.

↓]TIONES

. . .

164

Inv.no.85.032.a. 78 x 186 mm. Plate VI. Bowman and Thomas (1987), no.4 and Plate XVC. R.E.Birley (1990), fig. 23. *VRR* II, Plate VII.

This diptych contains six lines of writing on one face of one half of the tablet. There is neither a heading nor any other indication of the nature of the document but we cannot exclude the possibility that it is only part of a text the rest of which was written on other leaves (if so, presumably the end, judging by the fact that the lower quarter of the upper half of the leaf and the whole of the lower half is blank). The hand is a reasonably lucid cursive, not unlike that of **291**, but less elegant. Interpunct is employed several times. The indentation in lines 4 and 6 is odd and we can see no obvious reason for it.

Our best guess is that this is a military memorandum of some kind which describes the fighting characteristics and qualities of the native Britons with particular reference to cavalry. It might be an intelligence report directed to the commanding officer by *exploratores* (cf. Rankov (1987)), or possibly a piece of information provided with a view to the recruitment of natives, attested in the time of Agricola (Tacitus, *Agr.* 29.2). There is evidence for a British *ala* in Dacia in AD 110 (*CIL* 16.163; but note the remarks of Kennedy (1977) and cf. Reynolds, Beard and Roueché, *JRS* 76 (1986), 136). The first appearance of *numeri Brittonum* coincides with earliest occupation of Hesselbach on the Odenwald Limes *c.* AD 95-105 (see Hassall (1978), 45, Baatz (1973)). This suits the date of the Vindolanda text very well; in the *ed. pr.* we noted that its archaeological context placed it *c.* AD 92 but it has subsequently been reattributed to Period 3.

A more attractive alternative is to envisage it as a note or a draft of a note left by a departing commanding officer (cf. line 1 note) for his successor. This kind of instruction is recommended in a letter of AD 344 from Valacius the *dux* of Egypt to Flavius Abinnaeus, an *ala* commander, as he was about to relinquish his post (*P.Abinn.* 2.6-7): *de singulis etiam pro tutela publica obseruandis instruere [cura] ne quam sub primitiis saltem suis erroris titubantiam incurat* ("take care to instruct him in all the rules to be followed to guarantee public safety, in order to safeguard him from liabilities and mistakes, at any rate in the early days of his tenure").

The cursive hand and the fact that the text is written across the grain of the wood and *transversa charta* makes it unlikely that it is a literary text (cf. A.R.Birley (1991), 99, note 54), but it is perhaps worth bearing in mind that we do have Greek narrative texts on papyrus which describe military engagements, see Turner (1950) and cf. *P.Ross.-Georg.*III 1.

Especially noteworthy in the Vindolanda text is the occurrence, for the first time, of the patronising diminutive *Brittunculi* (line 5, contrast *Brittones* in line 1). This remains the only published text from Vindolanda which refers explicitly to the native Britons collectively or individually (cf. **180**, introduction and note Inv.no.1108, *VRR* II, 29). The information which the text offers is of some interest in view of the paucity of evidence for native British cavalry in this period. Our literary sources describe British *essedarii*, charioteers who went into battle with *pugnatores* whose role was to leap from the chariot at the appropriate time and engage on foot (Caesar, *BG* 5.16, 4.24.1, 32.5, 33, Pomponius Mela 3.6.52, Silius Italicus 17.417, Arrian, *Tact.* 19.2-3), cf. Stead (1965). That these were still prominent in Agricola's time (presumably only in the newly acquired or unconquered regions) is indicated by Tacitus' account of the battle at Mons Graupius (*Agr.* 35.3) and he elsewhere notes that the *essedarii* were persons of higher rank whilst the *pugnatores* were their *clientes* (*Agr.* 12). But it seems reasonable to assume that if our text were referring to these they would have been described as such in more detail. Tacitus certainly implies the presence of conventional cavalry too in the British forces at Mons Graupius (*Agr.* 36) and our Vindolanda text might be taken as an additional important indication of their prominence and character in the frontier region at the end of the first century AD.

. . . .

↓ nenụ . . . [.]ṇ Brittoneṣ
nimium multi · equites
gladis · non ụtụṇtur equites · nec residunt
Brittunculi · ụt · iaculos
mittant

"... the Britons are unprotected by armour (?). There are very many cavalry. The cavalry do not use swords nor do the wretched Britons mount in order to throw javelins."

1. The reading of the first three letters appears certain; the next letter is quite unlike all other examples of *u* in this hand but it is like *u* as made elsewhere in the tablets and we cannot think of any other way to read it. The next letter is wholly uncertain; what follows is a letter with a long descender, therefore *a*, *i*, *q* or *r*; the letter before *Brittoneṣ* could be

c or *e*, but we believe that *t* is also possible if all trace of the cross-bar has disappeared; note that there may well also be interpunct here. Our earlier suggestions, *-ne nuḍị s[u]nṭ Brittoneṣ* or *ne nuḍị ṣ[i]nṭ Brittoneṣ*, are therefore both acceptable readings, with the latter having the advantage that we do not have to suppose a word broken over two leaves, but the disadvantage that it is harder to make sense of it (except as the end of a sentence beginning on a previous leaf). If *nuḍị* is correct it is more likely to mean "unprotected by armour" than, literally, "stark naked" (cf. *OLD*, s.v. 4, citing Quadrigarius, *Hist.* 10b, *Gallus quidam nudus praeter scutum et gladios duos*, and Caesar, *BG* 1.25.4, *nudo corpore pugnare*; note also Tacitus, *Ann.* 12.35 on the Britons having *nulla loricorum galearumue tegmina*).

2. For *nimium* meaning "very" rather than "too" see *OLD*, s.v.; for its use in the latter meaning with *multus* cf. e.g. Cicero, *Planc.* 84, *quod nimium multos defenderem.* It does not seem difficult to understand a verb here (probably *sunt*) if there is a break in the sense after *Brittoneṣ* in line 1.

3. *gladis*: for *gladiis*. The contraction is common, cf. *Tab. Vindol.*I, p.73, **343**.i.9.

4-6. It is unclear from the syntax whether *nec residunt Brittunculi* etc. is intended to add further detail about the cavalry or whether it is to be taken as referring to the British fighting men in general, but the general sense of the passage perhaps favours the former. For the meaning of *residunt*, rendered in the *ed. pr.* as "take up fixed positions (*or* stay seated)", see now Adams (1994). On cavalry tactics in general see Arrian, *Tact.* 42-4.

5. *Brittunculi*: the word is new. For the formation Adams compares *homunculus*, *uirguncula*, *latrunculus*, *tirunculus*, etc., noting that the last two examples have the same type of base as *Brittunculus* (*latro/*, *tiro/*, *Britto/* + *-unculus*).

iaculos: Adams notes that the masculine is unattested but that there are other confusions of gender in our Vindolanda texts (e.g. *modiola*, *bruscas* in **309**.i.4, 10). Here the masculine may be due to the gradual loss of the neuter. For references to *iaculatio* in relation to cavalrymen it is interesting to compare Hadrian's remarks to the troops at Lambaesis, *ILS* 2487, 9134, 9135a.

165

*Tab. Vindol.*I 16.

Presumably the heading of a military document, probably a report of the same type as **127-53** or **155-7**.

xvi K(alendas) Mar[tias

. . . .

166

Inv.no.85.006. 70 x 22 mm.

This fragment is almost certainly complete at the top and the right.

]danus (centuriae) Felicionis
[ro]go domine Cerialis
traces
. . . .

" ...danus of the century of Felicio. I ask, my lord Cerialis ..."

1. *]danus*: *RNGCL* offers about a dozen possibilities for names with this ending. Possible alternative readings are *]ormus* and *]ornus*; for *cognomina* with the first termination *NPEL* offers only Hormus and Euhormus, both very rare; for the latter the possibilities are again limited: Necornus (*NPEL*), Cornus (?), Capricornus (*LC*).

The century of Felicio occurs in another *commeatus* request (**168**) and in a report (**138**). *Felicio (centurio)* also occurs in two accounts (**182**.i.6 and **193**.1), but the name is common and we cannot be certain that we have the same Felicio in all these texts.

2. The *g* of *ro]go* is very large and rises well above the line. The first three letters of *Cerialis* are almost completely abraded but the slight traces favour this reading as against *Genialis*.

3. Only sporadic traces of the tops of letters remain. If this line was indented, as seems to be the norm, the traces could fit the reading *di[gn]um [m]e hab[e]as*.

167

Inv.no.85.082. 102 x 25 mm.

This fragment is complete at the left-hand margin, where there may be the remains of one or two v-shaped notches; it may also be complete at the top (see line 1 note). A tiny scrap with exiguous traces of letters from two lines, which we have not attempted to transcribe, cannot be placed with any confidence.

traces?
rogo domine Cerialis
dignum me h[abeas
. . . .

"... I ask, my lord Cerialis, that you consider me a worthy person ..."

1. There may be faint traces of two or three descenders, but see **170** which appears to begin with *rogo*.

2. The first letter of *rogo* is enlarged. Only the bottoms of the letters in the name survive, but there is no real doubt about the reading.

3. Only the tops of the first five letters survive but *dignum* fits the traces very well. Thereafter only very faint marks are visible which are compatible with *me h[*. This line was certainly indented (cf. **174**.2).

168

Inv.no.85.236. 50 x 30 mm.

] (c̣ẹnṭuṛiạẹ) Felicionis
[rogo domi]ṇe Cerialis
[di]gnum me habeaṣ
[cu]ị ḍẹ[s comm]ẹạṭum
. . . .

"... of the century of Felicio. I ask, my lord Cerialis, that you consider me a worthy person to whom to grant leave ..."

1. For the century of Felicio see **166**.1.

2. This line must have projected at the left, as seems to be normal in these applications.

4. *[cu]ị*: there appears to be a dash over the end of this word; perhaps an abnormally long top-stroke of *c*, for which cf. **149**.2.

169

Inv.no.80.275. 116 x 45 mm.

Two joining scraps containing the beginning of a request for leave. A third scrap containing three letters (*ịus*), possibly in the hand of Cerialis (cf. **225-32**), does not belong to this text.

Gannallius (c̣ẹnṭuṛiạẹ) .ṛ. . .[
[rogo domi]ne Cerialis
. . . .

"Gannallius of the century of ... I ask, my lord Cerialis ..."

1. The name Gannallius is not attested but the reading is very clear. *NPEL* cites two occurrences of Gannicus, in Gallia Belgica and Noricum; *AS* I 1982, Ganapo at Nemausus in Narbonensis; note also Gannascus of the Chauci, Tacitus, *Ann.* 11.18. Cf. *LAN* 307-8.

.*ṛ*. . .: apart from *r*, only exiguous traces of the bottoms of letters remain. These would suit the reading *C̣ṛẹṣc̣[entis* (cf. **128**.4 for the century of Crescens) but there are other possibilities.

170

Inv.no.85.286.a. 123 x 34 mm.

There is a considerable amount of blank space above the writing on this fragment, which suggests that the name of the applicant might not have been written at the start (cf. **167**, **173** and perhaps **175**).

rogo dom<i>ne Cerialis
. . . .

1. *dom<i>ne*: the *i* has clearly been omitted. This may be an error but the form *domnus* is well-attested, see *OLD*, s.v., *TLL* V 1907.

171

*Tab.Vindol.*I 35, Plate VII, 3. *CEL* 103.

The pattern of applications for leave suggests that this text, tentatively assigned to the correspondence of Genialis in the *ed. pr.*, is another such, despite the difficulties inherent in reading and interpreting the two lines on fragment (b). The three fragments were found together, however, and there is every reason to think that they belong to the same tablet. It is notable that the lines are widely spaced and we think that the fragment (b), which we identified as containing part of column ii, perhaps fits below the major fragment (a), thus giving a text written on a half leaf (but there may be something missing in between). The two small fragments, of which the larger contains two letters (*ut*?), the smaller only one unidentifiable trace, cannot be placed with any confidence. The centurial symbol in a.1 has an unusually long tail.

a.
]ḍịtus (centuriae) Vern..[..].
[rog]ọ domine Cerialis
. . . .

b.
. . . .
]....ḅẹ....[
]..s.erḷer.[
. . . .

c.
. .
uṭ[
. .

"I, Expeditus (?) of the century of Vern.., ask, my lord Cerialis ..."

a.1. *Expe]ḍịtus* seems the most promising restoration. For the name see **161**.5.

Vern ..[..] .: the initial *V* is somewhat odd but *uern-* is a common Celtic prefix, see *AS* III 223-8. The completion of the name depends on the number of following letters of which traces survive. There seems to be too much ink for *Verni* which is the commonest name with this element. We now suppose that the faint marks after *s* which we interpreted as *uo* in the *ed. pr.* are not ink. We could read *Vernịạ[..]ṛ[*, suggesting a genitive of *Verniator* or *Verniatorius*, but have not been able to find these names attested. Alternatively, *Vernịọ[ni]ṣ* might suit (a rare name, normally held by freedmen, see *LC* 314, but note *CIL* 2.2361 [Baetica]); *Vernọ[ni]ṣ* does not seem so plausible.

b.1-2. The placement of this fragment is uncertain but we think that it perhaps fits below (a). In the middle of the surviving traces of line 1 *e* is virtually certain and *b* very probable before it. In view of this we have tried to follow the normal pattern and we think it just possible to read *dignum] ṃẹ ḥạḅẹạṣ c̣ụị [*. It is difficult to read the end of *des commeatum* plus a place-name in the line below. Perhaps we should restore *des com-* in line 1, with *meatum* followed by a long place-name or a place-name and indication of purpose in line 2. An alternative possibility is that fragment (c) is to be placed at the left of b.1, giving *uṭ [dignum] ṃẹ ḥạḅẹạṣ* etc., although *ut* does not occur in the other applications which are preserved at this point. If that were correct it might then be possible to restore *des* at the end of b.1 and the whole of *commeatum* at the beginning of b.2, with a long place-name following; *-erḷerọ* (or *-erḅerọ*) could certainly be a locative ending.

172

Inv.no.87.751. 85 x 30 mm.

The attribution of this text to Period 2 means that it should predate the other requests for leave. As far as it takes us, however, there is no reason to think that it deviated from the normal pattern. The person to whom the application is made is called Flavianus. This is a very common *cognomen* but it is difficult to avoid connecting its occurrence here with Hostilius Flavianus, a correspondent of Cerialis (see **261**.1). If this is the same person, the request for leave suggests that he was a prefect at Vindolanda during Period 2. The centurial symbol is more rounded than the usual angular symbol shaped like a figure 7.

Aueṇṭịṇụṣ (c̣ẹṇṭụṛịạẹ) .u.eḷi
rogo domine Flauiane
ḍ[ignum
. . . .

"I, Aventinus, of the century of ..., ask, my lord Flavianus ... a worthy person ..."

1. *Aueṇṭịṇụṣ*: the last five letters are very abraded but the reading is compatible with the traces and the name is reasonably common in the Gallic provinces (*NPEL* cites 8 instances in Gallia Belgica).

.u.eḷi: the first letter is very abraded but *eḷi* looks secure and before it *s* is probable; *c̣uṣeli* is possible, perhaps a derivative of *Cuses*, the name of a man with the ethnic Regus

(therefore from *castra Regina* = Regensburg), attested in an inscription from Mainz (*CIL* 13.7048). Note also the *cognomen* Sucelus attested in Italy and Noricum (*NPEL*); Cusedus, also attested in Italy, probably cannot be read. A possible though very difficult alternative is *ḷup̣eḷi*. For this form of the fairly common name Lupulus see *LC*, 128, 328 and note the occurrence of the name Lopolus in an inscription from Trier, *CIL* 13.3854; see also *VRR* II, 73, no.1, *Lupul(us)*.

173

*Tab.Vindol.*I 55. *CEL* 122.

The evidence for the pattern of texts requesting leave was not available when this fragment was first published, but it is now obvious that it must belong to this category. The name of the recipient of the application is certainly not Cerialis or Flavianus; we think it is probably Priscinus, probably at some time prefect of the First Cohort of Tungrians (for whom see **295**-**8**).

rogo ṭe domi[ne
P̣ṛịṣc̣ịṇẹ dignuṃ [
. . . . . .

"I ask you, my lord Priscinus, ... a worthy person ..."

1. It is possible that this is the first line of the text (cf. **170**, introduction). For another possible example of a request which includes *te* as the object of *rogo* see **175**.3 and introduction.

2. Despite the fact that the bottoms of the letters are lost and the first and last letters have virtually disappeared, we are reasonably confident of the reading. The reading of the second letter as *ṛ* compares very well with *r* of *rogo* in the previous line; *ịṣc̣ị* looks very good and *ṇ* before the final *ẹ* looks plausible.

174

Inv.no.85.146.a. 90 x 47 mm. *VRR* II, Plate X.

This fragment is complete at the left-hand edge, where there is a v-shaped notch, and probably at the foot. It is noteworthy that the applicant specifies the place at which he wishes to spend his leave. The blank space thereafter suggests that this was the end of the document.

ṛ[ogo
dig̣[num me habeas
cui des commeatum

Ụḷucịo *uacat*
uacat

" ... I ask ... that you consider me a worthy person to whom to grant leave at Ulucium (?)."

1. Only the foot of a descender survives and this is likely to belong to an enlarged initial *r* (cf. **167**.1).

2. The form of *g* is interesting since it has a descender curling to the left and resembles the alternative form in ORC (illustrated in Bischoff (1990), 64) which was not attested in the Vindolanda texts from the 1970s, but now appears also perhaps in **178** (see introduction) and **344**.i.6 (see introduction).

4. *Ụḷucịo*: we regard the reading as almost certain and it is likely to be a place-name, by analogy with **175**.3; A.R.Birley (1990a), 18 suggests that the name may be a corruption of *Viuidin*, for which see *PNRB* 507. If we were looking for a name lying behind a possibly corrupt version in the Ravenna Cosmographer, Cicucium might be a possibility (= ?Brecon Gaer, see *PNRB* 307 and note the relevant comment on *-ucium* as a latinised version of a Celtic suffix); it is not possible to read *Cicucio* in our text, however. It seems less likely that we have a form of Verlucio, located by *PNRB* 494 at Calne in Wiltshire, which appears as *Verlucione* in the Antonine Itinerary. It is perhaps worth noting that in *P.Mich.*VIII 466 Apollinarius promises to come from Bostra in Arabia to visit his family in Egypt when he gets leave and we might even consider the possibility that Ulucium (?) is to be found further afield, in Gaul, cf. **255**.i.3-4, **154**.12 note. See also **311**.back 1 note.

175

Inv.no.85.151. 92 x 45 mm. Plate VII.

The text on this tablet may be complete but this is far from certain. What is certain is that the text does not conform to the normal pattern, though the difference may be confined to the word order. There is a problem both at the beginning and the end, the former the more serious (see notes to lines 1 and 3-4).

The use of interpunct and apices is noteworthy.

.....[.] ḥạ[b]eas · cui ·
des · commeatum
Córis Messicus t[..
rógo · domine [
. . . .

Back:] Ṃessic̣ .

"I, Messicus ..., ask, my lord, that you consider me a worthy person to whom to grant leave at Coria. (Back) ... of (?) Messicus."

1. The small fragment must fit at the start of the first preserved line since it contains the top of *des* from the line below, but it is very hard to read the remains of the letters it contains, as they are somewhat obscured by dirt. What we require to fit the normal pattern is *dignum me habeas*, but there does not seem to be room for more than six letters before *ḥạ[b]eas*. If the first preserved line is not the first line of the document, we could simply read *num me* in this line with *dig* on a previous line; possible restorations before this would be *rogo domine Cerialis* or just *rogo domine* (see below). In which case the name of the applicant may have preceded and we would have to suppose that the tablet contained *two* requests for leave, the second of which came from Messicus (unless Messicus submitted his request in duplicate, which seems unlikely). It is perhaps more likely that the whole of *dignum me habeas* stood in this line; it might just be possible to read *ḍịg̣ṇụ[m me]* before *ḥạ[b]eas* but there seems scarcely to be room for the letters supplied in the lacuna. If this is correct, the tablet may well be complete as it stands; it then conveys exactly the same sense as the other requests but with a different word-order. It is not essential for the name of the recipient to have been included after *domine* (it is omitted in **176**), but it could of course have come in a further line not now preserved.

3. *Córis*: the apex mark here and in line 4 is slightly curved. For its use with short vowels cf. **291** and **265**, introduction and above, pp.59-61. For the identification of Coria as Corbridge see **154**.7 note.

Messicus: the name is not in *LC*; *NPEL* and *RNGCL* cite only one instance, from Noricum (*CIL* 3.11502). For another possible Norican connection in the Vindolanda texts see **184**.i.1 note.

3-4. At the end of line 3, after *Messicus*, *t* is certain and there is not room for more than two or at most three letters lost after this. One possibility is to read *t[e*, cf. **173**.1, where, however, *te* comes between *rogo* and *domine*. More seriously, however, this leaves us without any indication of Messicus' unit.

4. *rógo*: for the apex see note to line 3.

Back. The trace after *ṃessic̣* is so slight that it permits either the reading *Ṃessic̣ọ* (so probably just *a] Ṃessic̣ọ*) or *Ṃessic̣ị*, which might have been preceded by a noun meaning "request". We do not think that the apparent traces thereafter are ink. The writing on the back of what was evidently the first part of the text supports the idea that these requests were normally written on half-leaves.

176

Inv.no.85.187. 110 x 42 mm. Plate VII.

The text on this fragment may be practically complete. It appears to be the only case in which the applicant specifies the purpose of the leave as well as his destination (see notes to lines 4-5), which is of some interest in view of Vegetius' statement about the difficulty of obtaining leave (2.19, quoted above, p.77). Both the destination and the purpose are, however, unfortunately obscure. A small scrap with a tie-hole and the remains of a v-shaped notch may contain a few letters from the beginning of a line (unless the marks are dirt), possibly line 5. The back is blank.

Buccus t ̣[
rogo doṃiṇẹ ḍịgṇụṃ
me habeas cui des c̣[o]ṃ-
[m]eatuṃ p ̣r ̣ṣọ ut p̣oṣṣị[m
[*c.6*]ẹ ̣eṛe fa ̣[

"Buccus ... I ask, my lord, that you consider me a worthy person to whom to grant leave at ... so that I might ..."

1. *Buccus*: see *LC* 225, *TLL* I 2230.40-44, citing *CIL* 13.5730. The Latin word *bucca* means "cheek" but this name is generally regarded as Celtic (e.g. *AS* I 626); André (1991), 37 explains it as onomatopoeic, however, and appears to doubt the Celtic origin of the word.

t ̣[: in view of the occurrence of a centurial sign plus name at the corresponding point in **166**, **168**, **169**, **171** and **172** it is tempting to suppose that we should restore *tụ[rmae* followed by a name. It should be noted that this text is attributed to Period 3 and that there is no evidence that the Ninth Cohort of Batavians was an equitate unit (see above, p.23). It is not certain, however, that this text is connected with that unit or directed to Cerialis (for the Third Cohort of Batavians see **311**.back, **263**.ii.5 and for a *turma* **159**.1, all attributed to Period 3). Another possibility is that the name was followed by a rank, e.g. *tẹ[sserarius*; *tụ[*, however, is a very much easier reading than *tẹ[*.

2. This line is slightly indented, the following one slightly more so. It is noteworthy that the applicant does not add the name of the recipient after *doṃiṇẹ*.

ḍịgṇụṃ: only the bottoms of letters survive; these permit the reading given but cannot be said to compel it. But there cannot be any doubt about what is required.

3. Only faint traces remain at the end of the line, which are not easy to reconcile with *com*; *c̣[o]ṃ* is perhaps the least difficult reading. The word *commeatum* must have been divided between two lines since the presence of the whole word in line 4 would cause it to commence further to the left than the preceding lines.

4. *p ̣r ̣ṣọ*: this must be understood as a place-name, see **174**.4, **175**.3. It does not seem possible to read *coris*; the first letter looks much more like *p*, though *c* or *t* is not impossible; although the fifth letter could well be *s*, there seems to be a trace of one more letter following it; *p ̣r ̣ṣọ* does not suggest any known place-name (we note the Parisi of east Yorkshire, *PNRB* 435-6, but it is impossible to read the second letter as *a*; it looks more like *u*).

ut p̣oṣṣị[m: none of the other Vindolanda applications gives any clue to what we might expect after a place-name, but the reading is compatible with the traces and we think it likely to be correct. See *ChLA* XI 467.2-7, *P.Wisc.*II 70 and cf. Speidel and Seider (1988), quoted in the introduction to this section.

5. *]ẹ ̣eṛe fa ̣[*: the gap after *]ẹ ̣eṛe* suggests the end of a word, so if the reading of line 4 is correct we might expect an infinitive, with something preceding it. *ẹṃeṛe* is a possible reading and makes good sense. Following *fa* there is a high mark which may or may not be ink; if it is, it is probably *b* or *l*. In that case we might have *ut poṣṣi[m / ...] eṃere faḅ[as* (cf. **302**.1) or *faḷ[cem*, for example. If it is not ink, we could imagine a noun preceding *eṃere* and *fa[mili-/ari meo* or *fa[mili-/aribus meis* following.

177

Inv.no.85.186.a. 65 x 24 mm.

A fragment of a leaf with two lines of writing. There may be a notch in the right-hand edge. There is certainly a reference to *commeatus* (see note to line 1) and it is possible that this is part of a request for leave, with an additional detail which the others appear not to have. Thus one might envisage something like *rogo me dignum habeas cui des commeatum et scribas ...no praefecto* [at the place where I wish to spend the leave]. The fact that this text was found in close proximity to some of the other requests for leave (note particularly **176**) perhaps favours this notion. Alternatively, it might simply be a letter from someone mentioning that he intended to obtain leave and had written or was about to write to the prefect of his unit.

. . . .
]mmeatum et scri-
]. . ṇo praefecto
. . . .

1. *]mmeatum*: the restoration of *co]mmeatum* is inescapable. Following that, *scri-/[bas]* would fit as a parallel to *des*, if what we have is a request for leave.

2. *praefecto*: on either of the reconstructions suggested above, the prefect would be somewhere other than Vindolanda. *]f̣ịno* (e.g. *Ru]f̣ịno*) is compatible with the traces; another possibility is *]ẹ.uo*; this could be the end of name, but if the last three letters were the dative or ablative of *tuus*, this would suggest a different construction.

ACCOUNTS AND LISTS
(Nos. 178-209)

The attributions of the texts which we have grouped under this heading cover the pre-Hadrianic levels 2, 3, 4 and 5. In *Tab.Vindol.*I we grouped military reports and accounts together under the general heading "Documents" (*Tab.Vindol.*I 1-20). We now feel confident that in almost all cases we can distinguish the military reports and documents (**127-77**) from the accounts. More precise classification of the accounts and lists still presents difficulties, however. We are quite certain that we have, on the one hand, accounts which relate to the administration of the unit as a whole (e.g. **178**) and, on the other, lists which are concerned with the domestic administration of the *praetorium* (e.g. **194-6**). There are, however, a great many cases in which it is impossible to be certain to which of these categories (if, indeed, they are exclusive) the text ought to be assigned.

We have ordered the texts, very tentatively, into three groups. The first group consists of accounts which appear to relate to the administration of the military unit(s) or the position and military duties of soldiers, and accounts which relate to soldiers and personnel outside the context of the *praetorium* (**178-89**). The second group consists of texts which appear to relate to the domestic administration of the *praetorium* and the personnel in it (**190-9**). The third, quite substantial group, includes texts which we do not feel that we can place with confidence in either of the first two groups (**200-09**).

It is important to re-emphasise that we have classified these texts on the basis of content rather than archaeological attribution. We might expect that tablets attributed to Periods 2 and 3 will reflect activity in the *praetorium*, while those in the barracks/workshop of Periods 4 and 5 will relate to soldiers and personnel outside it. For reasons already explained (p.19), we have used these chronological indications only as a general guide and not as a basis for deducing the nature of any particular text.

(a) Accounts relating to the administration of the unit etc.

The only text which explicitly relates to the administration of the fort or the unit as a whole is **178**, recording the *reditus castelli*; **179** may be a text of the same type. It should be noted that, if we exclude receipts and pay-records, of which we have no examples at Vindolanda, the number of Latin military accounts which might properly be described as official is very small indeed - we have noted only *RMR* 74, 82, 83, *ChLA* XI 506 and *Doc.Madasa* 723.

There are several accounts which clearly relate to individual soldiers or groups of soldiers, and to people outside the context of the *praetorium*. In several cases it is impossible to be sure whether the transactions or activities which they represent should be seen as official (relating to their position and military duties) or personal; it may be that in reality, the distinction was not always clear-cut (cf. the note to *ChLA* III 204). The most important sub-group in this category consists of the accounts which were found in the area which has been identified as the centurions' quarters in the Period 4 barracks (**180**, **181**, **182**) and which certainly have links with the entrepreneurial letter of Octavius to Candidus (**343**) and the petition about maltreatment (**344**, written on the other side of **180**). The difficulty over the distinction between official and personal matters may be illustrated by the fact that **180** records wheat dispensed *militibus legionaribus* [sic] *iussu Firmi* (lines 22-3, whether regular military rations or not it is impossible to tell) and to a certain Lucco *in ussus* [sic] *suos* (line 30). We think it likely that this group of accounts represents transactions involving both civilian entrepreneurs and soldiers (and perhaps also connected non-military personnel such as female companions and slaves). The same may be true of an account assigned to Period 5 (**184**), in which the records of purchases or sums owed for such things as towels, cloaks and tallow (*sebum*) are organised by century. A somewhat different kind of activity may be attested by **185** if we have correctly interpreted it as a record of expenses incurred on a journey between Vindolanda and the south, perhaps for food and drink, clothing, stabling and axles for a carriage. The latter invites comparison with a letter which contains an embedded account recording the transport to Vindolanda of the components of wagons (**309**). **186**, the only text from Vindolanda with a consular date (AD 111), records quantities of beer, nails for boots, salt, wheat and perhaps pork and goat-meat. **187** is a cash account which probably includes the names of a woman and a veteran, and the names in **188** suggest ordinary soldiers rather than officers.

(b) The *praetorium*.

The accounts which most obviously suggest the existence of a substantial body of material relating to the administration of the *praetorium* are **190** and **191** which we originally regarded as likely to relate to the military unit. It now seems obvious that many of the accounts from Periods 2 and 3 must also be related to the *praetorium*. Texts which list some of the more unusual foodstuffs and commodities (such as **192** and **193**) may well belong to this category and it should be noted that there are three letters, two probably connected with slaves of Genialis and Verecundus respectively (**301**, **302**), which refer to the provision of foodstuffs in this context. A third, a copy of a letter from Cerialis (**233**), seems to contain an earlier, brief account of a similar kind. Equally interesting are the lists of household equipment and clothing, more likely to be inventories than accounts, which presumably reflect the possessions and the lifestyle of the equestrian officer class (**194**, **195**, **196**, **197**); these may well be written by the same hand as **191**.

(c) Uncertain

Two texts well exemplify the difficulties of classification which we have mentioned. **207**, assigned to the Period 3 *praetorium*, contains a record (not a cash account) of clothing, in which the highest number of an individual type of garment is 15; the name of the supplier, Gavo, appears in an account probably relating to the *praetorium* context (**192**) but the quantities in **207** might suggest that these could be cloaks intended for soldiers in a particular *contubernium*. Second, a fragmentary cash account which may be a record of repayment of loan or interest thereon (**206**). Such transactions between ordinary soldiers are known (cf. **312**, Tomlin (1992)), but it is equally possible that it might relate to a slave in the commander's household or, indeed, that it relates to a transaction between a resident of the *praetorium* and a member of the unit outside it.

There is another account of food written on a tablet containing a draft letter of Flavius Cerialis (**233**). For other accounts see: **375**, **380**, **387**, **411**, **428**, **439**, **440**, **479**, **493**, **495**, **500**, **510**, **512**-**18** (some doubtful).

We should explain the convention we have followed in resolving symbols and abbreviations. In some cases the text itself allows us to deduce which case of the noun we should understand, e.g. **180**.6 requires *m(odii)*, **181**.11-15 and **182**.i.9 require *(denarios)*. Where we have *summa* we have resolved in the nominative case. **185**.20-1 shows the use of the accusative in a list of items and on this basis we have followed the practice of resolving symbols and abbreviations in the accusative where we have no other indication, except in **178**, a simple list of amounts under the heading *reditus castelli*, which might be a nominative plural. The accusative could be justified on the ground that the writer of an account might normally assume that the items and amounts in his list were objects of some unstated verb.

178

Inv.no.85.043. 89 x 69 mm. Bowman and Thomas (1987), no.3, Plate XVC.

This account is written along the grain on a half-diptych and is probably complete. The back of the leaf is blank. The heading *reditus castelli* is followed by five consecutive dates in July of an unnamed year, each related to a sum in cash. The final line offers a total which must be in excess of 80 *denarii* (see note to line 6). The existence of daily accounts of income or revenues of the fort is of some interest, though one can only speculate on general grounds as to what their source may have been; perhaps the sale to the surrounding populace of foodstuffs or manufactured items.

The hand is a very competent cursive with several features of interest. The form of *g*, especially in line 2 and line 5, is new at Vindolanda (see **174**.2 note). In the dates the initial *i* is large (cf. **291**.i.3); *u* is sometimes made in two straight strokes, the first a long diagonal and the second a vertical.

↓ reditus castelli
vi K(alendas) Aug(ustas) (denarii) xxxvi s(emis)
v K(alendas) Aug(ustas) (denarii) xxvii
iiii K(alendas) Aug(ustas) (denarii) [
iii K(alendas) Aug(ustas) (denarii) ṿ[
pr(idie) K(alendas) Aug(ustas) (denarii) xv . [
sụmma (denarii) ḷx[

"Revenues of the fort:
27 July, *denarii* 36½
28 July, *denarii* 27
29 July, *denarii* ..
30 July, *denarii* 5+

31 July, *denarii* 15+
total, *denarii* 80+."

6-7. *xv.[*: marks at the right which in the *ed. pr.* we considered to be dirt now seem compatible with the reading of a numeral. If we have interpreted the traces correctly, the total in line 7 must be in excess of 80 *denarii* since the surviving figures add up to at least 83½ *denarii*.

179

Inv.no.85.252. 180 x 37 mm.

Two fragments of a diptych which is probably complete at all sides except the top. There is one notch and one tie-hole in each margin. The left-hand side contains what appears to be the end of an account (cf. **178**.7, **181**.16) written along the grain.

. . . .
summa (denarii) cclxxiiii s(emis) (as i)

"... total *denarii* 274½ and 1 *as*."

180

Inv.no.88.943. 77 x 264 mm. Plate VIII.

This document consists of three sections of a tablet (designated (a), (b) and (c) for the sake of clarity) each approximately the size of a normal half-leaf. On one side is the present text, an account, and on the other is a draft petition (**344**). The fact that the account occupies all three pieces whereas the petition only covers two suggests that it is probably correct to regard the latter as secondary, but our designation of the account as the front and the petition as the back can only be offered with caution. The format naturally invites comparison with **190** (see *Tab. Vindol.*I, pp.38-44 and Bowman (1975)). The offsets show that the fronts of (a) and (b) were folded face-to-face and that the back of (c) faced the back of (b). This tablet differs from **190**, however, in that there are apparently no tie-holes or notches. This may well mean that we have a large leaf which was cut and folded into a triptych, concertina-fashion; there is no other tablet like this but it should be noted that the vertical dimension of the whole tablet which this hypothesis implies is smaller than that of **154**. We would still have to suppose, however, that the beginning of the petition was on another tablet, now lost. The alternative is that we have two diptychs of which the lower half of the second has completely disappeared; this would make it more difficult to explain the offsets in **344**. Grouped with (c) there are 5 unplaced scraps of which 3 may each have remains of one letter.

The tablet is one of a group found together and attributed to the Period 4 building; see also **181**, **182** and **343**, the first of which is undoubtedly written by the same hand as **180** and **344**. Some of the names in this account also occur in other texts in this group (Primus, line 28 and **181**.6; Spectatus, line 5 and **343**.iv.42; Firmus, line 23 and **343**.iv.43; Candidus, line 24 and **181**.3, **343**.i.1). The name of the person who compiled this account is not known, but several deductions can legitimately be made from it and from the related documents (cf. Bowman, Thomas and Adams (1990), 43). The familiar and familial tone of some of the entries (*mihi*, *tibi* in lines 3, 20, 25 etc., *patri* in lines 7, 16, 33) suggests that this is not an official account but a private one made by one person for a close associate; it seems possible that we have two partners (perhaps brothers) and the father of one or both of them. It is certain that the draft petition on the other side was written by the same hand (the idiosyncratic form of *f* in lines 23, 25 and **344**.i.10 is particularly distinctive) and since the author refers to trade (*mercem*, line i.2) and describes himself as a *hominem trasmarinum* (line ii.15), it is very likely, as the whole tone of the petition suggests, that he was a civilian trader and that his associates were also. The account shows that wheat was supplied to military personnel, including a *beneficiarius* (line 18) and some legionary soldiers (line 22). Spectatus and Firmus, on whose instructions the disbursements in lines 5-6 and 22-3 were made, were surely military personnel. The nature of the business and the find-spot of the tablets suggests that they are likely to have been either centurions or *optiones* (the latter perhaps slightly preferable since these are known to have had responsibilities for matters connected with the food-supply in their units, see *RMR*, p.311, 81.ii.5-12; cf. A.R.Birley (1990a), 17, suggesting that they might be legionary centurions). If these inferences are justified, they leave us with the need to explain how non-official accounts generated by a civilian trader came to be discovered in a room of a barrack-block. Any such explanation can only be speculative, but it is perhaps worth noting that some of the footwear discovered in the same context also implies the presence of non-military personnel (*VRR* III, 44-6).

The evidence for the involvement of civilians in army supply, and especially in the supply of wheat, the basic commodity, is of considerable importance and contributes to filling an important gap in our knowledge (Breeze (1984), 58-9). The unknown author of this account must have been a crucial link between the producers and the army personnel who authorised the distribution within the unit; contrast *O.Bu Njem* 74-109 and pp.57-63, "lettres de voiture", sent to a *praepositus* by soldiers detached to producers of wheat, via transporters, stating the quantity carried. At the same time, several of the entries incidentally bear witness to a certain amount of agricultural activity in the penumbra of the fort: line 9, *bubulcaris*; line 27, *ad porcos*, cf. **183**.4; line 33, *ad i[uu]ẹncoṣ*.

The account itself does not concern itself with money and gives no indication how the wheat was paid for (it is to be noted that the entry in lines 5-6 is described as a loan). The traders might have been working under some kind of contractual arrangement. An arrangement of this sort might be inferred from **343**.i.6-ii.14 where Candidus at Vindolanda is asked to send Octavius the considerable sum of 500 *denarii* to help him avoid financial embarrassment over an amount of 5000 *modii* of (unthreshed?) grain which he specifically says that he has bought.

The dates in the present account (lines 11, 17) fall between 6/11 and 26 September, appropriately close to harvest-time. The total disbursement in the account is 320½ *modii* and the largest surviving individual entry is 26 *modii*. Some idea of the scale of this operation may be obtained from the calculation that if a very active male requires 3822 calories per day for subsistence (Foxhall and Forbes (1982), 48-9), the wheat equivalent needed to supply this would be about one seventh of a *modius*. This account therefore represents the wheat equivalent of a day's calorie requirements for more than 2000 soldiers (cf. **343**.i.7-8).

↓ ratio frumenti eṃ[ensi ex quo
ipse dedi in cupaṃ [
mihi ad panem [
Macrino ṃ(odii) vii
Felicio Victori iussu Spẹctati
comodati m(odii) xxvi
in follibus tribus patri ṃ(odii) xix
Macrino m(odii) xiii
bubulcaris in siluam m(odii) viii
item Amabili ad fanum m(odii) iii
[..]. Idus Septem(bres) Crescenti
iussu .[.]..ị m(odii) iii
item .[*c.6*]ẹ[ ]..
Macṛ[..]..uṣ[ ]. ṃ(odii) x̣ṿ
item ma.[*c.6.*] m(odii) [ ]iii
patri ad [*c.6*].as m(odii) ii
vi Kal(endas) [O]c̣tobṛ[es
Lu[..].[.. ben]ẹficịar[io] m(odii) vi
Felicio Victori m(odii) xv
ad turṭas tibi m(odii) ii
Crescenti m(odii) ix
militibus legionaribus
iussu Firmi m(odii) xi[
Candido m(odii) [
tibi in folle br.gẹse [
tibi [
Lucconi ad porcos [
Primo Luci [
tibi [
Lucconi in ussus suos [
item [.]ụọs m[.]..ị.[
in [.]uọtur[.].
patri [a]d ị[uu]ẹncoṣ [
item inter metrum [
libr.s xv redd. libraẹ x̣v[
fiunt m(odii) [
item mihi ad panem m(odii) i[
sumṃạ f̣rumẹnṭi m(odii) cccx̣x̣ ṣ(emis)

"Account of wheat measured out from that which
I myself have put into the barrel:
to myself, for bread ...
to Macrinus, *modii* 7
to Felicius Victor on the order of Spectatus
provided as a loan (?), *modii* 26

in three sacks, to father, *modii* 19
to Macrinus, *modii* 13
to the oxherds at the wood, *modii* 8
likewise to Amabilis at the shrine, *modii* 3
.. September, to Crescens
on the order of Firmus (?), *modii* 3
likewise ..., *modii* ..
to Macr... ..., *modii* (?) 15
likewise to Ma... (?), *modii* ..
to father ..., *modii* 2
26 September
to Lu... the *beneficiarius*, *modii* 6
to Felicius Victor, *modii* 15
for twisted loaves (?), to you, *modii* 2
to Crescens, *modii* 9
to the legionary soldiers
on the order of Firmus, *modii* 11+
to Candidus, *modii* ..
to you, in a sack from Briga (?), ...
to you, ...
to Lucco, in charge of the pigs ...
to Primus, slave (?) of Lucius ...
to you ...
to Lucco for his own use ...
likewise that which I have sent ... *modii* .. (?)
in the century of Voturius (?)
to father, in charge of the oxen ...
likewise, within the measure ...(?)
15 pounds yield 15+ pounds (?) ...
total, *modii* ...
likewise to myself, for bread, *modii* ..
total of wheat, *modii* 320½."

1. *eṃ[ensi*: only the first part of the letter after *e* is preserved and this is compatible with either *m* or *n*. *eṃ[pti* is the obvious alternative (cf. **343**.i.7, *spịcas me emisse*, **181**.3, *ḷignis emtis*) but we prefer *eṃ[ensi* on the ground that the account is not a record of purchase but of amounts of wheat disbursed; cf. Augustus, *RG* 3.12, *duodecim frumentationes .... emensus sum*. For the passive meaning of the participle see *OLD*, s.v.

ex quo: there is room for this restoration at the end of the line but *quod* is also possible and would give the same general sense, see line 2 note.

2. *in cupaṃ*: we are confident of the reading despite the fact that the writer has curiously left a rather large space between *u* and *p* (he also does this elsewhere for no apparent reason, cf. line 3, *mihi*). See Frontinus, *Strat.* 3.14.3, *salem ... cupis conditum*, Alfenus, *Digest* 19.2.31, *quod si separatim tabulis aut heronibus aut in alia cupa clusum uniuscuiusque triticum fuisset*. For the use of *dedi* see perhaps *OLD*, s.v. *do* 9a. The leaf is broken after the middle of *ṃ* and we cannot tell whether the line will have contained anything

else. This is a point of some importance since it materially affects the meaning. If we have lost *m(odios)* plus an amount, the sense would be: "Account of wheat measured out, from which I myself have put into the barrel x *modii*". But we regard this as less attractive.

3. *ad panem*: for this use of *ad* see *OLD*, s.v. G44. The entry is duplicated in line 37. Since the amount of wheat is not preserved in either case, it is impossible to tell whether the bread was for personal consumption or for re-sale. For supply of loaves to a military unit cf. *O.Claud.* 3-5 and note Rustius Barbarus sending loaves in *O.Wâdi Fawâkhir* 1.4-7 (= *CEL* 73). For bread in the military diet see Davies (1989), 191.

5. *Felicio Victori*: the name occurs again in line 19. For an occurrence of the *gentilicium* in Britain see *RIB* I 690 (York), Felicius Simplex a soldier of *Legio VI Victrix*. For Spectatus see **343**.iv.42 and introduction, above.

6. *comodati*: perhaps read *co<m>modati* but the form *comod-* is cited by *TLL* III 1993.43. The noun *commodatum* usually refers to a loan of imperishables, but it could be used of a valid loan of perishables, see J.A.C.Thomas (1976), 274-6. Here we can hardly have the noun in the genitive and we suppose that we must have the participle, agreeing with *m(odii)*; the verb can be used of things provided but not necessarily as a loan (see *OLD*, s.v.3).

7. We have considered the possibility that *patri* (cf. lines 16, 33) is to be taken as a proper name but we have not found it attested as such.

9. *bubulcaris*: for *bubulcariis*, for which see *CGL* II 259.44; it seems likely to refer to rations for oxherds, perhaps non-military personnel, working in woodland.

in siluam: for the use of *in* see *OLD*, s.v.A8.

10. *item*: the force and referent of this word is unclear here and in several other entries (lines 31, 34, 37). Contrast **182**.i.7 and note.

Amabili: there appears to be an extra stroke after *m* which suggests the reading *amiabili*, but such a name is not attested and an earlier photograph makes it clear that this is an offset.

ad fanum: this might refer to a local shrine and its guard or caretaker (who might perhaps be a civilian, compare the use of non-military personnel to man watchtowers in Egypt, *O.Flor.*, pp.25-6). Alternatively, it is worth considering whether it might be a reference to Fanum Cocidii (we note that Caesar, *BC* 1.11.4 refers to Fanum Fortunae as Fanum). If the identification of Fanum Cocidii with Bewcastle is correct (*PNRB* 363), this suggestion must be abandoned, since the Bewcastle site is not pre-Hadrianic, see Austin (1991), 41-3. If Fanum Cocidii is Nether Denton, however (see Jones and Mattingly (1990), 275 and cf. Jones (1991)), it would be an appropriate place to which supplies from Vindolanda might have been sent.

11. Only a trace of one digit of the numeral survives; it might be *ị* or *ṿ*, slightly inset. There is no abbreviation mark for *Septem(bres)*. It is very odd that there are two dates in the middle of the account but none at the beginning. The only area in which there might have been a date, now lost, is at the end of line 2, but the space would only allow something short, e.g. *K(alendis) Septem(bris)*.

Crescenti: the name occurs again in line 21. A *centuria Crescentis* occurs in **128**.4 and **148**.2.

12-3. There is a loose fragment which might be placed so as to supply the bottom of the letter after *iussu* and part of the first letter after *item* in line 13. Of the names which survive in this text *F̣[i]ṛṃị* could be restored.

item might here refer to *iussu* plus name in the previous line but the word seems to be used rather capriciously in this account (see line 10 note).

14-5. *macr[*: the reading of the surviving letters is virtually certain. What follows, after a gap of not more than three letters, seems to rule out a restoration of *Macr[ino* (cf. line 4, above). Therefore, perhaps e.g. *Macr[i(ni)]o Ius[to*; for *gentilicium* and *cognomen* see lines 5 and 19. Both Macrius and Macrinius, though fairly rare, are attested in Gallia Belgica (see *NPEL*).

15. *ma.[*: the third letter cannot be read as *c*; note e.g. *Marino*, **343**.i.3.

In the photograph of this leaf there is a tiny scrap with part of one letter which is misplaced after *item* in line 13.

16. *].as*: most probably *]tas*.

18. *ben]eficiar[io*: this is likely to be the *beneficiarius praefecti* and may well be the same person as the *beneficiarius* mentioned in **344**.i.10; cf. the later inscription from Housesteads (*RIB* I 1619) commemorating Hurmius son of Leubasnus, *beneficiarius* of the *praefectus* of *cohors i Tungrorum*. There is a small fragment with traces of two letters which may fit in this area. If the first letter, which is likely to be the foot of *r*, belongs to *[O]ctobr[es* in line 17, the second might allow us to read *b]e[n]eficiar[io* here. The spacing would allow a restoration of *Lu[cconi* or *Lu[cc]o[ni* before it, cf. lines 27 and 30, but it is surely very unlikely that a *beneficiarius* would be looking after pigs.

19. *Felicio Victori*: cf. line 5 and note.

20. *turtas*: palaeographically, only two readings seem possible, *turias* and *turtas*, and we think *turtas* more probable, accepting that only a vestigial trace of the cross-bar survives. *turtas* is an explicable alternative spelling of *tortas*, see Adams (1994); for *torta* meaning a "twisted loaf", see *Vg.Exod.* 29.23, *Num.* 6.19, *1.Sam.* 2.36, 10.3, (*1.Chr.* 16.3 *1.Par.* 16.3), *Jer.* 37.20 and cf. *tortula*, *Vg.Num.* 11.8.

21. *Crescenti*: cf. line 11 and note.

22-3. *militibus legionaribus*: for the change of suffix in the adjective see Adams (1994) and note that at Caesar, *BC* 3.2.2 there is a variant reading *legionarium militum*, cited at *TLL* VII.2 1109. The entry is important since it proves the presence of a group of legionaries at or near Vindolanda in the period before the building of Hadrian's Wall. Given the evidence for movement and fragmentation of units, this is not surprising. For an early legionary tombstone at Carvoran see *RIB* I 1862.

iussu Firmi: there may be a short apex mark after *iussu* but the writer does not use this elsewhere and it may well belong to the foot of *s* in *militibus*. He has left a large space between *r* and *m* in *Firmi*; since the leaf has split down the grain at this point it may be that there was a fault or irregularity in the surface which he was avoiding (though he has not done so elsewhere). The name Firmus occurs in the tablets only here and in **343**.iv.43 (but see above, lines 12-3 note), where it may well refer to the same person; see introduction, above.

24. *Candido*: a Candidus is the recipient of **343** and the name occurs elsewhere at Vindolanda in this group of texts and outside it (see introduction, above and **181**.2 note). Since it is a very common name it would be unwise to attempt to identify the recipient of wheat with any of the other Candidi.

25. *in folle br.gese*: for *folle* see above, line 7. The word which follows must be an adjective agreeing with *folle* but we are unable to explain it satisfactorily. The third letter is damaged by a break in the leaf but is most likely to be *i*; the fourth is quite certainly *g*; after that *ese* is virtually certain. If we have *brige(n)se*, could it be a sack from Briga or a particular kind of sack associated with the place? For Briga see **190**.c.38, **292**.c.v.2 and note

that *AS* I 542 records an adjective *Brigiensis*, cf. Pliny, *NH* 5.30, *Tagasense* (wrongly recorded in *LS* as *Tagastense*).

27. *Lucconi*: *NPEL* cites six instances from Italy and the Danubian provinces; cf. note to line 18, above.

ad porcos: see also **183**.4 and cf. line 33, below. This will mean that Lucco is in charge of the pigs, not that the wheat is to be used to feed them (cf. line 30 note).

28. *Primo Luci*: the second name could be a patronym but it is also possible that Primus is a slave (*LC* 291 shows that it is a common servile name) and that Lucius is the name of the owner; perhaps Lucius the *scutarius* (**184**.ii.22) or Lucius the *decurio* (**299-300**). The name Primus also occurs in **181**.6, where it may refer to the same person.

30. *in ussus suos*: for the geminate *s* see *Tab.Vindol.*I, p.73. The phrase implies personal use and should presumably be contrasted with the entry in line 27 which might, for instance, be issued as rations for Lucco and his (agricultural?) workers.

31-9. The writing on this, the third, section of the tablets is more abraded than that on the other two, as is natural if it was unprotected by a facing leaf (see introduction).

31-2. The indentation of line 32 suggests that these two lines should be taken as one entry, with the amount missing at the end of line 32, but we have not been able to solve the problems of reading and interpretation.

]ụọs: there cannot be more than two letters lost before this and there is unlikely to be more than one lost here or after *m*. The reading can hardly be doubted and it seems equally certain that a new word begins with *m*; this seems to reduce the possibilities to *duos*, *quos*, *suos*, *tuos* or *uos*. Then we could read a name such as *M[a]ṭtiạ[no* but we cannot see how to make sense of it. As a possibility we tentatively suggest *item [q]ụọs m[i]ṣṣị ṃ(odios)[* followed by a number.

32. *in[ ]uọtur[ ].*: there may, but need not be, a letter lost after *in* and the same applies after *r*. The last letter in the line looks distinctly like a centurial symbol. We could perhaps read *in uọtur[i] (centuria/-am)*? The name Voturius is cited as a *gentilicium* in Narbonensis by *NPEL* and it is also a Gallic tribal name; for *Viturius* (*sc.* Veturius) in Gallia Belgica see *CIL* 13.6391, but the reading is not as attractive. We cannot explain it, however. It should be noted that Speidel (1984), 107 is unable to cite a single instance of the name of the commander preceding *centuria*, but see *RMR* 9.9.f-n.

33. *[a]d ị[uu]ẹncoṣ*: we are certain of the ending, the initial *i* suits the traces and there is room to restore *[uu]*; we are therefore confident of the reading especially when we compare line 27, *ad porcos*.

34-6. These lines are difficult to understand both in detail and in the context of the account as a whole. *item* (cf. line 10 note) suggests that a new entry begins in line 34 but it is less clear whether this line is a complete entry on its own, or whether it is to be taken with line 35 or line 35 and line 36.

34. *inter metrum*: the reading is clear. There is a space between *inter* and *metrum* which might suggest that we have two words, but this writer is rather inconsistent about his spacing (cf. line 2 note). We have no example of it elsewhere (either as one word or two) nor do we see what the force of *inter* is likely to be. It is difficult to see what it could mean, although *TLL* VIII 899 suggests that *metrum* might be used in later Latin to mean "measure" and cites its use with *frumentum* (Rufinus, *Hist.* 3.6.3). We have translated it literally and wonder whether it might mean something like "on average", to be taken with what follows (see note to line 35).

We have considered another possible interpretation in the light of *C.Theod.* 13.5.38 and 13.9.5, where *epimetrum* and *diametrum* are found with reference to ships' cargoes, apparently meaning, respectively, something over and something under the correct amount. This perhaps suggests that in the Vindolanda text *intermetrum* is to be taken as a single word meaning something like "balance". Elsewhere we have found the terms only in *ChLA* X 436, a third-century account of *annona militaris*, where they are abbreviated to *diametr* and *epimetr*, which might, in a papyrus from Egypt, be resolved in the Greek form *-metron*. Both ἐπίμετρον and διάμετρον occur in Greek and it may be that *intermetrum* is the Latin equivalent of διάμετρον. One meaning of ἐπίμετρον is, as might be expected, an additional tax. In *P.Hib.*I 110.14 (cf. *P.Tebt.*I 91.11, 92.11) the meaning of διάμετρον is unclear (see note *ad loc.* and cf. *P.Cair.Zen.*IV 59669.2 note), although it is translated "difference on measure". This does not seem very promising.

35. At the beginning of the line we have either *librịs xv* or *librạs xv*, at the end *librạẹ* (or possibly *librạṣ* or *librịṣ*) followed by a number which might be read *iv* or *lv[* or *xv[*; of these, the first would be an unexpected form since *iiii* is much commoner in the tablets, the second is palaeographically the easiest and the third necessitates taking as a cross-stroke a mark which may not be ink. In between *redd* is certain and we might have *reddọ* or *reddị*. The point of this passage might be explained with reference to Pliny the Elder's calculations of the amount of bread which is yielded by various types of cereal and methods of baking, particularly *NH* 18.88, *siliginae farinae modius Gallicae xx libras panis reddit*; 18.62, *Galliae quoque suum genus farris dedere, quod illic bracem uocant, apud nos scandalam, nitidissimi grani. est et alia differentia quod fere quaternis libris plus reddit panis quam far aliud*; 18.67, *lex certa naturae ut in quocumque genere pani militari tertia portio ad grani pondus accedat, sicut optumum frumentum esse quod in subactum congium aquae capiat.* If this were a notation calculating the yield of bread, we might expect something like *librịs xv reddị(tae) librạẹ ẋv[iiii*, i.e. 15 pounds of cereal yield 19 (?) pounds of bread, which is within the range suggested by Pliny (the reading of the first numeral is certain and it therefore seems impossible to make sense of the second as either *iv* or *lv[*). This would seem to demand a preposition with *librịs* and some mention of *panis,* which could be accommodated by supposing that *ex* is lost at the end of line 34 and *panis* at the end of line 35. These two lines, taken together, might then mean "likewise, on average 15 pounds (of wheat) yield 15+ pounds of bread."

36. The suggestion made in the previous note does not take account of this line which is indented and looks as if it ought to belong with what precedes it. The reading is clear and it must mean "that makes nn *modii*", but we are not attracted by the notion that line 34 calculates *modii* of wheat, line 35 weight of bread made from weight of wheat and line 36 reverts to *modii* of wheat. For a combination of *librae* and *modii* in the same context, though not the same commodity, see Suetonius, *Iul.* 38.1, *frumenti denos modios ac totidem olei libras*.

37. See line 3 note.

38. A total is appropriate and *sum* at the start of the line is convincing. There is a gap between *sum* and *ma* and the two letters following are very spread out, cf. line 2 note.

181

Inv.no.88.944. 70 x 137 mm. Plate X. *VRR* II, Plate XVI.

A diptych containing a cash account recording sums received and debts outstanding. The leaf is complete at the right and left margins. The beginning of the text is lost, but the account ends before the broken edge at the foot. This tablet was found in the same place as **180/344**, **182** and **343** and it is undoubtedly written by the same hand as **180** and **344**. The writing at the right in lines 3-9 is very abraded and the figures are all more or less dubious.

. . . .
↓]̣ndi ̣[*c.6*]ṛ ̣ ̣
uacat?
̣ṣ ̣ ̣[̣ C]andid ̣ (ḍẹṇạṛịọṣ) ịị
lịgnis emtis (ḍẹṇạṛịọṣ) ṿịị
sticam (ḍẹṇạṛịọṣ) ịịị
ab Tetrico [(denarios)] ̣
ab Primo (ḍẹṇạṛịọṣ) ịị ṣ(emissem)
ab Alione ueterinario (ḍẹṇạṛịọṣ) x̣ ̣
ab Vitale balniatore (ḍẹṇạṛịọṣ) ịịị
summa (denarii) xxxiiii s(emis)
reliqui debent
Ingenus (denarios) vii
Acranius (denarios) iii
equites Vardulli (denarios) vii
contubernalis Tagamatịṣ
ụexṣịllari (denarios) iii
summa (denarii) xx

"...
... Candidus, *denarii* 2 (?)
for timbers purchased, *denarii* 7 (?)
a tunic, *denarii* 3 (?)
from Tetricus, *denarii* ..
from Primus, *denarii* 2½ (?)
from Alio the veterinary doctor, *denarii* 10+
from Vitalis the bathman, *denarii* 3 (?)
total, *denarii* 34½
the rest owe:
Ingenuus, *denarii* 7
Acranius, *denarii* 3
the Vardullian cavalrymen, *denarii* 7
the companion of Tagamatis (?) the flag-bearer, *denarii* 3
total, *denarii* 20."

1. It is possible that this line contains a heading comparable to that in **180**.1 and the traces at the end of the line do not seem to be compatible with a *denarius*-symbol and a

number. In that case, it might have begun with *ratio* followed by a gerund(ive). There is probably a *uacat* of one line following this. There is a mark at the broken edge of the leaf towards the left, but it seems likely that if there were an entry here we would see more traces to the right of it and there does not seem to be an amount of *denarii* at the far right.

2. *C]andiḍ*: the last letter is the merest trace and could be read as either *i* or *o*. Before the break there is too much space and ink to allow simply *ab*, and *s* as (probably) the second letter is virtually certain. Within this group of texts, a Candidus is the recipient of the letter from Octavius (**343**) and the name occurs in **180**.24; for occurrences outside the group see **146**, **148** (an *optio*), **301** (a slave), **183**.

3. *emtis*: for epigraphic examples of the form see *TLL* V.2 511.2-3. Since this entry clearly falls under receipts, the implication must be that the wood was purchased from the person responsible for the account. For concern with timber in the Vindolanda texts see also **215**, **309**.

4. *sticam*: the word does not appear in *OLD* or *LS* but the word *στίχη* is attested in *Ed. Diocl.* 19 etc. It is glossed as *tunica* in *CGL* II 593.62.

5. *Tetrico*: the name occurs in **346**.ii.3 and it is possible that this is the same person. *NPEL* cites four instances of the name in Gallia Belgica.

6. The name Primus, followed by *Luci* (slave of Lucius?), occurs in **180**.28.

7. *Alione*: *NPEL* cites one instance of this *cognomen* (in Italy). It also cites one instance of the *cognomen* Allo in Spain. We cannot absolutely exclude the reading *Alḷone* but *Alione* is a much better reading in this hand. Note *CIL* 6.37194, *[dis m]anib. [A]llio Quartion[i] medico coh.1 pr. ueterinario*. For another *ueterinarius* see **310**.i.10-12 (some additional comments in Bowman, Thomas and Adams (1990), 39).

8. The name Vitalis is very common (at Vindolanda in **263**.back 3). The term *balniator* does not occur elsewhere in the tablets (but see **322**.2 note); for the baths see **155**.3 and for appropriate footwear cf. **197**.3 note.

11. *Ingenus*: cf. *ṛẹḷicum*, **206**.back, margin 2 note and see Adams (1994). The name also occurs in **187**.i.11.

12. *Acranius*: the reading seems clear but the name is not attested elsewhere. Perhaps cf. Akanius (*CIL* 12.4378, cited by Weisgerber (1969), 140), Acratus (once in Italy), Acratianus (once in Pannonia), Acratianis (once in Dalmatia) cited by *NPEL*.

13. *equites Vardulli*: the presence of the Spanish *cohors i fida Vardullorum* in Britain is attested for the pre-Hadrianic period in diplomas of AD 98 and 105 (*CIL* 16.43, 51 = *RIB* II 2401.2), when it was quingenary and presumably equitate; it had become milliary by AD 122, cf. E.Birley (1988), 356 and *VRR* II, 5. This entry must surely indicate the presence of some personnel from that unit at Vindolanda; the movement of groups and detachments causes no surprise (see **154** introduction, with Bowman and Thomas (1991)). See also note to lines 14-5, below.

14-5. *contubernalis Tagamatịṣ*: the word *contubernalis* can mean either mess-mate in the military sense (cf. **310**.i.2) or, more generally, a partner, concubine or *de facto* wife/husband, see *TLL* IV 789-90. R.E.Birley (1990), 30 plausibly suggests that since soldiers were not allowed to contract legal marriages, this entry is a covert description of the "wife" of Tagamatis. The presence of women in military circles at a level below that of the officer class is also suggested by **310**.ii.16-7.

Tagamatịṣ: the name is unattested; the final *s* is fairly secure and it could be preceded by either *i* or *o*, but it is difficult to see how the latter could be a genitive form. *Tagamatis* could be a genitive form of either Tagamatis or Tagamas. Compare Tagarminis in **184**.i.3

and note. Although there is no direct link between this entry and the preceding *equites Vardulli*, it may be more than a coincidence that *Tag-* as a name element has a Spanish connection. He could conceivably be the *uexillarius* (cf. Breeze (1974), 282-3) in charge of Vardullian cavalry detached from the parent unit to Vindolanda.

182

Inv.no.88.947. 174 x 77 mm. Plate IX.

A diptych containing an account written in two columns along the grain. On the back of each half of the leaf are a few lines written by the same hand which probably belong to the same account. The text, which is virtually complete, records cash sums, in most cases for specified goods, notable among which is a horse (ii.12); these could well be sums still owed by individuals for the goods, those deleted with horizontal lines representing debts repaid. Since this text is attributed to Period 4 it presumably reflects a level below that of the officer class and may be a compilation by a civilian trader doing business with soldiers or a mixture of soldiers and civilians (see **180**, introduction, **184**, introduction).

The hand is a respectable cursive which uses an idiosyncratic form of *o*, open at the right and therefore looking more like *c*.

i

[*c.5* ⟦c]ọrnicen pretio
[*c.4*]ṣ m(odiorum) xv (denarios) xii (assem i) s(emissem) (quadrantem)⟧
[re]ḅus minutis (denarios) ii (asses ii)
⟦Sabinus Treuer (denarios) xxiix s(emissem) (asses ii)⟧
Ịṛcucisso ex pretio lardi (denarios) xiii s(emissem)
Felicio (centurio) lardi p(ondo) xxxxv
item lardi pernam p(ondo) xv s(emissem)
f̣ịun{n}t p(ondo) lx s(emissem) (denarios) viii (asses ii)
item accipi . reb<us> miṇụṭis (denarios) ṿi (asses ii) s(emissem) (qụạḍṛạṇṭẹṃ)

ii

Vattus [
⟦Victor ua . [⟧
⟦pretio caballi [⟧
⟦Exomnius (centurio) (denarios) [⟧
Atrectus ceruesar[ius
ex pretio ferri (denarios) i[
pretio exungiae (denarios) xi (asses ii)
Andecarus (denarios) *uacat*
Sanctus (denarios) *uacat*

Back: i

] . is
⟦] . . ẹ . arius (ḍẹṇạṛịọṣ) ịị ṣ(emissem) (assem i) .⟧

⟦ *traces* ⟧
[.]fịc̣....b.ụ.... (denarios) ii s(emissem) .
Ṣautenus (denarii) s(emissem) (assem i) (quadrantem)
Varia..uṣ [
uacat

ii
Traces of three lines

"⟦..., bugler, for the price of
... *modii* 15, *denarii* 12, *asses* 1¾⟧
likewise, for sundries, *denarii* 2, *asses* 2
⟦Sabinus from Trier, *denarii* 38½, *asses* 2⟧
Ircucisso, as part of the price of bacon, *denarii* 13½
Felicio the centurion, bacon, 45 pounds
likewise, bacon-lard, 15½ pounds
total, 60½ pounds, *denarii* 8, *asses* 2
likewise, he (?) has received for sundries *denarii* 6, *asses* 2¾
Vattus ...
⟦Victor ...⟧
⟦for the price of a horse ...⟧
⟦Exomnius the centurion, *denarii* ...⟧
Atrectus the brewer,
as part of the price of iron, *denarii* ..
for the price of pork-fat, *denarii* 11, *asses* 2
Andecarus, *denarii*
Sanctus, *denarii*
(Back) ...
...arius, *denarii* 2½, *asses* 1+
...
..., *denarii* 2½+
Sautenus, *denarii* ½, *asses* 1¼
Varia..."

i.1-2. We regard these lines as containing a single entry.

1. *c]ọrnicen*: we are not certain whether this should be taken as a name or a title but prefer the latter. It specifies a function ("bugler", see e.g. *ChLA* X 443.10 and cf. Speidel, (1984), 40-2); *LC* 319 cites it as a *cognomen*, but only in the Republican period. There is probably room for 5-6 letters before it, so we might have a very short name, followed by the title.

2. The line presumably began with a short noun in the genitive, e.g. *sali]ṣ*. The abbreviation of *m(odiorum)* is, unusually, marked by an almost vertical stroke above *m*. For the symbols at the end of the line see above, pp.54-5.

3. The restoration of *re]ḅus* is not in doubt, cf. i.9. For the usage see Cicero, *Cluent.* 180, *recordatus est se nuper in auctione quadam uidisse in rebus minutis aduncam serrulam*.

4. This is the only Vindolanda text which specifies the origin of an individual. Trier is particularly appropriate for the Batavian and Tungrian units which are known to have been at Vindolanda in the pre-Hadrianic period (especially for the latter, for which see **154**), but it is unsafe to use this text as firm evidence for the presence of any particular unit at the period to which this tablet is attributed.

For the form of the numeral cf **309**.i.5 and note.

5. *Ịrc̣ucisso*: the name, which must be assumed to be in the nominative case, is problematical. The second letter is clearly *r* so we must read *ịr* even though the first letter could be *l*; this diminishes the possible relevance of the name Laxtucissa (Stanfield and Simpson (1958), 184). *CIL* 16.61.23, a diploma of AD 114, attests the name Irducissa, which has a Boian origin (cf. Weisgerber (1969), 88). In order to read *Ịrḍucisso* as a version of this we would have to assume that the writer intended a *d* but omitted the vertical, or that the vertical has completely disappeared. Perhaps it is better to take what we can read at face value and accept *Ircucisso* as a hitherto unattested name.

6-8. We clearly have two quantities of bacon which are totalled in line 8.

6. For a centurion named Felicio see **166**.1 and note.

7. In this account the word *item* seems clearly to signify a further entry relating to the same person (contrast **180**.10 and note).

lardi pernam; the genitive is one of material, "bacon (consisting of) lard"; for the connection see Plautus, *Menaechmi* 209-10, *aliquid scitamentorum de foro opsonarier, glandionidam suilliam, laridum pernonidam* and cf. André (1991), 107-8.

9. *accipi* ̣: this must be either *accipiṭ* or *accipiọ*, in either case presumably an historic present. If *item* refers to Felicio, *accipiṭ* would construe and mean that he had had an advance of cash from the author of the account.

reb<*us*>: this may be a simple mistake or the writer might have meant to abbreviate; but he does not do so elsewhere, cf. i.3.

ii.10. *Vattus*: the name is very uncommon; not in the index of *LC*, and *NPEL* cites only one instance, from Italy. *AS* I 127 cites Vatta and Vattia, both feminine, as well as Vatto (*CIL* 13.5035).

11-2. These lines may well constitute a single entry, cf. i.1-2.

11. *ua* ̣[: this is most likely to be the beginning of a patronym.

12. *caballi*: for the use of this word as an alternative for *equus* see Rittweger and Wölfflin (1892), esp. 316-8. For the purchase of a horse in a military context see *ChLA* XXV 782.

13. The name Exomnius is reasonably common but, like the names in ii.14, 17, and 18, does not occur elsewhere in the Vindolanda texts. *NPEL* cites five instances of its use as a *cognomen* in Gallia Belgica.

14. *Atrectus ceruesar[ius*: the name is reasonably common and *NPEL* cites seven instances in Gallia Belgica (for an example from Trier see *CIL* 13.3707). For *ceruesarius* see *CIL* 13.10012.7, 11319 and note the discharged soldier of the fleet doing business as a *negotiator ceruesarius* on the Rhine frontier in *AE* 1928.183 (cf. Davies (1989), 199). It is probable that he both brewed and sold the beer, in which case he might have been a civilian. For *ceruesa* see *Tab.Vindol.*I, p.91. The entries in the two lines following are presumably payments made by Atrectus.

15. *ferri*: cf. **183**.2.

16. *exungiae*: cf. **190**.c.29 and the notes in *Tab.Vindol.*I, p.92. For the form, *TLL* II 1642.29-32.

17. *Andecarus*: this Celtic name is attested in Gallia Belgica (*NPEL* cites three occurrences); see also *AS* I 140, Weisgerber (1969), index, s.v., Evans (1967), 136-41.

17-8. Both these entries have a *denarius*-symbol with no sign of an amount. We presume that this is deliberate and that the intention was to add the sums later.

Back i.2. Possibly *te]sserarius* preceded by a name; if so, the only occurrence of this title in the tablets, but the auxiliary *tesserarius* is generally very poorly attested, see Holder (1980), 95, Breeze (1974), 282.

5. *Ṣautenus*: see **188**.7 note.

6. Of the names in *NPEL* Varianus is the most common and *nu* could easily be read, but the position of the stroke which seems to be the top of a final *s* would require three letters between *a* and *s*; we can find no attested name which would fit this (*Variarius*?). There is presumably an amount lost further to the right.

183

Inv.no.89.978. 47 x 68 mm.

A fragment of a leaf containing five lines of an account. This may be intact at the top and left but it seems unlikely that what we have is the beginning of the account. It is possible that it was the right-hand part of a diptych with the account written in two columns along the grain, like **182**.

. . . .
.utori (centurioni) *uacat*
ferri p(ondo) lxxxx [
Ascanio (denarios) xxxii[
Candido ad porco[s
.u.ae uector[i
. . . .

Back:]....re....

"to ...tor, centurion,
iron, 90 lbs ...
to Ascanius, *denarii* 32+
to Candidus, in charge of the pigs ...
to ..., transporter ... "

1. *.utori*: in view of the centurial sign, which is certain, we must have a name preceding and the termination seems secure. The reading of *t* is not easy; the alternative is *n* but we have not been able to find a suitable name with this ending. The beginning of the name is obscured by dirt but there does not seem to be room for *Adiutori* (cf. **199**.2, **214**.1) or another name of similar length. Perhaps *Tutori*.

2. *ferri p(ondo)*: there appears to be too much ink simply for *p* and it would be possible to imagine *(denarii) clxxxx[*; but it seems very unlikely that such a large sum would

be involved (cf. **182**.ii.15 where the amount for *ferrum* is less than 5 *denarii*).

4. The name Candidus occurs in several texts from different periods (see **181**.2 note) but the name is so common that it is pointless to hazard identifications.

ad porcọ[s: cf. **180**.27.

5: *.ụ.ae uectoṛ[i*: the name appears to begin with a large *ḷ* and we could read *Ḷục̣ae*; for the name Luca (gender uncertain) see *RIB* I 867; *NPEL* also cites Luca... (in Gallia Belgica) and Lucas. For *uectura* at Vindolanda cf. *VRR* II, 29.

Back. The surviving letters are faint and abraded. We might have a name in the genitive, preceded by *ratio* in the lost portion, cf. **192**.back, **207**.back.

184

Inv.no.87.622. 210 x 70 mm. (approx.). Plate XII. *VRR* II, Plate XVII.

There are 27 fragments of a double leaf which contains an account written in three columns along the grain of the wood. The configuration of the text enables us to place most of the major fragments with relative confidence (although very few of them are directly contiguous, which accounts for the approximation in calculating the size of the diptych). The text transcribed as (a) accounts for 14 of the fragments, (b) and (c) for another 2. Of the remaining 11 scraps, 9 contain exiguous traces and 2 appear to be blank. This is one of the few ink texts attributed to the later part of the period of occupation when the area may have been occupied by a workshop (although the distinction between barrack-block and workshop may not always be clear-cut, see Glasbergen and Groenman-van Waateringe (1974), 11, 25).

The account in (a) consists of 40 or 42 lines of text (see below) arranged in three columns. The format is not paralleled elsewhere in the tablets and is unexpected because the middle column straddles the central fold. The text is written in a competent cursive hand and is neatly arranged, with commodities and names aligned and the former regularly indented with respect to the latter. It is probable that in columns i and ii (though not in column iii) names and commodities alternate line by line.

Columns i and ii record names, commodities and amounts of money under the heading "century of Ucen(i)us (?)" and Col.iii has similar entries under the heading "century of Tullio". Among the commodities listed are over-garments, pepper, tallow, towels, thongs and items of footwear and clothing, and they might thus be described as a miscellaneous collection. Some of the entries have check marks before them which we have tried to indicate in our transcript (for a possibly comparable phenomenon see *O.Claud.* 83). One or two of these appear to be simply horizontal dashes but most have in addition a vertical or slanting stroke at the left and they appear before both names and commodities. In some cases there are horizontal lines which might go right through the entry (ii.28, 29, iii.36, 37) and may indicate that the account for that particular item had been settled. It is not clear whether we should classify this account as "official". Unless we suppose that the entries in i.2 and iii.32-4 record dealings with a century as a whole, it looks as if the commodities and their costs are to be referred to the names following them (see notes to lines i.17 and ii.29). They might thus represent transactions between soldiers and a civilian entrepreneur (cf. **180**, introduction); it is in no way surprising to find that soldiers had cash with which to purchase such items. It seems clear, at any rate, that it takes us to a level below the officer class and the personal names in the account (several of which are hitherto unattested) are of considerable value from that point of view.

There are two lines of writing at the foot of col.iii, written by the same hand but upside down in relation to the main text; it is unclear whether these are connected or not. The back contains abraded remains of seven lines of an account which may be written by the same hand. We have not been able to extract any coherent sense from this but it is possible that the first line has a centurial sign followed by a name (ending *-lis*?) and that the second reads *per[na]m (denarios) ii s(emissem)*; if this is correct it might be part of the same account as the text on the front.

a. i

(centuria) Uceṇi
⊢ superarias (denarios) xiii.[
⊢ Tagarminis ⟦.⟧
⊢ piper (denarios) ii
G̣ambax Tapponis
ṣ[udari]ụṃ (denarios) ii
].mni..[.].ubar[
⊢ ampullam [
.ụṛịọ Ṣṭ..ọnis
⊢ sudarium (denarios) ii
- Ammius [
]xxiix
].i
]ṃ (denarios) iii (asses ii) (quadrantem)
].s
]..i (denarios) i s(emissem) (assem i)
].armal *traces?*

ii

coturnum (denarios) iii ṣ(emissem)
Messor ⟦......⟧
- sagaciam (denarios) v (asses iii)
Luc̣ius scutarius
sebum (denarios) [
U]xperus
ị[
Agị.[
ṣ[
Huep..[
sudạṛ[ ] (denarios) ii
Tullio Carpẹnṭạri
uacat of 2 lines
(denarios) xḷ *traces*

iii

(centuria) Tullionis
corrigia (denarios) ii s(emissem)

- sebum (denarios) ii
sudari(um) (denarium) i
Butimas
sebum (denarios) ii[
d sudar(ium) (denarios) ̣[
]ọ subạrṃalọ
sebum (denarios) [
[C]aleḍus
uacat
uell[*c.8*]. . . . .
ue ̣[*c.8*] ̣aliator

b.

. . .
↓ ⟦]ṣẹḅ[⟧
]ạḅ[
. . .

c.

. . .
↓]ar ̣[
. . .

d-l. 9 tiny scraps with exiguous traces of writing.

(i.1-12)
"Century of Ucen(i)us (?)
overcoats, *denarii* 13+
Tagarminis
pepper, *denarii* 2
Gambax son of Tappo
towel, *denarii* 2
Sollemnis (?) ...
a flask ...
Furio (?) son of Stipo (?)
towel, *denarii* 2
Ammius ...
... 28 (?)"
(ii.18-iii.40)
"buskin, *denarii* 3½
Messor
a *sagacia*, *denarii* 5, *asses* 3
Lucius the shield-maker
tallow, *denarii* ..
... Uxperus
...
Agilis (?)
tallow (?), ...
Huep...

towel, *denarii* 2
Tullio son of Carpentarius
denarii 40+
century of Tullio
thongs, *denarii* 2½
tallow, *denarii* 2
towel (?), *denarius* 1
Butimas
tallow, *denarii* 2+
towel, *denarii* ..
...
tallow, *denarii* ..
Caledus"

i.1. *Uceṇi*: the reading of the name is not straightforward. Palaeographically *ucersi* is perhaps preferable but we can find no parallel for a name of this kind. Pliny the Elder mentions an Alpine tribe called the Ucenni, in his quotation of the text of the Tropaeum Augusti (*NH* 3.137, cf. *EJ*² 40). If we can accept the reading of a rather elaborate *n* as the penultimate letter, we might postulate a personal name derived from this tribe. *CIL* 14.3718 (Latium) has a name *Ucena Victoria*; its editor considered the *gentilicium* corrupt but the present text perhaps suggests that *Ucenus* or *Ucenius* is acceptable. Note also *Ucenteus* in Schallmayer *et al.* (1990), 595. The nomenclature of the western provinces otherwise offers only the *gentilicium* Usenius (*CIL* 3.5162, 5166) but it does not seem possible to read the second letter of our name as *s*.

2. *superarias*: the word occurs in *ChLA* III 204.4 and should be restored in *ChLA* I 12.8-9. It is defined in *CGL* IV 180.15 etc. as *uestis quae superinduitur*. The trace at the break might be either *i* or a fraction.

3. *Tagarminis*: the reading seems beyond doubt but the name is not attested (but cf. *contubernalis Tagamatis* in **181**.14). It looks like a genitive form, whereas the other names in this account are in the nominative. However, it is perhaps best not to be too dogmatic with such unusual and ill-attested formations. Tag- as a personal name element would be appropriate to an origin in either Gaul or Spain. *NPEL* cites Tagadunus and Tagadunius once each in Belgica and Tagnius in Spain. *AS* III 1700 connects Tagana with the R.Tagus in Spain and cites Tagassus at Nimes. There is something which looks like an ink-mark following, perhaps an erased centurial symbol.

4. *piper*: the occurrence of this item is somewhat surprising, especially in an account which appears to concern people of humble rank, since it must have been an expensive imported luxury. Pliny *NH* 12.28 gives the price of *piper nigrum* as 4 *denarii*/lb. See further Schwinden (1985), 123-9. Pepper is not mentioned as part of the military diet by either Davies (1989), 187-206 or Dickson (1989). It is known as an ingredient in oculists' salves, see Nielsen (1974), 22-3, 53. Is it possible that these were being made at Vindolanda (see **154**.24 and cf. *RIB* II 2446, A.R.Birley (1992))?

5. *G̣ambax Tapponis*: the first letter in the line is damaged but the reading is not in doubt. Tappo is reasonably well attested, Gambax not at all. *NPEL* cites Gamburio once in Belgica, Gambugius once in Noricum. Gamba occurs at Salona (*CIL* 3.13904); Weisgerber (1969), 141, 137.

6. *ṣ[udari]ụṃ*: the spacing of the traces rules out *s[eb]um* (see ii.22 note) and *s[udari]um* (see i.10 note) is therefore the obvious restoration.

7. This line seems likely to contain a name and there is no trace of the *denarius*-symbol or a numeral at the right. The traces of the first word are compatible with a restoration of *Soll]ẹmniṣ* but the following word is difficult to explain. Since the difficulties of reading and interpretation in lines i.17 and iii.38 may be related, it seems best to discuss all three cruces together.

In i.7 *.ubar* seems secure, but there appears to be nothing following it. The letter before *u* looks most like *i* but *s* (or even *l*) cannot be excluded. If what precedes it is a *cognomen*, the pattern of the text suggests that we should have either a patronym or perhaps a trade-designation; we have considered *tubarius*, listed by Tarruntenus Paternus among the *immunes* in *Digest* 50.6.7(6) but it is very difficult to read the first letter as *t*.

In i.17 we have *].armal* with possible traces following, but the alignment and the traces do not suggest a *denarius*-symbol and number. The letter before *armal* is probably *b*. There is a small fragment with remains of two letters, probably *ṣụ*, which could be placed at the left of *]ḅarmal*, but equally it might belong in i.16 (see note).

In iii.38 we have *]ọ subạṛmalọ*; the first trace is doubtful and the last could be a medial point, but the alignment suggests that we cannot have had a cash sum at the right.

In none of these three lines do we seem to have a commodity. We may have the same word in all three cases, probably so in i.17 and iii.38 at least; if so, perhaps *subar( )* or *subarmal( )*. Nevertheless, given the context, it is perhaps worth noting the evidence for the word *subarmale* as a substantive = *subarmalis vestis*. The word is used in *HA*, *Sev*. 6.11, *Claud*. 14.8 and *Aur*. 13.3, and in the first passage cited it refers to soldiers (*praetorianos cum subarmalibus inermes sibi iussit occurrere*). We can hardly envisage a descriptive title such as *subarmal(iator)*, however.

8. *ampullam*: this can be either a flask for oil or unguents, or a drinking vessel, see *TLL* I 2018. The word also occurs in **201**.8 and perhaps **439**.6 (and cf. *ChLA* VI 306).

9. *.ụṛịọ Sṭ..ọnis*: this line is likely to contain a name. The *cognomen* Furio, though rare, suits the traces. For what follows, we have considered names Stilo (*RNGCL*), Stico and Stipo (*NPEL*, Spain and Pannonia respectively). *il* is not at all easy to read; *ic* could be read but we note that the reading in *CIL* 2.2006 is questioned; *Ṣṭịp̣ọnis* suits the traces and is perhaps the most attractive possibility.

10. *sudarium*: the last letter is on a separate fragment, but it is certain that *sudarịạ.* cannot be read. A *sudarium* is a towel or napkin, perhaps for use in the baths, which could be worn around the neck like a scarf (cf. Suetonius, *Nero* 51, quoted in **196**.8 note). The price in lines i.6, i.10 and ii.28 seems clearly to be 2 *denarii* whereas in iii.34 it is equally clearly 1 *denarius* (the prices in other entries are uncertain or incomplete). In view of this we think it likely that the noun is used collectively. For towels and shoes and slippers for the baths see *P.Oxy*.XXXI 2599.24-5, 31-2 and cf. **197**.3 note.

11. *Ammius*: for this *gentilicium* see *LE* 121, 423. This might well have been followed by a *cognomen*, now lost in a gap between the fragments.

12-7. If the pattern in this column is that commodities alternate with names line by line and that the names follow the items to which they refer, we can easily envisage line 13 as the end of a patronym and line 15 as a *cognomen*.

16. See note to i.7, above. If the scrap with *ṣụ* belongs here we may have *ṣụ[d]ạṛị*.

17. See note to i.7, above.

ii.18. *coturnum*: traditionally seen as the raised boot, but it is difficult to understand how this might fit the context at Vindolanda. *TLL* IV 1086-7 cites Servius on *Aeneid* 1.337, *calciamenta etiam uenatoria crura quoque uincientia quorum quiuis utrique aptus est pedi*. For possible evidence of hunting interests at Vindolanda see **233**.i.4 note. The second part of Servius' comment would explain why it might make sense to purchase one *coturnus*, presumably as a replacement, but it is perhaps better to suppose that the singular is used collectively for a pair, see *P.Mich.* VIII 477.27 note, 508.5 note and cf. i.10 note, above. Carol van Driel Murray (*per litteras*) warns us of the danger of applying the description of a fourth-century commentator to second-century footwear since its technology underwent radical changes in the interim. She further remarks that there is no Roman archaeological evidence for what we would expect a *cothurnus* to be and it may be that provincials used cloth or leather bindings in conjunction with ordinary boots to extend them.

19. *Messor*: see *LC* 82, 361.

20. *sagaciam*: see **255**.i.8-ii.10 note.

21. *Luc̣ius scutarius*: the reading of the name as Lucius assumes a noticeable serif on the right-hand upright of *u*, of which we have an example in ii.27, *Huep..*. There is no difficulty in treating Lucius as a *cognomen*, cf. **156**.2 note. *scutarius* is attested as a *cognomen* (*LC* 320), but the occurrence of *praenomen* plus *cognomen* would not fit the pattern of names in this text and we prefer to take *scutarius* as indicating a craft; the word occurs in *CEL* 26. The first name might be read as *Luṭius* (*NPEL* cites Luteus in Gallia Lugdunensis and Luttius in Aquitania and Narbonensis).

22. *sebum*: animal suet or tallow; perhaps also in **319**.3. For its preparation see Pliny, *NH* 28.143, cf. Hodgson (1976), 7-8. For medicinal uses see Pliny, *NH* 22.59, Celsus, 2.30.2; for candle-making, Columella, 2.21.3. It also occurs in *P.Ryl.*II 223.4 (= *RMR* 82), along with oil and pitch, in an account of naval supplies.

23. *U]xperus*: The name is very rare, only a single instance, in Gallia Belgica, cited by *NPEL* (*CIL* 13.10017.937). We have found no other name with this ending, so the restoration seems probable. The alignment suggests that it was preceded by a *gentilicium*.

25. *Agị.[*: the alignment makes it clear that this must be a name. *Agịḷ[is* is a possible reading, cf. **329**, but not the same man since the latter belongs to a *turma*.

27. *Huep..[*: the first four letters appear to be certain although we know of no name beginning with these letters. *Hue-* does not seem to be a Celtic or Gallic name element. If it phonetically represents *Ve-*, as it clearly does in dedications to the *di Hueteres* (sc. *Veteres*, see *RIB* I, indexes, p.68 and perhaps cf. **187**.ii.3 and note), we could read *Huepịṭ[ta* as a version of the *cognomen* Vepitta (*CIL* 3.11234, Pannonia).

29. *Tullio Carpẹnṭạri*: *NPEL* cites Tullio only twice for Gallia Belgica; see also **312**.back 4. Names beginning *Cara-* are common in that province but we cannot read the fourth letter as *a*. For Carpentarius as a *cognomen* see *LC* 322. The fact that there is no commodity following this name and that the next column begins with the name of a century strongly suggests that the names are to be taken with the items preceding them (see introduction and cf. i.17, iii.40).

30. This sum is written right at the bottom edge with a significant gap after line 29. If we are correct in thinking that the commodities and amounts precede the names to which they refer it cannot be relevant to Tullio in line 29, and the *uacat* suggests that this is correct. It would be natural to take it as a note of the total for the century of Ucen(i)us (?) which occupies the whole of columns i and ii but 40+ *denarii* is not large enough to cover the sums which are preserved.

iii.31. This is presumably a different Tullio from the one in line 29.

32. *corrigia*: we expect an accusative and *TLL* IV 1032 attests a neuter form *corrigium*; at the end *a* is perhaps a correction written over *l*.

34. *sudari*: there is no sign of anything after *i* and it does not look as if the surface is abraded. We would expect an accusative (cf. note to iii.32) but it seems that we must have an unmarked abbreviation (cf. iii.37). For the price see i.10 note.

35. *Butimas*: the name is unattested. Note Butes, *CIL* 3.7893 (Dacia) and cf. Boutius, *CIL* 3.9834 (Dalmatia, but the person is from Spain), *CIL* 12.5686 (C.Bou..., Vienne), *CIL* 7.1336.174 (Bouti, London). Boutius occurs in Gallia Belgica (*ILB* 74) and *NPEL* indicates that it is common in Spain.

37. There is a clear *d* to the left of this entry. It is possible that it is deleted in which case we assume that the writer simply made a false start. For the abbreviation cf. iii.34 note.

38. See i.7 note.

40. The *cognomen* Caledus is very uncommon (see *LC* 178) but the reading of *aledus* is easy and we can suggest no other plausible restoration.

41-2. If the two fragments at the bottom right are correctly placed, we have the beginnings and ends of two lines written upside down in the same hand but it is unclear whether these are connected with the main text.

41. *uell[*: this might be the beginning of a name.

42. The remains of the third letter are compatible with *m* or possibly *n* or *r*.

]ạliator: it seems unlikely that we should understand the noun *aleator* here. *aliator* appears once as a name (*NSA* 1916, 108) but the preceding letter, which looks very much like part of *m*, seems to belong to the same word. Perhaps *ṃaliator*, given by *TLL* as an alternative spelling of *malleator*.

185

Inv.no.88.950. 60 x 171 mm. Plate XI. *VRR* II, Plate III.

A diptych which is only partially preserved at all margins, and has lost a good deal near the top. There are two fragments with traces of writing which may belong in this area but we are not able to place them securely nor do we have any confidence in our readings of the traces. We may well have the whole account, however. The writing, particularly in the upper part, is very abraded and difficult to read and there are a number of readings and interpretations with which we remain unsatisfied. This is the more frustrating because the account has several features of interest. It seems to record expenditure for a variety of items including food, perhaps clothing, equipment for a carriage (*raeda*, see note to lines 20-1) and perhaps also accommodation (see note to line 24). Some of the purchases or payments are connected with place-names, Isurium (Aldborough, line 23, cf. line 6), Cataractonium (Catterick, line 24), Vinovia (Binchester, line 26, cf. line 2), and this leads us to wonder whether we have an account of expenditure incurred on a journey. It is interesting that the order in which Isurium, Cataractonium and Vinovia occur towards the end of the account is the order in which they would be reached by a traveller coming from York to Vindolanda via Corbridge. The first part of the account could relate to an outward journey (see notes to lines 2, 4, 6) and the second part to the return. It must be admitted, however, that if this is close to the mark, the account cannot be regarded as a meticulous record of expenditure such as we find in the papers of Theophanes (*P.Ryl.*IV 627-38), for there are no dates at all in the second half of the text.

The hand is an unremarkable cursive. In line 24 note the use of *o* open at the right.

↓ [..].ạ...ạṣ.[*c.4?*].i
]. uis
[*c.3*]. *traces* (quadrantem)
[*c.3*]ḷ.ạ..ạṣḍuṃ
f̣ạẹc̣i (denarii) s(emissem)
[.] Ịdus Iulias i...ịọ
f̣ạẹc̣i (denarii) (quadrantem)
I]dus Iuliaṣ *traces*
f̣ạẹc̣i (denarii) (quadrantem)
[..] Iduṣ Ịulias ạ[
traces of six lines
⟦ *c.*12 ⟧ c̣[*c.3*] *traces* viii[
f̣ạẹc̣i (denarii) (qụạḍṛạṇṭẹṃ)
hordei m(odium) i (denarii) s(emissem) (assem i)
axes carrarios
duos ad raeḍaṃ (denarios) iii s(emissem)
sal auẹ.am (denarium) i
Isụrio f̣aẹc̣i (denarii) (quadrantem)
C̣ạtaractonio locaṛịọ (denarii) s(emissem)
f̣aẹc̣i (denarii) (quadrantem)
Vinouis subunc.lon.s (denarii) (quadrantem)
frumenti *traces*
f̣ịunt (denarii) lxxiix s(emis) (quadrans)
summa omnis (denarii) lxxxxiiii s(emis) (quadrans)
[*c.12*]..[*c.3*]ụṭị

(lines 5-10) "For lees of wine (?), *denarii* ½
July (8-13), at Isurium (?)
for lees of wine (?), *denarii* ¼
July (9-14), ...
for lees of wine (?), *denarii* ¼
July (10-14), ..."
(lines 17-29) "... 8 ..
for lees of wine (?), *denarii* ¼,
of barley, *modius* 1, *denarii* ½, *as* 1
wagon-axles,
two, for a carriage, *denarii* 3½
salt and fodder (?) ..., *denarius* 1
at Isurium, for lees of wine (?), *denarii* ¼
at Cataractonium, for accommodation (?), *denarii* ½
for lees of wine (?), *denarii* ¼

at Vinovia, for vests (?), *denarii* ¼
of wheat, ...
total, *denarii* 78¾
grand total, *denarii* 94¾.
..."

1. The reading given represents traces which seemed to be visible on an earlier photograph. Only the last two traces can be seen in the Plate. If this is the beginning of the account we would expect it to begin with a date, or perhaps *ratio* followed by a name in the genitive, or *a* plus ablative (cf. **192**.1, **207**.1), but the traces are too exiguous to suggest a reading.

2. The first surviving letter, of which only the lower part remains, is most easily read as *d*; *-ḍuis* might perhaps be the end of a place-name but the name Ardua is very doubtful, see *PNRB* 257, and we have found no other British place-name with this termination. Alternatively, it might be read as *-ọuis* and we might have *Vin]ọuis*, which is repeated in line 26 (for the *-ouium/-ouia* termination see *PNRB* 297, 389-90). This would fit the idea that the account records expenses on a journey from Vindolanda to York and back (see introduction), but this is very hypothetical; see also notes to lines 4 and 6.

4. We might have a date in this line but the traces are not easy to reconcile with a month-name; *maias* might just be possible. This makes it difficult to explain *ḍuṃ* at the end. If it were a place-name we would expect a locative (*]duiṣ* might be a possible reading but see note to line 2); Virosidum (Brough by Bainbridge) lies on the route from Carvoran to Catterick via Bravoniacum (Kirkby Thore), but that would exclude the possibility of an outward journey from Vindolanda via Vinovia.

5. *fạẹc̣i*: we believe that the same word occurs also in lines 7, 9, 18, 23 and 25 and it presents a serious problem of reading and interpretation. It is clearly a five-letter word of which the last letter is *i*. The first letter is most easily read as *s*, especially in line 7, but elsewhere, at any rate in lines 9, 23 and 25, it could be read as *f*. The second letter must be *a*. The third might be read as *c* in some cases (lines 5, 7, 9, 18) but in lines 23 and 25 it is unquestionably *e*. The penultimate letter in all cases is most naturally read as *c* but the form would perhaps admit *p* and we note that there is no other clear example of *p* in this text with which to compare it.

The reading which this most readily suggests is *saeci*, but we cannot derive any sense from this. The few Latin words beginning with *saec-* are all connected with *saeculum*. Since the form of the entries demands either accusatives or datives we cannot have a personal name (e.g. Saecus, or even Saccus). We can only suggest known Latin words if, despite the palaeographical difficulties which we have indicated, we read either *faẹc̣i* or *ṣaẹp̣i*. The latter would be taken as the dative of *saepes*, meaning "fencing". This would be unexpected in the context and even if we envisaged the purchase of such an item, it is hard to see why there should be six separate purchases at different times and places. *faeci*, the dative of *faex*, normally means "lees" or "dregs" and the cheapest kind of wine is something which travellers might purchase at various stopping-places; for its various uses see Cato, *Agr*. 96, Horace, *Sat*. 2.4.55, Celsus 4.29, cf. *TLL* VI.1 169.42-4. Note also the use for lees of beer described by Plin., *Med*. 3.6, *ebuli folia ... mixta cum faece ceruesiae ... in linteolo alligantur*.

6. *i..iọ*; if we have correctly identified the pattern of the text this might well be a place-name, and it seems just possible, though not easy, to read *Iṣụṛio* (cf. line 23), which

would support the idea that this account records expenses on a journey from and back to Vindolanda.

10. There may be an interpunct after *Iulias*. The *a* following might again be the beginning of a place-name but we have found no attested name beginning with A- between Vindolanda and York.

17. The four digits are written much further to the right than anything else in this text. The writing which occupies the left-hand half of the line looks as if it has been erased and it must have caused the writer to put the correct version further to the right. The numeral might then be part of the quantity and there will have been room for the *denarius*-symbol and another numeral in the lost part at the right.

18. Everything except the *denarius* symbol is very abraded; the amount may well be the same as is recorded for this item in lines 7, 9, 23 and 25, ¼ *denarius*; if the horizontal stroke belongs with the *denarius*-symbol, we would read *s(emissem)*, cf. line 5.

19. There may be an abraded flat dash over *m*. The digit is somewhat elongated and curved to the left. The amount after the *denarius*-symbol is probably to be interpreted as *s(emissem)* followed by a horizontal tick which we take to indicate one *as*, rather than *s* with a cross-stroke. This is important since it offers one of the few clear attestations of a price: 9 *asses* for a *modius* of barley. See further notes to lines 27-8.

20-1. For *axses carrarios* cf. **309**.i.5 and see note *ad loc*. in Bowman and Thomas (1987), 142. The reading of *raedam* is inescapable although the *d* is difficult; for the term as denoting a common type of transporter see Adams (1993), 49, note 26.

22. *sal auẹ.am*: this entry is difficult to elucidate. The letter after *ẹ* looks like *x* but we think that it might well have been corrected to *n*. An accusative form is appropriate and it would be possible to understand *sal* ("salt") as an accusative and to justify the case by the fact that it is reckoned by cost rather than quantity. If we are correct in thinking that this account is concerned with travel, it would make good sense to suppose that there is asyndeton and to interpret this as a purchase of salt and fodder for animals, i.e. *sal (et) aueṇam* (cf. Dixon and Southern (1992), 209).

23. The initial *i* is enlarged and aligned slightly to the left. Although the writing is abraded we are reasonably confident of the reading and the site of the former capital of the Brigantes (Aldborough, Boroughbridge) is a plausible stopping-place on a journey to or from Vindolanda. The name does not occur elsewhere in the tablets.

24. For contact between Vindolanda and Cataractonium (Catterick) see **343**.ii.15-6.

locaṛiọ: although the final letter is difficult we think that the reading is possible and that the word can be interpreted as a charge for lodging or accommodation either for people or for animals, see Varro, *LL* 5.15, *in<de> locarium quod detur in stabulo et taberno ubi consistunt*.

26. *Vinouis*: this must be understood as the locative form of the place-name Vinovia (Binchester). This reference is important because it clearly implies that the name is treated as a neuter plural rather than feminine singular, a possibility not envisaged in *PNRB* 504-5.

subunc.lon.s: the reading of the second part of this word poses difficulties. The letter after *c* is very difficult to read as *ụ*, unless it has been corrected; perhaps *o*. The penultimate letter might be *ị* or *ẹ*. This yields *subuncọlonịs* or *subuncọlonẹs*. The beginning of the word puts us in mind of "vests" but we would expect *subunculas* (cf. *RMLW*, s.v.), *subuculas* or *subuclas* (the last occurs in **196**.11). We could have either an accusative plural, or perhaps a dative (cf. line 24), but we can find no support for this form.

27-8. It seems clear that these lines contain a calculation of the price of an amount of wheat which was purchased, the total expenditure being given in line 28. Uncertainty about the details of the calculation results from the fact that the quantity in line 27 is difficult to read and the price per *modius* which seems to have been quoted at the end of the line is completely abraded. The reading of the quantity of wheat is doubtful but *lxxi* is compatible with the traces; thereafter we may have a fractional symbol, perhaps a quarter; after this perhaps *m(odius) i*. It seems possible to calculate orders of magnitude, however, using as a base the price of 9 *asses* for one *modius* of barley in line 19. The cost ratio of wheat to barley ought to be about 2:1, a proportion which is close to the nutritional ratio (see Bagnall (1985), 4). The price of wheat ought then to be somewhat over 1 *denarius* per *modius* (comparing well with the prices attested at Rome, see Duncan-Jones (1982), Appendix 8); calculation of any individual price always has to allow a good margin for regional or season distortion and it would not be surprising if the prices were a little higher in July, almost a year after harvest. The sum given in line 28 suggests a quantity of just over 70 *modii* at a price of just over 1 *denarius* per *modius*. If this is more or less correct, it will mean that a large proportion of the total account was spent on wheat. This may not simply be for provisions en route, if we are concerned with a journey; it might have been desirable or necessary to purchase wheat at the end of the season and transport it back to base.

29. For *summa omnis* cf. *RMR* 68.ii.24, iii.12.

30. The first surviving trace in the middle of the line is compatible with the top of a *denarius*-symbol. If so, we should have a number following (though the trace following the symbol is difficult) and it is possible that the end of the line should be read as *]vii*.

186

Inv.no.87.567. 60 x 167 mm. Plate VIII. *VRR* II, Plate III.

This double leaf contains 25 lines of an account. Much of the writing is abraded. The tablet is complete at the right-hand margin and probably at the foot, where the bottom third of the second half-leaf appears to be blank. There is some loss at the beginnings of lines. The top of the first half-leaf is physically intact and comparison with line 17 suggests that there is room for a date in the missing portion at the left; this may therefore have been the beginning of the text, but we cannot exclude the possibility that there may have been one or more leaves preceding (cf. **190**).

The account covers a period of some weeks at the end of AD 110 and the beginning of AD 111. It is of the greatest importance that it contains a reference to the consuls of AD 111 at the point at which the account goes from one calendar year to the next (lines 13-4). It is the only text from Vindolanda to carry a year date and is thus a crucial element in the dating of the occupation levels. Its location in the building of Period 4 suggests a connection with the centurions or *optiones* of the unit(s) at Vindolanda.

The account records miscellaneous commodities (nails for boots, salt, Celtic beer, pork) with quantities and cash value or cost. The names Gracilis, Audax and Similis (see line 22 note) occur with the preposition *per*, suggesting that commodities were purchased through them. The entry in lines 7-8, however, records 100 nails with the name of Gracilis in the dative, which indicates sale or disbursement to him. It seems plausible that the account was compiled by someone responsible for acquiring and re-selling or redistributing supplies. The names of Gracilis and Audax do not occur elsewhere and that of Similis, if correctly read, is unlikely to have any connection with Flavius Similis (**235**, **254**, **286**, cf. **347**). There is no indication of the status of these persons and we cannot exclude the possibility that they were slaves (cf. Privatus in **190**.c.26 etc.). This is the only account which reckons in *asses* alone rather than *denarii* or *denarii* and *asses*, and it seems to do so consistently.

The hand is rather ugly and sprawling. The form of *p* in line 4 and elsewhere is noteworthy and might perhaps be termed old-fashioned; the same may be true of *a* which often has two obliques at the left (see Fig.1 on p.53).

↓ [ ] per *traces*
[ ]. m(odios) xxx[..] ......
[Decem]bres pẹr G̣racịlem
[ ]. p(ondo) c ..[
[...]..[Dece]ṃbres per Grạc̣ịḷẹm
[..].. p(ondo) xxịị (asses) ..
[*c.3*] Ḳ(alendas) Ịạnuarias Gracili clauos
caligares · n(umero) c (asses duos)
[K(alendas) I]ạnuarias per Audacem
salis p̣(ondo) lx̣xxv[ ].ii.
[K(alendas) I]anua{ui}riaṣ cẹr[u]ẹse
ṃetretam (asses) viii
[CAL]PURNIO PISONE VETTIO
[B]ỌLANO CO(N)S(ULIBUS) *uacat*
[*c.5* Ia]nuariạṣ p̣ẹṛ ...a..m
[*c.6*].......c̣.ṇẹ (assem i) .
[*c.5* Feb]ṛuuaris pẹṛ Gracilem
[*c.7*]..met.r.[*c.3*]s ...cum (asses) .
[*c.4*] Februuar[i]ạs per G̣racịḷẹṃ
[*c.4*]..m e. poṛc.. *traces*
[p]ẹr Audacem pọṛciṇe p(ondo) xị ..
[..Id]ụs Februuarias pẹṛ Simịḷẹm
c̣eruese metrẹṭam ...
[*c.7*]aṣ per Auḍa[c]ẹṃ
[*c.8*]m *traces*
uacat

"... through Gracilis (?)
... *modii*, 30+ ...
.. November/December, through Gracilis,
..., pounds 100 ...
.. November/December, through Gracilis,
... pounds 22, *asses* ..
00 December, to Gracilis, nails
for boots, number 100, *asses* 2
00 December, through Audax,

of salt, pounds 85+, *asses* 12+ (?)
00 December, of Celtic beer,
a *metretes*, *asses* 8
In the consulship of Calpurnius Piso
and Vettius Bolanus:
00 January, through Audax (?),
goat-meat (?), ..., *as* 1 (?)
00 January (?), through Gracilis,
..., *asses* ..
00 January (?), through Gracilis,
... pork (?) ...,
through Audax, of pork (?), pounds 11+ , ...
0 February, through Similis,
of Celtic beer, a *metretes*, ...
00 February (?), through Audax
..."

1-2. It seems likely that this entry occupied two lines, as do all the other entries in the text except lines 19-21. There is room for a date in the missing portion at the left (cf. line 17). The writing after *per* is very abraded; *m* is fairly clear as the last letter and the rest is not incompatible with *Gracilem*.

The name of a commodity has been lost at the left in line 2. As is common, the abbreviation of *m(odios)* is marked by a superscript bar and the number may have lost one or two digits at the end. The abraded traces which follow may begin with the symbol for *asses*.

3. Here and in line 5 we have restored the month-name as December, but in theory it is of course possible that the month-name was *Nouembres*.

4. The traces at the right are presumably the remains of the price. The weight (100 lbs) suggests that we might perhaps be dealing with *ferrum* (cf. **182**.ii.15, **183**.2).

5-6. We have placed here a small detached fragment which contains parts of two lines and must belong at the left. It could in theory belong anywhere between lines 1 and 6, however. If we are correct, the reading in line 5 could be .. *N]ọṇ[(as) Dece]ṃbres*.

6. The name of the commodity at the left perhaps ends *]ịṣ*. There appears to be an interpunct after *p(ondo)* but it would be one of only two possible instances in this text (cf. note to line 8). If the small piece at the left does not fit here, we might have had *sal]ịṣ*.

7-8. This is the only entry in which there is a name in the dative (cf. introduction).

clauos caligares: there appears to be an interpunct following (cf. note to line 6). For military footwear in general see van Driel-Murray (1985). A very great deal of footwear has been found in the excavations at Vindolanda, see *VRR* III, 31-47; it is certain that the facilities for repair existed in the workshops at Vindolanda (cf. **155**.2). It is noteworthy that in *P.Ryl.*II 223 (=*RMR* 82) nails are measured by weight rather than number, as here.

Line 8, like 10, 12 and several others, is indented.

10. *salis*: salt also occurs in **191**.5 and perhaps **185**.22 (see note) and **202**.a.8; cf. note to line 6, above. For salt extraction in Britain see Bradley in De Brisay and Evans (1975), 20-5, Jones and Mattingly (1990), 224-8, and for its importance in the military diet Davies (1989), 188-9. Presumably the symbol for *asses* is lost in the gap. The numeral may well be *ẋii*, followed by a symbol which must be a fraction of an *as* (cf. **182**.i.2, 9).

11-2. This seems to be the only entry without *per* plus name or a name in the dative.

11. *I]anua{ui}rias*: there is no doubt about the writing of the extra syllable which is presumably simply a mistake (cf. lines 17, 19, 22), though a surprising one.

cer[u]ese: for Celtic beer see **190**.c.6 etc. with *Tab.Vindol.*I, p.91 (line 12 note) and for a *ceruesarius* in the writing-tablets **182**.ii.14.

12. *metretam*: this is a vessel of known capacity (100 *sextarii*, see *TLL* VIII 894) and is appropriate to the context here and in line 23. Here it is possible that it was followed by the digit *i*. It occurs nowhere else in the Vindolanda texts. In **190** *ceruesa* is measured in *modii*.

13-4. Calpurnius Piso and Vettius Bolanus are the consuls of AD 111. These lines must have been slightly indented if, as is surely the case, there was nothing before *[Cal]purnio*. The names are written in capitals, as is not uncommon with headings in military records (see Bowman (1994b)). For consular dates in capitals see e.g. *RMR* 70.b.i.6, ii.6-7 (= *P.Aberd.* 133). The form of *R* which is closer to the cursive than the capital form is noteworthy.

15. The format of the entries suggests that we should have a date followed by *per*; the traces would perhaps allow *Audacem* although it is not an easy reading.

16. This line is very abraded. At the left we may have *]ari* or *]rni*. Following that there are 7 or 8 letters of which the last 4 appear to be *cine*. If this were an adjective ending with *-cin(a)e* we might conceivably have *ca]rnis porcine* or, perhaps better, *hircine*. The difficulties with this are: (1) almost all sign of the *s* at the end of the first word has disappeared, though there may be a top-stroke visible; (2) we would have to imagine *p(ondo)* plus a numeral after *-cine*, all trace of which has disappeared. For pigs at Vindolanda see **180**.27, **183**.4, **191**.6 and cf. Hodgson (1976), (1977), *VRR* III, 113; for goatskins see **309**.ii.14.

17. *Feb]ruuaris*: it is noteworthy that *-uu-* is used consistently in the spelling of this month-name; see Adams (1994).

18. At the beginning of the line perhaps *]bum*. There is more than one way in which the words could be articulated. We might have e.g. *]bum et .r.[...]s*; this might suggest *se]bum* (cf. **184**.ii.22) followed by *et* and another word which ends with *s* just after the hole (cf. *CIL* 3^2, p.953, no.XV, pag. posterior, line 25). We would then expect a quantity and a sum, but the traces before the *as*-symbol look like *alcum*.

19-21. It seems that the entry for this date occupies three rather than two lines and includes two commodities obtained (?) through different individuals.

20. This line is very difficult. The first two letters could be almost anything; *m* is then certain as is *e* following it; then after one more uncertain letter we seem to have *po* and a descender of *r*. This suggests two nouns (cf. line 18 and note), the latter connected with pork, but neither *porci* nor *porcelli* is plausible. *porcine* (cf. line 21) might be better. The first word ought then also to be a genitive but we cannot suggest anything suitable.

21. *porcine*: see notes to lines 16 and 20, above.

22. *Similem:* we are confident of the reading of this name although it probably does not occur elsewhere in this account.

23. See notes to lines 11-2.

24. The spacing suggests *Marti]as* at the left. The commodity presumably follows in line 25.

187

Inv.no.87.704. 100 x 55 mm.

This half-diptych has one tie-hole and perhaps a v-shaped notch at the left-hand side. The only part preserved intact is the lower section which probably constituted about one third of the whole piece. There is a smaller, contiguous fragment from the upper left side. The writing is badly abraded and difficult to read, and the character of the hand adds to the problems since the letter forms are inconsistent, sometimes fairly normal cursive, sometimes approaching capital forms.

The text is an account written in two columns along the grain. In no other account do we have two columns on a single half-diptych, but compare **184** which has three columns on a complete diptych. The surviving text, insofar as it is legible, contains only one possible reference to goods or commodities (line i.7). The other entries may simply be sums owed or paid by various individuals to the person who compiled this account.

i

. . . .
.ṛ[
Vale.[
Fruẹ.[
.res.[
.ịḍḍi[
traces [
ṣụd · (denarios) (*traces*)
.ạg̣aṇ..
iii Iḍụs Martias ..
Crispa Poḷịonis (ḍẹṇạṛịị) (qụạḍṛạṇṭẹṃ)
Ingenuus uet(eranus) (ḍẹṇạṛịị) s(emissem) (assem i) .

ii

. . . .
Ṿ.ge *traces*
Ṃasuetus ex..iṣ *traces?*
Ḥụẹṭẹ *traces*

i.2. *Vale.[*: the last trace is compatible with *n*. *Valeṇ[tinus* could be read, a name which occurs in **255**.i.3, but since this is a letter sent to Flavius Cerialis it is not probable that this is the same man.

3. *Fruẹ.[*: the name Fruendus is reasonably well-attested in Gallia Belgica (see *NPEL*) and it is a good possibility here. We may have the name Frumentius in **160** (see *Tab.Vindol.*I, p.83, A.10 note) but there does not seem to be room for *m* before *ẹ* here.

4. If the initial letter is *C* we may have *Ḅresc̣[ens* or *Ḅresc̣[entius*; if *P*, probably *Ṗresẹ[ns* or *Ṗresẹ[ntius*, (*ae*>*e*).

5. The beginning of the line is smudged but there may well be a letter before *i* and, if so, it is most probably *V*. *Viddic* occurs in *CIL* 13.10010.2038, cf. perhaps *Viducus*, attested as a *cognomen* in Gallia Belgica and cf. *RIB* II 2463.59; if there is not a letter before

i, we wonder whether we might have the African name Iddibal which is used as both a *gentilicium* (P. Iddibalius Victorinus, *CIL* 8.859) and a *cognomen* (*IRT* 273, 300, 324). We note Imilco is attested as the name of a freedman in *RIB* I 193 (Colchester) and there is no guarantee that all the names in the present account must be those of military personnel (see note to line i.10). The reading *Ṿiḅḅi[* is less attractive but might suggest *Vibbianus* (for *Vibianus*).

7. *ṣụd* · : the reading appears to be very probable and *sum(ma)* is not possible. We can only suggest an abbreviation for *ṣụd(arium/-aria)*, cf. **184**.i.10 etc.

8. The reading is very difficult, especially at the beginning where there may be some smudging or correction and at the end where there is abrasion. The second and third letters could well be *rc* and *n* could be *ṛ*.The almost capital form of the *a* between *g* and *n* is noteworthy. If the first letter were *t*, which is not impossible, we might have a name beginning *Taga-* (cf. **181**.14, **184**.i.3).

9-11. In these lines we appear to have amounts at the right but no clear *denarius*-symbol, in contrast to line i.7. The amount in line 9 might belong with the name (?) in line 8. Perhaps the sums were added later (by a second hand?).

9. The reading of *Martias* is secure and this indicates that we must have a date. Although the reading of *Idụṣ* is difficult we can see no other possibility.

10. *Crispa*: the reading of the last two letters is difficult but the amount of writing and the spacing suggests that we have two names or words and it is impossible to read a termination in *-us*. For Pol(l)io see *LC* 164, *RIB* II 2491.114. The implication of reading the name of a woman in an account is not impossible to accept, cf. **181**.14-5 note. We suppose that the simple genitive could be taken to mean "daughter of", "wife of" (cf. **291**.back 15-7 note), whether legally recognised or not, or "slave of" (cf. **301**.back).

11. For the abbreviation *uet* for *uet(eranus)* see e.g. *RIB* I 517, 887, *CEL* 217.1 (= *ChLA* XI 477). This seems more probable than *uet(erinarius)*, cf. **310**.i.11, **181**.7. If this is correct, it is the only explicit evidence in the tablets for the presence of a veteran, but it is hardly surprising to find one in the vicinity of an important fort (cf. the diploma, *RMD* II 97).

ii.2. *Ṃasuetus*: the reading of initial *M* is not easy but we think it likely to be correct. For the form see Marichal (1988), index s.v. The name Mansuetus probably appears in **188**.12. It is a common servile name, suggesting that what follows may be the name of the owner.

3. We suppose that this is a name and that we should understand *Ḥụẹ-* as *Ve-*, see **184**.ii.27 note.

188

Inv.no.85.016. 22 x 87 mm.

A fragment which is complete only at the left-hand side and possibly the top. There are three other apparently blank fragments catalogued under this inventory number but their relationship, if any, to the piece with the account is not clear. The text appears to consist of names (lines 2, 5, 7, 10, 12) followed by words which are indented (lines 3, 4, 6, 8, 9, 11).

This layout suggests that the text is an account or a list of items ordered or purchased by various individuals rather than a simple name-list.

. . .
↓ a..[
Seṇe.[
ue[
ạ[
Andle.[
ṣ.[
Sautẹ.[
.[
equ.[
Bri ⸢gị⸣ o..[
et m.[
uacat
Ṃansueṭ[
. . .

1. *a*..: it is not possible to read the first letter as *r* (e.g. *rạṭ[io*); the second might be *n* and we certainly cannot read *a Gau[uone* (cf. **192**.1, **207**.1). Furthermore, the line is indented, which suggests that it is not the beginning of the text. In that case we may have a word for something ordered or purchased, if our hypothesis about the nature of the text is correct. Although we may have the top edge of this leaf, there is no reason why it should not be the lower half of a diptych, with the account beginning on the preceding half.

2. The *cognomina* Senecio and Senecianus are well-attested (see *NPEL*); the trace before the break is compatible with *c*. Names beginning with Sen- are particularly common in Gaul and Britain (cf. Inv.1091.a, *VRR* II, 58).

3-4. We take these letters to be the beginning of words for items ordered or purchased by Senec-, but there are clearly many possible restorations. An alternative for line 4 is *ṃ[*.

5. There is a mark at the edge of the leaf but it is impossible to be sure whether or not it is ink; if so, it might be part of the cross-bar of *e*. *Ande-* is a common prefix (*AS* I 139) and Andecarus occurs in **182**.ii.17, but the reading *Andle-* here is certain. *AS* I 148 cites Andlis as the name of a Spanish female deity. Perhaps a more promising parallel is *Adled[us* in *CIL* 13.5278 (Germania Superior); in order to read *Andle[dus*, however, we would certainly have to ignore the mark at the edge of the leaf.

7. Cf. **182**.back 5, *Ṣautenus*. Sautenius occurs once as a *nomen* in Gallia Belgica (*AE* 1968.335) and the remains of the last surviving letter are compatible with *n*. Note also Sau... (*CIL* 13.676) and the *cognomen* Sautus in the Trier region (*CIL* 13.4123).

8. There is a possible trace of a letter at the edge of the leaf and the spacing suggests that there ought to be a line of writing here.

9. *equ*.: the last surviving trace is compatible with *e* or *i* or *a* but not with *u*; therefore we cannot read *equụ[m* but the entry is probably something to do with horses (cf. **182**.ii.12).

10. The writer appears to have written *brio* and inserted *gi* with a ligature above the line. For the name Brigio, see the note on Brigionus in **250**.i.3. The traces following are difficult to read (the second might be *m*) but it does not look as if Brigionus was written

here. Nevertheless, it seems possible that the two references are to the same man, with the name given a Latin termination in the more formal context of a letter of recommendation.

et m.: the last surviving letter clearly seems to be *r* and it is possible that a vowel has simply been omitted in error (e.g. *m<u>r[ia* cf. **190**.c.27); otherwise we might have a conjoint *ur* as in **190**.c.27, in which case the reading here would be *aur[*. If we have correctly identified the nature of this text, we should have two items or commodities, linked by *et*, with the first directly following the name in line 10.

11. The names Mansuetus and Mansuetarius are very common. The first may occur in the form Masuetus in **187**.ii.2.

189

Inv.no.88.955.a-e. (a) 43 x 21 mm. (b) 62 x 30 mm. (c) 70 x 25 mm. (d) 46 x 14 mm. (e) 54 x 30 mm.

Six fragments, two of which join, form an account written along the grain. The two joining fragments are designated as (a) and may well form the top of the document. (b) is apparently complete at the left.

a.]ṿiii K(alendas) Februar[ias

. . . .

b.

. . . .

]ruṇ.ḷu.[
Idibus Iunis p̣e.[
].ị ạdṃen[

. . . .

c.

. . . .

]..us..s uiṇịaṣ eṃṭas
]ṣ ḷxx̣xvi s(emissem)

. . . .

d.

. . . .

subṭị..[
traces

. . .

e. *traces of 2 lines*

a.1. *]ṿiii K(alendas) Februar[ias*: less likely is *]x̣iiii*.

b.1. There may be the bottom of a letter before *r*. We could perhaps read *p̣runọluṃ*, a form of the diminutive of *prunus*, but if correct it would have to be understood as collective (cf. **192**.3 note).

3. Perhaps *ad men[sam/-as*.

c.1. At the end of the line *emṭas* makes good sense (cf. **181**.3) but it is hardly credible that we have a reference to vines before it.

2. The trace preceding the numeral is less likely to be a *denarius*-symbol. What we have read as the first digit (*l*) might alternatively be read as *p* for *p(ondo)*.

d.1. After *sub* we might alternatively have *n* which would imply two words here. *subṭi..*, if correct, would presumably be an adjective or, again, two words. *subpạen[ulas* (cf. **196**.9, 13) is hardly possible; equally hard is *subṭun[icas*.

e. It is impossible to be sure that this fragment belongs to this account.

190

*Tab.Vindol.*I 4, Plate II.1-2. R.E.Birley (1990), fig. 21.

The essentials of our analysis and our view of the format of this unique wooden notebook remain unchanged (cf. the remarks of Tjäder (1986), 301). The evidence of the tablets discovered in the 1980s strongly suggests, however, that this account belongs to Period 3 and should be re-interpreted in the context of the domestic administration of the *praetorium* rather than as an official account of supplies dispensed to the military unit or constituents of it. As a corollary we must also abandon the suggestion that the supplies of barley provide evidence for the view that the *cohors viiii Batauorum* (previously identified as *cohors viii*) was *equitata*, see p.23, above).

The tablet contains accounts, which may well be separate, of cash sums connected with some religious purpose (c.1-3) and of food supplies over a period of several days in June. It is impossible to be certain whether the account records supplies obtained or used. The fact that there are no costs recorded in this part of the account suggests that (unlike **191**) this is not an account of supplies purchased; we think that, with the exception of the entry in c.16, the account probably records commodities used or disbursed and that the entries for June 24 probably reflect the celebration of a religious festival. The prominence of barley in the account may be in its capacity as fodder for animals belonging to the *praetorium*. The evidence for slaves at Vindolanda makes it probable that this account was compiled by a slave member of the Cerialis household and certain that the Privatus mentioned in lines c.26, 28, 31 and 35 will have been a slave (see c.26 note). If it was a relatively informal household account book, its somewhat cryptic nature will be easier to understand. Finally, we now have a clearer notion of the meaning of lines c.38-9, even if the circumstances remain obscure; they are likely to refer to a visit made by Cerialis and members of his family to Briga (see note).

For additional evidence on matters related to foodstuffs and the Roman military diet see now Dannell and Wild (1987), 66-70, Dickson (1989), Davies (1989), 187-206, M.Jones (1991), King (1991).

It should be pointed out that the lines are numbered separately in each of the fragments and the numeration consequently differs slightly from that adopted in the *ed. pr.*

a.

. . . .

↓   ] (denarios) iii s(emissem)

].
]. ẹ
. . . .

b. . . . .
↓].s
] m(odios) [.]iị (denarii) s(emissem)
].i..m (denarii) s(emissem)
uacat

c. . . . .
↓ a]ḍ sacrum (denarios) [
]ṃ ạḍ sacrum (ḍẹṇạṛịọṣ) [
]ạtaṃ ad sacrum [
uacat
m^{2}? xiii K(alendas) Iuliḷ[as
hordẹ[i
ceruesạ[e
x̣[ii] K(alendas) Iuliạṣ
hordei m(odios) iiii [
ç̣eruesae m(odios) ii
[xi K(alendas) Iu]ḷias hordei [
].m ad hoṛ[
].tum
]ṃ(odios) ii
x K(alendas) Iulias
hordei m(odios) v s(emissem)
allatus ụini ..ssec[
viiii K(alendas) Iulias
hordei m(odios) v s(emissem)
uini m(odium) i (sextarios) xiiii
ceruesae m(odios) iii
viii K(alendas) Iulias
hordei m(odios) vị.[
ç̣ẹṛụẹṣạẹ m(odios) iii (sextarios) ...
uini m(odium) i (sextarios) xii
aceti (sextarios) ii
per Priuatum
muriae (sextarium) i s(emissem)
per P̣riuatum
axungiae (ṣẹx̣ṭạṛịọṣ) x mut[(uo)
domino ad stipes
per Priuatum
uini m(odium) i ad saç̣ṛụṃ
d<i>uae
uini (sextarios) xii
per Priuaṭụ[m
vii K(alendas) Iuliạs

hordei (sextarios) .ị.
domịni Brigae ṃạṇ[se-
runt
uacat

Unplaced fragments:

d.

. . .
↓] . . iaṣ
] .
] . i
] . ụṛ
. . .

e.

. . .
↓]ṣ i[
]iis
. . .

f.

. . . .
↓]. . .
](sextarios) ṿ s(emis)
] . ii .
. . . .

g.

. . .
↓]ṣi . is
. . .

(b) "… *modii* 3 (?), *denarii* ½
… *denarii* ½"
(c) "… for the festival, *denarii* ..
… for the festival, *denarii* ..
… for the festival …
19 June
of barley …
of Celtic beer …
20 June
of barley, *modii* 4+ (?)
of Celtic beer, *modii* 2
21 June, of barley …
… to the granary (?) …
…
… *modii* 2
22 June
of barley, *modii* 5½ (?)
Allatus (?), of Massic wine (?) …

23 June
of barley, *modii* 5½
of wine, *modius* 1 *sextarii* 14
of Celtic beer, *modii* 3
24 June
of barley, *modii* 6+
of Celtic beer, *modii* 3 *sextarii* ..
of wine, *modius* 1 *sextarii* 12
of sour wine, *sextarii* 2
through Privatus
of fish-sauce, *sextarii* 1½
through Privatus
of pork-fat, *sextarii* 10 as a loan (?)
to the lord for charitable donations
through Privatus
of wine, *modius* 1 for the festival
of the goddess (?)
of wine, *sextarii* 12
through Privatus
25 June
of barley, *sextarii* 11½ (?)
the lords have remained at Briga."

a.1. For the resolution of abbreviation and symbols in the accusative case see above, p.120 and cf. c.16 note.

c.1-3. We are not able to improve on our general interpretation of these lines but we are more inclined to think that they are to be seen as separate from what follows. For religious observances on New Year's Day see **265** and for a payment in connection with the Saturnalia see **301**.

6. It seems likely that *ceruesa* was brewed locally. For a *ceruesarius* at Vindolanda see **182**.ii.14 and for *bracis*, the cereal from which it was made, see **343**.iii.25-8.

12. We might have *per Priu]ạtum*.

16. We remain unhappy with the reading and interpretation of this line but we cannot improve on the suggestions made in the *ed. pr.* for the reading of the words after *allatus*. In view of clear evidence for the presence at Vindolanda of imported items such as pepper (**184**.i.4) and olives (**302**.margin 3) it now seems less improbable that Massic wine was to be found in Cerialis' household. As for *allatus*, the reading of which is certain, we now think it more likely that this is to be taken as a personal name, probably servile (see *LC* 349), in view of the fact that Privatus in lines 26, 28, 31 and 35 must be a personal name (see next note). For another possible case of a nominative personal name in an account see **199**.2 note.

26. It is now beyond reasonable doubt that Privatus will be the name of a slave in Cerialis' household (cf. perhaps *ChLA* X 409, *seruo in p[)*. The name occurs also in **199**, a fragment of an account from the same period (therefore probably referring to the same person) and in **303**.a.1, as the author of a letter sent to Vindolanda and therefore no doubt a different person. See also **415**.

27. For *muria* cf. **202**.5, **302**.margin 2 and see Curtis (1991), 79-85, esp. 80.

28. It is noteworthy that the final *i* from *aceti* in line 25 descends as far as this line.

29. In the *ed. pr.* we read *(sextarios) xv* but failed to note clear traces of two more letters at the right. It now seems clear that we should read *mut[(uo)* or *mut[(uum)* at the end of the line. This looks as if it could have been preceded by *ex* but *mutuo* seems normally to be used without a preposition (see **193**.1 note), and these letters must refer to the quantity of *axungia* since there is no other place in which this could have been stated. If *domino* in the following line refers to the prefect of the unit, however, it is difficult to understand why he should be credited with a loan of a commodity in an account which concerns his own household. For *axungia* cf. **182**.ii.16.

30. *domino ad stipes*: see lines 38-9 note.

32-3. The reading at the end of line 32 is very uncertain and it is unsatisfactory to suppose a scribal error in line 33, but we are unable substantially to improve on the suggestions in the *ed. pr.* *-duae* could perhaps be the end of a name (of a deity, cf. Viduus?). For the expression cf. perhaps Frontinus, *Strat.* 3.2.8, *omnis multitudo ad celebrandum Mineruae sacrum urbe egressa erat.*

37. The number might be *xi s(emissem).*

38-9. The reading *man[se-/runt*, suggested in the *ed. pr.*, note *ad loc.*, now seems to us correct (for the way in which *ma* is written cf. c.2) and we suppose that this notation, made by a member of Cerialis' household, refers to a visit by Cerialis and members of his family to Briga (the suggestion made by Harvey (1985), 69 must be abandoned in view of **292**.c.v.2). The single other attestation of the name in Britain probably refers to a place in Hampshire which must be too far away to be relevant to Cerialis' household (*PNRB* 277-8). A.R.Birley (1991), 101, note 70 suggests Kirkbride or Newbrough, both of which are fairly close to Vindolanda. The evidence of a woman named Brica (*RIB* I 744, Greta Bridge) and of a *civitas Bricic* (? *Brig{ig}*, *RIB* I 2022, Bleatarn between Castlesteads and Stanwix, perhaps fourth century) should also be noted. For comments on this place-name element see *PNRB*, *loc.cit.*, Piggott (1965), 172-4, with a distribution map. Piggott notes classical occurrences mainly in Spain with a few in the Rhine/Meuse area, post-classical occurrences in Gaul generally and postulates the influence of units raised in Celtic-speaking areas whose commanders are Celtic-speaking Roman citizens, which might be relevant to the present case. For the connection of Aelius Brocchus and Claudia Severa with Briga see **292**.c.v.2 note. If lines 29-30 be taken to indicate that *axungia* was given to Cerialis at Vindolanda on June 24, perhaps to take to Briga as some kind of a charitable donation, the note that he remained at Briga on June 25 (even if added later than that date) implies that it was close to Vindolanda.

191

*Tab. Vindol.*I 5, Plate II.3.

The accumulated evidence now makes it very likely indeed that this account of meat relates to the domestic administration of the *praetorium* and that the words in lines 8 and 11 should be understood as *in praetorio* (note *ChLA* X 409, *seruo in p[*). For the main hand see **194**, introduction. For animals at Vindolanda see the references given in **190**, introduction, *Tab. Vindol.*I, p.94, Hodgson (1976), (1977), *VRR* III, 108-13 and cf. King (1991).

. . . .
↓] in p̣[
]ṣ (denarios) [
condimen[t-
capream [
salis .[
porcellum [
pernam .[
in p[
frumen[ti
ceruin[am
in p.[
ad condiṭ[
caprea[
⟦s(umma) (denarii) [⟧
m^{2}? s(umma) (denarii) xx [
m^{1} braciṣ .[
(denarios) ị[
.ụm[

"in ...
... *denarii* ...
spices ...
roe-deer ...
of salt ...
young pig ...
ham ...
in ...
of wheat ...
venison ...
in ...
for pickling (?)
roe-deer ...
⟦total, *denarii* ...⟧
total, *denarii* 20+
of emmer ...
denarii ...
total (?) ..."

2. There may be a medial point after *s*, cf. note to line 14.

3. For *condimenta* see also **193**.3.

5. *salis*: see **186**.10 and note. The trace at the edge could be part of a superscript bar over *m* (i.e. *m(odi-)*).

6. *porcellum*: it is clear from **180**.27, **183**.4 and **186**.20-1 that pigs were kept as livestock either under military supervision or at least in the close vicinity of the fort.

7. *pernam*: cf. **182**.i.7. It does not seem likely that we have the remains of a *denarius* symbol at the edge but we might have *p(ondo)* followed by a number, then a cash sum.

12-3. *ad cotidia[n / caprea[m*, *ed. pr.* We originally understood this as a reference to daily needs or use. Our improved reading rather suggests a reference to pickling or preserving and we suggest as a possible restoration *ad condiṭ[um* (or *-uram*) / *caprea[e*.

14. There may be a medial point after *s(umma)*.

16. *braciṣ .[*: *bracịṣ* [, *ed. pr.* Cf. **343**.iii.25 and the note *ad loc.* in Bowman, Thomas and Adams (1990), **348**.2.

18. *ṣum[ma* is an attractive possibility and it might be the global total of individual sums, cf. **185**.29.

192

Inv.no.85.010.b. 66 x 90 mm. Plate XI.

This account is written on the upper half of a double leaf which has a v-shaped notch and a tie-hole in the top edge. The lower half is blank. As the first line and the docket on the back make clear, the account records items received from Gavo (see also **207** and cf. **218**.3) and contains a miscellany of edible and textile commodities which appears more likely to relate to the domestic needs of the *praetorium* than to the official requirements of the unit. Gavo seems to be an entrepreneur or supplier of goods, whether military or civilian is not clear; there is no evidence for his whereabouts.

The hand is a well-formed cursive. In its general character it is very similar to the hand responsible for **207**, which is also an account from Gavo, and one might expect them to be the work of the same writer, especially in view of the fact that in both texts the name is written as *Gauuo* on the front and as *Gauo* on the back; but we are less than certain since, for example, the form of *u* employed in *Gauuone* in the first line of the two texts is very different.

↓ a Gauuone
bedocem (ḍẹṇạṛịọṣ) [
fabae m(odios) .v (ḍẹṇạṛịọṣ) [
lanae p̣(ondo) xxxiix[
p(ondo) . (ḍẹṇạṛịọṣ) xiị s(emissem) (assem i) [
ṭosseas iii [
mellis m(odios) [
sagum [
s(umma) ⟦(denarii) lxx[⟧
(denarii) [

Back: ratio Gauonis

"From Gavo
a coverlet (?), *denarii* ...
of beans, *modii* 55 (?), *denarii* ..
of wool, 38 lbs, [
.. lbs, *denarii* 12½, *as* 1 ...

bedspreads 3, *denarii* .. (?)
of honey, *modii* .. *denarii* .. (?)
a *sagum*, *denarii* .. (?)
total, ⟦*denarii* 70+⟧
denarii ..
(Back) Account of Gavo."

1. The name Gavo is unattested but the reading here and in **207**.1 is clear; in **218**.3 the name *Gauoṇị* appears and the identification is very tempting. It is presumably a Celtic name. *AS* I 1992 cites Gavolus (*CIL* 5.337, Aquileia), *NPEL*, Gauua (*CIL* 13.3409, Gallia Belgica) and cf. Cauua (Weisgerber (1968), 232, 236).

2. *bedocem*: Adams drew our attention to *Ed. Diocl.* in which the Greek text records the word *βέδοξ* (once with the adjective Γαλλικός) at 19.56 and 58; in Lauffer's edition the word is restored in the Latin in the transliteration *fedox* (a word which does not appear elsewhere in Latin). We suggest that *bedox* is the correct transliteration and is what we have here. Dr. Wild takes it to be a bedspread or the like and notes that in the Edict it is half the price of the so-called *banata* listed with it. It seems to be the practice in these accounts not to include the number when the form of the word made it obvious that only one was meant, cf. *sagum* in line 8. We thus interpret the mark on the edge of the leaf as part of a *denarius*-symbol.

3. *fabae*: for the collective singular see *OLD*, s.v.1 and cf. **302**.1. The *modius* abbreviation is marked here and in line 7 by an almost vertical stroke above *m* rather than a flat dash; cf. **182**.i.2. There is a possible trace of a letter before *v* which might be *l*. The mark at the edge might be the remains of a *denarius*-symbol. For beans in the military diet see Davies (1989), 199.

4. *lanae*: the way in which the *l* is written above the other letters is noteworthy and its apparent ligature to *a* is remarkable.

4-5. These lines are difficult to interpret. *p* is very hard to read in line 4, although it looks virtually certain in line 5. There it is followed by one letter, after which a *denarius* symbol is possible, followed by the numeral and more symbols. If the deleted total in line 9 (between 70 and 99 *denarii*) is in the right area, we can hardly have *p(ondo) i (denarii) xii s(emissem)*, i.e. 38 lbs of wool at 12½ *denarii* per lb., a price which in any case seems far too high (cf. *Ed. Diocl.* 21.1-4 where the prices for wool range between 15 and 40 *denarii* per lb., 200 years later and after a period of inflation). The digit after *p* might be *l* (cf. the form of the letter in line 7, *mellis*), giving a price of 12½ *denarii* and 1 *as* per 50 lbs, which might then have been followed by an actual cost of about 9½ *denarii* in the missing portion further to the right. The presence of this item in the account suggests the possibility of textile production on-site at Vindolanda, cf. *VRR* III, 85-6. It is notable that there is plenty of evidence for the presence of sheep at Vindolanda (*VRR* III, 110-11), but it is noteworthy that lamb or mutton does not occur in any of the accounts of foodstuffs, probably reflecting the Celtic dietary preference for pork and beef, perhaps also in evidence at Valkenburg; cf. Trow (1990), 107, King (1984) and (1991), Dannell and Wild (1987), 68.

6. *ṭosseas*: the initial *t* is enlarged and the central part of the horizontal has all but disappeared. The reading is supported by the hitherto unique occurrence of *tossia Brit(annica)* in the Thorigny inscription (*AJ* 140.13), where the context suggests some kind of a coverlet or rug, cf. André (1966-7), arguing that the word is British Celtic representing the old Breton *toos* (we are grateful to Dr. Wild for drawing our attention to this article).

The word also occurs in **439**.10 and there appears to be a third British attestation in a writing-tablet from Carlisle, see Tomlin (1992), 148.

10. The account probably ends here with a revised total but there could have been another line in the missing lower part of the half-leaf.

Back 1. This is written along the grain from top to bottom of the leaf. The same notation occurs on the back of **207** and it is noteworthy that the name is spelled in the same way there, in contrast to the spelling in line 1. Cf. the notation *rationes C(ai) Calpur(nii) Ptol(emaei)* on the back of a papyrus (Coles (1981)) and the account headed *ratio Ḷạẹḷị* in *P.Qasr Ibrîm* 34.

193

Inv.no.85.111.a. 91 x 35 mm. Plate XIV.

This leaf or half-diptych is incomplete at the top and bottom. There may be a notch in the left-hand edge. It should be noted that lines 3-5 begin much further to the left than lines 1-2 and 6. The reading and interpretation of lines 1-2 and 6, where the writing is extremely abraded, is very difficult. The first line, which may refer to the remainder of the account indicates a loan. The account then appears to have date-headings in lines 2 and 6, the second perhaps one month after the first. The notations at the left which may have been added later in a second hand might indicate recovery of the items which were lent out (see note to line 3).

The form of *u* in line 3 (almost a flat dash) is noteworthy, as is that in *oua* (line 5) which lacks its right-hand side and perhaps is in ligature with *a*.

. . . .

Feḷịc̣ioṇi (c̣ẹṇṭụṛịọṇị) ṃutuo [
xịị K(alendas) Ịụnias
m^2? rec( ) · (*m*^{1}) condimẹntorum (sextarii) s(emissem) (denarii) s(emissem)
m^2? rec( ) · (*m*^{1}) halicae (sextarii) s(emissem) (denarii) (quadrantem) .
m^2? rec( ) · (*m*^{1}) oua ṇ(umero) ịịx · (denarii) (quadrantem)
xịị K(alendas) Ịụḷịas

. . . .

"... to Felicio the centurion as a loan ...
21 May (?)
(2nd hand?) received, (1st hand) of spices, *sextarius* ½, *denarius* ½.
(2nd hand?) received, (1st hand) of gruel, *sextarius* ½, *denarius* ¼ +
(2nd hand?) received, (1st hand) eggs, 8, *denarius* ¼
20 June (?) ..."

1. There may be a trace of a descender from a previous line but there are so many marks on the photograph that it is impossible to be sure. At the right *utuo* would appear to be certain and *m* is possible before this; we think it most probable that we have the word *mutuo*, which we should take to be the dative or ablative of *mutuum*; *TLL* VIII 1737 quotes

several examples where the predicative dative of the neuter means "for/as a loan" (cf. **190**.c.29 and note). For the name see **166**.1 and note; it is quite common and there may well be more than one Felicio in the Vindolanda texts. It does not seem possible to connect this with the name (?) in **206**.margin 1, which also begins *Fe-*.

2. It seems unlikely that there was any writing at the left and the date was probably centred.

3. *rec* here and in lines 4 and 5 is followed by a medial point to mark the abbreviation. It may well be in a second hand and could have been added as a later notation. For a verb expressing simple receipt, we would expect *accipio*, normally abbreviated as *acc*; perhaps some sense of reciprocity or return is intended; therefore *rec(epi)* or *rec(ept-)*, or, if recovery of a loan is involved, *rec(iperaui/at-)* (see *OLD*, s.v.1); for a loan of wheat cf. **180**.5-6 and cf. **190**.c.29. For *condimenta* see **191**.3.

4. *halicae*: cf. **233**. A.1. This is said to be gruel made from pounded wheat or emmer (see Pliny, *NH* 3.60, *in delicias alicae politur messis*, cf. Sallares (1991), 320, André (1981), 58)). There may be a second symbol at the end of the line but the trace is very abraded and we cannot elucidate it.

5. The number of eggs is expressed by three digits followed by a medial point, of which the last is certainly *x*. It might be read as *c̣ḷx* or *c̣ịx*, but if the cost is as small as it seems to be we ought to have a small number and *ịịx* is compatible with the traces. For eggs compare **302**.4-5 where the writer is asking for 100 or 200.

6. Only the tops of letters survive, but we are confident that we have a date which is centred (as in line 2).

194

Inv.no.86.597.a-b. (a) 32 x 60 mm. (b) 21 x 50 mm.

Two fragments of a leaf containing writing on both sides, the text on the one side being upside down in relation to that on the other. Both sides are written by the same hand and probably form part of a single text. Since the order is uncertain it should be noted that our designation of the sides as A and B is arbitrary and is used only for convenience of reference. A third fragment which was inventoried under this number (**195**) contains a text of a similar kind and at least one side of it may be written by the same hand, but it is impossible to establish that it belongs with **194**; **196** may also be at least partly by the same hand but has likewise been treated as part of a separate list. This hand may also be responsible for **197** and **191**.

Fragments (a) and (b) do not join directly but can be positioned side by side with a small gap between (large enough to accommodate one or two letters). The placing of the fragments and the reconstruction of the text is based on our understanding of lines B.1-2, although there is a problem with both reading and meaning in line 1 (see note), and is strongly supported by line A.8, if it is correctly read.

The text is a list of household objects which are almost all related to cooking, eating or drinking. The content is appropriate to the find-spot of these tablets; Room VIII of the Period 3 *praetorium* has been identified as a kitchen and the text must surely be part of an inventory of equipment. In some cases (e.g. lines A.7-8) we only have single objects; even where the gap between the fragments makes it impossible to be certain of the exact number of items involved, the order of magnitude seems to be small (see line A.3 note). We can hardly suppose therefore that this represents the complete stock of equipment for a substantial establishment such as the *praetorium* must have been, and it may be that this is part of a much longer list which the writer compiled by walking round and listing items in different locations in the room (see line A.6 note). Lists of this kind are not uncommon in the papyri; see for example, *P.Wash.Univ.*I 59, *SPP* XX 67, *BGU* III 781, *ChLA* XI 485. The terms for the different kinds of eating and drinking vessels, several of which appear in our list, are discussed by Strong (1966), 128-30 and by Oliver and Shelton (1979) with reference to *BGU* III 781, a long inventory of a very valuable collection of plate which totals over 300 Roman pounds of silver. This makes an interesting comparison with the Vindolanda list, especially, perhaps, if some of the silver in *BGU* III 781 was the property of the late and disgraced prefect of Egypt, Cornelius Gallus, a considerably wealthier Roman *eques* than Flavius Cerialis will have been, cf. Shelton (1977), 69. Most of the objects at Vindolanda are perhaps more likely to be ceramic than silver but there is some evidence for utensils of bronze at Vindolanda (cf. *VRR* II, 91) and a bronze lamp is listed in B.2 (see also note to B.1).

A.

. . . .
↓ .[
scuṭụḷ[as] ịi[
paropsiḍeṣ [ ] ṿ ⟦ii⟧
acetabuḷ[a]iii
ouaria · ịii
in laterar[..].
lanceṃ
scutul[a]ṃ

B.

↓ compenḍ[iá]rium et
lucerṇ[am] ạeneam
panaria · [ ]iiii
calices · [ ]ii ·
in ṭhẹ[ca]
trullas · [ ] theca
s[
[
. . . .

(A) " ...
shallow dishes, 2 (?)
side-plates, 5 (?)
vinegar-bowls, 3 (?)
egg-cups, 3
on the purlin (?)
a platter
a shallow dish"
(B) "a strong-box (?) and

a bronze lamp
bread-baskets, 4 (?)
cups, 2 (?)
in a box
bowls, 2 (?) in a box ..."

A.1. Since we are uncertain which side of the leaf to read first the order of the entries in the list is therefore also uncertain. It is clear that we have the cut edge of the leaf below line 8 and above B.1.

At the left there is the bottom of a letter hooked to the left, probably *c* or *e*.

2. *scuṭụḷ[as*: only the bottoms of the last three letters survive but the first three are clear and we are confident of the reading. The word recurs in line 8, apparently in the singular; see also **208**.a.1. The precise characteristics of these dishes, which are also listed in *BGU* III 781.IV.8, are not known (see Oliver and Shelton (1979), 26). On the reading and interpretation of the numbers see the notes to line 5 and B.3.

3. *paropsiḍeṣ*: common in the graffiti from La Graufesenque (see Marichal (1988), index, s.v.). These seem to be side-plates, perhaps for fruit or vegetables, see *BGU* III 781.I.14 (*BL* 1, 66) with Strong (1966), 129, Oliver and Shelton (1979), 23-4. The numeral was originally written as three digits but the last two seem to have been crossed out; it is possible that the uncorrected digit at the left is *ị* rather than *ṿ* but if so, the writer has not taken the trouble to correct the noun to the singular (cf. line 7 note).

4. *acetabuḷ[a*: also common at La Graufesenque (Marichal (1988), index, s.v.). See Oliver and Shelton (1979), 25-6.

5. *ouaria*: presumably egg-cups, for which see Strong (1966), 128 and Plate 42B. He also identifies an egg-phiale which holds a dozen eggs (98 and Plate 26B). The only citation of the word *ouarium* in *OLD* and *TLL* is *CIL* 8.9065.3, referring to the structure which held the *oua* used for recording the laps of chariot-races, but it must here describe either the egg-cup or the egg-holder. That it is the former rather than the latter is suggested by the occurrence of the word in its Greek form (ὀάρια) in *BGU* III 781.IV.6, with Oliver and Shelton (1979), 28, where there are 20 of these items. After the word there is an interpunct and then a possible faint trace at the right-hand edge of the leaf, but we are very uncertain whether this should be taken as *ṇ(umero)*, cf. B.3 note.

6. *in* projects to the left, which suggests that it might have been added after the second word had been written. There is an ink trace at the left-hand edge of the second fragment which could be either the top-stroke of *s* or an apex mark, of which there is one other example in this text (B.1). The top-stroke, together with the size of the gap, suggests *laterar[i]ó*, *laterar[i]á* or *laterar[ii]ṣ*. Of the possible words offered by *OLD* and *TLL*, *lateraria* ("a pottery") does not seem promising. We can derive sense from the use of *laterarium* in Vitruvius 10.14.3, 15.3 where it appears to mean "cross-beam" or "purlin" if we can envisage that the objects listed below (at least those in lines 7 and 8) were placed or stored on a cross-beam in the kitchen, cf. B.5 note.

7. *lanceṃ*: the word can perhaps be restored in **208**.4; cf. Oliver and Shelton (1979), 28. Here and in the following line the writer seems to have followed the practice of not specifying the number when only one item was meant, cf. **192**.2 note and note to line 3, above.

8. See note to line 2, above.

B.1. *compenḍ[iá]rium*: the high stroke, the top of which is visible, must be taken as an apex mark. The letter below it is lost but no other suitable word exists and the restoration, which enables us to fix the size of the gap between the two fragments, is certain. The precise meaning is uncertain. "Short-cut" offers no sense in this context; the word occurs in the context of granaries (*CIL* 6.33860, 33747) where Rickman (1971), 197, explains it as meaning "safe-deposit". Here it seems likely that it indicates some kind of container.

3. There appears to be an interpunct after *panaria* and then a possible trace at the left-hand edge of the second fragment, but it is doubtful whether we should take this as *ṇ(umero)*, cf. line A.5 note.

5. We must have *in ṭhẹ[ca]* (cf. *BGU* III 781.V.16, 18), presumably ending in the gap, but there may be a faint trace of *a* on the right-hand fragment. This is indented and probably refers to the item or items preceding (cf. B.6 and note). The word seems to be a general term for containers or receptacles, cf. *Digest* 33.9.3.11, *nec frumenti nec leguminum thecae (arculae forte uel sportae)*, "receptacles for grain or vegetables (such as boxes or hampers)".

6-7. In view of the plural noun there must be a number and *in* seems to be required before *theca* (cf. B.5); the size of the gap might just about allow us to restore *trullas · [ii in] theca*. For *trullas* see Strong (1966), 130, noting that the *trulla* might be the "very popular saucepan-shaped vessel which is found throughout the period of the Roman empire" and referring to *Digest* 34.2.36; cf. also *SPP* XX 67, ὀξυβάφια τρύλλια κασσιτ(εριvά), presumably shallow vinegar-bowls made of tin.

s[: this is indented suggesting that it might belong with what precedes; it must have been a short word or an abbreviation since there are no traces on the right-hand fragment; *s[ec(unda)*?

195

Inv.no.87.597.c. 30 x 45 mm.

A fragment of a leaf with writing on both sides, that on the one side upside down in relation to the other. The large space below the single line of writing on one of the faces suggests that this ought to be taken as the back. It is not possible to establish whether **195** belongs to the same text as **194**; on the hand see **194**, introduction. The items in the list include clothing and a knife.

↓ tunicạ . [
  pater[
ịu . ịolạ[
abollam [
abollạṃ [
. . .

Back:

. . .
*m*²?] c̣ultruṃ [

"Tunic(s) ...
...
...
an *abolla* ...
an *abolla* ...
...
(Back, 2nd hand) ...
a knife"

1. The size of the initial letter, the blank space above it and its position at the top left of the leaf strongly suggests that this was the beginning of the text. Of the last letter only a vertical survives and the length of the tail suggests that *tunicaṃ* is marginally preferable to *tunicaṣ*.

2. This line is considerably indented. If we have a miscellany of clothing and utensils (cf. back 1 and *P.Wash.Univ.*I 58) we might restore *patera[m / -s*, but the identation perhaps suggests that the word might be part of a name (cf. *Paternus* in **218**.3) or an adjective qualifying the word in the preceding line. If the latter, we might note *Digest* 34.2.23.2, *uirilia sunt (*sc. *uestimenta), quae ipsius patris familiae causa parata sunt.*

3. The reading of the second and the last three letters seems certain. The first letter appears to be a large *i* (or *s* but with no sign of the top-stroke; *l* is much less plausible). The third letter looks most like *c* but could be the short form of *l* (not elsewhere apparent in this hand, however). There is a word *culleum* (a leather wineskin, cf. van Driel-Murray (1985), note 29) and we might imagine a plural diminutive form *culiola*, but it is very hard to read the initial letter as *c̣*; note that the word *culliolum* is attested with a different meaning, see *OLD*, s.v., citing Paul. *Fest.* p.50M, *culliola cortices nucum uiridium.* The only other suggestion we can make is *ịuc̣ịola* for *iunciola*, which we would take to mean a pallet or small mattress made of rushes; this could certainly be read but the word is unattested.

4-5. In line 5 *b* has been corrected. The repetition of *abollam* suggests that the two entries might have been qualified by different adjectives, cf. *abolla cenatoria* in *CIL* 8.4508. Since it is difficult to distinguish between the various kinds of cloaks (see **255**.i.8-ii.10 note) we have not attempted a translation.

196

Inv.no.87.598. 46 x 186 mm. Plate X.

This diptych is complete at the top, bottom and left-hand edge. There are two tie-holes and one notch at the top and the bottom. The tablet was found in Room VIII, identified as a kitchen in the Period 3 *praetorium*, but the text on the front is a list of textile items. It indicates (lines 12, 15) that some items were obtained from Tranquillus and some from Brocchus. The missing right-hand side of the leaf presumably contained the numbers of the different items. The use of interpunct is noteworthy, particularly since it occurs consistently except after monosyllables. The text on the back which lists a miscellany of non-textile items may be written by a different hand (see **194** introduction) and may well not be part of the same list as that on the front (see back 1 note).

We think it likely that, like the other lists of utensils and clothing (**194**, **195**, **197**), this text records property in the household of Flavius Cerialis and thus reflects the milieu of the equestrian military officer in the late first and early second century. For lists of clothing in the papyri see *P.Wash.Univ.* II 104 and introduction. For clothing in the north-western Roman empire, see Wild (1985). In cases where the differences between the various kinds of cloaks are obscure or unknown, we have not attempted to translate the terms (cf. **255**.i.8-ii.10 note).

↓ cubitorị[a
lodicum · pạ[r
paenulas · caṇ[
de synthesi · [
paenulas · e ̣[
et laenam · e[t
cenatoriạ[
sunthesi[
subpaenụ[l
ḷiạ ̣[
subuclas · b[
á Ṭrạnqụ[illo
subpaenu[l
⟦á Ṭranqụịḷḷ[o⟧
á Brocchó [
tunicas · im[
simicị ̣[
tunicas · cẹn[

Back: ↓ *m*²? ç̣erui[
membra n(umero) [
cataçysẹn [
ansatam
anulos · cum l[

"...
for dining
pair(s) of blankets ...
paenulae, white (?) ...
from an outfit:
paenulae ...
and a *laena* and a (?) ...
for dining
loose robe(s) ...
under-*paenula(e)* ...
vests ...
from Tranquillus
under-*paenula(e)* ...
⟦from Tranquillus⟧

from Brocchus
tunics ...
half-belted (?) ...
tunics for dining (?) ...
(Back, 2nd hand?) ...
branches (?), number ...
a vase ...
with a handle
rings with stones (?) ..."

1. *cubitori[a*: the only other occurrence of the word in Latin is at Petronius, *Sat.* 30.1, also in the context of clothing where it appears to refer to dining-clothes. This seems to rule out the possibility of taking it, in conjunction with the following line, as "bedding". Unless it is a heading, which seems unlikely, it would have to be taken as an adjective qualifying a noun at the foot of a preceding leaf. The occurrence of the word *cenatoria* in line 7 and probably in line 18 must also indicate dinner-wear.

2. We suggest the restoration of *pa[r* but we could also have *pa[ria* followed by a number; we do not know why blankets should be recorded in pairs rather than simple numbers (cf. *CIL* 13.5708, quoted in the note to back 1, where *ceruicalia* ("cushions") are listed in pairs).

3. In *paenulas a* is corrected from *e*; this could be simply a slip but it might indicate that the writer originally intended to write *penulas* (cf. **186**.21, 23). The *paenula* is the Italian cape, a standard item of military attire.

can[: the *n* is more or less certain. The noun in line 9 is perhaps followed by a word which ends in line 10, that in line 11 appears to be qualified by a word which is mostly lost. In lines 16-7 *tunicas* may be qualified by two words (see note) and in line 18 it is probably followed by *cenatorias*. In lines 5 and 6 we may have adjectives but more probably just *et* (see lines 5-6 note). Some of the adjectives describing these garments may be colour-words which are common in such contexts, e.g. *SPP* XX 41.5, *P.Wash.Univ.*II 104.5, *ChLA* XXV 783 (cf. Wild (1985), 407-9), cf. *Digest* 47.2.19. We suggest that *can[didas* should be restored here, cf. *TLL* III 243.36, quoting its use of *tunicae lintes* in Livy 9.40.3.

4. *de synthesi*: for the partitive use of *de*, see *OLD*, s.v.10. It is interesting that in line 8 the writer spells the same word, or a cognate, with *u* rather than *y* (cf. also back 3 note). A *synthesis* is a set of items, often but not exclusively used of clothing. In *Digest* 34.2.38 a query about a will asks whether a woman can choose *an ex uniuersa ueste id est an ex synthesi tunicas singulas et palliola*, thus equating *synthesis* with *uniuersa uestis* and regarding it as including *tunicae* and *palliola*. See also *SPP* XX 41.5, listing a συνθεσίδιον κόκκινον σκουτούλα[τον ("a bright red check-patterned little synthesis") and cf. *P.Mich.*VIII 468.16 (= *CEL* 142, and see Cugusi's note *ad loc.*), *BGU* III 781.I.5 for its use in the context of utensils and silverware.

5-7. It seems likely that these lines, which are indented, specify at least three items or groups of items which belong to the *synthesis*. It would be possible to read *et [* after *paenulas* but we would then have to assume that the number was given *before* the noun; it is therefore perhaps better to suppose that we have an adjective beginning *e .[*.

6. *laenam*: it is impossible to specify the distinctive characteristics of the different types of cloak mentioned here and in other Vindolanda texts. Note that in *Tab.Sulis* 62 the editor takes *la[enam pa]lleum sagum* as three names for the same thing.

8. *sunthesi[:* this line commences further to left than lines 5-7 and we suppose that this indicates that it does not belong with the sub-heading in line 4 (see note). If this is correct it should mean that the word simply indicates a garment or garments, and we suggest that *sunthesi[nam/nas* should be restored, cf. *OLD*, s.v. *synthesina*, citing Suetonius, *Nero* 51, *plerumque synthesinam indutus ligato circum collum sudario prodierit in publicum sine cinctu et discalciatus* (cf. Dio 62.13.3).

9. *subpaenụ[l*: the restoration of *subpaenu[las/-lam* is certain both here and in line 13. The word is an *addendum lexicis*. Dr. Wild comments that it is difficult to imagine what specific type of garment would be worn *sub paenula*, noting that on tombstones a soldier will often wear a thick scarf beneath the *paenula*, visible at the neck, and that at *Not.Tir*. p.157, *suppaenulare* might agree with *focale*; for *suppaenulare* see *TLL* X.1 70.58. The adjective cannot have stood here or in line 13 since adjectives always follow nouns in this list.

10. This line is markedly indented. The first letter is very likely to be *l*, of which the top is visible at the bottom edge of the upper half-leaf. The most likely explanation is that we have an adjective ending *-liaṣ* and qualifying *subpaenụ[las*.

11. *subuclas*: the correct form is *subucula*. **185**.26 appears to have *subunc.lon.s* (see note). *b[* is presumably the beginning of an adjective which might be connected with bathing (see **197**.3 and note). It is perhaps worth noting that the Vulgate, *Levit*. 8.7 refers to priests wearing this garment with a *balteus* and that *TLL* II 1711.15 cites the word *balteatus*.

12. The apex mark appears only here, in the erasure in line 14 and twice in line 15. The name Tranquillus, which is erased in line 14, does not appear elsewhere in the tablets. If Brocchus of line 15 is the officer Aelius Brocchus (see note), Tranquillus was perhaps also a unit commander from whom Cerialis' household received supplies of clothing.

15. This might well be Cerialis' regular correspondent, the equestrian officer Aelius Brocchus (**243-8**; see also perhaps **207**.4 and note).

16. The word beginning *im[* presumably qualifies *tunicas* and distinguishes these from the *tunicas ceṇ[atorias* in line 18. We cannot suggest what it might be, however.

17. *simicị.[*: this word is markedly indented, which suggests that it belongs with the entry beginning in the previous line (cf. line 10 note). It is quite impossible to read the fifth letter as *l* (i.e. *simili*) and *c* looks virtually certain. The next letter is probably *i* and following that is a vertical at the broken edge. We suggest that we might have a misspelling of the word *semicinctium*, a narrow belt or girdle of some sort (see Martial 14.153 and Petronius, *Sat*. 94.8, from which it is clear that it is something with which it would be possible to hang oneself). If this is correct we might then have *tunicas im[cum] / simicịṇ[ctio* (or *-is*). Wild (1985), 410 notes that the tendency in the provinces was to wear the coat ungirt.

18. The most attractive restoration is *ceṇ[atorias*, cf. line 7. Dr. Wild suggests that the *tunica cenatoria* was of fine (wool) fabric with tapestry-woven decoration and notes that there are examples among textile finds at Vindolanda.

Back 1. There are some marks at the left but it is not clear that they are ink. If they are not, this line is indented. If *c̣erui[* is correct it might suggest *ceruical(ia)*, "cushions", (cf. *CIL* 13.5708, *ii lodices et ceruicalia duo par cenator et abollet ii tunica* [sic]), a restoration which would be more attractive if it were clear that the text on the back had some connection with that on the front (see introduction). Another possibility would be the adjective *ceruinus*. If the first letter were *p*, which we find less attractive, we might have *p̣er* plus a name.

2. *membra*: see **198**.2 note. This can hardly be a reference to human or animal limbs

and the only other possible meanings appear to be "branches" or parts of a catapult or a ballista. None of these seems to suit the context very well but we have no other suggestion to offer.

3. *cataçyseṇ*: we take this to be a transliteration of the Greek word κατάχυσιν but it has not so far been attested in Latin. We assume that it is qualified by something lost at the right (e.g. *aeneam*) and by *ansatam* in line 4.

5. We suggest the restoration *cum l[apide /-ibus*, which seems appropriate for rings.

197

Inv.no.87.602.a. 42 x 70 mm.

A fragment from the top left-hand corner of a leaf containing a list perhaps comparable to **195** and **196**; on the hand see **194** introduction. The large blank space at the top is noteworthy. The first two lines of the list are concerned with footwear rather than textile or household and culinary utensils. On Roman leatherware and footwear see van Driel-Murray (1985) and (1987) and on the finds at Vindolanda, R.E.Birley (1977), 125-6, *VRR* III, 1-75, esp. 31-47.

↓ calceos [
gallicuḷạ[s
neariá [
. . . .

"shoes
Gallic shoes
... for the baths (?)"

1. For *calcei* at Vindolanda see R.E.Birley (1977), 125.

2. *gallicuḷạ[s*: well-attested as the diminutive of *gallica* (for which see Cicero, *Phil.* 2.30.76, *cum calceis et toga, nullis nec gallicis, nec lacerna, Ed. Diocl.* 9.12-4); cf. *RIB* I 323 (Caerleon), *do tibi palleum et galliculas*.

3. *neariá*: we suggest that we have the end of the word *bal]nearia*, for items of bath wear. For the apex mark over a short vowel (though here it might just conceivably be a large interpunct) see above, pp.59-60. The word is used absolutely in *CIL* 13.5708 and *Tab.Sulis* 63.2 (but not neuter) and in agreement with *paxsa* in *Tab.Sulis* 32 (cf. **196.**11 note). Here, however, it might refer to footwear, see Charisius, *Gramm.* 1.77.2, *balnearius fur, balnearis autem urceus erit et solea balnearis*. We would need a neuter plural, perhaps *calceamenta*, Dionisotti (1982), 102, lines 55-6, *deferte res ad balneum mutatoria, tollite soleas et caligulas et calciamenta. ... tolle res et balnearia*. We might then restore *gallicula[s* (number) *et calceamenta bal-/nearia*. Other neuter words for footwear are *calceamen* and *sandalium*. R.E.Birley (1977), 125-6 suggests that wooden-soled slippers found in the pre-Hadrianic area at Vindolanda were for use in the bath-house. For an illustration of cork slippers of a later period van Driel-Murray refers us to Esperandieu (1922), 3127. Cf. *P.Oxy*.XXXI 2599.31 and **184**.i.10 note.

198

Inv.no.85.081.a. 52 x 32 mm.

This text is on one side of a fragment of a leaf which has writing on both sides. These three lines are clearly part of a list or account; on the other side are three lines which look like part of a letter (**371**). The two texts may be written by the same hand since they both have examples of the apex mark over final *a*. Comparison with **309** might suggest that the list could have been embedded in a letter. Since the better writing surface appears to be the side with the account, however, we prefer to suppose that this is the primary text and that the back was used for a draft letter.

. . . .
]..brá n(umero) x
]. membrá n(umero) v
]...ares n(umero) x
. . . .

1. Although it is possible to read *]ṃbra*, this suggests only *membra* and it seems unlikely that the account would record the same item with different quantities on consecutive lines. The alternative is *].ạbra*, which suggests e.g. *ḷạbra*, *cande]ḷạbra*.

2. For the use of the apex over a short vowel see above, pp.59-60. The most common meaning of *membra* which seems at all appropriate to the context is "branches", cf. **196**.back 2. However, it may be relevant that Vitruvius 10.11.1 and 7 uses it to describe part of a catapult and of a *bal(l)ista*; in the latter passage it is the equivalent of *χηλή*, regarded by *LSJ* as the "claws" of a military engine (see *σκορπίον*, 5); cf. *TLL* VIII 643.33.

3. *]...ares*: there appear to be three letters before *ares*, which is certain. *ca]ḷịg̣ares* (cf. **186**.7-8) is not possible. The letter before *a* looks like *i* and the one before that could be *t* or *s* or even *c*. We can find no word ending in *-tiares* or *-siares*; *-ciares* suggests *deliciares*, a word which occurs in connection with *tegulae* ("guttering tiles"), or *colliciares*, but the first *i* is very difficult and we might have to suppose *coll-/del]ẹc̣ịares*. Alternatively, if we could imagine *a* with two down-strokes (admittedly not elsewhere found in this hand), we might have *]c̣ṭares* (*lactares* = "suckling", but 10 animals seems a large number).

199

*Tab.Vindol.*I 7, Plate I.4.

. . . .
iiii Nonas
]. adiutor (denarios) .[
] p̣er Priuạṭ[um
. . . .

2. We assumed in the *ed. pr.* that *adiutor* was a common noun. It is well-attested as a name, however, and appears as such in **214**.1; it is obviously possible that it is a name here also. For another possible nominative name in an account see **190**.c.16 note.

3. See **190**.c.26 note.

200

Inv.no.87.547. 20 x 76 mm.

Part of a leaf, complete at the top and left-hand margin, containing the beginnings of 13 lines of an account. Apart from the heading, only dates with no observable pattern survive, offering no clue to the substantive content.

↓ Rati[o
viiii K(alendas) Dẹ[c
iiiị Ḳ(alendas) Dec [
Non(is) Dec[
iiii Idụṣ Ḍẹc̣[
pr(idie) K(alendas) I[a]ṇ [
xi K(alendas) Febr[
pr(idie) K(alendas) Febr[
iii Ịdụṣ Feb[
pr(idie) Idus Febr[
xiii Ḳ(alendas) Mart[
xvii K(alendas Apr[
pr(idie) Idus .[
. . . .

1-2. There is a large c-shaped mark at the left which we take to be the left-hand side of a large *v* at the beginning of line 2; for the enlarged initial digit cf. **291**.i.3.

3. There is a space between *c* and the edge of the leaf which suggests that the month-name is probably abbreviated here, as it probably also is in line 6. This cannot be proved in any of the other entries since the writing runs up to the edge of the leaf, but it is possible that the month-name was abbreviated in every case; February is often abbreviated as *Febr* (see *TLL* VI.1 412).

6. See note to line 3.

9. *Ịdụṣ*: the writing is very abraded here but the order of dates means that this is the only possible reading.

13. The final trace looks most like *m*, i.e. *Ṃ[aias*, but we cannot exclude *ạ* (*A[priles*).

201

Inv.no.87.570. 31 x 92 mm.

A fragment of an account covering a period during the first two or three months of an unspecified year. The leaf is probably physically complete only at the top but, if this were the lower half of a diptych, we would not have the beginning of the text. The writing is extremely abraded and very little can be confidently read. It is conceivable that it belongs with **202**, which will have followed **201** since it contains a date in late February or March (line 7).

. . . .
↓ ..[ ].ra..ạs ..[
x̣[..]ii K(alendas) Fẹbṛụ[arias
ṿ[ii]ị K(alendas) Fẹbruạ[rias
[..].ạx̣.ṛ..al[
[.]... *traces* [
[.]arp.ṛ..ṣ..[
K(alendis) Fẹbruari[is
[.]... ampuḷ[
.[.]..a maṣf̣[
[.]. Martiaṣ ..[
] fit sumṃ[a
]p̣ḷọmạdo[
traces of two lines
. . . .

1. We cannot read a date in this line.

8. *ampuḷ[*: cf. **184**.i.8.

12. The obvious way to break this would be between *a* and *d*, suggesting *di]ploma*. The word might refer either to a *diploma ciuitatis* (Suetonius, *Nero* 12.1) or to a travelling permit (Pliny, *Ep*. 10.64). But it does not fit well in an account.

202

Inv.no.87.568.a-e. (a) 24 x 67 mm. (b-e) small fragments.

This tablet consists of nine fragments, five of which can be joined (a). It could be the lower half of a diptych, perhaps belonging with **201** (see introduction) and it may be complete at the right. It contains an account of commodities and their cash prices. Of the four small unplaced fragments (b-e) only one (b) contains substantial traces.

a.

. . . .
↓]..i (sextarios) viii (denarios) ị..[
]..ṭ. (sextarium) i (denarii) (quadrantem)
].ẹti m(odium) i (sextarium) i [

⟦] (denarios) viiị⟧
].ṣ ṃuṛiaẹ [
] *uacat* (denarii) s(emissem)
]ṣ Martịạs
]lis
]..ri
]ịs
. . . .

b.

. . . . . .
↓]..[
] (denarios) [
].r.[
. . . . . .

a.1. *]..i*: these letters can be read in more ways than one. If we have the end of a commodity, it could be *]ṇṭi* (e.g. *frumenti*). It is not inconceivable, however, that we might have *] ṃ(odios) iii*.

2. The writing at the left is obscured by dirt adhering to the surface. We may have *a]c̣ẹṭị* (cf. **190**.c.25), perhaps repeated in line 3 (see note); *].eg̣ị* is a possible reading but it does not suggest anything suitable.

3. Perhaps *a]c̣ẹti*, cf. line 2. The *e* is made in three strokes with an oblique top-stroke. The dash over the following *m* extends on either side of the letter.

4. This entry appears to be erased with a single, horizontal line; perhaps a prematurely written total or subtotal?

5. Perhaps the end of a date at the left. For *ṃuṛiaẹ* cf. **190**.c.27 and note, **302**.margin 2. The letter read as *ị* is badly faded and appears to have a top-stroke. This is probably dirt, but if not, it would suggest *c̣*; however, it does not seem possible to make the traces at the left fit *ạmurc̣aẹ* ("lees of olive-oil").

8. *]lis*: perhaps the end of a commodity (e.g. *sa]lis*, cf. **186**.10 note) with the quantity at the right, if the leaf is incomplete at this margin, or at the beginning of the next line.

203

Inv.no.85.094.a. 60 x 25 mm.

Part of a leaf, complete at the top and left margin, containing an account of foodstuffs written along the grain. This may simply be a shopping-list or "menu" for a single meal and should perhaps be related to the domestic organisation of the *praetorium* (**284**, with which it was found, might well be a letter to Flavius Cerialis).

xviii K(alendas) Septembreṣ
offellam .[
panis ..[
uini (sextarium) i [

olei ..[

. . . .

"15 August
a pork cutlet (?) ...
of bread ...
of wine, *sextarius* 1 ...
of oil ..."

2. There may possibly be abraded traces of letters at the right and at the corresponding points in lines 3 and 5 where one would expect to find either quantities or cash sums.

offellam: the normal spelling is *ofella*. For the meaning adopted see Dunbabin (1935), 10 and cf. Adams (1994); note the comments of André on Apicius 7.4 (Budé ed., 1974) where the recipe given includes *ligusticum* and *amulum* (both perhaps found in **204**). The account in **191** also has the meat in the accusative case and other items in the genitive.

4. The symbol and the digit are further to the left than one might expect and it is possible that there was also a cash sum specified at the right.

5. Possibly traces of *m(odios)* and a numeral at the right.

204

Inv.no.85.052.a-b. (a) 25 x 53 mm. (b) 10 x 30 mm.

No join can be established between these two fragments. The larger (a) contains the remains of six lines of an account or a list written across the grain. The smaller (b) has exiguous remains of two lines which may well be in the same hand and might supply the end of the account. The list appears to contain foodstuffs and may concern the domestic organisation of the *praetorium* rather than the military unit as a whole.

a. ↓

ṃạṇḍạṭ[
.a...[
lent.s [
ligust..[
ạṃuli [
]...[
. . .

b. ↓

. . .
]ụri
uacat
]ṃma [
. . .

"Items ordered (?):
beans (?)

lentils
lovage
meal
...
butter (?)
total ... (?)"

a.1. The reading does not present any serious palaeographical difficulty and is suitable for the heading of an account or shopping-list, cf. **512**.1. A possible alternative reading would be *ạṃạ..ạ.[*, which would suggest *a* plus the name of the supplier of the goods (cf. **192**.1, **207**.1).

2. The traces are very abraded and only *a* is clear. We think it possible to read *f̣aḅạẹ* (for the collective singular cf. **192**.3, **302**.1) which fits the context very well (see line 3 and note and for beans and lentils in the military diet Davies (1989), 199), but the reading is highly conjectural.

3. There is a mark before *l*, but we take this as belonging to the line above. The penultimate letter is most easily read as *a* but *lentạs* seems unlikely; we think it possible to read *lentịs* (*lentẹs* is less likely), which we would regard as a collective singular (cf. *OLD*, s.v.1 and the references for *fabae* in the previous note) and assume that it was followed by a quantity or a sum of money. For lentils at military sites in Britain and Germany see Dickson (1989) and cf. Davies (1989), 199.

4. The traces are compatible with *ligustịc̣[*. On *ligusticum* see Pliny *NH* 19.165, 20.187; in the latter passage he notes that it is an ingredient in eye-salves which were perhaps in some demand at Vindolanda (see **154**.24 note). For a culinary use see Apicius 7.4 where it appears with *amulum* (below, line 5) in a recipe for cooking *ofella* (for which see **203**.2).

5. The last three letters are certain and *m* is probable. The trace of the first letter is compatible with *a*.

b.1. The form of *r* is very distinctive. *]ụri* could well be the end of *but]ụri*, for which see Dannell and Wild (1987), 69.

2. *su]ṃma [* looks an attractive restoration and suggests that this might be the end of a cash account, with the sums of money for individual items lost at the right.

205

Tab. Vindol. I 6, Plate III.1.

]vii K(alendas) · Ianuarias · in singulos dies
] (ṣẹx̣ṭạṛịị) iiii · f̣ịunt dies x̣ḷịị m(odii) x s(emis)
. . . .

"26 (?) December. Per day, 4 *sextarii*. Total for 42 days, *modii* 10½."

2. The interpretation of the calculation has been corrected from that in the *ed. pr.* where we suggested that the number of *sextarii* was 14 and the number of days was 12. *iiii*

is certainly an easier reading for the number of *sextarii* and the tall vertical after ẋ seems most likely to be *l*. We would now certainly reject the possibility that 24 *sextarii* might have been written; this would surely have been expressed as 1½ *modii*.

206

Inv.no.85.321.a. 33 x 58 mm. Plate XI.

This tablet, comprising three joining fragments of which one is probably blank, contains remains of accounts. It has writing on both sides, the text on one side being upside down in relation to the other except for two lines written in the right-hand margin, along the grain and running from bottom to top. We cannot be certain (1) whether both sides are parts of the same text and (2) if so, in what order we should read them. Our reconstruction is based on the supposition that the last two lines in the transcript might be some sort of summary at the end of the account and we have thus designated the side on which this is written as the back. These lines suggest that the text might be an account of repayments of interest on a loan. For another reference to a loan of money see **312**.ii.7 and cf. **193**.1; for other loans see **180**.6 and **190**.c.29. For a loan document from Carlisle and a list of other texts concerning loans in a military context see Tomlin (1992), 148, note 33.

The text is of some palaeographical interest (cf. Bowman (1994b)). The account written across the grain is in an ordinary cursive but the two last lines on the back are in a sort of capital script which becomes more formal at the end in *debet*, where *d*, *e* and *b* are clearly capital forms. The mixture of capital and cursive in one and the same text is noteworthy and perhaps evokes comparison with the headings in pay-records.

. . . .
↓] (denarios) ii ṣ(emissem)
]ṃe
] (denarios) ii (quadrantem)
] . ụm
] (denarium) i
]nti
] (denarios) i s(emissem)
. . . .

Back:
. . . .
↓] (denarios) .
uacat?
]be .
] (denarium) i s(emissem)
] (denarium) i s(emissem)
. f̣usci
](ḍẹṇạṛịọṣ) .
uacat?

R.margin: FENI . SOLVỊṬ (denarios) [
. Ẹ . . CUM DEBET [

2. *]ṃẹ*: *] .ạẹ* is also a possible reading.

Back 5. Perhaps the genitive of the common *cognomen* Fuscus, cf. **161**.3.

Margin 1. *FENI* seems clear, then one or two letters before *SOLV*. As there is not room for more than 2 letters between this and the *denarius*-symbol, only *soluit* is possible (for *SOLV* in capitals in an account cf. *P.Qasr Ibrîm* 38). Before it the reading looks most like *FENIỌ* or *FENIC̣Ị*. Fenius is attested as the name of a centurion in Britain (*AE* 1969.161a) and "he has paid [a certain sum] to Fenius" would at any rate construe. We would, however, prefer a name in the nominative. We have also wondered whether we might have a version of a name beginning *Phoen-* and note that Phoenix and Phoenicis are attested in Gaul (see *NPEL*). The name Fersio is attested on a inscription from Housesteads (*RIB* I 1620) but it does not seem possible to read *Fersio* here.

2. The alignment suggests that there may possibly be one or two letters at the left before *Ẹ* and there appears to be some dirt on the surface. What we can see is compatible with *. ẸḶỊCVM* and we suggest that *ṚẸḶỊCVM* (= *reliquum*) might be the solution.

207

Inv.no.85.018. 72 x 180 mm.

A diptych made up of fifteen fragments. There are two notches and two tie-holes at the top and bottom. The placement of two very small scraps in lines 2 and 3 is tentative and there is one other scrap with writing across the grain which must belong to a different tablet. As is clear from the notation on the back, the text is an account of Gavo, like **192**, but differs in that it appears to be concerned exclusively with clothing (*saga*, *sagaciae*, *tunicae*, *palliola* and at least two other items). It is possible that the account records supplies from Gavo which were then distributed or that there are sub-categories of items received from or distributed to other people (see notes to lines 4, 11). The highest number of items recorded is 15 (line 6) and this perhaps suggests that the clothes were for military rather than domestic use. On the hand see **192**, introduction.

↓ a Gauuone
sagá n(umero) ịịi
[[ṣag̣ạcias ṇ(umero) ṿịị]]
uacat
[*c.8*] .ó
]ṣ n(umero) v
]ụs n(umero) xv
[*c.3*]ṛal . [ ] ṇ(umero) .
[t]ụnicaṃ [
[e]ṭ palliolạ n(umero) vii
tunicas n(umero) v
a Mạṛco . [*c.4*] . .

palliola [n(umero)]x
ṭunicas [n(umero)]ii

Back: [ratio] G̣auonis

"From Gavo
saga number, 3
⟦*sagaciae* number, 7 (?)⟧
from (?) ...us
... number, 5
... number, 15
capes (?) number, ..
a tunic
and *palliola* number, 7
tunics number, 5
from Marcus the *optio* (?)
palliola number, 10 (?)
tunics number, 2 (?)
(Back) Account of Gavo."

1. For Gavo see **192**.1 note. Whether Gavo is collecting items from or distributing them to others depends on the reading and interpretation of lines 4 and 11 (see notes).

2. *sagá*: for the occurrence of the apex mark with short vowels see above, pp.57-61.

3. For *sagaciae* see **255**.i.8-ii.9, **184**.ii.20, **521**.2. It is unclear precisely what kind of cloak the word signifies; the noun had not occurred in Latin before the Vindolanda texts were discovered (Columella 11.1.21 has *sagaceus* as an adjective, see *Tab.Vindol.*I, p.74). The reading of the number at the right is uncertain. What appears to be a large *c* is certainly a crack in the wood. The rest of the top half of the diptych is lost after this line.

4. The first surviving letter appears to be *h* or, less probably, *n*. The former suggests that we might have *Brocc]ḥo*, possibly but not necessarily the prefect Aelius Brocchus (see **243-8**, **196**.15 note). Presumably the name was preceded by *a*, but it is also possible that the items following were destined for the person named (see line 11 note).

6. The easiest reading is *us* made in ligature (as in **248**.i.3, for example); a possible restoration would be *amict]us*. It is less likely that we should read *]ạs*.

7. We suggest the restoration of the word *[(h)ume]ṛaliị[a*, a kind of military cape, see *Digest* 49.16.14, *nam si tibiale uel umerale alienauit, castigari uerberibus debet.*

8. Since the entry is singular there is unlikely to be anything lost at the right (cf. **192**.2 note).

9. The broken letter at the start suits *t* and the spacing suits *e]ṭ*, even though there is no parallel in this account (but see **196**.6).

11. There are difficulties in the reading and interpretation of this line, which must be a sub-heading since it commences further to the left than the preceding and following lines. By analogy with line 1 it seems most likely that it begins with the preposition *a*, followed by a name beginning with *m*, though we cannot quite exclude a name in the dative beginning with *am* or *ma*. The next visible letter is *a* or *r*, although there could be a letter lost at the break in the leaf; there may then be traces of one more letter before *co* which is fairly certain. *a Marco* seems the most plausible reading; an alternative might be *a Mariço* (for

Mariccus of the tribe of the Boii see Tacitus, *Hist.* 2.61). The next letter is best read as *o* (assuming that the other marks are not ink) and there are some other marks further to the right which may or may not be ink. In between we may have lost some writing, for the corresponding area in the two following lines is abraded and *n(umero)* has disappeared. We tentatively suggest *ọ[ption]ẹ* or *ọ[ptio]ṇẹ*.

12-3. In both these lines there might be a digit lost, in addition to *n(umero)*, before the surviving traces.

Back 1. This is written along the grain from bottom to top of the lower half of the leaf.

208

Inv.no.87.596.a-c. (a) 36 x 60 mm. (b) 9 x 40 mm. (c) 12 x 25 mm.

Three fragments of a tablet written in a cursive hand of good quality which uses interpunct fairly frequently. The largest piece has a notch and tie-hole, which the writing avoids, in the bottom edge, but it is probable that the text does not end here. Unfortunately, we have not succeeded in joining the fragments, but the content suggests that all the pieces belong to the same text. It is clearly concerned with foodstuffs but does not seem likely to be an account. We suggest that it might be a culinary recipe, a hypothesis supported by the fact that it was found in Room VIII of the Period 3 *praetorium* which has been identified as a kitchen (see *VRR* I). For a text which is perhaps comparable see *P.Heid.* 1001.a-b (=*CPL* 318). The occurrence of the word *batauicọ* in line 2 might indicate that the Batavian officers' families brought some of their culinary customs with them (cf. Trow (1990), 107). It is impossible to be certain of the precise nature of the recipe but the presence of a garlic mixture (*alliatum*) and spiced wine or pickling liquor (*conditum*), perhaps also salt and olives (see notes to b.2, c.2), suggests a preserve of some kind (cf. Apicius 3.9).

a.

. . . . . .
↓]. . . scutul . [
]m batauicọ[
]m · alliatum
]ṇce · *uacat*
]ụlum · condit[
]. ip̣e
. . . . . .

b.

. . .
↓]en . [
]eolị[
]tul[
. . .

c.

. . .
↓]um[
]ḷ eṭ [
]..[
. . .

a.1. There is a possible trace of a letter at the right-hand edge of the leaf but not enough remains to identify it. *iṇ scutulạ/-ịļs* is possible; alternatively, perhaps *mi]ṭṭẹ scutulạ[m* followed by a noun in the genitive. For *scutula* = a small dish see **194**.A.2. The word may occur again in b.3

2. There is a significant gap between *batauic* and *ọ*, which is odd. It is not possible to read *batauicụ[m* as an adjective agreeing with a preceding noun. We might envisage *cu]m batauico* plus a noun, or a noun followed by something like *batauico [more paratum*.

3. *al(l)iatum* appears to be a sort of garlic paste, see André (1981), 20 and cf. *TLL* I 1553 citing Plautus, *Most*. 48, Donatus on Terence, *Phorm*.318.

4. If *scutulạ/ị[s* is correct in line 1, we could well have *in la]nce* here; for *lanx* = platter, see **194**.A.7.

5. The last surviving letter in the line is clearly *t*, thus ruling out *condimenta*. *conditum* is a spiced liquor used in preserves see *Ed.Diocl*. 2.17, Apicius 4.2.29, 7.6.4 etc. and we may well have an adjective from this word here; if so *poc]ụlum* would be an attractive restoration at the start of the line.

6. There is a v-shaped notch between *i* and *p̣e*; this was clearly cut before the text was written and the writer has avoided it. The penultimate letter does not look like *c* in this hand, but there is no other *p* to compare. This seems most likely to be the end of *acc]ipe*, a word which occurs in the recipe in *CPL* 318. If the ending were *ce*, we might have *la]ṇc̣e* (cf. line 4).

b.1. The last surviving letter is likely to be *t*, suggesting e.g. *condim]enṭ[a* (cf. **191**.3), but there are obviously other words for foodstuffs which include this group of letters (e.g. *lentes*, *polenta*).

2. The *e* might be the end of an imperative such as *mitte*. The last letter does not suit *e* (which would suggest *oleum*); *oli* suggests *oliuas* (used in a recipe for preserving cabbages, Apicius 3.9.4), for which there is evidence in another Vindolanda text (**302**.margin 3).

3. Another reference to a *scutula*, cf. a.1?

c.2. If *l* is correctly read we might have *sa]l*; it is possible to envisage a nominative but the accusative in the neuter form would be more comfortable. *c(a)epae* (onions) might be a plausible guess for what follows *et* (cf. Columella 6.6.5, *CIL* 3^2, p.953, no.XV, pag. posterior, line 25, *salem et cep(am)*).

3. The traces are very blurred and there might be an erasure.

209

Inv.no.87.596.d. 20 x 26 mm.

A fragment containing part of an account. There are two other scraps associated with this, one with a few letters, the other blank.

. . . . . .

↓]ụm[
] Ịanuarias [
]ạres n(umero) xii[
]ẹfectị[
traces?

. . . . . .

3. Perhaps the end of *caligares* (cf. **186**.7-8); but cf. **198**.3 and note.

4. A reference to the *praefectus* in the genitive is possible (i.e. something belonging to him) but equally this might indicate something repaired, *r]ẹfectị*, which might be either nominative plural or genitive singular.

CORRESPONDENCE OF VERECUNDUS
(Nos. 210-212)

There are two letters addressed to a prefect named Iulius Verecundus (**210**, **211**) and a third, of which we have only the opening, very probably belongs with this small group (**212**). **154**.1-3, which is probably to be assigned to Period 2, attests Iulius Verecundus as prefect of the First Cohort of Tungrians and **313**, which is written by the same hand as **213**, a letter to Cassius Saecularis, refers to a prefect named Verecundus. It is overwhelmingly probable that the recipient of these three letters is the same Verecundus. If so, the balance of probability is that he was at Vindolanda in Period 2.

In none of these letters is the content well enough preserved to give us anything of real substance but what does survive suggests that they were all written by people of similar rank.

It should be noted that **302** is a letter probably addressed to a slave of Verecundus; this is likely to be the same Iulius Verecundus. **326** (a third person reference), **455** (a draft letter?) and **457** (an address to the wife or a slave of Verecundus?) may relate to the same person, but the *cognomen*, which is all we have in these texts, is very common. See also **385**, which may have the remains of an address to a Verecundus, and **283**.2 note.

210

Inv.no.87.711. 96 x 18 mm.

The foot of what must have been the right-hand portion of a diptych containing the conclusion of a letter with an address on the back. The reading of the name is not absolutely certain but it is very probable that the addressee is the prefect Iulius Verecundus. Since the sender uses the term *col(lega)* of himself he too was probably a *praefectus* of a unit.

. . . .

].ẹ desiderio mẹo
ṇẹquẹ adhuc plus uerḅ.ṛ..
Ṣ..ạṃ..ạ mea te salụ[tat
m[2] bene uale frater [

. . . .

Back: *m*[1] Iulio Vẹṛẹc̣ụṇ[do
praef(ecto) coh(ortis)
]ịọ c̣ọl(lega)

"... my desire ... nor as yet (has there been) any more talk (?). My ... greets you ... (2nd hand) Farewell, brother ... (Back, 1st hand) To Iulius Verecundus, prefect of the cohort, from ...ius, his colleague."

1-2. It is difficult to see how to make sense of these lines. We could imagine something like some part of *scribo* followed by *] ḍẹ desiderio mẹo* or *indul]gẹ desiderio mẹo*, cf. *ChLA* X 434 (= *CEL* 175).

2. *uerḅọṛụṃ* is a possible reading at the right. The sense given in the translation is suggested only with diffidence. Adams points out that *neque (non) adhuc* is a standard combination, meaning "not as yet" and that *uerba* can mean "talk". In *ṇẹquẹ* the final *e* is very difficult.

4. This seems to be the work of a second hand. The alignment suggests that it has been rather squeezed in at the end and it is uncertain whether a line is lost after this, although one might envisage e.g. *karissime* in the missing portion at the right or below.

Back 1. *Iulio* is certain, as is *V* following it; the letters following are incomplete but all suit the reading, which we suggest with confidence because of the *gentilicium* and the fact that Iulius Verecundus is attested as prefect at Vindolanda.

2. It is noteworthy that the abbreviation of *coh(ortis)* is marked by *h* with an exaggerated curve and tail, cf. **295**.i.3.

211

Inv.no.88.951. 77 x 36 mm.

Part of what must have been the right-hand portion of a diptych containing five lines of a letter and, on the back, an address to Iulius Verecundus. The lines are complete at the left but we cannot be sure how much is lost at the right. The surviving text does not give any clue to the substantive subject-matter but merely refers to a conversation which the author is about to have, apparently at Luguvalium, and to the possibility of a visit from the addressee. The imperative *perueni* (line 4) can only have been used by an equal or a superior.

The form of *a* in *hac* (line 1) is notable - the left-hand stroke has a hook at the top and then descends vertically. It is noteworthy that interpunct is used in the first two lines of the text. The abrasion of the surface and the writing makes it impossible to be sure whether it is used thereafter.

. . . .
de hac · re · c ̣mpṛ[
ram c̣ṛas · Lugụ[ualio
locuturus sum si ẹṛ[go
uidetur perueni ad me [

traces

. . . .

Back: [I]ụḷị[o] Verecundọ
[pra]ẹf̣(ecto) c̣[o]ḥ(ortis)

. . . .

"... about this matter ... tomorrow I shall speak to ... at Luguvalium. If you approve, therefore, come to me ... (Back) To Iulius Verecundus, prefect of the cohort from (?) ..."

1-2. *c.mpṛ[*: there is no doubt about the reading of *c* even though most of the vertical has disappeared. There is some smudging between *c* and *m* and either *cọm* or *cụm* is possible. We prefer the former and can envisage *cọmpr[ehende-/ram*; this is perhaps unlikely to mean "understand" without some further qualification (see *OLD*, s.v.11), but it might well mean that the author had detained or arrested someone *de hac re* (see *OLD*, s.v.5).

2. *c̣ṛas*: the reading is not easy but if the pieces are moved flush most of the difficulty is removed by the recognition that the writing is fouled by the hook of a long descender from *r* in line 1.

Lugụ[ualio: the initial letter is crossed by the top-stroke of the preceding *s* and the last surviving letter is not easy, but it has probably been fouled by a descender from the previous line. For the locative place-name cf. **250**.i.9 and see Adams (1994). There is no difficulty in supposing that the sender might be intending to speak to a prefect of a unit at Luguvalium or perhaps someone in a higher position.

3. It is possible that *tibi* was written in the lost section at the right.

Back 2. The surviving tops of letters are consistent with *[pra]ẹf̣(ecto)*; further to the right there are exiguous traces which must belong to *c̣[o]ḥ*. Below this line there is an apparent trace of ink at the bottom right of the small piece which, if it is to be taken seriously, might be from the end of the name of the sender, written with an upward slant.

212

Inv.no.85.157. 118 x 28 mm. Plate XIII.

A half-diptych which must have constituted the left-hand portion of a letter. It is complete at the top and right-hand edge and contains the opening of a letter to Verecundus from a person whose name is uncertain. The hand is an elegant one which twice uses apex marks in line 1. It is noteworthy that the whole of the opening address is written in line 1, which is unparalleled in the tablets. It is overwhelmingly likely that the addressee is the prefect Iulius Verecundus, but Verecundus is a very common *cognomen* and we cannot prove it.

].o...ụs Verecundó suó salutem
occasion]em nactus sum scribendi
]..[

. . . .

"...us to his Verecundus, greetings. I have obtained the opportunity of writing ..."

1. *].o..ụs*: it is uncertain how much is lost at the left (see note to line 2 below). We assume the commonest pattern which would include the *gentilicium* and the *cognomen* of the sender. What survives is likely to constitute all or most of the *cognomen*. If the reading of the last two letters is correct we must assume some thickening of the first stroke of *u*; but we cannot rule out *-ḷịs*. At the left, the first surviving letter may well be *u*, with the characteristic serif at the top of the right-hand stroke. Following that, *o* is certain and *c* looks possible. The trace following is uncertain but if the name ends with *-us*, it ought to be either *]ụoc̣.ịṛụs* or *]ụoc̣.ẹṛụs*; alternatively *]ụoc̣..ạḷịs*. But we have found no names which fit these letters.

2. The restoration of *occasio]nem* seems inevitable, cf. **225**.4-5. The previous line will presumably have projected further to the left than this one but we cannot calculate the size of the missing portion at the left with any certainty since there might have been a preceding word (e.g. *hanc*). On this phrase see Adams (1994).

CORRESPONDENCE OF SAECULARIS
(Nos. 213-216)

There are two letters, both attributed to Period 2, which are addressed to Cassius Saecularis (**213**, **214**). A third (**215**), which substantially preserves only the *gentilicium* and the first two letters of the *cognomen*, very probably belongs with this group. A fourth letter (**216**), is included in this group because it is certainly written by the same hand as **214** and its semicircular notches strongly suggest that it comes from the same batch of writing materials, if not the same letter. It should also be noted that **313**, which does not preserve the name of the addressee, is written by the same hand as **213**.

The warm and familiar terms in which Saecularis is addressed by a legionary *aquilifer* in **214** suggests that he is not of equestrian officer status (for the conjecture that he might be a half-brother of the *aquilifer* see A.R.Birley (1990b), 7, *VRR* II, 29); the concern with equipment and supplies shown in the subject-matter of the other two letters suggests that he might be an *optio*, a *decurio* or a centurion. The balance of probability would place him at Vindolanda in Period 2, but if he was of centurial or similar rank he might have been there for an extended period of time.

213

Inv.no.88.865. 169 x 36 mm. Plate XIII. *VRR* II, Plate IV.

Part of a diptych, complete at the top and both margins, containing a letter from Curtius Super to Cassius Saecularis. Curtius Super does not appear elsewhere in the tablets (for another person with this *cognomen* see **255**.i.1). What is preserved of the substance of the letter concerns a transaction involving barley which has been purchased and Super seems to be suggesting that some persons or group should obtain it from Saecularis (see ii.2-3 note). This concern with supplies would fit the hypothesis that Saecularis was perhaps an *optio*. It is noteworthy that, despite the fact that both the *gentilicium* and the *cognomen* of the addressee are given on the back, the opening of the letter simply has *Cassio suo*. There is no precise parallel to this in the openings of the Vindolanda letters, nor have we found one in *CEL* (it is unclear whether Valerius of *P.Qasr Ibrîm* 30 = *CEL* 4 had a *cognomen*). In **291**.ii.9 Claudia Severa refers to her husband Aelius Brocchus as *Aelius meus*. In **343**.i.1 the writer calls himself Octavius only, but this could be a *cognomen* (*NPEL* s.v., cf. A.R.Birley (1991), 94).

The hand, a practised one writing rapidly, is of some palaeographical interest and can also be identified in **313**. The use of ligature is frequent, particularly notable in *Super* (i.1).

Letter-forms of interest are *o* left open at the right, *n* which is made in a single stroke in ii.1 (contrast ii.3) and *i* with a serif at the right and not always at the top of the vertical; *b* in *habeant*, which seems to be ligatured to *a* preceding, has almost completely lost its bow. The writing in column ii slopes up to the right in relation to the grain of the wood.

i

Curtius Super Cassio suo
salutem
].[..].[..].[..].[
. . . .

ii

ut interpreteris
et ut hordeum commer-
cium habeant a te [
[...]...ḷ.be.ṃ...uạ.ẹ
]ẹ.ḍạ
. . . .

Back:

Cassio Saecu-
[lari]
. . . . . .

"Curtius Super to his Cassius, greetings. ... so that you may explain and so that they may get from you barley as commercial goods ... (Back) To Cassius Saecularis."

i.3. Only the tops of letters survive of which the penultimate is either *l* or *b*.

ii.1. *interpreteris*: one meaning of *interpres* is "agent" or "go-between" (*OLD*, s.v.1); it would make good sense if Saecularis were being asked to act as go-between but the citations in *TLL* VII.1 2250.3 suggest that it is only used thus with reference to verbal or written communication. Alternatively, it may be that the verb has a general sense and that Cassius Saecularis is simply being asked or told to explain something. We should presumably not rule out the possibility, however, that he is being asked or instructed to act as interpreter (*OLD*, s.v.6) in some transaction with non-Latin speakers. In that case the implication would be that military personnel are selling barley to the natives.

2-3. *hordeum commercium*: the reading of *commercium* is secure (cf. A.R.Birley (1990b), 6); there is not room for *a* and the form of *i* with an emphatic serif at the right is well exemplified elsewhere (i.1.*Cassio*, ii.1 second *i* in *interpreteris*). *commercium* is, however, normally a noun and we presume that it is here used in apposition, "barley as commercial goods", in distinction to something for personal use. For this meaning see *TLL* III 1874.11 (*merces, res emptae uenditaeque*). Note *P.Mich.*VIII 469.4 = *CEL* 144, where Cugusi, following the original editors, suggests the restoration *ut emas illẹ[i al]ịqụạ [co]ṃṃercia* and notes that this would constitute the earliest example of *commercium* in this sense; the Vindolanda text is roughly contemporary.

3. There is a piece of the tablet missing after *te*.

4. At the left perhaps *libe*. No writing is visible after *e* at the right but there is room

for up to three letters and the surface may simply be abraded here; *uạṛẹ* is possible, *uạḷẹ* is not.

5. The line might end with *-enda*, possibly a gerundive, but if so the form of *d* is different from that in ii.2.

Back 1. The address is written on the back of the right-hand portion and the left-hand portion is blank, making it clear that the *cognomen* did not overrun on to this side. For another example of the name running on to a second line see **221**.

214

Inv.no.88.940. 100 x 26 mm. Plate XIII. A.R.Birley (1990b). *VRR* II, Plate IV.

The top of the left-hand portion of what was presumably a diptych, with probable remains of a notch in the left-hand edge. It contains the opening of a letter to Cassius Saecularis from a legionary *aquilifer* whose *cognomen* is Adiutor and it is the longest and most elaborate example of such an opening. The warm and familiar tone in which Adiutor addresses Saecularis suggests that the rank and status of the correspondents is comparable. The content of other letters to Saecularis (**213** and **215**) fits the hypothesis that he might have been a centurion, a decurion or an *optio* in a unit stationed at Vindolanda.

A.R.Birley (1990b) has transcribed this text, reading the name of the *aquilifer* as *Vettius Adiutor* and his unit as *leg(io) ii Aug(usta)*, and arguing that Vettius Adiutor might be one of two brothers attested on inscriptions from Pannonia. The identifications of the individual and the unit are obviously attractive but attention needs to be drawn to a difficulty in the reading of the *gentilicium* which we prefer to read as *Vịttius* (see further note to line 1). As for the identity of his legion, the numeral is very badly abraded but *ii* is the most plausible reading. It is, of course, the case that *legio ii Augusta* is the only legion with this epithet stationed in Britain (at Caerleon) in this period; there is, however, evidence for the presence of an individual from *legio iii Augusta* and a vexillation from *legio viii Augusta* in Britain probably in the Hadrianic period (see further note to line 2).

216 is also written by the same hand and the tablet has similar semicircular notches in the edge (as does Inv.no.87.809, which has only illegible traces).

Vịttius Adiutor aqui-
lifer leg(ionis) · ịị Aug(ustae)
Cassio Saeculari fra-
terclo suo plurimam
]...
. . . .

"Vittius Adiutor, eagle-bearer of the Second Augustan Legion, to Cassius Saecularis, his little brother, very many [greetings] ..."

1-2. *Vịttius Adiutor*: only the second letter of the *gentilicium* is uncertain. This letter has a noticeable serif at the top left, exactly like the serif in *i* elsewhere in this text, notably the second *i* in *aquilifer* and in *plurimam*; the form also occurs in **216** (see introduction), cf.

ChLA V 294. There is also a vestigial trace halfway up the vertical, which might be thought to point to *e* but which, we think, is not ink. There are two texts, probably the work of the same hand, but a different one from that of the present text, in which *e* is made in this way (**302**.4, back 1, **498**); elsewhere in the present text *e* is made in a completely different and much more normal way. *Vịttius* therefore seems to us a much more satisfactory reading, although we would not wish to exclude altogether the possibility of reading *Vẹttius* which is, of course, a much commoner *gentilicium*.

Adiutor: the word appears in **199**.2, where we originally assumed that it was a common noun (see note); if a name, it can hardly be the same person since it presumably refers to someone at Vindolanda.

aquilifer: see Breeze (1974), 269, 272, Speidel (1984), 3-6, 23-7. This was a senior staff post from which promotion to the centurionate was normal.

2. *leg(ionis) · ịị Aug(ustae)*: the spacing in this part of the line is very generous. The clear medial point after *leg* must mark the abbreviation. Thereafter the numeral is very abraded and the reading is complicated by the descender of *r* from the line above, between it and *aug*. The reading of the latter is secure, although there is no sign of a medial point following. In the numeral, traces of at least two digits are clear and the reading *ịị*, which would identify Adiutor's unit as *legio ii Augusta* based at Caerleon (so Birley, 1990b), is the most plausible. It is perhaps worth noting, however, that *ILS* 2726 (cf. 2735) contains evidence for the career of Pontius Sabinus, a *primus pilus* of the African *legio iii Augusta* who was *praepositus uexillationibus milliariis tribus expeditione Britannica*, among which was one vexillation from *legio viii Augusta* from Upper Germany (see also *CIL* 7.495, the inscription on the shield-boss of a soldier of *legio viii*, found in the Tyne, and *RIB* I 782). This *expeditio* is traditionally dated in AD 122 (for a summary of the evidence see Tomlin, *Britannia* 23 (1992), 318 and cf. Frere (1987), 123) and would therefore probably be too late to be relevant to the Vindolanda text.

3-4. *fraterclo*: this fairly rare diminutive (see *TLL* VI.1 1258) does not appear elsewhere in the openings of the Vindolanda letters nor can we find any instance in *CEL*. Note Cicero, *Verr*. 3.155, *uolo, mi frater, fraterculo tuo credas*.

4. *plurimam*: cf. **309**.i.1, **310**.i.2-3, **311**.i.1-2.

215

Inv.no.86.447+448. 114 x 79 mm. Plate XIV.

Three joining pieces survive from the right-hand half of a diptych, with probable remains of notches in the right-hand edge. The leaf contains the second column of a letter, which may be missing something at the end (see notes to line 8 and back 2). At the left there are some traces of the ends of lines of the left-hand column which, as often happens, overran the fold; they are so exiguous that we have not attempted to transcribe them. Unusually, the first line of the right-hand column projects at the left. It is noteworthy that the closing greeting is written by the same hand as the rest of the text, but it is possible that a final greeting was added by another hand below this. The name of the addressee on the back clearly begins with *Cassio*, a *gentilicium* which occurs elsewhere in the tablets only in the case of Cassius Saecularis, and the remains of the beginning of the *cognomen* leave us in no doubt that the addressee is Cassius Saecularis (see note to back 1). If the attributions of **213** and **214** to Period 2, and of **215** to Period 3 are correct, it is nevertheless possible that a centurion or decurion or *optio*, or someone holding a "senior staff post" (cf. Breeze (1974)), might have been at Vindolanda and generated correspondence over a number of years (or have been there on more than one posting, separated by some years). The subject-matter of the present letter, the supply of timber, compares well with the evidence in **213** for Cassius Saecularis' role in supplying barley.

The right-sloping hand is one of some character. *i* with a foot (approaching the shape of *L*) is interesting as is *r*, close to the capital form.

i

. . . .

traces of ends of lines

. . . .

ii

dịc̣ẹs si qui sunt iṇ[*c.7*
habebunt auctoritatem
Seuerini ego eṇịṃ ab illo
accepi si qui uolet uenịṛẹ
et quọ lignum et materiem
seruant aequọ́ perfereṭ
opto felicissimus bene
ualeas *vacat*
traces?

. . . .

Back:

Cassió Ṣạ *traces*
uacat
]ẹ c̣ọṛniclario

"... if there are any ... they will have the authority of Severinus. For I have got [it?] from him, if anyone wants to come, and he will not mind where they are storing the wood and timber. I pray that you are enjoying the best of fortune and are in good health ... (Back) To Cassius Saecularis, from ... *cornicularius*."

ii.1. *dịc̣ẹs*: we have considered as an alternative *dụịs*, which cannot be ruled out. In the context, however, a restoration such as *iu]/dịc̣ẹs*, or *in]/dịc̣ẹs*, from the verb *indico* rather than *index*, would be attractive (cf. **334**.2). The spacing suggests that *si qui* begins a new sentence.

After the break at the end of the line, a place-name or location would be appropriate; alternatively we might have had a perfect participle beginning *in-*. If the sense we envisage is on the right lines, *qui* could refer either to people who will have the authority or the objects which someone might obtain "if there are any in (place)". Since *qui* must be plural here it is impossible to tell whether we have an example of contamination of *quis* and *qui*, see note to line 4. On *si qui* for *si quis* see Löfstedt (II, 1942), 79-96.

3. *Seuerini*: the name, which is reasonably common (e.g. *RIB* I 1212, 1267), does not occur elsewhere in the tablets and the position of the person is unknown. There is a larger than normal space between this and *ego* which is appropriate to a break between sentences.

4. *si qui*: in view of *uolet* this must be taken as *si quis*, although it cannot be explained in the same way as *P.Mich.*VIII 468.41 (= *CEL* 142) where there is a following *s*. See Adams (1977), 30, note 112, 47.

uenịṛẹ: this is the least unlikely reading, but *i* is not quite like the other examples and not much survives of *e*; *uenịạṃ* is more difficult.

5. *quọ*: the final letter looks somewhat like *i* but it is unlike other examples in this hand and is harder to construe.

materiem: cf. *materias*, **309**.i.3. On the distinction between this and *lignum* see *TLL* VIII 449.64-9, Furneaux on Tacitus, *Ann.* 1.35.1.

6. *aequọ́ perferẹṭ*: the final trace does not look easily compatible with either *perferẹṭ* or *perfereṇṭ* but the former makes better sense and assumes less missing at the right where there should be no loss (cf. **260**, introduction). The obvious reading of the preceding word is *aeque*, but the final *e* would be unlike *e* elsewhere in this text and we do not see how to make sense with it. We think it just possible to read *aequo* with an apex over *o* (cf. back 1), which we suggest is to be understood as for *aequo animo* (cf. **302**.5, *aequo emantur*, i.e. *aequo pretio*).

8. It is possible that a second hand has added (e.g.) *uale frater* below this, cf. **250**.ii.17.

Back 1. *Cassió*: the apex is clear. It is curious that the *cognomen* is so badly abraded when the *gentilicium* just before it is very clear. The long diagonal ascender in the first letter can hardly be anything but *s* and the second could well be *a*.

2. *]ẹ c̣ọṛniclario*: this is written with a pronounced slant from bottom left to top right which is quite normal in this position. The first four surviving letters are abraded and obscured by dirt but the reading is not in any real doubt. *cornic(u)larius* unlike *cornicen* (see **182**.i.1 note) is not attested as a name (Cornicula, *LC* 331, is not related to the military title) and it must therefore indicate the writer's position. For legionary and auxiliary *cornicularii*, characterised as "senior staff officers", see Breeze (1974), 267-76, 280-86; in the legions this was a position from which men were regularly promoted to the centurionate. An auxiliary *cornicularius* appears in *CEL* 140.27 (= *P.Oxy.* VII 1022, AD 103). There is no way of knowing whether we are here dealing with a legionary or an auxiliary *cornicularius*. The title will have been preceded by a name, for which *ẹ* is a suitable termination. This must mean that something has been lost from the bottom of the leaf, cf. note to line 8.

216

Inv.no.87.737. 96 x 35 mm.

Five lines of a letter, with some use of interpunct. The writing in **214** and **216** is certainly the work of the same hand; the form of *i*, with a serif at the top left, is very interesting. It is striking that both leaves have semicircular indentations at the left margin which are presumably notches (also in Inv.no.87.809). Since these leaves are both left-hand portions they could only belong to the same letter if it had been written on more than one diptych (cf. **292**, **343**), but it is very likely that both letters come from Adiutor (even if the hand is not his own) and that both tablets come from the same batch of writing-material.

. . . . . .
rent [
si · e[*c.6*] *traces*
ui · et te t. . . ẹṛe. . . [
conserụent sc̣. . [
p̣ot.ra. emeram[
. . . . . .

4. *conserụent*: *ụ* is difficult but there seems to be no other possibility.

5. The reading *poteṛaṃ* can be envisaged (e.g. "I bought as much as I could"); *ẹ* can be read if we assume that the top has disappeared; the last letter is quite obscured by dirt.

CORRESPONDENCE OF GENIALIS
(Nos. 217-224)

The coherence of this group of texts and the identity of the persons or persons concerned is problematical and the difficulties are compounded by the fact that Genialis is a common *cognomen*.

There are two texts addressed to Flavius Genialis, both assigned to Period 3 (**218**, **221**). Another letter, also from Period 3, was sent to Flavius Cerialis by Flavius Genialis and the address on the back shows that this was not a draft or copy (**256**). There are two letters to a Genialis in which the *cognomen* only is preserved (**217**, **219**). In three other letters which contain the *cognomen* only the readings are too dubious to be used as evidence (**220**, **222**, **223**). **224** now appears likely to be the opening of a letter rather than a list, but only the first letter (*g*) of the name of the addressee is preserved; Genialis is no more than a possibility. Another letter which was assigned to this group in *Tab. Vindol.*I can now be seen not to belong (**171**). Finally, a letter assigned to Period 2 and addressed to Candidus, a slave of Genialis, is also relevant (**301**).

If we ignore the evidence of **256**, it is possible to suppose that there are 7 or 8 letters addressed to the same (Flavius) Genialis and that he was at Vindolanda at some time in Period 2 or 3 or both (cf. A.R.Birley (1990a), 20, suggesting that he was a predecessor of Flavius Cerialis). The combination of evidence in **220** and **301** makes it likely that he was a prefect, as was suggested in *Tab. Vindol.*I. The content of **218**, and of the other letters in so far as they are preserved, is not inappropriate. **256**, however, attests a correspondent of Cerialis named Flavius Genialis who was presumably somewhere other than Vindolanda at some point in Period 3. If this is the same man, we must suppose that he had moved on. On the difficulties of interpretation see further **256**, introduction.

217

Inv.no.85.242.b-d. (b) 40 x 27 mm. (c) 30 x 27 mm. (d) 15 x 25 mm.

Two joining fragments (b) from the left-hand portion of a diptych contain the beginning of a letter to Genialis. Two other substantial fragments appear to be by the same hand and their shapes suggest that they were folded face-to-face with the two fragments of (b) and, if so, they must join (possibly flush, but there may be a small gap between them) and will form part of the right-hand column of the letter. There is a detached fragment with a trace which is probably in a different hand. The large *G* in *Genial[i* is noteworthy, as is the large initial *C* in *Crescen[te]m*.

b.

i

].tilis Geniaḷ[i suo
ṣ[alutem
] Crescen[te]m cuṃ [
. . . .

c-d.

ii

. . . .
].abu[ ]ạe *uacat*
].em..ui..lin[
] ut cụm illo coṇ[
]uḅe.[..]..ra ịạṃ [
traces
. . . .

1. *].tilis*: *cognomina* with this ending given in *NPEL* are Adretilis, Gratilis, Gentilis and Utilis of which the last two are the most common. The trace surviving before *t* would certainly not allow *u* but is probably compatible with *n*; so we should perhaps restore *Ge]ṇtilis*.

3. The sense is likely to be "I have sent Crescens to you with ...". One of the other fragments inventoried under this number (**128**) has a reference to a *(centuria) Crescentis* and this is likely to be the same man.

ii.1. Perhaps restore *] ṭabu[l]ạe*, cf. **283**.6. For the *uacat* at the right cf. **291**.ii.8, **257**.6, **379**.

4. Perhaps a present subjunctive of *iubeo*, e.g. *i]ubeạ[s*, *i]ubeạ[t*, followed by (e.g.) *[ce]ṭẹra*, *[al]ṭẹra*.

218

*Tab.Vindol.*I 34, Plate VII, 1 and 2. *CEL* 102.

. . . .
c̣is rogo si quid utile miḥi credịḍ[eris
aut mittas aut reserues quid nobis opụṣ
esseṭ Paterno n(ostro) m^2 ⸢et Gauoṇị⸣ m^1 ad te manda⟦re⟧ m^2 ⸢ui⸣ m^1 quem-
quẹm ịṭa exegeras statim ad te dimisi
traces
. . . .

Back: Flauio Geniaḷi
. . . . .

"... please either send or keep on one side anything which you believe useful for me. I sent word to you by our friend Paternus (2nd hand) and by Gavo (1st hand) as to what our needs were. Thus, anyone whom you had demanded I immediately sent on to you... (Back) To Flavius Genialis."

3. *ẹt gạ.o ..l*, *ed. pr.*, *Agauo m(i)l(iti)*, *CEL* 102. *Gauoṇị* is certain and suggests that this may be the same person as *Gauuo* who appears as a supplier of goods in **192** and **207**, especially in view of the rarity of the name (see note to **192**.1) and the fact that on the back of both texts the name is spelled *Gauo*. Cugusi's reading of the the initial *a* in *CEL* 102 is in fact the top of the *d* below. The evidence for the patterns of writing and composition which are attested by the new tablets make us more confident that the interlinear additions here and in line 4 are likely to be the work of the sender of the letter (see our note in the *ed. pr.*).

4. *exegeras*: cf. perhaps **262**.3.

219

Inv.no.85.085. 105 x 27 mm.

The upper part of the left-hand portion of a diptych containing the beginning of a letter to Genialis from a person whose name is probably Flavius Proculus. Nothing of the content survives.

Flaụịụs P̣rocuḷus Geniali sụ[o
saḷutem
traces
. . . .

1. *Flaụịụs*: the first three letters and the final *s* are certain. In between there is a mixture of exiguous traces and dirt. This person may also be the sender of **444**.

220

Inv.no.85.089. 43 x 17 mm.

A fragment containing part of an address on what is presumably the back of the right-hand portion of a diptych.

] G̣ẹṇịạ[li
pra]ẹf̣ẹ[c]ṭ[o
. . . .

2. The reading is very uncertain but is compatible with the traces. For some supporting evidence that Genialis was a prefect see **301**.back 8-9 note.

221

Inv.no.85.332.a. 86 x 30 mm.

A fragment of a leaf containing one line of a letter and, on the back, an address to Flavius Genialis. It is very odd that the address is written upside down in relation to the writing on the front, but so little survives of this letter that we cannot elucidate this.

. . . . .
ẹṭ ọm..ra ạ.....[
uacat

Back: Fláuio Geni-
ạḷ[i
. . . .

1. We expect some recognisable part of a closing formula but the traces do not suggest anything familiar.

Back. For the division of the *cognomen* between two lines cf. **213**.back; for the use of the apex mark see above, pp.57-61.

222

Inv.no.85.332.b. 90 x 20 mm.

A fragment presumably from the right-hand portion of a letter. The front is blank. The back may well read *Flauio G̣ẹṇị[*, perhaps in the same script as **221**, but with a large *o*.

223

*Tab.Vindol.*I 36. *CEL* 104.

. . . . . .
]..ṭes ụ[
]ri n(ostro) s.[
. . . . . .

Back: G]ẹnịạḷi
. . .

2. Perhaps *consula]ri n(ostro)* (cf. **248**.ii.9-10), but there are other possibilities, e.g. *frat]ri* or a name.

224

*Tab. Vindol.*I 10, Plate III, 5

Perhaps the beginning of a letter to Genialis, rather than part of a list of names (as was suggested in the *ed. pr.*).

Licinius Asper G[
 ]̣[..].̣[
. . . . . .

1. Licinius Asper does not appear elsewhere in the tablets.

CORRESPONDENCE OF CERIALIS
(Nos. 225-290)

By far the largest group of letters is the correspondence of Flavius Cerialis, prefect of the Ninth Cohort of Batavians at Vindolanda during Period 3. We are able to include in this group some 56 texts with certainty or probability (**225-80**) and there are another 10 texts which possibly belong (**281-90**). Note also that **347** might be a letter to a slave of Cerialis. In addition, at least six of the applications for leave (**166-71**) are addressed to him. This makes it very likely that a great deal of the Period 3 material, both documents and unattributed letters, should be connected with him (see also above, p.19, note 11). The find-spots of the texts indicate that they were spread over a large area of the Period 3 *praetorium*.

There are 17 letters which are or might be drafts or copies of Cerialis' own letters (**225-41**; on the grounds for this distinction see above, p.42) and one letter which seems to have been sent by Cerialis and brought back to Vindolanda by its recipient (**242**). In this sub-group the names of only four of his correspondents are preserved: September and Brocchus were certainly equestrian officers (**234**, **233**), Crispinus may have been more highly placed (**225**), and the position of Flavius Similis is unknown (**235**). Cerialis' letters cover both military/professional and personal matters. There are references to deserters (**226**), to a *numeratio* (**242**), and a request for personal support or patronage (**225**). Personal matters possibly include an illness (his own or that of a son, **227**), the purchase of some protection against bad weather (**234**), and a request for some hunting-nets (**233**). It is thus clear that Cerialis did not merely keep copies of letters relating to military business.

The identification of common hands is a hazardous procedure, but in the letters emanating from Cerialis the hand which we can most often identify probably occurs in 8 texts (**225-32**) and it is this which we have suggested is the hand of Cerialis himself, writing drafts. In the other copies we think that there is a common hand in **234** and **239** and another in **235** and **240** (plus, possibly, **233**). Thus, apart from his own hand there are four or five other hands at work in the writing of Cerialis' correspondence.

In the 48 letters sent to Cerialis we can name 18 correspondents. They include 10 who can be identified with certainty, or some degree of probability, as equestrian officers: Claudius Karus (**250-1**), Caecilius September (**252-3**), Aelius Brocchus (**243-8**, cf. **285**), Flavius Similis (**254**, **286**), Iustinus (**260**), Hostilius Flavianus (**261**), Oppius Niger (**249**), Valerius Niger (**248** cf. **465**), Flavius Genialis (**256**), and Pastor (**259**). There are two probable centurions, Clodius Super and Imber (**255**, **258**), and two decurions, Vitalis and Verus (**263**, **284**). It should also be noted that the hand in one fragment of a letter suggests that the sender was Chrauttius, known elsewhere as a correspondent of the governor's *equisio* (**264**). Of the others, Faber may be a decurion (**281**) and Valatta is presumably a woman (**257**); there is no clue to the position of Placidus (**262**).

The letters which Cerialis received deal with a range of military and professional matters, as well as personal issues. One writer sends something through a cavalryman (**252**, also perhaps in **268**), another requests clothing for his *pueri*, certainly slaves (**255**), there is a letter of recommendation (**250**, also perhaps **260**) and an expression of good wishes for Cerialis himself (**248**); the movement of personnel is mentioned in **236** and **266**, the despatch of letters in **263**; **256** is a curious missive which appears to concern the sender's personal safety and fear of being attacked. On the personal side we have a request for a favour (**257**), perhaps a personal appeal in **282**, New Year greetings and a reference to a celebratory sacrifice in **261** and **265** respectively.

In the letters received by Cerialis, we have not found any common hands, apart from those which can be identified in the correspondence of Brocchus and Severa, of which two occur more than once (see **243**, **292** introduction).

For other texts which may belong with this group see: **169**, introduction, **347**, **357**, **362**, **364**, **373**, **384**, **403**, **404**, **406**, **413**, **423**, **424**, **430**, **462**, **466**. Note also that *Tab. Vindol.*I 27 (= **519**), originally assigned to Cerialis, has now been removed from this group.

225

*Tab. Vindol.*I 37, Plate VIII, 1-2. *CEL* 105.

This text can now be recognised as a draft of a letter from Cerialis to Crispinus. The association with the correspondence of Cerialis is established by the identity of this hand with that of **227**, where the name of Cerialis is to be found in the nominative. There are six other fragmentary texts (**226**, **228-32**) written by the same hand, and it may also be at work in the closure in **242**.ii; see also **466**. The hand, discussed in detail in the *ed. pr.*, is very idiosyncratic and unlike those found in texts which we suppose to have been the work of "professional scribes"; for this reason we think it probable that it is the hand of Cerialis himself, although this cannot of course be proved.

Minor revisions of the readings in the *ed. pr.* are signalled in the notes. Our view of the general sense and purpose of the letter has not changed. A.R.Birley (1991), 95-100, has suggested that Cerialis is asking for a transfer or promotion; it is certainly possible that this is the implicit point of the request for patronage but there is nothing explicitly about promotion in this or the other letters of Cerialis. Nor is it clear that we should regard this as an example of *litterae commendaticiae* in which the writer recommends himself, cf. Speidel and Seider (1988).

We are confident that the name of the addressee in Cerialis' draft was correctly read as Crispinus. The *cognomen* is common and we cannot identify him. Our original view that the draft should not be associated with what we identified as the "Archive of Crispinus" has been proved correct by the recognition that the name of the principal person in that archive is, in fact, Priscinus (**295-8**). The terms in which Cerialis writes suggests that Crispinus is an important man (note line 6, *d]ọminum meum*) and well-placed to assist an equestrian prefect by interceding with the governor. He might therefore be of senatorial status, a laticlave tribune or a legionary legate (cf. **154**.5-6 note).

[ ] *uacat* Crispino suo [*uacat?*
[G]ṛattịo C̣rispino redeunte .[...
[*c.10*] ⟦non fui mihi⟧ et .ḍ.[..
[*c.7* li]benter amplexụṣ ṣ[um do-
ṃine ṣalutandi te oc̣c̣ạṣṣịọṇẹṃ
[d]ọminum meum et quem saluom
⟦ḥạbere⟧ esse et omnis spei
⟦suae⟧ compotem inter praecipuạ
uoti habeo hoc enim de
me semper meruisti usque
ad hanc ḍ[*c.4*].tem cuius fịḍ-
ục̣ịạ họ[*c.6*]e te primuṃ [...
[*c.4*]..[*c.6*].. ⌜ut⌝ ẹ.il[...

Back:
[....]m Marcẹllum clarissị[mum ui-
[rum] consularem meum quar.[....
[oc]c̣assionem nunc ut.[*c.11*
[...]. ṭibi amicorum dọ[*c.10*
sụạ [p]ṛạẹsentia quos tụ[*c.9*
illius scio plurimos haberẹ [....
quomodo uoḷes imple quidq[uid
de te exspecto et me .ḷụ.[.]...
aṃicis ita instrue ut beneficio
tuo militiam [po]ṣṣim iucundam
experiri ha[ec ti]bi a Vindolanda scribo .[*c.6*]. hibernạ [..
[.].ṇ.ụ. ḥ..[*c.6*].ius a.[
. . . .

"To his Crispinus. Since Grattius Crispinus is returning to ... and ... I have gladly seized the opportunity my lord of greeting you, you who are my lord and the man whom it is my very special wish to be in good health and master of all your hopes. For you have always deserved this of me right up to the present high office (?). In reliance on this ... you first ... greet (?) ... Marcellus, that most distinguished man, my governor. He therefore offers (?) the opportunity now of ... the talents (?) of your friends through his presence, of which you have, I know, very many, thanks to him (?). Now (?), in whatever way you wish, fulfil what I expect of you and ... so furnish me with friends that thanks to you I may be able to enjoy a pleasant period of military service. I write this to you from Vindolanda where my winter-quarters are (?) ..."

1. The omission of the name of the sender is unique in the tablets; it is understandable in a draft, however, especially if this is a draft jotted down by Cerialis himself.

2. We retain the reading of the *cognomen* as *Crispino*; *P̣risc̣ino* is less attractive palaeographically. Even if the latter were correct, he should probably not be identified with the principal person in the correspondence of Priscinus (**295-8**).

3. For similar erasures in draft letters see **227**, **232** and **317**, and for examples from elsewhere see e.g. Sijpesteijn and Worp (1977), Speidel and Seider (1988).

2-3. A possible restoration would be: *redeunte ạ [Vin-/dolanda] et ạd [te / ueniente].*

8-9. *inter praecipuạ uoti habeo*: cf. *O.Wâdi Fawâkhir* 2.2 (= *CEL* 74), *opto deos ut bene ualeas que mea uota sunt.*

11. We propose the restoration of *ḍ[ignit]ạtem* here, which might be the antecedent of the following *cuius*.

13-4. *il[.../....]m Marcẹllum*: we retain the reading of the *ed. pr.* despite the fact that A.R.Birley (1991), 96 proposes *N[e-/ratiu]m*. There is no doubt that the reference in these lines is to L.Neratius Marcellus, known to have been governor of Britain in AD 103. In the *ed. pr.* we suggested reading *il[lum / Luciu]m Marcellum*, while indicating in our discussion that we recognised the difficulties posed by this restoration. Birley has argued that instead of *il* it is possible to read *n* and that the correct restoration is *N[e-/ratiu]m Marcellum* (accepted in *CEL* 105). This removes the difficulties we indicated but we are unable to accept it for two reasons. First the word division: *ratiu]m* must have come in line 14 but there would have been ample room for *Nera* in line 13. Secondly, while we accept that *n* is not impossible at the end of the preserved part of line 13, the reading is much more likely to be *il* (*pace* Birley there is no other *n* in this text made in quite this way). However, study of many more Vindolanda letters than were available to us when we produced the *ed. pr.* has shown that writers sometimes began the first line of a second column further to the left than the subsequent lines (see **215**, introduction); if we imagine our writer as having done this in the first line on the back of his leaf, it would be possible to restore the whole of *Neratiu]m* in line 14.

Before it, we now think it possible that we should read *s]ạḷ ⸢ut⸣ ẹṣ* or possibly even *ṣạḷ ⸢ut⸣ ẹṣ*. The traces just after the break are indeterminate but *l* looks plausible; *ut* is written above the line and it is impossible to tell whether there is erasure below or just an irregularity in the grain of the wood which the writer has avoided.

15-8. The sense which we envisaged here in the *ed. pr.*is conveyed by a restoration such as: *quarẹ [dat / oc]c̣assionem nunc ut f̣[auoris sit gra-/ti]ạ ṭibi amicorum dọ[tes augendo] / sụạ [p]ṛạẹsentia.*

18-20. See *CEL* 105, where *[nunc]* is restored at the end of line 19 and the alternative reading *uoḷes* (for *uoụes*) which we discussed in the *ed.pr.* is preferred. This necessitates a different understanding of the preceding passage, for which Cugusi offers: *quos* (sc. *amicos*) *tụ [gratia] / illius* (sc. *Marcelli*) *scio plurimos haberẹ*. This seems to us a more attractive reconstruction than our original suggestion.

21. The reading of the word at the end of the line is difficult. *p̣lur[i]ṃiṣ* makes good sense and we now think that it might be possible to read it, although *ṃiṣ* is far from easy.

22-4. Compare Speidel and Seider (1988): *rogo domine dignum me iudices ut .... possim beneficio tuo ...* (a text also regarded by its editors as a draft letter).

25. *c̣[um ia]ṃ hiberna* (or *q[uom]*), *CEL* 105: this seems to us improbable.

226

Inv.no.85.001.a-c. Ten small fragments, the largest 48 x 39 mm.

These small fragments fall into three groups of which one (a) gives us the beginnings of 13 lines, the others, (b) and (c), the ends of 9 lines. We cannot establish the relationship between the three groups, however. We may have the beginnings and ends of lines in a single column of writing, with the middle of the lines missing (but we cannot match beginnings and ends of individual lines); or we may have the remains of a text in two columns, with the ends of lines in column i and the beginnings of lines in column ii surviving; or we may have drafts of two separate letters, possibly about the same subject, on the same leaf (cf. Sijpesteijn and Worp (1977), *RMR* 89 = *P.Dura* 66 = *CEL* 191).

There seems to be only one possible erasure, but the large diagonal strokes on the fragments containing the ends of lines suggest that the draft was crossed out. There are few clues to the subject-matter, but the occurrence of the word *desertores* is notable; perhaps Cerialis is writing to another unit commander about returning some deserters who have been apprehended (cf. a.10-12 note).

a.

illum .[
eṭ illi.[
traces
⟦ṛ⟧ ṣṭ..[
.ọlgi.[.]..[
..[
et[
f̣[ ]m..[
cui pr.[
desertoreṣ [
ad te cum [
mụs.. per .[
....ẹṭ[

b.

].. mili
]c̣ui
]m[.]..re.
]...
. . . .

c.

. . . .
] ad te ..
]gio suo
] per illum
]lum commị
].[..].

a.4. The deleted *r* (or possibly *a*) might be read as a *denarius* symbol, but this is palaeographically less plausible.

5. It is not clear how the first letter should be read, but *ụolgi* is impossible. Perhaps a centurial or *turma* symbol, in which case a name should follow; but we have found nothing suitable.

10-12. There appear to be traces of two letters after *mụs* in 12, of which the first might be *i* or *a*. If Cerialis were writing about apprehending deserters and sending them to a higher authority, these lines might be speculatively restored as follows: *desertoreṣ [ ] ad te cum [NN misi-]/muṣ*. For another possible reference to deserters see **320**.4 and note. For the treatment of deserters see *Digest* 49.16.5.1-8.

b.1. This might well be a reference to *mili[tes*.

3. The line might end *ọreṭ* or *ọreṣ*.

c.2. If we have drafts of more than one letter, it would be possible to see this as the end of an address to someone with a name ending *-gius*. Alternatively, it might be the end of (e.g.) *nauigio*.

3. *prop]ṭer* is also possible.

4. It is tempting to suggest *commị-/[lito(nes)*, cf. **318**.2 note, but we could just as easily have part of (e.g.) *committo*.

227

Inv.no.85.011.a-b. (a) 85 x 27 mm. (b) 85 x 30 mm. Plate XV.

These two fragments contain a draft by the hand identified as that of Cerialis. It is evident from the physical characteristics of the wood that they belong together, probably to half of a diptych, but they do not join. If the hand really is that of Cerialis (see **225**, introduction), the reference to *Cerialis mei* in b.2 presents problems of interpretation. The easiest solution is to suppose that Flavius Cerialis is writing about his son who is also called Cerialis. If the reference is to the prefect himself, the letter must be from Lepidina and so we must either have the hand of an amanuensis or, more probably, we must suppose that Cerialis drafted the letter for his wife. There is not enough surviving text to give much clue to the content. The substitution of *ualetudinem* for *natalem* in b.2 is odd and it looks as though it may be part of an excuse; that is, the writer cannot do something because of the birthday of Cerialis or, on second thoughts, his state of health. This is not easy; in particular it is difficult to see how to supply the negative which would be required with *licuerit*. The celebration of birthdays plays a significant part in the social life of the inhabitants of the *praetorium* in the frontier region (see **291**).

a. ⟦Flauius Cerialis⟧ *uacat*
uacat

b. . . . .
.[
⟦natalem⟧ ⸢ụaḷeṭuḍineṃ⸣ Cerialis mei
licuerit liquere
enim ⟦uobis⟧ ⸢tibi⸣ de animọ

a.1. The erased name is written at the top left of the fragment, as if this were the beginning of a letter, but the remainder of the surface, to the right and below, is blank.

b.2. *ụaḷeṭuḍineṃ* must be an interlinear addition and hence a substitute for the erased *natalem*. There is a trace to the left which could be read as *r* but this must belong to the preceding line, at the end of which we might restore *propter* to precede *ụaḷeṭuḍineṃ*.

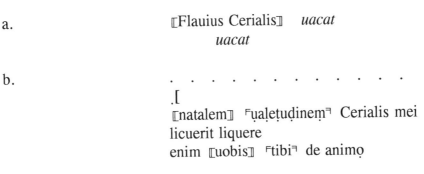

3. If there is a break in the sense after *licuerit*, what follows may mean something like "for I want you to be clear about my intentions", supplying *meo* (cf. *OLD*, s.v. *liqueo* 3b).

228

Inv.no.85.166. 42 x 32 mm.

A fragment, presumably of a letter, which is written in the hand identified as that of Cerialis.

. . .
traces
]ṣi quid
]iube
. . .

229

*Tab. Vindol.*I 51, Plate XI, 5. *CEL* 118.

A fragment containing two lines probably written by the hand identified as that of Cerialis.

. . . .
]. . .ạ quịc̣q[
]ṭeḷḷexcisse p̣[
. . . . .

2. Perhaps *in]ṭeḷḷexcisse*?

230

*Tab. Vindol.*I 52, Plate XI, 1. *CEL* 119.

Remains of three lines written in the hand identified as that of Cerialis.

. . . . .
traces
hoc coṇf̣ịṭẹọṛ [
]ẹ.ṣ f̣ạc̣ṭum[
. . . . .

231

*Tab. Vindol.*I 60. *CEL* 127.

Two joining fragments with some deletion, written by the hand identified as that of Cerialis.

. . . .
traces
]. enim [
] ⟦cetera⟧ [
]quem [
. . . .

232

*Tab. Vindol.*I 83. *CEL* 137.

A fragment written by the hand identified as that of Cerialis. Remains of four lines, with some deletion. Only *uig[* in line 2 is clear.

233

Inv.no.87.514. 176 x 34 mm. Plate XVI. *VRR* II, Plate X.

A diptych, complete at the top, left and right, containing a draft or file copy of a letter from Cerialis to Brocchus (B) and, at the right, written across the grain from top to bottom of the leaf, three lines of a list of foodstuffs (A). We think it most probable that (A) was written first and that the leaf, having been rotated through 90°, was then used for the draft of the letter without erasing the primary text. No doubt we have the end of the draft letter since there is a considerable space between the last line and the bottom of the leaf and we would not expect to find Cerialis' closing greeting. At least one line at the foot of the left-hand column must be lost, however, as is confirmed by the trace of one letter at the bottom edge; furthermore the items in (A) extend to the edge of the leaf and suggest the loss of part of the tablet which may have contained cash sums relating to the food items.

If, as seems likely, the two texts were written by the same hand, the list of foodstuffs suggests that the scribe may have been a member of Cerialis' household staff (perhaps a slave) rather than a member of the military unit. The hand may be the same as that in **235** and **240**; there is some use of ligature. Some examples of *o* are noteworthy, being made much like a small *c*; note in particular the first *o* in *Broccho*.

Cerialis asks Brocchus to send him some *plagae* (see note to line B.4) and, perhaps, to repair something (either the *plagae* or something else depending on what was in the missing part of the text).

A.

↓ ạḷịcas [
c̣ạḷlum [
uṇgellas [

"gruel ...
pork-crackling ...
trotters ..."

1. *ạḷịcas*: the reading is not certain, especially as it is impossible to be sure which ink traces belong to the list and which to the draft letter. The easiest reading of the last 4 letters is *-uias* but we know of no suitable word with this ending. If lines 2 and 3 are correctly read we expect a foodstuff and *alicas* would seem to fit the traces; for *alica* see **193**.4 note. However, if more of the traces at the left belong to this word (and not to the end of the letter), the reading may be *ḷạc̣ṭucas* (lettuces).

2. *c̣ạḷlum*: this is rind or crackling, usually of the pig, which Apicius, 7.1.5 associates with *ungellae* (see note to line 3). However, the same problem faces us as in the preceding line and an alternative reading which we cannot rule out is *ạḷịum* ("garlic").

3. *uṇgellas*: these are pigs' trotters, see Apicius 4.5.2 and cf. André (1981), 137, note 43. Pigs were certainly kept as livestock (**180**.27, **183**.4) and supplied meat (**191**.6, **186**.21), cf. *VRR* III, 113 .

B.

i
Flauius Cerialis Broccho
suo salutem
si me amas frater rogo
ṃittas mihi plagas
].[
. . . .

ii
fortissime *uacat*
frusta exeṛc̣ịas
uacat

"Flavius Cerialis to his Brocchus, greetings. If you love me, brother, I ask that you send me some hunting-nets (?) ... you should repair (?) the pieces very strongly."

i.2. For the position of *suo salutem* see **234**.i.2, **243**.2, **248**.i.2, **261**.2.

4. *plagas*: of the numerous meanings of *plaga* recorded in *OLD* only *plaga*², 3 and 4a ("counterpane" and "hunting-net") need be considered here. The text itself offers no basis on which to choose between these possibilities, but it is perhaps more likely that officers would be corresponding about hunting-nets than domestic soft-furnishings. For a similar preoccupation see *O.Wâdi Fawâkhir* 14.3-8 and, in this region of Britain, *RIB* I 1041 (Stanhope), I 1905 (Birdoswald); see *RIB* I 1005-6 (Cumberland quarries, a crude drawing of a stag) and the relief from Housesteads showing a stag confronted by a hunting-net (Bruce (1875), no.243 and cf. no.271 (Vindolanda)); in general see Davies (1989), 191-3, Hodgson (1976), 22, (1977), Dannell and Wild (1987), 68. In *P.Abinn.* 6.11-12 (mid-fourth century)

the writer notes that hunting-nets are stored in the fort at Dionysias "with the standards" and asks the officer Abinnaeus to send him some in order to deal with gazelles which are destroying crops. Furthermore, as *VRR* II, 38 notes, the dedication by Aelius Brocchus to Diana (*CIL* 3.4360) perhaps suggests a predilection for hunting. The only circumstantial evidence in favour of supposing that we are dealing with counterpanes is the possibility that some of the clothing supplied to Vindolanda came from Brocchus (**196**.15 note, **207**.4 note).

ii.1. Nothing is visible after *fortissime*, which may have been preceded by *quam* ("as strongly as possible").

2. *frusta exeṛc̣ịas*: see Adams (1994). There may be an interpunct after *frusta*, but since it would be the only example in this text it is perhaps better to regard it as unintentional. In the word which follows *exe* is certain as is *as* at the end of the line. The letter following *exe* has a long descender and must be *q* or *r*; *r* is difficult because we cannot see the head of the letter, but we have rejected *q* because it seems impossible to read the following letter as *u* or to supply a word which would make sense in the context. If our reading *exeṛc̣ịas* is correct, there is more space between *r* and *c* than might be expected; the explanation of this may be that the list (A) had already been written. The traces are compatible with our reading of *c̣ị*, though they hardly compel it. We suggest that this verb is to be taken as an alternative spelling of *exsarcias*, see *TLL* V.2, 1827. *Frusta* can then be understood as broken or torn sections; the word is used of torn pieces of clothing (Nepotianus 1.19, *cum frustis tunicae*).

234

Inv.no.85.118. 180 x 50 mm.

Six fragments of a diptych containing a draft of a letter in two columns from Flavius Cerialis to September, presumably Caecilius September of **252-3** (cf. A.R.Birley (1991), 98-9). The space after the last line in the right-hand column probably indicates that we have the end of the message proper, to which Cerialis would have added a closure in the fair copy. The left-hand column is broader than the right and overruns the fold. The hand is probably the same as that of **239**. The text appears to contain an interesting example of a phonetic error probably caused by dictation (see note to line ii.2); if so, this is the only clear evidence in the tablets for the use of dictation, which we suppose was common. If the content of the second column relates directly to what is in the first (which depends on how many lines are lost), Cerialis may be saying that tomorrow in accordance with September's wish he intends to buy, or to send the money for, some items in order to help them endure the stormy weather. The precaution is appropriate to October, the month in which Cerialis is writing.

i

Flauius Cerialis Septembri
suo saluṭem´
quod uis domine c̣ṛaṣ
id eṣṭ ịịị Ṇọnas Ọc̣[t]ó-
bres merc̣ . . pạ . . [
. . . .

ii

qui ferạmụṣ ṭeṃ-
pestates ⟦et hiem⟧ ⸢etiam⸣ si
molestae sint

"Flavius Cerialis to his September, greetings. Tomorrow, which is 5 October, as you wish my lord, I will provide some goods (?) ... by means of which (?) we may endure the storms even if they are troublesome."

i.1. *September*: for Caecilius September see **252** introduction and line 1 note.

2. For the mark after *salutem* see above, p.57.

3. For the sense in which we take *quod uis*, see perhaps Petronius, *Sat*. 137.9, *quod uis nummis praesentibus opta, et ueniet*.

4. *ịịị*: abrasion and dirt make the numeral very difficult to discern. We suggest what we think is the most probable reading.

Ọc̣[t]ó-: the ending *-bres* in line 5 requires one of the last four months of the year and only October and December are palaeographically plausible. The first letter shows no sign of the *hasta* of *d* and is much better read as *o*; the descender which can be seen must belong to the *r* of *c̣raṣ* in line 3.

5. *merc*..: the reading of the first four letters is secure and a reference to the purchase of some item is appropriate. Although *mercạṛ* is possible, it is very difficult to read *i* after this; other possibilities are *mercẹṃ* (the final *m* of *mercẹṃ* is not easy but it compares quite well with the last letter of *salutem* in line 2), *mercạṛẹṭ* or *mercạṛẹ* (but the non-deponent form is very rare, see *TLL* VIII 799.46).

pạ..[: the reading of *pa* presents no difficulty and thereafter we have the tops of two letters either of which might be read as *a* or *r*. We suggest the restoration *mercẹṃ pạṛạ[bo* and the interpretation that Cerialis is intending to supply September with some goods or with some money (if *mercẹṃ* is to be taken in the sense of *mercedem*, see *LS*, s.v., *TLL* VIII, 852) so that he can purchase something and send it back to Cerialis (for exchange between these two officers see **252**). For the verb *paro* cf. perhaps the metaphorical use of *merces* ... *parata* in Lucan, *Phars*. 7.303.

ii.1. We probably have the instrumental use of *qui* here, see Adams (1994).

f̣ẹṛạmụṣ: despite the abrasion of the writing, this reading is probable and allows space for the reading of *tem* in the very indistinct traces at the end of the line; palaeographically this can only be regarded as a guess but the beginning of line 2 allows no other plausible reading.

2. *pestates*: the first letter in the line is clearly *p*. The reading of *ṭẹṃpestates* is supported by the erasure ⟦*et hiem*⟧ which indicates that the scribe began to write *et hiemes*. *TLL* VI 2774.12-20 notes that grammarians and glossaries equate *hiems* and *tempestas* and gives the meaning *uentus fortis* (s.v.IA); the only citation with the words used together is Rufinus, *Hist.mon.epil.* 7, p.462a. The supralinear substitution of *etiam* strongly suggests that this was a phonetic dictation error (for which see Milne and Skeat (1938), 52, 55, and cf. Turner (1987), p.17).

3. For *molestus* used in relation to weather see e.g. Cicero, *Att*. 5.12.1.

235

Inv.no.86.358.a. 95 x 16 mm.

A fragment containing the first line of a draft or copy of a letter from Flavius Cerialis to Similis. He must surely be the same person as Flavius Similis, the writer of **254** and **286**; note also the letter from Rhenus, the slave of Similis, **347**. There is no evidence for Similis' rank or unit and these texts strongly suggest that he was not at Vindolanda.

The hand could well be the same as that in **240**, also a draft or copy of a letter from Cerialis. There are also similarities to the hands of **233** and **234** but we think the latter unlikely to be the same hand and we are unsure about the former.

F̣ḷauius Cerialis Simili sụọ
traces
. . . .

2. The top of an ascender is visible below *r* of *Cerialis* and this will belong to the first line of the body of the letter. Possible traces further to the right, may be part of *salutem*.

236

Inv.no.85.150.a-c. (a) 60 x 82 mm. (b) and (c) small fragments.

A draft or copy of a letter from Cerialis on what must have been the left-hand portion of a diptych. There are two tie-holes in the left margin and two notches in the left-hand edge. The name of the addressee has not survived (*fratẹṛ* in line 3 suggests that he might be another prefect), nor is there enough of the text to be sure of the subject. Cerialis seems to be saying that he has been waiting for someone or something to arrive. The hand bears some noticeable resemblance to that of **225-32** and it is therefore possible that this is Cerialis' autograph. The two small fragments (b) and (c) cannot be placed. The back is blank.

a.

Flauius Cerịa[lis
[salutem
iịị K(alendas) fratẹṛ .ụ.[
in horam [
exspectaui [
res mihi ..[
[*c.4*]..ọḥṇ[
[*c.5*]r.ṣ[
..[
. . . .

b.

. . .
]exig[

].sum[

. . .

c. . . .

].er[

. . .

"Flavius Cerialis to ..., greetings. On the 3rd (?) day before the Kalends, brother, I have been waiting ... until the *n*th hour ...... from our cohort (?) ... "

a.2. No trace of writing survives but the space between line 1 and the beginning of the message guarantees that the lost portion at the right will have contained *salutem* or *suo salutem*.

3. The remains of at least two letters are visible before *k*, of which the first has a complete vertical. The only plausible readings would seem to be *p̣ṛ(idie)* or *iịị*. As for the first, *p* is possible but *r* looks very difficult. We could have three digits but what looks like the top of the third may, in fact, be the misaligned top of the vertical of *k*. However that may be, we think it impossible that the word *fratẹṛ* could be placed in the middle of the date and therefore assume that the month-name was omitted because the recipient is expected to know which month Cerialis meant (cf. **199**.1, *O.Bu Njem* 91).

.ụ.: the first trace might be *i* or *d* and the third trace looks like *s*. If the first trace is dirt rather than ink, we might simply have *uṣ[que* (see note to line 4), though this would make the line very short.

4. *in horam* may well have been preceded by *usque* at the end of line 3 though this is not essential, see *B.Afr*. 78.9, *Caesar in horam decimam commoratus*. An ordinal number will presumably have followed.

5-7. One might imagine a restoration such as *[ut* (or *dum* or *si forte*) *mitte-]/res mihi* ("I waited for you to send to me ..." or "I waited in case you might send to me ..."). In line 7 *e]x̣ c̣oḥ(orte) ṇ[ostra* might be feasible.

237

Inv.no.85.180. 125 x 43 mm. *VRR* II, Plate X.

A fragment containing the beginning of a draft or copy of a letter. The hand, a very right-sloping cursive, cannot immediately be identified with any other in the archive, but it does bear some resemblance to **242**.

Flauius Cerialis

. . . .

238

Inv.no.85.186.b. 97 x 45 mm.

The beginning of a draft letter from Cerialis to a person whose name has not survived. The hand is not securely identifiable with any other in the Cerialis correspondence; it is similar in character to that of **248** and **291**, but cannot be the same since the latter come from Brocchus and Severa. The use of interpunct is notable. The draft seems to end with a deletion and to have been abandoned. There are traces of a few illegible letters on the back of the lower part of the leaf, but since a draft will not have contained an address, these probably belong to a different text or draft.

Flauius · Cerialis .[..]..[
salutem
si · sollicitudini · meae domin[e
explicạṭạ ẹsṭ ⟦..⟧
. . . .

3-4. If the readings are correct, the syntax would have demanded a feminine noun as the subject of *explicạṭạ ẹsṭ*, e.g. *cura* or *ratio*.

The whole of line 4 may be deleted with a single, horizontal stroke. If not, the last two or three letters are certainly struck through. At the end perhaps two digits with a superscript dash, or *n* with a dash, for *n(ostra)*, or *a*. if the apparent superscript dash is not ink.

239

Inv.no.85.194.a. 154 x 41 mm. Plate XVIII.

Two joining fragments containing the beginning of a draft or copy of a letter from Flavius Cerialis to a person only traces of whose name survive. It is probably written by the same hand as **234**, however, and may also be to September (see note to line 1). The back of the smaller fragment has traces of writing, apparently including *m* with a superscript dash (= *m(odius)*), which may suggest that this side was used for an account before or after the copy of the letter was written (cf. **233**, **299**). The writer appears to have used an apex over *a* in *Flauius*. There are three small scraps which probably do not belong with this text (see **402**).

Fláuius Cerialiṣ .[..].[*c.3*]ṛị sụó
salutem
.ẹṇ..unculam domine
. . . .

1. Traces of two letters of the end of the name of the addressee survive, of which the first is probably *r*, judging by the length of the descender; the descender of the first letter

of the name may be from *s*, in which case *S[ep]ṭ[emb]ṛị* suggests itself. On the small fragment the shape of the apex over *o* of *suo* compares well with that in *Fláuius*.

3. *.ẹṇ..unculam*: at the left there is a long horizontal bar which must belong to the first letter in the line and it can hardly be read as anything but *t*. The fourth and fifth letters are best read as *ṣị* although we cannot exclude *c̣ṭ*. This suggests *ṭẹṇṣịunculam* (*p̣ẹṇṣịunculam*, a rare word meaning "a small payment" seems to be excluded). We cannot explain this satisfactorily. *tensa* is a type of wagon (see *OLD*, s.v.) but this does not seem to be a legitimate formation of a diminutive. We note that the word *tensio* is used by Hyginus, *Gromat.*, *init.* with *papilionum* for pitching tents and we wonder whether we might have a diminutive indicating a pitched tent; for the derivation of a concrete meaning from an abstract noun perhaps compare *coriatio* in **343**.iv.40 and note. The word *tensio* is also well-attested in medical senses (*OLD*, s.v.) and that could be the meaning here (cf. perhaps **294**.6).

240

Inv.no.87.579. 51 x 30 mm.

A fragment of the left-hand side of a diptych containing the beginning of a draft or copy of a letter from Flavius Cerialis. The hand could well be the same as that which wrote **235** and perhaps **233**. The spacing suggests that the traces below the name probably belong to the first line of the body of the letter.

Flauius Cer[ialis
[salutem
].[.].[
. . . .

3. The traces below *Flauius Cer[ialis* are compatible with *ṣ[a]ḷ[utem* but their position on the line is much too far to the left for this to be possible.

241

*Tab. Vindol.*I 29. *CEL* 97.

The beginning of a draft or copy of a letter from Cerialis. We have been unable to identify the hand with any of those used in other letters which originate from Cerialis.

F̣ḷạuius Ceṛ[ialis
. . . .

242

Inv.no.85.160.a. 225 x 51 mm. Plate XVI. *VRR* II, Plate VII.

Two fragments of a diptych, containing a letter which presents problems of reading and interpretation. What is legible is only a small part of the text at the beginning of the main part of the letter and, if *ueni* (line 2) is to be taken as an imperative, the writer is instructing someone to come to Vindolanda in connection with a *numeratio*. The hand in which the text is written bears some similarity to that of **291**, **248** etc., but since the latter come from the household of Brocchus and Severa, it can hardly be the same hand (note, too, that it uses interpunct more consistently). The name of the sender, on the reverse, which suggests that the letter is not a draft or copy, is certainly not Brocchus. If it is Cerialis, as it seems to be, it is not easy to explain how a letter from him (a) ended up at Vindolanda and (b) was addressed to someone from his own cohort (see notes to ii.2 and back 2). Of the four lines on the right-hand portion, the first is so abraded as to be illegible for all practical purposes; the other three could well be written by the same hand as **225-32**, which we have identified as the hand of Cerialis. The message seems to be dated at the end (line ii.4) and this may be explained by the supposition that Cerialis was instructing someone to return to Vindolanda at short notice. In short, it is possible that we have a letter from Cerialis perhaps to a centurion of his own cohort, absent but not too far away, instructing him to return for some official duty; and that the letter was brought back to Vindolanda by its recipient and deposited there.

i

. . . . . .

c̣ṛạṣ · ḅẹne mane Vindo-
landam ueni · ut
numerationi · cen-

ii

. . . . . .

traces
*m*²? uale mi F̣elic̣ị..[
kạṛịṣṣịṃe *uacat*
...... Ṣẹpṭembṛẹṣ

Back:

. . . . . .

*m*¹? ṿịịịị Ḅạṭ(auorum)
[a] F̣ḷạụịọ C̣eṛịale *traces*

"Come to Vindolanda tomorrow, early in the morning in order to ... the payment (?) of the century (?) ... (2nd hand?) Farewell, my dearest Felicio (?) ... September. (Back, 1st hand) ... of the 9th Cohort of Batavians, from Flavius Cerialis, prefect (?)."

i.1. If the letter is from Cerialis (see note to back 2), there should be some chance that the missing opening address may survive on another fragment. We have considered **237** and **240**, of which the former was found in the same area as **242**. In the first, the size and lack of an addressee seem unpromising, although the hand is similar; the hand of **240** looks distinctly different.

This line commences further to the left than the two following lines which would normally suggest that it is the beginning of the message proper. At the beginning of the line only the bottoms of letters are preserved; *r* and *s* are virtually certain and the first trace is compatible with the bottom of *c*. If we read *c̣ṛạṣ*, which we think is the most attractive reading, we could envisage this as the opening of the message, albeit somewhat abrupt. We suggest that this message was sent to someone at a place very close to Vindolanda, perhaps an officer in charge of a small detachment outposted at a fortlet (see ii.2 note and cf. **154**, Bowman and Thomas (1991), 68 and note 35).

2. *ueni*: this could be either an imperative or a first person singular perfect. We prefer to suppose that we have an imperative and that the note was brought back to Vindolanda by its recipient.

3. *numerationi · cen[*: there may be an apex mark over the *a* of *numerationi*. The word can refer either to counting or, in a financial sense, to payment or accounting. Either would suit the context here. In the first sense, it might refer to a head-count on which strength reports such as **154** were based. *RMR* 65.10, a summary of dispositions from Dura-Europos (*c.* AD 240), *ṛel numerare*, might be such a reference (the *denarius* symbol at the end of the line does not look a plausible reading in this context). In that case *cen-/[turiae* or *cen-/[turiarum*, with the end of the word coming in the first line of col.ii, would seem the obvious restoration. In the financial sense, we note Tacitus, *Hist.*1.58, *Vitellius ... uacationes centurionibus ex fisco numerat* (cf. Frontinus, *Str.* 1.11.4) and the *Feriale Duranum*, *RMR* 117.i.6-7, *[vii Idus] Ianu[arias quod detur emeritis honesta missio cum usu priui]legio[rum] ụẹl numẹ[re]n[t]ụṛ [militibus stipendia ...]*. These would suggest the restoration *numerationi cen-/[turionum (-ibus)*, referring to payments made to the centurions either for special purposes, such as *uacationes*, or as *stipendium* (for the dates of such pay-days see *RMR* p.266). In either case, the sense which we envisage seems to require a verb such as *praesis* or *intersis*. The other possibility which we have considered is *cen[sus* (cf. **304**), but we have not found any example of the use of *numeratio* in this connection.

ii.1. Only the bottoms of letters survive.

2-3. *uale mi* is certain, as are the following *feli*. If this is the start of *feliciter* or *felicissime* (for which there is no exact parallel in the tablets), we should have to take *mi* as for *mihi*. The phrase does occur in *CEL* 7.ii.17, *uale mihi Macedo*, but it is much more likely that *mi* is a vocative as elsewhere in this phrase (e.g. **247**.2, **288**.4, and cf. Cicero *Verr.* 3.155, quoted in **214**.3-4 note). If so, we can only suggest that it was followed by a personal name (cf. *ChLA* X 417, where the emperor addresses the prefect of Egypt as *mi Maxime*). There is evidence in the tablets for a centurion named Felicio in the Ninth Cohort of Batavians, see **166**.1 and note. We are reasonably confident of *kạṛịṣṣịṃe* in line 3 and it may be that all we have is *uale mi Felicio karissime*.

4. We are confident of *bṛẹṣ*, which must mean that we have a date here, cf. *CEL* 8, and *ChLA* XI 488 (where the date is preceded by *dat(um)*). *ṣẹpṭem* best fits the preceding traces but the letters at the beginning of the line are very abraded; perhaps the most likely reading is a number followed by *nonas*.

Back 1. The name of the addressee presumably stood above this line on the lost part of the leaf. There is one possible trace of a letter at the extreme top left corner. The numeral is reasonably clear and may have a superscript dash above it. There is no sign of *coh* preceding.

2. If, as we think, this is the name of the sender, it is noteworthy that it is not written with an upward slant. *io* as the end of the *gentilicium* looks reasonably clear. In *C̣eṛịale* the end seems secure but *ṛị* are particularly difficult. The first letter could be read as *g* and this suggests the possibility *G̣ẹṇịale* (cf. **256** from Genialis to Cerialis), but *ṇị* is even more difficult than *ṛị*. What follows is probably compatible with the expected *p̣ṛạẹf̣(ecto)*.

243

Inv.no.86.500. 94 x 40 mm.

A fragment containing the beginning of a letter from Brocchus to Cerialis. We would normally expect this to be the left-hand side of a diptych but the right-hand edge appears to contain two v-shaped notches, which would indicate that this is the right-hand half. If these are deliberate, it may be that the message was a short one and was written on half a tablet (cf. **247**). An alternative explanation is that we have a letter like that of Octavius (**343**) which began on the right-hand side of the leaf. The hand which wrote this fragment, however, seems to us very likely to be that of **244**, **248** and **291**, and if this is correct, the scribe surely would not have begun at the right, contrary to his normal habit. That the writers of both **248** and **243** put the words *suo salutem* on the second line of the text is a further argument in favour of their identity.

[Aelius B]ṛocchus C̣eṛịali
suó saluṭem´
] ⸢fráter⸣ [
. . . .

2. *saluṭem´*: for the oblique mark after *salutem* (here not certain) see above, p.57.
3. *fráter*: there is no sign of writing in the line after *frater* which is placed very high in relation to line 2, and we suggest that it is an interlinear addition. The mark over *a* is almost horizontal but is probably deliberate in view of the use of the apex elsewhere.

244

Inv.no.85.092. 114 x 50 mm.

The right-hand part of a double leaf containing the end of a letter from Aelius Brocchus to Cerialis. Although so little of **244** survives for comparison, we are reasonably confident that the hand is the same as that of **291** even though the form of *u* is different and there are no apex marks. For the hands in the letters from Brocchus and his wife Severa see **243**, **292**, introduction. The lower part of the leaf, which no doubt contained the closing greeting, is lost.

. . . .
Seuera mea uos salutat
. . . .

Back: Flauio Cerialị *traces?*
. . . .

"... my Severa greets you. (Back) To Flavius Cerialis, prefect (?) ..."

1. Cf. **530**.

Back. The bottoms of all the letters of the name are lost but there is no doubt about the reading. We are not sure whether the following marks are ink but if so they can only be read as *p̣ṛạẹf̣(ecto)*.

245

Inv.no.85.193. 56 x 31 mm.

A fragment of the right-hand portion of a letter almost certainly written by the same hand as that of **292** to Lepidina from Severa. The address on the back may indicate that it was sent to Cerialis, not to Lepidina, and in that case it would be natural to suppose that it came from Aelius Brocchus. Not enough survives to indicate the subject of the correspondence. There are four other fragments which may be by the same hand and may be associated with this text, but we have failed to establish any convincing joins and have therefore treated them as parts of separate texts (**246, 403**, **404**, **406**).

. . . . .
[..]̣.[..]̣.[.]..[
..ró et ḍ[
tercurar[
. . . . .

Back: [Flauio Ce]ṛịạ[li
p̣raef(ecto) coh(ortis)
. . . .

2. There is also occasional use of the apex in **292** (e.g. *Brocchó*, a.i.3).

3. A possible restoration would be *fra]ter* followed by some part of the verb *curar[e*, but there are obviously other possibilities. At the left edge there may be a trace of a letter from the end of a line in the left-hand column.

Back 1. We have only the bottoms of letters but the restoration of *Ce]ṛịạ[li* is very probable, especially in view of the title following.

246

Inv.no.85.256. 82 x 23 mm.

A fragment containing what is presumably the beginning of a letter from Aelius Brocchus. It is written by the same hand as that of **292** from Severa to Lepidina, and may be in the same hand as **245** to Cerialis and a few other fragments (see **245**, introduction). Although we cannot prove that this fragment belongs to a letter to Cerialis, it is overwhelmingly probable that it does.

Aelius Bṛọc̣c̣ḥ[us
. . . .

247

*Tab. Vindol.*I 25, Plate V, 4 and 5. *CEL* 93.

Part of a leaf containing the foot of the right-hand column of a letter to Cerialis. The notch in the left-hand edge looks deliberate and probably indicates a letter written (or concluding on?) a half-diptych, cf. **243**. The evidence relating to Cerialis' wife Lepidina and the pattern of expression in **291** and **244** make it clear that the reading of line 1 in the *ed. pr.* was wide of the mark, as is that of *CEL* 93.1. The first hand is very idiosyncratic and we cannot parallel it in any of the other tablets; *a* in *tuam*, for example, is very odd.

. . . .
Ḷepidinam tuam a me saluṭa
m² ualẹ ṃị ḍomine
frater karissime

Back: *m¹* Flauio C̣ẹṛiali
traces
. . . . .

"Greet your Lepidina from me. (2nd hand) May you be well, my lord and dearest brother. (Back, 1st hand) To Flavius Cerialis ..."

1. *a me saluṭa*: cf. **260**.6.

2. The hand may well be the same as the second hand of **248**, in which case it is likely to be the hand of Aelius Brocchus (see **248**.ii.12-4 note).

ualẹ ṃị ḍomine: in the *ed. pr.* we hesitantly suggested *uaḷeạṣ*. The reading adopted, which was suggested by Cugusi (1987), 118 and *CEL* 93.2, is certainly preferable, although the form of *m* is decidedly odd.

Back 2. Below the address to Cerialis there are traces at the bottom edge of the fragment which we did not notice in the *ed. pr.* These are too exiguous to hazard a reading.

248

*Tab. Vindol.*I 21, Plate III,6, IV,2. *CEL* 89. R.E.Birley (1990), fig. 14. *VRR* II, Plate VIII.

This letter from Niger and Brocchus is almost certainly written by the same hand as that of **243** (from Brocchus), **291** (from Claudia Severa to Lepidina) and **244**. Whether it is in the same hand as **295** (Oppius Niger to Priscinus) is discussed in the introduction to **295**, where the identity of the various persons in the tablets called Niger is also discussed. We think that Niger in the present text is more likely to be Valerius Niger (**465**) than Oppius Niger.

i

Niger et Brocchus C̣eriạḷị
suo salutem´
óptamus frater it quot
acturus es felicis-
simum sit erit autem
quom et uotis nostris

ii

conueniat hoc
pro te precari et tú
sis dignissimus con-
sulari n(ostro) utique mạ-
turius occurres
m[2] op<t>amus frater
bene ụalẹṛẹ ṭẹ
domine *traces* ṇọ . ẹx̣ṣp̣ẹc̣

Back: *m*[1] [Fl]ạụ[io] Ceṛịạḷ[i
[prae]f̣(ecto) coḥ(ortis)
traces?

"Niger and Brocchus to their Cerialis, greeting. We pray, brother, that what you are about to do will be most successful. It will be so, indeed, since it is both in accord with our wishes to make this prayer on your behalf and you yourself are most worthy. You will assuredly meet our governor quite soon. (2nd hand) We pray, our lord and brother, that you are in good health ... expect ... (?) (Back, 1st hand) To Flavius Cerialis, prefect of the cohort ..."

i.2. For the high mark, like an apex, after the *m* of *salutem* see above, p.57.

3. With the additional evidence of the other texts written by this hand, we now regard the mark over *o* as a deliberate apex (likewise *tu* in line 8); see above, pp.57-61.

ii.9-11. A.R.Birley (1991), 89 suggests the possibility that the governor was in the region of Vindolanda, which is certainly plausible.

10. *n(ostro)* is abbreviated to *n* with a superscript dash, as happens frequently in the tablets. In the *ed.pr.* we stated that this was preceded and followed by a medial point but we

are now less confident that these marks are ink, although the same phenomenon may occur in **255**.i.3.

12-4. The reading and interpretation of the closure remains problematical. It is odd that *domine* is written further out to the left than the rest of the sentence and there seems to be a space between it and *bene*. A possible explanation of this is that the writer began to write a normal formula which would have fitted on two short lines but then decided that he wanted something longer; since he was very short of space, he began his third line (14) as far to the left as possible, but even so failed to get it all on the line. This involves understanding *domine* as the beginning of line 14 and supposing that there is continuous writing from *domine* to *exspec-* which has simply faded, and that the whole of lines 12-4 were written by the same hand. It is possible that this is the same hand as that of **247**.2-3, in which case it is likely to be the hand of Brocchus.

12. We now think *op<t>amus* preferable, surprising though the error is.

13. *ṭẹ* can be read provided that we accept that it was fouled by the subsequent writing below. The order is odd but not unparalleled, see **258**.4-5.

14. The traces after *domine* are very faint and the reading is uncertain. If it is correct, we must have part of the verb *exspecto*, but there is no room for anything after *exspec* in this line; there may be faint traces below on the broken corner of the leaf. Possibly the writer intended the imperative *exspecta*.

Back 17. There are possible traces of the name of the unit, which might be read as *ṿịịịị Ḅạ[t(auorum)*. There may be traces in the bottom left-hand corner which could be part of *a Broccho*, but we can see no sign of the name of Niger.

249

Inv.no.87.695. 75 x 22 mm.

Part of the left-hand side of a leaf containing the opening of a letter from Oppius Niger to Cerialis. Oppius Niger is the man who, apparently at a later date, sent **295** to Priscinus, but although the hand of the present letter bears considerable resemblance to that of **295**, it is probably not the same (*e* in particular being very different in the two texts). For discussion of the identity of persons with this *cognomen* in the tablets see the introduction to **295**.

[O]ppius Niger Ceriali suo
[salut]ẹ[m
]ẹ[
. . . .

1. There is a large space between the name of the sender and the addressee, cf. **259**.1 and note.

2. It is odd that there is no sign of the top of *s* in *salutem*.

250

*Tab. Vindol.*I 22, Plate IV, 1 and 3. *CEL* 90.

A letter of recommendation from Karus to Cerialis. In our commentary to the *ed. pr.* we suggested that the writer might be Iulius Karus of *AE* 1951.88. However **251** has now produced evidence for a correspondent of Cerialis with the name Claudius Karus and it is much more probable that this is our man; he is likely to be a fellow-prefect. On *litterae commendaticiae* note, in addition to the bibliography cited in the *ed. pr.*, Speidel and Seider (1988), Vendrand-Voyer (1983). In the *ed. pr.* (p.106) we stated that *Tab. Vindol.*I 54 (= **526**) and 55 (= **173**) might also be *litterae commendaticiae*; in neither case do we now think this probable and the latter is surely a request for *commeatus*.

Some significant changes from the *ed. pr.*, especially in lines 5-10, are signalled in the notes.

i

[*c.4*]ịus Karuṣ C̣[e]ṛ[iali
[su]ọ *uacat* ṣ[alutem
[*c.4*]brigionus petiṭ a ṃẹ
[domi]ne ut eum tibi coṃ-
meṇdareṭ rogo ergo do-
miṇẹ ṣị quod a te petieriṭ
[u]ẹḷịṣ ẹi subscribere
Anniọ Ẹquesṭri (centurioni) ṛegi-
onarịo Luguualio ro-
go ut eum commen-

ii

[*c.4*] ḍigneriṣ .[...
[...].que nom[ine
ḍebetorem m[e tibi
obligaturus ọp[to
te felicissimum
bene ⟦f⟧ ụạḷẹṛẹ
uacat
m² uale frater

Back: *m¹* [C]ẹriali
praẹf̣(ecto)

" ...ius Karus to his Cerialis, greetings. ... Brigionus (?) has requested me, my lord, to recommend him to you. I therefore ask, my lord, if you would be willing to support him in what he has requested of you. I ask that you think fit to commend him to Annius Equester, centurion in charge of the region, at Luguvalium, [by doing which] you will place me in debt to you both in his name (?) and my own (?). I pray that you are enjoying the best of fortune and are in good health. (2nd hand) Farewell, brother. (Back, 1st hand) To Cerialis, prefect."

i.1. For the position of *su]ọ* and *ṣ[alutem* cf. *ChLA* IV 245.

3. We noted in the *ed. pr.* that there is no guarantee that this is not the end of a longer name beginning in the lost part at the left. The name Brigio probably occurs in **188**.10, however, and this makes it probable that what we have here is a latinised version of this name, perhaps even referring to the same person. If it was preceded by a *gentilicium* here it must have been either short or abbreviated.

4-5. The writer must have intended *commendarem* (cf. the note in the *ed. pr.*).

5-10. Our doubts about the reading and interpretation of this passage were signalled in the *ed. pr.*, particularly the notes to lines 7 and 9-10. We remain doubtful that there is room to restore *ut* at the beginning of line 7. We now accept a suggestion of Adams that we understand *rogo* in line 5 to be followed by *si ... uelis*, and that we understand a break in the sense after *subscribere*, for which the meaning "write in support of to ..." is difficult to defend; we now think that the marks after *ro* in line 9 are not ink; *quod a te petieriṭ* will then be parenthetical, which removes the problem posed by *si quod* (see *Tab.Vindol.*I, p.73).

7. The reading *dign]eris* instead of *uelis*, proposed by Cugusi (1987), 116 (cf. *CEL* 90), is impossible.

i.10-ii.12. We still favour the restoration suggested in the *ed. pr.*, ... *ut eum commen-/[dare] ḍigneriṣ ẹ[ius / me]ọque nom[ine* etc., assuming that no line has been lost; *qu]ọque* (suggested by Cugusi (1987), 116, cf. *CEL* 90) is also possible.

15-6. A detached fragment from the end of the line, which does not appear in *Tab.Vindol.*I, Plate IV, has *um*.

Cugusi (1987), 117 and *CEL* 90 has suggested a different reading of line 16: *bene {f} ụ⟦ạḷẹṛẹ⟧*. We think it more likely that the writer began to repeat *felicissimum*, realised his mistake after writing *fel*, perhaps ineffectually rubbed out *f* and then corrected *el* to *ua* in order to begin *ualere*. It is not entirely certain that the majority of *ualere* has been erased (by mistake, according to Cugusi, *CEL*); the apparent crossing-out might simply be the wood-grain.

Back 18. The position of *[C]ẹriali* suggests that there was not room for *Flauio* to have been written before it, but this is the only clear example of omission of the *gentilicium*.

251

Inv.no.85.007. 81 x 15 mm.

A fragment containing the opening of a letter from Claudius Karus to Cerialis. It is very likely that Claudius Karus is to be identified with the writer of **250**, a letter of recommendation to Cerialis. Karus was presumably a prefect of another unit but cannot be further identified (see **250**, introduction). The hand of the present text is a very much better one than that of **250**. It is notable that it uses two distinct forms of *l*, the first angular, the second with hooks at top and bottom.

C̣laudius Karuṣ C̣eriali sụ[o

. . . .

1. Despite the faintness of the last two letters of *Karụṣ*, there is no doubt about the reading.

252

Inv.no.85.017. 160 x 30 mm. Plate XII. A.R.Birley (1991), 98-9 and Plate IIIa.

A diptych containing a letter from September to Cerialis, written in an interesting hand; noteworthy is the form of *a* (see Fig.1, col.2). It is also notable that the left-hand column extended well beyond the middle of the tablet. We have the end of the letter in the short, right-hand column. The loss of some of the address on the back of the right-hand side indicates that part of the leaf is lost at the foot, in which case we may have lost two to three lines in the left-hand column.

If the *gentilicium* is correctly read as Caecilius (see note to line 1), Cerialis' correspondent is probably identical with the man of the same name who is attested in command of a cohort in Syria in AD 88 (*PME* I, C26, A.R.Birley (1991), 98-9). September's reference to his having sent something *per equitem* may indicate that he had cavalry under his command, as a prefect of an *ala* or *cohors equitata*; it is possible, however, that he could have used an intermediary who was not a member of his own unit. For other texts possibly concerning this person see **234**, **253**, **298**.

i

C̣ạẹc̣ilius September Ceriali suo
salutem
].[*c.4*].....
. . . .

ii

per equitem
ad te mịsi
m^2 uale dominẹ fraṭẹr

Back: m^1 F̣ḷạuịọ C̣ẹṛịạḷị
. . . . .

"Caecilius September to his Cerialis, greetings. ... I have sent to you ... through a cavalryman. (2nd hand) Farewell, my lord and brother. (Back, 1st hand) To Flavius Cerialis."

i.1. The reading of the *gentilicium* as *C̣ạẹc̣ilius* is not entirely comfortable, principally because the spacing of the letters suggests that there ought to be either one broad letter or two letters between *a* and *c* and because we cannot see the top of *e*. *C̣ạṇc̣ilius* (*ILEsp*. 966) would perhaps be preferable palaeographically, but Caecilius is by far the commonest of the names ending in -cilius (see *RNGCL*).

September: the *cognomen* is not very common. *LC* lists 14 examples, *NPEL* only the Caecilius September mentioned in the introduction.

Back 1. Only the tops of letters in the address on the back are visible.

253

Inv.no.85.008. 55 x 20 mm.

The beginning of a letter addressed to Cerialis, perhaps from September (see note to line 1). The hand is probably not the same as that of **252**.

]ṃḅẹṛ Cerialị suọ

saluteṃ

. . . . .

1. The traces before *Cerialị* are very faint but suit the proposed reading well. If it is correct, the letter is probably from Caecilius September (cf. **252**, introduction), although September is, of course, not the only name with this termination (cf. **258**.back 8 note).

254

Inv.no.85.281. 115 x 24 mm.

A fragment containing the opening of a letter almost certainly from Flavius Similis (cf. **235**, **286**, **347**) to Cerialis. The left-hand edge may have the remains of a v-shaped notch. There is a smaller fragment of the same tablet with abraded traces which we cannot join to the main piece.

[Fl]auius Ṣiṃ[i]lis Ceṛ[iali

. . . .

255

Inv.no.85.033. 195 x 60 mm. Plate XV. *VRR* II, Plate VIII.

A complete leaf containing a letter in two columns from Clodius Super to Cerialis. Clodius Super may be a centurion (see note to line 20), in which case the somewhat familiar form of the closing greeting is interesting (cf. **242**.ii.2-3). We have not been able to identify him in any other texts, however, and there is no clue to his whereabouts. The main purpose of the letter is to record that the writer was pleased that Valentinus, just returned from Gaul, had approved some clothing and to request that Cerialis should send him (*sc.* Super) some cloaks and tunics for his *pueri* (see note to line 7). The right-hand side of the letter is rather abraded and lines ii.12-14 present problems of reading and interpretation which we have not been able to solve satisfactorily. If our suggestions are on the right lines, Super is saying that he has difficulty in procuring the clothing which his *pueri* may need in readiness for a transfer (?).

The hand is a good, regular cursive which uses two different forms of *d* (lines i.1, 4) and *l* (line i.3) as well as a very idiosyncratic *u*, which is almost a flat dash (line 4); *c* occurs in two forms, one like *p* (line 1), the other the more usual form (e.g. line 4).

i

[Cl]ọdius Super Ceriali suo
salutem
[V]alentinum n(ostrum) a G̣allia reuer-
sum commode uestem adprobas-
se gratulatus sum per quem
te saluto et rogo ut ea quae
ussibus puerorum meorum
opus sunt mittas mihi sa-

ii

gạc̣ias ṣẹx̣ sagạ [*c.3* pallio-]
ḷa septem tu[nicas se]x̣
qụạe scis c̣erte hịc me ṇọ[n
ṛịṭe impetrare c̣um simụṣ
nonạ ̣c̣usi etiam aḍ ẹọ[rum
traṇslationem m^2 uạḷẹạṣ
domine frater
c̣arissiṃẹ ẹṭ [*c.8*]ṣ
ṣịṃẹ *traces?*

Back: m^1 Flauió Ceria-
li praef(ecto)
ạ [C]ḷ[o]ḍio Supẹrọ (centurione)

"Clodius Super to his Cerialis, greetings. I was pleased that our friend Valentinus on his return from Gaul has duly approved the clothing. Through him I greet you and ask that you send me the things which I need for the use of my boys, that is, six *sagaciae*, n *saga*, seven *palliola*, six (?) tunics, which you well know that I cannot properly get hold of here, since we are ... ready (?) for the boys' transfer (?). (2nd hand) May you fare well, my dearest lord and brother, and ... (Back, 1st hand) To Flavius Cerialis, prefect, from Clodius Super, centurion."

1. The name has been quoted as Claudius or Cloudius Super (*VRR* II, 41) but the first surviving letter is much more easily read as *o*. Clodius and Modius would be possible restorations but the former is more common and much easier to reconcile with the traces on the back. We have found no other evidence for this man in the tablets and it is impossible

to read the nomen as Curtius (for Curtius Super see **213**).

3. The restoration of the very common *cognomen* Valentinus (cf. perhaps **187**.i.2) seems inescapable. *n* for *n(ostrum)* is surmounted by a horizontal stroke, as elsewhere, and it may be preceded and followed by medial dots (cf. **248**.ii.10 note).

Ġallia: the reading is not in doubt even though *g* is lacking its tail. Apart from the reference to Rome in **283**.4 and another possible reference to Gaul in **154**.12 (see note), this is the only mention in the tablets of a known place-name outside Britain.

6-8. *ea quae ... opus sunt*: for *opus* as predicative, agreeing with the nominative (in this case *quae*), see *OLD*, s.v. *opus* 13b and in particular the reference there to Quadrigarius, *Hist*.36, *res quae militibus opus sunt, ligna, aquam, pabulum*.

ussibus: as often the original geminate is retained after a long vowel, see *Tab.Vindol*.I, p.73, **309**.i.3 note (cf. Bowman and Thomas (1987), 141).

puerorum: it is very improbable that Super is referring to his own sons and the number of separate kinds of cloak required in batches of six and seven reinforces this. *puer* can mean "boy" in a colloquial sense among coevals, see Apuleius, *Met*.3.5, *heus, pueri, quam maribus animis ... dormientes adgrediamur*, cf. Catullus, 12.9, and note the use of the Greek equivalent *νεανισκοί* to refer to soldiers in Polybius 6.35.8. More commonly, however, it means "slaves" (see *OLD*, s.v.5 and e.g. Cicero, *Att*.3.7.1) and we suggest that this is the appropriate meaning here (cf. also **260**.7). This is also probably the meaning at *O.Bu Njem* 86.2-4 (cf. p.36), *trasmisi a<t> te domine item per puroṣ* (l. *pueroṣ*) *tuuos gura duua semis* (compare the editor's comment on *παιδάρια* in *O.Claud*. 151). Clodius Super is probably a centurion, but the numbers of garments involved are not appropriate to the members of a century and a centurion might well have several slaves, see *CIL* 3.8143 = *IMS* 2.325. It is perhaps worth noting that Cato, *Agr*.59 includes *tunicam* and *saga* among the clothing to be provided for agricultural slaves and that one of the categories of clothing (including *saga* and *tunicas*) specified at *Digest* 34.2.23 is *familiarica* (i.e. suitable for slaves).

i.8-ii.10. *sagaċias*: there is no serious doubt about the reading and the word also occurs in **521**.2 and **184**.ii.20, cf. *Tab.Vindol*.I, p.74. It evidently refers to some kind of a military cloak, as do the words *sagum* and *palliolum*. The precise differences between these different kinds of cloak are so unclear that we see no point in trying to translate the words.

sagạ: the two letters after *sex* are *sa* but the reading thereafter is very uncertain; as the traces might suit *b* we have wondered whether to read *sab̩[ana* (linen cloths), but the word is probably too long to leave enough space for a numeral; the same objection would apply to the reading *ṣeẋs ab̩[ollas*.

se]x̣: there remains only the bottom of a stroke sloping down from left to right which, by its position, ought to be the last letter in the line. If this is so, the restoration of *se]x̣* suits the trace far better than the ends of the other numbers up to 10.

11-4. Our reading and interpretation of this passage is offered very tentatively and should not conceal the difficulties in the readings at the beginnings of lines 11 and 12, and in line 13.

11. *q̣ụạe*: *q* has all but disappeared and it is not clear whether the apparent sloping stroke is in fact ink; if so, it is made differently from *q* elsewhere in this text. We think the reading of *uae* probable but the ligature of *ua* is unexpected.

scis ċerte: the order is unusual, but see Seneca, *Contr*. 10.5.2, *scis certe quam tristem illum emeris* (and cf. Seneca, *Ep*. 24.16). Palaeographically it would be equally possible to read *p̣er te*, but we have not been able to reconstruct a satisfactory sense along these lines.

hic: *hoc* is also a possible reading but we think *hic* preferable and it gives better sense.

no[n: the writing at the end of the line is abraded. The reading we have adopted is compatible with, but not compelled by, the traces.

12. *rite*: the reading is difficult but we do not think it possible to read *saepe*, which we have also considered; *sepe* (cf. *O.Wâdi Fawâkhir* 2.9-10 (= *CEL* 74), *sepius* for *saepius*) is even harder. For the sense in which we understand *rite* see *OLD*, s.v.3.

impetrare: cf. **269**.3.

simus: see note to line 13.

13. *nona.cusi*: this is a major crux. The reading of *non* is certain but *nonanis* quoted by A.R.Birley (1990a), 18 and implying a connection with a unit numbered ninth, is impossible since *us* is certain; although *nonanus* might be just possible as a reading, we cannot see how it could be construed. In addition, between *us* and *etiam* there is a very clear vertical stroke which, if it is ink as it appears to be, can only be read as *i*. This points to an adjective or participle ending *-usi*, to be taken with *simus*. It is, however, a major difficulty that the word order *cum simus non* followed by a participle or adjective is under most circumstances unacceptable; we should expect *cum non simus*, plus participle, or *cum non* (participle) *simus*. Even if we could accept the eccentric word-order the passage would still be difficult to explain. The letter after *non* resembles *a* and that before *us* most resembles *c*, but we cannot suggest a suitable word with these letters. We have considered the possibility of reading *excusi* and, since we do not see how the participle of *excudo* could make sense in this context, taking it as intended for *excussi*. However, this poses problems of both reading and interpretation: *x* is not easy to read and *e* is very difficult (as noted above, the letter looks most like *a*). Neither *OLD* nor *LS* suggests a suitable meaning but *TLL* V.2 1314 includes *promptus* among the synonyms for *excussus*. If the mark before *etiam* is, despite appearances, dirt, we might just be able to read *aptus* (though *p* is not easy and *t* is very hard). This would necessitate reading *sim* rather than *simus* in line 12 (the marks at the end could also be dirt rather than ink), but the sense conveyed would be the same. *Non liquet*.

ad eo[rum: *a* is certain, *d* followed by *e* possible; *o* is a mere trace which could be anything.

14. *translationem*: for the use of *translatus* in reference to the movement of personnel see e.g. *RMR* 63.ii.8, 64.ii.22, 25. No doubt *translatio* could also refer to the transport of clothing but we have not been able to find it attested in this sense, though *transfero* is well enough attested for transporting things from one place to another (*OLD*, s.v. 1a).

ualeas: the last three letters are severely abraded. *uale mi* (cf. **242**.ii.2-3 note, **247**.2) is not impossible.

15. This line and the two following are indented to the width of half the column; for a comparable layout in a Greek letter cf. *P.Herm.Rees* 5 (= Turner (1987), 70).

16-7. The ends of both lines are very abraded. In line 16 the first word does not look like *karissime* but the reading is plausible if it began with *c*. We might then have *et* followed by the beginning of another superlative (but *felicis-* looks too short).

Back 20. The centurial sign looks clear on the photograph and the original does not suggest that the mark is dirt rather than ink. If Clodius Super is a centurion, it might be thought surprising that in line 15 he uses the term *frater* in addressing the prefect Cerialis; he could easily have been a legionary centurion appointed *ex equite Romano*, however, and he would then be of the same social status as Cerialis (see E.Birley (1988), 189-205, citing e.g. *ILS* 2656, *CPE* 625-9, Dobson (1972)). There is very little documentary evidence for the language used in such contexts in military correspondence, see *RMR*, pp.348-9.

256

Inv.no.85.055. 214 x 36 mm. Plate XVI.

Four joining fragments of a diptych containing a letter to Cerialis from a certain Genialis. Although only *]auius* survives of the sender's *gentilicium* and there are a number of *gentilicia* with this ending, we need hardly hesitate to supply *[Fl]auius* in our text. If this is correct, it is natural to suppose that the sender is identical with the Flavius Genialis of **217-24**. There is some reason for uncertainty, however; the latter may have been prefect at Vindolanda in Period 2; the present text is from Period 3 and although we do not know where Genialis is writing from, it is most unlikely to have been Vindolanda. Furthermore, both elements of the name are very common. It is possible, however, that this is the same person writing during a posting elsewhere, subsequent to a period of duty at Vindolanda.

The right-sloping hand has proved particularly difficult to read and restore, partly because the ink is in places very faint and in others smeared; the latter feature is particularly troublesome. The writer also sometimes leaves sizeable gaps between words but he does this very inconsistently. The tablet is certainly broken at the foot, below line i.5, where at least one line is lost; the address on the back might have contained some 2-3 lines more than the one line preserved. The problem with the right-hand half is that it can be read and restored in such a way as to construe as a piece of Latin, but the sense produced is to say the least unexpected: Genialis appears to be admitting that he has behaved unacceptably towards someone and is afraid that he may have to suffer for it if his victim is released (or sent back) by Cerialis. It seems difficult to believe that a Roman prefect can have written in these terms (which would be a further argument for doubting the identity of the present Genialis with the recipient of **217-24**).

i

[Fl]auius Genialis Ceriali suo
salutẹm
ex coṇ.[..].[.]ṣ[..]eọs quọḍ p̣enes te
reṃ[*c.7*].ạcio tibị ..ṭ
Genịtọ[r *c.5*].em si enim
] *traces?*

. . . .

ii

mihi quia aliqua[n]ḍọ ṣọṛ.[
ḍe ịll. feci eọ adhuc per
siluolas repto tutiọr illo
futurus si remisserịs
*m*² uale domine
traces?

Back: *m^1* Flauio Ceriali

. . . . .

"Flavius Genialis to his Cerialis, greetings. ... because it is in your power to ... to you ... Genitor (?) ... For if ... to me, because I once (?) treated him in a niggardly fashion (?); for that reason I am still lingering in the thickets to be safer from him (?) if you release (?) him. (2nd hand) Farewell, my lord. (Back, 1st hand) To Flavius Cerialis ..."

i.1. For Flavius Genialis see the introduction.

3-5. Too much is missing in these lines for us to be able to restore what is lost with any confidence. All we offer are some suggestions for possible interpretations. At the start *ex coṇ* is more probable than *ex coṃ*; the trace following, if it is ink, is indecisive. There may also be traces of ink above this, which would have to be an interlinear addition. Following this the tops of two tall letters are visible, of which the first might well be *i* and the second seems most likely to be *s*; there may be no letter lost between them. We have considered the expressions *ex consilio*, *ex continenti* and *ex consuetudine* but we do not think it possible to fit any of them to the spaces and the traces remaining. We have also considered the possibility that we might have a place-name (Concangis is not too far from Vindolanda) but we are again unable to suggest anything which fits the traces and the spacing. After this *eọs* looks virtually certain but is perhaps not a word by itself; if so, the only possibilities which occur to us are *[m]eọs* and *[r]eọs*. If nothing is lost between the tops of the two tall letters, *m]iṣ[i r]eọs* could be read but we cannot suggest anything for what precedes.

Line 4 might begin with *rem* as a word by itself, or we may have some form of *remanere*, a verb which is often found with *penes*; in view of *remisseriṣ* in line ii.4, we have also thought, for example, of *rem[issio est*, "because it is in your power to release them/send them back". After the gap it is very difficult to read *f*, but we can think of no plausible alternative (*so]ḷạcio* is not a possible reading) and *f̣ạcio* is probably to be accepted. If we read *m]is[i* in line 3, *f̣ạcio* no doubt belongs to a different sentence; alternatively we may have the common phrase *[r]eos facio*. At the end of the line *t* appears certain, but there is too much ink before it for the reading to be just *tibị ụṭ*; *tibị ạụṭ* is possible (cf. below).

At the start of line 5 *gen* is a certain reading; only the feet of the following letters survive and *ịṭọ* is no more than consistent with the traces. It seems impossible to read anything other than a proper name in the present context but the case in which *Genịṭọ[r-* should be restored is unclear. A new sentence will have begun at *si enim*, with the previous sentence ending *-em*. A possible supplement would be *Genịṭọ[rem equi]ṭem*, although we cannot suggest how it would construe, and in such a broken context we cannot exclude the possibility that *em* is a 1st person verbal ending. If at the end of the previous line we read *tibị ạụṭ* (cf. above), we must supply *Genịṭọ[ri*; but we cannot suggest any coherent sense. We have also considered reading *tibị ạp̣ụṭ*; *reos ... facio ... aput Genitorem* makes very good sense and we could have *iudi]c̣em* to follow (cf. Suetonius, *Tib.* 8, *reum maiestatis apud iudices fecit*); but we cannot suggest how to fit in *tibi* or the *quod*-clause.

ii.1-2. The reading of the right-hand half of the first line is most uncertain; if *ḍọ* is right it seems inevitable that we should read *aliqua[n]ḍọ* but there is a lot of space in the lacuna for *n* alone and it may be that *aliqua* is a word on its own. The letter after *ḍọ* must be *s* or *f*; thereafter we do not attain certainty until we reach *e* in line 2. The letter before it is unlike *d* elsewhere in this text (cf. line ii.2, *adhuc*, line i.3, *quod*) and might be *b*, but we cannot suggest how the latter might construe. There is a space after this and before *feci* which suggests that the letters in between constitute a separate word, of which the two middle letters are clearly *ll*; it is not easy to read the initial letter as *i* but there seems to be no alternative; the final letter looks superficially like *o* but we believe that *i* could also be read. Because we can see no obvious way to make sense with *de illo* we very tentatively suggest reading *ṣọrḍ[i/ḍe ịllị feci*. *sordide* is most uncertain but not inconsistent with the traces; for its use with *facio* cf. e.g. Quintilian, *Decl.* 345 (p.364, 30), *si quid tu priuatus liberaliter fecisti, uniuersam ciuitatem uis facere sordide?* Note that here, as often, *sordide* is used of a mean or ungenerous action, a sense which might fit the context we envisage in our letter. There is a mark following *feci* which might be interpunct, but it is rather elaborate for this and interpunct does not occur elsewhere in this text; however, it does not look like a letter. After this we prefer to read *eọ* but *o* is smudged and *eṭ* is not impossible.

3-4. The reading here seems clear. The only doubt concerns *p* in *rep̣to* but this is certainly preferable as a reading to the alternative *rec̣to* and we do not see how the latter could be construed. We must take *siluolas* for *siluulas* (cf. *paruolus/paruulus*), a rare word but attested, e.g., in Columella 8.15.4. The difficulty lies in understanding what the writer is talking about (cf. introduction). For the phrase *per siluolas repto* see Adams (1994). For *illo* after *tutior*, Adams notes that *tutus* + ablative is unusual (cf. *B.Alex.* 1.3); *illo* as an adverb ("there") is possible. *remisserịs* can mean either "send back" or "release"; for the geminate *s* see the references in **255**.i.6-8 note.

5. It is doubful whether the traces below *domine* are ink, but the closing greeting could well have continued in the lost portion.

257

Inv.no.85.117. 96 x 52 mm.

Part of the beginning of a letter on the left-hand side of a diptych from a person named Valatta, probably a woman (see note to line 1). Two small fragments with writing have become detached and their placement has to be deduced (see notes to lines 1 and 3). There are two tie-holes at the left-hand side. The hand bears some resemblance to that of **311** but is somewhat cruder. The reference to Lepidina in line 5 leaves no doubt that the letter was written to Cerialis. This is the only letter to him which is apparently from a woman. What survives of the content suggests that she was asking for some favour or concession (perhaps compare **322**, **344**).

Ṿaḷatta [Ceriali suo
ṣ[alutem
rogo domiṇe ṛẹ[
teritat[e]m tuam [
et per Lepidinam quod [
mihi c̣oncẹdas *uacat*
].[
. . . .

"Valatta to her Cerialis, greetings. I ask my lord that you relax your severity (?) and through Lepidina that you grant me what I ask (?) ..."

1. The placing of one of the small fragments supplies the tops of *tta* and the reading seems secure. We have not been able to find the name in this form but note the female name Vallata in *CIL* 2.1798 (Baetica), cf. *LC* 357; we regard Valatta as an alternative spelling of this name.

2. We might equally well have *ṣ[uo salutem* in this line.

3-4. The reading and interpretation of these lines depends on the placing of the second small fragment at the right of line 3 and on the restoration of the word which ends *-teritatem*. The small fragment undoubtedly reads *].ẹṛẹ[*; if it fits flush to the broken edge, it will have the end of *domiṇe* followed by *ṛẹ*, as our reconstruction suggests. Of the nouns which terminate with *-teritas* only two seem worth considering in the context, *austeritas* ("severity") and *dexteritas* ("readiness to help"). The former would seem to make better sense in a context which refers to making a concession (line 6). As a possible supplement in lines 3-4 we suggest *ṛẹ[mittas aus-]/teritat[e]m* (cf. perhaps Pliny, *Ep.* 2.5.5), but we can envisage an alternative such as *ṛẹ[ddas* or *ṛẹ[feras dex-]/teritat[e]m tuam*. These suggestions imply that some 4 letters have been lost at the ends of lines 4 and 5 but we cannot be sure of this since it depends on the uncertain placing of *suo* in lines 1-2. To complete line 4 we might have simply *mihi*; at the end of line 5 *peto* would give good sense. A wholly different line of approach would be to suppose that the small fragment should be placed slightly further to the right, perhaps giving us *rogo domiṇ[e] peṛ ẹ[am dex-]/teritatem tuam et per Lepidinam* etc.

6. The space after *c̣oncẹdas* is unexpected, cf. **217**.ii.1, **291**.ii.8, **379**.

7. The trace, if it is ink, looks like the top of a centurial sign, but too little remains to propose this as a reading.

258

Inv.no.85.120. 86 x 33 mm. Plate XVII.

The lower part of what must have been the right-hand portion of a diptych, containing the end of a letter to Cerialis. Only the last few words of the message and the closure survive. The address on the back suggests that the letter is from a centurion with the *cognomen* Imber (see note to lines 8-9). We cannot accept the suggestion that this letter might be from Caecilius September (A.R.Birley (1991), 98, note 53). **252**.ii.3 must be September's autograph and the eccentric and crude hand of **258**.4-5, which must also be the author's autograph, is quite different. The letter might possibly concern the construction or provision of a bridge (see note to line 2).

. . . . . .
].\.[
..m ut p̣on.ẹ.[...].
praestarem *uacat*
m^2 opto bene ualere
te domine uale

Back: *m*[1] Fḷạuịọ C̣ẹṛịạḷị
praef(ecto) ·
a F̣.ṛ. . . .ḅre
. . . . .ne

"... so that I might provide you with a bridge (?). (2nd hand) I pray that you are in good health, my lord. Farewell. (Back, 1st hand) To Flavius Cerialis, prefect, from ..., centurion (?)."

2. *ịạm* is a possible reading at the beginning of the line. After *ut* it would be possible to read *c̣on.ẹ.* but we know of no suitable noun which begins thus to go with *praestarem*. We tentatively suggest *p̣onṭẹṃ*, taking *praestarem* in line 3 in the sense of "furnish", "provide" (*OLD*, s.v.8A). There is a trace at the right which could well be part of *i*; this suggests the reading *[tib]ị*.

4-5. This closure is written in a very difficult and idiosyncratic hand. *ualere* is possible only with an odd form of *u* with a stroke going down at the right and *a* with a sharp oblique stroke at the right, but it is made identically in line 5. The position of *te* is unexpected.

Back 6. Only the feet of letters survive and the reading of *C̣ẹṛịạḷị* is not wholly certain.

7. Unusually, the abbreviation of *praef(ecto)* seems to be marked by a medial dot after *f*. The apparent oblique stroke is not ink.

8-9. We think it unlikely that the correct reading is *a Septembre* (see introduction) and despite the uncertainty of the reading in line 9 we are fairly sure that the author cannot be another prefect. The first letter of the name seems to be *f* and it is possible that we have a *gentilicium*, perhaps followed by *Iṃḅre*. If this is correct there seems not to be room for *Fḷạuịọ*. Perhaps *Fụṛịọ*, a name which is reasonably common in the western provinces (see *NPEL*).

. . . .*ne*: only the last two letters are relatively clear but the preceding traces are not compatible with *ḍẹc̣ụṛịọne*; we therefore suggest that *c̣ẹnṭụṛịọne* should be read.

259

Inv.no.85.293.a-d. (a) 98 x 37 mm. (b)-(d) small fragments.

The left-hand side of a diptych containing the beginning of a letter from Pastor to Cerialis. The use of the term *frater* in line 3 suggests that Pastor may be of equivalent rank to Cerialis but there is no other reference to him in the tablets. There are two small fragments with traces of a few letters which we have not been able to place and have not attempted to transcribe. It is notable that the writer uses very tall ascenders (e.g. *bi* in line 3).

.[*c.4*]ụs Paṣtor Ceṛị[ali suo
salutem
misi tibi frater ṇọṭam ex qua

[*c.17*]....[.].
. . . .

"... Pastor to his Cerialis, greetings. I have sent you, brother, a sign from which ..."

1. There is a large space between the name of the sender and that of the addressee, cf. **249**.1, **321**.1, **347**.a.1.

3. *ṇọṭam*: the reading is somewhat uncertain since everything before *am* is very faint. The word apparently begins with *n*, and although *ọ* is not easy, *nọṭam* gives good sense (a "sign", "indication", or an agreed mark to indicate the genuineness of a letter, Cicero, *Fam.* 13.6.2 and cf. Youtie (1973)). We have also considered *c̣up̣am* which probably occurs in **180**.2 in connection with wheat (for physical evidence for wooden barrels at Vindolanda see *VRR* II, 76-81) and *ṣp̣ịc̣am* ("grain", cf. **343**.i.7 etc.), but neither reading is as convincing.

260

Inv.no.86.412. 117 x 74 mm. Plate XVII. R.E.Birley (1990), fig. 13. *VRR* II, Plate VIII.

The right-hand side of a diptych which contains the whole of the right-hand column of a letter from Iustinus to Cerialis. This seems to be guaranteed by the presence of notches in the right-hand edge and it is therefore odd that we seem to have lost one or two letters at the ends of some of the lines (cf. **215**.6). We can only assume that a small amount of the leaf has been lost by abrasion. Iustinus does not appear elsewhere, but his use of the terms *domine frater* in lines 4-5 and *col(lega)* in line 11 strongly suggests that he was a fellow-prefect. It is notable that the hand in which the text is written does not change in line 4 where the closing salutation begins; it is possible, therefore, that this is the hand of Iustinus himself, but it may be that we have lost a final *uale* in a second hand at the foot of the leaf. The content of the message proper suggests that this might possibly have been a letter of recommendation (cf. **250**).

. . . .
de op...[
esse scrị[*c.7* i]ṇ nọ[ti-
tiam tuam lụḅẹṇṭịṣṣi-
me perfero opto domin[e
frater felicissimus
bene ualeas saluta a m[e
Vindicem n(ostrum) et pueroṣ
tuos *uacat*

Back:
Flauio Ceriali praef̣(ecto)
coh(ortis) ·
a Iustino col(lega) ·

"... I have the greatest pleasure in bringing to your notice. I pray, my lord and brother, that you enjoy good health and the best of fortune. Greet from me our friend Vindex and your boys. (Back) To Flavius Cerialis, prefect of the cohort, from Iustinus his colleague."

1-2. There may be up to 14 letters missing in line 1. One way of supplementing and understanding this passage would be to restore *opịṇ[ione* followed by a short name (or possibly *te*) and adjective, followed by *esse scrị[psit quod i]ṇ no[ti-/tiam* etc.: "N has written about his opinion that N (*or* you) is (are) ..., which I have the greatest pleasure etc.". There are, however, alternative readings which are compatible with the traces, notably *opṭạ .[* or *opẹṛị[bus*.

2-4. For the phrase cf. Pliny, *Ep*. 10.75.2, *quod in notitiam tuam perferendum existimaui*. P.Vindob.Lat.Inv.126, line 12 (Sijpesteijn and Worp (1977), 92-4) may well contain the phrase *ad notitiam perfero*, or something like it.

lụḅẹṇṭịṣṣime: despite the damage at the beginning of the word, we are confident of the reading.

4-6. For the formula cf. **215**.ii.7-8 and **250**.ii.14-6.

7. *Vindicem n(ostrum)*: the name does not occur elsewhere in the tablets. Vindex must be assumed to be stationed at Vindolanda, and perhaps a member of Cerialis' cohort. The abbreviation of *n(ostrum)* is marked, as is normal, by a superscript bar (cf. **248**.ii.10).

pueroṣ: although there is no doubt of the presence of children in the *praetorium* during Cerialis' residence, we regard it as certain that the term here refers colloquially either to slaves or to fellow-soldiers as "the boys" (see **255**.i.7 and note). Greetings to members of the family normally take a different form and would surely be expected to include Cerialis' wife Lepidina if their sons were mentioned, cf. **291**.ii.9-10.

Back 10-11. It is noteworthy that *praef(ecto)* is, unusually, on the same line as the name and that the abbreviations of *coh(ortis)* and *col(lega)* are marked by medial points.

261

Inv.no.86.501. 102 x 33 mm. Plate XIX. *VRR* II, Plate IX.

Part of the left-hand side of a diptych containing the beginning of a letter from Hostilius Flavianus to Cerialis, sending a New Year's greeting. Hostilius Flavianus' status and whereabouts are unattested but it is possible that **172** is a fragment of a request for *commeatus* addressed to him. If so, it would suggest that Flavianus was at Vindolanda at some time and that he was a prefect (see above, pp.77-8). The social and religious prominence of the New Year is further emphasised by a letter to Cerialis referring to a sacrifice made on that occasion (**265**, see introduction and the references in notes to lines 3-4); note Pliny, *NH* 28.22, *primum anni incipientis diem laetis precationibus inuicem faustum ominamur*.

Hostilius Flauianus Cereali
suó salutem

annum ⸢nouọm⸣ f̣ạuṣṭum felicem
. . . .

"Hostilius Flavianus to his Cerealis, greetings. A fortunate and happy New Year ..."

1. *Hostilius Flauianus*: the *cognomen* may occur in **172** with reference to the same person but he does not appear elsewhere in the tablets. The *gentilicium* is fairly common in Italy and the western provinces (see *NPEL*).

Cereali: the name is spelled thus only here.

2. See **243**.2 and **233**.2 with note.

3. *nouọm*: although the last two letters of the word are somewhat abraded and may be obscured by dirt, the penultimate looks much more like *o* than *u*. The word is an insertion above the line. See Adams (1994).

f̣ạuṣṭum: despite the loss of the bottoms of letters, the reading is not in doubt. The phrase is formulaic and is frequently found on lamps and containers, see *CIL* 2.4969.3, *annum nouum faustum felicem mih(i) hu[n]c* (inscribed lamp; for *tibi* see e.g. *CIL* 10.8053.5.i) and cf. Seneca, *Ep*. 87.3. Flavianus' letter presumably contained a verb in the lost portion, cf. perhaps Fronto, *ad M.Caes*. 5.45 (Teubner ed., p.77), *annum nouum faustum tibi et ad omnia, quae recte cupis, prosperum cum tibi tum domino nostro patri tuo et matri et uxori et filiae ceterisque omnibus, quos merito diligis, precor*.

262

Inv.no.86.504. 88 x 32 mm. Plate XXVI.

A fragment of the left-hand portion of a leaf containing the beginning of a letter from Placidus to Cerialis. The name of the writer, which is an extremely common one, does not occur elsewhere in the Vindolanda tablets. The leaf is complete at the left which means that there was no *gentilicium*. Noteworthy features of the hand are the form of *r* with a foot which bends to the left at almost a right-angle to the descender, and *p* with a closed loop and a noticeable foot, with which the writer begins the letter (see *Tab. Vindol*.I, p.66 and above, p.51); since the more normal cursive form is used in line 3, it is obvious that the intention was to give the opening of the letter a more ornate appearance.

Placidus Ceriali suo
salutem
.[...]....ẹ.ẹ.eras domine
] ịnspice
] *traces*
. . . .

3. Before *domine* it is very likely that we have *ẹgeras* and possible that this is the end of *ẹx̣ẹgeras* (cf. **218**.4).

263

*Tab. Vindol.*I 23, Plate V, 1 and 2. *CEL* 91

The right-hand portion of a diptych containing the end of a letter to Cerialis. A re-reading of the text on the back indicates that the letter was from a decurion named Vitalis. Other changes from the *ed. pr.* are signalled in the notes, but particular attention should be drawn to the new readings of the numerals associated with the Batavian cohorts (line ii.5 and line 2 on the back).

i

Ceriali su]ọ
3? lines lost
].
]si
]ṃ

. . . .

ii

c̣[*c.9*].e tuó c̣om-
ṃ[*c.6*].[.]..[.]eṭ epịstu-
las .[..].s · quas ac̣cepẹraṣ
ab Equestṛe centụrịone
coh(ortis) · iiị · Bạṭạụorụṃ .[.].ị
aḍ tẹ pṛ(idie) K(alendas) Ma.... .nọs
..e.[.]benẹ .[*c.4*]ạṃụṣ
m[2]? dominam [*c.5*]..[.].aḷ.
ṭạ o............
ụịṭạli[..]............

Back: *m*[1] Flauịo C̣ẹrịali
praẹf̣(ecto) coh(ortis) viiịị Ḅat(auorum)
a Vitale dec̣ụrịone
a...[

" ... to his Cerialis ... ... and those letters which you (?) had received from Equester, centurion of the 3rd Cohort of Batavians, I sent (?) to you on 30 April (?) ... (2nd hand?) ... my mistress (?) ...(Back, 1st hand) To Flavius Cerialis, prefect of the 9th Cohort of Batavians, from Vitalis, decurion ..."

i.6. *]si*: we originally thought that these letters belonged to line ii.6 and completed the verb *misi* which began in ii.5. It now seems more likely, given that they stand to the left of the beginnings of lines in col.ii, that they belong to a line in col.i which overran the fold.

ii.1. *tuó*: we previously read the last letter as *e* made in two semicircular strokes, but we are now confident that it should be read as *o* with an apex mark (see above, pp.57-61), even though there is no other apex preserved in this text.

2. The spacing of the descenders visible before *et* is not decisive enough for us to calculate the number of missing letters here. We would not wish to rule out the reading *com-/m[endaue]ras et*.

3. *epistu/las* might perhaps be followed by *i[ll]as* or *m[e]as* (or even *d[u]as*), depending on the reading of the verb at the end of the line. The interpunct before *quas* appears to be deliberate although it is the only clear example in the text, except with the numeral in line 5 and the abbreviations in line 6. We are still uncertain whether to read *acceperam* or *acceperas* (either is palaeographically possible). If the latter, the writer would have to be understood as making a point about the date on which he had sent the letters which Cerialis had received; *m[e]as* would, of course, only make sense with *acceperas*.

5. In the *ed. pr.* we prefered *viii* to *iii* as the reading of the numeral but now that evidence for the Third Cohort of Batavians has appeared in **311**.back 2 we are quite sure that this is to be read here. The number, which is surmounted by a saucer-shaped mark, is preceded and followed by medial points. The first could indicate the abbreviation of *coh(ortis)* but such medial points appear in MSS to indicate that a number follows; this also seems to be the case in **295**.4 and is therefore likely here.

CEL 91.5-6 reads *[re]mi-/si* but since we now take *si* to belong to a line in col.i, we prefer to read *m[i]si* in line 5 which would fill the space available.

6. *ad te*: *ad te* now seems a more defensible reading despite the fact that there is no sign of a vertical.

It is quite likely that there are medial points after *pr* and *k* to indicate abbreviation; if there is a point before *pr* it must be interpunct.

ma.....: *maias* with a short word following (e.g. *et*) seems to suit the traces but *martias* cannot be excluded.

8. The hand appears to change at this point, in which case the last three lines must constitute the closure of the letter. We did not attempt to read these in the *ed. pr.* but we now think that we can read *dominam* and at least a few other letters. This line may well therefore begin with a reference to Cerialis' wife in the accusative (or the writer's wife, *domina m[ea*, but perhaps less likely coming from a decurion, see note to back 3). At the end of the line we might have *salu*, followed by *ta* at the beginning of the following line, but *dominam [tuam] a m[e] salu-/ta* is not at all easy.

9. The third letter in the line is clearly *o*, which could be the beginning of *opto*.

10. This line is still a complete mystery. It might begin with the word *uitalis*, either in the dative or nominative case, but the reading is really very uncertain and is somewhat awkward in view of our new reading of the address on the back (line 3). If it is correct we would have to suppose either that it is the adjective *uitalis* or that the writer, Vitalis the decurion, is referring to himself in the nominative or to some other person also named Vitalis (the name is common and occurs in **181**.8 as the name of a *balniator*).

Back 2. Palaeographically, the reading of the numeral as *viii* is easier, but in view of the additional evidence now available it must be read as *viiii* (see **151**.2 note). It is surmounted by a mark like that over the numeral in line ii.5 (see note).

3. The accumulated evidence for the pattern of addresses on the backs of the leaves, which was not available to us when the *ed. pr.* was written, makes it certain that we have *a* followed by the name of the sender. The reading of the name is not problematical. In the title, the abraded letters *uri* must have been rather crushed, but we see no other plausible reading.

4. *a...[*: we cannot elucidate this. The possible trace after the break looks like a high horizontal stroke. The letter before the break looks like *g* but the top stroke is probably dirt rather than ink. Therefore *aụṭ.[* or *aḍṭ.[* or *aụẹ.[*? If we have the name of a second writer we would expect *et*; if the place from which the letter comes, we have no parallel in the tablets. We cannot see how to read it as the identity of the sender's unit. We have considered whether it might be the date of receipt (i.e. *acc(eptum)* followed by a date, cf. *RMR* 89 = *CEL* 191), but we cannot see how to read it as such and, more significantly, the hand does not seem to change at this point.

264

Inv.no.85.084. 78 x 47 mm.

The end of a letter to Cerialis, with an address on the back. Only exiguous traces of the main part of the message remain but we have the complete closure written by a second hand. We think that this is likely to be the same as the second hand of **310**, in which case Chrauttius will be the correspondent of Cerialis in the present text. The identification of the hands rests on the palaeographical similarities (note particularly *o, e, l* and *c*) and is supported by the fact that both letters use the formula *opto sis felicissimus*, which does not occur in exactly this form elsewhere in the tablets. Since Chrauttius is likely to be of similar rank or status to his correspondent Veldedeius the *equisio* in **310**, the addition of the respectful *domine* and *quo es dignissimus* in the present text is appropriate to the address to a prefect. The position of the greeting, in the bottom right-hand corner of the tablet, is noteworthy.

. . . .
]. . *uacat*
].ṛạṇ[.]. *uacat*
m^2 opto domine sis
felicissimus quo
es dignissimus

Back: m^1 Flauio Ceriali
. . . . . .

" ... (2nd hand) I pray, my lord, that you enjoy the best of fortune, of which you are most worthy. (Back, 1st hand) To Flavius Cerialis."

2. We could equally well read *].ṇạ...*.

3-5. For the position of the closing greeting at the right cf. **255**.ii.15-7 and note.

Back 1. The loss of the bottoms of the letters in the address on the reverse shows that some part of the tablet has been lost. It is possible that there are some traces of writing at the broken edge on the front. Note that in **310**.ii.21 Chrauttius adds a concluding *uale*.

265

Inv.no.87.599. 96 x 50 mm. Plate XIX.

The top portion of the left-hand side of a diptych containing the beginning of a letter to Cerialis. The top left-hand corner, where the name of the sender will have been, is missing; three small scraps, each containing parts of letters, probably come from this part of the leaf but cannot be accurately positioned. The writer informs Cerialis that, in accordance with the latter's wish, he has marked the *dies Kalendarum* (New Year's Day) by a sacrifice. **261** contains a New Year's greeting from Hostilius Flavianus to Cerialis but there is no reason to connect **265** with Flavianus and the hand of **261** is certainly different. A notable palaeographical feature is that the writer several times marks the letter *a* with an apex, without regard to the quantity of the vowel (see above, pp.57-61). There is also a high apex-like mark over the *m* of *salutem* in line 2, on which see above, p.57.

]..ṣ Ç̣ẹṛịạḷị suọ
salutem´
ego, fráter, sácrifició dieṃ
Kálendarum sic-
ut uọluerás dẹdi-
traces
. . . .

"... to his Cerialis, greetings. Just as you wished, brother, I have consecrated the day of the Kalends by a sacrifice ..."

1. Not enough remains to hazard a guess at the identity of the author of the letter (*frater* in line 3 suggests a status similar to that of Cerialis).

3-4. *dieṃ Kálendarum*: this is frequently used without the name of the month, to refer to New Year's Day. For its general significance see Rea (1988) and *P.Oxy*.LV 3812.5-6 note, *CPR* VIII 52.6-8 note, Pliny, *NH* 28.22 quoted in **261**, introduction; and for the military significance, Fink, Hoey and Snyder (1940), 50-1.

5. *dẹdi-*: the reading *deos*, quoted by A.R.Birley (1990a), 18, looks possible at first sight but we do not think it can be read and are at a loss to see how it would make sense grammatically. Nor does the 1st person singular of the perfect tense of *dare* seem promising. We think it much more probable that we should supply some part of *dedico*, probably *dedi[caui]*. It should be noted that the ligatures of *edi* are remarkable and also that there is a stroke after *i* which looks like a hyphen; but we have seen no other example of this in the tablets and believe the use of hyphens at line-ends to be a much later development. If this reading is correct, *dieṃ* must be the object of the verb, although *die* would give better sense ("I dedicated (something) by sacrifice on New Year's Day"); despite the loss of half of the final *m*, which has overrun the fold, the reading is inescapable. Perhaps the meaning is that Cerialis' correspondent has consecrated the day to some deity. Compare Augustine, *de civ. dei* 7.7, *duos menses ... dedicatos ... ianuarium iano februarium termino*, Cassiodorus, *in psalm. praef.* 10[c], *ipsi nobis primam diei horam dedicant*, Ausonius, *Ep.* 21.25, *Octobres olim genitus Maro dedicat idus*.

266

Inv.no.86.496.a. 88 x 20 mm.

A fragment from the right-hand side of a leaf containing part of a letter with an address to Cerialis on the back. The writer expresses the wish that someone should come to him at Coria and receive something.

. . . .
uolọ ueniat · ad me
C̣ọris · et accipiat
. . . .

Back: Flauio Ceriali
. . . . .

"... I want him to come to me at Coria and receive ... (Back) To Flavius Cerialis."

2. *C̣ọris*: we are confident that the mark after the word is a deliberate interpunct (also possible after *uolọ* and probable after *ueniat* in line 1). For Coria as the Roman name for Corbridge see **154**.7 note, cf. **175**.3, **412**. The form here should again probably be regarded as a locative (= *Coriis*); if the writer had meant *from* Coria we would expect him to have used a preposition (cf. *Tab.Vindol.*I, pp.72-3). For the locative place-name in addresses see above, pp.43-5.

267

Inv.no.86.496.b. 53 x 22 mm.

A fragment from the right-hand side of a leaf containing the abraded remains of three lines of a letter, mostly illegible apart from *tui* in line 2. On the back there is an address, probably to Cerialis.

Back: [Fl]ạui[o] C̣ẹṛ[iali
p̣ṛạẹf̣(ecto) c̣ọ[h(ortis)
. . . .

1. The remains of the *cognomen* are exiguous. We read *C̣ẹṛ[iali* because of the find-spot, the *gentilicium* (which is, of course, not certain) and *p̣ṛạẹf̣* in line 2, which is very probable.

268

Inv.no.85.188. 64 x 47 mm.

Three joining fragments of a leaf containing part of a letter to Cerialis. It seems probable that we have the ends of some lines in the left-hand column, which overran the fold, and the beginnings of lines in the right-hand column. What is preserved of the address on the back shows that between a third and a half of the line length in the right-hand column is missing. The preserved part of the text seems to be referring to the despatch of something. The hand uses a high percentage of ligatures which, in view of the small amount remaining, make it very difficult to read.

i

. . . .
[ ].
[ ]ṇo
[ ]
[ ]i
. . . .

ii

. . . . .
comṃ[
tibi missi [
ẹqụịṭem ex ṭ[
goressẹt [
traces
. . . . .

Back: [Flauio] Cerialị
[praef(ecto)] c̣ọh(ortis)
. . . . . .

"... I have sent to you ... through (?) a cavalryman from ... (Back) To Flavius Cerialis, prefect of the cohort."

i.1. It is not certain that the marks at the edge of the leaf are ink.

ii.2. *missi*: see the references given in **255**.i.6-8 note.

3-4. *ẹqụịṭem*: only the tops of the first two letters survive. *e* is not difficult, though *f* is possible; *q* is very difficult indeed and virtually nothing survives except the top of a vertical, meeting the cross-bar of the previous letter. We have considered *f̣ụịṣṣem* as an alternative, but while the rest of the letters are possible *u* is impossible. If *ẹqụịṭem* is correct, one can imagine, e.g., *[*noun*] tibi missi per [N] / equitem ex turma [N]* or *tibi missi N / equitem ex turma [N]* (though the second name would have to be short); but this does not take account of the difficulty of articulating the word or words in line 4.

goressẹt: there is a space between *o* and *r* which suggests a division between words, and the penultimate letter might be *i* (e.g. *si ergo res sit ...*); if it is *gor essẹt* we must have a noun-ending, e.g. *fulgor*.

Back 2. The *c* has apparently been corrected, perhaps from *f*.

269

Inv.no.86.429.a-b. (a) 55 x 36 mm. (b) 25 x 22 mm.

A substantial fragment and two small joining pieces from the right-hand side of a leaf containing part of a letter to Cerialis. The small pieces do not directly join the larger, but the configuration of the address on the back shows that they must be placed to the left in the lower section and we have hypothetically reconstructed lines 2-4 on this basis. There is a v-shaped notch in the edge of the large fragment.

. . . .
]̣mus sẹdetsimi
.[ ]ṃp..bo quod
aụ[tem im]petrem rescribe
mị[hi *c.3*].ịṃ.. ....
. . . .

Back: Flauiọ [Ce]ṛịạḷị
traces
. . . . .

1. This could be articulated *sed etsi mi-* but perhaps better is *sed et simi-*. There is no particular reason to connect this with Flavius Similis of **235** and **254**.

2. There is only room for two letters between *mp* and *bo* and we suggest that the likeliest readings are *i]ṃpḷẹbo* or *co]ṃpḷẹbo* ("but I will also complete/fill similar ...").

3. The first letter on the small fragment to the left is certainly *a*, the second very probably *u*; *aụ[tem]* is the right length and makes good sense. For *petrem* the only plausible supplement seems to be *im]petrem* (perhaps "write back what it is you want me to get"); cf. **255**.ii.12.

Back 1. Only the middle sections of the letters *ṛịạ* are preserved and there are only very abraded traces of what follows, but in view of the *gentilicium* and the location of the tablet we are confident of the reading.

2. The line below presumably has *praef(ecto) coh(ortis)* but the traces are not substantial enough to suggest a reading.

270

*Tab. Vindol.*I 24, Plate V, 3. *CEL* 92

Fragments of a double leaf containing parts of two columns of a letter to Cerialis. The hand bears some resemblance to that of **249** (from Oppius Niger), though the *e* in the latter is somewhat taller.

i

]. Ceriali suo
saluṭem
]rḍịam agere
]c̣ulus ṇe cuiquam
]d mọṛạm fecit
].ṛ.ṣ..ṛd[
. . . . . .

ii

aspr[
sebam[
cum h[
tuu[
as r[
sub[
. . .

i.3. *].ntiam*, *ed. pr.* The earlier reading cannot be ruled out but we now prefer *]rḍịam*.

4. *]culus*, *ed. pr.*, *]sulus*, *CEL*. The latter is a possible reading.

ii.1. Perhaps cf. Licinius Asper (**224**), but the word division may be *-as pr[*.

271

Inv.no.85.222. 117 x 29 mm.

Three fragments of the right-hand portion of a diptych which appear to join, although this creates problems with the reading on the back nor can we suggest any connected sense for what we can read on the front. The letter is probably addressed to Cerialis.

. . . .
quae mịṣẹṛạṣ .mạu.f.b..
apụạṭ.ṇ...ụṃ...anum
. . . .

Back: ui *traces*
F̣ḷạụịọ C̣ẹṛịạḷị
. . . . .

1. There may be traces of a line above this.

2. *apua*, which appears to be a good reading, is a general term for "small fish", see Saint-Denis (1947), 8; cf. *VRR* III, 114.

Back 1. *ui*: in this position this can hardly be anything other than part of the name of the place to which the letter is being sent (cf. above, pp.43-5). *ui* is a good reading but it is very hard to read what follows as part of *Vindolandae*.

272

Inv.no.85.004.a-b. (a) 63 x 26 mm. (b) 28 x 10 mm.

Two fragments of which the larger contains the beginning of a letter, probably to rather than from Cerialis. Although the two pieces probably belong to the same text, it is not possible to establish a join.

a.]..[...].. Ceriạḷị [
]. dariṣ.[
. . . .

b. . . . .
traces
].uos ṇọ..[
. . . .

a.1. The letters preceding *Ceriạḷị* might be *ụṣ*. We have considered reading *F̣[l]ạ[ui]ụṣ Ceriạḷiṣ* but *F̣[l]ạ[ui]ụṣ* is very difficult and there is no trace of *s* following *Ceriạḷị*. It is noteworthy that there is no trace of *suo* or *salutem* below this; cf. **212**.1.

273

Inv.no.85.036.a. 85 x 60 mm.

Only the right-hand half the diptych survives, with an address to Cerialis on the back. The front is probably blank, which must mean that the message was a short one.

Back: Flạuio Ceriali
] *traces*
. . . .

2. We may have *[pra]ẹf̣* and, if the apparent trace further to the right is *o* rather than the bottoms of descenders from the previous line, *[c]o[h]*.

274

Inv.no.85.048.b. 88 x 22 mm.

The end of a letter to Cerialis which transmits a greeting to Lepidina. Compare **247** which may be from Brocchus. The present letter may also be from Brocchus, but the hand cannot securely be identified with any of those which occur in his correspondence and it is likely that other correspondents of Cerialis will have sent greetings to Lepidina. It is noteworthy that, in relation to the grain of the wood, the writing slopes markedly down to the right. There is an interesting ligature of *u* and *a* in line 3 (cf. above, p.52).

. . . .
].[
ịnteresse c...areạṣ *uacat?*
Lepidinam tuam saluta
. . . .

2. The traces are compatible with the reading *interesse cụị p̣areas*, e.g. "it makes a great deal of difference (*or* no difference) whom you obey".
3. Cf. **247**.1: *Lepidinam tuam a me saluta*. The greeting may be in a different hand from that of the previous line.

275

Inv.no.85.077. 30 x 15 mm.

A fragment of the beginning of a letter to Cerialis. It is noteworthy that *salutem* in line 2 is not justified at the right.

].ris Ceriali su[o
salutem
. . . .

1. The reading of *ris* is almost certain and before it *a* is probable. *RNGCL* lists about 40 names with this ending. *Singul]aris* is the restoration which most readily springs to mind, but the name does not occur elsewhere in the tablets.

276

Inv.no.85.211.a. 30 x 38 mm.

A fragment from the beginning of a letter addressed to Flavius Cerialis.

].ṣ Cẹrịalị
s]ụọ sạḷ[utem
. . . . .

2. Alternatively, *suo* might come at the end of line 1, with the traces at the left being part of the beginning of the message.

277

Inv.no.80.265. 108 x 30 mm.

Part of the right-hand side of a letter containing remains of three lines and on the back an address to Cerialis. Not enough survives to offer any clue to the content of the letter. There may be the remains of a notch in the right-hand edge of the leaf.

. . . . .
traces ṃus non
ideo *traces*
peṛẹ.ạ[
. . . .

Back: F̣ḷạụ[i]ọ C̣eriaḷi
. . . . .

278

Inv.no.85.285. 63 x 26 mm.

A fragment containing the beginning of a letter to Cerialis.

].o..ṣ Ceriali ṣ[uo
. . . . . .

1. The letter preceding *o* may be *i*, *p*, or *t*.

279

Inv.no.85.329. 60 x 15 mm.

A fragment from the beginning of a letter addressed to Cerialis. It is notable that in lines 1 and 2 *l* has a long diagonal for the foot.

]...nụṣ Ceriali suo
ṣalutem
]....[
. . . .

1. The traces are too faint to allow any suggestion for the reading of the name. If the termination is correctly read, we may note three possible names which turn up in Cerialis' correspondence: Crispinus (**225**.1), Iustinus (**260**.back 11), Hostilius Flavianus (**261**.1).

280

*Tab.Vindol.*I 26, Plate VI, 2 and 3. *CEL* 94.

This scrap contains, on one side, the beginning of what is probably a letter to Cerialis and, on the other, the remains of three lines of which the last two are written upside down in relation to the front. The first line may be the remains of an address script and this suggests that the two following lines may be part of a different text, perhaps a draft, on the back of a discarded letter, written over the top and upside down. The two texts thus may well not be connected. The hand of the Cerialis text bears some resemblance to that of **233**, which also has a second, apparently unconnected text.

]ụịus Ceriali [
].[
. . . . . .

Back:
. . . . . .
traces
].missi ạd c̣ul.[
traces
. . . . . .

1. In the *ed. pr.* we took this to be *Fla]ụius Ceriali[s*, but if the writing on the back includes remains of an address to Cerialis (see note to back.1), this could only be the case if Cerialis used a discarded letter for a draft. It is more likely that the first word is the end of the name of the sender followed by *Ceriali [suo*.

Back 1. The traces may be the remains of an address *]ạḷị*, written upside down in relation to the two following lines.

2. *].missiṣ ọculi.[*, *ed. pr.* We suggested the phrase *demissis oculis*, which occurs

commonly but not exclusively in poetic texts, but now think that the reading is not correct.

3. *]...ṭ.ạṃụ..[*, *ed. pr.* We no longer feel confident enough to offer even a tentative reading of these traces.

281

Inv.no.87.607. 172 x 36 mm. Plate XVIII.

The lower part of a diptych containing part of a letter. On the left-hand side are three lines of the first column. On the right there are only exiguous traces, perhaps belonging to the closing greeting; *saluta* in i.3 seems likely to come towards the end of the message and it is therefore reasonable to suppose that it ended in the upper, lost portion of the right-hand half. The attribution to the correspondence of Cerialis is not certain; it is suggested by the occurrence of the Ninth Cohort of Batavians in the address on the back (see note to back 2). Of particular palaeographical interest is the form of *e*, made in three distinct parts (e.g. line 2, *ipse*).

i

. . . .

]...bẹ..os
ḥabeo quos ipse tib[i
aḍferam saluta .[

. . . .

ii

. . . .

traces

. . . .

Back:

traces
]. viiii Batạụọ[rum
a Cluụịo Faḅro
]. P̣ẹṭri

"I have ... petitions (?) which I myself will bring to you. Greet ... (Back) To .... of the 9th Cohort of Batavians, from Cluvius Faber, ... of Petrus."

i.1. *]...bẹ..os*: the first surviving trace is compatible with *ṣ*; thereafter we ought to have a noun or an adjective to which *quos* in line 2 refers and the verb *adfero* in line 3 suggests that we ought to think of objects rather than persons (cf. **327**.1). We suggest the reading *ḷibeḷḷos*, which is compatible with the traces and could be understood either in the literal sense of "little books" (cf. *libros*, **333**.2) or "petitions" (of which we have possible examples in **322** and **344**, cf. **257**). There may be ink traces after this word, in which case a number might be appropriate.

3. It is uncertain whether there is ink after *saluta*. If so, probably *ạ*, the beginning of a name or of *a me*.

Back 1. There are traces of the bottoms of a few letters which would be compatible with the reading/restoration of *Flauio Ceriali praef(ecto)*, but they by no means compel it. Alternatively, *c[o]h(ortis)*, but that makes it difficult to see how we could read the trace at the beginning of line 2 (see note).

2. It is very difficult to see how the ink mark at the broken edge before the numeral can be read as *h* of *co]ḥ(ortis)*, nor is it obvious that the missing piece could have accommodated *co*; if it were an abbreviation mark we would certainly expect to see some part of *coh* before the break. There may be an oblique mark over the last digit of the numeral.

4. The reading of *P̣ẹṭri* is uncertain but we can think of no military rank or title which suits the traces. The name Petrus does occur in Gallia Belgica (*CIL* 13.1443, 1547) but not until the Christian period. There is, however, an earlier occurrence of the female *cognomen* Petra in Germania Superior (*CIL* 13.11672, cf. Weisgerber (1968), 241-2) which might justify our reading. What precedes it looks most like *l* but we do not find *co]ḷ(lega) P̣ẹṭri* persuasive; perhaps *(turmae)* or *(centuriae) F]ḷ(auii) P̣ẹṭri* (for the abbreviation of the *gentilicium* cf. **291**.i.1). Alternatively, we might have a reference to the *ala Petriana* (see *CIL* 16.43, 69) in which case the line might read *dec(urione) a]ḷ(ae) Petri(anae)*, cf. **284**.back 3 note.

282

Inv.no.87.563. 193 x 63 mm.

A complete diptych with remains of two columns of a letter. The left- and right-hand edges contain remains of notches and tie-holes. The left-hand column contains six lines of writing and the right six or seven. The address is written, as is usual, on the back of the right-hand portion. The writing is very abraded, particularly on the left-hand portion. It is nevertheless clear that the letter did not begin here and it seems evident that it must have been written on more than one diptych (cf. **292**, **343**). No substantive idea of the content can be gleaned. The letter may be addressed to Flavius Cerialis.

i

...... et habet
aḅ *traces*
traces eraṣ
]...squaṃ
traces ṇobis te
]ẹx̣..ṇṣue-

ii

tudine ama nos ..
exibe ṇobis .c̣.....
tat[*c.3*] *traces*

ṭuarum *traces*
traces
.ṛ.fịc *c.11* ạle
traces?

Back: *traces*
] viiii Bạṭ(auorum)
traces

"... as is your custom (?), love us and show ... to us ... of your ... (Back) To ... of the 9th Cohort of Batavians."

i.6-ii.7. *ṣue/tudine* is certain and the traces would permit *ẹx̣ c̣ọṇṣue-/tudine* (cf. *OLD*, s.v.1b).

ii.7. There appear to be traces of three letters after *nos* of which the first is *e* or *f*; *fra* could be read but there is no room for the rest of *frater*. We think that the best solution is to suppose that some of the traces are not ink and to read *ẹṭ*.

8-9. We expect a noun ending *-tatem* but the traces are too exiguous for us to suggest anything with confidence.

12. At the beginning *p̣rọfic* looks possible and some part of *proficiscor* seems more likely than part of *proficio*. The reading at the end of the line strongly suggests *ụale* and this could be the end of the letter; but we cannot say whether or not this is written by a different hand.

Back 1-2. Only the numeral *viiii* in line 2 is comparatively clear; there is room for *coh(ortis)* before it and *Bạṭ(auorum)* after it is just possible, though very little is visible. Of the name in line 1 we can really see only *la* and *i* in the *gentilicium*; the traces would just about support *Flauio* but it is difficult to see *Ceriali* in what follows (*Geniali* is certainly even harder).

283

*Tab.Vindol.*I 40, Plate IX, 3 and 4. *CEL* 107.

A fragment of what must be the right-hand portion of a diptych containing seven lines of a letter and on the back remains of an address to a prefect who could well be Flavius Cerialis.

. . . .
...[
peruer......[
quos si ......[
Ṛọmam petere .ọ.[
quitur uiatico ....[

quod .i.si ṭabuḷaṣ a..[
traces
. . . .

Back: [F]ḷ[au]iọ Ċẹṛiạḷi p̣raef(ecto)
. . . .

2. *peruer.......*: only the bottoms of letters survive at the right. We hesitantly suggest that a possible reading is *per Verẹcụndụṃ*, but note that the name is very common and need not refer to the prefect Iulius Verecundus (for whom see **210-12**).

3. *.at....*, suggested in *CEL* 107, is impossible.

4. *Ṛọmam*: the reading of initial *r* is probable and only *imam* or *omam* could follow; we therefore still consider the reading likely to be correct.

At the end *ẹọ.[* or *ṣọ.[*, suggested in *CEL* 107, is impossible.

5. *quitur*: probably *se]quitur* or a compound.

uiatico: also in **330**.2.

6. In the *ed. pr.* we suggested *f̣ibuḷạṣ* but now think that the second letter is better read as *a*. We might have *quod fiṭ si ṭabuḷaṣ a..[*, cf. **217**.ii.1.

Back 1. In the *ed. pr.* we suggested that a name such as *Liburno* would suit the traces. Only *r* is certain but *ċẹ* preceding it looks plausible and we now think it is possible, though difficult, to read it as an address to Flavius Cerialis.

284

Inv.no.85.094.b. 55 x 25 mm.

A fragment of the right-hand portion of a diptych containing part of a letter with an address on the back. This is complete at the right and suggests that nothing is lost at the left of the column on the front. The writing on both sides is very abraded and difficult to read. The text provides a clear attestation of the *cohors viiii Batauorum* and is addressed to its prefect, whose name should probably be read as Flavius Cerialis (see back 1 note). The sender of the letter was probably a decurion with the *cognomen* Verus. It is not possible to obtain any substantial idea of the subject of the letter. If there is a reference to the *clementia* of the recipient in line 2 (see note) it is possible that we have a petition or an appeal of some sort (cf. **257**, **281**.i.1 note, **322**, **344**).

. . . . . .
ạgas ṣị.ụom.[
rẹ ẹt ẹam cleṃ[
lo exsigas ịḍ..[
. . . . .

Back:]..[.].. ....
p̣raef(ecto) coh(ortis) viiii Bat(auorum)

].dio Vero dẹcụṛịọne ...ẹ

. . . .

" ... (Back) To Flavius Cerialis (?), prefect of the 9th Cohort of Batavians, from Claudius (?) Verus, decurion of the *ala* (?) ..."

1. Perhaps *ṣị ḍụo m.[*. An alternative might be *ṣạḷuom*, cf. **225**.6.

2. There is a space after *ẹt*; *ẹam* following it is plausible if we assume that the mark before *ẹ* is not ink. Following that, the reading *clem* looks good and suggests a reference to the recipient's *clementia*.

2-3. The restoration of *uo/lo* is plausible and fits the subjunctive following.

exsigas: see Adams (1994).

Back 1-2. The reading of line 2 is secure and the recipient must be a *praefectus* of *cohors viiii Batauorum*. Flavius Cerialis is the only person attested as such in the tablets. There are substantial traces of the letters of the name and we think it difficult though just possible to read *[F]ḷạ[u]ịọ C̣ẹṛịạḷị* without doing too much violence to the traces. We cannot exclude the possibility that we have Cerialis' predecessor or successor but we do not find it any easier to read (e.g.) *[F]ḷạ[u]ịọ G̣ẹṇịạḷị* (but there is no clear evidence which connects him with the Ninth Cohort of Batavians, cf. above, p.194). The numeral has a superscript dash.

3. It is noteworthy that this line is not written on an upward slant, as is often the case, but it must be the name of the sender. For the *gentilicium* the most obvious restoration is *Cla]ụdio* and the exiguous trace of the first surviving letter is compatible with the right-hand stroke of *u*. Of *dẹcụṛịọne* only the first *ẹ* is really difficult and the reading is credible if we assume that the word has been crushed in. Following that there are traces of 3 or 4 letters which could be read as *ạḷạe*; if that is correct, the name of the unit will presumably have come in the next line.

285

Inv.no.80.152. 79 x 34 mm.

A fragment containing the closure of a letter with part of the address on the back. There is no conclusive evidence that this belongs to the correspondence of Cerialis. It is included because the address possibly indicates that it was from Brocchus and because the hand in which the closure is written might be the same as the second hand in **247** and **248**.

. . .

m^2]e ḍọmiṇe
] karissime

. . .

Back:

. . .

m^1 *traces*
praẹ[f(ecto)
aḅ...[

1. This might begin *ual]e* or *opto t]e*, or *bene ualer]e*. The reading of *ḍomịne* is not certain (the ligature of *om* looks odd).

Back 3. *a Ḅṛọc̣[cho* is a possible reading, in which case the hand of lines 1-2 on the front will be the same as the second hand of **248** and probably **247** (see **248**.ii.12-4 note); alternatively, *aḅ* could be taken as the preposition.

286

Inv.no.86.444.a-b. (a) 65 x 17 mm. (b) 52 x 16 mm.

The larger fragment belongs to the left-hand side of a leaf and contains the opening of a letter from Flavius Similis. The name of the addressee is lost (what appears on the photograph to be ink is in fact dirt), but it is possible that it was sent to Cerialis; see **254**, probably written by a different hand, and **235**. The smaller fragment appears to belong to the same tablet but does not join the larger.

a. Flauius Similis [
. . . .

b. . . . .
].mm..[*c.10*].ṃ[
. . . .

287

Inv.no.85.099.a. 62 x 13 mm.

A fragment perhaps containing the end of a letter and an address to Cerialis.

. . . . . .
.[
saluta ạ...[
.onistụ.[
. . . . . .

Back:]... C̣ẹṛịạḷi
[p]ṛạef(ecto) coh(ortis)
. . . .

2. *saluta ạ ṃẹ* does not seem a probable reading.

3. The line seems to begin with *h*; *TLL* VI 2901 cites one example of *honestus* spelt *honistus*, *CIL* 16.108.extr.12 (AD 158).

Back 1. The reading of *C̣ẹṛịạḷị* is compatible with the traces but it is very difficult indeed to read the end of *Flauio* preceding it.

2. *coh* appears to be followed by a diagonal stroke, perhaps a mark of abbreviation.

288

Inv.85.035. 80 x 55 mm.

A fragment of the right-hand portion of a letter containing the end of the message proper and a closing greeting. The surviving text gives little clue to the content; it is possible that the sender is asking for instructions on how to reach the recipient. The possible attribution to the correspondence of Cerialis depends on the reading of line 3 (see note).

. . . .
r]ọgo ẹṛgo [
qu]omodo ueni
]. . .ṇam tuam
]. m^2 ụạle ṃi dọmine
ḳạrissime

"... I ask therefore ... how I might come (?) ... Greet (?) your ... . Farewell, my dearest lord."

3. *]. . .ṇam*: the traces are compatible with *]ịḍịṇam* which suggests that we should restore *Lep]iḍịnam*, the name of the wife of Cerialis. If this is correct, and assuming about 9 letters lost at the left, one might tentatively restore what remains along the following lines: *r]ọgo ẹṛgo [re-/scribas qu]omodọ ueni-/[am ad te Lep]ịḍịṇam tuam /[a me salut]ạ* etc.

4. *ụạle ṃi dọmine*: cf. **247**.2 and see **242**.ii.2-3 note.

289

Inv.no.85.237. 68 x 43 mm.

A fragment of the right-hand portion of a diptych containing five lines of the end of a letter and traces of an address on the back. The hand does not change in line 3 where the closure begins. The leaf is probably complete at the right and missing 3-4 letters at the left.

. . . .
] minoṛasc̣ri
].er sụọṣ ṇotum
] uoluị opto do-
[min]e frater ḅeṇ[e
[ual]ẹạṣ

Back: F̣ḷạụịọ C̣ẹṛ[iali

. . . . .

" ... I wished to make it known (?). I pray, my lord and brother, that you are enjoying good health. (Back) To Flavius Cerialis (?) ..."

1. The word division could come before or after *a*. After *s* we cannot rule out *t* or *p* (cf. the name Asper in **224**.1).

2. Before *sụọṣ* the most attractive reading is *p̣er*, but *prop]ṭer* or *in]ṭer* is possible.

Back. The reading is plausible, but far from certain.

290

*Tab. Vindol.*I 28. *CEL* 96

A fragment of a letter containing abraded and illegible traces of two lines on the front. The reading of the address to Cerialis on the back is not certain.

Back:]. C̣ẹṛịạḷị

. . . .

CORRESPONDENCE OF LEPIDINA
(Nos. 291-294)

Sulpicia Lepidina was the wife of Flavius Cerialis, prefect of the Ninth Cohort of Batavians, stationed at Vindolanda in Period 3. She received two letters from Claudia Severa, wife of Aelius Brocchus (**291**, **292**), and one from a woman whose name is perhaps Paterna (**294**). Another scrap with a closure written in Severa's hand must also be assumed to belong to a letter to Lepidina (**293**). These tablets are all assigned to Period 3 but it is noteworthy that they were not found together (one in Room IV, two in Room VIA and one on the *via principalis*). The subject-matter of the letters is social and personal and it is notable that Claudia Severa herself writes very full and intimate closures in her own hand. The evidence for correspondence between literate women of the equestrian officer class is of no less interest than their presence itself at Vindolanda.

It should be noted that Lepidina is mentioned as an intermediary, presumably for Cerialis, in **257** and as the subject of standard greetings in letters to Cerialis (**247**, **274**, cf. **263**.ii.8 and **288**). It is possible that **227** is a draft written by Cerialis for Lepidina.

291

Inv.no.85.057. 223 x 96 mm. Plate XX. Bowman and Thomas (1987), no.5. *CEL*, Appendix Vindol. γ. R.E.Birley (1990), fig. 15. *VRR* II, Plate XI.

This diptych contains a letter to Sulpicia Lepidina from Claudia Severa, wife of Aelius Brocchus, sending Lepidina a warm invitation to visit her for her (Severa's) birthday (on the celebration of birthdays by private individuals see *RE* VII, 1142-4) and appending greetings to Cerialis from herself and greetings from her husband.

The elegant script in which this letter is written is also probably to be recognised in **243**, **244** and **248**. The letters are slim, with marked ascenders and descenders, and very little use of ligature. There is occasional use of the apex mark for which see pp.57-61, above. In the present text the use is not always in long quantities. It is quite certain that the author is Severa herself, adding a brief message and the closing greeting in her own hand as she also does in **292** and **293**. Almost certainly, therefore, these are the earliest known examples of writing in Latin by a woman.

i

Cl(audia) · Seuerá Lepidinae [suae
[sa]ḷ[u]ṭẹm

iii Idus Septembṛ[e]ṣ soror ad dieṃ´
sollemnem nạtalem meum rogó
libenter f̣aciás ut uenias
ad nos iụcundiorem mihi

ii

[diem] interuentú tuo facturá si
[.].[*c.3*]ṣ *uacat*
Cerial[em t]ụum salutá Aelius meus .[
et filioḷụs ṣalutant *uacat*
m^2 *uacat* sperabo te soror
uale soroṛ anima
mea ita ụạḷeam
karissima ẹt haue

Back: m^1 Sulpiciae Lepidinaẹ
Cerialịṣ
a Ṣ[e]ụerạ

"Claudia Severa to her Lepidina greetings. On 11 September, sister, for the day of the celebration of my birthday, I give you a warm invitation to make sure that you come to us, to make the day more enjoyable for me by your arrival, if you are present (?). Give my greetings to your Cerialis. My Aelius and my little son send him (?) their greetings. (2nd hand) I shall expect you, sister. Farewell, sister, my dearest soul, as I hope to prosper, and hail. (Back, 1st hand) To Sulpicia Lepidina, wife of Cerialis, from Severa."

i.1. *Cl(audia)*: this is the only certain example of the abbreviation of a *gentilicium* in the tablets (but see **294**.1 note and **281**.back 4 note). The medial point following is the only example in this text and must be intended to mark the abbreviation. The name suggests that Severa's family acquired citizenship in the reign of Claudius, a generation before that of Cerialis and his wife.

2. On the right-hand half of the diptych there may well be the foot of an oblique stroke after *sa]ḷ[u]ṭẹm*; for such a mark see above, p.57.

3. *iii*: the first digit is enlarged; on this phenomenon see *O.Bu Njem*, p.38.

dieṃ´: the *m*, which is broken between the two halves of the diptych, is followed by an oblique stroke similar to an apex or to the stroke which follows *salutem* in one or two texts and may occur here (see preceding note). After *dieṃ* it cannot represent an apex or be intended to mark punctuation and we are unable to explain it (see above, p.59, note 48).

4. *sollemnem*: for the use of this word in connection with birthdays cf. Horace, *Od.* 4.11, and Fronto, *ad Ant.imp.* 1.2 (Teubner ed., p.87): *te mihi ab deis die tibi sollemnissimo natali meo precatum.*

ii.7. *interuentú tuo*: for the sense of *interuentus* here see *OLD*, s.v.1; cf. Cicero, *Att.* 4.2.5: *interuentu Varronis tui nostrique.*

7-8. The sense needed is not in doubt. There appears to be a descender from this line visible above the *r* of *Cerialem*. In the *ed. pr.* we chose to ignore this and supplied (*exempli gratia*) *[uenie]ṣ* (a restoration which we would still prefer to *[uenia]ṣ* of *CEL*). If this is part of a letter and not just a stray mark, we must have a different verb, since none of the letters in *uenie* descends below the line in this hand. The trace could be from the foot of *a* and we now think that *ạ[deri]ṣ* is a better restoration (there may just be room for four letters in the lacuna); in which case either this line was indented compared to the lines before and after it, in alignment with line 10, or we could restore *[tu] ạ[deri]ṣ*. It is strange that the rest of the line is blank, even though there is an obvious break in the sense; there may be a parallel in **217**.ii.1; the *uacat* in **258**.3 comes after the message proper and before the greeting added by the second hand; see also **257**.6, **379**.

9-10. A.R.Birley (1991), 101 proposes the reading *Aelius meus [te] et filios salutat* (accepted by Cugusi, *CEL*), cf. *VRR* II, 39 where *[uos]* is restored in place of *[te]*. We retain our original reading of line 10 which we are confident is correct. *salutant* is certain (Birley suggests that the *n* is really the tails of *l* and *a* from the line above but this is unacceptable: *n* is clear and is made exactly as elsewhere in this text, e.g. *uenias* in line 5). Given that the reading is *salutant* we must have a noun in the nominative to precede. There is room for 3 letters between *filio* and *sal* of which the last is certainly *s* and the first almost certainly *l*; this points unequivocally to *filioḷụs*. The only problem is the end of the preceding line where there is a trace of the foot of a letter after *meus*. Despite the odd word-order, we cannot see what this can be other than the object of *salutant*. As we stated in the *ed. pr.*, *u[os* cannot be read and we must choose between *ṭ[e* and *ẹ[um*; in the *ed. pr.* we inclined to prefer the former but we now think *ẹ[um* more likely. Regardless of the reading of this passage and the interpretation of *pueros* in **260**.7 (see note *ad loc.*), the archaeological evidence makes it probable, as Birley remarks, that Cerialis and Lepidina had children with them in the *praetorium* at Vindolanda (see *VRR* III, 44-6).

11. *sperabo te*: Adams comments: "*spero* does not seem to be used elsewhere in the active with a personal object in this sense (the Plautine *sperare deos*, "put one's trust in the gods", is different), but compare the use of *speratus* "longed for", of a person, in comedy: e.g. Plautus, *Amph.* 676, *Amphitruo uxorem salutat laetus speratam suam*, *Stich.* 583, Lodge, *Lexicon Plautinum* II, 668. *sperabo te* represents a transfer into the active of this idiom. Cicero might have used another verb (cf. e.g. *Att.* 4.1.8, *uehementer te requirimus*)." See now Petersmann (1992), 289, citing Terence, *Eun.* 193-5, *dies noctesque me ames, me desideres, me somnies, me exspectes. de me cogites, me speres.*

12-4. *anima mea*: the expression should be compared with Severa's closure in **292**.back 2-3 (see note). Adams comments: "This endearment is not found in comedy, where however the comparable *mi anime* is put regularly into the mouths of females (12 examples in Plautus and Terence, 9 of them spoken by women; similarly *mi animule* is uttered twice by women in Plautus; details in Adams (1984), 71). Cicero uses *mea anima* twice (in the plural) when addressing women (*Fam.* 14.14.2, 14.18.1)."

It may be added that *anima* in this usage is not confined to females: in Fronto, *ad M.Caes.* 2.10.3 (Teubner ed., p.30), Marcus Aurelius describes Fronto as *anima dulcissima*. The expression is also used on a gold ring found in the fourth-century vicus at Vindolanda: see *Britannia* 2 (1971), 301 no.72.

13. *ita ụạḷeam*: we have little doubt about the reading, although we cannot exactly parallel the expression. *ita ualeas* in *CIL* 5.1490 and in the letter quoted in Suetonius, *Aug.* 69.2 seems to have a rather different sense. What we have in the present letter, if it is to be taken closely with *karissima*, may be similar to some of the usages indicated in *OLD*, s.v. *ita* 17; cf. *ita uiuam*, used in Cicero, *Fam.* 16.20.1, *Att.* 5.15.2, Valerius Maximus 9.13.3, 16.20.3, etc., and *ita sim felix*, found in Propertius, 1.7.3 and Suetonius, *Tib.* 21.4, where a letter from Augustus ends *iucundissime et ita sim felix uir fortissime......uale*; cf. also the

examples quoted in *OLD*, s.v. *ualeo* 2d of *ne ualeam* used in asseverations. See Adams (1994).

14. *haue*: it is odd to find this word used when *uale* has preceded; for its use as a salutation at the end of a letter *OLD* quotes only *haueto* in Sallust, *Cat.* 35.6.

15-7. The use of a word for "wife" in such an address is not necessary and is also omitted in **292**.back (cf. the address to the slave *Candido Genialis* in **301**.back).

15. *Lepidinaẹ*: no doubt because of lack of space, the *a* and *e* are very cramped and are written almost as a conjoint letter, as they frequently are in inscriptions.

16. *Flaui]ị*, *ed. pr.*: we now think that the mark which we thought was *i* is probably not ink. **292** is addressed on the back to *Sulpiciae Lepidinae Cerialis*.

17. *[a Se]ụerạ*, *ed. pr.*: traces of the first two letters now seem to us clearly visible. The second letter might be read as *c* but the mark following (which might be *l*, suggesting *Cl(audia)*) is probably not ink. There might be an apex mark over the final letter of *Ṣ[e]ụerạ*.

292

Inv.no.85.042.a-c. (a) 190 x 31 mm. (b) 193 x 36 mm. (c) 96 x 32 mm. Plates XX, XXI. *VRR* II, Plate XI.

This letter and that of Octavius to Candidus (**343**) are the only examples in which more than one diptych survives (cf. **282**). The layout and organisation of the text of Severa's letter is even more curious and idiosyncratic than that of Octavius. The first double leaf (a) contains the beginning of the letter. This, like the other leaves, is probably complete at the foot and both margins but is incomplete at the top. It is unique in that the text of the letter, instead of being written in the usual two columns, is written in one very broad column across the whole width of the double leaf, a format to which we can quote no parallel elsewhere in the collection; and enough survives of the opening for us to be confident that this was written in the same format. In addition, while it is usual for the first line of the letter proper to commence further to the left than the following lines, the extent to which line 2 is set out to the left in comparison with lines 3-4 is remarkable. On the second double leaf (b), which must have been placed below (a) when the letter was completed and folded, the scribe has reverted to the two-column format. Here, too, there must be one or two lines missing at the beginning of each column. Despite the fact that the main text of the letter continues on another leaf (c), the closing greeting, comparable to that in **291** and also clearly written by Severa in her own hand (cf. also **293**), is on the back of the right-hand half of (b). This may well be because the back of (c) was occupied by the address. Of the third leaf (c), only the right-hand half survives. We must assume, therefore, that we have lost whatever was on the left-hand side and a line or two from the top of the leaf. The last line on (c) suggests that nothing is lost between it and Severa's closure on the back of the right-hand half of (b); this is the only certain example in the tablets of a closure written on the back of a leaf (but cf. **303**, **305**). The back of (c) contains, as we would expect, the address to Lepidina. All the leaves contain remains of notches and tie-holes in the usual places.

The text is personal and intimate in tone. Severa has asked her husband Brocchus for permission to visit Lepidina. He has apparently agreed and Severa intends to make the visit, perhaps saying that there are essential matters which she does not want to deal with by correspondence (see a.i.4 note). She speaks of her intention to remain or lodge at a place called Briga (see c.v.2, note), before sending greetings to Cerialis. Unlike the birthday invitation (**291**), this letter gives a clear indication of the regularity of correspondence between Severa and Lepidina.

The hand in which this letter is written is one of at least three which appear in letters emanating from the household of Brocchus and Severa. This hand is also found in **246** (the opening of a letter from Brocchus), probably **245**, and perhaps **403**, **404** and **406**. It is a rather elegant, squarish hand which shows occasional use of ligature and apex (a.i.3, 4, b.ii.4). Noteworthy are the long *i*, two forms of *l* (e.g. c.v.3) and *u* written as a shallow curve (c.v.2, cf. b.ii.4).

a. i

. . . .

ṣạḷụṭẹṃ
ẹgo soror sicut tecum locuta fueram et promiseraṃ
ut peterem a Brocc̣hó et uenirem at te peti
et reṣ[po]ṇdit mihi <i>tạ corḍe semp̣[er li]c̣ịtum unạ́

b. ii

. . . .

traces
quomodocumque possim
at te peruenire sunt enim
necessariá quaedam qua[e]

iii

. . . .

traces?
rem meum epistuḷas ṃẹaṣ
accipies quibus scies quiḍ
sim actura haec ṇọbiṣ

c. v

. . . .

traces
.ṛạ eram et Brigạe ṃansụṛạ
C̣erialem tuum a me saluta
uacat

b. Back: m^2 [ual]e ṃ. . ṣọror
ḳarissima et aṇịṃạ
ma desideraṭissima
uacat traces

c. Back: m^1 Sulpic̣iaẹ Ḷẹpidịnae Ceriạ[li]ṣ *traces?*
a Seuerạ Ḅ[rocchi

" ... greetings. Just as I had spoken with you, sister, and promised that I would ask Brocchus and would come to you, I asked him and he gave me the following reply, that it was always readily (?) permitted to me, together with .... to come to you in whatever way I can. For there are certain essential things which .... you will receive my letters by which you will know what I am going to do .... I was ... and will remain at Briga. Greet your Cerialis from me. (Back, 2nd hand) Farewell my sister, my dearest and most longed-for soul. (1st hand) To Sulpicia Lepidina, wife of Cerialis, from Severa, wife of Brocchus (?)."

a.i.1. *ṣạḷụṭẹṃ*: this is written at the right-hand end of the line and we assume that a preceding lost line contained the beginning of the letter, *Claudia Seuera Lepidinae suae*, written across the whole width of the double leaf (*Claudia* is abbreviated in **291**.i.1, written by a different hand).

2. *ẹgo*: *go* is certain; before it we should probably simply read *ẹ* and take the other marks as offset. For another letter beginning with *ego* see **265**.3. We would not rule out as an alternative reading *ẹṛgo*; its position at the beginning of a sentence is quite normal, cf. *P.Mich.*VIII 469.17 (= *CEL* 144); at the beginning of a letter it suggests response to, or resumption of, something discussed in an earlier letter (*OLD*, s.v. 5).

locuta fueram: see Adams (1994). There is a mark over *locuta* which is not ink.

3. *at te*: also in ii.3, cf. *P.Mich.*VIII 472.4, 17 (= *CEL* 147), Adams (1977), 25-9.

4. *mihi <i>tạ corḍe*: we have been unable to find a way of resolving the difficulties in this line without supposing a scribal error due to haplography. The reading of *mihitạ* is virtually certain (there is no serious doubt about *ạ*). Following that *cor* is clear and, after a doubtful letter, *esem* is equally clear; as the broken letter thereafter suits *p* very well, we think *semp[er* is certain. The doubtful letter after *cor* could be *t*, but we cannot suggest what *corte* would mean (unless it were to be understood as being for *corde*; the scribe does write *at te* in lines a.i.3 and b.ii.3 but this use of *t* for *d* is much less surprising). We think *corḍe* defensible as a reading; for *d* written with a very small bow cf *quaedam* in b.ii.4. Since *tacorde* makes no sense and *ita* fits very well, we can only suppose that this was what was intended and that the second *i* has been omitted. For *corde* perhaps see Virgil, *Aen.* 6.675, *si fert ita corde uoluntas*, Plautus, *Capt.* 420, *uideas corde amare inter se*, and cf. *TLL* IV 940 which seems to suggest that it could mean *ex animo*.

li]c̣ịtum unạ́: only the top of the letter which we have read as *c* is visible but it compares well with the example in *actura* (b.iii.4) and the word fits the context very well. We imagine that the following line (b.ii.1) began with *cum* plus name or description or both (e.g. *cum Candido seruo*, or perhaps joining a military party, *cum militibus/centurionibus cohortis*). An alternative way of reconstructing the sense of what follows is to suppose that *li]c̣ịtum* is the end of a sentence and that in the subsequent sentence Severa is saying "therefore I shall try to visit you, in company with X, by whatever means I can". It seems less likely that *unạ́* is nominative (to which the apex is no objection cf. *necessariá*, b.ii.4), meaning "alone". In what follows she could be saying either that there is some essential business which she needs to discuss with Lepidina face-to-face rather than by correspondence or that there is some essential business which prevents Brocchus from accompanying her.

b.ii.3. *at te*: see a.i.3 note.

4. There is a mark on the right-hand half of the leaf, after the gap, which cannot be the top of *e* in this hand; it can hardly be the top of *c* or *s* either (which in any case make no sense here). Unless it is just an offset, which looks improbable, it is an apex. For an apex

over a diphthong see *CEL* 72.7, 81.11. Alternatively, there might perhaps be enough space to accommodate *qua[e á]*.

iii.1. Perhaps a gerundive (e.g. *agenda sunt*) to end the sentence, then a new sentence beginning, for example, *per frat]/rem* or *per familia]/rem*.

2. *ṃẹaṣ*: this seems to us the likeliest reading although only *a* is clear; neither *a me* nor *duas* can be read.

4. *sim actura*: for the future-exponent see Adams (1977), 49. There might be an apex over the *a* at the end of *actura*, though this may be just offset.

c.v.2. Col.iv will have been written on the left-hand half of this diptych and is wholly lost. We must therefore reckon with the loss at this point of 4-5 lines in col.iv before the first line of col.v (of which only exiguous traces remain).

.ṛạ: there is a mark, like an apex, over the *r* but we think this is probably not ink. In view of *ṃansụṛạ* following we expect another future participle here; although we could just possibly read *ụra* the word division is unlikely.

For Briga cf. **190**.c.38-9 and note, *domịni Brigae ṃạṇ[se-]/runt*; it is obviously the name of a place in the vicinity of Vindolanda. It remains uncertain whether Briga was the home base of Brocchus and Severa; the fact that Severa explicitly states her intention to remain there might suggest that Lepidina would not necessarily expect her to be there. It should also be noted that *ṃansụṛạ* might mean "intending to stop off at" or "intending to lodge at" (*OLD*, s.v.2a) and, if this were the case, it would imply that Briga was not her home base.

3. Cf. **291**.ii.9, where *a me* is omitted.

b.back. It is very unclear on the photograph which marks are ink and which are not and this makes the readings particularly difficult.

1. The first visible letter is certainly *e* and the spacing permits *[ual]e* (cf. **291**.ii.12, **293**.1). The next letter is almost certainly *m* and the line clearly ends *ror*; we therefore expect *mea soror*, but it is very hard to read this.

2-3. *ḳạrissima*: the reading of the first two letters is most uncertain.

et aṇịṃạ / ma: we expect *et anima mea* or *et mea anima*, but find it impossible to read either. We give what we think is the least problematical reading but would stress that it is very hard to read the dotted letters. For the possessive adjective in this form see Adams (1994). For the use of *anima* in the closure see **291**.ii.12 with the note, cf. **293**.1 note. For *desideratissima* see *CIL* 6.21974.6-8, *coniugi carissim[ae] animae desideran[tissi]mae* (cf. *TLL* VI.1 710).

4. The traces might belong to *[ua]ḷẹ*.

c.back 2. As in **291**.back 16, *coniugi* is omitted. It is noteworthy that the last three letters of *Ḷẹpidịnae* are written in ordinary cursive, whilst the first six letters in the previous line are in the spindly script associated with addresses. There may be traces further to the right; if so, presumably from *praef(ecto) coh(ortis)*.

3. *a Seueṛạ*: only the tops of the last two letters survive. Thereafter there is a trace of the top of an ascender which is compatible with *b* and it is difficult to imagine that we could have anything other than *Ḅ[rocchi*.

293

Inv.no.8.160.b. 88 x 36 mm. *VRR* II, Plate XI.

A fragment of what must have been the right-hand side of a diptych containing the closure of a letter written in the same hand as the closures of Claudia Severa in **291**.ii.11-4 and **292**.b.back 1-3. The back contains traces which can be reconciled with an address to Lepidina.

. . . .

m[2] uaḷe ......[
soror kạṛịṣsimạ
traces

. . . .

Back:

. . . .

m[1] *traces*
[a] Ṣẹụẹṛạ

1. After *uaḷe* there are clear traces which should probably be read as *ạṇ*, suggesting *anima mea* (cf. **291**.ii.12-3, **292**.b.back 2-3).

Back 1. The traces are very exiguous. No doubt the address was *Sulpiciae Lepidinae Cerialis* as in **291-2** but we do not feel confident enough to fit the traces to any satisfactory reading. At the right before the break we may have *ịṇ[*. It seems possible that this hand, which will have been the hand of the main part of the letter, is the same as either that in **292**, **245** and **246**, or that in **291**, **243**, **244** and **248**.

2. *a] C̣ḷ(audia) Ṣẹụẹṛạ* is possible but not probable.

294

Inv.no.85.056.a. 65 x 65 mm. Plate XIX.

Part of a diptych containing the left-hand column of a letter to Lepidina. It is complete at the top and almost complete at the left, but there may be some lines lost at the foot. There are probably some 6-8 letters missing at the right, an estimate based on the restoration of *suae* in line 1 and *ṣ[alutem* in line 2. We assume that the letter continued in another column on the lost right-hand portion of the diptych.

The occurrence of *salua* in line 3 makes it certain that Lepidina's correspondent is a woman. Her name is difficult to read but it cannot be Claudia Severa; see further line 1 note. The surviving part of the letter does not enable us to be certain about the subject-matter. If line 6 has a reference to a fever or a cognate word (see note), it may be that the writer is promising to bring Lepidina some drugs or remedies (for concerns about health in Cerialis' household see **227**).

This hand is an interesting one, using two forms of *l*, a very upright and narrow *e*, an elaborate curve at the top of *b* and a flat *u*.

].ạ. . .ṇa Lepidiṇ[ae suae
ṣ[alutem
ita sim salua domi[na
ut ego duas aṇ.[
f̣ẹṛaṃ ṭịbị alteṛ[am
alteṛam febric̣.[
et ideo me tibi ẹ[
sed quatẹnus m.[
. . . .

" ... Paterna (?) to her Lepidina, greetings. So help me God, my lady [and sister?], I shall bring (?) you two remedies (?), the one for ..., the other for fever (?) and therefore ... myself to you ... but insofar as ..."

1. There is a clear *a* in the middle of the line which we take to be the end of the name of the sender (we think the traces between this and *Lepidiṇ[ae* are not ink). Before this there are traces of some 5-6 letters and in the lacuna at the left not more than two or three letters can have been lost. As there appears to be a medial point after the first letter, we have considered the possiblity that there was an abbreviated *gentilicium*, perhaps *C]l* · (= *Cla(udia)*, cf. **291**.i.1) or *F]l* · (= *F]l(auia)*). If this is correct, the only two instances of abbreviation of a *gentilicium* in the tablets concern women. In what follows, the first surviving letter looks most like *p* or *c*, the second is very probably *a* (though *r* may also be possible). Two or three uncertain letters follow before what looks most like *na*, which we take to be the ending of the name. We think it is possible, though difficult, to read the name as *P̣ạṭẹṛṇa*.

3. *ita sim salua*: a comparable phrase, *ita sim felix*, is attested in Propertius 1.7.3 and Suetonius, *Tib*. 21.4; cf. also Cicero, *Att*. 16.13a.1, *ne sim saluus si aliter scribo ac sentio*, and Terence, *Phormio* 807, *ita me seruet Iuppiter ut proprior illi quam ego sum nemost*. This last example is also a parallel for a wish introduced by *ita* followed by *ut* (see *OLD*, s.v. *ita* 17). Since we appear to need nothing more at the end of line 3 to complete the sense, the solution may be to supply *soror*.

4-6. The restoration and interpretation of this passage depends on three cruces: the words at the end of line 4, the beginning of line 5 and the end of line 6. The suggestions which follow can only be tentative.

4. *aṇ.[*: the final trace is faint and exiguous, but the letter preceding must be either *n* or *m* and the former is preferable. A feminine noun is required and if our suggestions for lines 5 and 6 are on the right lines, something with a medical connotation would be appropriate. Thus, perhaps, *anṭ[idotos* (a feminine form), meaning remedy (*TLL* II 168-9). Alternatively, if *aṃ.[* is to be read, *aṃp̣[ullas* (for the medical use see *TLL* I 2018.64).

5. Of the reading *f̣ẹṛaṃ* only *r* is certain, though *e* before it is probable; the initial letter must be *f* or *s*. A first person verb is needed and the start of this line seems the most probable place for it. The traces after *r* could be almost anything. We tentatively suggest reading either *ṣẹṛaṃ* (presumably the end of an epistolary pluperfect) or *f̣ẹṛaṃ*; in either case it could be the end of a compound verb, depending on the length of the supplement in line 4. The reading of *ṭịbị* assumes that the mark between the first and second letters is either dirt or a smudge.

alteṛ[am: the foot of the exaggerated descender of *r* can be seen at the end of line 6.

6. *febriç.[*: the penultimate letter could be *p* (there is no other *c* in the text for comparison); following that we have the descender of *r* in the previous line running through the next letter which might be *i*, *a* or *u*. If we read *ụ*, we can restore *febricụ[lae*, giving the sense suggested in the translation. Alternatively we could have part of the verb *febricito*, though we do not see how it would construe. We have considered the possibility that we have a name here, but we have not found one which begins Febri-. *antidotus* is normally followed by *ad* or *aduersus* plus the name of the disease, but it is found with the genitive *amoris* in Augustine, *Medit.* 7. Another possibility would be to supply *ançillas* in line 4 with *febri ça[rentes*, meaning "I will bring two servant-girls, one for you and the other for X, free from fever" (for *febri careo* cf. Cicero, *Fam.* 16.15.1); or we might begin a new sentence with *febri* (though one misses a connecting word) reading, e.g., *febri ça[reo*; *febri p̣ṛ[ostrata sum* is a less likely reading.

CORRESPONDENCE OF PRISCINUS
(Nos. 295-298)

In *Tab. Vindol.*I we identified four texts (I 30-33) as connected with a person named Crispinus whom we identified as a probable prefect of the First Cohort of Tungrians *c.* AD 105. **296** now enables us to see clearly that the correct reading of the name is Priscinus and this can be read with little difficulty in the other letters (we consider that the two persons named Crispinus in **225**.1 and 2 are different people, see notes *ad locc.*). We have been able to identify a fragment discovered in the 1980s as probably belonging to the letter originally published as *Tab. Vindol.*I 31, but we now regard the attribution of *Tab. Vindol.*I 32 (= **520**) as extremely doubtful and have consequently removed it from this section. The combination of *Tab. Vindol.*I 33 and 82 (now **298**.b) offers us the probability that Caecilius September, known as a correspondent of Flavius Cerialis (**234**, **252-3**), also wrote to Priscinus; another fragment, overlooked in *Tab. Vindol.*I, may or may not belong to the same letter (**298**.a). **173**, an application for leave, also appears to be directed to Priscinus.

The identification of Priscinus as prefect of the First Cohort of Tungrians still rests on the evidence of **295** alone (though **173** also supports the view that he was a prefect). None of the other letters preserves enough content to add anything substantive. The archaeological context of the tablets points to Period 4, which would put Priscinus at Vindolanda after *c.* AD 104; the presence of his correspondence in a barrack-building would be a little surprising if he were a prefect.

See also **448**.

295

*Tab. Vindol.*I 30, Plate VI, 1. *CEL* 98.

A complete letter from Oppius Niger, who must surely be a unit commander, to Priscinus. Niger appears to be telling Priscinus that he (Niger) had sent on their way from Bremetennacum (Ribchester) the two soldiers of the First Cohort of Tungrians, whom Priscinus had despatched with letters to the governor.

Since the *ed. pr.* we have accumulated further evidence which necessitates discussion of individuals in the tablets with the *cognomen* Niger. The following texts are relevant: (1) the present letter from Oppius Niger to Priscinus; (2) **249**, the beginning only of a letter from Oppius Niger to Cerialis; (3) **248**, a letter from Niger (no *gentilicium* given) and Brocchus to Cerialis; (4) **465**, the beginning only of a letter from Valerius Niger to an unidentified addressee.

It is immediately evident that we must surely have the same Oppius Niger in (1) and (2), writing to two different people at Vindolanda, one certainly and the other probably a prefect, perhaps at different periods. Our interpretation of **295** suggests that Oppius Niger was himself stationed at Bremetennacum when he wrote it; that need not necessarily imply that he was at Bremetennacum when he wrote **249**. Is Niger of **248** the same Oppius Niger? The evidence of the hands in **248** and **295** is crucial, though the main texts of both were written by scribes rather than their authors. If we were confident that the same scribe was at work in both that would be a strong argument in favour of identity. In fact, although the hands look superficially similar we cannot convince ourselves that they are the same, for there are some important technical differences (see the introduction to the *ed. pr.*). Nor is there any conclusive evidence in the second hands, in **295** that of Niger and in **248** that of either Niger or Brocchus. On balance it seems to us probable that Niger of **248** is not Oppius Niger of **295** and **249**. It should be noted that, even if he were, we should not draw any conclusion about his location (nor, as a consequence, about that of his co-author Brocchus, presumably Aelius Brocchus, on which see **292**.c.v.2 note). Niger of **248** may, then, be identical with Valerius Niger of **465** (both letters are attributed to Period 3) but we know nothing more about him.

i

Oppius Niger Priscino [suo
ṣ[alutem
Crispum et .ẹ[*c.8*]ṣ ex̣ coh(orte)
·i· Tungrorum quos cum
epistulis ad consularem n(ostrum)
miseras a Bremetennaco

ii

].[..].[.]..[*c.3*
.[.].[.]..um Kal(endis) F̣[eb]ṛ[
*m*² ụale dọmịṇẹ
frateṛ

Back: *traces of 2 lines*

"Oppius Niger to his Priscinus, greetings. Crispus and ... from the 1st cohort of Tungrians, whom you had sent with letters to our governor, [I have straightaway sent on (?)] from Bremetennacum to ... on 1 February. (2nd hand) Farewell, my lord and brother."

i.1. In the *ed. pr.* we considered the possibility that the *gentilicium* of the author should be read as *Oc̣c̣ius* but we now regard *Oppius* as certain in view of **249**.1.

3. Harvey (1985) suggests *ṛẹ[liquo]ṣ*. Although he is correct to observe that *r* in this hand does not always have an exaggerated descender, we think it impossible to read it here and it does not resemble the *r* in *consularem* (line 5) which Harvey compares. We prefer the suggestion that we have a name beginning with *P̣e-* or perhaps *Ṭe-* (cf. Tertius, **343**.ii.21). We may well have a short name followed by *milite]ṣ*, cf. **300**.i.3-4.

3-4. For the *cohors i Tungrorum* see **154**.1-2 and above, pp.22-3.

ii.7. The sense required seems clear. It might be possible to restore *stati]ṃ [p]ṛ[a]ẹṃ[isi* (cf. *CEL*, note *ad loc.*), but the traces are very ambiguous.

8. *]. [ ]. [ ]ạum Kal( ) F̣[ebr*: *CEL* 98. In *CEL 98* Cugusi mistakenly quotes the reading of the *ed. pr.* as *]rum*. We could in fact envisage reading *]ẹṛum* or *]ọṛum*, which we would now regard as likely to be the end of a place-name rather than the end of an ordinal number, since these numbers are never fully written out in dates (see the note in the *ed. pr.*). A more attractive alternative is *]. ḍum* and we think it may be possible to read *ạ[d] Ḷ[i]ṇḍum* (Lincoln), although the use of *ad* with a place-name does not occur elsewhere in the tablets (see *Tab. Vindol.*I, p.72). We are now more confident that the month-name was February and take the last trace in the line as the foot of *r* rather than the top of *e* in the line below.

9. For the form of *e* at the end of *ụale* cf. now **300**.ii.12 note. The reading is unquestionably correct (cf. the note to the *ed. pr.*).

Back. There seem to be sufficient traces for a *gentilicium* followed by *Priscino*, which is what we would expect, and for a second line, but the traces are too slight for us to offer a reading.

296

Inv.no.85.046+047. 107 x 34 mm.

Two joining fragments of the left-hand portion of a diptych containing the opening of a letter from Flavius Conianus to Priscinus. It is the very clear and distinctive *p* at the beginning and *c* in the middle of the name of the addressee on which we base our view that the name of the person with whom this small group of letters is associated is Priscinus rather than Crispinus (contrast *Tab. Vindol.*I 30-33).

[F]ḷạuius C̣oniaṇus Priscino [suo
ṣạḷ[utem
. . . .

1. *C̣oniaṇus*: we could perhaps read *C̣oniaṛịus* but it is less attractive. The form of *c*, with a diagonal stroke at the bottom, is unusual. The *cognomen* Conianus is unattested but note the rare *gentilicium* Conius, attested in Spain, Dalmatia and Sardinia (?) (*NPEL*); there is also a *gentilicium* (?) Coriarius, *AE* 1978.123 (Puteoli), but that might be a misreading. This name does not appear elsewhere in the Vindolanda tablets.

297

(a): *Tab. Vindol.*I 31, Plate VII, 4. *CEL* 99. (b) and (c): Inv.no.85.316.a-b. (a) 23 x 17 mm. (b) 29 x 15 mm.

This letter to Priscinus from a person named Firminus is remarkable for its frequent use of interpunct. We have included two fragments found in 1985 since they are certainly written by the same hand as the earlier piece, also using interpunct, and the name of the sender on the back suggests that they are likely to be part of the right-hand portion of the letter. What is left of the content suggests that the sender might be expressing indignation at having been accused of sharp practice.

a.

i

Fi]ṛminus · Priscino · suo ·
salụtem ·
] niḥil · malo · animo · feci
] · ego · idem in contractụ [
] · fecisse umquam noṇ e.[
] · te aliquid · e.[
. . . .

. . . . . .
q]uod fạcṭuṃ [
]mea · e.[
]esti · pudọ[
. . . . . .

b.

ii

. . .
] f̣raṭẹr · .[
].dạs · me[
traces
. . .

Back:

Pr]ịṣc̣ịṇ[o
. . . .

c.

. . . . .
]ṣque ad me.[
].ṇtas · ex eiṣ [
].[..]ḷẹ f̣ṛạ[
. . . . .

Back:

a] Firmino

a.1. Only the foot of a letter is visible before *minus*; this is compatible with *ṛ* and we are now confident of *Fi]ṛminus*, which we suggested in the *ed. pr.*, in view of the name on the back of (c). The evidence of the new tablets makes it likely that there was a *gentilicium* preceding, which means that there will be a few letters lost at the left of lines 3ff.

4. We are now confident of *contractụ* (what we took as a possible *i* is in fact part of *e* in the line below). For the phrase in legal texts see *TLL* IV 753.39.

5. At the start a restoration of *iuro me* or *affirmo me* would suit the sense we envisage. At the end perhaps *eṣ[t*.

9. The broken letter at the right will not allow *ị* but suits *ọ*; therefore, presumably,

some case of *pudor*. Perhaps a reference to the *pudor* of a *hominis modesti*, cf. *OLD*, s.v. *pudor*, 2c.

There are three scraps with traces of writing which cannot be placed (see note in the *ed. pr.*, line 9).

b.back. None of the letters survives complete but the reading fits the traces very well.

c.1. Probably restore *u]sque ad me*.

3. Perhaps *ua]ḷẹ fṛạ[ter*, which is compatible with a position at the bottom of the right-hand side of a leaf suggested by the content of the back, but note that this is written by the same hand as the rest of the text.

Back. This must be the name of the sender of the letter and, together with the hand, suggests the connection of these two fragments with the main portion of the letter.

298

(a): Inv.no.197. 110 x 30 mm. (b): *Tab.Vindol.*I 33+82, Plate X, 1 and 2. *CEL* 101, 136.

The first of the fragments published under this number (a) was overlooked in editing the tablets from the 1970s. In *Tab.Vindol.*I text no. 104 is incorrectly identified as Inv.no.197, hence our reference to this text as *Tab.Vindol.* 104 in Bowman and Thomas (1987), 129, note 10. It preserves part of the beginning of a letter to Priscinus; it may thus belong to the same letter as the other two joining fragments (b) but this is very uncertain. It is noteworthy that *suo* is more or less aligned with the end of *Priscino*, with *sal[* written to the right of this. Unless *salutem* extended well beyond the centre of the diptych the word must have been abbreviated; there is no certain parallel for this in the tablets, but elsewhere *sal* for *salutem* is of course common (e.g. *ChLA* IV 224). The other joining fragments (b) were originally catalogued under the same inventory number but were published separately. It is suggested in *VRR* II, 40 (cf. A.R.Birley (1991), 98 note 53) that the name on the back of the fragment published as *Tab.Vindol.*I 82 should be read as *Septembre* and that the sender of the letter is Caecilius September who appears as a correspondent of Flavius Cerialis (**234**, **252-3**). This is likely to be correct and the association of the fragments shows that September is on this occasion writing to Priscinus. If this letter does come from September the writing by the second hand on the front ought to be the same hand as that of the second hand in **252**.ii.3 (cf. our remarks on **258**), but there is not enough surviving to allow a proper comparison. If the fragments are correctly joined, there is a large gap between the end of the message proper and the closing greeting, probably *uale frater kari]ṣsime*. Furthermore, there are two small joining fragments with traces which appear to fit below this; there is no real difficulty in envisaging an addition to the closure. There is another small fragment with a trace of one letter on each side but we have not been able to place this.

a.] Priscino
] ṣuọ ṣal[
. . . . .

b.

. . . . . .

m[1] *traces*

uacat

m[2] kari]ṣsime

]m

].

. . . . . .

Back: *m*[1]]ọ P̣ṛịṣc̣ịṇ[o

a Ca]ẹc̣ịḷịo Septembre

b.1. Perhaps *opto] ṭẹ ḅẹṇẹ ụạḷẹṛẹ*, *ed.pr.* We now think this unlikely to be right, although it would not be impossible to envisage the phrase closing the message proper and being followed by something else in the sender's autograph (cf. **300**.ii.10-12).

4. The remains of a diagonal stroke which could be the top of *ṣ*.

Back 2. The reading of the *cognomen* is certain. In the *ed. pr.* we suggested that the tops of letters below *P̣ṛịṣc̣ịṇ[o* might be read as *p̣ṛạẹf̣*, but if the two fragments are correctly joined these traces must belong to the *gentilicium* of September.

CORRESPONDENCE OF LUCIUS
(Nos. 299-300)

The two letters addressed to Lucius are assigned to different periods (3 and 5 respectively), but we are tempted to refer them to the same individual, who might have been at Vindolanda for a period of several years, or on more than one posting. One of the letters gives him the title of *decurio* (**299**); the subject-matter of the other, the despatch of two cavalrymen, would be appropriate to a decurion (**300**). Note also **180**.28.

299

*Tab.Vindol.*I 39, Plate VIII, 3 and 4. *CEL* 139.

The back of the left-hand portion of the diptych has abraded traces of five lines, written across the grain, perhaps a casual account (cf. **233**).

i

. . . .
quod est principium epistulae
meae te fortem esse a Cordono-
uis amicus missit mihi ostria
quinquaginta quo uelocius fir-
. . . .

ii

].[*c.3*]ạṛ.....[
uacat

Back: Lucio decurion[i
]..tẹṛi

"... which is the principal reason for my letter (to express the wish?) that you are vigorous. A friend sent me fifty oysters from Cordonovi (?). In order that ... more speedily ... (Back) To Lucius, decurion from ..."

1. *principium*: translated in the *ed. pr.* as "first point" but see *OLD*, s.v. 7b.
2-3. For oysters in Britain see Winder in Milne (1985), 91-5 and cf. Dannell and

Wild (1987), 69, *VRR* III, 114. In the *ed. pr.* we suggested *Cordonoui* or *Cordonouae* as the nominative form of the place-name but it could also be *Cordonouia* (cf. Vinovia, **185**.26 note). There is still no firm evidence for its location, but the Thames estuary on the north Kent coast would be a suitable area.

3. *missit*: see **255**.i.6-8 note and the references there given.

ii.1. Perhaps *c]ạṛịṣṣịṃ[e* rather than *k]ạṛịṣṣịṃ[e*, since we would be more likely to see some part of the bottom of a *k*, cf. *ed. pr.* The latter is adopted by *CEL*.

Back 2. The evidence now available for the form in which addresses were written on the backs of the leaves makes it certain that is part of the identity of the sender, slanting upwards from left to right. The reading of *i* at the end seems quite secure; rather than an ablative of the type found in **311**.back 4 (*Sollem̩ṇị*), **312**.back 4 (*Tullioni*), we may have the end of a genitive which will have followed the symbol for *centuria* or *turma*.

300

Inv.no.87.608.a. 165 x 68 mm. Plate XXII.

This diptych preserves parts of the top, bottom and right-hand edges. The letter is written to Lucius, but the name of the sender, of which only the end survives, seems to be irrecoverable. The writing is generally very abraded and we can make nothing of the last part of col.i and the first part of col.ii. The part of the message which has survived records that the sender has despatched two *equites* to camp. This is appropriate to the identification of the addressee as Lucius the decurion (see back note).

i

] *c.8-9* Lucịo suo
salutem
]ạ..um et Fṛọntinum
equites remisi ad
castra iiii · K(alendas) Martias
[..]....lleg̣ạs tibi ṛ..

ii

c.4 [*c.5*] *c.8*
.u qui ... laḅọre .....[
⟦.⟧hic ut scires scṛ....[
tibi opto fraṭẹr beṇ[e
ualeas
uacat
m² uale

Back: *m¹* *traces*

. . . .

"... to his Lucius, greetings. I sent back ... and Frontinus the cavalrymen to the camp on 26 February ... so that you might know I have written to you. I pray, brother, that you are in good health. (2nd hand) Farewell. (Back, 1st hand) To Lucius, decurion (?)."

i.1. It is common, but not universal, for the opening line of a letter to project further to the left than the first line of the main message (line 3) which, in turn, is often set further to the left than the lines following. The loss at the left is therefore uncertain but we should probably allow for at least 13 or 14 letters, including the traces, for the name of the sender, which no doubt included both *gentilicium* and *cognomen*. For Lucius as a *cognomen* see *RMR* 82.3, **184**.ii.21 and note and cf. **156**.2 note.

3. There appear to be two names, which is appropriate to what follows (cf. **295**.i.3). The first may have lost one or two letters at the left. The second name, Frontinus, does not occur elsewhere in the tablets.

5. Numerals are sometimes preceded and followed by medial points (e.g. **295**.i.4), a common phenomenon in later manuscripts, but in this case there is only one following.

6. The reading is very uncertain. If it is correct, the author may be referring to sending back some other colleagues (*collegas*).

ii.7. The traces are very abraded and obscured by dirt.

8. *qui* looks certain (but note that the form of *q* is quite different from that in line 4, cf. Fig.1 (p.53, above), cols. 1 and 2). After that we could read *ịṭạ* although *t* is not easy.

9. The reading may be simply *scṛịpṣị*.

10-12. It is noteworthy that the scribe has written the substantive closing greeting, leaving the author to add only *uale* in his own hand (cf. **250**.ii.17, **353**.ii.3).

12. *uale* is written in a quick scrawl; *u* is practically a flat dash; *l* has hardly any vertical; for the form of *e* see Fig.1 (p.53), col.3.

Back. It is difficult to read anything except *u* in the name. At the right we may have *d* followed either by an abbreviation mark or by *ec* (cf. **299**.back).

MISCELLANEOUS CORRESPONDENCE
(Nos. 301-353)

Under this heading we have collected 53 texts which merit a full edition and cannot be shown to belong with any of the groups of correspondence which we have identified; it is possible, however, that some of them belong with other groups, particularly the correspondence of Cerialis which is by far the largest. The range of correspondents and subjects is varied and there are several very interesting and important texts. **343** is the longest of all the letters found at Vindolanda and casts a valuable light on the economic and entrepreneurial activity in the frontier region; **309** attests the despatch of components for wagons and there are two texts which certainly or probably concern the quarrying of stone (**314** and **316**). A fragmentary text which is probably part of a letter clearly attests the very important fact that a census was being (or was to be) carried out, perhaps in the earlier part of the 90s (**304**), and military or official activities are also recorded in **345**. More intriguing is **344**, coming from the same milieu as **343** and three important accounts (**180-2**), in which the writer complains to a high official about maltreatment and beating, perhaps by a centurion. A more fragmentary text may contain a similar petition or appeal about the theft of a *balteus* (**322**) and judicial activity may also be mentioned in **317** (cf. **281**). **312** refers to a debt and to the imminent arrival of someone, presumably at the place to which the letter was addressed, perhaps Coria Textoverdorum.

More personal matters are reflected in **310**, to the governor's *equisio*, and **311**, in which the sender complains about the addressee's failure to write. **346** records the despatch of what are probably personal gifts of clothing. Domestic and social matters are represented in **301**, concerning items for the celebration of the Saturnalia, and **302**, the provision of foodstuffs, including chickens, apples, eggs and olives.

Equestrian officers are represented in this correspondence (**315**, **319**, **345**, probably **318** and possibly **305**). It is harder to be sure about the lower ranks: we have the governor's *equisio* in **310** and a *duplicarius* in **312**; **346** reads as if it concerns people of modest status but that cannot be proved. The servile sector is quite well represented (**301**, **303**, **347**, probably **302** and perhaps **311** and **341**). There is one letter which is probably from a woman and is certainly not addressed to Sulpicia Lepidina (**324**).

As for the hands, we have not been able to identify any groups of letters by common hands but it should be noted that **313** is written by the same hand as one of the letters to Saecularis (**213**), and the hand of Chrauttius, correspondent of the governor's *equisio* (**310**), is very probably also in evidence in the correspondence of Cerialis (**264**).

301

Inv.no.87.748. 182 x 76 mm. Plates XXIII, XXV. *VRR* II, Plate VI.

A complete diptych with notches in the left- and right-hand edges. The whole of the message is on the left-hand portion and the right contains only a brief closure. It is notable that the beginning of the message in line 3 is hardly at all indented (cf. **350**). The address is on the back of the right-hand portion and is written in fairly large but normal cursive, unlike the spindly script normally employed in addresses (for another example see **352**.back). It shows that the addressee was a slave of Genialis (see back 8 note); it is likely that the author of the letter was also a slave (see back 11 note). The closure is written in the same hand as the rest of the text, but more rapidly, and we assume it to be the hand of Severus himself, which is competent and fairly fast, with some word division.

The subject of the letter seems to be some payment for an item or items connected with the Saturnalia; the syntax is peculiarly compressed and our failure to understand the first word of the message makes it infuriatingly obscure. In view of the importance of the Saturnalia for people of servile status the subject of the letter is particularly appropriate. There is no other reference in the Vindolanda texts to this festival; for other religious observances see **190**, **265**, cf. **261** and perhaps **466**.

i

Ṣ[eu]ẹṛ[u]ṣ Candido suo
salutem
sọuxtum saturnalicium
(asses) iiii aut sexs rogo frater
explices et radices ne minus (denarii) s(emissem)

ii

uacat
uale frater
uacat

Back:
Candido Genialis
p̣ṛạẹf̣(ecti)
a Seuero
....ị ṣẹṛụọ

"Severus to his Candidus, greetings. Regarding the ... for the Saturnalia, I ask you, brother, to see to them at a price of 4 or six asses and radishes to the value of not less than ½ *denarius*. Farewell, brother. (Back) To Candidus, slave of Genialis the prefect, from Severus, slave of ..."

1. Apart from the final *s* only the bottoms of letters in the name of the author survive but the reading is guaranteed by line 10 on the back where the name is clear.

Candido: this common *cognomen* occurs at Vindolanda in several other texts (**343**.i.1,

180.24, **146**.2, **148**.1, **181**.3, **183**.4, **312**.ii.8) but in no case is it probable that the person bearing it was a slave.

3. *so̩uxtum saturnalicium*: the interpretation of the first word is particularly problematical. The last five letters seem absolutely certain; the only possible alternative would be *e* instead of the first *u* (cf. ii.7, *uale*) but this is very unlikely. If it is an attempt at *sextum* it can only be a mistake, but this seems very implausible. Before *u* we can hardly have anything but *o* and the first letter looks like a clear *s*; but *souxtum* suggests no attested Latin word nor a botched attempt at any word we can find used in connection with the Saturnalia (cf. Macrobius, *Sat.* 1.10.20). In fact, we find it difficult to see how it can be a botched attempt at any attested Latin word at all. If, like *radices*, it is a plant or the product of a plant (see note to line 5), we wonder whether it might be intended for *sucus/succus* (medicine, dye, perfume (?), cf. *OLD*, s.v.2) for which *RMLW* cites the form *suxus*. For *saturnalicium* in a military context see *RMR* 68.ii.8, iii.7, recording deductions from soldiers' pay for the *saturnalicium kastrense*. For the significance of the Saturnalia for slaves see Macrobius, *loc.cit.* For a request for items for festivities cf. *O.Wâdi Fawâkhir* 3.5 (= *CEL* 75), *in die festo mi opus est*.

4. The symbol at the beginning of this line must be either *asses* or *sextarii*. It has the slanting vertical common to both symbols (see e.g. **186**.6, 8 and **190**.c.19, **193**.3, 4) and it also has a stroke at the top which suggests *sextarii*; but the horizontal tick to the left of the vertical, which does not run through it, suggests *asses* and in a context with a clear reference to *denarii* this is perhaps preferable. Furthermore *(sextarii)* would need a genitive of the noun to which it referred, which *souxtum saturnalicium* (whatever the explanation) can hardly be; see further note to line 5. It is curious that the writer has used the numeral *iiii* but written out the word *sexs*.

5. We take the noun + *saturnalicium* in line 3 to be the direct object of *explices* and *(asses) iiii aut sexs* to be an accusative of price (cf. *Tab.Vindol.*I, p.93). For this verb in Vindolanda texts, with and without a financial implication, see **343**.i.4, with the notes *ad loc.* and in Bowman, Thomas and Adams (1990), **316**.margin 2-3.

radices: we have considered the possibility that this should be understood as part of a verb, *radico*; *LS* cites the active form as post-classical with the meaning "take root" but we cannot see how this could make sense. The only alternative seems to be to take it as plural of *radix*; this might mean "radishes" (*OLD*, s.v. 1c, cf. André (1981), 16-7); alternatively in this context it might be understood as the *radix Britannica* which had medicinal properties, see Pliny, *NH* 25.20-1 and Davies (1989), 219 and Plate 10.7. Note, however, the special connection of the Saturnalia with crops and plants (Macrobius, *loc.cit.* in note to line 3).

5-6. *ne minus*: see *OLD*, *ne* 3.

ii.7. The ligature of *u* and *a* is noteworthy, as is the form of *e*.

Back 8-9. For Candidus see note to line 1. Genialis is probably Flavius Genialis, for whose correspondence see **217-24** and cf. **256**.i.1 and note. The reading of line 9 is complicated by the presence of dirt and a knot in the wood. There are traces of four or five large letters at the right of the leaf and the writing which we have transcribed as lines 10 and 11 is more or less directly to the left of them. The traces are compatible with the reading given and the size of the letters suggests that this is Genialis' title; this is important since it is the strongest evidence we have for the fact that he was a prefect (cf. **220**). The address seems to follow the same pattern as that of **347**.back, where the name of the addressee is not followed by *seruo* but the name of the sender is, see note *ad loc.* and note to line 11, below.

11. The reading of this line is uncertain and is complicated by the presence of dirt and a knot in the wood.

The first letter of the name is probably *p* or *c*, the second *a* or *r*. *Parati* is perhaps compatible with the traces. It is not possible to read *Pacati*, a name which occurs in one of the stilus tablets (Inv.no.88.923, see *VRR* II, 62), cf. Pacata in **353**.ii.1.

ṣẹṛụọ: the reading is very difficult and it is difficult to tell what is ink and what is dirt, especially in the middle. There may be an apex over the last letter. We have considered as an alternative *cọṛṇic̣lạṛịo* and, palaeographically, this reading could be defended. It is certain, however, that Candidus is a slave (see the preceding note) and we think it inconceivable that a *cornicularius* would address a slave with the word *frater* (lines 4 and 7).

302

Inv.no.88.839. 107 x 40 mm. Plate XXIV. *VRR* II, Plate IV.

Part of what was presumably the right-hand portion of a diptych. On the front are five lines of a letter written along the grain and, at a right-angle in the left margin, parts of four more lines; these must have been written between the columns, as in **311** (contrast **316** where the notches in the left-hand edge show that the marginal writing must have been at the left of col.i). There is no sign of a closure, but it could have been written (if brief) in the left margin or below the lines which are along the grain, if something has been lost from the bottom of the leaf. On the back is the end of an address which suggests that the recipient was probably a slave of Verecundus (no doubt the prefect of **210**-**2**). The content of the letter, the acquisition of foodstuffs, is appropriate to a domestic slave in the *praetorium*. Not enough of the address on the back survives to give us any clue to the identity of the author but the negotiations about relatively perishable foodstuffs suggest that he cannot have been very far away.

The way in which the letter is set out is slightly odd. The beginning of the surviving part is written as a list, like that in **309** except that the numbers are written out rather than represented by digits. Thereafter, although the text still reads as a list with glosses, three lines are written continuously and the latter two are indented. There may be something missing at the bottom of the leaf. The hand is very like that of **498** and could well be the work of the same person.

. . . .
ḟạḅạe ḟrenṣaẹ   ṃ(odios) duos
pullos   uiginti
malạ ṣị potes formonsa inuenire centum oua centum aut
  ducenta si ibi · aequo emantur
. . . .

L.margin: ↓
]rio mulsi si ẹḅr .[
]mus (sextarios) viịi muṛịạẹ .[
] .ṣ modium oliuae [
] .ṇọ ⟦ . . ṃ⟧

Back: . . . .
traces
Verecundi
traces?

"... bruised beans, two *modii*, chickens, twenty, a hundred apples, if you can find nice ones, a hundred or two hundred eggs, if they are for sale there at a fair price. ... 8 *sextarii* of fish-sauce ... a *modius* of olives ... (Back) To ... slave (?) of Verecundus."

1. *fạḅạẹ frenṣaẹ*: only the bottoms of letters of *fạḅạẹ* survive but we are in no doubt about the reading. For the collective use see **192**.3. For *frensus* as an alternative form of *fre(s)sus* see *TLL* VI.1 1286 and for *fabae fressae* lines 68ff.; cf. *formonsa* in line 3. *TLL* shows that *faba fre(s)sa* is a well-known expression, found at *Ed. Diocl.* 1.9, 10 and several times in *CGL* (where the spelling *frensa* is found in the mss. at II 69.3, 314.1, V 60.28).

ṃ(odios): *m* is very faint but can certainly be read. There is no trace of a superscript dash. It is slightly odd that the number is written in full as *duos* rather than digits (so too *uiginti* in line 2), especially given the layout of the text. It looks less odd in lines 3-5 and (e.g.) **255**.ii.9-10 where the text is continuous.

2. *pullos*: for chicken and other domestic fowl in the military diet see Davies (1989), 195-6, Dannell and Wild (1987), 68, and for Vindolanda, Hodgson (1976), 25-6 and (1977), *VRR* III, 113.

3. *maḷạ*: only the bottoms of the last two letters survive but we are confident of the reading. Apples are not mentioned elsewhere in the Vindolanda tablets (for fruit in the military diet see Davies (1989), 198). *ṣị* has almost completely disappeared but the reading is surely inescapable. That the adjective *formonsa* is appropriate to apples is suggested by its use with *poma* (*TLL* VI.1 1112.57); for the form see Adams (1994). *formosa* is used of *pondera* by Rustius Barbarus in *O.Wâdi Fawâkhir* 1.11 = *CEL* 73.

4. *oua*: cf. **193**.5 and note.

5. There is a clear interpunct after *ibi*.

aequo emantur: we have not found an example of the use of *aequo* on its own with the verb *emo*, and *pretio* must be understood, unless it followed the verb; cf. perhaps *aequọ perferet*, **215**.ii.6 and note. For the phrase *aequo pretio* see *Digest* 30.66 and cf. *aequis pretiis* in *Digest* 47.11.6 *pr.*, Livy 7.21.8.

Margin. Our understanding of these lines is hampered by the fact that we do not know how long they were.

1. The reference to *mulsi*, a drink made from honey and wine, suggests that the word following might well be *ebrius* or a cognate. If there is a word division at the edge of the leaf, *ebri-* would be preferable and there may be a faint trace of *i*. Apart from the possible reading of a *titulus pictus* on the neck of an amphora from Masada (*Doc.Masada* 821) we have found no explicit reference to *mulsum* in the military context (not mentioned by Davies (1989), 187-206), but honey is attested at Vindolanda in **192**.7.

2. *]mus* is presumably the end of a verb, possibly *emere*.

3. *oliuae*: for the collective singular cf. line 1, *fạḅạẹ*. For olives in Britain see *Britannia* 21 (1990), 369-70 no.24.

Back 1. Only exiguous traces of the bottoms of letters.

2. If the recipient was a slave of Verecundus, *seruo* might have followed *Verecundi*, but it is not essential, see **301**.back 8-9.

3. There may be traces at the bottom left corner where one might expect the name of the sender of the letter.

303

Inv.no.88.845.a-h. (a) 54 x 23 mm. (b) 76 x 28 mm. (c) 22 x 16 mm. (d) 25 x 20 mm. (e-h) small scraps.

Eight fragments of a diptych of which five (a-e) have significant amounts of writing. All were found together and all are in the same hand; we therefore presume that they belong to the same letter. (a) and (b) clearly form part of the left- and right-hand halves respectively; (b) has the remains of the address on the back; (c), (d) and (e) each have writing on both sides. We have not been able to join these or to establish their relationship to the large fragments (a) and (b). We may have a letter which was continued on the back of the left-hand half of the diptych to which fragments (c-e) would then belong (cf. **292**). The difficulty with this is that the back of (a) is blank.

The tablet contains a letter from Privatus to Albiso but it has not been possible to extract any connected sense from the text. *seru[* in e.2 suggests that this letter might come from the servile milieu (cf. **301**, **302**).

a.

P̣riuatus Albisoṇ[i suo
[salutem
accep̣i superius ...[
]bis ...[
. . . .

b.

. . . .
traces ụḅ..met
traces tunt dom
traces illịs me nul
.ẹ.ṛụṃ..bi *c.6* ṃ.ṣe
. . . .

Back:

Ạlbisoni *traces* [
. . . .

c.

. . .
t..[
in.[
me.[
...[
. . .

Back:

. . . .
... coraạ.[
i]ụdịc̣aui[

]ndicabị[
traces

.   .   .   .

d.

.   .   .   .

]ṇdum ..[
]llum ...tem[
]ṣc.. *traces* [

.   .   .   .

Back:

.   .   .   .

uic....[
...hi quọd [
.....de.[

.   .   .   .

e.

.   .   .

].o seru[
]....[

.   .   .

Back: *traces of 2 lines*

a.1. *Priuatus*: the first letter is difficult; it may have been made in the tall, capital form but, if so, the top is abraded. The name, a common servile one, occurs in **190**.c.26, 28, 31, 35 where its bearer is probably a slave (see also **199**, **415**). The present text is attributed to a different period and since Privatus is the author of the letter he must be presumed to be somewhere other than Vindolanda.

Albisonị: after *o* there is only a trace of the bottom of a vertical, which is compatible with *n*. Albisius is attested as a *cognomen* in *CIL* 13.6237 and as a *gentilicium* in *CIL* 12.3394 but we cannot read this here. It is likely that we have the dative of the name Albiso, attested only by Sidonius, *Ep.* 150.6 (see *AS* I 77, *LAN* 33). See b.back note.

2. *superius*: cf. **334**.5. This may be followed by *iiị[*, which is most naturally taken as the beginning of a date.

b.2. *dom* looks like a line-ending; no doubt part of *domine* but the word division is unexpected.

4. .ẹ rụm .bi: *ṭibi* is possible.

Back. The traces after *Ạḷbisoni* might be the beginning of the name of the owner if Albiso is a slave; it might be possible to read *Gẹ....[* ("slave of Genialis" (?), cf. **301**.back 8-9).

c.back 3. Probably part of the verb *indico*, cf. **334**.2, but there are other possibilities.

d.back 2. *mịhi* is possible.

e.1. Since there are traces of writing below *seru[* it is unlikely to be part of an address.

304

Inv.no.87.767. 92 x 10 mm. Plate IX.

A fragment of a leaf containing three lines, presumably of a letter. It is important because it contains a clear and unequivocal reference to the organisation of a census, which must be taken to apply to the frontier region. For arguments in favour of the universality of the provincial census see Brunt (1990), 329-35, citing evidence for the involvement of military personnel, which the Vindolanda text must also be taken to illustrate. The evidence for census procedures in Britain in this period is discussed by Frere (1987), 188-9; note particularly *ILS* 1338, the *censitor Anauuorum* in the north (cf. also Southern (1989), 97, *PNRB* 249-50), and *ILS* 2740, a *censitor* at Colchester.

. . . .

traces

censús · administret · ụṇam

traces

. . . .

2. There appears to be an apex mark over *u* of *census* (see above, pp.57-61). The interpunct after *census* is very clear; at the left of *ụ* after *administret* there is a mark which appears to be a serif but could easily be interpunct; for this reason we incline to prefer the reading we have given to the alternative *administretuṛ ịam*. *census* could then be understood as genitive singular and we could envisage it as part of a phrase such as *ut actionem census administret*. *unam* is then best taken as the beginning of a new sentence.

305

Inv.no.88.828. 186 x 56 mm.

A diptych containing remains of two columns of a letter. The left-hand portion preserves remains of 5 lines of the first column and the right much abraded traces of 7 or 8 lines of the second. The back of the left-hand side also has abraded traces of 4 lines which indicates that the letter was continued on the reverse of the leaf (cf. **292**, **303**). The address as usual is written on the back of the right-hand portion. We have been unable to read anything except odd letters of the text on the front of the right-hand side or the back of the left. On the latter, it looks as if we might have a second hand, although what can be made out does not suggest any of the familiar closing formulae. The main hand is an unremarkable cursive which uses the apex mark in the address.

i

. . . .

traces

c.5 ḥaḅẹṣ quid ergọ

a te ịṃpetrauerim re-

scribe mi ut ...[.]....
ḥis.ḅ[.]..[
. . . .

ii
traces of 7/8 lines

Back:

i
m²? *traces of 4 lines*

ii
m¹? Vettió Seueró
..[
. . . . . .

i.3. The very long tail of *a* at the beginning of the line is noteworthy.

ịṃpetrauerim: although the first two letters are very faint, the reading is not in doubt (cf. **255**.ii.12).

4. *mi*: for the contracted form cf. **343**.i.10, ii.23. After *ut* only the tops of letters survive.

5. *ḥis .ḅ[*: the last letter might be *l*. Thereafter only traces of the tops of letters survive.

Back ii.1. Both elements of the name are extremely common. For Vettius cf. **214**.1 note; Severus occurs in **349**.6 and **301**.i.1 (the latter probably a slave). Vettius Severus does not occur elsewhere in the Vindolanda texts and is not likely to be identical with either of the other individuals with this *cognomen*. The attestation of T.Vettius Severus, the prefect of *cohors iv Hispanorum* (*PME* V81), is too late to be relevant. See next note.

2. *..[*: the only certain traces are of the tops of two letters (there may be some further traces to the right but it is impossible to be sure whether these are ink). It is probable that these belong with the name of the addressee rather than the sender, since they are not written on an upward slant. The traces are compatible with *p̣ṛ* and the spacing would allow *p̣ṛ[aef(ecto) coh(ortis)*. It must be stressed, however, that this is extremely uncertain (cf. *VRR* II, 27, 30).

306

Inv.no.85.067. 63 x 55 mm.

A fragment of a leaf containing part of the right-hand side of a letter with traces of address script on the back. Since we have neither the left- nor the right-hand edge intact it is impossible to establish the line length. The first hand writes a nice, right-sloping cursive.

. . . .
]. li.iuga[
].nis acuṭa[

].s. . .ṇ.st.aẹ
]. . . . . *m²* uale. . domi[ne
] *uacat?* f̣ṛater caris-
] *uacat?* ṣime
]. . . . ḥaec
] *traces*
. . . .

Back: *traces?*

1. *iuga* might suggest a reference to yoked animals.
2. There might be a letter or, more likely, an interpunct after *nis*.
3. At the right *ṇọṣṭraẹ* might be read.
4. The message might end with *ṭịḅị*.

5-6. The writer appears to have left spaces at the left, aligning these lines with the beginning of his closure part-way through line 4, cf. **255**.ii.15-7, **264**.3-5.

carisṣime: for *c* rather than *k* see **299**.ii.1 and cf. the note on *CEL* 139, *ad loc.*

7-8. There are traces of two more lines of which we can make nothing coherent. For an addition after the closure see **248**.ii.14.

307

Inv.no.85.318.a-d. (a) 43 x 29 mm. (b) 17 x 11 mm. (c) 28 x 9 mm.

One substantial fragment of a letter (a), written on both sides of a leaf (cf. **340**). There are two smaller fragments, also with writing by the same hand on both sides (b, c) which may fit together. It is not clear how they may relate to (a), but the sloping writing on one side of the smallest fragment suggests that it belongs to the address on the back. There is no clear indication as to which side is the front and which the back of (a); we have designated as the back the text in which there are spaces at the right of the lines of writing, which seems to us slightly to predispose in favour of this. The content is exiguous but what there is suggests a concern with legal matters (cf. perhaps **317**, **339**).

a.

. . . . . .
iṇạ[.]ṛ[
pi⟦.⟧gṛị.[.].[
a uobis omn[
exoró d.[
].[..].[
. . . . . .

Back:

. . . .
].er
]ṣc̣ribti
].e ad accụs-

a]ṇtium
traces
. . . .

b.
. . .
]. siue
. . .

Back:
. . .
libe[
. . .

c.
. . .
]uiṇ[
. . .

Back:
. . .
.qu..[
. . .

a.2. Perhaps some case of *piger* or *impiger*. We are confident that *g* is correctly read; it has a remarkably long tail (as does *r* in this hand).

4. It is not possible to read *dọ[mine* after *exoro*.

Back 2-4. *scribti-/[o]ṇe* seems a plausible restoration; for the spelling cf. **339**.4. This would suit the context if the reading *accụs/[a]ṇtium* (in which the first *c* is re-made) is correct. A noun in the accusative would then follow.

b. If fragment (c) does not fit below, this piece may belong with a.1.

308

Inv.87.780. 98 x 15 mm.

Two joining fragments which preserve parts of three lines from the start of a letter. It is remarkable that the writing slants upwards and is not written, as usual, straight along the grain.

traces? Atto Atṭ..ịi...[
salutem
].[.].[.]ạḷere
. . . .

1. For the name Atto see **345**.i.1-2, ii.3 (cf. **320**.2). Note that here there may be traces of two to three letters before *Atto* which could be the end of his *gentilicium*. What follows should be the name of the recipient and it is very strange that it too appears to begin Att-; indeed a possible reading is *Attọṇị* (though *n* is difficult). No doubt it is just possible

that this is correspondence between two men both of whom had a fairly uncommon *cognomen*, but in view of the possible repetition, it is perhaps worth considering whether this is just a draft or writing-exercise in which the writer has used a name, perhaps his own, *exempli gratia*.

3. *b]ẹ[n]ẹ [u]ạlere* could be read but would be unexpected at the beginning of a letter (cf. perhaps **311**.i.3)

309

Inv.no.85.051. 167 x 86 mm. Plate XXVI. Bowman and Thomas (1987), no.6, Plate XVII. *CEL,* Appendix Vindol. α.

The tablet survives in a number of fragments and the placing of some of the smaller of these is somewhat uncertain. The text is complete except that the beginnings of lines at the start of col.ii are lost. Though couched in the form of a letter, it is in fact no more than an inventory of goods despatched. Most of these are wooden items - components of carts etc., which are being sent to the recipient in relatively large numbers (compare *Ed. Diocl.* 15). It seems likely that both the sender and the recipient were civilians working for the military rather than soldiers, and the transport of such manufactured wooden objects to a military post is of considerable interest (cf. **185**.20-1). For additional comments on possible evidence for civilian trading activity at Vindolanda see **180**, introduction.

The hand responsible for the body of the letter is rather inelegant, whereas the second hand, that of the author himself, has some style to it. There are faint traces of an address on the back.

i

Meṭṭo Aduẹcto plurimam sụo
salutem
missi tibi materias per Saconem
modiola n(umero) xxxiiii
axses carrarios n(umero) xxxiix
inibi axsis tornaṭus n(umero) [i
radia n(umero) ccc
axses ad lectum n(umero) xxṿi
sessiones n(umero) viii
bruscas [n(umero)] ịị
pluṭeạ ṇ(umero) x̣x̣[

ii

]. n(umero) xxix
]. . ilia n(umero) vi
] ṃissi tibi pelliculas caprinas n(umero) vi
uacat
m^2 [opto] bene ualeas frater

Back: *m*[1] *traces of 2 lines*

"Metto (?) to his Advectus (?) very many greetings. I have sent you wooden materials through the agency of Saco:
hubs, number, 34
axles for carts, number, 38
therein an axle turned on the lathe, number, 1
spokes, number, 300
planks (?) for a bed, number, 26
seats, number, 8 (?)
knots (?), number, 2 (?)
boards (?), number, 20+
..., number, 29
benches (?), number, 6
I have sent you goat-skins, number, 6
(2nd hand) I pray that you are in good health, brother."

i.1. *Metto*: the name seems to be without parallel, though Mettus is not uncommon. Either of the dotted letters could be read differently (e.g. *Melco*), but we cannot suggest a known name which suits what is written.

Aduecto: *[Ad]uectus* occurs once in Nash-Williams (1950), no.215 and this seems the most plausible reading here; *Aduesto* is easier palaeographically, but we know of no example of this name.

plurimam suo salutem: the order is strange; *plurimam salutem* also occurs in **310**.i.2-3, **311**.i.1-2 and probably **214**.4-5 (where *salutem* is lost), but there the words are in the expected order.

3. *missi*: cf. **255**.i.6-8 note and see Adams' comment in the *ed. pr.* (note *ad loc.*). He points out that the spelling *missi*, which is poorly attested, must largely have disappeared by the beginning of the second century AD and is not found in the letters of Claudius Terentianus. There are several other examples at Vindolanda see **268**.ii.2, **299**.i.3, **314**.2, **318**.4, **268**.ii.2, **344**.ii.19.

materias: this is here used in its basic meaning of timber (as used for building, etc.); cf. *materiem*, **215**.ii.4 and note. The layout of the letter, with a repeated *missi tibi* in line 14, strongly suggests that all the items listed below, down to line 13, are made of timber, as opposed to the hides in line 14.

per Saconem: we suppose this to be the name of the agent through whom the goods are being despatched (cf. perhaps **252**.ii.1-2). Once again we know of no example of the name in this spelling, although Sacco occurs (see *NPEL*); *sacco* is also attested as a common noun ("sack"), see *OLD*, s.v., but the context suggests this is not what we have here.

4. *modiola*: *modiolus* is well attested as the nave or hub of a wheel, e.g. *Ed. Diocl.* 15.3. The neuter is not attested in the classical period, but is given in *RMLW* s.v., and *TLL* VIII 1239.39-40 cites Constant. Porph., *Caer. aul. Byz. 1,91m p.414, 17, μοδίολον χρυσοῦν*.

5. *axses carrarios*: cf. *axes carrarios*, **185**.20. Apart from the Vindolanda references, the word *carrarius* is apparently only found once in the classical period, in *RMR* 58.ii.6, where it is a noun meaning "a man who makes wagons". As an adjective it is cited in *RMLW*

in the phrase *uia carraria*. *Ed. Diocl.* 15.30 has the expression τροχοῦ καρραρικοῦ. For *axses* see Adams (1994).

xxxiix: *xxxxiix*, *ed. pr.* Cf. **182**.i.4. The form of the numeral is reasonably well attested, e.g. *xxiix* is used of a man's age in *RIB* I 673. For a discussion of the subtractive system of numeration see Marichal (1988), 41-7.

6. *axsis tornatus*: cf. *Ed. Diocl.* 15.1a where the Greek entry is paralleled by the Latin *axis tornatus*. The mark which we originally read as the digit *i* now seems to us not to be ink, but in view of the singular noun no other number is possible.

7. *radia*: as with *modiola* the word in a masculine form occurs with the meaning required here, "spokes" (e.g. *Ed. Diocl.* 15.5). For the neuter we may compare the entry *certides* (= *cercides*) *radia* in *CGL* III 195.53.

ccc: *ccc[*, *ed. pr.* We now think it likely that nothing is lost at the right.

8-ii.13. It may be that in these lines we have some items intended for furniture-making, rather than the components of vehicles.

8. *axses ad lectum*: this entry is a puzzle as we cannot imagine why axles should be needed for a couch or bed. It hardly seems likely that it is used to indicate a vehicle or carriage in which one could sleep, i.e. a *dormitorium* (see *Ed. Diocl.* 15.35 and Lauffer's note *ad loc.*). It does not seem possible to take *lectum* to mean "litter" nor have we found any evidence for couches or beds with wheels, see Richter (1966), 105-10, Ransom (1905). The latter does not cite the word *axis* in her appendix of technical terms (109-12). Since *axis* can mean "board" or "plank", see *OLD*, s.v. *axis* 2 and Fordyce's note to Catullus 17.3, we should perhaps so understand it here, even though it must be used in the meaning "axles" in lines 5-6. We note that some Roman couches have cross-pieces between the feet (Richter (1966), fig.530, 532) but it would be odd to call these *axes*.

xxṿi: *xxv[*, *ed. pr.*

9. *sessiones*: also listed among items needed for building carts in *Ed. Diocl.* 15.7.

viii: *[.]ṿiii*, *ed.pr.* One of the detached fragments can justifiably be placed so as to supply the right-hand part of *v* and the remaining digits of the numeral and there is probably nothing lost.

10. *bruscas*: for the knot on the maple producing figured wood used in furniture manufacture see Pliny, *NH* 16.68, and cf. the entry in *CGL* IV 594.31: *brustum* [sic] *materiae genus*. In Pliny, *NH* 16.68 *bruscum* is mentioned along with *molluscum*; of *bruscum* Pliny remarks *e brusco fiunt et mensae*. *TLL* II 2211.78 cites *CGL* III 571.44 for a masculine *bruscus*. The form *brusca* meaning "brushwood" is found in the medieval period (*RMLW*, s.v.) but that can hardly be the meaning here.

11. *c̣lu.e [*, *ed.pr.* We now think that the reading *p̣luṭeạ*, which we considered in the *ed. pr.* as offering good sense, is possible. The main problem is that it is very difficult to see *a* at the end, but it may be that a trace survives. It can simply mean "board" (see *OLD*, s.v.3), but in view of *lectum* in line 8, we note that it may mean the end-rest or back of a bed or couch (see Ransom (1905), 109, 111, notes 16a, 17, citing *CGL* II 152.39, Propertius 4.8.68, Martial, 3.91.10, Suetonius, *Cal.* 26).

ii.12. The first surviving trace might be *s*.

13.]..*ilia*: in Bowman and Thomas (1986), 123 we tentatively suggested *strigilia*, but the word is attested only in the feminine form *strigilis*, "scraper" (of which several examples have been found at Vindolanda). It now seems possible that the traces immediately after the break, which look like a clear *g* at first sight, might be read as *ẹḍ*, suggesting *s]ẹḍilia* ("chairs", "benches"), although it is not clear how these would differ from *sessiones* (line

9). If *g* is the correct reading, the only possible word we have found is *tegilia* ("coverings" once dubiously in Apuleius, *Met.* 9.12), but these do not fit into a list of wooden items.

14. The leaf is broken at the left and it is possible that *et* may be lost.

pelliculas caprinas. The same expression occurs in Pliny, *NH* 30.99. After this line the *uacat* would accommodate four lines, not one as stated in the *ed. pr.*

Back. There are traces of a line in large letters which must be the name of the addressee, and of a second sloping up from left to right, which must be the name and description of the sender. No letters are legible, however.

310

Inv.no.86.470. 189 x 70 mm. Plates XXVIII, XXIX . Bowman, Thomas, Adams (1990), no.1, Plates V, VI; *CEL*, Appendix Vindol. η. *VRR* II, Plate XII.

A complete diptych with tie-holes and notches visible at both the left and right. The address is written, as is normal, on the reverse of the right-hand side of the leaf.

The writer of the letter is Chrauttius, the recipient Veldedeius or Veldeius (see line 1 note). Chrauttius twice addresses Veldedeius as *frater*, which is very common in Latin letters and need imply no actual relationship. But the reference in line 6 to *parentibus nostris* would at first sight suggest that the two were, in fact, brothers. This, however, raises two problems. First, that the term *contubernali antiquo* in the opening (line 2) would then seem inappropriate. Secondly, the name Veldedeius has a suffix which is non-Germanic and generally regarded as Celticised, whereas there is reason to think that the name Chrauttius is Germanic (see the note to line 1). It is very hard to believe that we are dealing with two brothers one of whom had a Celtic and the other a Germanic name. For both these reasons - and given that the word *parens* can mean not only "relative" but also "elder" in a more general sense - it is no doubt better to assume that Chrauttius and Veldedeius were not related; see further the note to lines 1-2.

The content of the letter is fairly routine: admonition for not having written for a long time, enquiry about the *parentes* and the military unit in which a mutual acquaintance is serving, a financial transaction involving a pair of shears supplied by a *ueterinarius*, and greetings to other friends. The mention of the *ueterinarius*, Virilis, is of some interest, as is the occurrence of a woman named Thuttena who is referred to as *soror*.

The spellings in the letter are generally correct, with no sign of changes affecting the Vulgar Latin vowel system or final consonants. Chrauttius admits one noteworthy lexical vulgarism (*tot*, line 5), and writes largely in epistolary clichés. The probable appearance of a second hand in lines 20-1, which we must assume to be that of Chrauttius, shows that he used a scribe for the main part of the text.

The body of the letter is written in a large, sprawling and rather ugly hand. There is often differentiation between thick and thin strokes, but this is far from creating an elegant effect. Several of the letters occur in different forms, e.g. *o* can be quite large or a mere blob, and *p* can be close to the form P or almost indistinguishable from *t*. *b* is noteworthy, since the loop is often placed directly underneath the curve, so that the letter comes close to resembling a modern lower-case b. There is occasional use of ligature. Lines 20-1, the closing greeting, are written in a very similar hand, so similar in fact that we cannot be certain that the whole letter was not written in the same hand. The probability is, however, that this greeting was added, as was normal, in a different hand, the hand of the sender of the letter, Chrauttius. This hand, and a similar closure, may be identified in a letter to Cerialis (**264**) and strongly suggests that Chrauttius was one of his correspondents. There is an interesting ligature in the *us* of *felicissimus*, line 20.

In the *ed. pr.* we commented on the difficulties raised by the presence and interpretation of the word *Londini* on the back of the right-hand side of the leaf. We are now confident that this is to be understood as the address to which the letter was sent and we assume that Veldeius received it in London and brought it to Vindolanda at some point (cf. pp.43-5, above). Two possible explanations for this may be envisaged. The first is that he was there as part of the entourage of the governor during a visit to the fort. The second is that he belonged to a unit at Vindolanda and was detached for duty with the governor in London, where he received this letter from Chrauttius; on his return to Vindolanda he brought the letter back with him. Some circumstantial support for this hypothesis comes from **154** which records that personnel from the First Cohort of Tungrians, which was no doubt stationed at Vindolanda at that time, were detached for duty in London. We do not know to which unit Chrauttius and Veldedeius belonged and we can see no justification for describing them as "former members of a Batavian unit" (so *VRR* II, 51).

i

Chrauttius Veldeio suó fratri
contubernali antiquo plurimam salutem
et rogo te Veldei frater miror
quod ṃihi tot tempus nihil
rescripsti a parentibus nostris si quid audieris aut
Quoṭ.m in quo numero
sit et illum a me salutabis
⟦s⟧ uerbis meis et Virilem
ueteriṇarium rogabis
illum ut forficem

ii

quam mihi promisṣịt pretio
mittas per aliquem de nosṭṛịṣ
et rogo te frater Virilis
salutẹs a me Ṭhuṭteṇam
sororem Velbuteịụm
rescribas nobis cụṃ . . .
se habeat *uacat*
m^2? opt<o> sis felicissimus
uale

Back: *m^1* Londini
Veldedeio
equisioni co(n)s(ularis)

a Chrauttio
fṛạtre

"Chrauttius to Veldeius his brother and old messmate, very many greetings. And I ask you, brother Veldeius - I am surprised that you have written nothing back to me for such a long time - whether you have heard anything from our elders, or about ... in which unit he is; and greet him from me in my words and Virilis the veterinary doctor. Ask him (*sc.* Virilis) whether you may send through one of our friends the pair of shears which he promised me in exchange for money. And I ask you, brother Virilis, to greet from me our sister Thuttena. Write back to us how Velbuteius is (?). (2nd hand?) It is my wish that you enjoy the best of fortune. Farewell. (Back, 1st hand) (Deliver) at London. To Veldedeius, groom of the governor, from his brother Chrauttius."

i.1. *Chrauttius*: we have been unable to find this or a similar name elsewhere; but note the Tungrian named *Chartius*, Weisgerber (1969), 279 (= *AE* 1968.412); also *Rautio*, *RIB* I 1620, *Crotus*, *RIB* I 1525, 1532. Prof. R.E.Keller and Prof. N.Wagner very kindly supplied us with extensive philological information, but were unable to establish a decisive etymology. Prof. Keller notes that "<ch> is the general Latin transliteration of Gmc. /x/ before liquids and nasals" (e.g. *Chlotharius*, *Chnodomarus*). *LAN* 214-6 cites names beginning Chrod-.

Veldeio: here and at line 4 the addressee is named Veldeius, but at line 23 Veldedeius. The name was probably Veldedeius, with Veldeius a syncopated form. This is supported by the fact that the form *Veldedii* occurs on a leather offcut from Vindolanda (*VRR* II, 94 no.12), discovered on the floor of a room near to the find-spot of this tablet and identified as belonging to equestrian equipment, which is entirely appropriate to our *equisio consularis* (see line 24 and note). The name *Vilidedius* occurs in *RIB* I 1420, reported as coming from Housesteads; this might be the same name, and even the same person, as that here. It seems likely that this name is Celtic: the suffix *-eius* is common in Celtic names, note *Nammeius* at Caesar *BG* 1.7.3 and see Evans (1967), 369 and the collection of such forms by Glück (1857), 102, note 3, 140. Note also *Velbuteius* in line 17. Many Celtic names begin *Vel-* (see *AS* III 139-55), and there is a place-name *Veldidena* (Wilten bei Innsbruck), see *AS* III 142. On the etymology of *Vel-* see Evans (1967), 272-7, especially 275-6.

suó: this appears to be the only use of the apex in this letter; see above, pp.57-61.

1-2. *fratri contubernali antiquo*: for *antiquus* of an old acquaintance see Cicero *Fam.* 11.27.2, *nemo est mihi te amicus antiquior*; cf. too Lactantius, *Mort.* 20.3, *ueteris contubernii amicum*. It seems very unlikely that Chrauttius would address a real brother as his "old comrade-in-arms" (*antiquus* would be particularly out of place), but highly likely that he would address an old comrade with the term of affection *frater* (for *frater* as an "*appellatio blanda*" see *TLL* VI.1 1256.22; the idea behind the usage is illuminated by *O.Wâdi Fawâkhir* 2.6-9 = *CEL* 74, *ego te non tanquam amicum habio set tanqua fratrem gemellum qui de unum uentrem exiut*). If Veldeius is not the real brother of Chrauttius (cf. the introduction), it follows that the *parentes nostri* of line 6 cannot be their real parents. Just as *frater* could be addressed as a term of affection to a coeval, so *parens* could be used as a term of affection or respect for someone older (see *TLL* X.1 361.73 and *HA*, *Did.Iul.* 4.1, *unumquemque, ut erat aetas, uel fratrem uel filium uel parentem adfatus blandissime est*; cf.

Horace, *Epist.*, 1.6.54, *"frater" "pater" adde; / ut cuique est aetas, ita quemque facetus adopta*).

2-3. The form of the address is unusually full. *plurimam salutem* is paralleled in **309**.i.1-2 and **311**.i.1-2.

et rogo te Veldei frater: for *rogo te frater*, which was no doubt a cliché of private letters, see line 15, *rogo te frater Virilis*; cf. *O.Wâdi Fawâkhir* 1.10 = *CEL* 73. Twice in the letter the writer has used the vocative *frater* along with a name (here and in line 15). Usually *frater* as a term of address occurs on its own (see, e.g. *O.Wâdi Fawâkhir* 1.10, 2.19, 4.2 = *CEL* 73, 74, 76). Presumably the fuller expression, being less hackneyed, was more affective.

4-6. *miror...rescripsti*: this parenthetical clause has interrupted *rogo te ... si quid audieris*. For parentheses in *rogo*-constructions in colloquial texts cf. Petronius *Sat.* 75.3, *P.Mich.*VIII 467.17ff. = *CEL* 141, and note the examples of interposed *si*-clauses quoted at *Tab.Vindol.*I, p. 124.

5. *tot tempus*: *tot* (sing.) = *tantum* does not seem to be attested. For an analogy compare the singular use of *paucus* = "small" (e.g. *P.Mich.*VIII 471.10, 13, 31 = *CEL* 146; cf. Adams (1977), 79), a sense which passed into the Romance languages (Meyer-Lübke (1935), 6303: e.g. Fr. *peu*). It is a question of a plural ("count") adjective (*pauci*, *tot*) acquiring a singular ("mass") usage. Various adjectives have a singular "mass" meaning which contrasts with a plural "count" meaning (e.g. *omnis* "whole" compared with *omnes* "all"; in colloquial and later Latin note *toti* "all" compared with *totus* "whole"; for *omnis* in this sense see **185**.29).

6. *rescripsti*: for a large collection of examples of such haplology (on which see Leumann (1977), 234) see Neue and Wagener (1892-1905), III 500-06.

8. *Quoṭ.m*: there is a marked thickening of the strokes in the last three letters, but we think it unlikely that an erasure is intended. What is needed at this point is a personal name to which *illum* in line 9 can refer (for the accusative case see the note in the *ed. pr.*). See perhaps *Qutos* (= *Qu(in)tos* or *Qu(ie)tos*?) in Marichal (1988), no.28.14 and cf. Evans (1967), 465.

8-9. *in quo numero sit*: presumably *numerus* in the military sense "any unit, or part thereof" (see Speidel (1984), 119-21, Davies (1989), 17, "*in numero referri*" etc.). The word also occurs in **344**.ii.12 in this sense.

9-10. *illum a me salutabis* ⟦*s*⟧ *uerbis meis*: the idiom *a me salutabis* also occurs at **311**.ii.3-4, *salutabis a me Diligentem* (cf. *rogo ... salutes a me Thuttenam* in lines 15-6 of the present text); see also **509**. *salutabis* displays the colloquial use of the future expressing a command (Hofmann and Szantyr (1965), 311; cf. the more usual *saluta* in e.g. **353**.ii.1, cf. *P.Mich.*VIII 467.33 = *CEL* 141, 468.48ff. = *CEL* 142, *O.Wâdi Fawâkhir* 1.19 = *CEL* 73, 3.16 = *CEL* 75).

⟦*s*⟧ *uerbis*: the writer appears to have written the initial *u* over an *s*, perhaps because he mistakenly began to write *salutabis* a second time. For the expression "greet someone *meis/nostris uerbis*", see also **353**.ii.1, **509**, Tomlin (1992), 151, note 55 and Cicero, *Fam.* 7.29.2, *Tironemque meum saluta nostris uerbis*; for *meis uerbis* with different verbs cf. Cicero, *Att.* 5.11.7, *Fam.* 5.11.2, 15.8.

10-12. In view of *forficem* in line 12 it is clear that Virilis must be the source of the shears, but it is difficult to elucidate the syntax. We have assumed that *et Virilem ueteriṇarium* is added as an afterthought, as a second object of *salutabis* in line 9, and that *illum* in line 12 must refer to Virilis. The word *ueterinarius* is attested in **181**.7, *ab Alione* *ueterinario*, cf. *O.Flor*.15. Virilis and Alio were presumably military *ueterinarii*. The description *ueterinarius* (or *medicus ueterinarius*, for which see *CIL* 5.2183, 6.37194) is found elsewhere of veterinarians serving with the army: see *CIL* 3.11215, 6.37194, cf. *IGRR* I.1373, *Digest* 50.6.7. On the veterinary service in the Roman army, see Davies (1989), 209-36 esp. 212, 214. *ueterinarius* was not, however, an exclusively military term (cf. Columella 6.8.1, 7.5.14, 11.1.12); see Adams (1992b). A military *ueterinarius* will have dealt largely with the equine animals, see Dixon and Southern (1992), 23-9.

forficem: see Adams (1990b).

ii.13. *promiṣịt*, *ed. pr.*: the reading of the end of this word is doubtful since we cannot be certain how many of the traces are really ink; we now prefer the alternative reading *promissịt* (for the geminate *s* see **255**.i.6-8 note, **309**.i.3 note).

pretio: this is an ablative (of price) used idiomatically (see *ed. pr.*, note *ad loc.*).

14. *mittas per aliquem*: for this idiom in letters see, e.g., **309**.i.3, *P.Mich.*VIII 467.19 = *CEL* 141, 468.5, 8 = *CEL* 142, *O.Wâdi Fawâkhir* 1.4, 7f. = *CEL* 73, 2.12 = *CEL* 74, *O.Bu Njem* 76.4-5, 77.3, 79.3-4, cf. Cugusi (1983), 278-9.

15. *frater Virilis*: the word order here should be contrasted with that in line 4. In third person reference the term of affection *frater* (so too *soror*) is regularly placed after the name (see lines 1, 16-7, and 25-6, *O.Wâdi Fawâkhir* 1.1 = *CEL* 73, 2.1 = *CEL* 74). But in the vocative *frater* is sometimes placed before the name as here; cf. Fronto, *ad Amicos*, 2.4.1 (Teubner ed., p.188), Calpurnius Siculus, *Ecl.* 1.8. This is the marked word order, suited to affectionate address.

rogo te frater Virilis: in lines 11-2 Chrauttius asks Veldedeius to convey a message to Virilis. Here he apparently imagines himself as addressing Virilis directly. The switch into direct address of someone who is not the addressee of the letter is striking and unannounced, but it raises no great difficulty, particularly since Chrauttius has asked that the greeting to Virilis should be *uerbis meis*. Cf. Apuleius, *Met.* 3.12, where Lucius addresses the absent Byrrhena directly when sending a message to her through a slave.

15-6. *rogo ... saluteṣ*: for *rogo* + subjunctive see **291**.i.4-5, **311**.ii.5-6 and **314**.4-5, cf. Petronius, *Sat.* 49.6; further examples in Kühner and Stegmann (1955), II 229.

16. *Ṭhuṭteṇam*: a probable though by no means certain reading: the second *t* is particularly uncertain and the initial letter could just possibly be *c* or even *p*.

17. *sororem*: for the affectionate term *soror* see **291**.i.3, ii.11, 12, **292**.a.i.2, **293**.2. The occurrence of a woman in this military context is noteworthy (cf. **181**.14-5 note).

Velbuteius is presumably a Celtic name (see above, line 1 note). In the *ed. pr.* we took this to be governed by *saluteṣ* in line 16 but we now think it more likely that this is an accusative of the type we have in lines 8 and 10 (so *CEL*); on this see Adams' notes in the *ed. pr.*, *ad locc.*

18. *cuṃ* . . .: the letters *c* and *m* are reasonably certain and there appears to be a *u* between them; the traces in the rest of the line are unclear. We have suggested in the translation the way in which we should like to understand these words. The obvious word to appear at this point is *quomodo* but this cannot be read. We have considered the spellings *cuomodo* and *comodo* (cf. *Tab.Sulis* 4.2, *com[o](do)*), but we do not find either of these a convincing reading.

20. *optọ*, *ed. pr.*: we now prefer to read *opt<o>* rather than suppose that the final *o* ran into the following *s*, where there is a blob of ink at the point at which the two strokes meet. For epistolary closing formulae see Cugusi (1983), 47-64, *CEL* I, pp.20-5. For *sis felix*

see *TLL* VI.1 444.24. For the formula employed here **264** has the only exact parallel, *opto domine sis felicissimus quo es dignissimus*; this is probably written by the same hand as the closure in the present letter, which suggests that Chrauttius was responsible for both.

21. The small fragments which were reversed in the plates accompanying the *ed.pr.* are now correctly placed in Plates XXVIII and XXIX.

Back 22. *Londini*: see the introduction and above, pp.43-5. *RIB* II 2443.7 (= Richmond (1953), 206-8. No.3.8 = *CEL* 87) has *Londinio* on the back, which Cugusi (*CEL*, note *ad loc.*) takes to mean that it was written at London; since the tablet was found in London this does not seem likely.

23-4. These lines are written in larger letters than those preceding and following, but it is not a capital script and in fact does not differ except in size from the cursive script used in the rest of the letter, cf. **352**.back.

24. *equisioni*: more usually *equiso*, see *TLL* V.2 726.39. *Equisio* is found mainly in glosses but see also *CIL* 3.13370 (= *equiso*: *TLL* V.2 726.33) where the *equisiones* were attached to *legio II Adiutrix*. Dixon and Southern (1992), 157 suggest that the *equisio* may be more than just the governor's personal groom.

6. *fṛatre*: see note to line ii.21.

311

Inv.no.85.100+108. 220 x 87 mm. Plates XXIV, XXV.

Three joining fragments of a diptych containing a letter from Sollemnis to Paris with an address on the back. The left-hand portion is complete and probably contains remains of two notches in the left-hand edge; the right is missing a line at the top and probably one or two lines at the foot. It is noteworthy that there are three lines of writing, probably by a second hand, at a right-angle to the main text in the margin between the columns; the first two of these lines are on the right-hand portion, the last on the left.

The text of the letter is of some interest for its style and latinity but its substance is not very informative. Sollemnis complains that Paris has not written to him, sends greetings to three friends and asks for a list of names. The address connects Paris with the *cohors iii Batauorum*, part or all of which may therefore have been at Vindolanda in Period 3 (see above, p.24); this is one of only two pieces of evidence for the existence of this unit (cf. **263**.ii.5 and note). It is difficult to be certain of the nature of that connection, however, because parts of the address are difficult to read. It is possible that Paris was a slave of the commander or another officer of the unit and this would make it likely that Sollemnis was also a slave (cf. **301**). The Greek name of the addressee, as well as the names in lines ii.3-5, might seem to support this (see note to line i.1). However, the evidence for Batavians in the imperial guard shows that Greek names are not at all unusual in that Batavian context (see Bellen (1981), but this particular name is not attested.

The main hand is a very competent and interesting, squarish cursive which spaces the words carefully and uses few ligatures. Interpunct appears only once (i.5) although the state of preservation of the writing, particularly in col.ii, might well not allow us to see it, were it there. It is noteworthy that the writer four times uses an apex mark over the final letter of a 1st person singular verb (i.5, 8, 9, ii.5); cf. above, pp.57-61. The form of *e* is noteworthy as is *u* in *ualere* (line 3); note in particular *d* in *Paridi* which ends with the curve normally diagnostic of *b* in ORC (also in *Diligentem*, ii.3).

i

Sollemnis Paridi fratri plurimam salutẹ[m
ut scias me recte ualere
quod te inuicem fecisse
cupió · homo inpientissi-
me qui mihi ne unam e-
pistulam misisti sed
putó me humanius
facere qui tibi scribó

ii

. . . .
ṭibi f̣ṛaṭẹṛ [..]..[
contubernalem meum
salutabis a me Diligen-
tem et Cogitatum et
Corinthum et rogó
mittas mihi nómina
traces
. . . .

Margin: ↓ m^2?]m.
]ter
]mẹ

Back: m^1 P̣ạṛịḍị ..lục..oṛ.[
coh]ọrtis iii Batauo-
rum
a Sollemṇị
]....o

"Sollemnis to Paris his brother, very many greetings. I want you to know that I am in very good health, as I hope you are in turn, you neglectful man, who have sent me not even one letter. But I think that I am behaving in a more considerate fashion in writing to you ... to you, brother, ... my messmate. Greet from me Diligens and Cogitatus and Corinthus and I ask that you send me the names ... Farewell, dearest brother (?). (Back, 1st hand) To Paris ... of the 3rd Cohort of Batavians, from Sollemnis ..."

i.1. For Sollemnis in a Batavian context see *AE* 1952.146 (Bellen (1981), no. 13). The name Paris is fairly uncommon in this region. It occurs in Germania Superior as the name of a slave (*CIL* 13.6423, cf. 13.11015, Aquitania).

1-2. *fratri plurimam salutẹ[m*: *fratri* is not common in the Vindolanda texts at the start of letters (an example in **310**.i.1 and cf. **214**.3-4; in both these texts *plurimam* is also used, see also **309**.i.1), but is often found elsewhere, see e.g. *CEL* 73-80, 157. The omission of *suo* is unparalleled at Vindolanda but it occurs elsewhere, e.g. *CEL* 72, 73 (*fratri* is used in the latter).

3. *ut scias*: for the freestanding *ut* introducing a wish ("know that ...") see Adams (1994).

recte ualere: see *OLD*, s.v. *recte* 9.

4. The sense must be "I hope you are well too"; on this use of *facere* see Adams (1994).

5-6. *inpientissime*: for this formation see Adams (1994) and cf. *RIB* I 1829, *pien[tis]sime et [des]id[eratissime*.

6. *ne*: this usage for *ne ... quidem* also occurs at **343**.i.5 (see note and cf. Quintilian 1.5.39, Petronius, *Sat*. 47.5, *OLD*, s.v. *ne* 7).

ii.1. Despite the loss of the tops of letters, the reading of *tibi frater* is certain. In the line before it one might imagine something like *gratias agam* and following it *si salutes*; there would not be room for a name, however, and it seems awkward to suppose that Diligens is the name of the *contubernalis* with the two other names added as an afterthought. Alternatively, we might imagine something like *commendo tibi, frater* [name], with a new sentence beginning in line 3.

2. *contubernalem*: this term may have a military connotation but it can also be used in a general sense in a servile context, cf. Seneca, *Ep*. 47.1, and note that *TLL* IV 791 cites *conseruus* as a synonym. Cf. back 5 and note.

3. *salutabis*: for the colloquial use of the future expressing a command see **310**.i.9-10 and note.

3-5. The name Diligens is uncommon in the area covered by *NPEL* (only one example cited, a tribune in Britain, *RIB* I 1237); *LC* 259 cites 9 examples and 2 freedmen/slaves. For Corinthus in an Ubian context see *AE* 1952.145 (= Bellen (1981), no.12). Cogitatus is more common (3 occurrences in Gallia Belgica according to *NPEL*).

Margin. The closure appears to be written by a second hand in three short lines. We suggest restoring *uale] mị / fra]ṭer / karissi]mẹ*, cf. **242**.ii.2-3 note, **247**.2-3, **288**.4-5

Back 1. The tops of the letters are lost, more seriously at the left than the right. The beginning of the letter guarantees that the name Paris must appear and *P̣ạṛịḍị* can be read at the left (note that *d* has an unusual curve, cf. introduction). If this is correct, it should be noted that there is no *gentilicium*. Thereafter we have remains of some ten letters and room for up to three more on the fragment which has been broken off. We think it possible that Paris was a slave of someone belonging to the Third Cohort of Batavians (see note to line 5, below and cf. **301**.back) and it may be that we should look for the name of his owner in this line. Alternatively, immediately following the name it may be possible to read *ụḷục̣ịọ*, as a locative place-name (cf. **174**.4 and note), as suggested in *VRR* II, 37; this would then indicate the place to which the letter was sent (see above, pp.43-5). For a place-name immediately following the name of the addressee see *Britannia* 19 (1988), 496, no.32 (cf. above, p.44, note 24), and perhaps *RIB* 2443.11. The difficulty with this is that what follows ought to be a rank, or description of the position of the recipient which continues in line 2, and it is hard to imagine the place-name coming between the name of the recipient and his description. A possible alternative is suggested by *ChLA* III 200, a slave-sale which has the notation *actum Seleuciae Pieriae in castris in hibernis uexillationi clas(sis) pr(aetoriae)* and *P.Diog*.1, *actum castris hib(ernis) coh(ortis) s(upra) s(criptae) contra Apollonospoli Magna Thebaidis*; *c̣ạṣ[tris* would make sense in our text, but the difficulty of the reading must be emphasised (*s* is particularly hard). If this were correct, it would weaken the case for the presence of the Third Cohort at Vindolanda. We have no other suggestion as to how the traces at the end of the line might be read; they do not suggest any familiar military title.

2. *]ọrtis*: it is extremely odd that there is no sign of *coh* before this, but the explanation can only be that the surface is more badly abraded here than elsewhere.

4. For the ablative ending cf. *Tab.Vindol.*I, p.74.

5. Traces of several letters, of which the last is certainly *o*. *(con)s]ẹṛụo* would make sense but we doubt whether it can be read; see notes to i.1 and ii.2.

312

Inv.no.88.935. 183 x 93 mm. Plates XXVII, XXIX.

A diptych which is complete at the foot and is lacking the top and part of the left side of both the left- and right-hand portions; there are two tie-holes and two notches in the right-hand edge. It contains a letter from Tullio to a *duplicarius* whose *gentilicium* is Cessaucius. The hand is rather crude and sprawling, sometimes leaning to the left, sometimes to the right; *o* is sometimes interesting, especially in *non* (line i.5, where *n* is also noteworthy), as is *g* in *rogo* (ii.3); *r* and *q* frequently have very long descenders.

i

. . . .

traces

[*c.9*] ad quem cum pṛịṃuṃ

[potes r]ọgo uenias habemus eniṃ

[*c.3*].[*c.4*].ạreṃ de rebus quas ṃiḥ[i

ṃịsseras non q.... ille sciat

.ẹ.... scṛị[p]sisseṣ.c̣. *traces*

ii

[*c.7* d]ẹḅeo tibi (denarios) x

[*c.6* Can]diduṃ et Natạlem

[*c.5*]..ụm rogo aliquiḍ

[*c.4*]ọrum mihi mịṭṭas

ṛ[ogo] Vir..cium exc̣ịpịas beṇe

uacat

*m*²? opto bene ualeaṣ uaḷ(e)

Back: *m*¹ Coris t..sṭ *traces*

Cessaucio Ni.ṛịn[

dup(licario)

a Tullioni

"... I ask you to come to him as soon as you are able. For we consider him a friend of ours (?). About the things which you had sent me ...why he should know (?) ... you (?)

had written ... I owe you 10 *denarii*. ... Candidus and Natalis ... I ask you to send me some ... I ask you to give Viriocius (?) a warm welcome. (2nd hand?) I pray that you enjoy good health. Farewell. (Back, 1st hand) (Deliver) at Coria of the Textoverdi (?), to Cessaucius Nigrinus (?), *duplicarius*, from Tullio."

i.2. We are reasonably confident of the reading, although *p* and *r* of *primum* are abraded and difficult (and the final *m* is probably crossed by a descender from the line above).

4. *].arem*: the trace after the break can be read as *i* and we suggest the restoration *[eum] f[amil]iarem*.

At the end of the line, where the writing is very blurred, we could read *sub* as an alternative, but do not see how to construe *sub-/misseras* here. We can read the vertical as the left-hand stroke of *h* and *mihi* is to be expected if *misseras* in the following line is correct.

5. The first two letters of *misseras* are difficult to read, especially *m*. After *non* we could read *quare* which would justify the subjunctive *sciat* and might suggest something like "I see no reason why he should know ...". Such a broken context requires great caution, however.

ii.7. For debts between soldiers see Tomlin (1992), 148, note 33 and perhaps cf. **193**, **206**.

8. We could supply *per* at the beginning of the line and suppose that the debt was to be returned through Candidus and Natalis, but this would certainly not account for all the loss. We might obtain a better fit by supposing that a new sentence began here, e.g. *[(re)mittam Can]didum et Natalem*, and perhaps a third name at the beginning of the next line. For persons in the Vindolanda text with the common name Candidus see **301**.i.1 note; the name is far too common to allow any identification and this Candidus may well come from elsewhere. The name Natalis does not occur elsewhere in the tablets.

11. *Vir..cium*: the most plausible reading is *Viriocium*; this is reported by A.R.Birley (1991), 89 as *Viriocus*; the closest parallel we have found for this is *CIL* 13.4514, *Viriaicus* (cf. Birley, *loc.cit.*, Weisgerber (1969), 232).

excipias bene: cf. Petronius, *Sat.* 100.4, *quam bene exulem exciperem*.

Back 1. *corist..st*: A.R.Birley (1990a), 18 (cf. *VRR* II, 37) reads "*Corieptusti(um)* (?)". The reading is difficult since the traces after the first six letters are very abraded and it is uncertain how much more writing there is. We regard the reading of *Coris* followed by *t* as quite certain; *coriep-* results from taking the left-hand part of the top of *t* as the cross bar of an *e*. Since the word or words are placed in the top-left corner of the leaf it is natural to take them as a place-name in an address (see above, pp.43-5). *Coris* with something following suggests a name of the pattern *Coria* plus a tribal name, of which several are attested (see *PNRB* 317-20, arguing that all the *coria*-names in Britain and on the continent derive from the Celtic word for "hosting-place, tribal centre" and that some eventually became assimilated to Latin *curia*). If this is correct, it is very tempting to connect the name on the Vindolanda letter with Curia Textoverdorum, attested by *RIB* I 1695 and certainly in the region of Vindolanda, perhaps its *vicus* (see *PNRB* 470-2). The form of the name is problematical (see *PNRB* 471), but it is possible to suggest that we here have *Coris Texsto* followed by indeterminate traces.

2. *Cessaucio*: the reading is certain, but the *gentilicium* is unattested. We have found: Cessicius (*NPEL*, *CIL* 3.7448 (Moesia)); Cassicius (*CIL* 6.2675); Cessitius (*LE* 428);

Cacussius, Weisgerber (1969), 141. A.R.Birley (1991), 92 (cf. *VRR* II, 37) cites the *cognomen* as *Morin[o* (attested once in Gallia Belgica, see *NPEL*), which might evoke a connection with the Morini of north-west Gaul, but this reading is very difficult. The second visible vertical has no slant and suggests that we should read *Ni* rather than *M*; the two letters before the break do seem to be *in*; perhaps *Nigṛịn[o*, although there hardly seems to be room for *g*.

3. *dup(licario)*: this does not occur elswhere in the Vindolanda texts; cf. *CEL* 83 = *ChLA* X 424. For auxiliary *duplicarii* see Breeze (1974), 278-86.

4. *a Tullioni*: the form of *a* is interesting because a second descender is written more horizontally than is normal and almost makes a cross-bar. For the ablative in *-i* see *Tab.Vindol.*I, p.74. A.R.Birley (1990a), 18 (cf. *VRR* II, 37) has cited the name as Pullio but this is not correct; the cross-stroke at the top extends on both sides of the vertical. The name Tullio occurs twice in **184**.ii.29, iii.31 presumably borne by people at Vindolanda. The name is reasonably well-attested but occurs only twice in Gallia Belgica according to *NPEL*.

313

Inv.no.88.929. 86 x 37 mm. Plate XIV.

A fragment of a tablet containing part of a letter written by the same hand as **213** which is a letter from Curtius Super to Cassius Saecularis. It is very cursively written with numerous ligatures. The presumption is that this letter is from the same person, whether or not he wrote it himself, but the recipient and the time of writing may be different.

. . . .
sacerdoṭem quem
rogo ut ad Verecun-
dum p̣raef(ectum) de f̣es-
. . . .

"... the priest whom I ask that you send (?) to Verecundus the prefect about the festival (?) ..."

1. *sacerdoṭem*: this could be a *cognomen* and it does occur as such, although only twice, in the area covered by *NPEL*. In view of *f̣es-* in line 3, however, it seems more likely to refer to a priest.

2-3. *Verecundum*: it is possible that the reference is to Iulius Verecundus, prefect of the First Cohort of Tungrians (see **154**.2-3 and **210-2**), although the *cognomen* is very common. The presence of the letter at Vindolanda suggests that Verecundus ought to be somewhere else; since it is attributed to Period 3 and it is probable that the evidence for his presence at Vindolanda belongs in Period 2, it may well be that he and his unit had moved on or that he had moved to a different unit.

3. *p̣raef(ectum)*: the initial *p* is obscured by dirt but there is no doubt about the reading. Abbreviation of the word in the body of a letter is noteworthy.

de fes-: it is likely that we have a noun in the ablative case and the most probable restoration must be *festo* or *festis*.

314

Inv.no.85.107. 112 x 46 mm.

A fragment of the left-hand side of a diptych with a notch in the left edge. It contains six lines of a letter concerning the transport of lime which the addressee is being asked to despatch speedily. The fact that the recipient of the letter, who is presumably at Vindolanda, had guaranteed or approved supply of the lime and that the sender of the letter anticipates its arrival *primo mane* suggests that it must have been quarried in the vicinity (see Bruce (1978), 43, *RIB* I 1007-15, Davies (1968)). See also **156** and **316**. It is noteworthy that the writing slopes down across the grain. Word division is good but is not observed after monosyllables.

. . . .
]..[.].......[
miṣsi quae calcem petereṇ[t
quam nobis commoḍasti
quas rogo continuo
iubeas onerari ut prim[o
mane nobis itemṃ ...[
. . . .

"... I have sent ... to get the lime which you have provided for us. I ask you to order them to be loaded without pause so that ... to us early in the morning in turn (?) ..."

1. In view of *quas* in line 4, which is certain, the object of *misṣi* in this line must be feminine. The animals used for draught-work of this kind would be oxen (therefore a masculine word or a neuter like *iumenta*) or mules. It does not seem possible to read *mulas* at the end of the line but it is possible that there was a noun, now lost, followed by a number (perhaps *qụịnqụ[e)*. On the feminine form see Adams (1993) and for the use of mules as pack-animals and draught-animals see Toynbee (1973), 185-92, esp. 191-2 and for oxen 152-62, esp.161-2. An alternative might be *raedas* (which is also incompatible with the traces at the end of the line) followed by a number; for their use in routine transportation see Adams (1993), 49, note 26 with further references.

2. *misṣi*: see **255**.i.6-8 note, **309**.i.3 note.

calcem: cf *RMR* 9.6k, where the reading printed in the text is *calceṃ*. Fink comments in his note that the suggestion *cal(ceamenta) cen(turionis)*, "working on foot-gear of the centurion" is attractive but we think that *calcem* is preferable; cf. **156**.4 and note.

4. For the construction perhaps cf. **326**.ii.1.

315

Inv.no.85.121. 97 x 25 mm. Plate XXIII.

A fragment of a letter, which probably belongs to the left-hand side of a diptych, referring to the despatch of wagons (cf. **314**, **316**). The hand bears some similarity to that of **213** and **313** but it is slower and more careful and is probably not the same. Interpunct is found everywhere except after monosyllables and after *carrula* in line 2.

. . . .
traces
ut carrula uobis · den-
tur · et alias · ad Vocusium
Ạf̣ṛicanum · praefectum
]....ṛ.ṛum
. . . .

"... in order that wagons may be given to you and ... other ... to Vocusius Africanus the prefect ..."

2. *carrula*: there is a neuter by-form *carrum* of the more commonly attested masculine form *carrus* (see *B.Hisp*. 6.2, *carra complura ... retraxit*). *OLD*, *TLL* and *LS* record only a masculine form of the diminutive *carrulus* but refer only to *Digest* 17.2.52.15, *carrulorum uecturas*. The evidence of the present text suggests that this might better be understood as a neuter, *carrulum*. We note also that the glossaries record a neuter Greek diminutive *καρρίον* cf. *LSJ*, s.v.

3-4. *alias* should perhaps be taken as an adjective agreeing with a noun such as *epistulas*; alternatively, the adverb, meaning "besides".

Vocusium Ạf̣ṛicanum: despite the loss of the bottoms of the first three letters of the *cognomen* there is no doubt about the reading. This person does not appear elsewhere in the tablets.

5. *...ṛ.ṛum*: *...ṛọṛum* is a possible reading and this suggests that we might have the name of the unit of which Africanus was prefect. Of the units attested in Britain in this period whose names have this ending, *cohors i Celtiberorum* (*CIL* 16.51 = *RIB* II 2401.2, AD 105), *cohors iii Bracarorum* (*CIL* 16.69, AD 122) and *cohors i Afrorum* (*CIL* 16.69, AD 122) can be ruled out on palaeographical grounds. The traces would just accommodate *T]ụṇgṛọṛum* and *cohors i* and *cohors ii Tungrorum* (see above, pp.22-3 and Smeesters (1977), 180-1) and *ala i Tungrorum* are attested in Britain. *alae i* would not fill the space at the start of the line; neither would *coh i* or *ii* but *cohortis* written in full would be suitable (the word is normally, but not always, abbreviated, see **311**.back 2, **318**.3). The context makes it clear that Vocusius Africanus is not at Vindolanda, but this does not rule out a reference to the First Cohort of Tungrians since the unit could have been elsewhere when this letter was written.

316

Inv.no.85.183.b. 100 x 50 mm. Plate XXXII. R.E.Birley (1990), fig.12. *VRR* II, Plate IX.

Part of the left-hand portion of a diptych with two notches in the left-hand edge. The configuration of the text, in which the single trace of the first line stands well to the left of the beginning of line 2 and the latter, in turn, commences to the left of the following 5 lines, indicates that we very probably have the beginning of the letter minus the opening address. It is uncertain whether there is anything missing at the bottom of this column; the whole of col.ii is lost. There are six lines written by a second hand in the left margin at a right-angle, across the grain. The last line in the margin contains a closing greeting and must be presumed to be the end of the letter.

The subject of the letter is the transport of stone; for this activity in the region of Vindolanda see also **314** and cf. *P.Mich.*VIII 466. The first hand is a rather elegant cursive with squarish letter-forms, which does not use ligature.

.[
quem modum carrulorum
missurus sis domine
deliberare tecum debes
ad lapidem portandum
Ṿoconti enim centụ[
carruḷis uno die la.[
. . . .

L.margin: ↓*m*[2]
nisi rogas Vocontị[
ut lepidem exp̣[
non explicabi[
rogo ụṭ rescri[bas
quid uelis me [
opto benẹ [ualeas

"... you ought to decide, my lord, what quantity of wagons you are going to send to carry stone. For the century of Vocontius ... on one day with wagons ... (2nd hand) Unless you ask Vocontius to sort out (?) the stone, he will not sort it out. I ask you to write back what you want me to do (?). I pray that you are in good health."

1. Only the trace of a descender remains, at the far left. This is likely to be first line of the letter and therefore a name; the trace is compatible with *f* (e.g. *F̣[lauius*) but there are obviously other possibilities.

2. *carrulorum*: cf. **315**.2 and note, where it is suggested that the word is *carrulum* rather than *carrulus*.

4. Cf. *OLD*, s.v. *deliberare* 1b.

6-7. We have considered two ways in which these lines could be restored and understood. The first is to take *Ṿoconti* as the genitive of the personal name Vocontius (not very common, but for an occurrence at Carlisle see Tomlin (1992), 153, note 60; for Germania Inferior see *CIL* 13.8655 and cf. *CEL* 62 (Vindonissa)) and to restore *centụ[ria* at the end of the line. If the high hook at the end of line 7 indicates *laḅ[*, therefore from *labor* or *laboro*, the meaning will be that the century of Vocontius has worked or will work with wagons to move stone on one day. Against this is the fact that we would expect a reference to the century of Vocontius to come in the form *centuria Voconti* (probably with the symbol rather than the word written in full), see Speidel (1984), 107 who points out that this order is universal, but cf. *RMR* 9.9.f-n.; the reversal of the normal order need not unduly worry us in a letter as opposed to a formal document.

The alternative is to take *Ṿoconti* as referring to the men of a Vocontian unit; the *ala (Augusta) Vocontiorum c.r.* is attested in Germania Inferior in the Flavian period but was in Britain by AD 122 (see *VRR* II, 4, Holder (1980), 222). Then we might restore *centụ[m* at the end of the line and envisage the meaning as "the Voconti with 100 wagons on one day have worked *or* will work, *or* by their labour have moved..."; note that it is not possible to read *carrulọs*. Against this is the text in the margin, lines 1-3, which very strongly suggests that we should there restore the accusative singular *Vocontị[um* (see note *ad loc.*) to follow *rogas*, in which case the reference here must surely be to the same person.

Margin 1-2. The restoration and interpretation of these lines is uncertain and affects the understanding of lines 6-7 above. The main problem is the restoration of *Vocontị[* in line 1. Either *Vocontị[um* or *Vocontị[os* is possible. If we restore the singular as a personal name we can then restore *exp̣[licet* in line 2 and *explicabi[t/(ur)* in line 3 and take these lines to mean "unless you ask Vocontius to sort out the stone, he will not sort it out *or* it will not be sorted out". If we restore the plural, we would then restore *exp̣[licent* in line 2 and, necessarily, *explicabi[s/-itur* in line 3: "unless you ask the Vocontians to sort out the stone, you will not sort it out (i.e. get it sorted out) *or* it will not be sorted out". For the meaning of *explico* = "sort out" cf. **343**.i.4, **301**.i.5. The switch from active to passive is unlikely, however, and with either version we prefer the active. The strongest argument for the first alternative is that we think it much more likely that *rogo* would be followed by the name of a single person than *Vocontios*.

2. There is no doubt that *lepidem* has been written. This is surely a simple error for *lapidem* in view of line 5, but it is worth noting that the transliterated Greek word λεπίς (several meanings, including "metal plate", see *LSJ*, s.v.) is attested (see *TLL* VII.2 1173; the normal accusative is *lepida* but a latinised form is no doubt possible, cf. **346**.ii.2).

3. It is possible to envisage *quare* or *ergo* at the end of the line.

4. There will have been room for *mihi* at the end of this line.

5. *facere* is the obvious restoration.

317

Inv.no.86.458. 87 x 43 mm.

This fragment belongs to the right-hand portion of a diptych with two notches in the right-hand edge. We may have virtually the whole of the half-leaf; we have considered, but are inclined to reject, the possibility that we may have the ends of lines of col.i at the left. The leaf contains part of a draft of a letter with erasures, corrections and interlinear additions. These make it difficult to be sure of the line divisions or of the articulation of words and phrases, especially since so little of the content is preserved. There seem essentially to be six lines of writing, well spaced out with good word division. The draft is of interest for the insight it provides into the process of composition of a letter and it might possibly be the work of the hand of Cerialis (see **225-32**; the form of *n* with a long descender at the right in line 3b is very like the eccentric *n* in **225**.back 24). In so far as we have any clue to the subject-matter, the occurrence of the words *cognitionem* and *misi* suggests that the writer may be informing a higher official that he has sent a miscreant to be dealt with; cf. **322**, **344**.

. . . .
].ṛạ. ⟦.ṛ.mur⟧ detu
]...[*c.4*] ita ut iuss⟦eraṣ⟧ ⸢isti⸣
3a].om[.].o..ṇti.*traces* c̣ọm...
3b] ạḍ ⟦cogṇitiọṇem⟧ inscriḅ-
]ḍam cogṇitionem
]ṃ misi ⟦a...⟧
].eṭ *c.9* ṃenṭuṃ
traces
. . . .

1. *detu*: this might be part of the verb *defero* which looks suitable in the context (cf. **127-9**) but the traces at the left of the next line are not easy to reconcile with an appropriate verbal ending.

3a. We take this to be an interlinear correction to line 3b. If *].om* is the end of a word cf. *saluom*, **225**.6.

3b. *ạḍ* is very uncertain.

3-4. *inscriḅ[en]ḍam* looks a likely restoration, perhaps erased. If the context is legal it might be connected with *cognitionem*, whether the bungled attempt before it or the word after it, which has clearly not been erased. *inscriptio* in its legal sense, however, means "accusation" and the verb *inscribere* is not used with *cognitio* as a direct object (see *TLL* VII.1 1848 and perhaps note *Digest* 48.5.2.8, *si libellos inscriptionum deposuerit*). We cannot elucidate the supralinear addition at the end of line 3a; the last three (or four) letters are very obscure indeed and may themselves have been erased.

5. *misi* has not been erased (the horizontal line through *mi* is the grain of the wood). What follows has certainly been erased. It might begin with *ad*.

318

Inv.no.85.171. 80 x 26 mm.

Part of a portion of a diptych containing four lines of a letter. The first surviving line, of which only the bottoms of letters remain, appears to commence further to the left than the subsequent lines. It is thus likely that it will have been the first line of the message proper if this is the left-hand column of the letter; there may, in fact, be a v-shaped notch in the left edge. The loss of part of the letter *m* at the end of line 3, where it seems to have overrun the fold, supports this. The author was in command of a cohort and it is possible that he was prefect of an auxiliary unit; alternatively, he might be a legionary centurion (see line 2 note). The recipient is likely to have been a prefect.

. . . .
traces
domine comm...[
ex cohorṭe cui praesuṃ
missi ad te ideo ut poss[
. . . .

"... my lord, I have sent ... from the cohort of which I am in command to you so that you (?) might be able ..."

1. For the probability that this is the beginning of the message see introduction. If this is correct we might expect it to begin with a name or names (cf. **295**.i.3, **300**.i.3). The traces of 8-9 letters at the left might end with *-um*.

2. *comm...[*: it is difficult to envisage any restoration other than *commịḷị[tones/onem* (cf. **226**.c.4 note) and there is room to restore it, assuming that we have a left-hand column. If this is correct it is possible to imagine that it was written by an auxiliary prefect, cf. Suetonius, *Caes*. 67.2, *nec milites eos pro contione, sed blandiore nomine commilitones appellabat*. Alternatively, it might have come from a centurion commanding a cohort in a legion (see Breeze (1969) and cf. **255**.back 20 note).

4. *missi*: see **255**.i.6-8 note, **309**.i.3 note.

poss[: *poss[is* is the likeliest restoration but we cannot exclude *poss[im*.

There are no tops of letters visible below this line, which suggests that the letter was a short one with not more than 5 lines in this column.

319

Inv.no.85.274. 109 x 30 mm.

A fragment containing the beginning of a letter to a *praefectus* of a cohort. Very little of the message survives but the tablet is unusual in that the address has been written on the back of what would normally be expected to be the left-hand portion of the diptych rather than the right. Alternatively, we may have a letter which began on the right-hand portion, like **343**. We prefer the first hypothesis but it cannot, of course, be proved. Neither the sender nor the addressee can be identified elsewhere in the tablets.

Libṛ.... Ṿeraniọ ṣuọ
salutem
..bi aliquanḍọ .....ṛaṃ
..qu......[

traces

. . . .

Back: *traces*

praef(ecto) coh(ortis)

ạ Ḷịḅ..... (c̣ẹṇṭụṛịạẹ) ......

1. *Libṛ....*: we are confident of the first three letters and if the fourth is *r* rather than *a* (note that *RNGCL* cites Libanius) we can see no possibility other than that this is a contraction of *Liber-*. Of the *cognomina* listed in *NPEL* and *RNGCL*, Lib(e)ranus, Lib(e)ratus (or -ius), Lib(e)rarius and Lib(e)rinus, the last seems to us least awkward for both front and back.

Ṿeraniọ: there is very little trace of the last letter but it may have an apex mark over it, as may the following *ṣụọ*. The first five letters are reasonably secure and Veranius is attested as a *cognomen* (for an occurrence at Trier see *CIL* 13.11888); Cleranius is also attested (see *RNGCL*) but only as a *gentilicium*.

3. *..bi*: *ṭibi* is what we might expect but the second letter looks like a clear *e* and *ṣẹbi* looks like a plausible reading (cf. **184**.ii.22 etc.).

Back 1. The traces are not substantial enough to enable us to suggest a reading. Their position implies rather a large gap on the front above the first line, which is odd.

3. The traces at the left are compatible with *ạ Ḷịḅṛịṇo*. The following letters presumably belong to his title or position, perhaps beginning with a centurial sign and followed by a name of 5 or 6 letters of which the second may be *x*.

320

Inv.no.86.422. 106 x 43 mm.

Part of the right-hand portion of a diptych containing line-ends from the first column, which we have not transcribed, five lines of the second column of a letter, and remains of an address on the back. This hand is very difficult to read and we have little notion of the content. There may be a reference to three people, at least one of whom might have a female name (line 2), and this may be followed by a reference to the release of deserters. The closure, which is probably in a second hand, consists only of *uale*.

i

traces of 5 lines?

ii

. . . .

libenti ḍẹḷecṭor .[.].[

ạtọnem ẹṭ pactam et ru .ṛ[

deịnḍe omịṣẹṛas .ḍ.[

deṣẹṛṭores *traces*

m[2] uale

Back: m^1 *traces*

]. . . ḅḷ. . ọ

ii.1. The tops of some letters are missing in the second word. We think it most likely that we have the verb *delector* in a middle sense, perhaps preceded by a phrase such as *animo libenti*. An alternative would be to take *libenti* as a name, followed by *defectori* or *defectores*, but we can see nothing after *r* which resembles *e* or *i*.

2. *ạṭọnem*: the trace before *t* is definitely ink and this must be the beginning of the line. We can only suggest that this is a name (see *Attonem* in **345**.ii.3 and cf. **308**), or possibly the end of a name.

p̣actam: this looks certain and if it is preceded by *et* (obscured by dirt), we must have a female name, perhaps *Pac<a>tam*, cf. **353**.ii.1; the only alternative we can envisage is *sactam* (for *Sanctam*, a well-attested name (cf. **182**.ii.18)).

ru.ṛ: the doubtful letter, of which only the bottom survives, might well be *b*; *LC* cites the *cognomina* Ruber and Rubrianus; *RNGCL* offers Ruta, which is also possible.

3-4. We appear to have an abrupt change of subject here. There seems no possible reading other than *deịnḍe* for the first word. *omes* appears to follow but suggests nothing; we therefore prefer to read *omịṣ*, although *i* is very difficult. There is a gap before the next group of letters and the writer may have avoided a knot. In line 4 *de* and *ores* are certain and if *deṣẹṛṭores* is correct, we may have a reference to the release of some deserters who had been apprehended (cf. **226**.a.10).

Back 1. Traces of the bottoms of letters in address script.

2. This is doubtless the name of the sender. The traces would be compatible with *ạ P̣ụḅḷịc̣ọ*.

321

Inv.no.86.507. 90 x 21 mm. Plate XXVII.

Two joining fragments from the top of the left-hand portion of a diptych containing the opening of a letter to a person called Fadus. There is a tiny scrap with traces of a few letters which we cannot place; it might supply part of the name of the sender. Only the first line of the message survives and, rather surprisingly, it seems to express the wish that something might turn out badly for the recipient. The hand is a reasonably competent but not very elegant cursive.

].ṣ Fado suo
salutem
opto male tibi eueniaṭ uṭ peṛ
traces
. . . .

"... to his Fadus, greetings. It is my wish that it might turn out badly for you ...."

1. The space at the left suggests that the *gentilicium* and *cognomen* of the author will have been written. There is a large gap between the end of the *cognomen* and the name of the addressee, cf. **347.**a.1 and note.

Fado: there is no doubt about the reading despite the fact that the lower part of the oblique of *a* has been abraded. For the *cognomen* Fadus, which is not common, see *LC* 178; it is held by a legionary soldier in *CIL* 6.3618. It does not occur elsewhere in the Vindolanda texts.

322

Inv.no.88.966. 97 x 28 mm. Plate XXVIII.

A fragment of a leaf containing remains of four lines. There may be remains of notches in the left-hand edge, in which case the fragment will belong to the left-hand part of a diptych. This is supported by the fact that the ends of the lines seem to overrun the edge of the leaf. The content suggests a petition or appeal, perhaps directed to the prefect since it is attributed to the Period 3 *praetorium*, about the theft of a *balteus* (cf. **344**). Word-division is good. The form of *a* in *balteum* (line 3) is interesting.

. . . .

traces

traces . . .neo seruoṛụ[m

traces et balteum me[

mihi subripuerunt

. . . .

2. Nothing can clearly be seen before *neo* but there are few words possible; of these *balneo* is the most attractive and can probably be read. For the presence of slaves see **190**, **301**, **303**, **347** and above, p.29. If the *balteus* is an item of military equipment (see note to line 3), it may be that the author is suggesting that the slaves are involved in the theft or that there is some connection with the slaves' quarters. If this is right it suggests that the slaves have a separate bathing establishment in the *praetorium* or the fort.

3. *balteum me[*: the obvious supplement is *me[um* and the sense requires nothing more before *mihi* in line 4. The *balteus* might be a cross-belt from which a short sword or knife was suspended or a waist-belt (later more commonly called *cingulum*), see Robinson (1975), 169, 171, Bishop and Coulston (1993), 96-8. A *b[a]ltẹu ṃịli[ta]re* [sic] is among the items of clothing and equipment requested by Claudius Terentianus in *P.Mich.*VIII 470.6 = *CEL* 145, cf. *P.Mich.*VIII 464.18, 474.8-9, III 217.19. If the word is used in a more general sense as "belt", the author need not be referring to an item of military equipment and might not be a soldier (i.e. perhaps a slave).

323

*Tab. Vindol.*I 41, Plate VII, 5. *CEL* 108.

] · offici · erat · inposuisse
]ụilitatis · est · quas · tamen
]ḥi ternis · uictoriatis
]ṇtatas · ẹx̣ ratiunculis
].[*c.5*].[..]..ḅimo
. . . .

2. *ụilitatis*: this could be left as it stands or supplemented as *ci]ụilitatis*.

3. *mi]ḥi ternis uictoriatis*: we considered this reading in the *ed. pr.* and it is adopted in *CEL*; it now seems more plausible though the absence of interpunct is noteworthy for this hand. For the phrase *ternis uictoriatis* see Cicero, *pro Font.* 9.19. For a reference to "small change" (*aere minuto*) see **327**.2-3.

4. *]ṇtatas*: there are many possible supplements, e.g. *arge]ṇtatas*.

ẹx̣, which we suggested in the note to the *ed. pr.*, is adopted by *CEL* and we think it likely to be correct.

5. At the end *]..limo* is also possible.

324

*Tab. Vindol.*I 42, Plate IX, 5, 6 and 7. *CEL* 109.

i

. . . .
quẹ[
res scriberẹ ụ[
peruenisses Vin[
ṛọg.[.].c[..].....[
. . . .

ii

. . . .
].[..].....ọ
]is felicissima
]na et nos amare
]..ṣ *uacat*
. . . .

Back:

. . . . . .
..[.]ạ..[...
]...ịnná

i.2. *resscriberẹ*, *CEL*. This may well be right since the word occurs elsewhere in the tablets (e.g. **269**.3) and the spelling would not be unexpected.

3. We must surely have a place-name and *Vin[dolandam* is attractive, but there are other possibilities, e.g. Vinouia (see **185**.26).

4. *ṛọgọ .ṛṣ. . . . . .*, *CEL*. This may be correct.

ii.1. *] . . .ṣ. . . . .ọ*, *CEL*. This does not seem to us likely to be correct.

1-4. In the *ed. pr.* we tentatively suggested *opto utaris felicissima fortuna*, but in view of the evidence in the new tablets for correspondence between women we now think it much more probable that we should restore something like *ọp̣ṭo /[ut s]is felicissima / [domi]na.*

For what follows we tentatively suggested *et nos amare / [te cre]das*, but Cugusi has correctly pointed out (*CEL* 109, *ad loc.*) that *nos/me* is regularly found as the object of *amare* in Cicero's letters and elsewhere. This is no doubt the case here, but the traces in line 4 are too slight to suggest any clear reading. Its position would suggest that this is the closure added by the sender, but it is noteworthy that the writing on the back is almost certainly by the same hand.

Back 1. *. . .ạụ. . .*, *CEL*. This must be part of the name or description of the recipient. If it matches the pattern of addresses in letters to Lepidina (**291-2**), we would expect the name of the woman's husband here. It is very difficult to fit the traces to *Cerialis*; the first two letters might be *Pa*.

2. There is a clear apex mark over the *a* which we did not recognise in the *ed. pr.* The writing slopes upwards from the left and this must be the name of the sender of the letter, e.g. *ab Erinnna*. The masculine name *Cinna* cannot be read here. Note the personal name Senna on the back of a tablet from Carlisle, *Britannia* 21 (1990), 367, no.17, but it is not possible to read *] . .enná* here.

325

*Tab. Vindol.*I 43, Plate X, 4, 5 and 6. *CEL* 110.

i

]̣.ius Fontanus [su]o
[salut]ẹṃ
traces
. . . .

ii

piscam te p.[
quam me ipṣ[um
instruere ṃẹ[
. . . .

Back:].s. .nió Ni. .o[
. . . .

i.2. *sa]l[utem*, suggested in *CEL* 110, is impossible because of the spacing.

ii.1. Presumably we have the first person singular of the future indicative or present subjunctive of *concupisco*. *TLL* IV 106.21-4 gives examples of this verb with accusative and infinitive.

Back. *]issinio Ni..o*, *ed. pr.* The second surviving letter is certainly *s* and this seems to be followed by *i* corrected to *c*; the first surviving letter must be *i* or *u*, and this suggests that either Priscinius or Fuscinius is possible; *NPEL* cites both for Gallia Belgica. *Nis.o*, suggested in *CEL* 110, looks plausible; of the *cognomina* cited in *NPEL* we note Nisus and Ninsus; *Nisso* could be read, perhaps as a form of one of these names. It is not possible to read the name of the recipient of **312**.

326

Inv.no.85.020.a. 230 x 30 mm. Plate XVIII.

A diptych which is complete only at the right and left edges. It contains part of a letter which we find very difficult to elucidate. The first line of the left-hand portion, which is clearly not the opening, begins further to the left than the subsequent lines and may well be the beginning of the message proper. There is some use of interpunct.

i

. . . .

c.18 n...ul.i.[
c(larissim-) · u(ir-) · de....us · enim illis · Verecundi furis · mal.risp[

. . . .

ii

. . . .

c.11 dicun....uas rogo
sicut here coepisti inquiras
in q[u]a ..*traces* [

. . . .

i.1-3. The reading *c · u ·* is quite clear and we can see no other way of resolving this than as some case of *clarissimus uir*; the clear medial point between *c* and *u* rules out the possibility of reading it as the number *cv* (105). If this is right it ought to be preceded by a name (cf. **225**.14-5); it might refer to a governor (it is impossible to read *Marcelli*) but could refer to someone else of senatorial status, e.g. a legionary legate. The traces at the end of line 1, which overruns the fold, are difficult to interpret; *ul* are certain but we cannot suggest a *cognomen* which is compatible with the traces.

What follows is very obscure. There seems no possibility of doubting the reading *enim illis Verecundi furis*, and, since there are several references in the tablets to at least two people called Verecundus (**154**.2-3, **210-12**, **127**.7), it seems almost certain that the word here is also to be taken as a personal name. *furis* might equally be the genitive of *fur* or the second person of the verb *furo*, though neither word looks attractive. The reading of the six to eight letters before *enim* is unclear. The first two letters can hardly be anything other than *de*; the next letter looks most like *m*, but there is a slightly oblique stroke over it such as is used elsewhere to mark an abbreviation (see also above, p.57). We do not see what possible abbreviation can have come at this point. The next letter is most like *s* but *e* is possible if all trace of the horizontal stroke has been lost. This is followed by either one or two letters before the last letter which is certainly *s*. If we have a single letter it must be *n*; if two letters, the second must be *u*. The stroke before this curves in a way which hardly suits *i* or the start of *n* in this hand, though neither reading can be excluded; also possible is *t* if the cross-bar is no longer visible. We have considered no less than four possibilities. (1) *deṇṣịus*: this could make sense with the meaning "more frequently" or the like, but it is very hard to read the third letter as *n*. (2) *de ịpṣịus*: the second half of the supposed *m* could indeed be read as *p*, but it is hard to read *i* preceding this. Nor do we see how to make sense of this; *de* would have to go with *illis* and *ipsius* presumably with *Verecundi*; but the word-order surely makes this impossible. (3) *deṃẹṇs*: the difficulty in reading *en* before final *s* has been indicated above and the word hardly makes good sense. It would presumably have to be taken with *furis*, understood as the verb, with the meaning "you are furiously angry with those (men?) of Verecundus". One argument against all the above suggestions is that they involve ignoring the apparent stroke over the third letter. It is hard to see what this can be, though it might possibly be the top of *c* if this example is made somewhat differently from the one earlier in the line. We have therefore also considered (4) *dec̣ṛẹtus*, but again it is not easy to turn the apparent *m* into *cr* (a descender from the line above complicates the reading). This would have to mean something like "appointed to (do something in respect of) those (men?) of Verecundus"; it would perhaps look more attractive if we took *furis* as a slip for *fueris* (cf. *locuta fueram* in **292**.a.i.2), but we are naturally reluctant to suggest a scribal error in such a broken context.

A possible alternative reading for the end of line 3 is *maṭẹrịs* (though *t* and *e* are not easy), but it is still hard to see how it can be construed so as to agree with *illis*.

ii.1. *dịcunṭ* is possible, but not *dịcuṇṭụṛ*. What follows looks like *quas* and may be paralleled by a similar construction with *rogo* in **314**.4-6, although it is not clear how *inquiras* could have a direct object in the accusative ("please, just as you started doing yesterday, make enquiries ...").

327

Inv.no.85.028. 88 x 32 mm.

A fragment of a leaf containing three lines of a letter. It is not clear whether it belongs to the left- or right-hand portion of a diptych. The text mentions *aes minutum* ("small change") and it is possible to imagine that the sender is informing the recipient that he has despatched someone carrying the money; cf. **323**.3 for a reference to the coins called *uictoriati*. For the function of coinage in this respect see Howgego (1992).

. . . . .

et aḍ. . runṭ

secum in aere
minuto quia gr.[
. . . . .

"... and they are bringing (?) it with them in small change because ..."

1. *adferunt* fits the traces reasonably well and makes good sense here (cf. **281**.i.1 note and 3).

2-3. For *aes minutum* see *TLL* I 1075.25.

328

Inv.no.85.053.b. 73 x 40 mm. Plate XXII.

A fragment of a letter from the right-hand side of a diptych. There is a tie-hole (perhaps two) and probably the remains of a notch in the right-hand margin. The hand is an untidy one which writes rapidly and with a fair number of ligatures.

. . . .
dicebas te debere
potes si uis cras
id est .[
. . . .

"... you said that you ought to ... You can, if you wish, tomorrow, that is ..."

2-3. For the expression cf. **234**.i.3-5.

329

Inv.no.85.122. 85 x 14 mm.

A fragment containing two lines of a letter. If the lines are complete, as they appear to be, the column will have been quite narrow and this suggests that we may have part of the right-hand portion of a diptych. A trace at the top left corner may either belong to a previous line in this column or to the end of a line in the left-hand column which overran the fold. The content, though exiguous, is important since the reference to a *conturmalis*, who is most naturally taken to be at Vindolanda, provides evidence for the presence of cavalry (cf. **159**.1 and the correspondence of Lucius the decurion, **299-300**).

. . . . . .
.[
iubeas Agilem

conturmalem

. . . . .

2. Agilis is a very common *cognomen*; note *Agị.[* in **184**.ii.25.
3. *conturmalem*: the word does not occur elsewhere in the tablets but cf. **159**.1 note.

330

Inv.no.85.131. 70 x 13 mm. Plate XXIX.

A fragment containing three lines of a letter. It is not clear whether it belongs to the left- or right-hand side of a diptych. Apart from the reference to *uiaticum* we have no clue to the content. The text is remarkable for its regular use of interpunct (cf. **345**) and also for the form of *a*, approximating to the capital, in which the second descender has virtually become a cross-bar.

. . . .

traces

]ṃạ...m · uiatico · meó

]....re · quod · ante ⟦an[⟧

. . . .

2. For *uiaticum* cf. **283**.5 (= *Tab.Vindol.*I 40, where see our note). There may be an apex mark over the final *o*.

3. The last two letters in the line are emphatically erased and it looks as if the writer may have begun to write *ante* again. There is an apparent horizontal stroke through *ante* preceding them but this is not ink.

331

Inv.no.85.137. 100 x 15 mm. Bowman and Thomas (1987), no.1. *CEL*, Appendix Vindol. ζ.

This must be a draft of a letter, perhaps with a line containing the names of sender and recipient missing at the top. It is clearly only a draft since the writer has had two attempts at the first line (cf. perhaps *ChLA* XI 493) and may have abandoned his text before completing the word *karissime* (no trace of final *e* is visible on the photograph); he has also corrected the *f* of *frater*, probably from *k*. The hand is a rather inelegant, but nonetheless competent cursive. The other side of this fragment contains a line of Virgil (**118**).

. . . .

ṣaluṭẹṃ

rogo ..g *uacat*

rogo frạter karissim
. . . .

332

Inv.no.85.163. 111 x 18 mm.

A fragment of the left-hand portion of a diptych with remains of a notch in the left-hand edge. It contains the beginning of a letter, but the opening line is lost.

. . . .
salutẹm
summas tibi domine gratias
. . . .

"... greetings. [I send] you warm thanks, my lord ..."

333

Inv.no.85.196.b. 68 x 20 mm.

A fragment of a leaf with two lines of a letter. The content is exiguous but the reference to *libros* in line 2 is interesting and perhaps provides some context for the literary knowledge at Vindolanda attested in **118**.

. . . . . .
] ạb Arcano an-
]̣set librọs exse-
. . . . . .

1. *arcano*: this word occurs in **162**. *ab* here suggests strongly that it is a personal name. It seems likely that we have the right-hand edge of the leaf with *an* the start of a word which continued in the next line.

2. The first trace does not look like *s*; perhaps we have a word ending in -*s* followed by *et*.

librọs: before the first letter there is the descender from *r* in the previous line. Given the knowledge of Virgil, and perhaps of Catullus, attested at Vindolanda (**118**, **119**), there is no reason to doubt the availability of books.

exse-: this suggests part of the verb *exsequor*, continuing in the next line (see line 1 note).

334

Inv.no.85.230. 71 x 66 mm. Plate XXXII.

Three joining fragments of a letter. Little can be gleaned from the content. The somewhat "old-fashioned" hand is of palaeographical interest, especially the form of *r*.

. . . . . .
traces
]. saluto et indico [
] ạudientibus cụm p̣[
sc]ripseras p̣ạ.[
] superi uịs[
].ụịsmiṭẹṛdi.[
. . . . . .

3. *cụm p̣[*: alternatively perhaps *c̣ọmp̣[*.

5. There seems to be more than *superius* (which would be more likely to be the adverb than the rare *gentilicium*); *superi* might be the genitive of the *cognomen* Super (cf. **213**.1, **255**.i.1).

335

Inv.86.352. 68 x 24 mm.

Two joining fragments from what appears to be the end of a letter, perhaps to a woman (see note to line 4). We should therefore expect to see something of an address on the back, but nothing is visible. The writing on the right-hand fragment has mostly disappeared and no connected sense can be obtained. Word division is good.

. . . .
f̣ẹro sed cṛạ *c.10* [
ịdeo esse sc̣ịr *c.9* u.ad.[
torio ḍẹ c̣eṣṣe *c.10* em *uacat*
m²? uale..ṣ.[

1. *craṣ* is possible.

2-3. Presumably *adi[u-]/torio* (cf. P.Brooklyn 24.iii.5, Thomas and Davies (1977)), probably not preceded by *cum*.

4. It is not clear whether this greeting is in a different hand, which is what we should expect. The last visible letter is either *d* or *o*; the former suggests *ualeạṣ ḍ[omine*, but the traces perhaps suit *ualeạṣ ṣọ[ror* better.

336

Inv.no.86.367. 52 x 26 mm.

Part of the right-hand portion of a diptych containing the ends of four lines of a letter, written in a rather crude hand with thick strokes and much use of serifs; those on *i* and *u* are noteworthy. There are remains of an address on the back.

. . . . . .
]ṛunt fạṭịg̣ạṭ.e
]milare ad usum
].t enim aḍ ca⟦.⟧s.r
]ẹraṃ ạḍịṛe Vin-
. . . . . .

Back: *traces*
. . .

1. *fạṭịg̣ạṭ.e*: the reading is uncertain but is compatible with the traces. Possibly *e]ṛunt fạṭịg̣ạṭạe* with reference to mules, see **314**.1 note.

2. Perhaps the end of *similare* (for *simulare*) or a compound. The *m* at the end of *usum* has a long tail.

3. *ca⟦.⟧s.r*: the letter between *s* and *r* looks like *i* but might be read as *t*. We would expect *castra* but there is no sign of final *a* even though there would have been room to squash it in; a word division with *a* on the next line is not credible. We might have a simple error of omission (*castr<a>*) or an unusual word-division *castr/orum* followed by an accusative noun with *ad*. The alternative reading *adcasịr* seems to lead nowhere.

4. We could envisage *ạḍịṛe Vin-/[dolandam*, but there are other possibilities (e.g. *Vin-/[ouia*, cf. **185**.26).

Back. Tops of letters at the beginning of the name of the addressee. It may be just possible to reconcile the traces with *F̣ḷạụị[o*; thereafter no reading can be offered.

337

Inv.no.87.546. 75 x 33 mm.

A fragment of a leaf with four lines of writing. There are possible traces on the back which suggests that this was part of the right-hand half of a diptych.

. . . . . .
]e.ura[ ]n....ụm
] ṇon secatur ..
]ra castresia eu..[
]um t.. nec mi
. . . . . .

1. At the beginning *]ec̣ura[* is possible; alternatively perhaps *]eṭur a[*.

3. Perhaps *sac]ra castresia*, cf. **190**.c.1-3, 32-3; for the form see *TLL* III 544, citing *CIL* 3.12376 etc. At the end of the line possibly just *euṃ*.

338

Inv.no.88.884.a. 49 x 29 mm.

A fragment which belongs to the right-hand portion of a diptych and may have remains of a notch in the right-hand edge. On the front are abraded remains of four lines of a letter and on the back remains of an address.

. . . . .
traces
ạliquẹ...ẹm
traces ṛm..ị
traces quam
. . . . .

Back: Vindol · ..[
traces
. . . .

Back 1. *Vindol* is followed by a medial point, which makes it impossible to read *Vindolạṇ[*. The *l* has a very long descender. For the abbreviation cf. **343**.back 46.

2. Only the tops of letters survive; they are compatible with *F̣ḷạ[uio* but do not exclude other readings.

339

Inv.no.85.207. 50 x 45 mm.

A fragment of a tablet containing the remains of four lines of a letter written in a good hand. The fragmentary content suggests a possible legal context (see line 4, note). There is an interpunct between *me* and *ba* in line 3 and another before *et* in the same line. The form of *a*, with a hook at the top, at the end of line 3 is notable.

. . . .
].[
]f̣.ṣ..ṛṭitionem
]. · et suasit me · ba-

]..scribtio

. . . .

2. The word *subscriptionem* (cf. line 4) cannot be read here. The traces after *]f̣.ṣ* are compatible with *p̣ạṛṭịtionem* but there are other possibilities.

4. Before *scribtio* we have what is very probably the top of *b* and the traces before this permit *s]ụḅscribtio* (for the orthography see *OLD*, s.v.). This suggests that the content may be connected with legal matters (cf. perhaps **317**).

340

Inv.no.85.210. 66 x 22 mm.

A fragment of a tablet containing part of a letter. Though the content is exiguous, the tablet is of some interest because it has writing on both sides of the leaf, almost certainly by the same hand. There is no way of knowing, however, which is front and which back, or whether it was a letter sent to Vindolanda, or a draft written by someone at Vindolanda.

A.

].[
]ạ..ụṭẹṃ
]ḅ..am libente[r
] *traces* [
. . . . . .

B.

. . . . . .
].ị.ẹṇ.ṃ *traces* [
].s praestare parati
]..... duos .antum
].[.].[.]ẹ..us
. . . . . .

A.2. It does not seem possible to read *salutem* here.

3. *ti]ḅị ṭam libente[r* might be envisaged but it is not clear what is ink and what is dirt.

B.1. *q]ụịḍ ẹṇịṃ* is possible.

3. Presumably *ṭantum* at the end but the first *t* is difficult; the tall second *t* is an interesting form, with a curved cross-stroke.

341

*Tab. Vindol.*I 45, Plate X, 7 and 8. *CEL* 112.

. . . . . .
traces
]imọ karisime

Back:

. . . . . .
]....[
ab Trophim[o
conlega

2. *]imọ* is unlikely in this position (so *CEL*) but we do not think it is possible to read *dom]iṇẹ* (*CEL* 112, note *ad loc*.).

Back 1. *Trophimọ*, *CEL*. We can see no trace of *o*.

2. *conlega*: see our note in the *ed. pr.* and the note on *CEL* 177.3. It is clear that the term can be used between officers (cf. **260**.back, **345**.back) or others of equal rank or status. Trophimus is a common servile name and we wonder whether *conlega* is here used between slaves (cf. Plautus, *Asin.* 556, 576).

342

*Tab. Vindol.*I 46, Plate X, 9. *CEL* 113.

Perhaps part of the left-hand side of a letter.

. . . .
traces
].aṃus rogamus
].f̣ec̣tu nec̣ẹssita-
].ṭṛis ịgnoscạs
]s..e........
. . . .

3. Perhaps *a]ḍf̣ec̣tu*, with the meaning "intention" or "purpose" (see *OLD*, s.v.7), which we prefer to *defectu* or *profectu* suggested in *CEL*.

4. *ue]ṣṭṛis* or *no]ṣṭṛis* is possible. The sentence *rogamus ut adfectu necessitatibus nostris ignoscas* would make good sense.

5. *[ ]s.ẹṭ......ṣ*, *CEL*. This reading is possible but does not seem to us probable.

343

Inv.no.88.946. 182 x 79 mm. and 179 x 79 mm. Plate XXX. Bowman, Thomas and Adams (1990), no.2, Plates VII, VIII. *CEL*, Appendix Vindol. *θ*. R.E.Birley (1990), fig. 16. *VRR* II, Plate XIII.

This letter consists of two complete diptychs which have been scored and folded in the usual manner. Each of the diptychs has notches and tie-holes in the left- and right-hand margins. The surfaces of both are much defaced by offsets, indicating that the ink was still wet when the leaves were folded. This also makes it apparent that the two leaves were folded independently. There is no proper address on the reverse (a feature to which we have no parallel in the Vindolanda tablets), merely the abbreviated word *Vindol* written diagonally across the top corner on the back of the right-hand side of the second diptych. This would only be visible if the second leaf were placed beneath the first after they had been folded. The most natural assumption is that *Vindol* indicates the destination of the letter (see above, pp. 43-5 and note to iv.42-3) and the lack of a full address presumably implies that the letter was to be delivered by someone who was personally known to the recipient, or that the letter was to form part of a batch of letters, all of which were being sent to Vindolanda. The presence of a closing greeting indicates that it is not a draft or file copy.

The letter is written in the familiar two-column format, but with one striking oddity: the letter begins with col.i on the right-hand portion of the first diptych and continues with col.ii on the left-hand side; col.iii is on the right of the second diptych and col.iv on the left. The normal pattern is thus completely reversed. The most obvious explanation for this is that the writer was left-handed and adopted this device in order to be able to read what he had written in the first and third columns as he continued in the second and fourth. Since the closing section (iv.42-5) is written by the same hand as the rest of the text, we must assume that Octavius wrote the letter himself.

The script has numerous cursive tendencies, including occasional ligatures and distortions of the letter forms. Individual letters are often crudely made, notably *h*, *m* and *n*. *o* is made in two halves and the right-hand half is at times curved in the "wrong" direction so as to make a ligature with the following letter (see, e.g., *coria* in lines iii.31 and 33). The impression one forms, however, is that the somewhat clumsy appearance of the writing is less due to the writer's incompetence than to his desire to write quickly. In general this is not always an easy script to read, and it is frequently made much more difficult by the presence of the offsets mentioned above.

There are a great many points of linguistic interest, details of which may be found in Adams' notes to the *ed. pr.*; many of these are reproduced below but some have been omitted or abridged. The style is colloquial with occasional vulgarisms and phonetically inspired misspellings. One of these vulgarisms (*quem* for *quam*, line 40, if the text has been interpreted correctly) can be paralleled in another recently discovered document of early date (a legal contract of AD 39 from Murecine, see iv.38-41 note). This usage has hitherto been regarded as a late phenomenon (fourth-century); it is interesting to note that both examples are perpetrated in business contexts. Octavius uses a variety of financial idioms and a few technical terms. This is presumably the sort of unpretentious latinity we should expect in a business letter.

The whole letter is replete with signs of entrepreneurial initiative. The sums of money and goods involved are very considerable: Candidus is asked for 500 *denarii* and Octavius has laid out 300 (a year's pay for a *miles gregarius* in this period). The natural conclusion is that Octavius and Candidus are involved in the supply of goods in a military context on a large scale. 5000 *modii* of cereal and hides numbering in the hundreds can hardly be intended for any other market. Octavius (wherever he was) presumably purchased the cereal from local sources. The hides will have come from the military sector since it is surely inconceivable that tanneries operating on this scale can have existed outside it. The reference to the presence of hides at Cataractonium (Catterick, lines ii.15-6) is of great interest and well fits the archaeological evidence for a large tannery there in the period between *c.* AD 85 and 120 (see Butler (1971), 170, Burnham and Wacher (1990), 111-7). The reference to credit arrangements with a certain Tertius, albeit for a small sum, is also of interest. The evidence for the operation of a cash economy on this scale and for the sophistication of the financial dealings in this region is in general supported by the evidence of the accounts from Vindolanda.

We cannot be certain of the identity of either Octavius or Candidus nor do we have any indication of Octavius' whereabouts (see ii.15-18 note). Both names are common, but Octavius does not occur elsewhere in the Vindolanda texts. The name Candidus occurs in several other Vindolanda texts (and there are many others, including some centurions of the Hadrianic period, cited by A.R.Birley (1991), 93) but it is such a common *cognomen* that we cannot assume identity. Candidus, the slave of Genialis (**301**), a prefect who seems to have spent some time at Vindolanda but probably in an earlier period than that of the present letter, is one possible candidate. A much more likely candidate for identification with the recipient of the present letter here is a man of that name mentioned in two accounts (**180**, **181**) found in close proximity to this letter. One of the accounts, which seems likely to have been compiled by a civilian trader (**180**, introduction), also contains the names Spectatus and Firmus, whom Octavius greets in lines iv.42 and 43 of the present letter. The account makes it clear that they have been responsible for ordering the dispensation of supplies, in the case of Firmus to legionaries. Spectatus and Firmus were no doubt military personnel and the same is likely to be true of Candidus. A.R.Birley ((1990a), (1991), *VRR* II, 60) has suggested that some or all of them might be legionary centurions and the location of the tablet in the rooms at the end of the barracks-building might support that. On the other hand, if the involvement in the administration of military supplies is a good indicator, at least some of them might have been *optiones* (note Candidus the *optio* in **146**.2, **148**.1). As to Octavius, we see no way of deciding whether he was a civilian entrepreneur and merchant, or a military officer responsible for organising supplies for the Vindolanda unit; in the latter case he might have been a member of the unit himself or someone with a broader responsibility for units in the area (in general cf. Davies (1989), 52-3, 200-1).

For further comment on this text see A.R.Birley (1991); some of his points are discussed in the notes below.

i

Octauius Candido fratri suo
salutem
a Marino nerụi pondo centum
explicabo e quo tu de hac
re scripseras ne mentiọnem
mihi fecit aliquotiens tibi
scripseram spịcas me emisse

prọp̣e m(odios) quinque milia propter quod (denarii) mihi necessari sunt
nisi mittis mi aliquit (denariorum)

ii

minime quingentos futurum
est ut quod arre dedi perdam
(denarios) circa trecentos et erubescam ita rogo quam primum aliquit
(denariorum) mi mitte coria que scribis
esse Cataractonio scribe
dentur mi et karrum de quo
scribis et quit sit cum eo ḳarro
mi scribe iam illec p̣eṭissem
nissi iumenṭa non curaui uexsaṛe
dum uiae male sunt uịde cum Ṭertio
de (denariis) viii s(emisse) quos a Fatale accepit
non illos mi *uacat* accepto tulit

iii

scịtọ ṃae explesse [[exple]] coria
clxx et bracis excussi habeo
m(odios) cxix fac (denarios) mi mittas ut possị-
ṃ spicam habere in excusso-
rio iam autem si quit habui
p̣erexcussi contuber-
nalis Fronti amici hic fuerat
desiderabat coria ei ad-
signarem et ita (denarios) datur-
{ur}us erat dixi ei coria intra K(alendas) Martias daturum Idibus

iv

Ianuariis constituerat se uentur-
um nec interuenịt nec curauit
accipere cum haberẹt coriạ si
pecuniam ḍaret dabam ei Frontinium Iulium audio magno licere pro coriaṭione quem hic
comparauit (denarios) quinos
saluta Spectatum I . . . -
ṛiuṃ Firmum
epistulas a Gleục̣one accepi
uạḷ(e)

Back: Vindol

"Octavius to his brother Candidus, greetings. The hundred pounds of sinew from Marinus - I will settle up. From the time when you wrote about this matter, he has not even mentioned it to me. I have several times written to you that I have bought about five thousand *modii* of ears of grain, on account of which I need cash. Unless you send me some cash, at least five hundred *denarii*, the result will be that I shall lose what I have laid out as a deposit, about three hundred *denarii*, and I shall be embarrassed. So, I ask you, send me some cash as soon as possible. The hides which you write are at Cataractonium - write that they be given to me and the wagon about which you write. And write to me what is with that wagon. I would have already been to collect them except that I did not care to injure the animals while the roads are bad. See with Tertius about the 8½ *denarii* which he received from Fatalis. He has not credited them to my account. Know that I have completed the 170 hides and I have 119 *modii* of threshed *bracis*. Make sure that you send me cash so that I may have ears of grain on the threshing-floor. Moreover, I have already finished threshing all that I had. A messmate of our friend Frontius has been here. He was wanting me to allocate (?) him hides and that being so, was ready to give cash. I told him I would give him the hides by 1 March. He decided that he would come on 13 January. He did not turn up nor did he take any trouble to obtain them since he had hides. If he had given the cash, I would have given him them. I hear that Frontinius Iulius has for sale at a high price the leather ware (?) which he bought here for five *denarii* apiece. Greet Spectatus and ... and Firmus. I have received letters from Gleuco. Farewell. (Back) (Deliver) at Vindolanda."

i.1. For Octavius and Candidus see the discussion in the introduction.

3. *a Marino*: the name is well attested, but has not so far appeared elsewhere in the Vindolanda texts. We have considered and rejected the possibility of reading a name *Amarino*.

nerụi: presumably genitive singular, the use of the word indicating "animal tendon etc., used as material" (*OLD*, s.v.2): cf. Vitruvius 1.1.8, *per quae tenduntur suculis et uectibus e neruo torti funes*; Tacitus, *Ann.* 2.14.3, *non loricam Germano, non galeam, ne scuta quidem ferro neruoue firmata*. One hundred pounds of this material seems a considerable quantity but it is not out of keeping with the quantities of other commodities mentioned in this letter. A.R.Birley (1991), 92 raises the possibility that we should read *neruiọ* and understand it as an ethnic. The putative *o*, however, is demonstrably an offset from *q* of *quam* in ii.14.

4. *explicabo*: our statement in the *ed. pr.* that this is a problematical usage was perhaps over-cautious and the evidence of its use in other Vindolanda texts (see below) provides some reassurance. *explico* had a well-established financial use (*TLL* V.2 1731.17) of sorting out, settling a debt, financial obligation or difficulty, which would fit the context here. The letter is full of financial terminology (cf. lines 12, 23, 39ff., perhaps 31-2). In this sense *explico* is used absolutely, or with a sum of money as object, or with a variety of words as object, indicating the debt, burden, account, etc. It is common in Cicero's letters to Atticus, e.g. 5.5.2, 12.24.3, 12.31.2, 13.29.1, cf. *B.Alex.* 34.2, Suetonius, *Dom.* 12.1, *Digest*, 42.1.31. There is a good deal of flexibility to this usage. The object of the verb need not define the debt in strict financial terms, but may merely express the general "burden" or "business" to be "sorted out" financially (note Cicero, *Att.* 12.24.3). It occurs, moreover, in this sense in two other contexts in the Vindolanda texts with reference to items which cannot, literally, be unravelled (note especially **301**.i.5, **316**.margin 2, 3). This, together with the recurring preoccupation with financial matters in the present text, weakens

the suggestion by A.R.Birley (1991), 92 that we should understand the verb in its literal sense.

4. *e quo*: sc. *tempore*, "from the time when"; Augustan and later, cf. *TLL* V.2 1090.65. The end of the line after *hac* has been left blank because of the tie-hole; similarly lines iii.29 and iii.31. Lines ii.16, 19, iv.40 and 42 are indented at the start for the same reason.

5. *scripseras*: epistolary pluperfect, cf. line i.7, *scripseram*, line iii.30, *fuerat*, line iv.35, *constituerat*.

ne: = *ne ... quidem*, a vulgarism mentioned by Quintilian 1.5.39, who calls it *detractio*. It is also found in **311**.i.6.

mentiọnem: the reading is inevitable, although *on* is somewhat difficult; *o* is made in three, rather straight strokes, left open at the bottom and ligatured to *n*, which makes the letter combination look rather like *cul*; but no such word exists.

7. *spịcas*: the reading is not quite certain - *i* is not easy and *p* is very oddly written if correctly read; nevertheless the word must be accounted very probable in the context. Normally it means ears of corn, which we assume to be meant here, but it can refer to other cereals (see *OLD*, s.v.). Does he use this rather than *frumentum* because he is buying it unthreshed (cf. lines iii.26-9)?

8. *p̣rọp̣e*: the reading of *ọp̣* is far from certain because the leaf is badly defaced by offsets at this point; indeed of the word as a whole only the final *e* is beyond question. 5000 *modii* is a very large quantity of grain (though he may have bought it unthreshed, see previous note). It is unfortunate that there is no indication as to where Octavius got it from, but the quantity and the financial transaction suggest that army supply was not always a straightforward matter of requisitioning *annona*. For some further evidence in the Vindolanda texts see **180**, **213**.

9. *necessari*: = *necessarii*. A standard contraction in the colloquial language: for further examples in the Vindolanda material see *Tab.Vindol.*I, p.73, and *gladis* in **164**.3.

10. *nisi mittis mi aliquit*: in the *ed. pr.* we considered *mittas* a possible but less good alternative; we are now confident that *mittis* is correct. The future *mittes* might have been expected, but in fact conditionals of this type (with present indicative in the protasis and future in the apodosis) are not uncommon, particularly after *nisi*. The present stresses the need for immediate action to avert disaster; it is well-suited to threats and warnings, e.g. Cicero, *Verr.* 4.85, *Rab.Post.* 18, Nepos 15.4.3.

ii.12. *quod arre dedi perdam*: for the monophthongisation of *ae* in *arre* cf. *que* (ii.15), *illec* (ii.19) and probably *male* (ii.21, see note *ad loc.*). The terminology is financial. For *arram perdo* see *Digest* 18.3.8 *ut arram perderet*, and for *arra* associated with *do* see Gaius *Inst.* 3.139 ... *cum de pretio conuenerit, quamuis nondum pretium numeratum sit, ac ne arra quidem data fuerit. nam quod arrae nomine datur....*

13-4. *erubescam*: no doubt idiomatic (if to be understood as financial embarrassment), but we have found no precise parallel.

14-5. *ita rogo ... mi mitte*: *rogo* + imperative is colloquial syntax, with the direct construction (the imperative) used instead of subordination, see e.g. Petronius, *Sat.* 67.1, 75.3, Martial 2.14.18, *P.Mich.*VIII 469.17 = *CEL* 144, *[m]erca minore pretium* [sic], *rogo.*

15-8. A.R.Birley (1991), 94 infers from this passage that Octavius was writing from somewhere to the north or west ("east" is a typographical error, as Prof.Birley kindly pointed out to us) of Vindolanda since the latter lay between him and Catterick, but what Octavius writes here need only imply that Candidus was in a position to instruct someone at Catterick to send the hides and the wagon to Octavius; one possible explanation for this is that Candidus was in the military and Octavius was not.

15. For *que* = *quae* see above, ii.12 note.

16. *Cataractonio*: see *Tab.Vindol.*I, pp. 72f. on *Luguualio* in **250**.i.9 and cf. above, pp.43-5 and Adams (1994). For Catterick as a centre for leather-processing see the introduction.

16-8. *scribe dentur mi et karrum de quo scribis*: the plain (jussive) subjunctive without *ut* follows the governing verb; for another example in this letter see lines iii.31-3, *desiderabat coria ei adsignarem*. If the meaning is "write that they should be given to me, and that the *carrus* about which you write (should be given to me)", *karrum* could be the neuter by-form of the usual *carrus* (see *B.Hisp.* 6.2 *carra complura ... retraxit* and cf. **315**.2 note). Alternatively, if it is masculine accusative, the construction would be a *constructio ad sensum*, with the accusative determined by the underlying idea that someone should "give" the *carrus* to Octavius.

18. *quit*: cf. *aliquit* (i.10, 14), *si quit* (iii.28), contrast *d* in *quod* (i.9, ii.12).

19. *illec* = *illaec*, neuter plural, cf. ii.12 note.

p̣eṭissem: in the *ed. pr.* we preferred to read *c̣ep̣issem*; there is little to choose but we now think that the third letter looks more like *t* than *p*. Either offers acceptable sense.

20. *nissi*: for this spelling see also *Tab.Sulis* 32.7 and 65.10 and notes *ad locc.*

iumenṭa non curaui uexsaṛe: for *curo* with the infinitive (as distinct from *ut*) see *TLL* IV 1499.43ff. and cf. iv.36-7, *nec curauit accipere*. *uexo* was idiomatic of a horse or other quadruped hurting itself in the course of work or a journey, see *Schol.Iuu.* 8.148, Pelagonius 216.2, *Mulomedicina Chironis* 671. In *uexsare* the *a* and *r* are written very close together and there is some abrasion, but there is no doubt that both letters are there (*pace* A.R.Birley (1991), 95).

21. *dum uiae male sunt*: we take *male* as a misspelling of *malae* (see note to i.12). It is unlikely to be the adverb: the usual complement of *male est* is a dative (of a thing or person affected), expressed or understood (*TLL* VIII 237.7, *OLD*, s.v. *male* 1b).

21-2. *uide ... de*: for this idiom cf. Cicero, *Att.* 11.24.2, 12.6.1, 15.8.2.

Ṭertio: a possible alternative reading is *C̣ertio* but the name Tertius is very common (see A.R.Birley (1991), 94).

Fatale: perhaps the same person as *] .io Fatale*, the sender of **349**. A.R.Birley (1991), 93 suggests an identification with Claudius Fatalis who is known to have served three terms as a centurion in British legions, but if so he is not identical with the sender of **349** since his *gentilicium* cannot be Claudius (see back 1 note).

23. *non illos mi accepto tulit*: between *mi* and *accepto* the writer has left a blank space of 30 mm., presumably because the piece now missing from the bottom of the tablet was already missing when the letter was written. The expression is a variant of the classical financial formula *aliquid mihi acceptum (re)ferre* (for which see *TLL* I 314.13, *OLD*, s.v. *fero* 24b). *accepto* is the substantivised participle, *acceptum* = "thing received", *pecunia accepta* (so *TLL* I 321.82). The case can only be predicative dative.

iii.24. *sciṭọ ṃae explesse*: the reading of the first two words is far from certain, but the sense produced is exactly that required. For spellings showing *ae* for *e* see Coleman (1971), 186-90, esp. 189, citing *sae* = *se* in *CIL* 3.8412, cf. *ChLA* X 416.ii.19 and *Tab.Sulis* 94 with Adams (1992a), 10. For *scito me* in letters cf. Cicero, *Fam.* 2.15.1, *O.Wâdi Fawâkhir* 1.14-5 = *CEL* 73. For *explesse* cf. *O.Wâdi Fawâkhir* 1.7 = *CEL* 73, *explesti iiii matia*.

25. *bracis*: for other examples of this Celtic word at Vindolanda see **191**.16, **348**.2. It is a kind of cereal used in making Celtic beer (see *Tab.Vindol.*I, p. 96, cf. Pliny, *NH* 18.62), but of "genre inconnu" (André (1985), 37).

excussi: *excutio* (lit. "shake, strike (something) out of (something else)") could be used of threshing, cf. *TLL* V 2 1309. 32-6: see especially Columella 2.10.14 *nam semina excussa in area iacebunt, superque ea paulatim eodem modo reliqui fasciculi excutientur*, cf. Varro, *Rust*. 1.52.1. It was not a technical term for one particular method of threshing, but a general term for the separation of one part of a crop from the rest by shaking, striking or the application of pressure.

26. In the *ed. pr.* we were fairly confident about the reading of the numeral as *cxi*, written twice, although we pointed out that the dittography is unexpected (the dittography in lines 32-3 is much more easily explicable). We now think it possible that most of the extra traces which we were reading are offsets and that *cxix* is more likely.

fac ... mi mittas: *fac* + subjunctive is common in the colloquial language and epistolography from early Latin onwards; see e.g. Cicero *Att*. 2.14.1, cf. *CPL* 256, *fac itaque emas*.

26-7. *possị/m̤*: the word is inescapable in the context but the ending is difficult to read. If we suppose the writer put *im* at the beginning of line 27, both the letters are oddly made (for the word division cf. *uentur/um* in lines 35-6). We now prefer the alternative possibility which is to take the trace at the end of line 27, which goes through the *o* at the end of the line below, as ink (and not offset) and read *possị/m̤*; such a word division is very bizarre but perhaps credible in a letter written by someone of limited literacy.

27. *spicam*: at i.7 the plural was used but here the writer prefers the collective singular. Botanical terms are frequently used in the collective singular (e.g. *faba*: for singular and plural examples see *TLL* VI.1 2.52 and for singular examples at Vindolanda **192**.3, *fabae*, **302**.1, margin 3, *fabae* and *oliuae*).

27-8. *in excussorio*: *excussorium* is a neologism but its formation is regular and its meaning clear. It is synonymous with *area*, indicating the place where the act of separating *grana* from *spicae* takes place; at Varro, *Rust*. 1.52.1 *excutio* is used of this process, and *area* is used of the place where it is carried out.

autem: here it seems to be close to *enim* in meaning. On *autem* = *enim* (mainly in later Latin) see Hofmann and Szantyr (1965), 490-1.

29. *p̣erexcussi*: a possible alternative reading is *ter excussi*, which is supported by the gap the writer has left between the *r* and the *e*, but which is, we think, on other grounds a less attractive reading. This is by far the earliest occurrence of *perexcutio*.

31. *ei*: in the *ed. pr.* we understood this as = *sibi* (so also *CEL*, note *ad loc.*); for another example at Vindolanda see **250**.i.4. A.R.Birley (1991), 93 points out that it could equally well be taken as referring to Frontius, i.e. Frontius' *contubernalis* asked for the hides to be assigned to Frontius. We see no way of deciding between these alternatives.

iv.36. *interuenit̤*: this seems to mean "(did not) turn up", though it usually refers to an unexpected or chance arrival (e.g. Terence, *Phorm*. 91, cf. *TLL* VII.1 2299.73). In **291**.i.5-ii.8 Severa looks forward to the *interuentus* of Lepidina.

38-9. *Frontinium Iulium*: a new sentence must begin at this point. In the *ed. pr.* we understood the name as an example of the archaising inversion of *gentilicium* and *cognomen*, but A.R.Birley (1991), 91 points out that Frontinius is a good example of a "fabricated" *gentilicium* and that Iulius is often found as a *cognomen*.

38-41. This sentence is baffling. *pro coriaṭione* is a major crux and it is by no means the only difficulty.

There is an active *liceo* and a deponent *liceor*. The active has two main uses: (a) = "to be for sale" (*TLL* VII.2 1357.61), e.g. Cicero, *Att.* 12.23.3, *de Drusi hortis, quanti licuisse tu scribis, id ego quoque audieram*; with the genitive of value *quanti* here, contrast the ablative of price at Seneca, *Contr.* 1.7.3, *magno licet* (*magno* in iv.39 must be this same usage); (b) with a personal subject = "have for sale", with accusative of the thing offered for sale (*TLL* VII.2 1357.71), e.g. Pliny, *NH* 35.88 *quanti liceret (pictor) opera effecta.* The deponent means "bid for" (at auction) (*TLL* VII.2 1357.81), e.g. Seneca, *Contr.* 1.2.4, *in auctione nemo uoluit liceri.* Octavius has presumably used the first verb (rather than the deponent in an active form). If *comparauit* means bought, as seems likely (for this common sense see *TLL* III 2011.26, *OLD*, s.v. 3b; cf. e.g. Spanish *comprar*), there must be a contrast expressed between buying at a certain price and selling, offering for sale, at a different (higher) price. If so, the meaning of *magno licere pro* (assuming that *pro* is the preposition) would be something like "is asking a high price for". It is a difficulty that *liceo* is not attested with a *pro*-expression as complement, but on the other hand the verb is not frequent, and one cannot be certain about its range of uses.

coriaṭione would then have to be explained as the ablative of a noun *coriatio*, unattested in Latin at this date. The word *coriatio* is cited in *RMLW* (15th cent., no reference given), with the meaning "covering with leather". This is discussed by Petersmann (1992), 288, leading A.R.Birley to withdraw his suggested emendation ((1991), 95, *VRR* II, 60). The word would presumably have to be understood as an abstract verbal noun which had taken on a concrete meaning, a commonplace semantic development. Compare, e.g., *uulneratio*: this will at first have meant literally "the making of a wound", and then have acquired the concrete sense "a wound that is made" = *uulnus*; similarly *coriatio* (which would be a derivative of **corio(r)*) might originally have meant "the making of leather" (abstract) and then acquired the concrete sense "leather that is made"; perhaps cf. also *tensiunculam*, **239**.3 and note. There still remains the problem of *quem* following. This would have to be taken as a masculine relative form used for the feminine. It used to be thought that this usage was late (see, e.g., Löfstedt (1911), 132). However, there is now a parallel in one of the tablets from Murecine, dated to AD 39 (*TP* 18.2.8.-9, Wolf and Crook (1989), no.5), in which C.Novius Eunus writes "*quem suma iuratus promissi me ... redturum*" [sic], where *quem suma* = *quam summam*, an expression which occurs in the more correct version of the document (*TP* 18.5.7). The masculine form was eventually to replace the feminine entirely (cf. Fr. *qui*, masc. and fem.). See also *CEL* 7.II.20 with Cugusi's note *ad loc.*

The expression *comparauit (denarios) quinos* seems to contain an accusative of price ("which he bought for five *denarii* apiece"), a construction which occurs at Petronius, *Sat.* 43.4, *uendidit enim uinum, quantum ipse uoluit*, and perhaps in *P.Mich.*VIII 469.17 = *CEL* 144, with Adams (1977), 40-2, where further bibliography is cited. It is odd that the distributive *quinos* is used in association with the singular relative *quem*, though the antecedent may have a collective sense, and the relative clause would then contain a sort of *constructio ad sensum*. In any case distributives were by this time used for cardinals.

This explanation of these lines was offered in the *ed. pr.* with some diffidence but we cannot suggest any substantive improvement. It is far from satisfactory to have to bring into existence at this date a verbal noun with concrete meaning which is attested only later (based moreover on an unattested verb *corio(r)*), a new use of *licere*, and an early example of *quem* = *quam*. The discovery of a fifteenth-century example of the word unfortunately throws no light on the major problems posed by our passage, namely the sense of the whole sentence and the presence of the masculine relative form immediately after *coriatione*. The reading of the lines seems more or less certain, but it is possible that a different word-division might throw new light on the passage. In the *ed. pr.* we considered the possibility of taking *cori* in *coriatione* as a genitive, but saw no obvious noun which could be extracted from the following letters on which *cori* might depend.

42-3. *Spectatum*: A.R.Birley (1991), 94 points out that there are no other examples known in Britain. This strengthens the case for identifying this man with Spectatus of **180**.5, who must have been at Vindolanda. If this is correct, it makes it virtually certain that the letter of Octavius was sent *to* Vindolanda (see above, pp.43-5).

I . . . /ṛiuṃ: no doubt another proper name. In the *ed. pr.* we read the second letter as *ṃ* and we still think this is what it most resembles; however, the only name we find attested which would suit this beginning and ending is Imbrius and this is certainly not a plausible reading here. A.R.Birley (1991), 91 has suggested the very common *cognomen Iạṇụạrium*, accepted in *CEL*. The writing after *i* could be taken as *a* in this hand but it is very hard to reconcile what follows this with *nua*. Despite the palaeographical difficulties we would not wish to discount the possibility that *Iạṇụạ/riuṃ* should be read and we have nothing else to suggest.

Firmum: presumably to be identified with Firmus of **180**.23.

44. *Gleục̣one*: cf. A.R.Birley (1991), 94.

45. *uạḷ(e)*: probably this is all that was written in this line. The traces of ink at the right are offset and it is almost certain that the word was abbreviated, cf. **312**.ii.12, **349**.margin 1, **505**; see also *ChLA* X 428.10, on which Schubart's original view is preferable to that of Marichal (so also *CEL* 3).

Back 46. *uindol*: we are now uncertain whether this is written by the same hand as the letter on the front. The abbreviation is paralleled in **338**.back 1 (see note).

344

Inv.no.88.943. 171 x 77 mm. Plate XXXI. *VRR* II, Plate XIV.

This text is written on the other side of two of the three leaves which contain an account of dispensations of wheat (**180**). For the physical characteristics of this leaf, the format and the question of which is the primary and which the secondary text see the introduction to **180**. It is certain that both texts were written by the same person; compare the idiosyncratic form of *f* in lines i.3, 10 and ii.16 here and in **180**.23 and 25. Note also the form of *a* with two descenders (line i.8, *quia*, *ua-*) and the *g* in *uirgis* and *castigatum* (line i.6) not unlike that in **174**.2 (see note). Word division is often indicated.

The reconstruction of this text involves the placing of some small fragments, details of which are discussed in the notes. The maximum line length, for purposes of restoration, is 26 letters (line 6), but there may be as few as 18 (line ii.15, where the writer does not go all the way to the edge). The text is repetitive and the word order is awkward (especially line i.7). The use of the other side for an account points to the conclusion that this was a draft which was never sent. The space after *commississem* (ii.19) suggests that we have the end of the substantive part of the text (though it lacks a closure); this is confirmed by the fact that the back of the first part of the account (**180**.1-15), which would have been the last of three faces used in writing the petition, is blank. It seems obvious, however, that there must have been something substantial before the first surviving line and this suggests that the draft was begun on another leaf which we do not have.

The content is exceptionally interesting. The writer is appealing to someone in addressing whom he uses the term *maiestatem* (see i.4-5 note). This is surely unlikely to be anyone of lower status than the provincial governor, especially since he indicates that he has been unable to complain to the prefect of the unit and has perhaps failed to gain satisfaction from the *beneficiarius* or the centurions. It seems very unlikely that he is addressing the emperor. He asks that as an innocent man he should not be allowed to suffer beating as if he had committed some crime. The language in i.6-7 and ii.17-9 is ambiguous and could mean either that he has been punished and is asking for redress or that he was expecting to be punished and is asking for prevention, but on balance the former seems more probable. The whole tone of the appeal suggests that the author was a civilian and his description of himself as *hominem trasmarinum*, which may be intended to emphasise that he is not just a local *Brittunculus* (cf. **164**.5), strongly supports this (cf. *VRR* II, 59). The reference to *mercem* (i.2), in combination with the account of wheat on the other side of the leaf, suggests that he is very likely to be a trader. In that case, the quality of the latinity (repetitive though it is) is worth emphasis, as is the fact that the text appears to contain no erasures. If *numeri eius* (ii.12) refers to the unit of his persecutor or assailant, it may be that he is complaining about being victimised by a member of the military and is even perhaps being detained in the fort. Centurions were certainly able to inflict flogging on other soldiers (cf. Tacitus, *Ann.* 1.23) and may well not have hesitated to extend such treatment to those outside the military; compare *O.Flor.* 2 in which a decurion writes to a *curator praesidii*, requesting the despatch of a civilian who had set fire to some reeds near the *praesidium*. The evidence for civilians, including traders, in contact with the military is very welcome and does not present a serious problem (see also **309**, introduction, **343**, introduction and for civilians in a legionary *fabrica* cf. *ChLA* X 409), but the hypothesis that the author had been flogged by a centurion may help to explain the puzzling fact that a civilian text, if that is indeed what it is, was deposited and found in the barrack-block within the fort.

For another possible petition among the Vindolanda texts see **322** (cf. **257**) and compare *ChLA* X 434 (with further references to comparable texts).

i

eo ṃagis me ca[*c.12*
d . . . [.]em mercem [*c.8*
r[.] uel effunder[*c.3*]ṛ[
[. .]ṃine probo tuam maies-
[t]atem imploro ne patiaris me
[i]nnocentem uirgis caṣ[t]igatum
esse et domine proụ[.]. prae-
[fe]c̣ṭo non potui queri quia ua-
[let]udini detinebatur
queṣ[tu]s sum beneficiario

ii
[*c.8* cen]turionibụ[s
[*c.7*] ṇụmeri eius [
[*c.3* tu]ạm misericord[ia]m
impḷoro ne patiaris me
hominem trasmarinum
et innocentem de cuius f[ide
inquiras uirgis cruenṭ[at]u[m
esse ac si aliquid sceler[i]ṣ
commisissem *uacat*

"... he beat (?) me all the more ... goods ... or pour them down the drain (?). As befits an honest man (?) I implore your majesty not to allow me, an innocent man, to have been beaten with rods and, my lord, inasmuch as (?) I was unable to complain to the prefect because he was detained by ill-health I have complained in vain (?) to the *beneficiarius* and the rest (?) of the centurions of his (?) unit. Accordingly (?) I implore your mercifulness not to allow me, a man from overseas and an innocent one, about whose good faith you may inquire, to have been bloodied by rods as if I had committed some crime."

i.1-4. This passage presents the most difficult problems of restoration and interpretation. Fundamental to our understanding of it is the placement of a small fragment so as to supply the beginnings of lines 1-3. We are confident that this is correct and it is supported by the fact that the first of the three lines commences slightly to the left of the others and is thus likely to be the first line in the column; the placement also suits the text of the account on the other side.

1. *eo ṃagis me ca[*: the readings seem certain, despite the loss of the left part of *m*. Given the repetitiveness of the text (compare lines i.5-6 and ii.13-4), it is attractive to restore some part of the verb *castigo*, most probably *ca[stigauit*.

2. *d . . .[ ]em*: at the left, *dị* (less probably *dẹ*) looks the most likely reading, then the tops of two letters which would suit *c* or *s* or *g*, followed by *e*. We could plausibly restore *dịc̣ẹ[r]em* or *-dịg̣ẹ[r]em*. Then *mercem* is certain; what appears to be a supralinear addition following it is in fact an offset. *mercem* may refer to merchandise or goods (see **234**.i.5 note) and a reference to a reduction in its worth would be suitable, but it does not seem that *redigo* can mean this without some further qualification (e.g. *ad nummum*, *ad assem*).

3. *effunder[*: it is a little surprising to find the verb *effundo* in this context but the reading leaves no room for doubt. We tentatively suggest that it is to be understood in the literal sense of "pouring down the drain".

If the stroke between *mai* and *es* in line 4 is a descender from this line (see note to lines 4-5), the letter can only be *r* in this hand.

4. *[. .]ṃine p̣robo*: *m* is far from certain but we can see no better reading. *probo* is reasonably secure despite the horizontal split running through the word. Unless *probo* goes with *tuam maies[t]atem* and *imploro* begins a new sentence, which seems most unlikely, *[do]mine* must be ruled out and it is probable we have the phrase *[ho]mine probo*, which seems likely to refer to the petitioner. We could make sense of this by supposing that the phrase including *[ho]mine probo* begins a new sentence (we owe this point to Prof. H.M.Hine). As a possible reconstruction we offer, with diffidence and *exempli gratia*: *eo ṃagis me ca[stigauit dum] / dịc̣ẹ[r]em mercem [nihil uale-]/r[e] / uel effunder[em. p]ṛ[o] /*

[ho]mine probo etc. This is admittedly somewhat awkward. If it is plausible, however, it may be suggested that the small fragment with *ḷe* (not shown in Plate XXXI) may belong to *ualere*. For this meaning of *pro*, "as befits", see *OLD*, s.v. 16b.

4-5. *tuam maies[t]atem imploro*: the position of *tuam* before its noun is probably paralleled in the similar phrase in lines 13-4; although the tablet is split horizontally through this word there is no doubt about the reading. After *mai* there is a letter which descends below the line with a hook to the left. Two explanations are possible. Either it is an extraordinarily long descender of *r* in the previous line (of which this section is lost) and the writer has simply jumped over it in writing *maies* (the closest parallel for such an *r* is in *misericord[ia]m*, line ii.13); or he has written *maiiestatem* with the second *i* different in form from the first. The spelling is possible, see *CIL* 13.3672 and the discussion of this and analogous forms by Leumann (1977), 127; see also e.g. Priscian, *Gramm.* 2.14.6, *antiqui solebant ... "maiius" ... scribere quod non aliter pronuntiari posset, quam si ... proferretur ut "mai-ius"*. We prefer the first explanation.

For *maiestatem imploro* cf. the petition from the *coloni* of the *saltus Burunitanus* to Commodus, II.19-20 (most recent edition by Flach (1978), 489-92), *im]ploratum maiestatem tu[am*.

6-7. *uirgis caṣ[t]igatum esse*: there is a horizontal stroke between *i* and *r* which makes it look as if *uergis* might have been written but the mark is an offset (there is no doubt about the reading in line ii.17). In general compare the *saltus Burunitanus* inscription (cited in the previous note), II.11-16, *missis militib(us) [in eu]ndem saltum Burunitanum ali[os nos]trum adprehendi et uexari, ali[os uinc]iri, non<n>ullos ciues etiam Ro[manos] uirgis et fustibus effligi iusse[rit]*, cf. *Acts* 16. The trademark of the vicious centurion was the *uitis*, with which floggings were inflicted (see Tacitus, *Ann.* 1.23, cf. Juvenal 14.193, Livy, *Epit.* 57), but the use of the word *uirgis* does not seem a sufficient reason to exclude the possibility that the victim's persecutor was a centurion (see note to lines 10-12). The perfect participle passive (also in lines ii.17-8), makes the writer's current position ambiguous; by asking the recipient not to allow him to have been punished, he might be asking either for prevention or redress. We prefer to suppose that the latter is the case (cf. our suggested restoration of *ca[stigauit* in line 1).

7. *proụ[ ].*: the letter after *pro* is most like *u* and we wonder whether the reading is *proụṭ*. To this there are both palaeographical and linguistic objections: the trace before *prae* is very high for the top of *t* (though cf. perhaps *potui* in the following line) and would better suit *c*, *e*, *g* or *s*, and there seems to be room for another letter between *u* and *t*. In addition *prout* does not seem to be the right word in the context; if we have interpreted the sense correctly it is difficult to see why the writer could not simply have used *cum*, *quia* or *quod*. A.R.Birley (1990a), 18 has suggested *Proc̣[ul]ẹ*; it is not impossible to interpret the traces in this way, but there does not seem to be room for two letters in the gap between them; if this is right the next sentence follows in asyndeton. If *proụṭ* is right we suppose that it means "inasmuch as".

8-9. *quia ua/[let]udini detinebatur*: we have considered the possibility that we have the locative of a place-name *Va[...]udinium* before *detinebatur*, but, especially in view of the phrase *quia perpetua ualetudine detinetur* in *CIL* 6.100234.17 (AD 153), the restoration of *ua[le]tudini*, with the meaning "bad health" (cf. perhaps **227**.b.2) seems inescapable, despite the fact that we expect the ablative *ualetudine*. There is not room for more than three letters at the left of line 9. Both examples of *i* at the end of the word are tall and slightly bowed (the first more than the second) but there is no sign of a cross-bar on the second. It is perhaps best to regard it as a simple error.

i.10-ii.12. There are two small joining fragments which, by a process of elimination, are most likely to belong at the beginning of either line 10 or line 11 and the offsets show that the former is correct. This means that the restoration *quẹṣ[tu]s sum* seems inevitable and the sense would be "[inasmuch as] I could not complain to the prefect ... I complained to the *beneficiarius* ...". If our understanding of the writer's drift, that he is making his present appeal because previous efforts to obtain redress have failed, is correct a possible restoration would be: *quẹṣ[tu]s sum beneficiario / frustra et ce]ṇturionibụ[s / ceteris] ṇụmeri eius* etc.

beneficiario: it is probable, since the writer seems to be referring to local military officers, that he is here referring to the *beneficiarius praefecti* of the unit at Vindolanda rather than a *beneficiarius consularis*. For a *beneficiarius praefecti* of the First Cohort of Tungrians, which could be the unit involved here (see above, pp.22-3), see *RIB* I 1619 (Housesteads, Hurmius son of Leubasnus). The account on the other side of this leaf records a dispensation of wheat to a *beneficiarius* whose name begins with *Lu-* (**180**.18) and there is no reason why the same person should not be involved in the matter described in the petition. There is little evidence for the functions of the *beneficiarii praefecti* but it is noteworthy that the *beneficiarii* of the governor often provide the link between the civilian population and the governor (see Rankov (1986), especially 254, 279-80 citing evidence for complaints to *beneficiarii*, assumed to be *beneficiarii* of the prefect of Egypt, e.g. *P.Amh.*II 77, *SPP* XXII 55). It seems reasonable to suppose that at Vindolanda the *beneficiarius* of an auxiliary prefect might provide the link between a complainant and a prefect of a unit who could not be approached directly. For a *beneficiarius* in a tablet from Carlisle see Tomlin (1992), 152, note 57.

cen]turionibụ[s / c.7] ṇụmeri eius: the restoration of *cen]turionibụ[s* is not open to doubt. Thereafter we propose to restore *ceteris* (or something with the same sense) in the lacuna, see above, and to understand *eius* as a pronoun referring to the assailant. *numeri* simply means "unit" in a general sense, see **310**.i.8-9 and note. There is abundant evidence in papyri from Egypt for petitions or complaints addressed to centurions (e.g. *P.Ryl.*II 141, AD 37).

12-3. *[proin- /de]* or *[qua- / re]* would supply the sense required. If *prouṭ* is right in line i.7 (see note) *[proin/de]* would be very suitable.

tu]ạm misericord[ia]m imp̣ḷoro: for the position of *tu]ạm* see note to line 4; there is a tiny fragment with the letter *m* which clearly belongs at the right-hand side and must supply the end of *misericord[ia]m*; for the phrase cf. Cicero, *pro Murena* 86, *uestram fidem obtestatur, <uestram> misericordiam implorat.*

15. *hominem trasmarinum*: for the omission of *n* cf. **187**.ii.2, *Masuetus*. Compare *ChLA* III 200, a sale of a slave from Seleucia Pieria, described as "*natione transfluminianum*". The writer is here likely to be a Gaul who wished to distinguish himself from the local natives. At *VRR* II, 59, however, it is taken as indicating the recruitment of Britons.

16. *f[ide]*: *f* is certain, the rest is conjecture and the word is suggested *exempli gratia.*

17. *cruent[at]u[m*: the leaf is broken diagonally at the right-hand edge. The reading is inescapable but we have to suppose that all or most of the *m* is lost. We have not been able to parallel the expression with *uirgis* but note *TLL* IV 1237, quoting Optatus 2.18 (p.52.4), *tegulis plurimi cruentati sunt.*

18. *aliquid sceler[i]ṣ*: the reading after *sceler* is uncertain since there is a piece of the

tablet missing; *aliquid* + genitive would be the most satisfactory reading, see *OLD*, s.v. *aliquis* B7a.

19. *commississsem*: see **255**.i.6-8 note, **309**.i.3 note.

345

Inv.no.88.949. 184 x 36 mm. Plate XXXI. R.E.Birley (1990), fig. 17.

A diptych containing the lower part of two columns of a letter. There is a notch in each edge. The text is remarkable for its regular use of interpunct, even after monosyllables, by both the scribe and the author who added the closure in his own hand. The letter is addressed to a prefect whose name is lost and comes from one Celonius Iustus who describes himself as *col(lega)* and must therefore also be a prefect. The surviving part of the letter is concerned with military business - the despatch and request for the return of a decurion named Atto, the removal or discharge of some persons, perhaps Atto and someone else named in the lost part of the tablet.

i

. . . .

traces [pe]ṛ Ạ[t-
tonem · decurionem ·
misi tibi · te · rogo · frater · continuo · illọs · expungas et · nulli · ali · quam

ii

. . . .

].ṛ.[
acceperunt rogọ ..[.]. ..[
dem · Attonem · remittas
m[2] bene · ualeas ·
frater · et · domine
opto

Back:

. . . .

m[1]].[
praef(ecto)
ab Celonio Iusto
col(lega)

"... I have sent you ... through (?) Atto the decurion. I ask, brother, that you immediately strike them off the list. And no others .... have received. I ask that you send that same (?) Atto back to me. (2nd hand) It is my wish that you enjoy good health, my brother and lord. (Back, 1st hand) To ... prefect, from Celonius Iustus, his colleague."

i.1-2. *Ạ[t-]/tonem*: this is no doubt the same person whose return is requested in ii.3, hence the restoration of the end of line 1. The long descender which can be seen before this must belong to *r* (*a* in this hand has one or two short descenders) and is most easily explained as the end of *per*.

3. It is notable that there is no interpunct between *misi* and *tibi*.

4-5. *illọs expungas*: the end of *illọs* is rather smudged but the accusative can be read and is what we would expect. It must refer to persons mentioned earlier in the letter. *expungo* means "remove from the list"; in a military context it can be used of deserters (*Digest* 49.16.15, cf. **226**.a.10) or of straightforward discharge (cf. ἐκσφουνγεύειν, *P.Oxy.* IX 1204.19); cf. *RMR* 47.i.16 note, Gilliam (1986), 113). See *O.Bu Njem*, p.90 and cf. *TLL* V.2 1833.

5. There is a clear interpunct between *ali* and *quam*, which means that *ali* must be taken as *alii* (the form is cited by *OLD* at *CIL* 2.6278.25).

ii.2. The restoration of the end of the line is problematical. After *rogo*, *ṃi̥[h]i̥* is compatible with the traces. Thereafter there may be very slight traces and a descender. If we read *ẹụ[n-]/dem* we would have to suppose that the descender belongs to a letter from the line above (cf. the long descender of *r* between *e* and *m* at the end of line i.2). The only plausible alternative which occurs to us is *ịḅ[i-]/dem* in the sense "at once" (*OLD*, s.v.3), in which case we would have to suppose that we have the descender of the first *i* but that the second example was shorter.

3. There is an interpunct between *dem* and *Attonem* guaranteeing that the name is Atto rather than Matto; both are attested but Atto is the commoner, see *NPEL*, citing 11 instances in Gallia Belgica. For the name at Vindolanda see **308** and cf. **320**.2 note.

Back 1. R.E.Birley (1990), 18 restores the name of Vettius Severus (**305**.back) as the addressee (*Vettio] S[euero*). The identification of Severus as a prefect at Vindolanda in Period 2 is very uncertain (see above, p.26). The descender which is visible is no doubt *r* in this hand. It can hardly belong to an initial *S* of *Seuero*; if it did we would be sure to see the descender of *r* further to the right and nothing is visible. Thus *Vettio Seue]ṛ[o]* would be a more attractive restoration, but this is entirely speculative.

3. *C̣elonio Iusto*: we have considered reading the *gentilicium* as *Velonio* (see *LE* 99) but *C̣* is a better reading. Celonius is not cited in *LE* but there is a dedication from Rovenich (Tolbiacum), now lost, by one Celorius Iustus, perhaps concealing a misreading of this name and referring to the same person (*CIL* 13.7937, *VRR* II, 31).

346

*Tab.Vindol.*I 38, Plate IX, 1 and 2. *CEL* 106. R.E.Birley (1990), fig. 18. *VRR* II, Plate VII.

i

. . . .

traces

rạm tibi paria udoṇ[um
ṭ. ab Sattua solearuṃ [
duo · et subligariorụm [
duo solearum paria dụ[o

traces

. . . .

ii

. . . .

]um ṣaluṭa...[
]ṇdem Elpidem Ịụ[
].enum Tetrịcum et omṇ[es
[c]ontibernales cum quibus
[o]p̣to felicissimus uiuas *uacat* [

. . . .

Back: *traces*

"... I have sent (?) you ... pairs of socks from Sattua, two pairs of sandals and two pairs of underpants, two pairs of sandals ... Greet ...ndes, Elpis, Iu..., ...enus, Tetricus and all your messmates with whom I pray that you live in the greatest good fortune."

i.2. The obvious restoration is *mise]ṛạm* (so *CEL*).

3. At the start *tri]/a* (so *CEL*) is impossible. *t* is very good and *i* is quite promising for the next letter; this suggests *uigin]/ṭị*, a large quantity but not all necessarily for the use of one person. We suggest that Sattua is best understood as a personal name and note the brand *Sattuo* on a leather patch (*VRR* II, 93 no.9.i). Fatua is attested as a personal name in Lusitania (*LC* 264) but we do not think *F̣attua* a preferable reading. *paria* is no doubt to be supplied after the break.

5. The double mention of the item is no doubt due to the fact that the second pair of sandals came from someone else (so *CEL*).

ii.1. *ṣaluṭaṛẹ .[*, *ed. pr.* We now think that *ṣaluṭa ạ ṃẹ* is a more plausible reading; the final trace is exiguous.

2. At the end *P̣ụ[* is also possible.

3. *R]ḥenum* (cf. **347**.a.1) is a possible restoration.

Tetrịcum: despite *CEL* we prefer to retain the reading, against *Tetrẹcum* (see our note *ad loc.* in *Tab. Vindol.*I).

5. The words *litterarum uestigia*, which appear at the foot of col.ii in *CEL*, should be at the foot of col.i.

347

Inv.no.86.346.a-c. (a) 90 x 23 mm. (b) 56 x 20 mm. (c) 56 x 23 mm.

Eight fragments of a diptych, of which three (one consisting of two joining pieces) have writing, two on both sides. It seems likely that we have two fragments from each half of a diptych, that (b) contains the top of the second column and that (c) is to be placed below it, but not immediately below. The tablet contains a letter from Rhenus, a slave of Similis (see c.back 2 note), to Primigenius who may be a slave of Cerialis (see note to b.back 1).

The closure is written in a hand similar to the main hand (a very good one) but possibly not the same one. For slaves in the military context see Speidel (1989).

a.

Rhenus Primigenio [
sa]ḷuṭeṃ
. . . .

b.

. . . . .
ualde desiderọ
traces
. . . . .

Back:

traces?
. . . . .

c.

. . . . .
ueniam max̣ị[
̣erte *uacat*
m²? optọ [
ter [
. . . . .

Back:

. . . . .
m¹]ạḷịṣ *traces?*
a Rh]ẹṇo Similis
seruo

"Rhenus to his Primigenius, greetings. ... I very much desire ... the greatest indulgence (?) ... through (?) you. (2nd hand?) I pray that you are in good health, dearest brother (?) ... (Back, 1st hand) [To Primigenius] (slave of) (?) ...alis, from Rhenus, slave of Similis."

a.1. For the *cognomen* Rhenus, which is not common, see *LC* 203 and cf. Rhenicus (*CIL* 13.11548). The name of the addressee, Primigenius, is very common and is much used by slaves and freedmen (see *LC* 290). The large gap between the name of the sender and that of the recipient is noteworthy (cf. **249**.1, **259**.1, **321**.1).

b. *ualde desiderọ*: there are apparently no traces of ink before this and the phrase is appropriate for the beginning of the letter. There appear, however, to be traces of writing on the back which must belong to the address; if this is so this fragment must belong to the right-hand portion of the letter.

Back. If the traces are ink, they must belong to the address; it is possible that we have traces of the end of *Primigenio* followed by *Ceri-*, with the end of the name on the back of (c), see note.

c.1-2. A.R.Birley (1990a), 19 cites this as referring to a despatch of wine, but the reading of *ueniam* leaves very little room for doubt. What follows, if correctly read, must be part of *maximus*, either the superlative or a name. *ueniam* could be the present subjunctive or future indicative of *uenio* or one of its compounds. An alternative solution is to take *ueniam* as the noun, followed by *max̣ị[mam*.

.er te: either *ṭer te* or *c̣erte* looks preferable to *p̣er te* from a palaeographical point of view, but there is a clear *uacat* following which indicates that this must be the end of the message and this seems a difficult position for either.

We can envisage the expression of a strong desire to see the addressee, followed by something beginning with a phrase such as *per]ueniam max̣ị[ma celeritate*; or, if *ueniam* is the noun, something like *ut / ueniam max̣ị[mam habeam/accipiam / p̣er te.*

3-4. *ter* can hardly be anything but the end of *frater*, in which case Primigenius must surely also be of servile status (see back 1 note). We can envisage *optọ [te bene ualere fra]/ter [karissime.*

Back 1. *]ạḷịṣ*: the reading is compatible with the traces. If it is correct, Primigenius might be a slave of Flavius Cerialis or of Flavius Genialis; the traces on the back of (b) are very uncertain but might favour the former. It is uncertain whether there are traces following but the name of the addressee could be followed by a simple genitive, without *seruo* (see **301**.back, *P.Oxy*.XLIV 3208 verso = *CEL* 10).

2. *Similis*: it is likely that this is the Flavius Similis attested as a correspondent of Flavius Cerialis in **254**, **235** and probably **286**.

348

Inv.no.87.728. 94 x 27 mm.

A fragment containing five lines of a letter, perhaps concerning the sale of the cereal *braces* (cf. **343**.iii.25, **191**.16).

. . . .
traces f̣ẹcisse c . . [
de brace qu . . adscrịbis uen-
dendam adhuc mem . . . em
c.15 u . . ạ
traces
. . . .

"... to have done ... about the *braces*, which you are assigning (?) for sale ..."

1. At the end it looks most like *cụ .*; there may be three or four letters lost after this.

2. *brace* is certain. After that, the construction seems to require *quam* but the reading of the letters after *qu* is extremely uncertain.

adscrịbis: this seems a slightly odd verb to use here. Note perhaps *Digest* 40.5.24.8, *si ita scripsit "ne eum alienes" "ne eum uendes", idem erit dicendum si modo hoc modo fuerit adscriptum, quod uoluerit eum testata ad libertatem perduci*, where the word seems to mean "to add as a title" to a sale or "write something additional".

349

Inv.no.87.806. 71 x 26 mm.

A fragment of the right-hand portion of a diptych containing seven lines of a letter. There are further traces at the left of two lines written in the margin at a right-angle to the main text and perhaps also of the ends of two lines of the left-hand column. There are remains of an address on the back. The name of the addressee does not survive but the sender of the letter has the *cognomen* Fatalis. He may be the same person as the Fatalis mentioned in **343**.ii.22 in the context of a financial transaction. A.R.Birley (1991), 93 suggested that that person might be Claudius Fatalis, who is known to have served three terms as a centurion in British legions; the hypothesis might equally be applied to the Fatalis of **349** but the traces of the antepenultimate letter of the *gentilicium* do not favour *d* (see note to the back). The content is obscure but Fatalis may be promising to be somewhere on the Nones of a month and asking the recipient to explain something to him and to a certain Severus.

ii

. . . .

traces
di propiti ṣuṇṭ .[
futurụs Nonis .[
uelim mihị ...[
ria explices ....[
Seuero expḷịca salụṭ[
tubẹrṇạ[

L.margin: ↓].ḅ.ṣ · ual(e)
]ẹ

Back: . . . .
].io Fatạḷe

"... if the gods are propitious ... I (?) will be ... on the Nones of ... Please explain to me ... explain to Severus ... Greet your (?) messmates ... Farewell, dearest brother (?). (Back) ... from ...ius Fatalis."

ii.2. *di propiti ṣuṇṭ*: there is no doubt about the reading of the first two words (cf. **466**) and they must be part of a standard expression of optimism; given that *propitius* is often used of the gods (cf. *OLD*, s.v.) it would be perverse to understand *di* as anything other than the contracted form of *dei*. What follows is less certain. The first two letters look like *fu* but what follows seems clearly to be *n* and after that *t* is possible; it may be that the apparent cross-bar of *f* is illusory.

3. *Nonis*: there is a very faint trace following which might be the beginning of a month-name (probably omitted in **236**.3, however) but no reading could be regarded as more than very speculative. We have no way of calculating the number of letters likely to be lost

at the right. The sender may be saying something like *Vindolandae, si di propiti sunt, (ego) sum futurus Nonis* [month-name].

4. *uelim*: see *OLD*, s.v.10. The traces at the end of the line are too exiguous to enable us to attempt a reading.

5. *explices*: for the uses of this verb in the Vindolanda texts see **343**.i.4, **316**.margin 1, **301**.i.5 and notes *ad locc*. The financial usage is well-attested but here it is perhaps safest to take it in its common meaning "explain". The traces at the end of the line are very faint; *ḟṛạṭ[er* may be possible.

6. *Seuero*: there are two other people with this name in the Vindolanda texts, Vettius Severus, the recipient of a letter and perhaps a prefect (**305**.back), and the writer of **301** who was a slave. Neither seems likely to be identical with the person here mentioned.

expḷịca: the reading of *l* is difficult; we would need to ignore apparent ink at the foot of *l* and assume that the mark at the top right of *i* is not ink.

salụṭ[: if this is correct we suggest restoring something like *salụṭ[a (a me) con-/tubẹrṇạ[les tuos/meos*.

Margin 1. The first traces appear to be *] .ḅạs* but *]ạḅịṣ* (*salut]ạḅịṣ*?) is perhaps not impossible. For the abbreviation of *uale* see also **312**.ii.12, **343**.iv.45, **505**.

2. Perhaps *frater karissim]ẹ*.

Back 1. This is written on an upward slant and must be the name of the sender. For Fatalis see the introduction. The trace of the first surviving letter looks most like *l*, which would rule out *Fla]ụio*, and would be very hard to reconcile with *Clau]ḍio*. Of the common *gentilicia*, *Iu]ḷio* is easier to read. Note the remark of Tomlin (1992), 151 that in Britain this *gentilicium* is almost always held by legionary centurions or rankers.

350

Inv.no.87.788. 88 x 28 mm.

Part of the left-hand portion of a diptych containing the opening of a letter from a person called Claudius Popa. Despite the fact that the half-diptych appears to be intact at both edges there is no sign of the name of the addressee or of *salutem*. The writing in the second line clearly overran the fold. This suggests that the letter might possibly have been written across the whole width of the diptych (cf. **292**.a.i.1-4). It is noteworthy that the second line, the beginning of the message proper, is not indented as it normally is in these letters.

Ç̣laudius Popa *uacat* [
ṃemoriam tuam dom[ine
. . . .

"Claudius Popa to ... The memory of you, my lord ..."

1. *Popa*: the reading is very clear but the *cognomen* seems to be extremely rare (one citation in *LC* 319, a freedman of the Republican period, and two in *RNGCL*); *VRR* II, 67

suggests the unattested name *Popio*, but we do not think this reading is possible. For the large gap after the name of the sender see **347**.a.1 note and the references there given.

351

Inv.no.87.796. 46 x 19 mm.

A fragment containing remains of three lines.

. . . .
.[
ḍa · tọ.[..].....[
Fortunati (centurionis) [
. . . .

3. There may be an interpunct after *Fortunati*. The *cognomen* is an extremely common one but it is perhaps worth noting that *RIB* I 1907 (Birdoswald) attests a centurion of the Sixth Legion named L.Vereius Fortunatus.

352

Inv.no.86.433. 81 x 12 mm.

A fragment of the right-hand portion of a diptych containing the remains of three lines of a letter, as well as some traces of writing at a right-angle in the left margin. The back contains part of an address to Marcus Cocceius Velox, who does not appear elsewhere in the Vindolanda texts.

. . . .
traces
re ne saltem quiuiṣ
traces
. . . .

L.margin: ↓].ra.[

Back: Marco Cocceio Vẹḷọc̣ị ..
traces
. . . .

1. *re ne saltem*: *re* is presumably the end of a word which began in the previous line. There is a gap between *n* and *e* because the writer left space to accommodate the descender from the line above.

Margin. Possibly *fraṭ[er*. For writing between the columns cf. **302**, **311**.

Back. It is noteworthy that this is *not* written in address script but in a largish, ordinary cursive; compare **310**.back 23-4. The traces after the initial *V* are very abraded. Velox is a fairly well-attested *cognomen*, but, perhaps surprisingly, not in Britain. Its first occurrence seems to be on a text from Catterick, *t(urma) Velo[cis* (*Britannia* 21 (1990), 374, no.60). The use of the *tria nomina* in full is not paralleled in either the addresses or the texts at Vindolanda and Velox is obviously not here using it himself (cf. A.R.Birley (1990a), 19, *VRR* II, 69). The attribution of the tablet to Period 5 would place it some 20 years later than the reign of Nerva which the *gentilicium* evokes. There appear to be traces of two more letters at the end of the line; perhaps the beginning of a title or rank.

353

Inv.no.85.069. 109 x 20 mm.

A fragment containing the ends of two lines from the left-hand column of a letter and three lines from the end of the right-hand column. The amount of space before the first line in the second column suggests either that the writer left a blank space between the end of the message proper and the closure, or that the three surviving lines came at the top of col.ii; if the latter is the case, as is suggested by the fact that *ụalẹ* at the end of line ii.3 is probably by a second hand, the letter must have been written on more than one tablet (cf. **292**, **343**), since the preserved line-ends in col.i clearly cannot belong to the opening of a letter.

i

. . . .
]. per
]ḅịṣ
. . . .

ii

. . . .
Pacatam saluta uerbis meis
et tuos omnes cum quibus optọ
domine bene ualeas m^2? ụalẹ

"... Greet Pacata in my words, and all your household with whom, my lord, I pray that you are in good health. (2nd hand?) Farewell."

ii.1. There is no clear evidence for Pacata elsewhere in the Vindolanda texts (but cf. **320**.ii.2). For Pacatus in a Batavian context see *CIL* 6.8807 (Bellen (1981), no.9); the *cognomen* is particularly common in Gallia Belgica (see *NPEL*).

uerbis meis: for the expression cf. **310**.i.9-10.

2. *tuos omnes*: cf. **260**.7-8, *pueros tuos*.

The ligature of *us* in *quibus* is noteworthy. The reading must be correct (cf. **346**.ii.4-5, *cum q̣uibus / o]p̣to felicissimus uiuas*) although no trace of the tail of *q* survives.

3. *ụalẹ*: the first letter is very difficult to read but it can hardly be anything else. It is difficult to be certain that we have a second hand here since the sample of writing is so small; on balance, however, it seems likely that *uale* was added by the author when the scribe had written the fuller closing formula (cf. **250**.ii.17, **300**.ii.12).

DESCRIPTA
(Nos. 354-573)

Under this heading we have described texts which do not merit full editions either because they are too fragmentary or because we have not been able to read or extract sense from the writing which survives. With very few exceptions we have described only those tablets on which we have been able to read something more than isolated letters. It should be added that there are very many fragments on which the photographs show abraded traces of writing or marks which might be writing. We have not thought it worthwhile either to describe these or to include them in our concordance. A full list of all the tablets and the reference numbers of their photographs can be found in *VRR* II, 109-22.

We have also included the minor texts first published in *Tab.Vindol.*I, the majority as *descripta*. We have omitted the stilus tablets.

All texts are written along the grain of the wood unless otherwise noted. The backs of all fragments are blank unless otherwise stated.

354. Inv.no.85.003. One line with possible traces of descenders from a line above: *] . ạresp̣alu . [*. The undotted letters appear certain but do not suggest any obvious articulation; possibly a reference to a *palum* ("stake"), but *m* is a very difficult reading.

355. Inv.no.85.010.a. Plate XXXII. Parts of three lines from the end of a letter; it is not clear whether the hand changes for the last two lines: *mihi fieṛi . [/ uale doṃ[in]ẹ / ka[ri]ṣsime*. The writing is very cursive and there is a remarkable ligature between *m* and *e* in *karissime*, made by adding a link stroke. Traces of one line of writing in address script on the back.

356. Inv.no.85.015. A fragment of the left-hand side of a letter with remains of 4 lines: traces / *ṇarum . [/ tibi feliciṇ[t]ạ[/ precatur ṣị ṛ . [*.

357. Inv.no.85.020.b. Two joining fragments with traces of three lines; of the first only descenders. Lines 2-3: *] . . . nuntiauerit [/] . . . . ụsẹṛẹ ṣị[*. The space before *nuntiauerit* suggests that the verb was not compounded. The writing is fairly cursive and has some resemblance to the hand of **225-32**, but not enough for us to be able to assert that it is the same hand.

358. Inv.no.85.020.c. A tiny scrap with remains of one line: *] . . cṛo*.

359. Inv.no.85.023. *VRR* II, Plate I. A complete diptych with notches and tie-holes; back blank. Abraded traces of several lines of script, though most of the lower leaf was probably blank. Written across the grain but not likely to have been an account (cf. **164**). The last line on the upper leaf ends *rus*.

360. Inv.no.85.024. Faint traces of two lines, of which the second may end *ṭiḅi ḥ[*.

361. Inv.no.85.026. Three joining fragments with a large blank at the left, therefore presumably the left-hand side of a letter; found with **327** but probably not part of the same letter. Only two descenders from line 1; lines 2-4 read: *deṭineạ[* (or *deṭineṛ[]*) / *.us .ieṇṣ[* / *cas batau .[*. Certainly a reference to Batavians; the last letter could be either *i* or *o*.

362. Inv.no.85.030. Abraded remains of a line of writing sloping up to the right: *a . . ṛ . ẹ . . ọc̣eriaḷi . [. .* We take this to be the name of the sender of a letter. *a Flauio Ceriali* is impossible and there is at least one letter after *ceriali*. As this letter is compatible with *s*, we suggest that we have an analogous text to **301**, i.e. a letter written by a slave of Cerialis; the name of the slave is irrecoverable. Below are traces of a further line, which is illegible but can hardly be anything other than part of *praefecti*, perhaps abbreviated. The other side is blank.

363. Inv.no.85.032.b. Two joining fragments no doubt from the end of a letter, since the smaller reads *]ẹụalerẹ .[*; probably *opto te ben]ẹ ụalerẹ f[rater*.

364. Inv.no.85.036.b. Abraded traces of two lines, no doubt of a letter; found with **273** and possibly part of the same letter. The first line may end *benḍum* (*ṣc̣ṛịbenḍum* or *ḥạbenḍum* is perhaps possible).

365. Inv.no.85.052.c. Remains of five lines written across the grain. Probably a list of names: traces / *.loṭi[* / *oṇno[* / *cano[* / *.ent[*. Line 2: first letter *c*, *g* or *p*. Line 3: possibly a letter before *onno*. Line 5: *ḷent[* is possible.

366. Inv.no.85.056.b. Faint traces of two lines written across the grain. The second appears to read *]ạḅịlis .[* and the rest of the leaf is apparently blank.

367. Inv.no.85.059.a. Four lines written across the grain, probably a list of names: *ṃ . . [* / *quaṛ[* / *lụb[* / *ṃas .[*. *NPEL* lists *cognomina* beginning with *quar* and *lub*, e.g. *Quartus*, *Luba*, *Lubitiatus*; in line 4 probably *masc̣[*, cf. **505**.

368. Inv.no.85.059.b. Remains of three lines from the left-hand side of a letter, with tie-hole visible. One descender only from line 1; lines 2-3: *p̣er qu[* / *abṛị . . [*.

369. Inv.no.85.061. Remains of a few letters written across the grain. In the top line *ḅa[* can be read and may have traces of *ii* preceding, i.e. a reference to a cohort of Batavians. It is doubtful whether anything was written above this, but there are faint traces of letters below it.

370. Inv.no.85.068. Remains of two lines from the start of a letter. *]....ci su[o / salute[m*. The traces might fit *Felici*, but the spacing does not suit.

371. Inv.no.85.081.a.back. Left-hand portion of three, possibly four, lines; written on the other side of **198** (see introduction): *..et[/ [ ]ecis da..[/ .amá [*. There may be traces of a line before line 1. Line 2: possibly *[f]ecis*; after this *dr* is equally possible. Line 3: the second *a* has an apex; the reading appears to be *sama*, which can hardly be right; perhaps *fama*?

372. Inv.no.85.081.b. Tiny scrap with traces of address script on the back; on the front part of one line: *]..er[*.

373. Inv.no.85.081.c. Parts of two lines of which the first reads *]usper[* or *]uscer[*. Conceivably *Flaui]us Cer[ialis* or *]us Cer[iali suo]*; but other restorations are possible.

374. Inv.no.85.081.d. Parts of three lines (written across the grain?) in quite an elegant script; the first reads *]ant[*.

375. Inv.no.85.081.e. Remains of several lines written across the grain, of which all but the last three are severely abraded. These three lines read: *] fr..[/]..gus[/].resa.[*. The first line may possibly contain a reference to *frumentum* or to the century of *Frumentius*, cf. **160**.A.10 note).

376. Inv.no.85.083. Somewhat abraded remains of the beginnings of eight lines written across the grain. Perhaps shorthand, see **122-6**.

377. Inv.no.85.093. Remains of two lines, with interpunct: *]. · scriberem · [/].nure · .: ..[*. Line 1: a long descender at the left, e.g. *tib]i*. Line 2: for *nure* also possible is *mire* (hardly *u]enire* even though the letters after this could be read *ad*, preceded and followed by interpunct).

378. Inv.no.85.098. Beginnings of three lines, no doubt part of a letter: *inspicere dic.[/ singulos ce.a.[/ me...[*.

379. Inv.no.85.099.b. Remains of two lines, no doubt part of a letter: *...ionem ut.re.isne.[/ inuenire*. In the first line *utereris* is a possible but not an easy reading. The second line is apparently blank after *inuenire* though there may well be an ascender from a line below visible; cf. **291**.ii.8, **257**.6, **258**.3.

380. Inv.no.85.099.c. Two non-joining fragments with writing along the grain; the smaller reads *ab[*, the larger has a *denarius*-sign followed presumably by a figure (if so, apparently *c* or *d*).

381. Inv.no.85.101.b. The top left-hand corner of a tablet which reads *cla[*; probably therefore a letter from someone with the *gentilicium* Claudius (or Claudia).

382. Inv.no.85.103. Part of one line: *]mul.cre.[*.

383. Inv.no.85.109. Remains of one line: *]ẹntabeṇ . . . ṭ .* (not *bene ualeas/ualere*).

384. Inv.no.85.111.b. Remains of one line in large letters: *]ṛia[*, conceivably part of the name Cerialis.

385. Inv.no.85.114. Remains of writing in address script: *] . . o . . ạ . ẹf . . [*. We could read *]ṇḍo* at the start, suggesting *Verecu]ndo*, but it is difficult to read *praef* after this. The other side is blank.

386. Inv.no.85.119.b. Remains of two lines of which the first reads *] . uli ẹgo*.

387. Inv.no.85.124. Abraded remains of at least eleven lines of an account written across the grain. The *denarius*-symbol occurs frequently, but otherwise only occasional letters are legible.

388. Inv.no.85.126. Possible descenders of one line with abraded traces of one further line: *] . siḍọ*, followed by traces of 6 or 7 more letters; *domine* cannot be read.

389. Inv.no.85.139. A small scrap which reads *] . agesor[ ] . [*, with traces of a second line below this; *sor[o]ṛ* is possible.

390. Inv.no.85.146.b. A scrap with remains of the ends of two or three lines, presumably of a letter. Only *] . rium* in line 1 is legible.

391. Inv.no.85.147. Ends of three lines, no doubt of a letter, in a neat script halfway between a cursive and a capital: *]ụtiussen /] . . ermitte /]ṛ . ịạ ạd*. Alternatively, line 1 may also begin *]ṇtius*; articulate *-tius sen-*? Line 2: *ṗermitte* is possible. Line 3: there may be an apex over the *a* in *ạd*.

392. Inv.no.85.164. A fragment reading *] . . uḷị hiber-*, no doubt a reference to winter or winter-quarters. Remains of address script on the back.

393. Inv.no.85.165. A fragment with remains of two lines. Possibly: *v N[onas / co[h*. This might be a report of the same type as **127-53**, but other types of document cannot be excluded.

394. Inv.no.85.168.back. On the other side of a leaf containing a military report (**135**), four lines of a text written in a tiny but neat script which appears to be unrelated to the report. We can make nothing of the traces in lines 3-4. Lines 1-2: *] . . las eṃe . . . [/ uiċṭọṛị ạḍ . . . ros . . . ẹ[*. Line 1: perhaps *emeṇḍạ[s*. Line 2: if *uiċṭọṛị* is correctly read it is likely to be a personal name, cf. **180**.5, **182**.ii.11; following that perhaps *ạḍ ċạṛros*.

395. Inv.no.85.170. Beginnings of two lines, no doubt of a letter: *ẹṭ alteros d[/ . ero uos sụ[*.

396. Inv.no.85.175. A small fragment with parts of two lines. The first has only one or two descenders in address script. The second reads: *chor viiii [*, clearly a reference to *cohors viiii Batauorum*; the numeral has a superscript bar. For the spelling *chor(tis)* cf. **127**.2.

397. Inv.no.85.177. Remains of five lines, no doubt of a letter. Very badly abraded. Only occasional letters legible, except at the end of line 4 which probably reads *quarṭa*.

398. Inv.no.85.181. Remains of two lines: *r . . [/ rariu[*.

399. Inv.no.85.182. A small fragment with remains of two lines of which the first reads *] . ṛaẹ . [*; possibly *p̣ṛaẹf̣*, in which case the traces beneath might be read as *[c]ọḥ*.

400. Inv.no.85.189. Beginnings of three lines; very abraded. The second may read *ṭṛab[*.

401. Inv.no.85.192. Abraded traces of a single line. Possibly shorthand, see **122-6**.

402. Inv.no.85.194.b-d. Three non-joining fragments, no doubt from a letter. It is unclear whether they all belong to the same text. They were found with **239** but probably do not form part of that text. b: a long descender from line 1 with the start of a second line, reading *bot . [* (e.g. *scri-]/bo tị[bi]*); traces on the back. c: on one side only *]m* remains, the rest being blank; on the other side probably an address, reading *]rị . [ ]ó*, e.g. *P]rịṣ[c]ó* (cf. **420**). d: front blank; back traces of address script.

403. Inv.no.95.195. Two fragments with parts of three lines of a letter, possibly in the same hand as **292**, **404** and **406**: (traces) *et res[/ alịos miseraṃ [/* (traces); the piece which we have transcribed as the first line may be incorrectly placed.

404. Inv.no.85.196.a. Start of two lines from the right-hand side of a letter, with a possible trace of the left-hand column visible; the hand resembles that of **292** and **406**. *ṣ . . ḍ fạ . [/ cos n c̣ . [*. Line 1: hardly *q̣ụọḍ*. Line 2: there is a superscript dash over *n*; most probably *ami-]/cos n(ostros)*, rather than *co(n)s(ular-) n(ost-)*; there is no abbreviation mark after *cos*. The tops of a line in address script are visible on the back; although this may be a name ending *li*, neither *Ceriali* nor *Geniali* can be read.

405. Inv.no.85.196.c. A scrap with remains of two lines from the closure of a letter and the name of the sender, written on an upward slant, on the back. Front: *u]ạleas /] .* (perhaps *e* at the end of *domine* or *karissime*). Back: *ạ Dione*.

406. Inv.no.85.199.b. Remains of one line, no doubt of a letter: *]etefe . . c̣[*; possibly *]e te felịc[-*. Perhaps by the same hand as **403** and **404**.

407. Inv.no.85.199.c. A scrap with remains of the end of a letter. On the front *] ḍominẹ [*; on the back, bottoms of six letters in address script. Perhaps part of the same letter as **406**.

408. Inv.no.85.201. A fragment with a notch and tie-hole and remains of the beginning of one line: *min . ur . . [*; the obvious reading is *minṇur*, but we do not see how this could be articulated.

409. Inv.no.85.202. A tiny scrap which reads: *q]uod ge[*. Possible traces on the back.

410. Inv.no.85.209.a. Remains of one line written along the grain: *.ṛ.dụṣ.[*; *pr(idie) Idus* is possible.

411. Inv.no.85.209.b. Parts of three lines written across the grain; probably an account. Line 3 reads *perce.[*; perhaps *per* followed by a name.

412. Inv.no.85.211.b. Two joining (?) fragments containing part of a single line, probably from the top right-hand side of a letter: *]..ḅisp̣alụ[..].corị.s*; *p* could be *c* or *t*, but none suggests any obvious articulation (for *palu* perhaps cf. **354**). *cor* may be followed by a short and then a long *i*; *corịịs*, if correct, would suggest a reference to Coria (cf. **154**.7 note). This was found with **276** but appears to be in a different hand.

413. Inv.no.85.214. Remains of one line which may well read *F̣lạuị[o* in address script. There are probably traces on the front.

414. Inv.no.85.219.a. Beginnings of three lines, no doubt from a letter; the second reads *dạ..profị.[*. Two lines of writing are visible on the back of which the second may read *cẹ..ạc..[*; as this is slightly on the slant and may be preceded by remains of *a*, it is possible that it is the name of the sender; it is not *a Ceriale* (cf. **242**) and the traces do not suit any other name known in the Vindolanda texts.

415. Inv.no.85.219.b. One line which reads: *]priụạṭị.r[*. Possibly but not necessarily a name (cf. **190**, **199**). Possible traces of a second line. Perhaps part of the same letter as **414**.

416. Inv.no.85.220. One line in address script, which may well read *c̣ẹr* (possibly with traces preceding), but it seems impossible to read *ceriali*; after *r* the traces are most like *g.[*.

417. Inv.no.85.223. Two very abraded lines, no doubt of a letter. Of the first only occasional letters legible; the second may read *]f̣rạṭer ṃ[*.

418. Inv.no.85.225. One line from the top left of a tablet, beginning *ṭr* or *p̣r*, followed by illegible traces. The latter suggests a date beginning with *pr(idie)* but we cannot read one which suits the subsequent traces.

419. Inv.no.85.229.a-b. Two non-joining fragments. The larger reads *].omṃuṣ.[*, with an ascender visible from a line below. Possibly the opening of a letter. The smaller may read *]ḍẹṃ[* and perhaps fits at the left or right of the larger piece.

420. Inv.no.85.240.a-d. Five fragments of a letter, of which two join. The joining fragments (a) contain the ends of five lines of the right-hand column: traces */].u..esṭ /].et se com-/]..isse eṭ /]...salutạ*. On the back, written on the slant, as usual for the name of the sender: *ab P̣risco ..[* (cf. **402**). The traces at the right do not suit *collega*; *f̣ṛ[atre* is possible although the first letter looks more like *s*. There are three more fragments with, respectively, traces of three lines, two lines and one line.

421. Inv.no.85.250. Three joining fragments, no doubt of a letter: traces *n..fr.[/].aṣ non poṣsum auṭeṃ [/]....[...]ṣsustineṛ.[*; tops of letters of one further line. In line 3 one expects some form of *sustineo*, but the broken letter at the right appears to be *a*.

422. Inv.no.85.264. One line which reads: *]r accipẹṛ..[*, perhaps *accipẹṛẹṇ[t*; also possible is *accipị* followed by interpunct.

423. Inv.no.85.267. On the front the beginning of one line only: *epistuḷ[*; thereafter apparently blank and so perhaps the end of a letter. The back has remains of two lines of which the first is in address script. The second may well read *pṛạef[*. There appear to be traces before this but not enough survives to be confident that we could justifiably suggest *Flauio Ceria/li*.

424. Inv.no.85.268. One line reading *]ụiọ collega* (*o* is a mere dot); no doubt this is part of the address of a letter, recording part of the name and description of the sender. There are descenders visible from a preceding line and it is quite possible that this fragment fits immediately below **423**. There may be much abraded traces of writing on the other side.

425. Inv.no.85.270.a-b. Two non-joining fragments. One has illegible traces of a line in address script; the other reads *]ḟes[*.

426. Inv.no.85.272.a. A small fragment which reads *Flaui[*, no doubt the start of a letter.

427. Inv.no.85.272.b. Two joining fragments containing the bottoms of letters from one line and a second line reading: *ficias · accipere · ubi*; the use of interpunct is noteworthy.

428. Inv.no.85.282.b. Remains of three lines, apparently from the top of a leaf, written across the grain: *]ioṛạ[/].irec.[/].mbịạ[* (not *m]embra*).

429. Inv.no.85.286.b-c. Two joining fragments and one larger fragment which does not join but which may well be in the same hand. One side of the larger fragment begins *cum*, but thereafter only traces of letters survive. Both sides of all three fragments bear writing, none of which is apparently in address script; but all the writing is much abraded and only occasional letters can be read.

430. Inv.no.85.292. Remains of three very abraded lines, no doubt part of a letter. The second may read: *]r..c̣ibị.[*. On the back traces of address script; *C̣ẹṛịạ[li* is not impossible, but the traces before it do not look like the end of *Flauio*.

431. Inv.85.294. Remains of two lines of which the first reads *]..c̣iterdomin[*; *fe]ḷịciter domin[e* is possible, suggesting the closing greeting of a letter, but there is no certain instance of *feliciter* elsewhere in the tablets. Only odd letters legible from the line below. Possible traces of writing on the back.

432. Inv.no.85.299. A tiny fragment with remains of one line: *c̣oriụ.[*.

433. Inv.no.85.306. Very abraded remains of four lines, no doubt of a letter. The second and third read: *]mul.[/]ṛesṭịb[*.

434. Inv.no.85.312.a-b. Two non-joining fragments which could well be in the same hand. One has remains of two lines of which the first reads *] .c̣c̣uprẹ.unc̣u.[* and the second preserves only the tops of letters. In the first line all the letters read as *c* could be *t*, and the line may end *ṣunṭ u.[*; but we cannot suggest how to articulate what precedes. The other fragment has traces of one line; only occasional letters legible.

435. Inv.no.85.314. Remains of one line; after traces of some nine letters this reads *c̣umc̣.[* (or *ṣumc̣.[*). Perhaps the right-hand column of a letter. On the back are the remains of one line apparently written upside down in relation to the front; possibly the tops of another line below.

436. Inv.no.85.316.c. Found with **297** but probably not part of the same letter. Remains of one line with the tops of letters from a second: *]ali..ep̣..[*.

437. Inv.no.85.317. Ends of three lines, no doubt part of a letter; several letters are clearly legible but as a whole the text is too abraded to give connected sense. Line 1 begins *]qui*, possibly *quiạ ṣụm*; line 3 begins *]..ṣsitu*, but nothing is clear after this.

438. Inv.no.85.318.e. Found with **307** but probably not in the same hand. Remains of a single line which reads *]es pro.[*; there are traces on the back.

439. Inv.no.85.321.b. A fragment of a tablet broken at all four margins, with remains of text on both sides. Probably in the same hand as **440** and perhaps part of the same account. Side A: *].aṣanḍ..[/].ẹn.ral.[/]ọ.eḷis ṭi[* / traces / [5] traces / *].ampul.[/]na..aṭu.[/]* uacat *ceruin[/]..al..s.[* /[10] ⟦*ṭọṣṣẹạ*⟧ / traces. 1: it does not seem possible to read a reference to *sandalia*. 2: the traces are perhaps compatible with the word *uentrale* ("money-belt"). 6: it does not seem possible to read *ampulḷ[a* or *ampulḷạ*; perhaps *ampulạ[*, a misspelling? Cf. **184**.i.9. 8: cf. **191**.10. 10: the word has a large initial *t*; for *tossea* see **192**.6 and note. Side B: illegible except for the occasional *denarius*-symbol.

440. Inv.no.85.321.c. A half-diptych complete at the left with a notch at the top in relation to the text on side A. Side A: remains of five lines with gaps between them. Side B: very abraded remains of 11 lines; only occasional letters legible. Probably in the same hand as **439** and perhaps part of the same account.

441. Inv.no.85.324. Much abraded remains of the start of four lines, probably from the left-hand column of a letter: *sị.ẹ.[/ meṃọ[/ quạ...[* / traces.

442. Inv.no.85.325. The bottoms of letters from one line and part of a second line, no doubt of a letter. Line 2 reads *]ạliter enim me [*. Written in a good right-sloping hand with a marked space before and after *enim*.

443. Inv.no.85.330. Much abraded traces of three lines, no doubt of a letter. Only one or two descenders from line 1 and line 3 is completely illegible. Line 2 may read: *].miṣị peṛ.*

444. Inv.no.85.331. Two joining fragments preserving the ends of three lines of a letter. Of line 1 only bottoms survive. Lines 2-3 read: *]. ndie · cum /]. aseris*. Neither *pridie* nor *meridie* looks likely (and *cot(t)idie* is impossible); interpunct after this looks clear. There may be traces of a line or two below line 3. On the back a line in address script: *.a...[; Flauio [* may be possible if we suppose that almost all trace of *l* has disappeared. Below this a line written on the slant, therefore the name of the sender: *.pro...o[; a Proculo* is likely (cf. **219**).

445. Inv.no.85.332.c. A fragment with remains of one line written in thick letters with some smudging at the end: *]abis .rol...*. There is a large blank space below the writing but it seems very unlikely that this is an address in the form *dabis* + dative name (see above, pp.43-5).

446. Inv.no.86.340. A fragment of the left-hand portion of a letter containing remains of two lines of the opening: *]..to r.[/ salute[m; to* appears to be the end of the name of the sender (not Atto or Metto, cf. **308**, **309**), *r.[* the beginning of that of the recipient.

447. Inv.no.86.349. Severely abraded remains of the beginnings of four lines. The first begins *co*; otherwise only occasional letters legible.

448. Inv.no.86.358.b-c. Two non-joining fragments of the right-hand side of a letter, with part of an address preserved on the backs. They were found with **235** and **449**, but seem unlikely to belong to either. The front of (b) has descenders from line 1 and an ascender from line 3; line 2 reads: *enim quidqui[*. The back is difficult: at the left are parts of two letters which appear to be written on a slant and are therefore perhaps part of the name or title of the sender (though they seem large for this); *co]ll(ega)* may be just possible. The letters to the right of this, in address script, may begin *lat* with remains of some five or six letters more before the break. The front of (c) reads *].omi*; as it is complete at the right, it could fit to the right of (b), but this does not suit the back; this appears to be complete at the left and then to read *pa.[* or *pr.[* (*pra[ef* is impossible, but *Pri[scino* could be read).

449. Inv.no.86.358.d. A long thin strip with remains of two lines on each side, neither of which appears to be an address. It is unlikely to belong with **235** or **448**. One side has descenders of one line and a second line which reads: *quid .e..omini mei te[; domini* seems inevitable, although it is difficult to read *d*. On the back only *e* at the end of the second line can be read.

450. Inv.no.86.380.a. A small scrap with remains of one line: *]ussis*; possible traces of ascenders of a line below. Also possible traces on the other side.

451. Inv.no.86.380.b. Writing on both sides: Side A has part of three lines: *].mama.[/]gram.seus.[* / traces. Line 2 could be read as *Gramaseus* (or *Gramasius*), but we have found no such name attested. Side B has the remains of two lines in a different script: *]..re.e.[/].uilionifr.[*. Perhaps *A]quilioni* followed by some case of *frater*; the name is not attested in this form but *NPEL* cites both Aquilius and Aquilo.

452. Inv.no.86.384.a. Two joining fragments with remains of two lines on each side, written in different hands. Side A no doubt preserves the ends of two lines of a letter:

]. . ẹrụṃquenạ . . br . . [/]ẹ . ṛ . . . . ạbriṣ. In line 1 *p̣ḷẹrụṃque* is possible; line 2 might end *ṃbriṣ*, but a month name is not possible. Side B preserves the bottoms of letters from one line and part of a second line beginning *. . roḷae . ụ . . . . [*; we would expect an address but cannot suggest anything plausible.

453. Inv.no.86.384.b. Two fragments which do not join. One is a tiny scrap which reads *coh[* ; the other has parts of letters from two lines, but the letters are too broken to permit any reading.

454. Inv.no.86.393. A tiny fragment with remains of one line in large letters, perhaps address script. The first letter is *o* and the second may be *p*, suggesting some case of *optio*. If this is an address one expects writing on the other side and this may indeed contain traces now illegible.

455. Inv.no.86.396. Two joining fragments containing one line which reads *] Verecundus*. This may be a draft of a letter from Iulius Verecundus (see **154**, **210-2**) but the name is so common that it need not be connected with this prefect.

456. Inv.no.86.399. Severely abraded traces of three, perhaps four, lines of a letter. The penultimate line may read in part *siḟṛa[* (*si fra[ter*?), and the last line may read *] . . ṇátoṛe[* with an apex over the *a*. On the back traces of one line in address script.

457. Inv.no.86.421. Remains of two lines, apparently from the top of a tablet. Line 1 reads: *Ṿerecundi[*; therefore this cannot be part of a letter to Verecundus (for whom see **154**, **210-2**); possibilities are the start of a letter to someone called Verecundi(n)us, or, if this is the back, an address to the wife or slave of Verecundus (cf. **302**). Only the tops of one or two letters of the second line survive.

458. Inv.no.86.423. A tiny scrap with part of one line: *] . ntp̣ṛu[*. If rightly read, no doubt divide *-nt pru[*. *r* could easily be *a* and we would not altogether wish to exclude the possibility of reading *ren]ụntịau[*, with a marked serif on *i*; if this is correct, the text is probably a military report like **127-53.** There are a few illegible traces on the back.

459. Inv.no.86.431. Three joining fragments with the remains of three lines. Almost totally illegible except the end of the last line which reads *q̣uicquam*.

460. Inv.no.86.432. Remains of two lines of a letter. Of the first, only descenders survive. Line 2: *] . n eị ictụ eḷ eṭ . . . ẹ .* ; the spaces might well be deliberate and the space between *u* and *e* would seem to rule out *uel*. There may be traces on the back.

461. Inv.no.86.434.a-c. Three fragments in the same hand, no doubt belonging to a letter. (c) consists of two joining pieces but there is no apparent join between (a) and (b). A number of individual letters are legible but no connected sense emerges. The last line of (a) reads *]c̣arum[*. Possible traces on the back of (b).

462. Inv.no.86.444.c. A small fragment with part of one line, perhaps from the top of a tablet: *]ụṭ . . . . ạḷisagạ . . . [*; *g* has a noticeably prolonged top stroke. Conceivably the beginning of a draft letter from Cerialis (see **233-241**). Under Aga- *NPEL* lists only names formed with the Greek Agatho-; *RNGCL* cites Agaso but is seems impossible to read *Agasoni*.

463. Inv.no.87.469. Beginnings of three lines; the second apparently contains the word *flammula[*. This is well-attested as the diminutive of *flamma* = "flame" (see *OLD*, s.v.) but it is also later used of a flame-coloured cavalry banner by Vegetius, 2.1 (cf. Milner (1993) *ad loc.*, citing Ammianus 20.6.3).

464. Inv.no.86.480. The ends of two lines. Of the first only descenders remain; the second appears to read *] marciá*, possibly preceded by *de*. There is an apex over the final letter. The name Marcius is well attested.

465. Inv.no.86.498. Two joining fragments with, in large letters, *Valerius Niger [*; no doubt the start of a letter. For Niger see the introduction to **248**. An ascender is visible below this; from its position it may well be from *s[uo*, placed as occasionally elsewhere towards the left on the second line.

466. Inv.no.87.499. A fragment with writing on each side. Side A reads: *] . . te et propit . [/] . . . nes celebr[*. Line 2 may have *] mines* (not *homines*). Perhaps a reference to religious celebrations, see **190**, **265**, **301**, **313**, **349**. The hand is cursive with noticeable use of ligature, especially in *celeb*; it resembles the hand of **225-32** and may be the same. Side B, in a different hand, also has parts of two lines, the first apparently with a large blank at the right. The second, after traces of some four letters, may read *maioris*, followed by interpunct; then *p[. .] . . [*.

467. Inv.no.86.502. Two joining fragments with one line of script in large letters. The first letter is probably *f* and the abraded traces following would permit, but certainly do not compel, the reading *Flauius*, then perhaps *. . aces[*. This suggests the start of a letter, perhaps an incomplete draft since there is a large space below this line which is apparently blank.

468. Inv.no.86.503.a. A small fragment of a letter which reads: *esse q[/ decimu[*. The end of a letter from a preceding column is visible at the left.

469. Inv.no.86.503.b. Found with **468** but probably not in the same hand. Abraded remains of the ends of two lines, no doubt of a letter; the second reads: *] futurus sum*.

470. Inv.no.86.506. A fragment perhaps containing the end of a line of the left-hand column of a letter (*] . n(ostr-)*, *n* with a superscript dash) and the beginning of another from the right-hand column (*rog[*).

471. Inv.no.86.508. Part of one line reading: *] . lisstrictis . . . [*; probably divide *] . lis strictis*, though *strictissim[e* is not impossible.

472. Inv.no.86.510. Parts of three lines in thick letters: *]r[/] . stet [/] . . quar . [*; no doubt part of a letter. On the back the tops of two letters which could be *fl*, i.e. an address beginning *Fl[auio*.

473. Inv.no.87.534. A fragment containing the beginnings of two lines of a letter, perhaps from the left-hand column: *pretium cor[/] nc [*. Perhaps a reference to the price of hides, cf. **343**.iii.30-iv.38.

474. Inv.no.87.538.a-b. Two non-joining fragments of a letter; (a) preserves the ends and (b) the beginnings of two lines. There is writing on the back of (a) which is in the same hand as the front and is not part of an address. a: *] . . ne /]e pro suis*; back: *] liber /] te occ .* In line 1 the traces would suit *do]mine*, though there are obviously other possibilities. b: *ides [/ ⸢quia⸣ hones[t. id est* is possible; *quia* has been inserted between the lines.

475. Inv.87.539. A small scrap with a tie-hole containing the beginning of one line: *decant [*.

476. Inv.no.87.552. Two complete lines and the top of a third written in a right-sloping cursive. It is noteworthy that the cross-bar of *t* does not continue to the right of the hasta. Since there are traces of address script on the back, this must come from the top of the right-hand column of a letter. Lines 1-2 read: *quidquid itaque potuero / ad uos ui [. .]dos festinabi-*. *uid[en]dos* is likely; after this one expects *festinabo*, but the last letter is clearly *i*; therefore presumably *festinabi-/[mus*.

477. Inv.no.87.573. Three lines of the right-hand column of a letter in a good, right-sloping cursive. For the most part severely abraded and only odd letters legible, except at the end of line 2 which reads: *usque u nd[*; *usque Vind[o-/landam* looks possible. Faint traces of one line in address script on the back.

478. Inv.no.87.583. Much abraded traces of two or three lines, no doubt of a letter. The last line appears to end *s[ ]obis*; perhaps *[u]obis* (the space seems less likely to accommodate *[n]obis*).

479. Inv.no.87.602.b-c. Two non-joining fragments of an account, both complete at the right. (b) comes from the top of a leaf, shows a notch and tie-hole and has parts of 10 lines. (c) may well be the bottom half of the same leaf and has parts of 9 lines. However, so little survives of each line that we cannot be certain that they are all in the same hand. It is possible, however, that they are, and that the hand is the same as that in **191**, **194**-**7**; but these fragments are probably not part of any of those accounts. The frequent use of the apex mark is noteworthy.

b. *] Ianuar( ) /]ná /]nst s / á /* [5] *m ´ / s in lan bá /]s /] /]st /]t*. Line 1: probably *Kalendi]s*, *Noni]s* or *Idibu]s*. Line 2: or *]ria*. Line 3: it would be also be possible to read *]nestu*, with a large apex mark over *u*. Line 5: we do not expect an apex-like mark after *m* in an account, and so we should perhaps read *] a*. Line 6: *in lancibus* does not seem a possible reading unless we suppose some correction or erasure at the end and an abbreviation, i.e. *in lancib*⟦ . ⟧*(us)*.

c: *] i . . /]ar /]s pru . . /] iiii /* [5] *]m cum /]ó /] ii /]orum /]ló*. Line 2: cf. b.1. Line 3: *]stru* is also possible, but hardly *]strum*. Line 4: perhaps *]viiii*. Lines 6 and 9: possibly a proper name; cf. **196**.12, 15 (though *cum* in the present text suggests a different construction).

480. Inv.no.87.603. A small scrap with the ends of two lines: *]ṇi /]rụm*. If correctly read, *u* has noticeable serifs.

481. Inv.no.87.604. Ends of two lines of a letter: *]ṇosti occupa /]. . eas . . uae*; perhaps *nosti* [= *nouisti*] *occupa-/[re*.

482. Inv.no.87.605. Part of the right-hand side of a diptych containing the ends of three lines from one column and two lines of a second. Use of interpunct is noteworthy. At the left: *] .t /]. . ṇị /] .ị ·* ; at the right: *de · guṭṭịs · ċeruesạ/rum ·* . *ceruesarum* seems inevitable although initial *c* is not an easy reading and the force of the plural is not obvious; for *ceruesa* see **186**, **190**. The letter after *gu* seems to be a correction, probably from *c*, and *guttis* ("drops") makes sense. *gusṭis* could be read (normally 4th declension, but *TLL* VI.2 2368 attests an alternative form *gustum*), suggesting a reference to the tasting of beers, but this is less likely. The rest of the tablet is blank, suggesting the end of a letter in the normal two columns. If this is the case, it is strange that there is no closure and no trace of an address on the back, and this suggests that it may be a draft.

483. Inv.no.87.608.b. A tiny scrap with remains of one line: *ca. . [*.

484. Inv.no.87.679. Remains of three lines of a letter: *] .ṣimos .u .ṣ / ep]ịstulas ḍuaṣ* ⸢*mihi*⸣ *misis-/[ti]. . . . . . in quibus*.

485. Inv.no.87.685. A small scrap, no doubt of a letter, with remains of one line: *.o .eo qui ex .[*. There is a large gap between *eo* and *qui* and a smaller one after the preceding *o*; there may be two letters between this and *eo*, but more probably we should read *ṃeo*.

486. Inv.no.87.694. Remains of one line, probably from the top of the right-hand column of a letter: *]bẹbim. . [*; *ha]bebimuṣ* is possible. On the back the tops of letters from a line in address script; what remains does not suit the name of any known addressee in the tablets.

487. Inv.no.87.714. A single line of writing, with blank spaces all round: *hẹrmẹs*. Since the undotted letters appear certain, there seems no other way to take this than the name Hermes, even though we should not expect a name by itself in the nominative. The name need occasion no surprise: there are other Greek names in the tablets and Hermes occurs in *RIB* I 195 (from Colchester); a further eight examples of Hermes are cited in *NPEL* from Gallia Belgica. The other side of the tablet is blank.

488. Inv.no.87.739. Half of a diptych with severely abraded traces of (probably) six lines of a letter. Mostly illegible. In the penultimate line *ad* can be read, and in the last line: *]ṭe caṛrum* traces.

489. Inv.no.87.764. Six joining fragments of a letter, probably belonging to the right-hand side; there are also traces on another small fragment. Abraded remains of four lines; good word division. Line 1: *]. . ịḅ. . . e .*; possibly a participle ending *-ibẹnṭem*, but perhaps better read *]. ḷibẹnṭeṛ*. Of line 2 only odd letters are legible. Lines 3-4: *] .ạ .ere quod tẹ . . . /]ẹcṭ .ṣe ç. . oṗ. . m. .* (hardly *opṭạmuṣ*).

490. Inv.no.87.766. A small scrap with part of one line: *]ụstus ma[*. The top of the tablet is preserved and the way this line is written strongly suggests that we have the first line of a letter, i.e. one being sent by a person whose name ended -ustus to a person whose name began Ma-.

491. Inv.no.87.769. A fragment with remains of four lines written across the grain in a script which uses some capital forms, notably *D* and *B*. Probably a list of names: *do . . [/ da . . [/ bog[/ . . n[*. Line 2: *d* is written in a normal cursive form, contrasting with the capital in line 1; probably *dau* or *dali* (*NPEL* cites some names beginning with *Dau-*). Line 3: for *Bog-* see *CIL* 7.1336.162 (London), *Bogi-*.

492. Inv.no.87.781. A small fragment from the top of a tablet. Since it reads *] . . ẹṛọ suo*, it is no doubt from the first line of a letter.

493. Inv.no.87.783.a-c. Three non-joining fragments of an account written across the grain. (a) has a tie-hole visible and is from the top of a diptych; it has parts of five lines. (b) is a small piece with remains of four lines. (c), which has two tie-holes, is clearly from the bottom; it has remains of (probably) eight lines, but is too abraded to be legible.
a: *]ṛ . . ṇo c̣[/]ẹb . ṛ . . . [* / traces / *] . oris in [/ ^{5}] (den.) i s(emissem) (assem i) [*. Line 1: *ṭio* could be read for *ṇo* but *ratio* is impossible. Line 2: perhaps no letter lost between *b* and *r*; *F]ẹbrụạr[i-* is therefore possible but is not an easy reading. Line 4: *c̣oris* (cf. **154**.7 and note) is not impossible but is not probable.
b: *] (denari-) s(emissem) (assem i) [* / traces / *] (denarios) vi [/] (asses) ịịi . [*. Line 4: the *as* symbol also occurs in c.3; here it appears to be followed by a symbol unlike any other we have seen in the tablets (but there is no certainty that all the traces on the photograph are ink).

494. Inv.no.87.792. Three joining fragments which contain the remains of three lines, presumably from the right-hand side of a letter since what survives on the back looks like part of an address. The writing has for the most part faded completely and only a few letters survive at the left; lines 2-3: *]ṣhọ* traces / *]eṛịṣ* (less likely is *ual]eạs . [*). The back may well be in address script. Part of one line survives: *. ẹṣṣị . . [*; we can only read *C̣ẹṣṣịọ* if we suppose that *o* is represented by a mere dot; if this is right, the *cognomen* after this may begin *F̣ịṇ[*.

495. Inv.no.88.830. Eleven abraded lines, written in a thick, rather ugly, script. Written across the grain and presumably part of an account, though we have been unable to establish anything definite (cf. also the note to line 11). *]* traces / *] . erịṃ[/]* traces / *] . e . ụr[/ ^{5}]cia · rogị[/]ṃṃạṇḍẹs[ ] . . niṭuọ[* / traces / *] . . simṃ . . [/ ^{10}]ạṃ · expḷ[/] . ụale [*. Line 2: *p̣er* and a personal name (cf. **186**) is not impossible. Line 5: the interpunct seems clear, but a word beginning *rogi* (or *roci*) is not attractive. Line 6: *ṃạṛịḍẹṣ* could be read but we can find no suitable word with such an ending. Line 9: the traces are so badly preserved that we would not wish to rule out the reading *p]ẹṛ Simiḷẹ[m* (cf. **186**.22), though it does not seem probable. Line 11: it is possible that nothing is written before or after *uale*, but it would be unparalleled for a letter to be written across the grain or for a writer to add *uale* at the foot of an account; we think it more probable that *uale* is part of a longer word.

496. Inv.no.88.840. A diptych with notches and tie-holes, complete at both sides. It appears to be complete also at top and bottom, but the end of the second line cannot read *salutem*; therefore either it is incomplete at the top or we have a letter written on more than one tablet. The left-hand side has remains of five lines and the right-hand at least three, but unfortunately so severely abraded that little remains legible; line 3 at the left ends *me · domi* (note the interpunct), but elsewhere only occasional letters can be read.

497. Inv.no.88.884.b. Abraded remains of four lines, no doubt from the left-hand side of a letter, written at an angle and not straight along the grain. Line 2 seems to read: *]libẹṛ* traces of c.6 letters *ṭibị* traces of c.6 more letters *[*. Otherwise only occasional letters legible.

498. Inv.no.88.897. One line from the end of a letter probably written by the same hand as **302**: *].ạẹ.ṭare* (m^2) *ọptọ bene ualeạṣ seṃpeṛ*. The second hand is interesting palaeographically, especially the form of the first *e* in *bene*.

499. Inv.no.88.905. Part of one line, no doubt of a letter and probably from the top of a tablet. Only the top parts of the individual letters are preserved: *]..ṣeṛạṇọṣ.rne..a..[*. There appears to be an apex over the first *a* and possibly over the *o*; we have wondered whether we have the remains of a name, but any reading would be extremely hazardous.

500. Inv.no.88.914. Severely abraded traces of perhaps six lines written across the grain. The first visible line may read *].mxx[*, and lower down a *denarius*-sign is probable.

501. Inv.no.88.933. Two non-joining fragments, each with the remains of the right-hand part of a single line; it is not clear whether they belong to the same tablet. Fragment (a) reads: *].oṛẹmno..* (traces below this may or may not be ink). Fragment (b), which has two noticeable notches, reads: *].ṛe*.

502. Inv.no.88.939. Part of the beginnings of three lines, no doubt of a letter. Of line 1 only descenders remain. Line 2 reads: *cumquaọ.[* or *cumquaḍ.[*. The former would have to be divided *cum qua o-*; the latter could read *cum quadṛ[-*. Of line 3 only two ascenders survive, the second probably *b*.

503. Inv.no.88.960. Feet of letters at top left: *ṣebẹ* traces *[*. The remainder of the tablet is blank which suggests the end of a letter, i.e. part of *opto te bene ualere*, but the letter at the start does not look like *t*.

504. Inv.no.89.970. Parts of four lines from the top of the left-hand side of a letter: *]* traces of c.5 letters *o suo* / uacat *salutem* / *].enisse x..* / *].ṇọẹ.o ṭibi eṭ*. Line 3: *ụenisse* (or a compound) is possible; the numeral following may be part of a date. In line 4 we give what is the most obvious reading, but would not wish to exclude the possibility we should read *ḥạḅẹḅo* before *tibi*.

505. Inv.no.89.980. Remains of the end of a letter with the name of the sender on the back. *domi]ne bene ualere*; then, after a space and in a second hand, *ual(e)*. This abbreviation of *uale* also occurs in **312**.ii.12, **343**.iv.45 and **349**.margin 1. The first hand is cursively written and the second even more so. Back (on the slant and probably in the first hand): *a Ma ... lo dec(urione)*; *Masculo* is possible, cf. **367**.

506. Inv.no.89.981.a-b. Two non-joining fragments; of the smaller only traces of two lines survive. The larger has the ends of the first seven lines of a letter. Lines 1-4: *]aeco /] salutem /] . equites .[/]ndam ...[*. The end of line 1 clearly has the name of the addressee: perhaps *C]aeco* (but an alternative possibility is *]afio*). *suo* must have been written on line 2 unless this line considerably overran the fold. Lines 3-4 may have contained a reference to the despatch of cavalrymen to Vindolanda, but there are clearly numerous other possibilities. Of lines 5-7 only odd letters can be read.

507. Inv.89.983.a-b. Two non-joining fragments, no doubt of a letter. (a) has abraded remains of three lines; in the second a word ending *rias* is preserved, but the traces before this do not permit a clear reading; the line below probably reads *duas et [*. On (b) only one or two letters are legible.

508. Inv.no.162. This tablet was discovered in the excavations of the 1970s but was overlooked in the compilation of *Tab.Vindol.*I. There are two fragments of a diptych with parts of two columns of a letter. Col.i: *enim d[/ tes mihi [/ postea qua[*. Col.ii: traces / *tare ut .[/ fratrem a[/ beam qua .[/* 5 *ibi habe[*. ii.1-2: possibly *salu-]tare*. 3-4: presumably *ha-]beam*.

509. Inv.no.171. This tablet was discovered in the excavations of the 1970s but was overlooked in the compilation of *Tab.Vindol.*I. It reads: *salut]abis uerbis [meis /] .m magis*; perhaps restore *magis-/[trum*.

The following ink tablets were originally published in *Tab.Vindol.*I. They are here given new publication numbers, in the present series. We cite the numbers assigned to them in *CEL* only in those cases where *CEL* reprints the text. We do not reproduce the texts (for which the reader should refer to *Tab.Vindol.*I or to *CEL*) but merely note changes from the *ed. pr.* or points on which our interpretation is now different.

510. *Tab.Vindol.*I 8. In line 6 we now read: *] s(emissem) (quadrantem) (asses iii) s(emissem)* . . The last trace may not be significant.

511. *Tab.Vindol.*I 9. The numeral should presumably be restored as *vii[ii*. This may be part of a report of the same type as **127-53**.

512. *Tab.Vindol.*I 13. In line 1 of the second fragment we now read *] n(umero) xxxx*.

513. *Tab.Vindol.*I 14. Note that in line 2 there may be an apex mark after *o*.

514. *Tab.Vindol.*I 15.

515. *Tab. Vindol.*I 17.

516. *Tab. Vindol.*I 18.

517. *Tab. Vindol.*I 19.

518. *Tab. Vindol.*I 20.

519. *Tab. Vindol.*I 27 = *CEL* 95. We originally assigned this tentatively to the correspondence of Cerialis, but we now think this less likely. One line survives on both front and back. On the back only the tops of some seven or eight letters in address script remain; the letters at the left could well read *F̣ḷạụịọ*, but what follows does not look like the start of *Ceriali*. On the front we read *].[.]cum de iniuria*. At the left the top of an ascender is preserved, probably *s*; there is a marked gap before *de*. After this *iniuria* is written above the line, even though it could easily have been written in alignment with *de*. This perhaps suggests a petition (cf. **281**, **322**, **344**).

520. *Tab. Vindol.*I 32 = *CEL* 100. A fragment from the top of a letter preserving the ends of two lines from the left-hand column (which overran the fold) and the start of three lines from the right-hand column. We previously regarded this as possibly belonging to the correspondence of Priscinus ("Crispinus"); this is still a possibility, but the doubtful reading of the end of the name of the addressee as *]ṇo* is insufficient evidence for including it with **295-8**. We now read: col.i, *]ṇo suọ / salute]ṃ*; col.ii, *ẹị fra .[/ exp̣lica[/ . . . .ṭ ex̣ .[*.

521. *Tab. Vindol.*I 44 = *CEL* 111. Line 1: *et ḷ[*, *CEL*. Line 2: *. . . .[.]. c̣ọtidian[*, *CEL*.

522. *Tab. Vindol.*I 48 = *CEL* 115. Line 2: there is an interpunct after *facis*.

523. *Tab. Vindol.*I 49 = *CEL* 116.

524. *Tab. Vindol.*I 50 = *CEL* 117.

525. *Tab. Vindol.*I 53 = *CEL* 120.

526. *Tab. Vindol.*I 54 = *CEL* 121.

527. *Tab. Vindol.*I 56 = *CEL* 123.

528. *Tab. Vindol.*I 57 = *CEL* 124.

529. *Tab. Vindol.*I 58 = *CEL* 125.

530. *Tab. Vindol.*I 59 = *CEL* 126.

531. *Tab. Vindol.*I 61 = *CEL* 128.

532. *Tab. Vindol.*I 62 = *CEL* 129.

533. *Tab. Vindol.*I 63.

534. *Tab. Vindol.*I 64.

535. *Tab. Vindol.*I 65 = *CEL* 131.

536. *Tab. Vindol.*I 67.

537. *Tab. Vindol.*I 68.

538. *Tab. Vindol.*I 69.

539. *Tab. Vindol.*I 70.

540. *Tab. Vindol.*I 71.

541. *Tab. Vindol.*I 72.

542. *Tab. Vindol.*I 73.

543. *Tab. Vindol.*I 74.

544. *Tab. Vindol.*I 75 = *CEL* 134.

545. *Tab. Vindol.*I 76.

546. *Tab. Vindol.*I 77.

547. *Tab. Vindol.*I 78.

548. *Tab. Vindol.*I 79.

549. *Tab. Vindol.*I 80.

550. *Tab. Vindol.*I 81.

551. *Tab. Vindol.*I 84.

552. *Tab. Vindol.*I 85.

553. *Tab. Vindol.*I 86.

554. *Tab. Vindol.*I 87.

555. *Tab. Vindol.*I 88 = *CEL* 138.

556. *Tab. Vindol.*I 89.

557. *Tab. Vindol.*I 90.

558. *Tab. Vindol.*I 91.

559. *Tab. Vindol.*I 92.

560. *Tab. Vindol.*I 93.

561. *Tab. Vindol.*I 94.

562. *Tab. Vindol.*I 95.

563. *Tab. Vindol.*I 96.

564. *Tab. Vindol.*I 97.

565. *Tab. Vindol.*I 98.

566. *Tab. Vindol.*I 99.

567. *Tab. Vindol.*I 100.

568. *Tab. Vindol.*I 101.

569. *Tab. Vindol.*I 102.

570. *Tab. Vindol.*I 103.

571. *Tab. Vindol.*I 104.

572. *Tab. Vindol.*I 105.

573. *Tab. Vindol.*I 106.

APPENDIX

The survey of the writing-tablets in *VRR* II, 18-72 offers summaries of the contents of a very large number of the texts with quotations of the readings. The references to the texts are by inventory number only, since the publication numbers of the present volume were not available when the survey was compiled. Not surprisingly, there are a number of places in which our readings differ from those suggested in *VRR* II. For the convenience of the reader we append below a list of texts where there are differences which seem to us substantive, quoting our publication number, the inventory number and the page reference in *VRR* II. This list is strictly confined to matters of reading and meaning in the texts themselves; matters of broader historical interpretation are not addressed.

119 (85.183), p.35.
137 (85.199), p.33.
156 (85.248), p.34.
167 (85.082), p.42.
180 (88.943), p.58.
182 (88.947), p.58, p.65.
184 (87.622), p.69.
185 (88.950), p.28.
187 (87.704), p.34.
188 (85.016), p.34.
193 (85.111), p.34.
206 (85.321), p.34.
213 (88.865), p.29.
214 (88.940), p.29.
215 (86.447+448), p.57.
225 (I 37), p.44.
226 (85.001), p.42.
234 (85.118), p.21, p.40.
239 (85.194), p.39.
258 (85.120), p.40.
263 (I 23), p.41, p.47 (where it is cited as "BT 22").
264 (85.084), p.42.
286 (86.444), p.42.
291 (85.057), p.39.
294 (85.056), p.39.
298 (I 33), p.56.
300 (87.608), p.35.
301 (87.748), p.28.

309 (85.051), p.35.
312 (88.935), p.37, p.50.
324 (I 42), p. 35, p.39.
325 (I 43), pp.35-6.
343 (88.946), p.59.
350 (87.788), p.67.
439 (85.321), p.34.
495 (85.830), p.28.
505 (89.980), p.29.

We offer a few additional comments on texts discussed in *VRR* II, in particular the stilus tablets.

p.4, p.35: we think it unlikely that there is any reference to the *ala Vocontiorum* in **316**.
p.21: the reference for the phrase *de carris Brittonum* should be to Inv.no.1108.
p.27: we are not sure that the letters *cos* can be read in **305** (88.828); but even if the reading is correct, it is most likely that they are part of a longer word.
p.29: 88.836, a stilus tablet in two pieces. The larger, probably palimpsest on the front, has *Cataractonio / Alḅano* on the back, which we take to mean that it was sent to Albanus at Catterick. The smaller piece, which is not palimpsest, may very well not belong with this. It has the opening of a letter and seems to us to read *Albinus Dẹḷị.o suo salutem* (there seems to be insufficient room for *Delicio*).
p.30: 88.851, a stilus tablet. The back is divided by a recessed strip and letters have been scratched both to left and right of this. We believe that they should be read in continuous lines across the recess (not in two columns as suggested in *VRR* II). This yields, we think, the reading *Vinouiṣ* in the first line (i.e. a place-name in the locative, cf. **185**). We cannot see the reading *Eburacum*, suggested for the following line.
p.33: for our suggested reconstruction of the formulaic reports with the *renuntium*-heading, see above, pp.73-6.
p.35: 87.725, a stilus tablet. We are unable to read the ink writing on the rim, but we do not think that the name Africanus is there.
p.43: 87.561, a stilus tablet. We are unable to confirm the readings suggested for the tablet and for the rim.
p.43: 87.722, stilus tablet. The reading *Cerial[* is suggested but the position of the scratches would better suit a place-name. Only *c* and *r* are certain but we think that *Cọriṣ* can be read (cf. **154**.7). For the name of the addressee we suggest *Rumano*.
p.45: Flavius Similis (cf. also pp.42 and 56). He is the addressee of a draft letter from Cerialis (**235**) and himself writes to Cerialis at Vindolanda in **254** (cf. **286**). In addition, it is probably a slave of his who writes to Vindolanda in **347**. All this clearly implies that Similis was *not* at Vindolanda.
p.45: Paternus (cf. p.31). We now think **283** (I 40) likely to have been addressed to Cerialis. Paternus in **218** (= I 34) is certainly not a prefect.
p.46: *[Perp]etuus*. The reading *]etuo praefecto* in **177**.2 is only one possibility.
p.51: we are sure that Chrauttius does not occur in **258** (85.120).
p.57: 87.689, a stilus tablet. Again we suggest that this is to be read in continuous lines, not in two columns (see above on p.30, 88.851). The first line has the place-name *Vindolande*

(= *Vindolandae*, locative). The next line has the name of the addressee, ending *-io Veceto*, and the third line has (presumably) the name of the sender, ending *-stio Optato*.

CONCORDANCE

The numbers and letters which identify the find-spots refer to the designation of rooms and areas in the structures of Periods 2-5; for further detail see *VRR* I. Other find-spots are designated by the following abbreviations:
WVIA: refers to the southern part of the *via principalis*, west of the yard designated "Room VIA" in the Period 3 building.
Ditch: refers to the Ditch of the pre-Hadrianic fort of Period 1; it is probable that the tablets found here in fact belong to Period 2.
SG: refers to the South Gate of the pre-Hadrianic fort of Periods 2-5.
N: refers to the site to the north

Inv.no.	Location/ Room no.	Period	Publ.no.
85.001	IV	3	**226**
85.003	IV	3	**354**
85.004	IV	3	**272**
85.006	IV	3	**166**
85.007	IV	3	**251**
85.008	IV	3	**253**
85.010.a	IV	3	**355**
85.010.b	IV	3	**192**
85.011	IV	3	**227**
85.015	IV	3	**356**
85.016	IV	3	**188**
85.017	IV	3	**252**
85.018	IV	3	**207**
85.020.a	IV	3	**326**
85.020.b	IV	3	**357**
85.020.c	IV	3	**358**
85.023	IV	3	**359**
85.024	IV	3	**360**
85.026	IV	3	**361**
85.028	IV	3	**327**
85.030	IV	3	**362**
85.032.a	IV	3?	**164**
85.032.b	IV	3?	**363**
85.033	IV	3	**255**

85.035	IV	3	**288**
85.036.a	I	3	**273**
85.036.b	I	3	**364**
85.042	IV	3	**292**
85.043	IV	3	**178**
85.046	III	4	**296**
85.047	III	4	**296**
85.048.a	VIA	3	**159**
85.048.b	VIA	3	**274**
85.051	VIA	3	**309**
85.052.a-b	VIA	3	**204**
85.052.c	VIA	3	**365**
85.053.a	VIA	3	**130**
85.053.b	VIA	3	**328**
85.055	VIA	3	**256**
85.056.a	VIA	3	**294**
85.056.b	VIA	3	**366**
85.057	VIA	3	**291**
85.059.a	VIA	3	**367**
85.059.b	VIA	3	**368**
85.061	VIA	3	**369**
85.067	SG	2	**306**
85.068	XVI	5	**370**
85.069	XVI	5	**353**
85.077	VIA	3	**275**
85.081.a	VIA	3	**198**, **371**
85.081.b	VIA	3	**372**
85.081.c	VIA	3	**373**
85.081.d	VIA	3	**374**
85.081.e	VIA	3	**375**
85.082	VIA	3	**167**
85.083	WVIA	3	**376**
85.084	WVIA	3	**264**
85.085	C	2	**219**
85.089	VIA	3	**220**
85.092	VIA	3	**244**
85.093	XVII	4	**377**
85.094.a	XVII	4	**203**
85.094.b	XVII	4	**284**
85.098	C	2	**378**
85.099.a	WVIA	3	**287**
85.099.b	WVIA	3	**379**
85.099.c	WVIA	3	**380**
85.100	WVIA	3	**311**
85.101.a	VIA	3	**131**
85.101.b	VIA	3	**381**
85.103	VIA	3	**382**
85.105	WVIA	3	**132**

85.107	VIA	3	**314**
85.108	WVIA	3	**311**
85.109	VIA	3	**383**
85.111.a	WVIA	3	**193**
85.111.b	WVIA	3	**384**
85.114	WVIA	3	**315**
85.117	WVIA	3	**257**
85.118	WVIA	3	**234**
85.119.a	WVIA	3	**121**
85.119.b	WVIA	3	**386**
85.120	WVIA	3	**258**
85.121	WVIA	3	**315**
85.122	WVIA	3	**329**
85.123	WVIA	3	**133**
85.124	WVIA	3	**387**
85.126	WVIA	3	**388**
85.131	WVIA	3	**330**
85.135	WVIA	3	**134**
85.137	WVIA	3	**118**, **331**
85.139	WVIA	3	**389**
85.146.a	WVIA	3	**174**
85.146.b	WIVA	3	**390**
85.147	WVIA	3	**391**
85.150	WVIA	3	**236**
85.151	WVIA	3	**175**
85.152	WVIA	3	**285**
85.157	Ditch	1	**212**
85.160.a	WVIA	3	**242**
85.160.b	WVIA	3	**293**
85.163	WVIA	3	**332**
85.164	WVIA	3	**392**
85.165	WVIA	3	**393**
85.166	VIA	3	**228**
85.168	WVIA	3	**135**, **394**
85.170	D	2	**395**
85.171	VIA	3	**318**
85.175	D	2	**396**
85.176	D	2	**136**
85.177	D	2	**397**
85.180	WVIA	3	**237**
85.181	WVIA	3	**398**
85.182	WVIA	3	**399**
85.183.a	WVIA	3	**119**, **122**
85.183.b	WVIA	3	**316**
85.186.a	WVIA	3	**177**
85.186.b	WVIA	3	**238**
85.187	WVIA	3	**176**
85.188	WVIA	3	**268**

85.189	WVIA	3	**400**
85.190	WVIA	3	**158**
85.192	WVIA	3	**401**
85.193	WVIA	3	**245**
85.194.a	WVIA	3	**239**
85.194.b-d	WVIA	3	**402**
85.195	WVIA	3	**403**
85.196.a	WVIA	3	**404**
85.196.b	WVIA	3	**333**
85.196.c	WVIA	3	**405**
85.199.a	WVIA	3	**137**
85.199.b	WVIA	3	**406**
85.199.c	WVIA	3	**407**
85.201	WVIA	3	**408**
85.202	WVIA	3	**409**
85.206	WVIA	3	**138**
85.207	WVIA	3	**339**
85.209.a	WVIA	3	**410**
85.209.b	WVIA	3	**411**
85.210	WVIA	3	**340**
85.211.a	WVIA	3	**276**
85.211.b	WVIA	3	**412**
85.214	WVIA	3	**413**
85.219.a	WVIA	3	**414**
85.219.b	WVIA	3	**415**
85.220	WVIA	3	**416**
85.222	WVIA	3	**271**
85.223.a	WVIA	3	**417**
85.224	WVIA	3	**129**
85.225	WVIA	3	**418**
85.229.a-b	WVIA	3	**419**
85.230	WVIA	3	**334**
85.236	WVIA	3	**168**
85.237	WVIA	3	**289**
85.240	WVIA	3	**420**
85.242.a	III	4	**128**
85.242.b-d	III	4	**217**
85.244	III	4	**162**
85.248	VIA	3	**156**
85.250	VIA	3	**421**
85.252	VIA	3	**179**
85.256	VIA	3	**246**
85.260	VIA	3	**139**
85.264	WVIA	3	**422**
85.265	WVIA	3	**277**
85.267	WVIA	3	**423**
85.268	WVIA	3	**424**
85.270	WVIA	3	**425**

85.272.a	WVIA	3	**426**
85.272.b	WVIA	3	**427**
85.274	WVIA	3	**319**
85.275	WVIA	3	**169**
85.276	WVIA	3	**140**
85.281	WVIA	3	**254**
85.282.a	WVIA	3	**141**
85.282.b	WVIA	3	**428**
85.285	WVIA	3	**278**
85.286.a	WVIA	3	**170**
85.286.b-c	WVIA	3	**429**
85.292	WVIA	3	**430**
85.293	WVIA	3	**259**
85.294	WVIA	3	**431**
85.299	WVIA	3	**432**
85.306	WVIA	3	**433**
85.309	WVIA	3	**142**
85.312	WVIA	3	**434**
85.314	VIA	3	**435**
85.316.a-b	SG	2	**297**
85.316.c	SG	2	**436**
85.317	SG	2	**437**
85.318.a-d	SG	2	**307**
85.318.e	SG	2	**438**
85.321.a	SG	3	**206**
85.321.b	SG	3	**439**
85.321.c	SG	3	**440**
85.324	SG	3	**441**
85.325	SG	3	**442**
85.328	SG	3	**143**
85.329	SG	3	**279**
85.330	SG	3	**443**
85.331	SG	3	**444**
85.332.a	SG	3	**221**
85.332.b	SG	3	**222**
85.332.c	SG	3	**445**
85.334	SG	3	**144**
86.340	II	5	**446**
86.341	WVIA	3	**145**
86.343	WVIA	3	**146**
86.346	XI	4	**347**
86.349	WVIA	3	**447**
86.352	VIA	3	**335**
86.358.a	VIA	3	**235**
86.358.b-c	VIA	3	**448**
86.358.d	VIA	3	**449**
86.360	VIA	3	**147**
86.364	VIA	3	**157**

86.367	WVIA	3	**336**
86.371	WVIA	3	**123**
86.380.a	II	5	**450**
86.380.b	II	5	**451**
86.384.a	XI	4	**452**
86.384.b	XI	4	**453**
86.393	XI	4	**454**
86.396	III	4	**455**
86.399	III	4	**456**
86.409	VIA	3	**120**
86.412	VIA	3	**260**
86.421	VIA	3	**457**
86.422.	VIA	3	**320**
86.423	VIA	3	**458**
86.426	VIA	3	**148**
86.428	VIA	3	**149**
86.429	VIA	3	**269**
86.431	XIV	5	**459**
86.432	XIV	5	**460**
86.433	XIV	5	**352**
86.434	XIV	5	**461**
86.444.a-b	WVIA	3	**286**
86.444.c	WVIA	3	**462**
86.447	III	4	**215**
86.448	III	4	**215**
86.458	II	3	**317**
86.469	III	4	**463**
86.470	VIA	3	**310**
86.474	VIA	3	**124**
86.479	VIA	3	**150**
86.480	VIA	3	**464**
86.496.a	IX	3	**266**
86.496.b	IX	3	**267**
86.498	IX	3	**465**
86.499	IX	3	**466**
86.500	IX	3	**243**
86.501	IX	3	**261**
86.502	III	4	**467**
86.503.a	V	3	**468**
86.503.b	V	3	**469**
86.504	IX	3	**262**
86.506	V	3	**470**
86.507	IX	3	**321**
86.508	VIA	3	**471**
86.510	VIA	3	**472**
87.514	II	3	**233**
87.515	II	3	**125**
87.534	III	4	**473**

87.538	III	4	**474**
87.539	III	4	**475**
87.546	IX	3	**337**
87.547	IX	3	**200**
87.552	IX	3	**476**
87.563	D	2	**282**
87.567	IV	4	**186**
87.568	D	2	**202**
87.570	D	2	**201**
87.573	V	3	**477**
87.579	IX	3	**240**
87.583	V	3	**478**
87.596.a-c	VIII	3	**208**
87.596.d	VIII	3	**209**
87.597.a-b	VIII	3	**194**
87.597.c	VIII	3	**195**
87.598	VIII	3	**196**
87.599	VIII	3	**265**
87.602.a	VIII	3	**197**
87.602.b-c	VIII	3	**479**
87.603	VIII	3	**480**
87.604	VIII	3	**481**
87.605	VIII	3	**482**
87.607	V	3	**281**
87.608.a	V	3	**300**
87.608.b	V	3	**483**
87.622	VII	5	**184**
87.679	X	3	**484**
87.684	X	3	**126**
87.685	X	3	**485**
87.694	X	3	**486**
87.695	IX	3	**249**
87.704	X	3	**187**
87.711	F/G	2	**210**
87.714	V	4	**487**
87.728	V	4	**348**
87.737	F/G	2	**216**
87.739	V	4	**488**
87.748	H/I	2	**301**
87.751	K	2	**172**
87.764	N/J	2	**489**
87.766	N/J	2	**490**
87.767	N/J	2	**304**
87.769	N/J	2	**491**
87.780	H/I	2	**308**
87.781	XV	3	**492**
87.783	XV	3	**493**
87.788	V	4	**350**

87.792	Ditch	1	**494**
87.796	XI	4	**351**
87.806	XVI	4	**349**
88.828	N/J	2	**305**
88.830	N/J	2	**495**
88.837	Ditch	1	**161**
88.839	Ditch	1	**302**
88.840	Ditch	1	**496**
88.841	Ditch	1	**154**
88.845	Ditch	1	**303**
88.865	N/J	2	**213**
88.884.a	XVII	3	**338**
88.884.b	XVII	3	**497**
88.897	N/J	2	**498**
88.905	XII	5	**499**
88.914	L	2	**500**
88.929	XII	3	**313**
88.933	XII	5	**501**
88.935	XVII	3	**312**
88.939	O	2	**502**
88.940	O	2	**214**
88.943	XIV	4	**180**, **344**
88.944	XIV	4	**181**
88.946	XIV	4	**343**
88.947	XIV	4	**182**
88.949	M	2	**345**
88.950	M	2	**185**
88.951	M	2	**211**
88.955	XX	3	**189**
88.960	XVIII	3	**503**
88.966	XVIII	3	**322**
89.970	XVIII	3	**504**
89.978	XXI	3	**183**
89.980	M	2	**505**
89.981	XXI	3	**506**
89.983	Q	2	**507**

Tab. Vindol. I

Inv.no.162	?	?	**508**
Inv.no.171	?	?	**509**
Inv.no.197	?	?	**298**
1	II	3	**155**
2	VIA	3	**151**
3	II	5	**160**
4	IV	3	**190**
5	VIA	3	**191**
6	II	4	**205**

7	VIA	3	**199**
8	II	4	**510**
9	II	4	**511**
10	II	4	**224**
11	II	4	**163**
12	II	3	**127**
13	II	3	**512**
14	II	4	**513**
15	II	4	**514**
16	II	4	**165**
17	II	4	**515**
18	II	4	**516**
19	II	3	**517**
20	II	3	**518**
21	II	3	**248**
22	VIA	3	**250**
23	II	3	**263**
24	VIA	3	**270**
25	VIA	3	**247**
26	II	3	**280**
27	VIA	3	**519**
28	VIA	3	**290**
29	VIA	3	**241**
30	II	4?	**295**
31	II	4?	**297**
32	II	4?	**520**
33	II	4?	**298**
34	VIA	3	**218**
35	II	3	**171**
36	VIA	3	**223**
37	VIA	3	**225**
38	II	4?	**346**
39	XV	5	**299**
40	II	3	**283**
41	VIA	3	**323**
42	VIA	3	**324**
43	VIA	3	**325**
44	VIA	3	**521**
45	VIA	3	**341**
46	VIA	3	**342**
47	VIA	3	**152**
48	VIA	3	**522**
49	VIA	3	**523**
50	VIA	3	**524**
51	VIA	3	**229**
52	VIA	3	**230**
53	VIA	3	**525**
54	VIA	3	**526**

55	VIA	3	**173**
56	VIA	3	**527**
57	IV	3	**528**
58	IV	3	**529**
59	IV	3	**530**
60	IV	3	**231**
61	IV	3	**531**
62	IV	3	**532**
63	IV	3	**533**
64	IV	3	**534**
65	XV	5	**535**
66	IV	3	**153**
67	II	3	**536**
68	II	3	**537**
69	II	3	**538**
70	II	5	**539**
71	II	3	**540**
72	II	3	**541**
73	VIA	3	**542**
74	VIA	3	**543**
75	VIA	3	**544**
76	VIA	3	**545**
77	VIA	3	**546**
78	VIA	3	**547**
79	VIA	3	**548**
80	VIA	3	**549**
81	VIA	3	**550**
82	VIA	3	**298**
83	VIA	3	**232**
84	VIA	3	**551**
85	II	5	**552**
86	II	5	**553**
87	II	3	**554**
88	II	3	**555**
89	VIA	3	**556**
90	VIA	3	**557**
91	VIA	3	**558**
92	VIA	3	**559**
93	VIA	3	**560**
94	IV	3	**561**
95	II	3	**562**
96	II	3	**563**
97	II	3	**564**
98	II	3	**565**
99	WVIA	5	**566**
100	II	3	**567**
101	II	3	**568**
102	II	3	**569**

103	II	3	**570**
104	II	3	**571**
105	II	3	**572**
106	VIA	3	**573**

BIBLIOGRAPHY

J.N.Adams (1977), *The Vulgar Latin of the letters of Claudius Terentianus*. Manchester

J.N.Adams (1984), "Female speech in Latin comedy", *Antichthon* 18: 43-77

J.N.Adams (1990a), "The latinity of C.Novius Eunus", *ZPE* 82: 227-47

J.N.Adams (1990b), "The *forfex* of the *veterinarius* Virilis (Vindolanda inv.no.86/470) and ancient methods of castrating horses", *Britannia* 21: 267-71

J.N.Adams (1992a), "British Latin: the text, interpretation and language of the Bath curse tablets", Britannia 23: 1-26

J.N.Adams (1992b), "The origin and meaning of Lat. *ueterinus, ueterinarius*", *Indogermanische Forschungen* 97: 70-95

J.N.Adams (1993), "The generic use of *mula* and the status and employment of female mules in the Roman world", *RhM* n.f.136: 35-61

J.N.Adams (1994), "The Latin of the Vindolanda writing-tablets", (forthcoming)

L.Allason-Jones (1989), *Women in Roman Britain*. London

R.D.Anderson, P.J.Parsons, R.G.M.Nisbet (1979), "Elegiacs by Gallus from Qasr Ibrîm", *JRS* 69: 125-55

J.André (1966/7), "Tossia: couverture de lit", *Etudes celtiques* 11: 409-12

J. André (1981), *L'alimentation et la cuisine à Rome*. 2nd ed., Paris

J.André (1985), *Les noms de plantes dans la Rome antique*. Paris

J.André (1991), *Le vocabulaire latin de l'anatomie*. Paris

P.S.Austin (1991), *Bewcastle and Old Penrith*. Cumberland and Westmorland Antiquarian and Archaeological Society, Research Series no.6. Kendal

D.Baatz (1973), *Kastell Hesselbach und andere Forschungen am Oldenwaldlimes. Limesforschungen, Studien zur Organisation der römischen Reichsgrenzen an Rhein und Donau* 12. Berlin

D.Baatz (1983), "Lederne Gürteltaschen römischer Soldaten", *Archäologisches Korrespondenzblatt* 13: 359-61

R.S.Bagnall (1977), "Army and police in Roman Upper Egypt", *JARCE* 14: 67-86

R.S.Bagnall (1985), *Currency and inflation in fourth century Egypt. BASP*, Suppl.5.

R.S.Bagnall (1986), "Papyri and ostraca from Quseir al-Quadim", *BASP* 23: 1-60

H.Bellen (1981), *Die germanische Leibwache der römischen Kaiser des julisch-claudischen Hauses*. Wiesbaden

J.Bingen, G.Nachtergael (ed. 1978), *Actes du XVe congrès international de papyrologie*. Papyrologica Bruxellensia 16. Brussels

A.R.Birley (1979), *The People of Roman Britain*. London

A.R.Birley (1981), *The Fasti of Roman Britain*. Oxford

A.R.Birley (1990a), "Vindolanda; new writing-tablets 1986-9", in Maxfield and Dobson (ed. 1990): 16-20

A.R.Birley (1990b), *Officers of the Second Augustan Legion in Britain.* Cardiff

A.R.Birley (1991), "Vindolanda: notes on some new writing tablets", *ZPE* 88: 87-102

A.R.Birley (1992), "A case of eye disease (*lippitudo*) on the Roman frontier in Britain", *Documenta Ophthalmologica* 81: 111-9

E.Birley (1988), *The Roman Army. Papers 1929-86.* Amsterdam

R.E.Birley (1977), *Vindolanda. A Roman frontier post on Hadrian's Wall.* London

R.E.Birley (1990), *The Roman documents from Vindolanda.* Newcastle upon Tyne

B.Bischoff (1986), *Paläographie des römischen Altertums und des abendländischen Mittelalters.* 2nd ed., Berlin

B.Bischoff (1990), *Latin palaeography, antiquity and the middle ages.* Cambridge [= English edition of Bischoff (1986), by D.Ó Cróinín and D.Ganz]

M.C.Bishop (ed. 1985), *The production and distribution of Roman military equipment.* British Archaeological Reports, Int.Ser. 275. Oxford

M.C.Bishop (1985), "The military fabrica and the production of arms in the early principate", in Bishop (ed. 1985): 1-42

M.C.Bishop, J.C.N.Coulston (1993), *Roman military equipment.* London

M.C.Bishop, J.N.Dore (1988), *Corbridge, excavation of the Roman fort and town 1947-80.* London

T.F.C.Blagg, A.C.King (ed. 1984), *Military and civilian in Roman Britain: cultural relationships in a frontier province*, British Archaeological Reports, Brit.Ser. 136. Oxford

T.F.C.Blagg, M.Millett (ed. 1990), *The early Roman empire in the west.* Oxford

A.Gonzáles Blanco, M.Mayer Olivé, A.U.Stylow (1987), *La cueva negra de Fortuna (Murcia) y sus tituli picti. Antigüedad y Cristianesimo* IV. Murcia

J.H.F.Bloemers (1983), "Acculturation in the Rhine/Meuse Basin in the Roman period: a preliminary survey", in Brandt and Slofstra (ed. 1983): 159-210

H.Boge (1973), *Griechische Tachygraphie und tironische Noten.* Berlin

G.C.Boon (1983), "Potters, oculists and eye-troubles", *Britannia* 14: 1-12

A.K.Bowman (1974), "Roman military records from Vindolanda", *Britannia* 5: 360-73

A.K.Bowman (1975), "The Vindolanda writing-tablets and the development of the Roman book form", *ZPE* 18: 237-52

A.K.Bowman (1981), *Roman Writing-Tablets from Vindolanda.* London

A.K.Bowman (1991), "Literacy in the Roman empire: mass and mode", in Humphrey (ed. 1991): 119-31

A.K.Bowman (1994a), *Life and letters on the Roman frontier. Vindolanda and its people.* London

A.K.Bowman (1994b), "The Roman imperial army; letters and literacy on the northern frontier", in Bowman and Woolf (ed. 1994): 109-25

A.K.Bowman, J.D.Thomas (1975), "The Vindolanda writing-tablets and their significance: an interim Report", *Historia* 24: 463-78

A.K.Bowman, J.D.Thomas (1983), *Vindolanda: the Latin writing-tablets.* Britannia Monograph 4. London

A.K.Bowman, J.D.Thomas (1986), "Vindolanda 1985: the new writing-tablets", *JRS* 76: 120-3

A.K.Bowman, J.D.Thomas (1987), "New texts from Vindolanda", *Britannia* 18: 125-42

A.K.Bowman, J.D.Thomas (1991), "A military strength report from Vindolanda", *JRS* 81: 62-73

A.K.Bowman, J.D.Thomas, J.N.Adams (1990), "Two letters from Vindolanda", *Britannia* 21: 33-52

A.K.Bowman, J.D.Thomas, R.P.Wright (1974) "Appendix to Roman Britain in 1973: the Vindolanda writing-tablets", *Britannia* 5: 471-80

A.K.Bowman, G.D.Woolf (ed. 1994), *Literacy and power in the ancient World*. Cambridge

R.Brandt, J.Slofstra (ed. 1983), *Roman and native in the Low Countries*. British Archaeological Reports, Int.Ser. 184. Oxford

D.J.Breeze (1969), "The organisation of the legion: the First Cohort and the *equites legionis*", *JRS* 59: 50-5

D.J.Breeze (1974), "The organisation of the career structure of the *immunes* and *principales* of the Roman army", *Bonner Jahrbücher* 174: 245-92

D.J.Breeze (1984), "Demand and supply on the northern frontier", in Miket and Burgess (ed. 1984): 32-68

D.J.Breeze, B.Dobson (1985), "Roman military deployment in north England", *Britannia* 16: 1-19

D.J.Breeze, B.Dobson (1987), *Hadrian's Wall*. 3rd ed., London

K.W. De Brisay, K.A.Evans (ed. 1975), *Salt: the study of an ancient industry*. Colchester

J.Collingwood Bruce (1875), *Lapidarium septentrionale*. Newcastle upon Tyne

J.Collingwood Bruce (1978), *Handbook to the Roman Wall*. 13th ed. by C.M.Daniels, Newcastle upon Tyne

P.A.Brunt (1990), *Roman imperial themes*. Oxford

B.C.Burnham, H.B.Johnson (ed. 1979), *Invasion and response: the case of Roman Britain*. British Archaeological Reports, Brit.Ser.73. Oxford

B.C.Burnham, J.S.Wacher (1990), *The "small towns" of Roman Britain*. London

R.M.Butler (ed. 1971), *Soldier and civilian in Roman Yorkshire*. Leicester

R.Cagnat (1914), *Cours d'épigraphie latine*. 4th ed., Paris

G.Calboli (ed. 1990), *Latin vulgaire - latin tardif II. Actes du IIème colloque international sur le latin vulgaire et tardif, Bologne 29 Août - 2 Septembre, 1988*. Tübingen

I.D.Caruana (1987), "A wooden ansate panel from Carlisle", *Britannia* 18: 274-7

I.D.Caruana (1992), "Carlisle; excavation of a section of the annexe ditch of the first Flavian fort, 1990", *Britannia* 23: 45-109

E.Casamassima, E.Staraz (1977), "Varianti e cambio grafico nella scrittura dei papiri latini, note palaeografiche", *Scrittura e Civiltà* 1: 9-110

P.J.Casey (1982), "Civilians and soldiers - friends, Romans, countrymen?" in Clack and Haselgrove (ed. 1982): 123-132

P.Castrén, H.Lilius (1970), *Graffiti del Palatino II, Domus Tiberiana*. Helsinki

G.Cencetti (1950), "Note paleografiche sulla scrittura dei papiri latini dal I al III secolo d.c.", *Memorie dell'Accademia delle scienze dell'Istituto di Bologna. Classe di scienze morali* V.1. [Published in 1951.]

P.A.G.Clack, "The northern frontier: farmers in the military zone", in Miles (ed. 1982): 377-402

P.A.G.Clack, S.Haselgrove (ed. 1982), *Rural settlement in the Roman north*. Durham

W.E.H.Cockle (1979), "A new Virgilian writing exercise from Oxyrhynchus", *Scrittura e Civiltà* 3: 55-75

R.G.G.Coleman (1971), "The monophthongization of */ae/* and the Vulgar Latin vowel system", *TPhS* 1971: 175-91

R.A.Coles (1966), *Reports of proceedings in papyri*. Papyrologica Bruxellensia 4. Brussels

R.A.Coles (1981), "A quadrilingual curiosity in the Bodleian Library in Oxford", *Proceedings of the XVI International Congress of Papyrology*: 193-7. American Studies in Papyrology 23. Chico

M.Della Corte (1940), "Virgilio nell'epigrafia pompeiana", *Epigraphica* 2: 171-8

G.Costamagna, M.F.Baroni, L.Zagni (1983), *Notae Tironianae quae in lexicis et in chartis reperiuntur novo discrimine ordinatae*. Fonti e studi del corpus Membranarum Italicarum, Ser.2, Fonti Medievali 10. Rome

H.M.Cotton (1981), *Documentary letters of recommendation in Latin from the Roman Empire*. Beiträge zur klassischen Philologie, 132. Königstein

P.Cugusi (1972-3), "Le piú antiche lettere papiracee latine", *Atti della Accademia delle Scienze di Torino* 107: 641-687

P.Cugusi (1981), "Gli ostraca latini dello Wâdi Fawâkhir", in *Letterature comparate, problemi e metodo, Studi in onore di E.Paratore* II: 719-753. Bologna

P.Cugusi (1983), *Evoluzione e forme dell'epistolografia latina nella tarda repubblica e nei primi due secoli dell'impero*. Rome

P.Cugusi (1987), "Leggendo le tavolette latine di Vindolanda", *RFIC* 115: 113-121

R.I.Curtis (1991), *Garum and salsamenta, production and commerce in materia medica*. Studies in ancient medicine 3. Leiden

C.Daniels (1989), "The Flavian and Trajanic northern frontier", in Todd (ed. 1989): 31-5

G.B.Dannell, J.-P.Wild (1987), *Longthorpe II: the military works depot*. Britannia Monograph 8. London

R.W.Davies (1967), "Ratio and opinio in Roman military documents", *Historia* 16: 115-8

R.W.Davies (1968), "A note on some Roman soldiers in quarries", *CW* n.s.68: 22-6

R.W.Davies (1974a), "A report of an attempted coup", *Aegyptus* 54: 179-196

R.W.Davies (1974b), "The daily life of the Roman soldier under the principate", *ANRW* II.1: 299-338

R.W.Davies (1976), "Singulares and Roman Britain", *Britannia* 7: 134-44

R.W.Davies (1989), *Service in the Roman Army*. Ed. D.J.Breeze, V.A.Maxfield. Edinburgh

H.Devijver (1989), *The equestrian officers of the Roman imperial army*. Amsterdam

H.Devijver, H. Harrauer, K.A.Worp (1984-5), "Eine lateinische Holztafel in Leiden", *Oudheidkundige Mededelingen uit's Rijksmuseum van Oudheden te Leiden* 65: 19-22

C.Dickson (1989), "The Roman diet in Britain and Germany", *Archäobotanik. Dissertationes Botanicae* 133: 135-54

A.C.Dionisotti (1982), "From Ausonius' schooldays", *JRS* 72: 83-125

K.R.Dixon, P.Southern (1992), *The Roman cavalry*. London

B.Dobson (1972), "Legionary centurion or equestrian officer? A comparison of pay and prospects", *Ancient Society* 3: 193-207

B.Dobson, J.C.Mann (1973), "The Roman army in Britain and Britons in the Roman army", *Britannia* 4: 191-205

S.Dow (1968), "Latin calligraphy at Hawara: P.Hawara 24", *JRS* 58: 60-70

C.van Driel-Murray (1985), "The production and supply of military leatherwork in the first and second centuries AD: a review of the archaeological evidence", in Bishop (ed. 1985): 43-81

C.van Driel-Murray (1987), "Roman footwear: a mirror of fashion and society", *Recent research in archaeological footwear*. Association of Archaeological Illustrators and Surveyors, Technical Paper No.8: 32-42.

R.L.Dunbabin (1935), "Notes on Lewis and Short", *CR* 49: 9-12

R.P.Duncan-Jones (1982), *The economy of the Roman empire; quantitative studies.* 2nd ed., Cambridge
E.Esperandieu (1922), *Recueil général des bas-reliefs, statues et bustes de la Gaule romaine* IV (1922). Paris
D.Ellis Evans (1967), *Gaulish personal names.* Oxford
D.Ellis Evans (1983), "Language contact in pre-Roman and Roman Britain", *ANRW* II.29.2: 949-87
I.M.Ferris, R.F.J.Jones (1991), Binchester - a northern fort and vicus", in R.F.J. Jones (ed. 1991): 103-8
R.O.Fink, A.S.Hoey, W.F.Snyder (1940), "The *Feriale Duranum*", *YCS* 7: 1-222
D.Flach (1978), "Inschriftenuntersuchungen zum römischen Kolonat in Nordafrika", *Chiron* 8: 441-92
P.Flobert (1990), "Le témoignage épigraphique des apices et des I longae sur les quantités vocaliques en latin impérial", in G.Calboli (ed. 1990), 101-10
L.A.Foxhall, H.A.Forbes (1982), "ΣΙΤΟΜΕΤΡΕΙΑ: the role of grain as a staple food in classical antiquity", *Chiron* 12: 41-90
S.Franklin (1985), "Literacy and documentation in early medieval Russia", *Speculum* 60/1: 1-38
S.S.Frere (1987), *Britannia, a history of Roman Britain.* 3rd ed., London
S.S.Frere, J.K.St. Joseph (1974), "The Roman Fortress at Longthorpe", *Britannia* 5: 1-129
S.S.Frere, J.J.Wilkes (1989), *Strageath, excavations within the Roman fort 1973-86.* Britannia Monograph 9. London
M.Fulford (1984), "Demonstrating Britannia's economic dependence in the first and second centuries", in Blagg and King (ed. 1984): 129-42
M.Fulford (1991), Britain and the Roman empire: the evidence for regional and long distance trade", in R.F.J.Jones (ed. 1991): 45-48
C.Gallazzi (1982), "P.Narm.inv.66.362: Vergilius, *Eclogae* VIII.53-62", *ZPE* 48: 75-8
D.Ganz (1990), "On the history of Tironian notes", in P.F.Ganz (ed. 1990): 35-51
P.F.Ganz (ed. 1990), *Tironische Noten.* Wiesbaden
J.F.Gilliam (1986), *Roman Army Papers.* Amsterdam
W.Glasbergen, W.Groenman-van Waateringe (1974), *The Pre-Flavian garrisons of Valkenburg Z.H.* Amsterdam
C.W.Glück (1857), *Die bei Caius Iulius Caesar vorkommenden keltischen Namen in ihrer Echtheit festgestellt und erläutert.* Munich
H.Görgemanns and E.A.Schmidt (ed. 1976), *Studien zum antiken Epos.* Beiträge zur klassichen Philologie 72. Meisenheim
A.E.Gordon (1958-65), *Album of dated Latin inscriptions*, I-IV. Berkeley
A.E.Gordon and J.S.Gordon (1957), *Contributions to the palaeography of Latin inscriptions*, University of California Publications in Classical Archaeology 3.iii. Berkeley
T.N.Habinek (1985), *The colometry of Latin prose.* University of California Classical Studies 25. Berkeley and Los Angeles
D.Hagedorn (1979), "Ein verkannter Vergilvers auf Papyrus", *ZPE* 34: 108
W.S.Hanson (1987), *Agricola and the conquest of the north.* London
B.R.Hartley, J.S.Wacher (ed. 1983), *Rome and her northern provinces.* Gloucester
D.Harvey (1985), "Nugae Vindolandenses", *Liverpool Classical Monthly* 10.5 (1985): 69
M.Hassall (1970), "Batavians and the Roman conquest of Britain", *Britannia* 1: 131-6
M.Hassall (1973), "Roman soldiers in Roman London", in Strong (ed. 1973): 231-7

M.Hassall (1978), "Britain and the Rhine provinces: epigraphic evidence for Roman trade", in Taylor and Cleere (ed. 1978): 41-8

M.Hassall (1983), "The internal planning of Roman auxiliary forts", in Hartley and Wacher (ed. 1983): 96-131

D.Haupt, H.G.Horn (ed. 1977), *Studien zur den Militärgrenzen Roms: Vorträge des 10. internationalen Limeskongresses in der Germania Inferior. Bonner Jahrbücher* Beih. 38

N.J.Higham (1991), "Soldiers and settlement in northern England", in R.F.J.Jones (ed. 1991): 93-102

J.G.F.Hind (1980), "The Romano-British Name for Corbridge", *Britannia* 11: 165-71

L.Hird (1977), *Vindolanda V: the pre-Hadrianic pottery*. Hexham

G.W.I.Hodgson (1976), *The animals of Vindolanda*. Haltwhistle

G.W.I.Hodgson (1977), *Vindolanda II: the animal remains from excavations at Vindolanda 1970-75*. Hexham

J.B.Hofmann (1951), *Lateinische Umgangssprache*. 3rd ed., Heidelberg

J.B.Hofmann, A.Szantyr (1965), *Lateinische Syntax und Stilistik*. Munich

P.A.Holder (1980), *Studies in the auxilia of the Roman army from Augustus to Trajan*. British Archaeological Reports, Int.Ser. 80. Oxford

P.A.Holder (1982), *The Roman Army in Britain*. London

R.P.Hoogma (1959), *Der Einfluss Vergils auf die Carmina latina epigraphica*. Amsterdam

N.M.Horsfall (1981), "Aspects of Virgilian influence in Roman life", *Atti del Convegno mondiale scientifico di studi su Virgilio, Mantova-Roma-Napoli, 19-24 Settembre, 1981*, II: 47-63. *Cultura e Scuola* 20. Rome

C.J.Howgego (1992), "The supply and use of money in the Roman world 200 BC - AD 300", *JRS* 82: 1-31

J.H.Humphrey (ed. 1991), *Literacy in the Roman world. JRA*, Suppl.4. Ann Arbor

M.Iliescu, W.Marxgut (ed. 1992), *Latin vulgaire - latin tardif III. Actes du IIIème colloque international sur le latin vulgaire et tardif, Innsbruck, 2-5 Septembre, 1991*. Tübingen

B.Isaac (1992), *The limits of empire, the Roman army in the east*. 2nd ed., Oxford

R.Jackson (1988), *Doctors and Diseases in the Roman Empire*. London

R.Jackson (1990a), "Roman doctors and their instruments: recent research into ancient practice", *JRA* 3: 5-27

R.Jackson (1990b), "A new collyrium stamp from Cambridge and a corrected reading of the stamp from Caistor-by-Norwich", *Britannia* 21: 275-83

G.D.B.Jones (1984), "'Becoming different without knowing it'. The role and development of *vici*", in Blagg and King (ed. 1984): 75-91

G.D.B.Jones (1990), "The emergence of the Tyne-Solway frontier", in Maxfield and Dobson (ed. 1990): 98-107

G.D.B.Jones, D.J.Mattingly (1990), *An atlas of Roman Britain*. Oxford

M.Jones (1991), "Food production and consumption - plants", in R.J.F.Jones (ed. 1991): 21-8

R.J.F.Jones (ed. 1991), *Britain in the Roman period: recent trends*. Sheffield

G.H.Karlsson, H.Maehler (1977), "Papyrusbriefe römisch-byzantinischer Zeit", *ZPE* 33: 279-94

D.L.Kennedy (1977), "The *ala I* and *cohors I Britannica*", *Britannia* 8: 249-55

A.C.King (1984), "Animal bones and the dietary identity of military and civilian groups in Roman Britain, Germany and Gaul", in Blagg and King (ed. 1984): 187-218

A.C.King (1991), "Food production and consumption - meat", in R.F.J.Jones (ed. 1991): 15-20

J.Kramer (1991) "Die Verwendung des Apex und P.Vindob. L 1 c", *ZPE* 88: 141-50.

R.Kühner, C.Stegmann (1955), *Ausführliche Grammatik der lateinischen Sprache: Satzlehre*. 3rd ed. revised by A.Thierfelder. Leverkusen

E.Lalou (ed. 1992), *Les tablettes à écrire de l'antiquité à l'époque moderne. Bibliologia* 12. Brepols-Turnhout

C.D.Lanham (1975), *"Salutatio" Formulas in Latin letters to 1200, Syntax, Style and Theory*. Münchener Beiträge zur Mediävistik und Renaissance-Forschung 22.

M.Leumann (1977), *Lateinische Laut- und Formenlehre*. 6th ed., Munich

N.Lewis (1989), *The documents from the Bar Kokhba period in the Cave of Letters, Greek papyri*. Jerusalem

A.Locher, R.C.A.Rottländer (1985), "Überlegungen zur Entstehungsgeschichte der *Naturalis Historia* des älteren Plinius und die Schrifttäfelchen von Vindolanda", *Lebendige Altertumswissenschaft. Festgabe zur Vollendung des 70. Lebensjahres von Hermann Vetters*: 140-7. Vienna

E.Löfstedt (1911), *Philologischer Kommentar zur Peregrinatio Aetheriae*. Uppsala

E.Löfstedt (1933-42), *Syntactica. Studien und Beiträge zur historischen Syntax des Lateins* I-II. Lund

London in Roman times (1930). London Museum Catalogues, no. 3

J.Mallon (1952), *Paléographie romaine*. Madrid

J.Mallon, R.Marichal, C.Perrat (1939), *L'écriture latine*. Paris

J.C.Mann (1974), "The northern frontier after A.D.369", *Glasgow Archaeological Journal* 3: 34-52

I. Di Stefano Manzella (1987), *Mestiere di epigrafista. Guida alla schedatura del materiale epigrafico lapideo*. Rome

R.Marichal (1979), "Les ostraca de Bu Njem", *Comptes-rendus de l'Académie des Inscriptions et Belles-lettres* 1979: 436-52.

R.Marichal (1988), *Les graffites de La Graufesenque. Gallia*, Suppl.47. Paris

R.Marichal (1992), "Les tablettes à écrire dans le monde romain", in Lalou (ed. 1992): 165-85

V.A.Maxfield (1986), "Pre-Flavian forts and their garrisons", *Britannia* 17: 59-72

V.A.Maxfield, M.J.Dobson (ed. 1990), *Roman frontier studies 1989, Proceedings of the XVth International Congress of Roman Frontier Studies*. Exeter

R.McKitterick (ed. 1990), *The uses of literacy in early medieval Europe*. Cambridge

A.Mentz (1944), *Die tironischen Noten*. Berlin

W.Meyer-Lübke (1911), *Romanisches etymologisches Wörterbuch*. Heidelberg

P.S.Middleton (1979), "Army supply in Roman Gaul: an hypothesis for Roman Britain", in Burnham and Johnson (ed. 1979): 81-97

R.Miket, C.Burgess (ed. 1984), *Between and beyond the Walls. Essays on the pre-history and history of north Britain in honour of George Jobey*. Edinburgh

D.Miles (ed. 1982), *The Romano-British countryside*. British Archaeological Reports, Brit.Ser. 103. Oxford

M.Millett (1990), *The romanization of Britain*. Cambridge

G.Milne (1985), *The port of Roman London*. London

H.J.M.Milne, T.C.Skeat (1938), *Scribes and correctors of the Codex Sinaiticus*. London

N.P.Milner (1993), *Vegetius: Epitome of military science*. Liverpool

A.Mócsy (1983), "The civilized Pannonians of Velleius", in Hartley and Wacher (ed. 1983): 169-78
R.W.Müller (1964), *Rhetorische und syntaktische Interpunktion*. Diss. Tübingen
V.E.Nash-Williams (1950), *Early Christian monuments of Wales*. Cardiff
F.Neue, C.Wagener (1892-1905), *Formenlehre der lateinischen Sprache*. 3rd ed., Berlin
C.Nicolet (1970), *Recherches sur les structures sociales dans l'antiquité classique*. Paris
H.Nielsen (1974), *Ancient ophthalmological agents*. Odense
A.Oliver, J.Shelton (1979), "Silver on papyrus", *Archaeology* 32: 22-8
R.A.Pack (1965), *The Greek and Latin literary texts from Greco-Roman Egypt*. 2nd ed., Ann Arbor
M.B.Parkes (1991), *Scribes, scripts and readers*. London
M.B.Parkes (1992), *Pause and effect*. Aldershot
D.P.S.Peacock (1992), *Rome in the desert: a symbol of power*. Southampton
H.Petersmann (1992), "Zu den neuen vulgärlateinischen Sprachdenkmälern aus dem römischen Britannien. Die Täfelchen von Vindolanda", in Iliescu and Marxgut (ed. 1992): 283-91
A.Petrucci (1962, 1963-4), "Per la storia della scrittura romana: i graffiti di Condatomagos", *Bulletino dell'Archivio palaeografico italiano*, Ser.3.1: 85-132; 3.2-3: 55-72
S.Piggott (1965), *Ancient Europe from the beginnings of agriculture to classical antiquity*. Edinburgh
R.Pintaudi, P.J.Sijpesteijn (1989), *Tavolette lignee e cerate da varie collezioni*. Papyrologica Florentina XVIII. Florence
N.B.Rankov (1986), *The beneficiarii consularis in the western provinces*. D.Phil. thesis, Oxford
N.B.Rankov (1987), "M.Oclatinius Adventus in Britain", *Britannia* 18: 243-9
C.L.Ransom (1905), *Couches and beds of the Greeks, Etruscans and Romans*. Chicago
J.R.Rea (1988), "On the Greek Calends", *Proceedings of the XVIII International Congress of Papyrology* II: 203-8. Athens
R.Rebuffat, R.Marichal (1973), "Les ostraca de Bu Njem", *Revue des études latines* 51: 281-286.
I.A.Richmond (1953), "Three Roman writing-tablets from London", *AJ* 33: 206-208.
G.M.A.Richter (1966), *The furniture of the Greeks, Etruscans and Romans*. London
G.E.Rickman (1971), *Roman granaries and store buildings*. Cambridge
K.Rittweger, E.Wölfflin (1892), "Was heisst 'das Pferd?'", *ALL* 7: 313-31
H.R.Robinson (1975), *The armour of imperial Rome*. London
A.Rosenfeld (1965), *The inorganic raw materials of antiquity*. London
M.M.Roxan (1990), "Women on the frontiers", in Maxfield and Dobson (ed. 1990): 462-7
N.Roymans (1990), *Tribal societies in northern Gaul, an anthropological perspective*. Amsterdam
E.Saint-Denis (1947), *Le vocabulaire des animaux marins en latin classique*. Paris
R.Sallares (1991), *The ecology of the ancient Greek world*. London
E.Sander (1963), "Die Kleidung des römischen Soldaten", *Historia* 12: 144-66
E.Schallmayer, K.Eibl, J.Ott, G.Preuss, E.Wittkopf (1990), *Der römische Weihebezirk von Osterburken I: Corpus der griechischen und lateinischen Beneficiarier-Inschriften des römischen Reiches*. Stuttgart
W.Schmitz (1893), *Commentarii notarum Tironianarum cum prolegomenis adnotationibus criticis et exegeticis notarumque indice alphabetico*. Leipzig

L.Schwinden (1985), "Römerzeitliche Bleietiketten aus Trier", *TZ* 48: 121-37
R.Seider (1976), "Beiträge zur Geschichte und Paläographie der antiken Vergilhandschriften", in Görgemanns and Schmidt (ed. 1976): 129-72
R.Seider (1983), "Beiträge zur Paläographie der altesten lateinischen Papyri der Sammlung Erzherzog Rainer der Österrreichischen Nationalbibliothek", *Papyrus Erzherzog Rainer. Festschrift zum 100-jährigen Bestehen der Payrussammlung der Österrreichischen Nationalbibliothek*: 135-44. Vienna
J.C.Shelton (1977), "Short notes on documentary texts", *ZPE* 24: 69-73
P.J.Sijpesteijn, K.A.Worp (1977), "A Latin papyrus from the Vienna collection", *ZPE* 24: 91-4
J.Smeesters (1977), "Les Tungri dans l'armée romaine, état actuel des nos connaissances", in Haupt and Horn (ed. 1977): 175-86
P.Southern (1989), "The *numeri* of the Roman imperial army", *Britannia* 20: 81-140
M.A.Speidel (1987), "Neue Inschriften auf Schreibtäfelchen aus dem Schutthügel des Legionslagers Vindonissa", *Jahresbericht der Gesellschaft pro Vindonissa 1986*: 49-64
M.A.Speidel (1991), "Entlassungsurkunden des römischen Heeres", *Jahresbericht der Gesellschaft pro Vindonissa 1990*: 59-65
M.A.Speidel (1992), "Roman army pay scales", *JRS* 82: 87-106
M.P.Speidel (1970), "The captor of Decebalus", *JRS* 60: 142-53
M.P.Speidel (1978), *Guards of the Roman armies*. Antiquitas, Reihe 1.28. Bonn
M.P.Speidel (1984), *Roman army studies* I. Amsterdam
M.P.Speidel (1985), "Furlough in the Roman army" *YCS* 28: 283-293.
M.P.Speidel (1989), "The soldiers' servants", *Ancient Society* 20: 239-47
M.P.Speidel, R.Seider (1988), "A Latin papyrus with a recruit's request for service in the auxiliary cohorts", *JEA* 74: 242-244.
J.A.Stanfield, G.Simpson (1958), *Central Gaulish potters*. London
I.Stead (1965), "The Celtic chariot", *Antiquity* 39: 259-65
J.Stevenson (1990), "Literacy in Ireland: the evidence of the Patrick dossier in the Book of Armagh", in McKitterick (ed. 1990): 11-35
K.Strobel (1987), "Anmerkungen zur Geschichte der Bataverkohorten in der hohen Kaiserzeit", *ZPE* 70: 271-92
D.E.Strong (1966), *Greek and Roman gold and silver plate*. London
D.E.Strong (ed. 1973), *Archaeological theory and practice*. London
A.U.Stylow, M.Mayer Olivé (1987), "Lectura y comentarios literario y paleografico", in Blanco (1987): 191-235
J.Svennung (1958), *Anredenformen, vergleichende Forschungen zur indirekten Anrede in der dritten Person und zum Nominativ für den Vokativ*. Lund
J. du P.Taylor, H.Cleere (ed. 1978), *Roman shipping and trade: Britain and the Rhine provinces*, CBA Research Report 24. London
J.C.Teitler (1985), *Notarii and exceptores*. Amsterdam
J.A.C.Thomas (1976), *Textbook of Roman law*. Amsterdam
J.D.Thomas (1976), "New light on early Latin writing: the Vindolanda tablets", *Scriptorium* 30: 38-43
J.D.Thomas (1992), "The Latin writing-tablets from Vindolanda in north Britain", in Lalou (ed. 1992): 203-9
J.D.Thomas, R.W.Davies (1977), "A new military strength report on papyrus", *JRS* 67: 50-61

J.-O.Tjäder (1954-82), *Die nichtliterarischen lateinischen Papyri Italiens aus der Zeit 445-700.* Skrifter utg. av Svenska Institutet i Rom 4°, 19. Lund

J.-O.Tjäder (1977), "Latin Palaeography, 1975-7", *Eranos* 75: 131-61

J.-O.Tjäder (1979), "Considerazioni e proposte sulla scrittura latina nell"età romana", *Palaeographica, diplomatica, et archivistica: studi in onore di Giulio Battelli*: 31-60. Rome

J.-O.Tjäder (1986), review of *Tab.Vindol.*I, *Scriptorium* 50: 297-301

M.Todd (1985), "Oppida and the Roman army. A review of recent evidence", *OJA* 4.2: 187-99

M.Todd (ed. 1989), *Research on Roman Britain 1960-89. Britannia*, Monograph 11. London

R.S.O.Tomlin (1986), "Roman Britain in 1985", *Britannia* 17: 450-2

R.S.O.Tomlin (1992), "The Twentieth Legion at Wroxeter and Carlisle in the first century: the epigraphic evidence", *Britannia* 23: 141-58

J.M.C.Toynbee (1973), *Animals in Roman life and art.* London

S.D.Trow (1990), "By the northern shores of Ocean: some observations on acculturation process at the edge of the Roman world", in Blagg and Millett (ed. 1990): 103-18

E.G.Turner (1950), "Papyrus 40 della raccolta Milanese", *JRS* 40: 57-9

E.G.Turner (1956), "A Roman writing-tablet from Somerset", *JRS* 46: 115-8

E.G.Turner (1957), "Half a line of Virgil from Egypt", *Studi in onore di A.Calderini e R.Paribeni* II: 157-61. Milan

E.G.Turner (1978), *The terms Recto and Verso, the anatomy of the papyrus roll*, in Bingen and Nachtergael (ed. 1978): 1e partie

E.G.Turner (1987), *Greek manuscripts of the ancient world.* 2nd ed., revised by P.J.Parsons. London

E.G.Turner, O.Skutsch (1960), "A Roman writing-tablet from London", *JRS* 50: 108-11

V.Väänänen (1966), *Le latin vulgaire des inscriptions pompéiennes.* Berlin

J.Vendrand-Voyer (1983), *Normes civiques et métier militaire à Rome sous le principat.* Clermont-Ferrand

G.R.Watson (1969), *The Roman soldier.* London

G.R.Watson (1974), "Documentation in the Roman army", *ANRW* II.1: 493-507

J.L.Weisgerber (1968), *Die Namen der Ubier.* Cologne/Opladen

J.L.Weisgerber (1969), *Rhenania Germano-celtica.* Bonn

C.R.Whittaker (1989), *Les frontières de l"empire romain.* Paris

L.Wierschowski (1974), *Heer und Wirtschaft, das römische Heer als Wirtschaftfaktor.* Bonn

J.-P.Wild (1977), *Vindolanda II: the textiles.* Hexham

J.-P.Wild (1985), "The clothing of Britannia, Gallia Belgica and Germania Inferior", *ANRW* II.12.3: 362-422

E.O.Wingo (1972), *Latin punctuation in the classical age.* The Hague

J.G.Wolf, J.A.Crook (1989), *Rechtsurkunden in Vulgärlatein aus den Jahren 37-39 n.Chr.* Abhandlungen der Heidelberger Akademie der Wissenschaften, Philosophisch-historische Klasse 1989.3

H.C.Youtie (1973), "ΣΗΜΕΙΟΝ in the Greek papyri and its significance for Plato, *Epistle* 13 (360a-b)", *Scriptiunculae* II, 963-75. Amsterdam

INDEXES

The indexes include all the texts published in this volume (with the exception of **118** and **121-6**), as well as the texts published in *Tab. Vindol.*I which have not been republished (**510-73**). A line number in square brackets indicates that the word is wholly supplied. Entries of the type "202.a.2n" mean that the word in question is suggested in the relevant note.

INDEX I Calendar

Calpurnio Pisone Vettio Bolano, consulibus = AD 111 186.13-14

Ianuarius 186.15 209.2 479
viiii Kalendas 143.1
]vii Kalendas 205.1
pridie Kalendas 200.6
] Kalendas 186.7, 9, 11
Idibus 343.34-5
Februarius 130.1 186.17, 19 493.a?
Kalendis 201.7 295.8
x[ ]ii Kalendas 201.2
xi Kalendas 200.7
v[ii]i Kalendas 201.3
]viii Kalendas 189.a
]v Kalendas 130.2
pridie Kalendas 200.8
iii Idus 200.9
pridie Idus 200.10
] Idus 186.22
Martius 186.24n 201.10 202.a.7
xvi Kalendas 165
xiii Kalendas 200.11
iiii Kalendas 300.5
intra Kalendas 343.33-4
Nonis 156.1
iii Idus 187.i.9
] Idus 135.1?
Aprilis
xvii Kalendas 200.12
vi Idus 136.1
Maius 147n 185.4n
vii Kalendas 155.1
pridie Kalendas 263.ii.6?
Iunius 127.1n
xii Kalendas 193.2
xv Kalendas 154.1
Idibus 189.b.2
Iulius 193.6
xiii Kalendas 190.c.4
xii Kalendas 190.c.7 193.6
xi Kalendas 190.c.10
x Kalendas 132.1 190.c.14
viiii Kalendas 190.c.17
viii Kalendas 190.c.21
vii Kalendas 190.c.36
pridie Nonas 151.1
] Idus 185.6, 8, 10
Augustus
vi Kalendas 178.2
v Kalendas 178.3
iiii Kalendas 178.4
iii Kalendas 178.5

INDEX II Personal Names

INDEX III Geography

INDEX IV Military and Official Terms

INDEX V Abbreviations and Symbols

INDEX VI General Index of Latin Words

233.B.i.4 236.a.6 255.8 256.ii.1 257.6 269.4 291.6 292.a.4 299.i.3 303.d.back 2n 310.5, 13 311.i.6, ii.6 312.4, 10 322.4 323.3n 343.6, 9 345.ii.2n 349.ii.4 355 484 508 523
nobis 218.2 282.5, 8 291.6 292.b.iii.4 310.18 314.3, 6
nos 263.ii.6 282.7 291.6 324.ii.3
emendo 394?
emetior 180.1
emo 176.5n 180.1n 181.3 189.c.1 216.5 302.5 343.7
enim 215.ii.3 225.9 227.b.4 231.2 256.i.5 292.b.ii.3 312.i.3 316.6 326.i.2 336.3 340.B.1n 442 448.b 508
eo, *adverb* 256.ii.2 344.1
epistula 263.ii.3 292.b.iii.2 295.5 299.i.1 311.i.6 343.44 423 484 536
eques: see Index IV
equisio: see Index IV
ergo 211.3 250.5 288.1 292.a.2n 305.i.2
erubesco 343.13
etiam 234.ii.2 255.13
euenio 321.3
excipio 312.11
excussorium 343.27
excutio 343.25
exhibeo 282.8
exigo 218.4 262.3n 284.3
exoro 307.a.4
experior 225.24
expleo 343.24
explico 238.4 301.5 316.margin 2n, 3 343.4 349.ii.5, 6 520
expungo 345.i.4
ex(s)arcio 233.B.ii.2
ex(s)equor 333.2n
ex(s)pecto 225.21 236.a.5 248.14n
exungia: see axungia

faba 192.3 204.a.2n 302.1
faber 160.A.8, 12, B.4, 9
fabrica 155.1
facio 156.3, 5 157.2 230.3 256.i.4?, ii.2 270.i.5 291.5, 7 297.a.3, 5, 7 311.i.4, 9 316. margin 5n 343.6, 26 348.1 371? 522.2
faex 185.5, 7, 9, 18, 23, 25
fama 371?
familiaris 312.4n
fanum 180.10
fatigo 336.1
faustus 261.3
febric[294.6
felicitas 356
feliciter 431?
felix 261.3
felicissimus 215.ii.7 248.4 250.15 260.5 264.4 310.20 324.ii.2 346.ii.5
felic[406?
fero 234.ii.1 294.5? 335.1? 343.23
ferrum 182.15 183.2
festino 476
festum 313.3?
-ficio 427
fides 344.16? 536.iii
fiducia 225.11-12
filiolus 291.10
fio 180.36 182.8 185.28 201.11 205.2 283.6n 355
fir[299.i.4
flammo 156.4
flammula: see Index IV
follis 180.7, 25
forfex 310.12
formo(n)sus 302.3
fornax: see furnax
fortis 299.i.2
fortiter
fortissime 233.B.ii.1
frater 210.4 233.B.i.3 236.a.3 243.3 247.3 248.3, 12 250.17 252.ii.3 255.15 259.3 260.5 265.3 289.4 295.10 297.b.1, c.3n 300.10 301.4, 7 306.5 309.15 310.1, 4, 15, back 26 311.i.1, ii.1, margin 2n 331.3 343.1 345.i.3, ii.5 347.c.3-4n 349.ii.5n, margin 2n, 352. margin? 363 417 420.back? 451.B? 456? 508

salus
salutem 212.1 213.i.2 217.i.2 219.2 233.B.i.2 234.2 236.a.[2] 238.2 239.2 240.[2] 243.2 248.2 249.2 250.2 252.i.2 253.2 255.2 256.i.2 257.2 259.2 261.2 262.2 265.2 270.i.2 275.2 276.2 279.2 291.2 292.a.1 294.2 295.2 296.2 297.a.2 298.a.2 300.2 301.2 303.a.[2] 308.2 309.2 310.3 311.i.2 319.2 320.2 325.i.2 331.1 332.1 343.2 347.a.2 370 446 504 506 520 532 534
saluto 210.3 225.5, 13n 244 247.1 255.6 260.6 263.ii.8n 274.3 281.i.3 287.2 288.4n 291.9, 10 292.c.3 310.9, 16 311.ii.3 334.2 343.42 340.ii.1 349.ii.6, margin 1n 353.ii.1 420 508? 509 530
saluus 225.6 284.1n 294.3
Saturnalicius 301.3
scelus 344.18
scio 225.19 255.11 292.b.iii.3 300.9 311.i.3 312.5 343.24
scribo 177.1 212.2 225.25 260.2n 289.1? 300.9 311.i.9 312.6 324.i.2? 334.4 343.5, 7, 15, 16, 18, 19 364? 377
scriptio 307.a.back 2-3n
scutarius 160.A.4n 184.21
scutula 194.A.2, 8 208.a.1, b.3n
se 310.19 343.35 420
secum 327.2
sebum 184.22, 33, 36, 39 186.18n 319.3n
seco 337.2
secundus 194.B.6-7n
sed 269.1n 294.8 311.i.7 335.1
sedile 309.13n
semis: see Index V
semper 225.10 292.a.4 498
septem 255.10
seruo (-are) 215.ii.6
seruus 301.back 11 303.e.1? 322.2 347.c.back 3
sessio 309.9
sex 255.9, 10 301.4
sextarius: see Index V
si 211.3 215.ii.1, 4 218.1 228.2 233.B.i.3 234.7 238.3 250.6 256.i.5, ii.4 283.3?, 6n 284.1n 291.7 302.3, 5, margin 1 310.7 328.2 343.28, 37 344.18 356 456?
sicut 265.4 292.a.2 326.ii.2
silua 180.9
siluula 256.ii.3 (siluol-)
simici[196.17
similis 269.1n
simulo 336.2n (simil-)
singularis: see Index IV
singulus 205.1 378
siue 307.b.1?
solea 346.i.3, 5
sollemnis 291.4
sollicitudo 238.3
soluo 120.2 206.margin
sordide 256.ii.1-2?
soror 291.3, 11, 12 292.a.2, b.back 1 293.2 310.17 335.4n 389?
souxtum 301.3
spero 291.11
spes 225.7
spica 343.7, 27
statim 218.4 295.7n
stica 181.4
stipendio(r) 154.14n
stips 190.c.30
strictis[471 cf.547
structor 155.3 156.3
suadeo 339.3
subarmal[184.7n, 17?, 38
subligar 346.i.4
subpaenula 196.9, 13
subripio 322.4
subscribo 250.7
subscriptio 339.4n
subucula 196.11
subunc.lon.s 185.26
sudarium 184.6, 10, 16n, 28, 34, 37 187.i.7n
sum
eram 292.c.2
erat 323.1 343.33
erit 248.5
erunt 336.1n

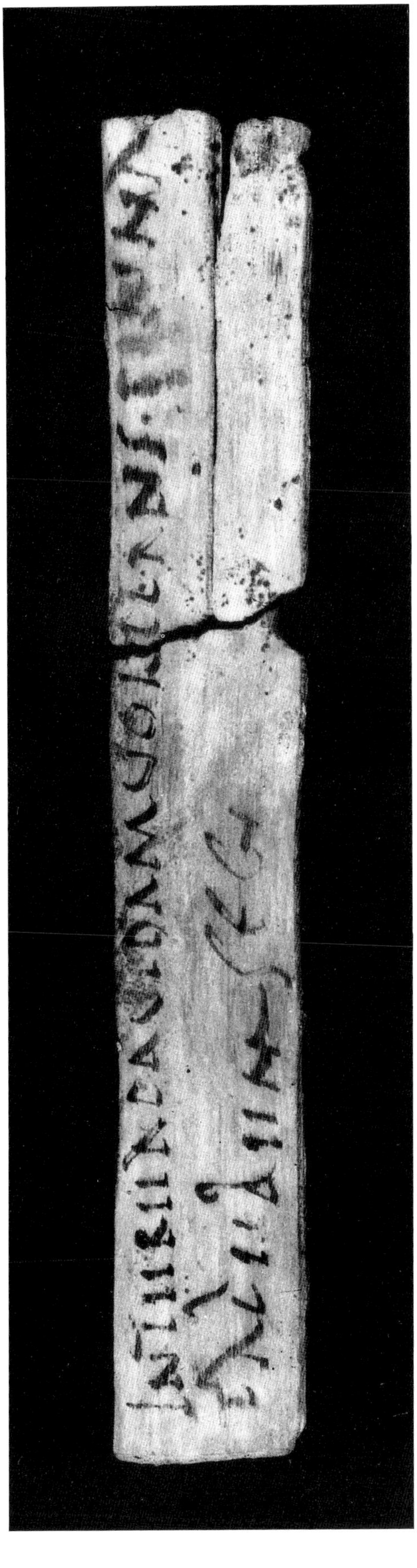

118 100 x 15 mm.

121 65 x 40 mm.

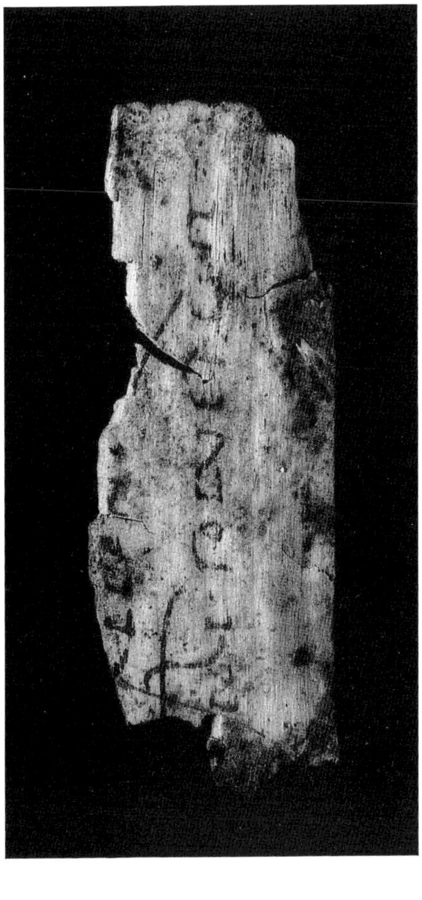

120 66 x 24 mm.

PLATE II

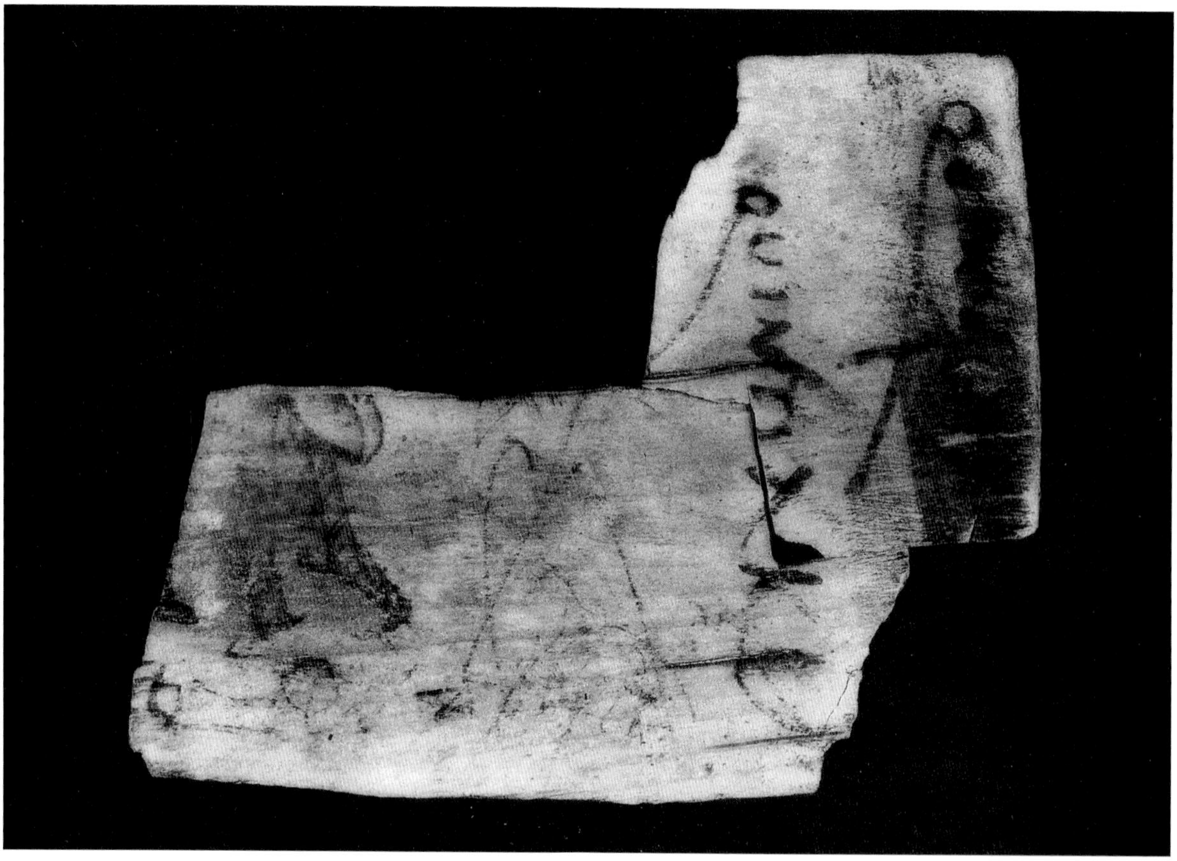

119 62 x 73 mm.

122 62 x 73 mm.

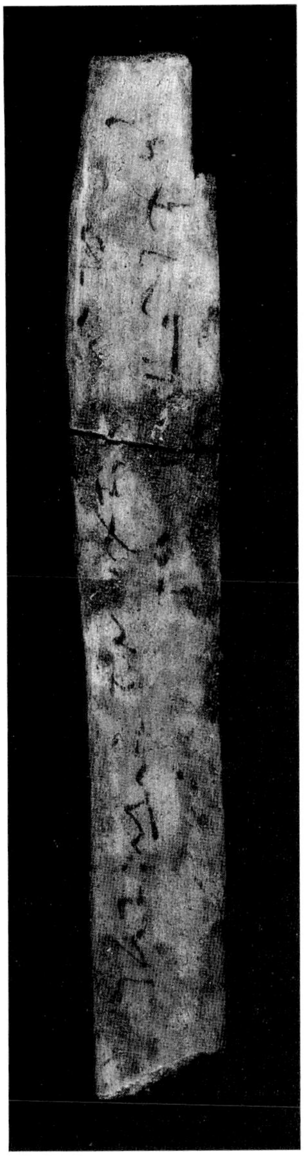

123 (side A) 90 x 114 mm.

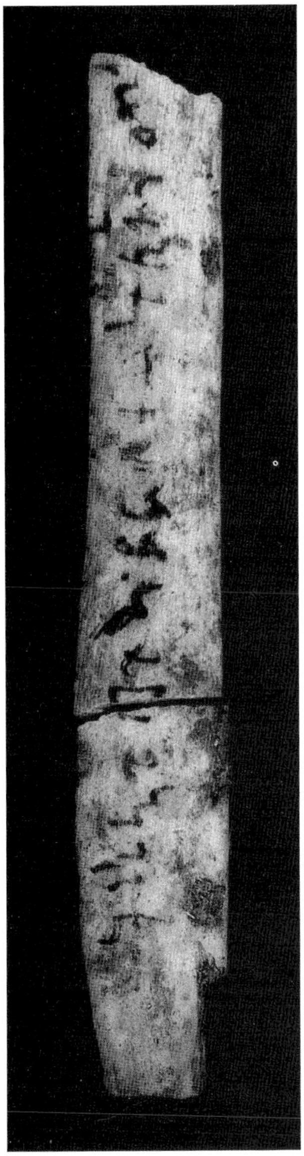

123 (side B) 90 x 114 mm.

147 75 x 20 mm.

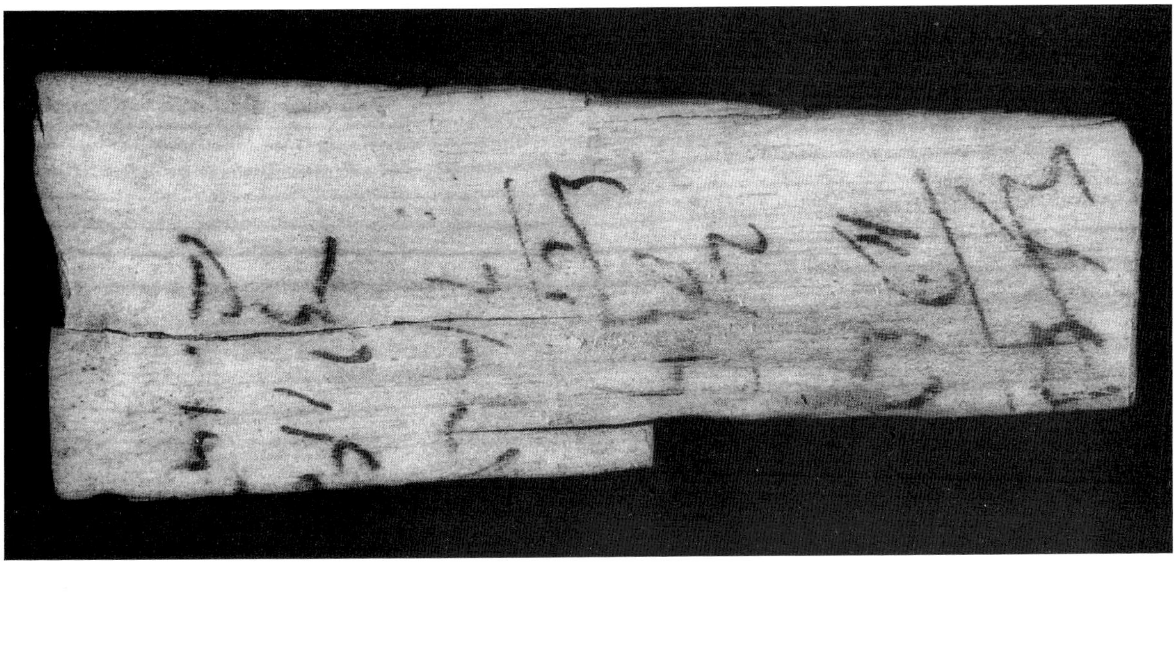

126 28 x 75 mm.

127 70 x 83 mm.

139 76 x 37 mm.

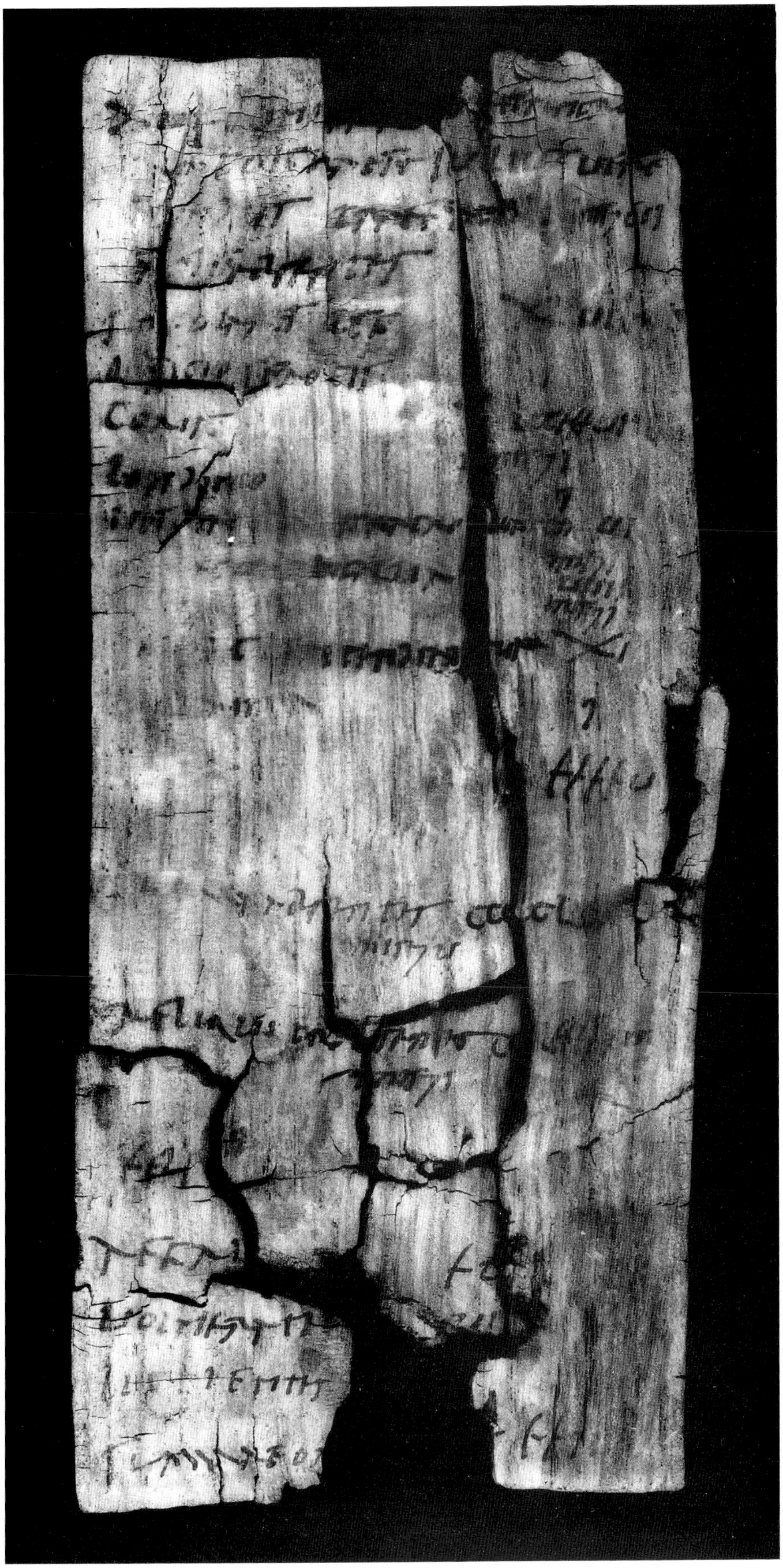

154 86 x 197 mm.

164 (upper half) 78 x 93 mm.

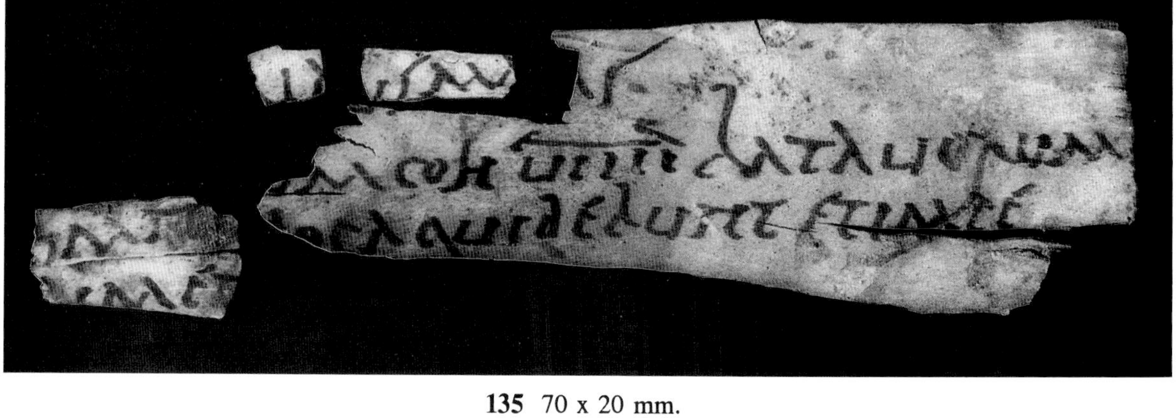

135 70 x 20 mm.

176 110 x 42 mm.

175 92 x 45 mm.

130 66 x 33 mm.

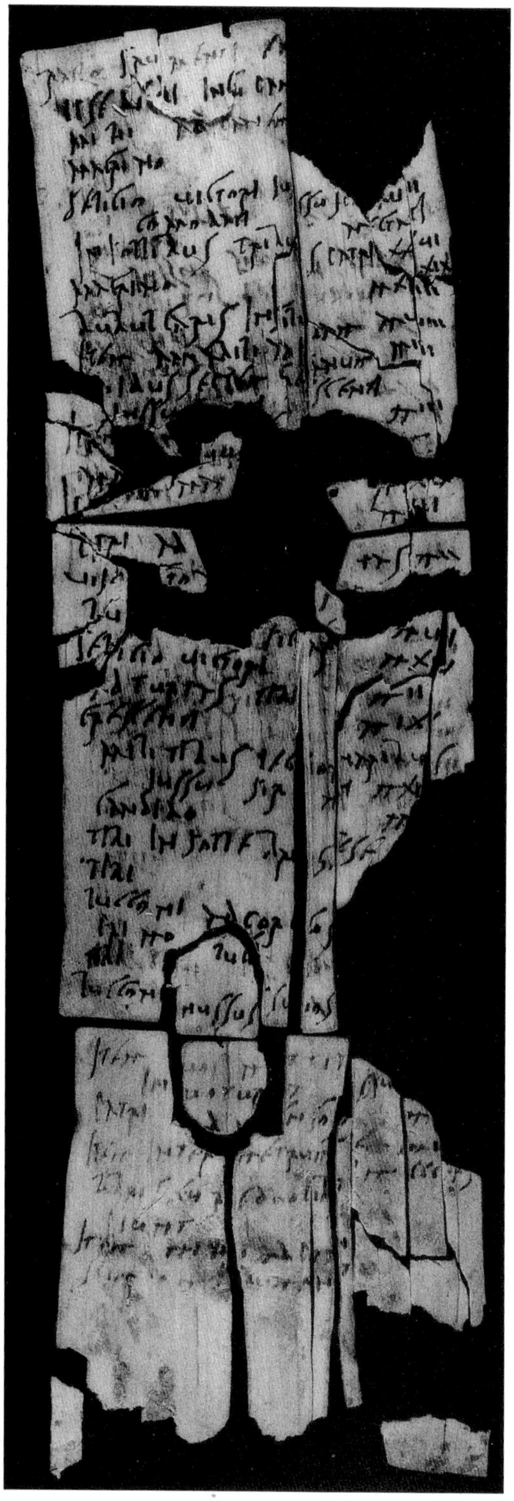

180 77 x 264 mm.

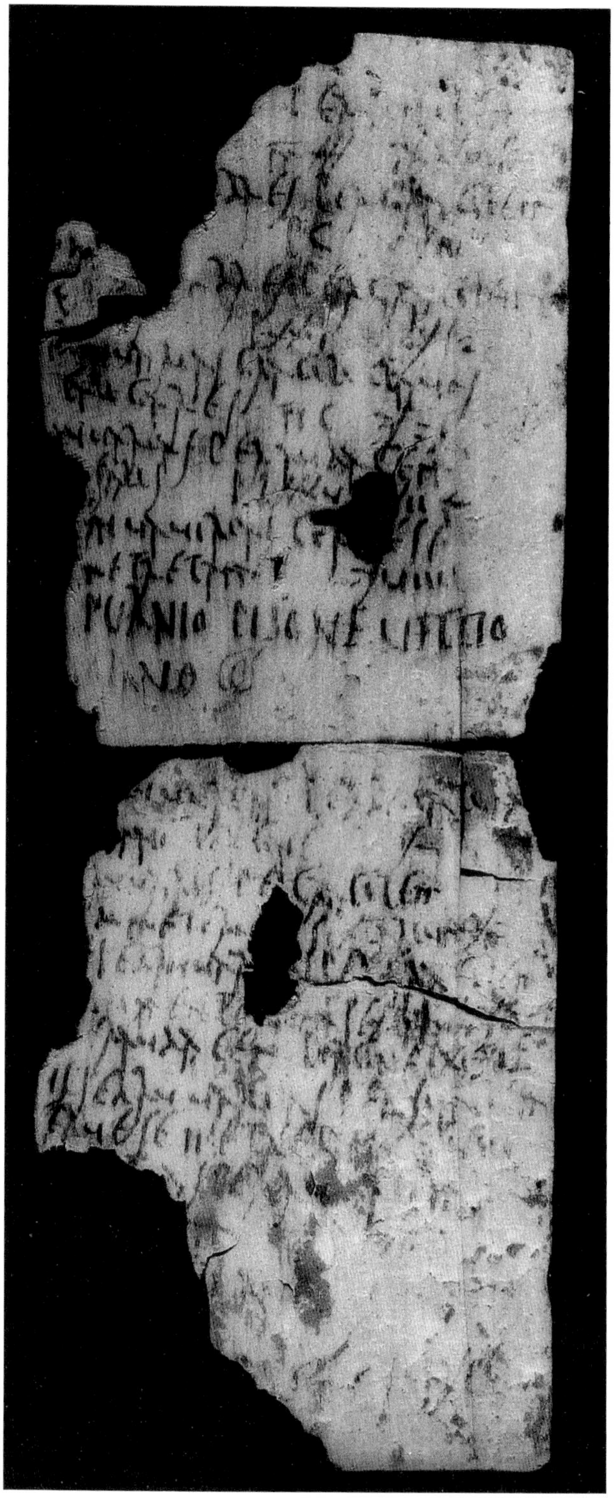

186 60 x 167 mm.

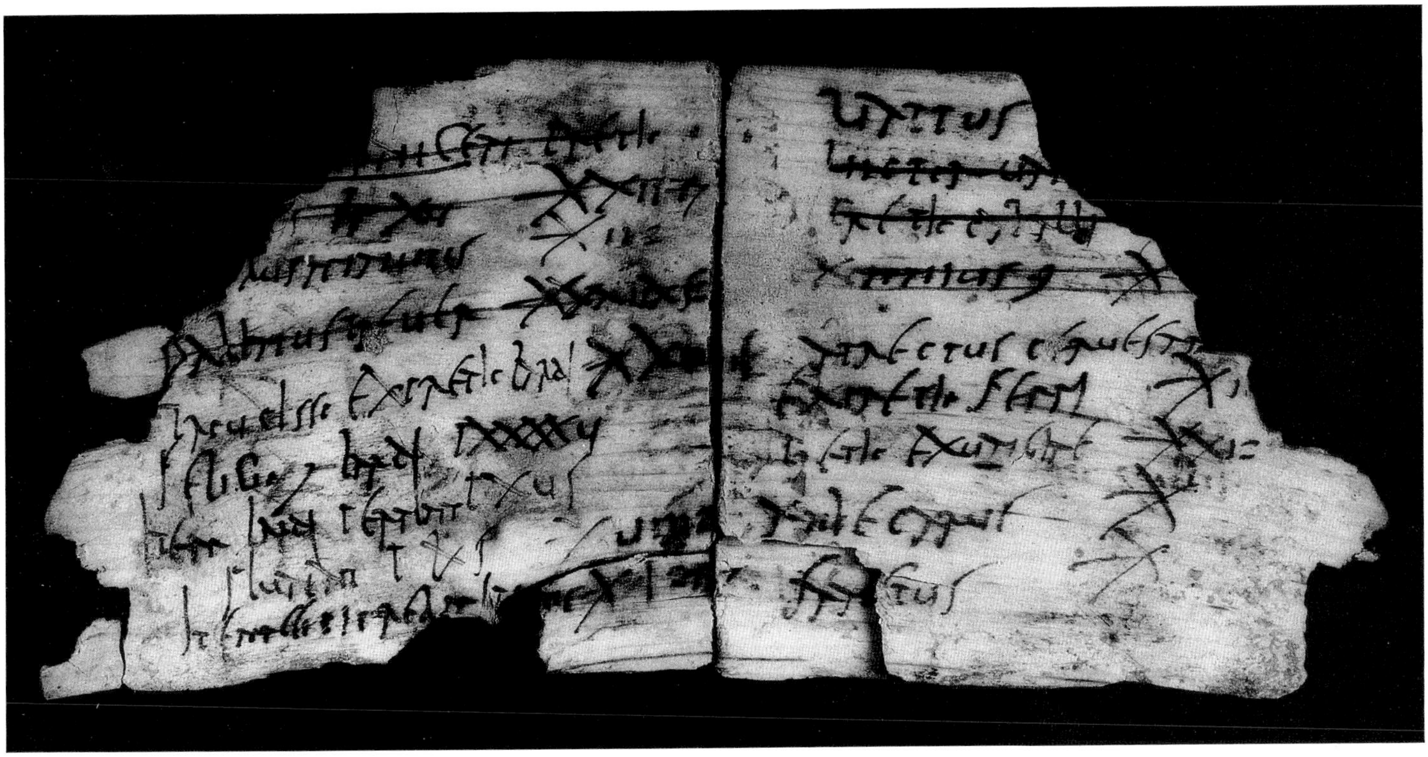

182 174 x 77 mm.

304 92 x 10 mm.

196 46 x 186 mm.

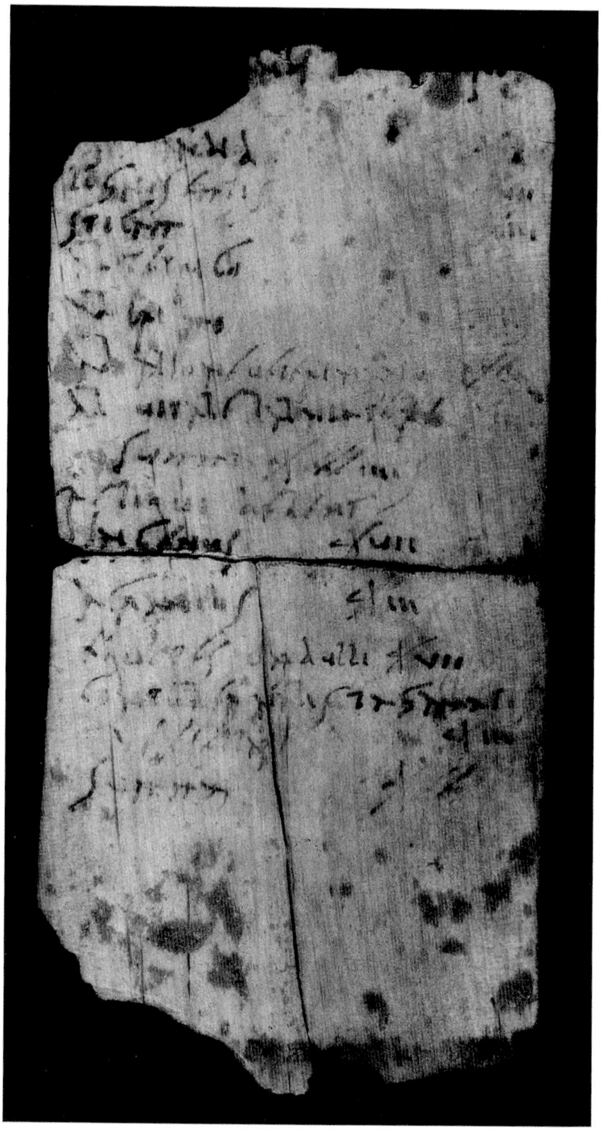

181 70 x 137 mm.

206 33 x 58 mm.

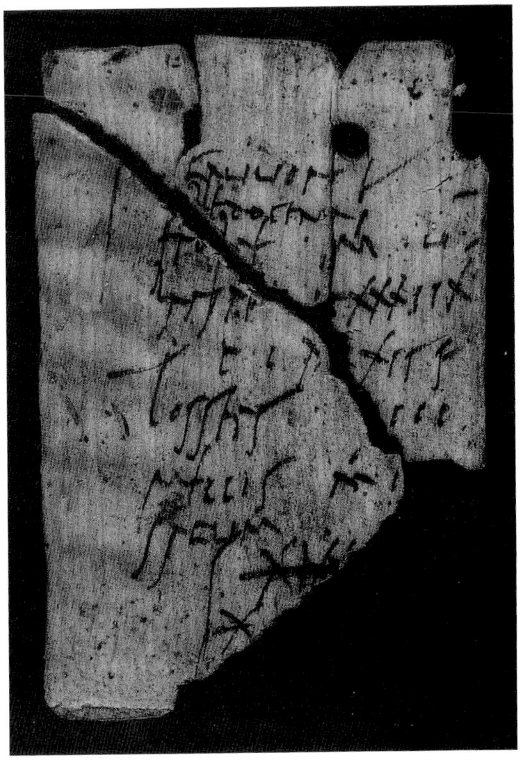

185 60 x 171 mm.

192 66 x 90 mm.

PLATE XII

252 160 x 30 mm.

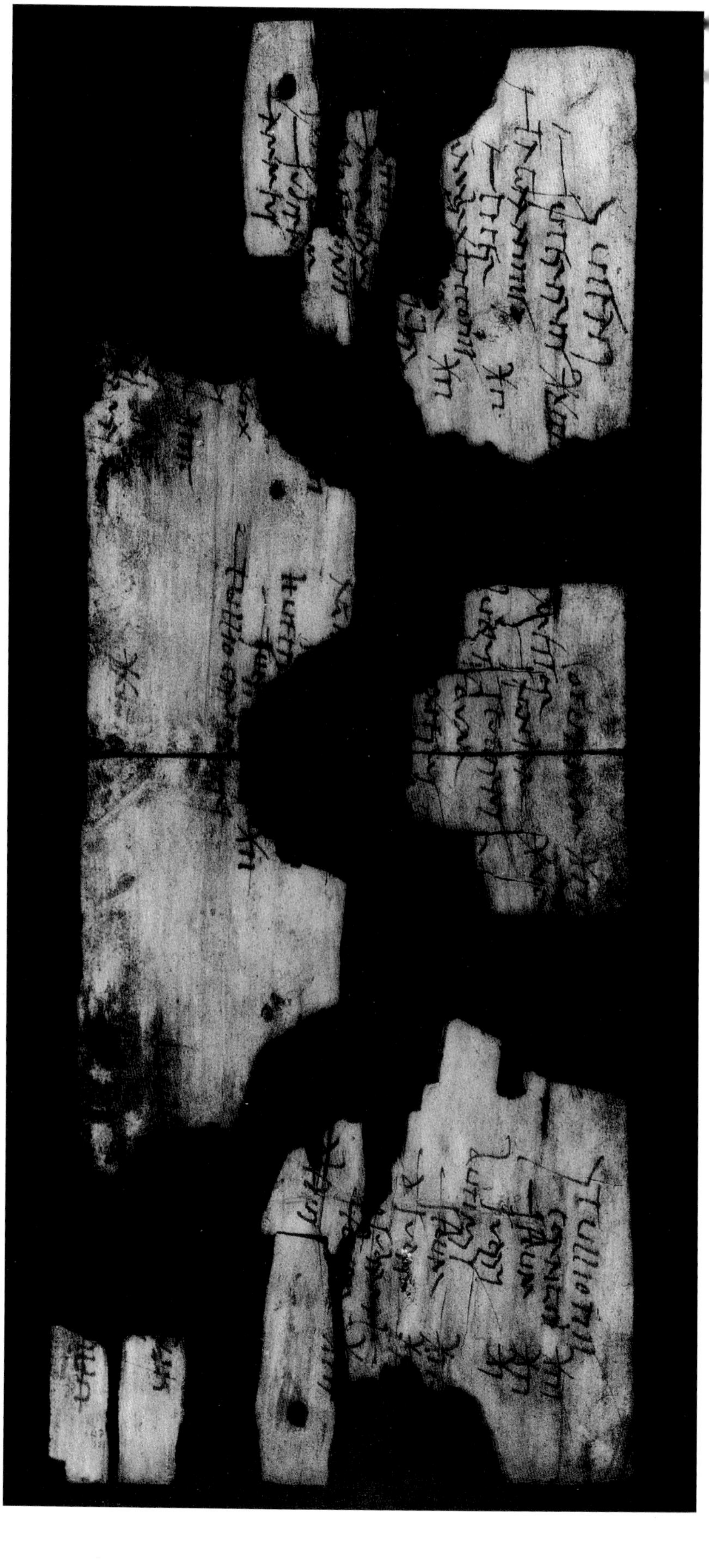

184 210 x 70 mm. (approx.)

213 169 x 36 mm.

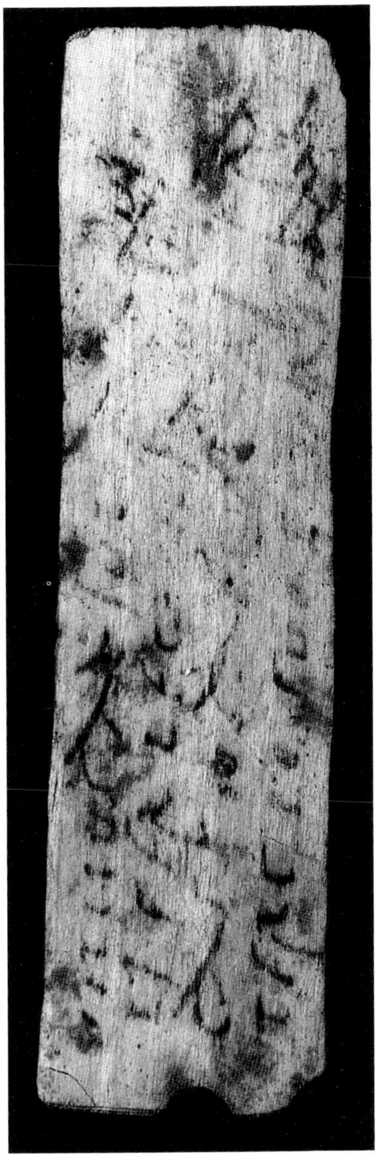

214 100 x 26 mm.

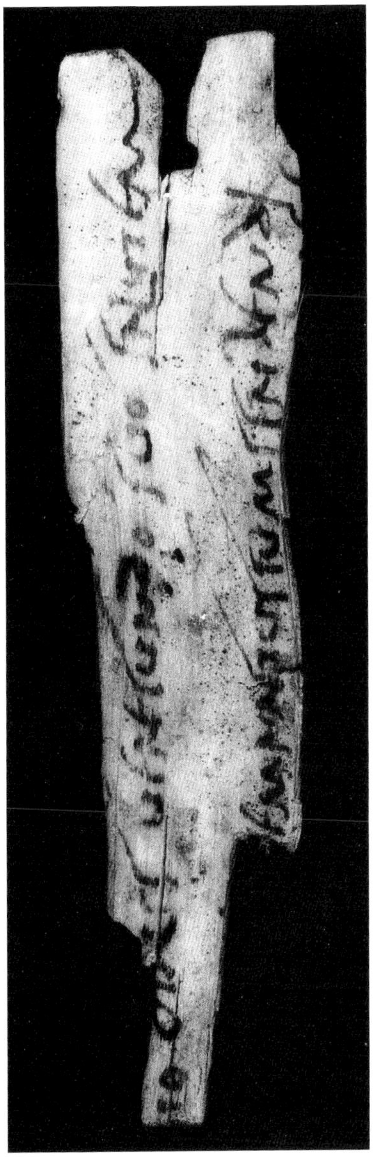

212 118 x 28 mm.

193 91 x 35 mm.

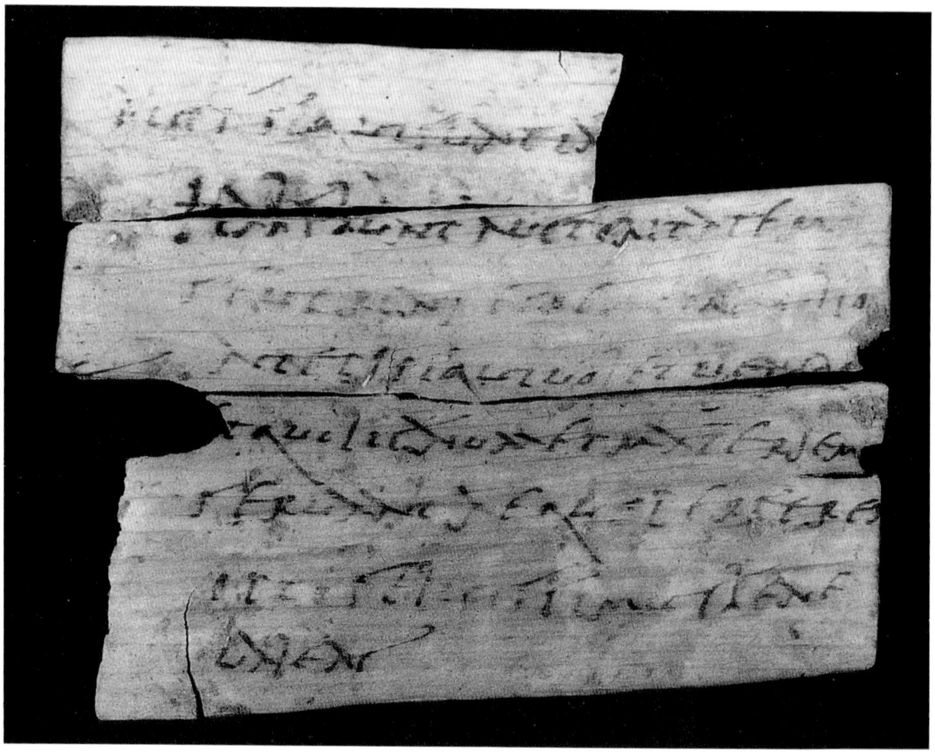

215 114 x 79 mm.

313 86 x 37 mm.

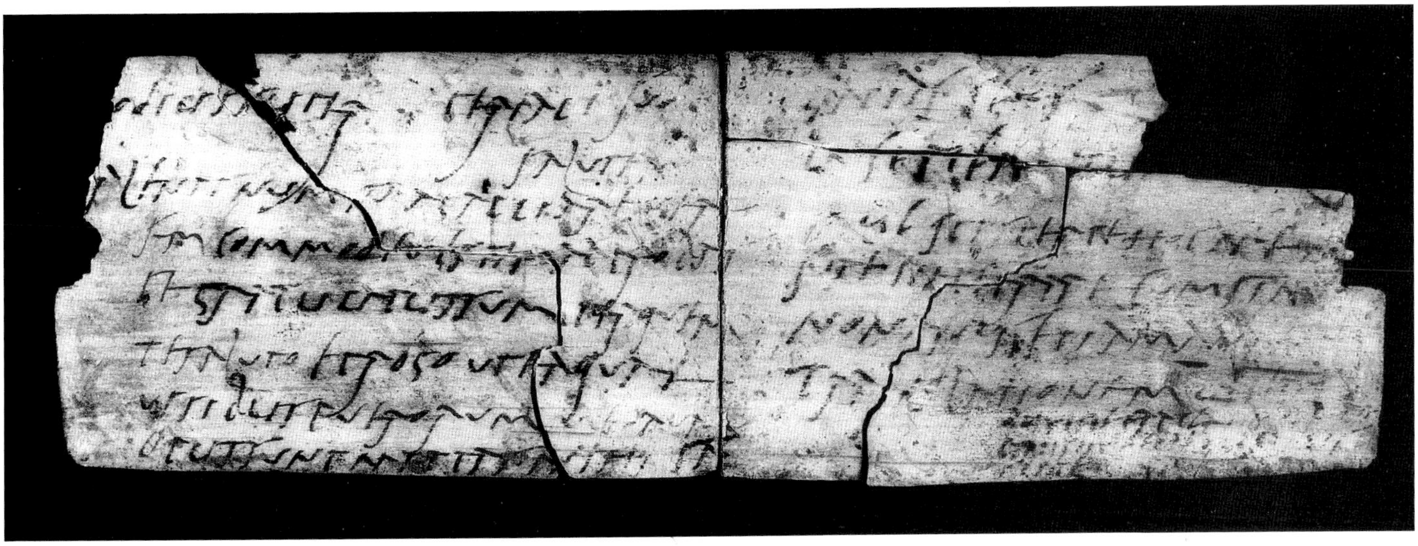

255 (front) 195 x 60 mm.

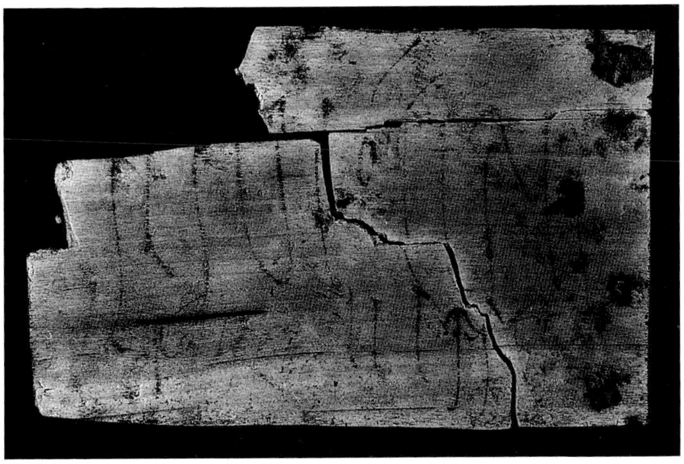

255 (back) 98 x 60 mm.

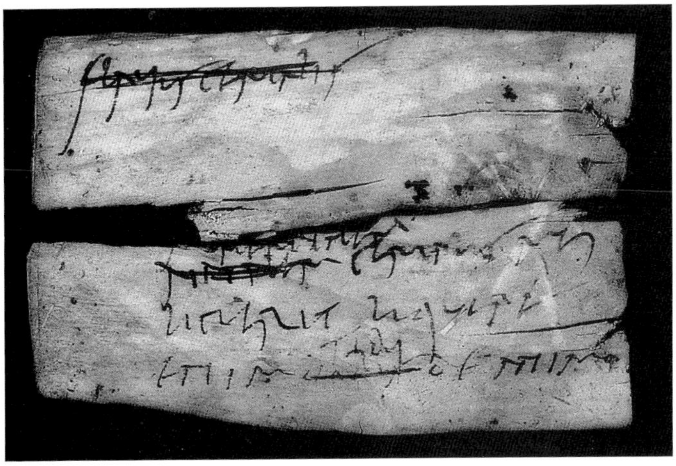

227 85 x 27 mm., 85 x 30 mm.

PLATE XVI

242 225 x 51 mm.

256 214 x 36 mm.

233 176 x 34 mm.

260 (front) 117 x 74 mm.

260 (back) 117 x 74 mm.

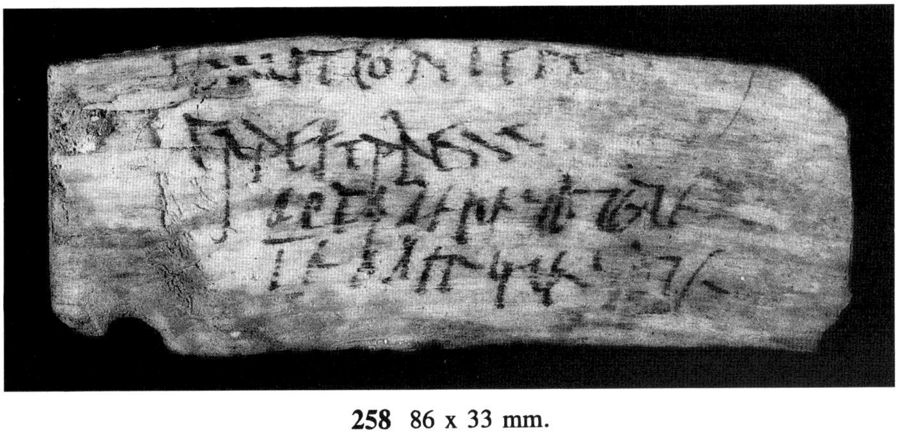

258 86 x 33 mm.

PLATE XVIII

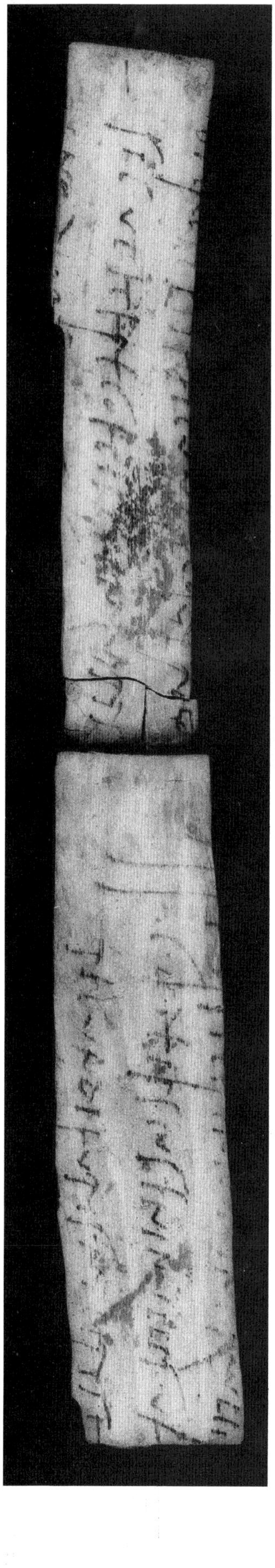

326 230 x 30 mm.

239 154 x 41 mm.

281 (left-hand side, front) 86 x 40 mm.

281 (right-hand side, back) 86 x 37 mm.

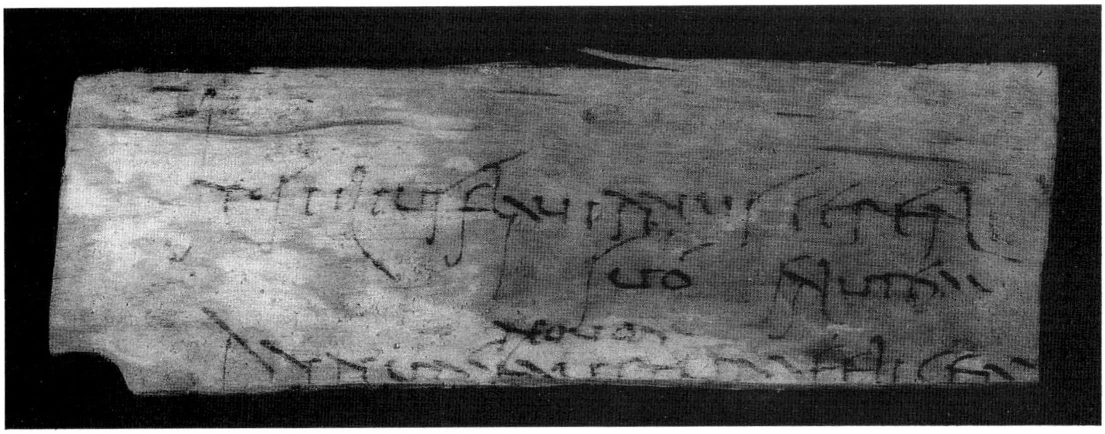

261 102 x 33 mm.

265 96 x 50 mm.

294 65 x 65 mm.

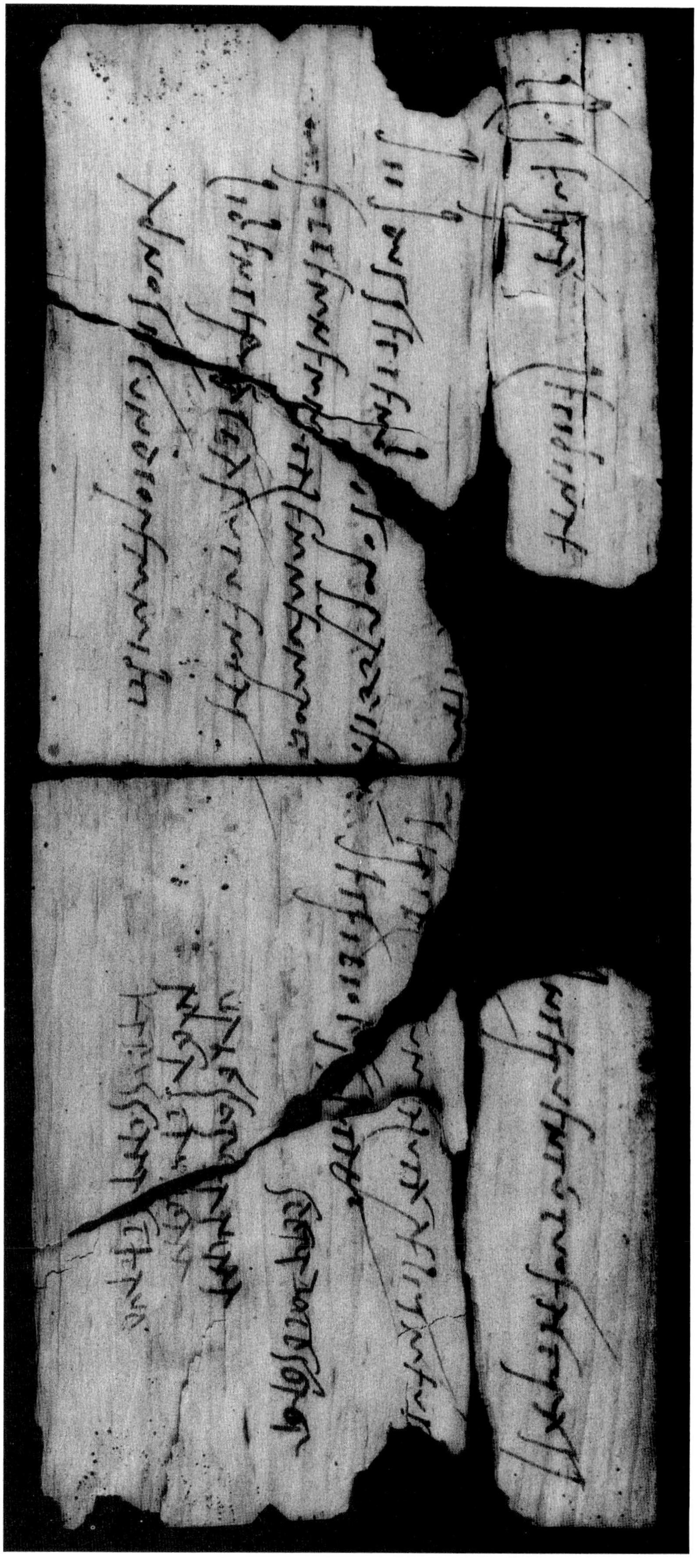

291 223 x 96 mm.

292.b (back) 94 x 36 mm.

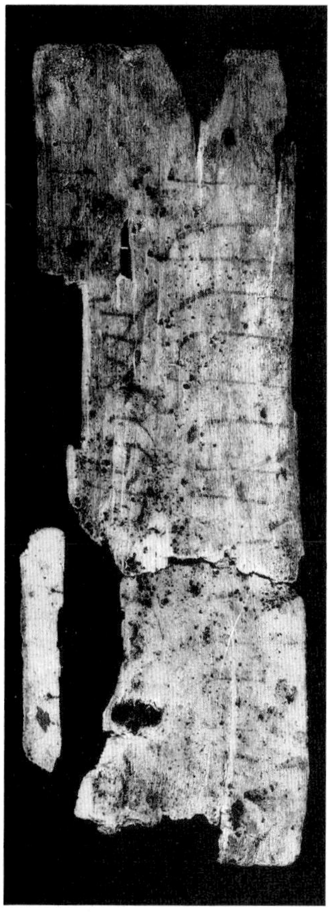

292.c (back) 96 x 32 mm.

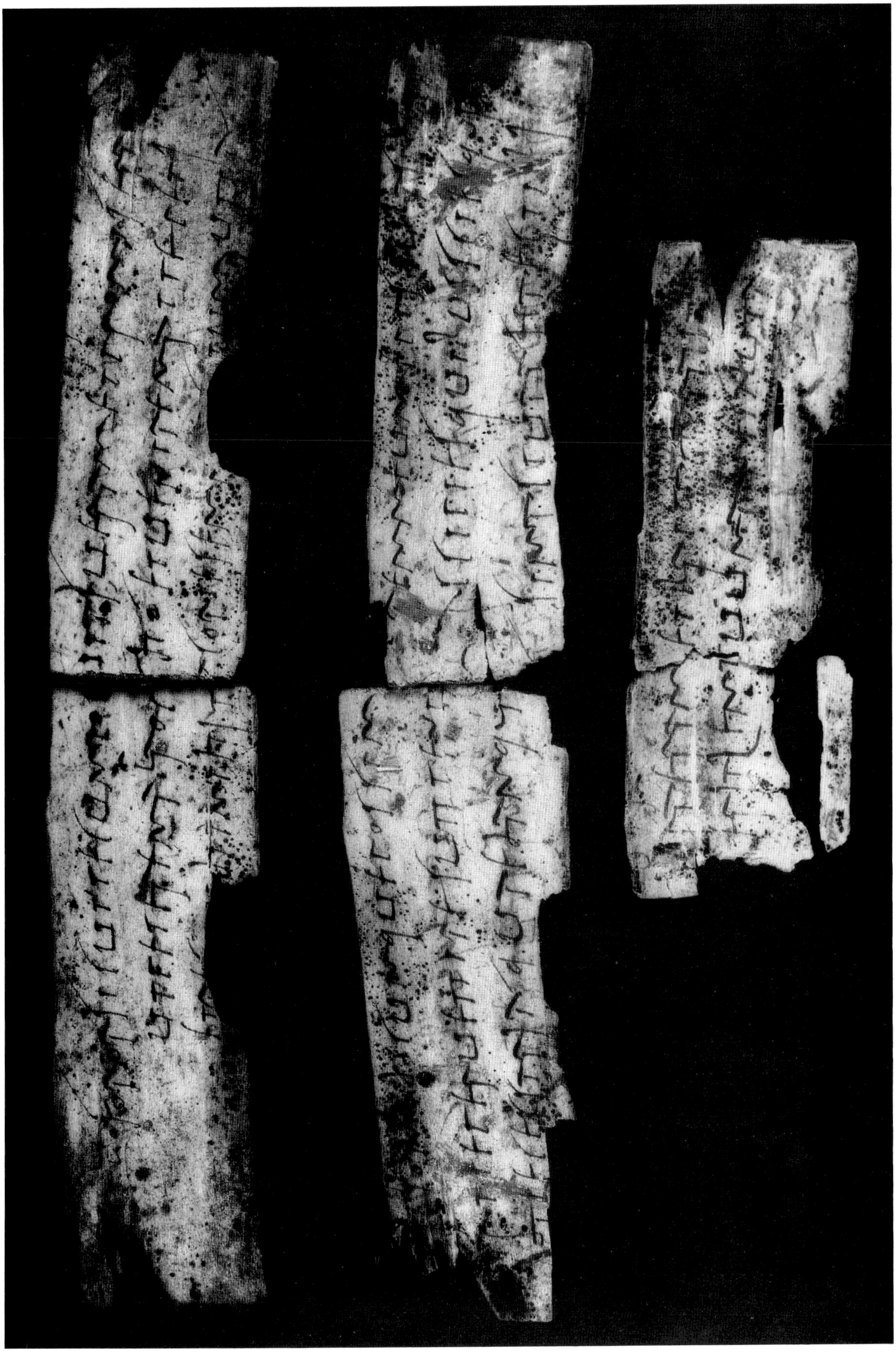

292 (front) 190 x 31 mm., 193 x 36 mm., 96 x 32 mm.

300 165 x 68 mm.

328 73 x 40 mm.

301 (front) 182 x 76 mm.

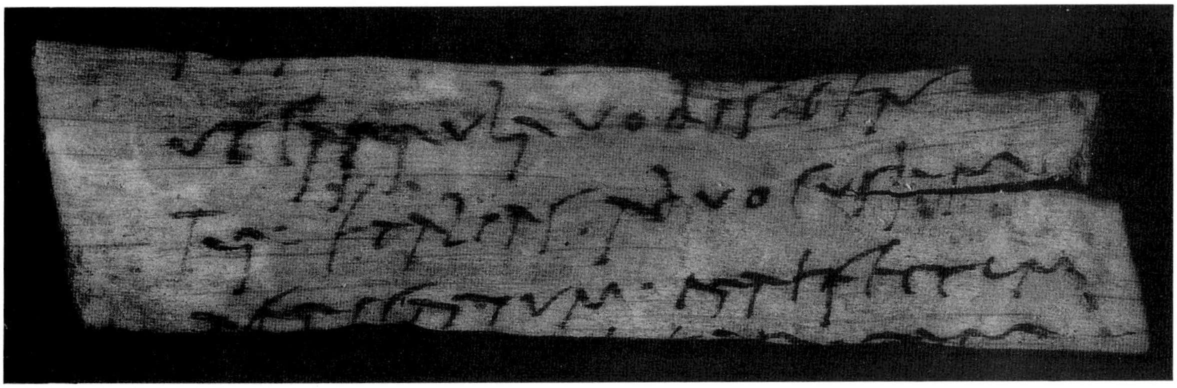

315 97 x 25 mm.

311 (front) 220 x 87 mm.

302 107 x 40 mm.

301 (back) 91 x 76 mm.

311 (back) 110 x 43 mm.

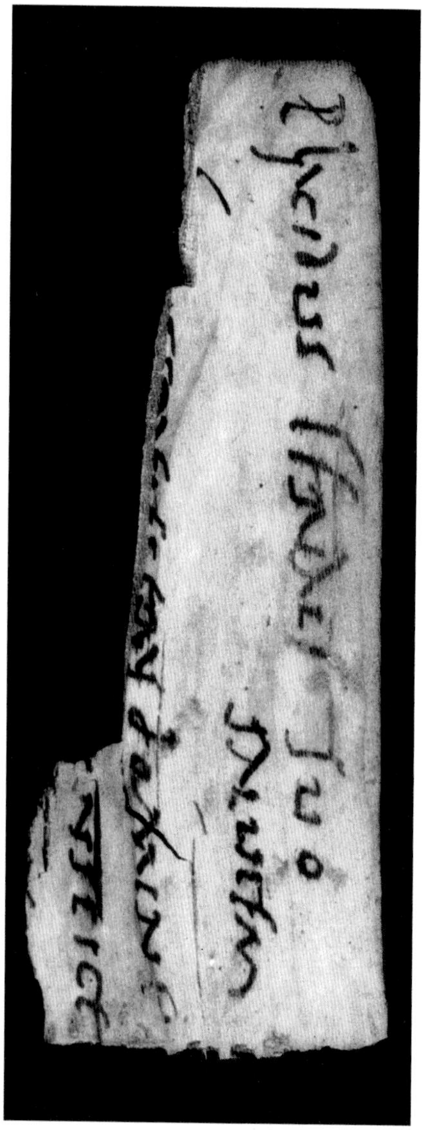

262 88 x 32 mm.

309 167 x 86 mm.

312 (front) 183 x 93 mm.

321 90 x 21 mm.

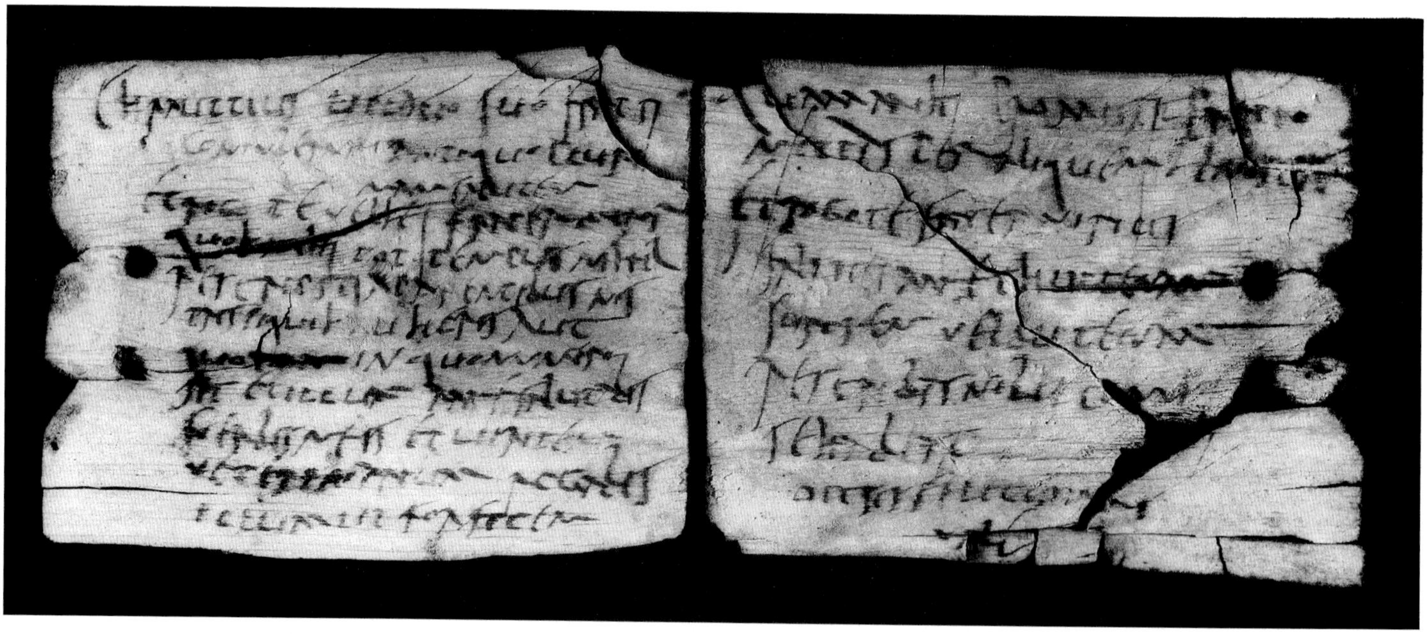

310 (front) 189 x 70 mm.

322 97 x 28 mm.

312 (back) 92 x 93 mm.

310 (back) 95 x 70 mm.

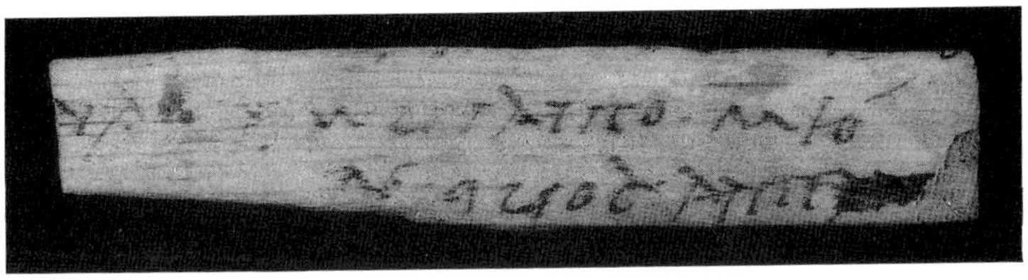

330 70 x 13 mm.

PLATE XXX

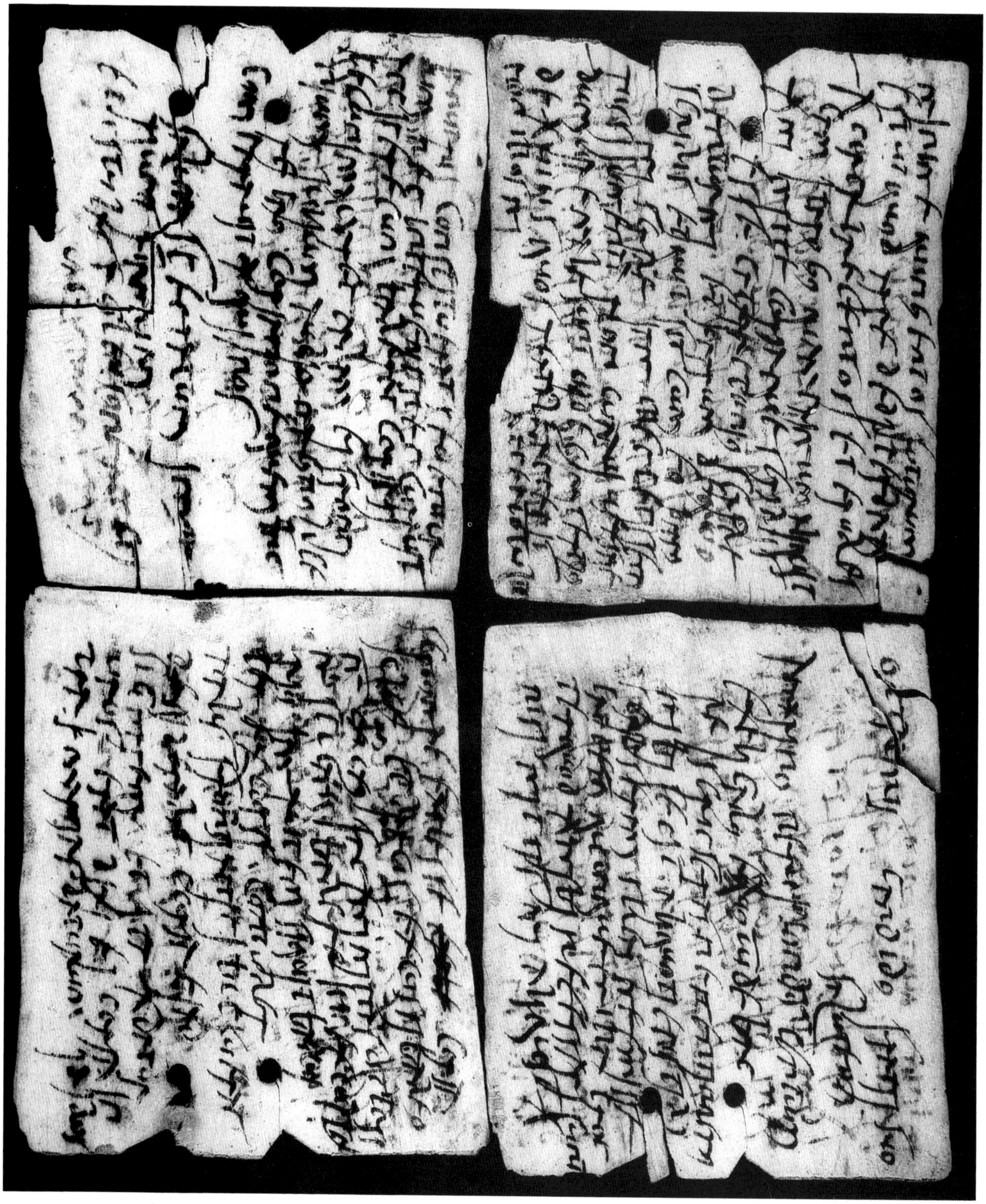

343 182 x 79 mm., 179 x 79 mm.

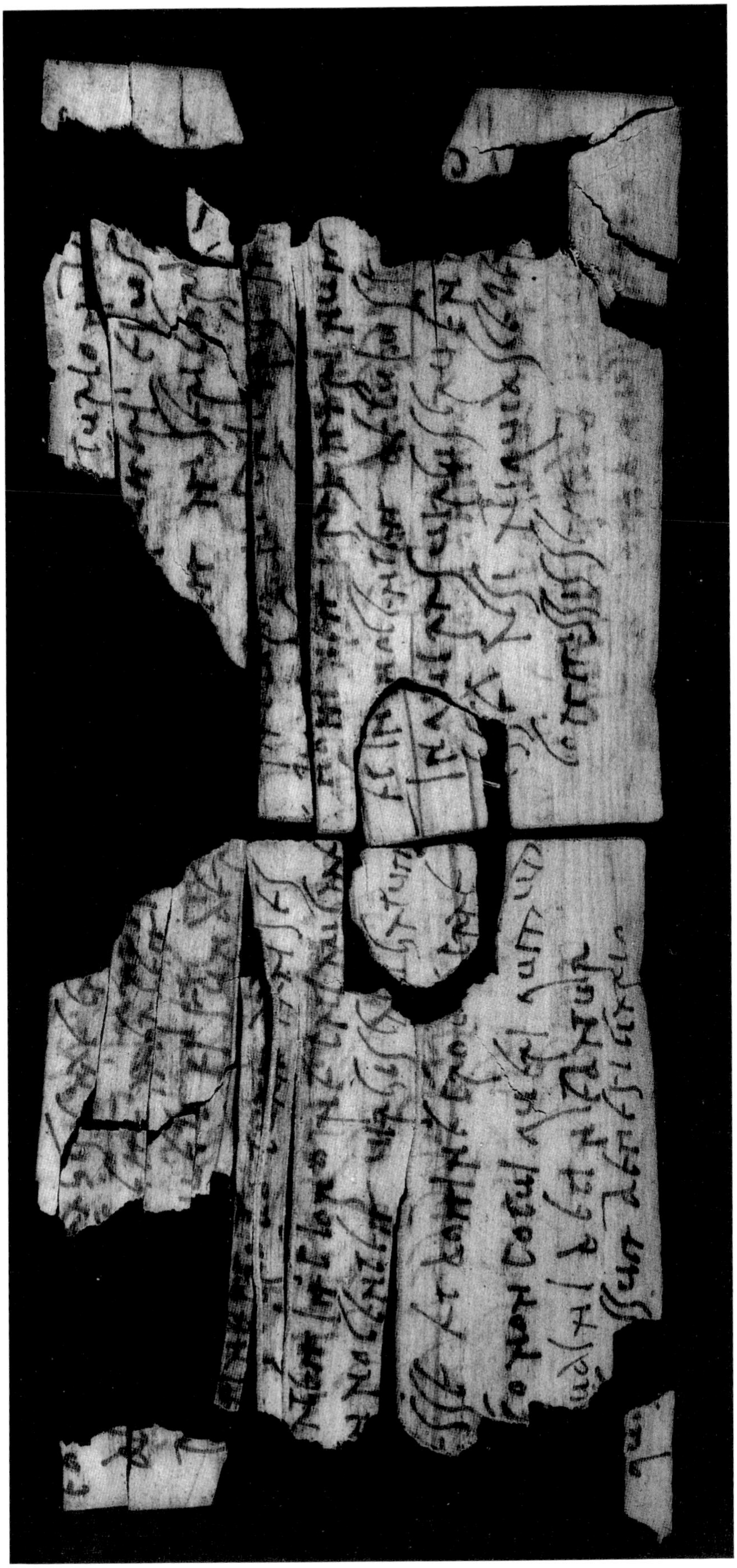

344 171 x 77 mm.

345 184 x 36 mm.

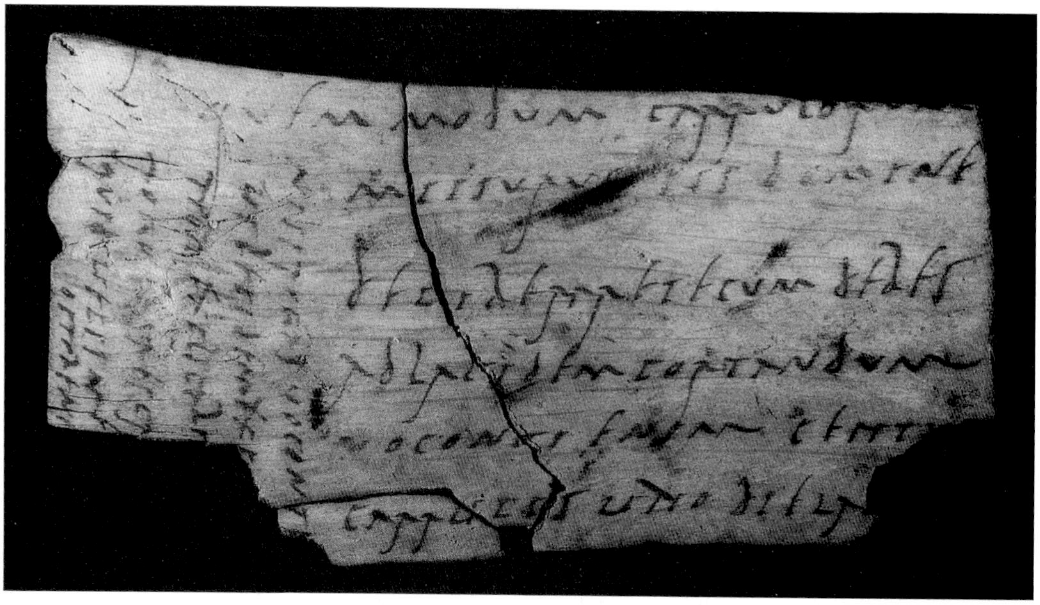

316 100 x 50 mm.

334 71 x 66 mm.

355 92 x 38 mm.